D0559944

THE ONE YEAR BOOK OF
Family Devotions

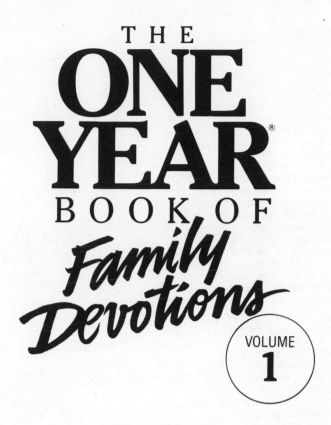

THE ONE YEAR® BOOK OF *Family Devotions*

VOLUME 1

Children's Bible Hour
Tyndale House Publishers, Inc.
Wheaton, Illinois

Stories written by V. Louise Cunningham, Cathy Garnaat, Jorlyn Grasser, Jan Hansen, Nancy G. Hill, Ruth Jay, Dean Kelley, Sherry Kuyt, Agnes Livezey, Deborah Marett, Hazel Marett, Sara Nelson, Raelene Phillips, Victoria Reinhardt, Phyllis Robinson, Deana Rogers, Catherine Runyon, Charlie VanderMeer, Geri Walcott, Linda Weddle, Barbara Westberg, and Carolyn Yost. Authors' initials appear at the end of each story. All stories are taken from issues of *Keys for Kids,* published bimonthly by the Children's Bible Hour, Box 1, Grand Rapids, MI 49501.

Library of Congress Catalog Card Number 88-71950
ISBN 0-8423-2540-9, cloth
ISBN 0-8423-2541-7, kivar

Printed in the United States of America

3 4 5 6 7 94 93 92 91 90 89

CONTENTS

OCTOBER

NOVEMBER

DECEMBER

YOU HAVE in your hands a year's worth of delightful stories, all of them taken from *Keys for Kids,* a bimonthly publication of the Children's Bible Hour. For years the Children's Bible Hour has made this devotional magazine available free of charge to any family requesting a copy. Their fine ministry to parents and children has been much appreciated over the years, and Tyndale House is proud to present in one volume this one year collection of the many stories made available through *Keys for Kids.*

Each day's story provides a contemporary illustration of the day's Scripture reading. Following each story is a "How About You?" section that asks children to apply the story to their own lives. And following this is a memory verse, usually taken from the Scripture reading. Many of these memory verses are taken from the King James Version of the Bible, but in many cases another version has been used for the sake of clarity. Each devotion ends with a "key," a two-to-five word summary of the day's lesson.

The stories here are geared toward families with children aged eight to fourteen. Children can enjoy reading these stories by themselves, but we hope that you will use them in a daily devotional time that involves the whole family. Like the many stories in the Bible that teach valuable lessons about life, the stories here are made to speak not only to children but to adults. They are simple, direct, and concrete, and, like Jesus' parables, they speak to all of us in terms we can easily understand. And like all good stories, they are made for sharing, so look upon them as the basis for family sharing and growth.

JANUARY

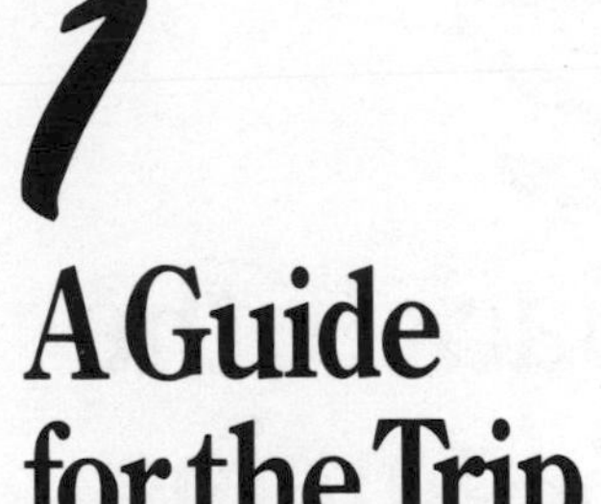

A Guide for the Trip

FROM THE BIBLE:

Your word is a lamp to my feet
and a light for my path.
I have taken an oath and
confirmed it,
that I will follow your
righteous laws.
I have suffered much;
preserve my life, O Lord,
according to your word.
Accept, O Lord, the willing
praise of my mouth,
and teach me your laws.
Though I constantly take my life
in my hands,
I will not forget your law.
The wicked have set a snare for
me,
but I have not strayed from
your precepts.
Your statutes are my heritage
forever;
they are the joy of my heart.
My heart is set on keeping your
decrees to the very end.

Psalm 119:105-112, NIV

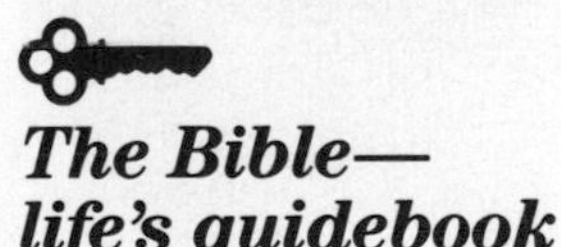

The Bible—life's guidebook

AS DAD REACHED for the Bible, Robbie sighed. He hated family devotions, but his parents thought it was so important. "The Bible is about now, tomorrow, and forever," Mother often said. "You can learn a lot from the past—like how not to make the same mistake others made."

Dad, too, encouraged Bible reading. "God's Son, Jesus, lived on earth without making one mistake. It's interesting to read about it in God's Word."

Robbie didn't agree. He thought the Bible was boring. "It's all about people who lived thousands of years ago," he said. "Things are so different now."

When Dad announced that he was going to Australia on business and his family could go along, Robbie was excited. One day he brought home books and maps from his schoolteacher. "Mr. Tucker's been to Australia," Robbie said. "He told me all about it. Lots of things are different there. Look! He loaned me a guidebook. It tells you things to do and what not to do and good places to go."

"That's great, Robbie," Dad told him, "but won't it bore you to read all this? And your teacher—didn't he make any mistakes and have any problems?"

"Oh, sure," laughed Robbie. "He told me about it so I won't make the same mistakes. And these books won't bore me. I'll learn how to have a good trip and how to get along in that country. It helped Mr. Tucker on his trip, and it will help me, too."

Dad nodded. "A guidebook is a good idea," he agreed, "but since you never seemed interested in reading the guidebook for your most important journey, I'm a little surprised that you're interested in this one."

Robbie stared at Dad. "What journey?" he asked. "What guidebook?"

"Your journey through life," answered Dad. "The Bible is the guidebook, and God—the author—is the best guide for that journey."

Robbie continued to stare. He had never thought of it that way. "You're right, Dad," Robbie agreed finally.

HOW ABOUT YOU? Are you trying to journey through life without a guide? The Bible is filled with instruction and help for you. It has all you need to know to make a good trip through life. A.L.

TO MEMORIZE: *"Your word is a lamp to my feet and a light for my path"* Psalm 119:105 (NIV).

JANUARY

Back to the Beginning

FROM THE BIBLE:

So if you are standing before the altar in the Temple, offering a sacrifice to God, and suddenly remember that a friend has something against you, leave your sacrifice there beside the altar and go and apologize and be reconciled to him, and then come and offer your sacrifice to God. Matthew 5:23-24, TLB

Restore friendships

"I CAN'T! I just can't do it!" Diana cried out. She wadded up the paper and burst into tears.

"What can't you do?" Dad looked up from his paper.

"I can't get these figures to balance," sniffed Diana. "Tomorrow when I turn in our club treasurer's report, everyone will think I'm dumb. And Janet will be happy!"

Dad looked at Diana's report. "Speaking of Janet, I haven't seen her lately. I thought she was your best friend. Why would she be happy if you make a mistake in your report?"

Diana hesitated. "Well, we both wanted to be treasurer, and we quarreled. I got elected, but she still tried to tell me how to do the job. I finally informed her that I'd do things my own way. Since then we haven't been speaking," Diana said sadly.

"I'm sorry to hear that, and I know God must be, too," began Dad. Suddenly he pointed to some of the figures on the report. "Say, Diana, go back to the beginning and add up your figures one by one. See what you get."

Diana tried it, and it worked. "I found my mistake, Dad!" she exclaimed. "In the beginning I multiplied by four instead of adding it. Now it's right."

"It usually helps to go back to the beginning," Dad said. "You know, Diana, I think it would be a good idea to go back to the beginning of your quarrel with Janet, too."

"What do you mean?" asked Diana.

"It sounds like both of you wanted your own way in the beginning. That was selfish. Then you hurt each other by using cutting words," Dad explained. "How about going to Janet and apologizing for wanting your own way? Listen to what she has to say. I'm sure she has some good ideas."

Diana sighed. "OK, Dad. She was wrong, but so was I. I'll go back to the beginning and tell Janet I was wrong. I want us to be friends again."

HOW ABOUT YOU? Is there someone with whom you've had a disagreement? Are you sure it was *all* that person's fault? Ask God to show you what you might have done wrong. Confess your sin to God; then go to the other person and apologize. A restored friendship will make you both happy. Don't carry old grudges into the new year. J.H.

TO MEMORIZE: *"You ought to forgive and comfort him, so that he will not be overwhelmed by excessive sorrow"* 2 Corinthians 2:7 (NIV).

JANUARY

3

More Than Forgiveness

FROM THE BIBLE:

And the Lord said to Moses, "If anyone sins by unintentionally defiling what is holy, then he shall bring a ram without defect, worth whatever fine you charge against him, as his guilt offering to the Lord. And he shall make restitution for the holy thing he has defiled, or the tithe omitted, by paying for the loss, plus a twenty percent penalty; he shall bring it to the priest, and the priest shall make atonement for him with the ram of the guilt offering, and he shall be forgiven. . . ." And the Lord said to Moses, "If anyone sins against me by refusing to return a deposit on something borrowed or rented, or by refusing to return something entrusted to him, or by robbery, or by oppressing his neighbor, or by finding a lost article and lying about it, swearing that he doesn't have it: on the day he is found guilty of any such sin, he shall restore what he took, adding a twenty percent fine, and give it to the one he has harmed; and on the same day he shall bring his guilt offering to the Tabernacle."

Leviticus 5:14-16; 6:1-5, TLB

ANDY LIKED PRAYING with his mother at bedtime. It helped to remind him that God was right there with him. One night after praying for the missionaries and for his mom and dad, he remembered something else. "Oh, forgive me, Lord," he prayed. "I didn't mean to run into Mrs. Evans's fence this afternoon. I guess I shouldn't have been cutting across her lawn. Forgive me for breaking her rosebush, too. Thank You. Amen."

After Andy's mother prayed, she kissed her son and covered him up. "Andy," she said, "you didn't mention anything to me about Mrs. Evans's fence. What happened?"

Andy frowned. "Do I have to tell you? God has forgiven me, hasn't He? I asked Him to forgive me."

"Certainly God has forgiven you," Mother assured him, "and you don't have to tell me what happened if you don't want to. But I might be able to help you make amends if you share what happened."

"Make amends? What do you mean?" Andy was puzzled.

"God's Word tells us that if our sin hurts someone else, then we must do our best to make amends—to make things right," explained Mother. "God forgives the sin if we're truly sorry and confess it, but it's up to us to do whatever we can to straighten out the situation. Perhaps you need to go and see Mrs. Evans and apologize."

Andy was quiet for a few moments. "I need to do more than that," he admitted finally. "She didn't see me break the fence or the rosebush, but I'll ask if I can pay for them."

"That's an excellent idea," Mother said. "Remember, when you ask God's forgiveness, your actions should show that you are truly sorry."

HOW ABOUT YOU? Is there someone to whom you have done something wrong? In Old Testament times, sacrifices had to be offered in such a case, and the situation had to be corrected. Since Jesus made the supreme sacrifice for all our sins, we no longer have to offer such sacrifices, but the principle of making amends is still the same. Sometimes it's embarrassing or inconvenient to make amends for our wrong actions, but it's something all Christians must do. God cannot accept our service and devotion if we refuse to correct our mistakes. C.R.

TO MEMORIZE: *"And he shall make restitution for the holy thing he has defiled"* Leviticus 5:16 (TLB).

Make amends

JANUARY

See No Evil

FROM THE BIBLE:
Do not love the world or anything in the world. If anyone loves the world, the love of the Father is not in him. For everything in the world—the cravings of sinful man, the lust of his eyes and the boasting of what he has and does—comes not from the Father but from the world. The world and its desires pass away, but the man who does the will of God lives forever. 1 John 2:15-17, NIV

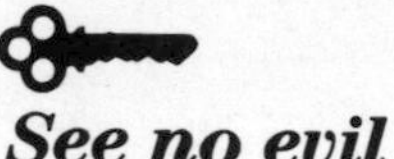

See no evil

HOLLY LOVED TELEVISION! She ran to the set and turned it on as soon as she awoke each day. When she came in from school, she watched it almost nonstop until bedtime. She didn't think TV harmed her in any way, and she wasn't very particular about what she watched. Her parents, who should have known better, didn't pay much attention to what she watched either. Many programs were bad!

After school she watched a couple of soap operas that were very immoral in words and actions. The clothing was indecent, and the people were always drinking alcohol. On Tuesday night, Holly watched a half hour comedy program in which there was a lot of swearing. When talk shows came on, Holly laughed with the audience at the dirty jokes that were told.

For the opening exercises at Sunday school one week, Holly's little sister sang, "Oh, be careful little eyes what you see. . . . For the Father up above is looking down in love, so be careful little eyes what you see!" Then the superintendent told the children they should never look at anything that they wouldn't want God to look at with them.

That week Holly didn't enjoy television so much. On one afternoon soap opera, an unmarried lady was trying to steal a married lady's husband. Holly knew God wouldn't like to look at that. She tried a game show, but her favorite celebrity was wearing a tee shirt with suggestive words on the front. God wouldn't like that either. On Tuesday evening the comedy program was only half over when Holly jumped up and turned off the set. She knew God wouldn't want to watch a program where men kept using His name in swear words. Holly felt ashamed because she suddenly realized that when she was hurt or upset, she'd been thinking dirty words. "It's because I hear them all the time on TV," she thought to herself. "Why, those programs I watch aren't good for me. From now on I'm going to be more careful about what I let my eyes see!"

HOW ABOUT YOU? Are you careful about what you let your eyes see on the television? You should choose programs that are clean and wholesome. And many times it is a good idea to turn the set off! R.P.

TO MEMORIZE: *"I will set no wicked thing before mine eyes"* Psalm 101:3.

JANUARY

5

Fox and Geese

FROM THE BIBLE:
So, if you think you are standing firm, be careful that you don't fall! No temptation has seized you except what is common to man. And God is faithful; he will not let you be tempted beyond what you can bear. But when you are tempted, he will also provide a way out so that you can stand up under it.
1 Corinthians 10:12-13, NIV

Escape from sin

AMY AND CARL had invited their friends to come over and play fox and geese. The children shuffled their feet into the snow to make a huge pie face design. It looked like a giant wheel with eight spokes running through it.

Ken volunteered to be the first fox. "Remember, the center is the safety spot," Carl instructed. "Run into it, and you are safe. But you have to use the escape spokes to get there. If the fox catches you, you're it."

The children romped in the snow until Amy and Carl were called in for lunch. "You seemed to be having a good time out there," observed Mother. "But why didn't you take turns being the fox?"

"We did," Amy said.

Mother looked surprised. "But every time I looked out, Bryan was it," she said.

Carl laughed. "That was Bryan's own fault. He always tried to get just as close to the fox as possible before he'd run. Then he got caught."

"And he never used the escape routes until it was too late," Amy added. "That was foolish."

Mother nodded. "You know," she said, "many people do the same thing in the game of life."

"The game of life? asked Carl.

"We face trials and temptations, but Jesus has given us escape routes," explained Mother. "We can run to Him for safety. But sometimes we try to get so close to sin before we run away that we get caught by that sin."

"Like the time I sat with the older kids at the assembly even though I knew they were troublemakers," Amy said.

"That's right," agreed Mother. "You could have escaped by sitting with Christian friends."

"And the time I listened to those bad jokes instead of walking away," Carl said. "Those bad thoughts hung in my mind for days."

"You've got the right idea," Mother said with a smile. "We are in the world, but we don't have to be of it. If we read God's Word, pray, and follow His commands, we'll understand the way to escape sin. We don't have to get caught."

HOW ABOUT YOU? Do you run away from sin before you get involved? You should. Ask Jesus for help. He will show you the way to escape. J.H.

TO MEMORIZE: *"God is faithful; he will not let you be tempted beyond what you can bear. But when you are tempted, he will also provide a way out so that you can stand up under it"*
1 Corinthians 10:13 (NIV).

6

How Many Bibles?

FROM THE BIBLE:

The law of the Lord is perfect,
reviving the soul.
The statutes of the Lord are trustworthy,
making wise the simple.
The precepts of the Lord are right,
giving joy to the heart.
The commands of the Lord are radiant,
giving light to the eyes.
The fear of the Lord is pure,
enduring forever.
The ordinances of the Lord are sure
and altogether righteous.
They are more precious than gold,
than much pure gold;
they are sweeter than honey,
than honey from the comb.
By them is your servant warned;
in keeping them there is great reward.
Psalm 19:7-11, NIV

Appreciate the Bible

"I'VE GOT the Gideon New Testament they gave us in school, and the Rainbow Bible Mom and Dad gave each of us when we turned five, and the ones they gave us at Sunday school when we got promoted from primaries to juniors," Tim called from his room to Tina's.

"Did you count the one you got for memorizing all those verses in vacation Bible school?" Tina yelled back.

"Twins! Twins!" called their father from the foot of the stairs. "What is all the shouting about up there?"

Tina ran to the top of the steps. "Oh, Daddy, the man who spoke to our Bible club today told us to go home and count the number of Bibles we have," she explained. "He said there are people in communist countries who would give a whole six months' wages just to get a part of the Scriptures in their own language. Tim has four Bibles of his own, and I've found three so far."

"Well, let's do it with a little less noise," suggested Dad.

Later, the twins came downstairs with a list they had made. "Daddy," Tim asked, "may we please go into your study to count your Bibles?"

"Yes," Dad said, "and don't forget that huge antique family Bible of Mother's."

That evening Tina and Tim told the rest of their family that they had discovered twenty-two Bibles in their home. "Tina thinks we have more than most people because Dad's a preacher," said Tim.

"Probably," Mother said with a nod, "but I'm sure most Christians in this country have several."

"It's hard to realize that some Christians don't have the freedom to read God's Word whenever they wish," said Dad. "And then we also have to remember that there are some countries where people can't have Bibles because it's never been translated into their language."

The children hadn't thought of that. How blessed they were! That night the family thanked God for all their freedoms and for the availability of God's Word. They prayed for Christians living in countries where God's Word is not honored. They also prayed that the Bible would be available soon to everyone in his own language.

HOW ABOUT YOU? Do you take your Bible for granted? Never forget to be thankful for the Bible. Pray for those who are not blessed as you are. R.P.

TO MEMORIZE: *"Humbly accept the word planted in you, which can save you"* James 1:21 (NIV).

JANUARY

7

The Strange Bird

FROM THE BIBLE:
Three years after King Jehoiakim began to rule in Judah, Babylon's King Nebuchadnezzar attacked Jerusalem with his armies, and the Lord gave him victory over Jehoiakim. Then he ordered Ashpenaz, who was in charge of his palace personnel, to select some of the Jewish youths brought back as captives—young men of the royal family and nobility of Judah—and to teach them the Chaldean language and literature. "Pick strong, healthy, good-looking lads," he said; "those who have read widely in many fields, are well informed, alert and sensible, and have enough poise to look good around the palace." The king assigned them the best of food and wine from his own kitchen during their three-year training period, planning to make them his counselors when they graduated. . . . But Daniel made up his mind not to eat the food and wine given to them by the king. He asked the superintendent for permission to eat other things instead.
Daniel 1:1-6, 8, TLB

Always stand for right

"HI, MOM," said Ryan as he hung up his jacket. "We had fun at Boy Scouts today. We're working on our bird badge. Did you know that a mockingbird has been known to change its tune eighty-seven times in seven minutes? What a strange bird!"

"That's amazing," agreed Mother. "Amazing and rather wonderful."

The next day Mother overheard two conversations while waiting for Ryan after his basketball game. Jim, one of Ryan's teammates, approached him. "Hey, Ryan, I stole a pack of my dad's cigarettes," said Jim. "Wanna meet me at that old empty ware house near my place for an after-dinner smoke?"

"Sounds like fun," said Ryan, "but I can't. I have to go some place." Jim ran off to find someone else to join him.

As Ryan turned, he bumped into Tad, a boy from his Sunday school class. "Hey, Ryan," said Tad, "you wanna hear something? Jim stole a pack of his dad's cigarettes."

"I know," interrupted Ryan. "And they call that fun?"

On the way home in the car, Mother asked, "How's my 'strange bird' doing today?"

"What do you mean?" Ryan looked confused.

"You know—my mockingbird," said Mother. Then she explained. "I'm really pleased that you didn't agree to meet Jim tonight, but I did hear a 'little bird' I know change his tune pretty quickly this afternoon. 'Sounds like fun,' he said one minute, and the next minute he said, 'They call that fun?' "

"Oh, that," replied Ryan sheepishly as he slid down in his seat a little. He knew he should have told Jim right out why he wouldn't come. He sat up straighter as they neared home. "I'm gonna tell Jim the real reason I wouldn't join him," he said firmly. "I'll call him as soon as we get home." And he did.

HOW ABOUT YOU? Do you change your tune like a mockingbird, depending on what other "birds" you are near? It's difficult to take a stand for what you really believe to be right when your friends don't agree, but with God's help, it is possible. Daniel did it. You can, too! P.R.

TO MEMORIZE: *"But Daniel made up his mind not to eat the food and wine given to them by the king"* Daniel 1:8 (TLB).

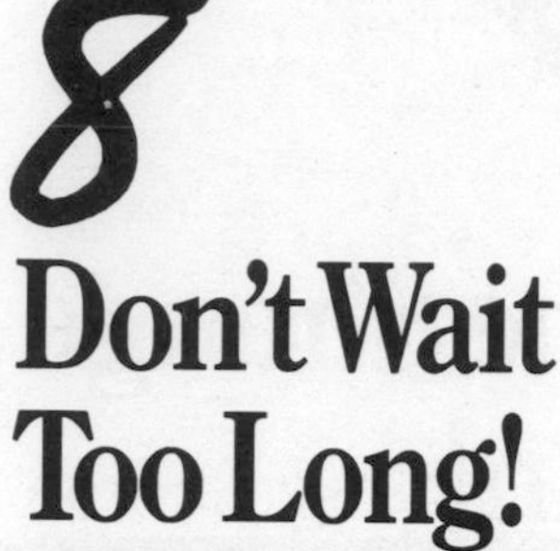

Don't Wait Too Long!

FROM THE BIBLE:
And since Christ is so much superior, the Holy Spirit warns us to listen to him, to be careful to hear his voice today and not let our hearts become set against him, as the people of Israel did. They steeled themselves against his love and complained against him in the desert while he was testing them. But God was patient with them forty years, though they tried his patience sorely; he kept right on doing his mighty miracles for them to see. "But," God says, "I was very angry with them, for their hearts were always looking somewhere else instead of up to me, and they never found the paths I wanted them to follow." . . . Beware then of your own hearts, dear brothers, lest you find that they, too, are evil and unbelieving and are leading you away from the living God. Speak to each other about these things every day while there is still time, so that none of you will become hardened against God, being blinded by the glamor of sin.
Hebrews 3:7-10, 12-13, TLB

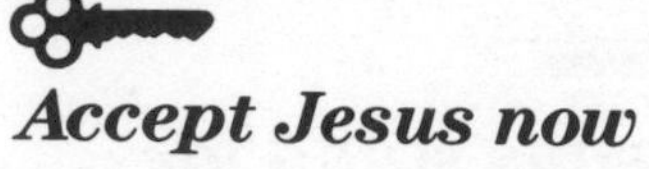

Accept Jesus now

ONE SUNDAY MORNING at the church Jeremy attended, the pastor made an announcement. "We have a visitor with us today, Mr. Peter Black," he said. "Mr. Black would like to share his testimony of what the Lord has done in his life."

As the middle-aged man stood up and began to speak, Jeremy could hardly believe his ears. Why, this man had been a criminal—in and out of prison for about twenty years! Now he was a Christian and spent most of his free time telling other people about Jesus. *How exciting!* thought Jeremy. *I wish I had a testimony like that!*

After church Jeremy's parents invited Mr. Black to their home for dinner. As they sat at the table, the guest smiled at Jeremy and said, "Your mother tells me that you're a Christian, too."

"That's right," said Jeremy, feeling embarrassed. "I was only five when I asked Jesus into my heart. I didn't have any really big sins in my life, so I don't have an exciting story to tell like you do."

A sad look came over Mr. Black's face. "Son, let me tell you something," he said. "I am forty-two years old. I have spent nearly half of my life in jail. Because of my prison record, I have a hard time finding a job. I have been married and divorced twice and have three children who hardly even know me. My health is poor because of all the drinking I did over the years. You see," he continued, "although I finally did accept the Lord, that didn't undo all the terrible consequences of the sins in my life. Be thankful that you came to know Him early!"

I do thank you, Lord, Jeremy prayed silently. *Thank You for saving me as a little boy—so that I have a whole life ahead to use for You!*

HOW ABOUT YOU? Did you accept Christ as your Savior at a young age? If so, take time to thank Him now, and determine to live your whole life in His service. If you've put off accepting the Lord, don't wait any longer. Accept Him today. You may not have another opportunity. If you wait, your sins may leave scars that you will carry with you all your life. Don't wait too long! S.K.

TO MEMORIZE: *"Behold, now is the accepted time; behold, now is the day of salvation"*
2 Corinthians 6:2.

JANUARY

Take the Garbage Out

FROM THE BIBLE:

Come and hear, all who fear God,
And I will tell of what He has done for my soul.
I cried to Him with my mouth,
And He was extolled with my tongue.
If I regard wickedness in my heart,
The Lord will not hear;
But certainly God has heard;
He has given heed to the voice of my prayer.
Blessed be God,
Who has not turned away my prayer,
Nor His lovingkindness from me.

Psalm 66:16-20, NASB

Leave sin, then pray

"IS DAD HOME yet?" Jason asked eagerly one afternoon. "Mr. Williams, down at the hardware store, is looking for someone to help with sweeping and cleaning for an hour or so after school each day. He said to talk it over with Dad, and if it's OK with him, the job is mine!"

Mother smiled. "Dad will be here soon, but before he comes you'd better take the garbage out. He told you to do it this morning."

"Yeah, OK," agreed Jason as he took off his coat and went to his room. Soon he heard Dad come in, so he hurried to the kitchen. "Dad," he said, "I want to ask you about something."

"All right," said Dad, "but I see you didn't take the garbage out yet. Do that first." Dad left to wash his hands.

As soon as Dad reappeared, Jason tried again. "I have a chance to get a job."

"I see the garbage is still there," came Dad's reply.

"I know. I'll get it in a minute. But—"

Dad frowned. "You've had lot of minutes already," he said as he began reading the newspaper.

"Dad, can't we talk?" whined Jason.

Dad looked up. "We can as soon as you take the garbage out," he replied firmly.

Jason stood silently for a moment, then he quickly got to work and took care of the garbage. "There. I'm sorry I didn't do it sooner," he said when the job was done. Dad smiled as he listened to Jason tell about his job opportunity.

For family devotions later that evening, Dad asked Jason to read aloud from Psalm 66. When he finished reading, Jason grinned at his dad. "I know what it means when it says God won't hear us if we have sin in our hearts. That's just like you, Dad. You wouldn't listen to me until I took out the garbage. And God won't listen to us until we get rid of the garbage of sin in our lives."

Dad grinned back at Jason. "You're right, Son," he said. "That's an important lesson for us to learn."

HOW ABOUT YOU? Does God seem far, far away? Do you feel like nobody is listening when you pray? Maybe God is saying, "Take out the garbage, and then I'll listen." Are you clinging to cheating? Swearing? Disobedience? Whatever it is, get rid of it. You cannot expect God to answer your prayers when you deliberately sin. H.M.

TO MEMORIZE: *"If I regard wickedness in my heart, the Lord will not hear"* Psalm 66:18 (NASB).

JANUARY

10

Well-Protected

FROM THE BIBLE:

He will cover you with his
feathers,
and under his wings you will
find refuge;
his faithfulness will be your
shield and rampart. . . .
If you make the Most High
your dwelling—
even the Lord, who is my
refuge—
then no harm will befall you,
no disaster will come near
your tent.

Psalm 91:4, 9-10, NIV

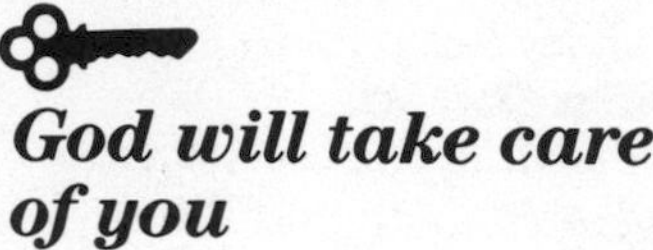

God will take care of you

"OOOOH! I don't feel good," moaned Shelly as she came to the breakfast table. "Can't I just stay home today?" She sat down and clutched her stomach.

"I don't believe you have a fever," said Mother as she felt her daughter's forehead, "but if you really don't feel well, I suppose you should stay home."

Later that morning Mother was making cookies, and Shelly joined her in the kitchen. "Oh, let me help!" she exclaimed. Putting on one of Mother's aprons, Shelly squealed as one of the eggs broke and slid down her arm and onto the floor. "Oh, I never will learn to do this right! It's a good thing I have a big apron on."

"It certainly is!" agreed Mother, laughing as she helped clean up the mess. Looking at Shelly thoughtfully, she said, "The stomachache seems to have disappeared." As Shelly nodded, Mother continued, "Do you think you really were sick, honey, or were you just nervous about going to a new school?"

"Oh, Mother," burst out Shelly, "I wish we had never moved! I feel so strange in this school, and I don't have any friends. I don't know *anybody.*"

"It will get better," Mother assured her. "You know, it's a good thing you had the protection of that apron as we made cookies. But are you aware that you also have protection as you go to school?" Shelly looked surprised as Mother continued, "You're a Christian, a child of God, and He is your protection. The Book of Psalms says, 'He shall cover thee with his feathers, and under his wings shalt thou trust.' God will take care of you, even in a new school and among many new faces. Remember, He is with you always."

Shelly nodded slowly. "Ann and Barb were really friendly yesterday. I guess I'll go this afternoon and take them a cookie," she decided. "It shouldn't be so bad if I just remember I'm well-protected."

HOW ABOUT YOU? What are your afraid of? A new school? A difficult class? A school bully? The dark? If you're a Christian, God is your protection in whatever situation you face. Trust Him. H.M.

TO MEMORIZE: *"The LORD is my light and my salvation; whom shall I fear?"* Psalm 27:1.

11

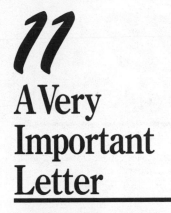

A Very Important Letter

FROM THE BIBLE:
I thank my God upon every remembrance of you, always in every prayer of mine making request for you all with joy, for your fellowship in the gospel from the first day until now, being confident of this very thing, that He who has begun a good work in you will complete it until the day of Jesus Christ; just as it is right for me to think this of you all, because I have you in my heart, inasmuch as both in my chains and in the defense and confirmation of the gospel, you all are partakers with me of grace.
Philippians 1:3-7, NKJV

Write to missionaries

SANDY-HAIRED JAMIE chewed the end of her pencil as she tried to think of something to write next. "Whatcha doin'?" asked her brother, Josh. "Is that your homework?"

Jamie shook her head. "No, I'm writing a letter to Mr. Sandborn," she said. "He's the missionary who came and spoke at our church last fall."

"He probably doesn't even remember you," said Josh.

"I know," replied Jamie, "but I thought he might like to get a letter since he's not married and works all alone in that village."

Some days later, in a small, run-down hut, a missionary sighed in the sweltering heat and sat down at the table. He was tired and discouraged. The work progressed so slowly, and sometimes it seemed that he might just as well go back home and give up his missionary work. He looked at the mail in his hand. Letters were scarce, and he especially wondered about the long envelope addressed in a child's unfamiliar handwriting.

He smoothed out the letter and began to read. "Dear Mr. Sandborn," it said, "I just wanted to tell you we're all thinking of you and praying for you. I liked it when you came to our church last fall. I hope you're having a good time there." The missionary smiled as he continued reading. "I remember the things you told us about having faith in God. I will try to have more faith. Because of you, I think I would like to be a missionary some day. Thank you for your help. Love, Jamie."

Mr. Sandborn sat for a few moments, and then he breathed a prayer of thanks for the encouragement of that simple letter. *Perhaps this is God's way of letting me know He intends to use my ministry here,* he thought. *Maybe I need more faith, too.*

He smiled as he looked out the window at the village children playing in the sand. Then he took out a piece of paper. He had to write a thank you letter to a very important person.

HOW ABOUT YOU? Have you thought about ways you could encourage the missionaries you know? Even a child can write a simple letter to a missionary. You may never know just how much it means to someone far away. Why not write one this week? S.K.

TO MEMORIZE: *"As cold waters to a thirsty soul, so is good news from a far country"* Proverbs 25:25.

JANUARY

12

Noisy Kids!

FROM THE BIBLE:

Guard your steps when you go to the house of God. Go near to listen rather than to offer the sacrifice of fools, who do not know that they do wrong. Do not be quick with your mouth, do not be hasty in your heart to utter anything before God. God is in heaven and you are on earth, so let your words be few. As a dream comes when there are many cares, so the speech of a fool when there are many words. When you make a vow to God, do not delay in fulfilling it. He has no pleasure in fools; fulfill your vow. It is better not to vow than to make a vow and not fulfill it. Do not let your mouth lead you into sin. And do not protest to the temple messenger, "My vow was a mistake." Why should God be angry at what you say and destroy the work of your hands? Much dreaming and many words are meaningless. Therefore stand in awe of God. If you see the poor oppressed in a district, and justice and rights denied, do not be surprised at such things; for one official is eyed by a higher one, and over them both are others higher still.

Ecclesiastes 5:1-8, NIV

Be polite in church

"I HEARD some sad news at the church board meeting last night," Mr. Lansing told his son, Gary.

"You did?" Gary looked up. "What was it, Dad?"

"It involves a family who moved into the yellow brick house on Elm Street," Dad told him. "Their name is Peterson. Last Sunday they attended our church, and on Monday night Pastor Helms visited them." That didn't sound sad to Gary. That sounded happy! It was neat to see new people come to church. Gary listened as Dad went on. "They said they liked Pastor Helms's message, at least what they heard of it. The sad part is that three boys were sitting behind them, talking and laughing during the entire service. The Petersons told Pastor Helms they were going to look for another church.

"That's too bad," Gary said. And then he remembered that some new people had been sitting in front of him and his friends this past Sunday! He slowly realized why his dad was telling him about the Petersons. He was one of those who had been talking!

"Son, we've told you before that it's not only important to listen for what you can get out of a message, but it is just plain bad manners to disturb those around you! For the next month you will sit with Mom and me. If you do sit with your friends again after that, you will sit farther front than Mom and I do, not behind us."

Gary nodded numbly. "Yes, Dad." For the rest of the day he thought about what had happened. He knew what he'd have to do. He'd have to go to the Petersons' house and apologize to them for making so much noise. He'd also invite them to come to church again.

HOW ABOUT YOU? Do you listen quietly during church? There have been many occasions when people haven't come back to a church because of the whispering during the service. Sit still. Be polite to those who are around you. Welcome new people instead of being rude to them! L. W.

TO MEMORIZE: *"Guard your steps when you go to the house of God. Go near to listen"* Ecclesiates 5:1 (NIV).

JANUARY

13

Noisy Kids!

(Continued from yesterday)

FROM THE BIBLE:

Teach me, O Lord, to follow
your decrees;
then I will keep them to the
end.
Give me understanding, and
I will keep your law
and obey it with all my heart.
Direct me in the path of your
commands,
for there I find delight.
Turn my heart toward your
statutes
and not toward selfish gain.
Turn my eyes away from
worthless things;
preserve my life according
to your word.
Fulfill your promise to your
servant,
so that you may be feared.
Take away the disgrace I dread,
for your laws are good.
How I long for your precepts!
Preserve my life in your
righteousness.
Psalm 119:33-40, NIV

Take sermon notes

GARY FELT GOOD. Even though it had been hard to do, he had gone and apologized to the Petersons and asked them to visit the church once again. They agreed, and they even gave Gary a friendly "Hi" as they walked in the door the next Sunday.

Before the service started, Gary's dad handed him a notebook and a pen. "I want you to write down ten truths that the pastor gives in his message today," Dad instructed him. "I think you'll find that note-keeping is helpful."

Gary was surprised. He didn't think he'd be able to understand the pastor's message, but he nodded and took the notebook. He listened attentively, and before long he found himself actually enjoying the sermon! By the end of the service, Gary had written down twelve important thoughts—two more than his dad had told him to write! He realized that he hadn't been able to understand before because he hadn't even tried to listen!

After church Gary showed the pastor his notes. "I'm going to do this every week, Pastor Helms," he said. "I'll suggest to the other kids that they try it, too!" Gary felt good. Not only had the Petersons come back to church, but he had learned a good way to listen to the pastor's sermons and to understand them.

HOW ABOUT YOU? Do you take notes on your pastor's sermons? Even if you just write down the Scripture he uses, or the main topic, it will help you to remember what he says. If he uses a word you don't understand, write that down on a piece of paper and ask him to explain it after church. He'll be glad to help you. You could also ask your dad and mom to discuss the message with you. They can help you understand, too. L.W.

TO MEMORIZE: *"Do your best to present yourself to God as one approved, a workman who does not need to be ashamed and who correctly handles the word of truth"* 2 Timothy 2:15 (NIV).

JANUARY

14

I'll Do It

FROM THE BIBLE:

"But what do you think about this? A man with two sons told the older boy, 'Son, go out and work on the farm today.' 'I won't,' he answered, but later he changed his mind and went. Then the father told the youngest, 'You go!' and he said, 'Yes, sir, I will.' But he didn't. Which of the two was obeying his father?" They replied, "The first, of course." Then Jesus explained his meaning: "Surely evil men and prostitutes will get into the Kingdom before you do. For John the Baptist told you to repent and turn to God, and you wouldn't, while very evil men and prostitutes did. And even when you saw this happening, you refused to repent, and so you couldn't believe."

Matthew 21:28-32, TLB

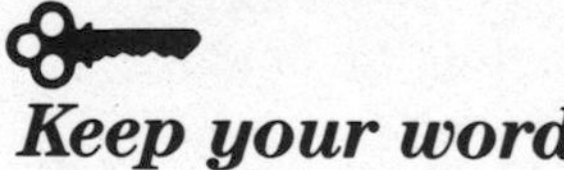

Keep your word

WHEN MRS. BROWN asked Paul to distribute invitations to the after-school Bible club in her home, he agreed readily. "I'd like these passed out today," explained Mrs. Brown. "The club starts the day after tomorrow."

"No problem," said Paul, and he took several invitations. "I can easily do it tonight."

Mrs. Brown looked grateful. "This really helps me out."

"I'm going to pass these out for Mrs. Brown," Paul told his mother when he got home. Then he laid the invitations on an end table and went out to play. After supper he did his homework and worked on his model car, completely forgetting about the invitations. The next day, while dusting the furniture, Mother found them.

After school that day, Paul came bursting into the house. Not noticing the stern look on Mother's face, he began to tell her his problem. "That Rick!" he exploded angrily. "He told me he'd return a book to the library for me, and he didn't do it! Now I have to pay a fine. I think he should . . ." His voice trailed off when he saw the invitations in Mother's hand. Before she could say a word, he murmured, "But, Mom, I forgot."

"Paul, I'm disappointed that you didn't do the job you said you'd do," said Mother. "I think your experience with Rick today is a good lesson on the importance of doing what you promise. If you can't or don't want to help, say so right away. Don't say you'll do something, causing someone to depend on you, and then fail him or her. When you do that, you're failing God, too."

"I know it's late, but I'll still run around the neighborhood with these right now—before I have a snack," said Paul. "I'm really sorry, and I'll apologize to Mrs. Brown, too. Be back soon, Mom."

HOW ABOUT YOU? Are you faithful to do whatever you said you'd do? It's easy to make quick promises, but not so easy to carry them out. Make sure you follow through on promises made to others. God always keeps His promises, and He wants us to be like Him. C.Y.

TO MEMORIZE: *"Dear friend, you are faithful in what you are doing for the brothers"*
3 John 5 (NIV).

JANUARY

15

Here's My Gift

FROM THE BIBLE:

"As for you, my son Solomon, know the God of your father, and serve Him with a loyal heart and with a willing mind; for the Lord searches all hearts and understands all the intent of the thoughts. If you seek Him, He will be found by you; but if you forsake Him, He will cast you off forever."
1 Chronicles 28:9, NKJV

And David said to his son Solomon, "Be strong and of good courage, and do it; do not fear nor be dismayed, for the Lord God—my God—will be with you. He will not leave you nor forsake you, until you have finished all the work for the service of the house of the Lord."
1 Chronicles 28:20, NKJV

Serve God cheerfully

CHRISTA ENJOYED occasionally playing the piano for the opening exercises in Sunday school. But then Ken asked her to accompany his trumpet solo at Bible club. "I suppose I can," she agreed reluctantly. Ken suggested times when they could practice, but she found she was either busy or unwilling to give up her free time. Finally she agreed to run over the piece just before the program.

During the next few months, Mother noticed that Christa was often invited to play for various groups. She usually agreed to play, but she did so without much enthusiasm. Her face often looked gloomy, and she grumbled about how busy it made her. "Is it really so bad?" Mother asked.

Christa scowled. "You always tell me I should use my gift of music for the Lord, but now that I'm using it, you're still not satisfied." She sighed impatiently and left the room.

That evening Christa spoke to her older brother, Bill, as he left the dinner table. "Would you help me with my math? I just don't understand it."

"I've got things to do," Bill replied.

"But I have a test tomorrow, and you explain it so well. Please help me," pleaded Christa.

"I want to work on my models tonight," protested Bill. "Call one of your friends to help you."

"I'm sure you can take a little time to help your sister," suggested Mother.

"Oh, all right," Bill growled. "I'll be in my room. Call when you need me." He stomped out.

"Oh, Mother!" wailed Christa. "When he's so grouchy about it, I don't even feel like having him help me. But I do need help. Why can't he be pleasant about it?"

"Are you always pleasant when people ask you to do something?" asked Mother gently.

Christa blushed as she remembered how unhappily she had promised to play for someone just that afternoon. "I know what you mean," she admitted. "I guess playing the piano unwillingly isn't really using my gift for the Lord at all, is it? I'm going to do it more cheerfully from now on!"

HOW ABOUT YOU? Are you grumpy when you are asked to serve in some way? Solomon was told to serve God with a "perfect heart and with a willing mind." That's good advice for Christians, too. You should be happy to serve the Lord who has done so much for you. H.M.

TO MEMORIZE: *"Serve the LORD with gladness"* Psalm 100:2.

JANUARY

16

PK

FROM THE BIBLE:

How we praise God, the Father of our Lord Jesus Christ, who has blessed us with every blessing in heaven because we belong to Christ. Long ago, even before he made the world, God chose us to be his very own, through what Christ would do for us; he decided then to make us holy in his eyes, without a single fault—we who stand before him covered with his love. His unchanging plan has always been to adopt us into his own family by sending Jesus Christ to die for us. And he did this because he wanted to! Now all praise to God for his wonderful kindness to us and his favor that he has poured out upon us, because we belong to his dearly loved Son. So overflowing is his kindness toward us that he took away all our sins through the blood of his Son, by whom we are saved; and he has showered down upon us the richness of his grace—for how well he understands us and knows what is best for us at all times.
Ephesians 1:3-8, TLB

Christians are privileged

PAUL HEADED for the church. The fellows there were talking loudly, but when he approached, they got quiet. "What's up?" Paul asked.

"Nothing, since *you* got here," Buck muttered. "We gotta be careful what we say or do around a PK—a preacher's kid. They're fragile—right, guys?" The boys laughed, but Paul was embarrassed.

That evening Paul complained to his dad. "I get tired of being teased and left out of activities just because you're a preacher," he said. "I wish you had some other job."

The following day, Paul had an accident with his bike and broke his leg. His parents stayed at the hospital with him as long as they could and prayed with him before leaving. By the next day, his bedside table was filled with cards, games, and books from people in the church. Others stopped to visit and pray with him. "You sure get a lot of attention," observed his roommate, Kyle.

"I guess it's because my dad's a preacher," Paul said, "and a lot of people know me."

"You're lucky to have a dad who prays for you," replied Kyle. "All my dad does is yell at me, and he's done plenty of that since this accident. You're a privileged kid, Paul."

Paul was quiet on his way home from the hospital a few days later. "What's wrong, Son?" asked his dad.

"Well, I've always thought that 'PK' meant 'preacher's kid,' and I've always complained a lot about that, especially when other kids made a big deal about it," Paul said. "But now I see that it means 'privileged kid,' too. I know now that I have special privileges that I've taken for granted."

HOW ABOUT YOU? Are you a PK—a privileged kid? You are if you're a Christian. Maybe you feel left out when you see some of the things other kids do. Maybe you sometimes think being a Christian is a chore, especially if kids make fun of you. Don't fret over the world's reaction to your faith, and don't envy the world's goods and pleasures. You are richly blessed. Your sins are forgiven, you're on your way to heaven, your heavenly Father cares for you, and He answers prayer. He's all you need. J.H.

TO MEMORIZE: *"But ye are a chosen generation, a royal priesthood, an holy nation, a peculiar people"* 1 Peter 2:9.

JANUARY

17

Is That Me?

FROM THE BIBLE:

Dear brothers, I have been talking to you as though you were still just babies in the Christian life, who are not following the Lord, but your own desires; I cannot talk to you as I would to healthy Christians, who are filled with the Spirit. I have had to feed you with milk and not with solid food, because you couldn't digest anything stronger. And even now you still have to be fed on milk. For you are still only baby Christians, controlled by your own desires, not God's. When you are jealous of one another and divide up into quarreling groups, doesn't that prove you are still babies, wanting your own way? In fact, you are acting like people who don't belong to the Lord at all. There you are, quarreling about whether I am greater than Apollos, and dividing the church. Doesn't this show how little you have grown in the Lord? Who am I, and who is Apollos, that we should be the cause of a quarrel? Why, we're just God's servants, each of us with certain special abilities, and with our help you believed.

1 Corinthians 3:1-5, TLB

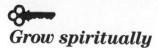

Grow spiritually

"I DIDN'T really understand the pastor's message," said Keith on Sunday afternoon. "He said the people in the church at Corinth were babies. Weren't there any adults?"

"I have something that might help you understand," Mom said, smiling. "I came across a cassette tape this week that you might like to hear." She put a tape in the player and turned it on.

Keith heard some giggles, and then Dad started talking. "Welcome to the Browns. It's September 16, and Keith is three years old. He's going to tell us what he did in Sunday school today."

Keith heard more giggles and then, "I builded with blocks, and . . . and we sanged, and I sanged loud, and my teacher telled a story."

"Is that really me talking?" Keith laughed as the babyish voice went on to recite the ABCs. "I sound so little!"

"You *were* little, Keith," agreed Mother.

"That's a funny tape," Keith said when it had stopped, "but what does that have to do with the pastor's message?"

"Well, Keith," said Mom, "it would be silly if you talked that way now, wouldn't it?"

"Sure." He grinned. "I've grown up since then."

"That's right," Mom agreed, "and now you talk and act differently from when you were little. You see, Keith, many of the people in Corinth had been Christians for a long time, but they still were acting like babies, spiritually. They had accepted Christ as Savior, but instead of studying the Scripture, they were arguing over whether Paul or Apollos was the better preacher. You see, Son, just as it's important to grow physically, it is also important to grow spiritually."

"Oh, I see," Keith said, nodding. He paused and then added, "I want to grow spiritually just like I've grown physically. I'd hate to sound like a baby Christian all my life."

HOW ABOUT YOU? Have you been a Christian very long? Have you been growing spiritually or do you still act like a baby in the Lord? You should know more about the Bible this year than you did last year. Spiritual growth comes by talking to God, reading your Bible, and serving the Lord. Make sure these things are part of your life. L.W.

TO MEMORIZE: *"Like newborn babies, crave pure spiritual milk, so that by it you may grow up in your salvation"* 1 Peter 2:2 (NIV).

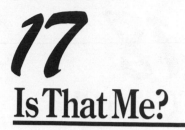

JANUARY

18

Cat in the Window

FROM THE BIBLE:
Don't worry about anything; instead, pray about everything; tell God your needs and don't forget to thank him for his answers. If you do this you will experience God's peace, which is far more wonderful than the human mind can understand. His peace will keep your thoughts and your hearts quiet and at rest as you trust in Christ Jesus. Not that I was ever in need, for I have learned how to get along happily whether I have much or little. I know how to live on almost nothing or with everything. I have learned the secret of contentment in every situation, whether it be a full stomach or hunger, plenty or want; for I can do everything God asks me to with the help of Christ who gives me the strength and power.
Philippians 4:6-7, 11-13, TLB

Be content with Christ

JUDY AND JACK were sitting together on the couch, looking at a new catalog. Mother sat in the armchair, knitting. After a while, Judy sighed and pointed to a picture. "Mother," she whined, "I still want an outfit like this one. Wouldn't my friends at church be impressed!"

"And I want one of these talking robots," said Jack, turning several pages. "See? It's voice-activated and everything! Couldn't you get one for me? It's not all that expensive!"

Just then, they heard a noise. "Meowrrr!" It was Fluffy, their cat, sitting on the windowsill.

"Look at him!" Judy laughed. "He's watching those birds out in the front yard again."

"That dumb cat," said Jack. "By this time he ought to know that he can't get those birds through the window."

Mother looked at Fluffy. The cat's tail was twitching with excitement as he stared intently at the birds he couldn't reach. "Fluffy *is* silly, isn't he," she agreed. Then she added, "Almost as silly as two children I know."

"Us?" asked Jack. "What do you mean?"

"Fluffy is making himself miserable by longing for something he can't have," explained Mother. "You and Judy have the same problem. You both know we can't afford to buy anything new right now because of Dad's job situation, yet you persist in thinking about the things you can't have instead of enjoying what you do have. I'd say you were at least as silly as Fluffy."

The children were silent for a moment. Then Jack put the catalog down. "We're sorry, Mom," he said. "Come on, Judy. Let's go play that new game we got for Christmas."

HOW ABOUT YOU? Are there things you would like, but you know you can't have them right now? Don't allow your mind to dwell on these things. God wants you to realize that He is enough to make you happy. Also, He sees the dangers and problems that would come if you always got your way. Be content with what He gives you. S.K.

TO MEMORIZE: *"Be content with such things as you have"* Hebrews 13:5 (NKJV).

JANUARY

19

Garbage In— Garbage Out

FROM THE BIBLE:

Jesus said to them, "I tell you the truth, unless you eat the flesh of the Son of Man and drink his blood, you have no life in you. Whoever eats my flesh and drinks my blood has eternal life, and I will raise him up at the last day. For my flesh is real food and my blood is real drink. Whoever eats my flesh and drinks my blood remains in me, and I in him. Just as the living Father sent me and I live because of the Father, so the one who feeds on me will live because of me. This is the bread that came down from heaven. Your forefathers ate manna and died, but he who feeds on this bread will live forever."

John 6:53-58, NIV

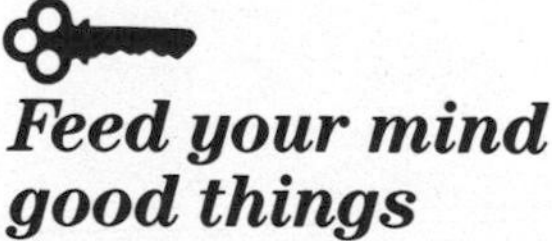

Feed your mind good things

BETH WAS UPSET with herself. She couldn't remember ever using bad words before. But lately whenever she got angry or things didn't go her way, the first thing that came to her mind was terrible, foul language. One evening Beth was helping Mom do the dishes, she dropped a glass and broke it, and a swear word slipped out.

Mom looked at her in shock! "Why, Beth! Whatever has gotten into you?"

Beth began to cry as she tried to explain. "I don't know! I *am* a Christian, but lately I can't seem to control what I think and say."

"Sounds to me like you're being programmed wrongly," suggested Mom.

"What do you mean?" asked Beth.

"Well, do you remember the first day you used a computer? I believe you were taught the concept of 'garbage in—garbage out.' "

"Sure," Beth answered. "The teacher said that if we put wrong information—'garbage'—into the computer, then all we can get out of it is wrong information. Once I was stuck on a problem because I had put wrong information into the computer."

Mom nodded. "It's the same with your mind," she explained. "What you program into it is what eventually comes out of it through your speech. In other words, if you read the wrong kind of literature, watch TV programs with foul language or immoral ideas, and run around with kids who swear, that's the 'program' going into your mind."

"Oooh," said Beth thoughtfully. "Just as I had to replace the 'garbage' program in the computer with correct information, so I have to replace the 'garbage' programs my mind has been receiving with good material. I guess I would do that by listening to good programs and running around with Christian friends."

"That's the idea," Mom said, smiling, "and also through Bible reading and prayer. Then I'm sure you won't have a problem with what comes out of your mouth."

HOW ABOUT YOU? Do you ever find yourself saying bad words when you really don't want to? Today's memory verse may sound strange to you, but it has a lesson for you. You "eat" by programming your mind with Jesus—through reading and meditating on the Bible and through prayer. Then He will help you to "live by" Him—in other words, live the way He wants you to. R.P.

TO MEMORIZE: *"The one who feeds on me will live because of me"* John 6:57 (NIV).

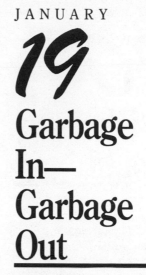

20

I Wish I Could

FROM THE BIBLE:

"Here comes that master-dreamer," they exclaimed. "Come on, let's kill him and toss him in to a well and tell father that a wild animal has eaten him. Then we'll see what will become of all his dreams!" But Reuben hoped to spare Joseph's life. "Let's not kill him," he said; "we'll shed no blood—let's throw him alive into this well here; that way he'll die without our touching him!" (Reuben was planning to get him out later and return him to his father.) So when Joseph got there, they pulled off his brightly-colored robe, and threw him into an empty well—there was no water in it. Then they sat down for supper. Suddenly they noticed a string of camels coming towards them in the distance, probably Ishmaelite traders. . . . "Look there," Judah said to the others. "Here come some Ishmaelites. Let's sell Joseph to them! Why kill him and have a guilty conscience? Let's not be responsible for his death, for, after all, he is our brother!" And his brothers agreed.

Genesis 37:19-27, TLB

Don't envy another's talent

JODY PUT her hands over her ears and intently read the bulletin on her lap. She didn't want to hear her friend, Laura, play the piano solo. After church everyone would talk about how Laura had mastered the piano, and Jody didn't want to hear that, either. She was envious, that was all there was to it! She wished *she* could play in church.

That week, the annual all-school track meet was held at Jody's school. All the classes were competing against one another in running events. Jody confidently waited on the sidelines. She had been chosen to run the cross-country race. She had always been the fastest runner in her class.

"You running the last event?" Jody turned to see Laura standing next to her.

"Probably."

"I wish I could run as fast as you do," said Laura. She sighed. "I can't even beat a turtle."

Jody looked at Laura in surprise. After a moment, she laughed. "That's funny. I always wished I could play the piano as well as you do, and at the same time you were wishing you could run as fast as I could."

Laura grinned. "I guess we've both been pretty silly."

"I even tried not to listen last Sunday," confessed Jody, "but I heard you anyway. You did a great job."

"Thanks," said Laura, just as Jody's teacher came to get her for the next race. "Hope you win your race."

When Jody got home that afternoon, she told her mother about her conversation with Laura. Mother smiled. "Our job is to use the abilities God gave us the best way we know how. We should not waste our time wishing we could do something someone else is doing," said Mother. "I think you and Laura both learned an important lesson."

HOW ABOUT YOU? Have you ever wished you could write, play an instrument, or draw as well as someone else could? Have you ever disliked someone because of his or her abilities? Today's Scripture gives an example of terrible sin that resulted from envy. Remember, God made each person unique and gave each one different abilities. Don't be envious of someone else's talent. Instead, be happy with the talent you have. L.W.

TO MEMORIZE: *"Love is kind and is not jealous; love does not brag and is not arrogant"* 1 Corinthians 13:4 (NASB).

JANUARY

21

Dangerous Games

FROM THE BIBLE:

You adulterous people, don't you know that friendship with the world is hatred toward God? Anyone who chooses to be a friend of the world becomes an enemy of God. Or do you think Scripture says without reason that the spirit he caused to live in us envies intensely? But he gives us more grace. That is why Scripture says: "God opposes the proud but gives grace to the humble." Submit yourselves, then, to God. Resist the devil, and he will flee from you. Come near to God and he will come near to you. Wash your hands, you sinners, and purify your hearts, you double-minded. Grieve, mourn and wail. Change your laughter to mourning and your joy to gloom. Humble yourselves before the Lord, and he will lift you up. James 4:4-10, NIV

AS CARRIE AND DAD drove slowly along, they saw some children dashing back and forth across the busy street. "It looks like those kids are having some kind of contest or game, trying to get as close to the cars as they can without getting hit!" exclaimed Carrie.

Dad shook his head. "What a dangerous game! I wonder if any of them have ever known someone who was hit by a car. Probably not, or I don't think they'd do that." A little farther along, Dad pointed to a liquor store. "That store reminds me of a dangerous game I used to play," he said. "I was a lot like those children playing in the street."

"What do you mean?" Carrie asked. "The people going in the store aren't running in front of cars."

"No, but drinking can be as dangerous as an oncoming car," said Dad. "When I was younger, I would go into bars with my unsaved friends, but I'd drink pop. I was trying to get as close as possible to the things in the world even though I was a Christian. Can you see why that was very dangerous?"

Carrie nodded. "You might have been persuaded to take a drink, and that could have led to taking more. You could even have gotten addicted to it."

"That's right," agreed Dad. "When I finally decided to give my life completely to Christ, I had to learn some new rules. My question no longer is, How close to the world can I get? In its own way, that's as dangerous as dashing in front of a car. My question now is, How close to *Christ* can I get while I live in this sinful old world?"

HOW ABOUT YOU? Do you think it might be fun to do things you've been told are wrong? Do you feel it's all right to be in places where un-Christlike activities are going on, as long as you don't join in? Sometimes it seems that people in the world—and Christians, too—are having a wonderful time, but they don't realize how close they are to disaster. Stay as far away from temptation as you can. C.R.

TO MEMORIZE: *"Don't you know that friendship with the world is hatred toward God?"* James 4:4 (NIV).

Run from temptation

JANUARY

22

Baby's First Steps

FROM THE BIBLE:

We who are strong ought to bear with the failings of the weak and not to please ourselves. Each of us should please his neighbor for his good, to build him up. For even Christ did not please himself but, as it is written: "The insults of those who insult you have fallen on me." For everything that was written in the past was written to teach us, so that through endurance and the encouragement of the Scriptures we might have hope. May the God who gives endurance and encouragement give you a spirit of unity among yourselves as you follow Christ Jesus, so that with one heart and mouth you may glorify the God and Father of our Lord Jesus Christ. Accept one another, then, just as Christ accepted you, in order to bring praise to God.

Romans 15:1-7, NIV

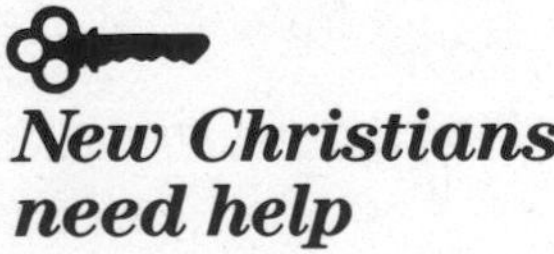

New Christians need help

"I GIVE UP!" exclaimed Ellen.

Mother looked up as she heard her daughter's words. "Give up on what?" she asked.

"Give up on Janet," explained Ellen as she tossed her school books on the kitchen table. "I was so glad when she became a Christian a month ago, but now she's getting tiresome! One day she acts like a Christian, and the next she lies or cheats or uses bad language. She'll never make a good Christian!"

"I hope you won't really give up on her," said Mother. "You need to pray for her and help her understand how to live for the Lord."

"Oh, I don't know," muttered Ellen with a sigh. "I think it's hopeless!"

After supper that evening, Ellen was playing with her baby brother. Suddenly she called out, "Mom! Look at Davy! He wants to walk!" Sure enough, when Ellen stood Davy on his feet, he took a tottering step toward her. "He took his first step by himself!" exclaimed Ellen. "I'm going to teach him to take more."

Ellen spent half an hour trying to teach her brother to walk. Mother smiled as she heard Ellen encourage and help the baby. "Come to Ellen, Davy," coaxed the girl. "Come on, honey. You can walk!" Over and over Ellen put the tottering baby back on his feet, for he was never able to take more than two steps before he tumbled to the floor.

"Better give up," advised Mother. "He'll never be able to walk. He just keeps falling down."

Ellen looked at her mother in surprise. "Give up? What do you mean?" she asked as she picked up the baby. "He just needs more help. Isn't that right, Davy?" Ellen put him down and patiently started to help him again.

Mother chuckled as she spoke. "You're exactly right, Ellen, Davy does need your help. And so does Janet. She's a 'baby' Christian. She's going to need lots of help in learning to walk spiritually, that is, to live as a Christian should live."

HOW ABOUT YOU? Do you know a Christian whose spiritual walk is not as good as you think it should be? Perhaps he is a baby Christian who is learning the first steps of Christian living. He needs your prayers, your encouragement, and your help, even as you need the help of older Christians. G.W.

TO MEMORIZE: *"We who are strong ought to bear with the failings of the weak"* Romans 15:1 (NIV).

JANUARY

23

Telltale Mirror

FROM THE BIBLE:

But be doers of the word, and not hearers only, deceiving yourselves. For if anyone is a hearer of the word and not a doer, he is like a man observing his natural face in a mirror; for he observes himself, goes away, and immediately forgets what kind of man he was. But he who looks into the perfect law of liberty and continues in it, and is not a forgetful hearer but a doer of the work, this one will be blessed in what he does.

James 1:22-25, NKJV

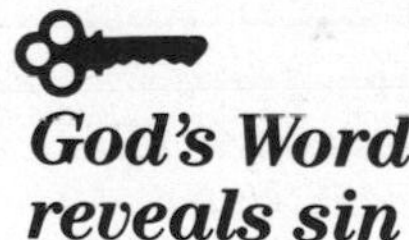

God's Word reveals sin

JASON CLIMBED into the car and slammed the door. "Why do you tell Miss Betty everything I do?" he grumbled.

"I didn't tell your Sunday school teacher anything about you," Mother answered calmly.

Dad slipped the car into gear. "And I know I didn't."

"Then how did Miss Betty know that I . . . I . . . " Jason stopped. Come to think of it, his folks didn't even know about some things Miss Betty had talked about. She had looked straight at him and read in the Bible about some of his secret sins. "I . . . ," Jason began again. Then he quickly changed the subject. "Look at Darci's face."

"What's wrong with my face?" Darci's lips puckered.

Mother smiled and handed the little girl a mirror from her purse. "What have you been eating?"

"Chocolate cake." Darci's voice quivered. "We had 'freshments in Sunday school."

As they gathered around the dinner table, Jason laughed. "Darci, don't you ever wash your face?"

Darci clicked her tongue. "I forgot."

"She saw herself in the mirror, but she still forgot," laughed Jason as his sister hurried to wash her face.

"Have you ever seen yourself in the 'mirror' of the Word of God, Jason?" Dad asked.

Jason gulped. "Yeah, I mean, yes, sir. But I never thought of the Bible as a mirror before."

"It's like a mirror," replied Dad. "It shows us our sin."

"But it doesn't do much good to see our faults if we don't correct them." added Mother. "We're like Darci if—"

"Let's eat," Darci interrupted as she came back to the table with water dripping off the end of her nose. "My face is clean now."

"Let's all make sure our hearts are clean, too." Dad smiled. "When the Lord shows us we have sinned, let's ask Him to forgive us and wash us clean."

HOW ABOUT YOU? When you look in the mirror of God's Word, do you like what you see? If you see sin in your life, don't forget it or try to hide it. Instead, confess it to God and ask Him to forgive you. He wants to cleanse you and help you live as you should. B.W.

TO MEMORIZE: *"Wash me thoroughly from any iniquity, and cleanse me from my sin"*
Psalm 51:2 (NASB).

JANUARY

24

Something Special

FROM THE BIBLE:
Likewise the Spirit also helps in our weaknesses. For we do not know what we should pray for as we ought, but the Spirit Himself makes intercession for us with groanings which cannot be uttered. Now He who searches the hearts knows what the mind of the Spirit is, because He makes intercession for the saints according to the will of God. And we know that all things work together for good to those who love God, to those who are the called according to His purpose. For whom He foreknew, He also predestined to be conformed to the image of His Son, that He might be the firstborn among many brethren. Moreover whom He predestined, these He also called; whom He called, these He also justified; and whom He justified, these He also glorified. What then shall we say to these things? If God is for us, who can be against us?
Romans 8:26-31, NKJV

All things work together for Good

JON PROPPED his chin in his hand as he watched his grandmother mix shortening and sugar. "I'm making your favorite cake, Jon—chocolate." As Jon smiled faintly, Grandma added, "Why so quiet? Is anything wrong?"

Jon snorted. "Everything's wrong! Dad's getting transferred, so I have to leave all my friends. Mom says I have to give up my dog, too. And the doctor says I have to wear a brace on my leg for two years. How can I ever make new friends wearing a metal monster? If God loved me, He wouldn't let all this happen to me." Jon slammed his fist on the table. "It's not fair!"

"Here, have a taste." Grandma handed him the cocoa.

"Yuck!" Jon drew back.

"Then how about this?" Grandma dipped a spoon into the shortening and sugar mixture.

Jon frowned. "No way am I going to taste that!"

Grandma raised her eyebrows. "Then how about some flour, or baking soda, or this egg?"

Jon grinned. "Awww, Grandma, you're teasing me."

Grandma smiled. "You know, the Bible says all things work *together* for good in the life of a Christian. It doesn't say all things *are* good. Cocoa or a raw egg isn't good alone, but when I mix all the ingredients together . . ."

"Yummmm, yummmm, good!" Jon sang.

"So in life," Grandma continued as she sifted flour into the batter, "when God gets through mixing a Christian's experiences together—the bitter, the sweet, the happy, the sad—life comes out good. Moving and wearing a brace are bitter experiences for you now, but trust God, Jon. He'll add some 'sugar' and some 'flavoring,' and in the end it will be good. Even better than my cake." Grandma laughed.

"Maybe so," Jon agreed. Then he grinned. "Grandma, may I lick the beater?"

HOW ABOUT YOU? Have you had to swallow some bitter experiences lately? Be patient. All the ingredients are not in yet, but God is making something special out of you. B.W.

TO MEMORIZE: *"And we know that all things work together for good to those who love God, to those who are the called according to His purpose"* Romans 8:28 (NKJV).

JANUARY

25

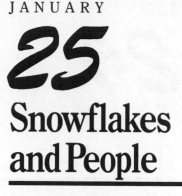

Snowflakes and People

FROM THE BIBLE:

As Peter was coming in, Cornelius met him and fell down at his feet and worshiped him. But Peter lifted him up, saying, "Stand up; I myself am also a man." And as he talked with him, he went in and found many who had come together. Then he said to them, "You know how unlawful it is for a Jewish man to keep company with or go to one of another nation. But God has shown me that I should not call any man common or unclean."

Acts 10:25-28, NKJV

God made everyone beautiful

JESSICA AND HER FRIEND, Jimmy, shouted with glee as they stood back to admire the snowman they were making. As they began to fashion some arms, a classmate, Aiko, came along. She grinned and stopped to help. "Go away," said Jessica with a scowl. "This is our snowman." Aiko's grin faded, and she slowly left. "She'd have wanted to give him slanting eyes," Jessica said loudly enough for Aiko to hear. At the window Jessica's mother frowned.

A little later Jason, another classmate, stopped to help, and he, too, was soon sent on his way. "You'd probably want to cover his face with mud and make him all black," Jessica laughed.

"Oh, who wants to help you anyway, Whitey?" Jason retorted.

Jessica angrily stomped her foot. "You stop calling us names!" she shouted. Still watching, Mother went to call Jessica in.

"Oh, Mother! Did you see our snowman?" Jessica asked as she came in the door. "We call him Mr. Snowflake!"

Mother smiled. "Really?" she asked. "Did you know there was once a man who was called 'The Snowflake Man'? Why don't you look him up in the encyclopedia? His name was Wilson Bentley."

Interested, Jessica hurried to see what she could find. Soon she returned to report to her mother. "I found him," she said. "He lived in Vermont, and his hobby was studying snowflakes. He found that each one was a perfect crystal, and no two were ever alike. But they were all beautiful!"

Mother nodded. "Kind of like people," she said. "They have different kinds of hair and eyes and skin. But they're all made by the great artist—God—and in His sight, each one is beautiful. So, unless we're going to disagree with God, we should consider them beautiful, too."

Jessica was quiet for a time. "Mother," she said finally, "may I have some kids over after school tomorrow? I need to apologize to Aiko and Jason, and I'd like to ask them to come help me build another snowman."

HOW ABOUT YOU? Do you think you're better than people who look different from you, are poorer, or don't seem as smart? God made everyone according to His own special plan. Be careful not to say He made anyone poorly. H.M.

TO MEMORIZE: *"And He has made from one blood every nation of men"* Acts 17:26 (NKJV).

JANUARY

26

Take Off the Labels

FROM THE BIBLE:

You have no right to criticize your brother or look down on him. Remember, each of us will stand personally before the Judgment Seat of God. For it is written, "As I live," says the Lord, "every knee shall bow to me and every tongue confess to God." Yes, each of us will give an account of himself to God. So don't criticize each other any more. Try instead to live in such a way that you will never make your brother stumble by letting him see you doing something he thinks is wrong.

Romans 14:10-13, TLB

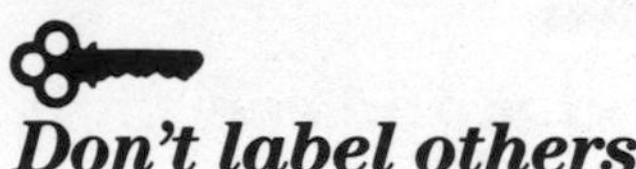

Don't label others

"WHO'S THAT beautiful young lady in the second row?" asked Dad as he pointed to Kara's class picture.

Kara giggled. "You know that's me."

"Let me see, too." Three-year-old Lance pulled at his father's leg, and Dad lifted him onto his lap. "Who's that?" Lance pointed at a dark-haired girl.

"Oh, that's Stephanie. Her family is rich, and she's so stuck-up." Kara wrinkled her nose and pointed at another girl. "That's Melissa. She's not stuck-up, but she's dumb."

Lance continued asking, "Who's this? What's that?" Kara answered, "That's Juan. He's a foreigner and he sure is strange." Or, "That's Kevin. He wears the thickest glasses I've ever seen, and he's a bookworm. He's the smartest one in our class, but he's so weird."

"Don't you like anyone in your class?" asked Dad.

Kara looked shocked. "Of course! I like all of them—well, almost all of them."

"I sure couldn't tell it by the way you were talking." Dad raised his eyebrows.

"Oh no!" exclaimed Mother just then. Everyone saw that she was holding two shiny cans. "Lance has taken the labels off some of the canned goods," she groaned. "Now I don't know what is what!"

Dad chuckled softly, then louder. Soon they were all laughing together. When Mother caught her breath, she said, "It looks like we'll have surprise meals for a few days. I had planned to have applesauce, but we'll have whatever is in this can." She held up one can, then opened it. "Green beans," she announced, looking at Lance, "and you, young man, are going to eat your share with no complaints!"

Later, as they sat down to eat, Dad said, "We have a tendency to label people like we do cans. We say the rich are stuck-up, the poor are dumb, the smart are weird, and foreigners are strange. Kara, I think you need to take the labels off your classmates. We should not label others."

Kara looked at the green beans. "I see what you mean, Dad," she said. "It's what's inside that counts, isn't it?"

HOW ABOUT YOU? Are you quick to judge people? Do you put labels on them? The Bible warns against judging others. Take off the labels. Accept them for what they are. B.W.

TO MEMORIZE: *"God does not show favoritism"* Acts 10:34 (NIV).

"STAND STILL, Staci, while I measure this hem," Mother ordered. Staci fingered the soft fabric. "Will my dress be finished by tomorrow night so I can wear it to Lydia's piano recital?"

Mother nodded. "Probably. Are you finished with your science project?"

"No." Staci shook her head. "I decided not to enter the science fair."

"But you spent hours on your project," Mother reminded.

Staci shrugged. "I know. But I'm tired of it."

Mother raised her eyebrows. "Just like you got tired of the pillow you were making Grandma for her birthday?"

"But she liked the scarf I bought her." Staci defended herself as she slipped the dress up over her head and handed it to her mother.

After school the next day, Staci skipped down the hall to the sewing room. In the doorway, she stopped and stared. "Mother," she wailed, "my dress isn't done!"

Mother shrugged. "I know. I got tired of it."

"Got tired of it!" cried Staci. "But, Mother, aren't you ever going to finish it? I mean, it's almost done now. You won't let it just go to waste, will you? Oh, won't you please finish it?"

"It would be foolish for me not to finish your dress, wouldn't it?" asked Mother quietly. "Just like it was foolish for you to stop working on your science project and your grandmother's pillow."

"Ooohhh," Staci moaned.

"Only when a job is finished does it bring satisfaction," continued Mother. "An unfinished job is time wasted. I don't believe the Lord is satisfied, either, when we leave a job half-done. He requires faithfulness even in small things."

Staci glanced at the clock. "Mother, if you'll finish my dress, I'll finish my science project."

Mother smiled. "I thought you might say that."

HOW ABOUT YOU? How many unfinished projects do you have? Start today to discipline yourself to complete what you start. Jesus finished the task He came to earth to do. The Apostle Paul finished his assignment. Before the Lord will trust you with a big job, He has to know you can finish little ones. B.W.

TO MEMORIZE: *"I have fought the good fight, I have finished the race, I have kept the faith"* 2 Timothy 4:7 (NIV).

JANUARY

27

The Finished Job

FROM THE BIBLE:

Later, knowing that all was now completed, and so that the Scripture would be fulfilled, Jesus said, "I am thirsty." A jar of wine vinegar was there, so they soaked a sponge in it, put the sponge on a stalk of the hyssop plant, and lifted it to Jesus' lips. When he had received the drink, Jesus said, "It is finished." With that, he bowed his head and gave up his spirit. John 19:28-30, NIV

I have fought the good fight, I have finished the race, I have kept the faith. Now there is in store for me the crown of righteousness, which the Lord, the righteous Judge, will award to me on that day—and not only to me, but also to all who have longed for his appearing. 2 Timothy 4:7-8, NIV

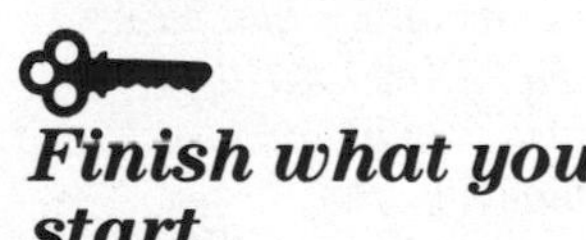

Finish what you start

JANUARY

28

I'll Do the Dishes

FROM THE BIBLE:

For the power of the life-giving Spirit—and this power is mine through Christ Jesus—has freed me from the vicious circle of sin and death. We aren't saved from sin's grasp by knowing the commandments of God, because we can't and don't keep them, but God put into effect a different plan to save us. He sent his own Son in a human body like ours—except that ours are sinful—and destroyed sin's control over us by giving himself as a sacrifice for our sins. So now we can obey God's laws if we follow after the Holy Spirit and no longer obey the old evil nature within us. Those who let themselves be controlled by their lower natures live only to please themselves, but those who follow after the Holy Spirit find themselves doing those things that please God. Following after the Holy Spirit leads to life and peace, but following after the old nature leads to death, because the old sinful nature within us is against God.

Romans 8:2-7, TLB

Serve God with love

JAN SAT at the kitchen table lost in thought, while her mother put away the dinner dishes. Finally Jan sighed. "My Sunday school teacher said something that I still can't figure out," she announced.

"Oh? What did he say?" asked Mother.

"Well," Jan replied, "he said the only way to be really happy as a Christian is to do what God wants us to do all the time, instead of doing what we want. It doesn't make sense. How can we be happy if we're always doing things we really don't want to do? I think that would make me miserable, not happy!"

"I understand what you're saying, and in a way, you're right," agreed Mother. "If the Christian life was just a matter of forcing ourselves to do unpleasant things, it certainly wouldn't be very enjoyable, would it? But it seems to me you're overlooking something important."

"What's that?" asked Jan.

Mother smiled. "Remember how you reacted when I asked you to wash the dishes after supper tonight?"

"Uh, I suppose I complained a little," Jan admitted sheepishly. "I'm sorry, Mom. I guess I just didn't feel like doing them."

"I know that doing dishes isn't your favorite job," Mother said with a chuckle, "but what about last night, when I wasn't feeling well? You came in from school and cleaned up the whole kitchen, just to surprise me. And after supper, you jumped right up and said, 'I'll do the dishes tonight.' "

"That's right," Jan grinned. "And I really didn't mind. But I did it to be nice, not because I had to."

"In other words, you did it out of love," explained Mother. "And that's the real secret of a happy Christian life. If we try to serve God in our own strength and out of a sense of duty, we'll never be truly happy. But when we serve Him out of love and gratitude to Him, He gives us joy and contentment. That's what makes the difference!"

HOW ABOUT YOU? Do you ever serve God grudgingly, just because you feel you have to? When you don't feel like doing the things you should, admit it to God and ask for the help of His Spirit. Then do what He wants you to do out of love for Him. That way you'll truly be a happy Christian instead of a miserable one! S.K.

TO MEMORIZE: *"So now we can obey God's laws if we follow after the Holy Spirit and no longer obey the old evil nature within us"* Romans 8:4 (TLB).

JANUARY

29

What Do You Hear?

FROM THE BIBLE:

Rejoice in the Lord, O you righteous!
For praise from the upright is beautiful.
Praise the Lord with the harp;
Make melody to Him with an instrument of ten strings.
Sing to Him a new song;
Play skillfully with a shout of joy.
For the word of the Lord is right,
And all His work is done in truth.

Psalm 33:1-4, NKJV

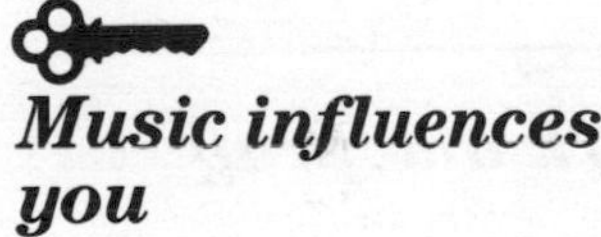

Music influences you

"RODNEY!" exclaimed Mrs. Thomas. "How many times must I tell you not to play that kind of music!"

"Aw, Mom, everybody listens to a little rock now and then," protested Rodney. "Besides, this don't hurt me."

"*Doesn't* hurt," Mother corrected. "But it does! Both the words and the music get into your mind and influence you whether you realize it or not."

Rodney sighed and picked up his new model ship. "Is Dad home yet?" he asked.

"Not yet," replied Mother. "Since he was made manager of Burger Haven, he has extra responsibilities. Shall we surprise him and meet him there?"

Rodney brightened. "Oh yeah! Can I have a large sundae?" he asked eagerly.

"You can't possibly be hungry, yet," laughed Mother, "but maybe a small one would go down. We'll see."

Rodney's father saw them come in and came to greet them. "I'll be with you in a minute," he said.

They sat down, and Rodney listened intently as Dad walked away. "What's Dad singing?" he asked.

"Come to Big Al's, bring all your pals." Dad's voice drifted back softly as he sang under his breath. "Our burgers are the best, in the east and the west."

Rodney gave a shout of laughter. "Dad, you're advertising for the competition!"

Dad grinned sheepishly. "I heard it on the radio while I was driving to work this morning, and it got into my head. I guess I'd better be more careful about what I listen to."

On the way home, Rodney was thoughtful. "I guess maybe you're right, Mom," he murmured finally. "If hearing that song could make Dad advertise for the wrong restaurant without even knowing it, maybe the songs I hear influence me more than I thought they did, too. I'm going to be more careful about what I hear."

HOW ABOUT YOU? How about the music you listen to? Do the words please God? Advertisers know that words set to music stay with you even longer than spoken words. And how about the music itself? Would you invite Jesus to listen with you? If you're a Christian, He *is* with you. Be sure that both the *words* and the *sound* of the music please Him, and that they don't hurt your testimony. H.M.

TO MEMORIZE: *"Take heed what you hear"* Mark 4:24 (NKJV).

JANUARY

30

Work and Pray

FROM THE BIBLE:

Now it happened, when Sanballat, Tobiah, the Arabs, the Ammonites, and the Ashdodites heard that the walls of Jerusalem were being restored and the gaps were beginning to be closed, that they became very angry, and all of them conspired together to come and attack Jerusalem and create confusion. Nevertheless we made our prayer to our God, and because of them we set a watch against them day and night. Nehemiah 4:7-9, NKJV

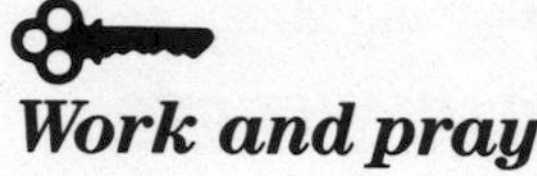

Work and pray

"SHOULDN'T YOU be studying your spelling?" asked Mother.

"Yeah, I s'pose," agreed Lynn. "I'll do it as soon as this program's done."

But just as the program ended, Marcia called, and Lynn spent the next half hour chatting on the phone. After that she had a bedtime snack, and then it was time to turn in. *No time to study now,* she thought sleepily. *I'll just have to ask the Lord to help me.* Jumping into bed, she murmured a prayer asking for help with her spelling.

As she took the test the next day, she again asked God to help her do well. She was disappointed in the results—a D! "Doesn't the Bible say that if we lack wisdom we should ask God for it?" she asked Mother that evening.

Before Mother could answer, the phone rang. Lynn ran to answer it. "That was Marcia," she said as she returned. "May I go to town with her? And may I have some money to buy a lock for my locker? Lots of kids are getting their pencils and things ripped off at school."

"Oh, that's a shame," said Mother. She reached for her purse, then changed her mind. "I have an idea. Why don't you pray about it? Ask the Lord to protect your things."

"Mother!" exclaimed Lynn. "It's all very well to pray about it, but it only makes sense to put a lock on, too."

"In other words, even though you pray, you should also do what you can to take care of the problem? You should do your part?" asked Mother. As Lynn nodded, Mother added, "And wouldn't that be true regarding your spelling test, too? You didn't study. You didn't do your part. Yet you expected God to help you remember things you never learned."

Lynn looked ashamed. "I guess I really knew better. After this I'll study hard. I'll do my part and then I know God will help me, too."

HOW ABOUT YOU? Do you pray about your schoolwork? About friends who need to know the Lord? About money you need for something special? Prayer is important, but it is only part of the battle. You also need to study. You need to witness. You need to look for ways to work and earn money. When the walls of Jerusalem were being built, God's people prayed *and* they set a watch. Jesus told His disciples to watch *and* pray. We, too, must pray, and we must also work. H.M.

TO MEMORIZE: *"Watch and pray"* Matthew 26:41.

JANUARY

31

Jonathan's Ministry

FROM THE BIBLE:

But Jesus called them to Himself, and said, "You know that the rulers of the Gentiles lord it over them, and their great men exercise authority over them. It is not so among you, but whoever wishes to become great among you shall be your servant, and whoever wishes to be first among you shall be your slave; just as the Son of Man did not come to be served, but to serve and to give His life a ransom for many."
Matthew 20:25-28, NASB

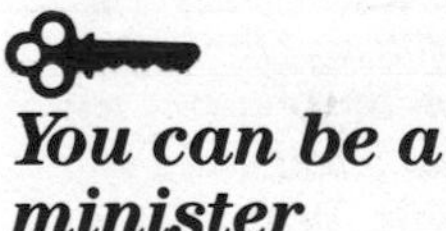

You can be a minister

"TODAY WAS Pastor Wilson's birthday, and we had a party for him," announced Jonathan on the way home from Sunday school. "It would be fun to be a minister. That's what I'm going to be when I grow up."

"I don't know how much fun it would be, but I'm sure it's rewarding," Dad said.

"Could we stop by Grannie Nelson's and check on her?" asked Mother.

"Do we have to?" groaned Jonathan. "I'm starved, and you know how she talks and talks and talks."

"She's lonely," replied Mother. "She needs someone to minister to her."

"Minister to her?" Jonathan echoed. "If she needs a preacher, tell Pastor Wilson."

"I didn't say she needs a 'preacher,' " Mother said, smiling. "What I said is that Grannie Nelson needs a 'minister.' We can't all be preachers, but we can all be ministers—even you, Jonathan!"

"Well, I am going to be one when I grow up if I don't starve to death first," Jonathan complained.

"You can be one now," Mother insisted. "A minister is simply a servant. You can minister to Grannie Nelson."

"Aw, you're just kidding. Pastor Wilson isn't a servant!" said Jonathan.

"He certainly is," Dad corrected. "He is God's servant."

"If you're not willing to serve others, you cannot be a minister," added Mother.

"Do you know how the child Samuel ministered to the Lord?" Dad asked as they turned into Grannie Nelson's driveway. "He ministered to the Lord by serving Eli. He lit the lamp in the tabernacle, swept the floors, and ran errands."

Jonathan took a deep breath, "Well, that isn't exactly how I had it pictured, but I guess I'd better start now. Maybe Grannie Nelson needs her sidewalk swept."

HOW ABOUT YOU? Did you know that Christians are to be ministers? As a servant of God, your job is to serve others. Look around you. Find one person today that you can serve. You'll be surprised how much fun it is! And as you serve people, you are actually ministering to the Lord. B.W.

TO MEMORIZE: *"But whoever wishes to become great among you shall be your servant"*
Matthew 20:26 (NASB).

FEBRUARY

1

It Ought to Hurt

FROM THE BIBLE:
O loving and kind God, have mercy. Have pity upon me and take away the awful stain of my transgressions. Oh, wash me, cleanse me from this guilt. Let me be pure again. For I admit my shameful deed—it haunts me day and night. It is against you and you alone I sinned, and did this terrible thing. You saw it all, and your sentence against me is just. But I was born a sinner, yes, from the moment my mother conceived me. You deserve honesty from the heart; yes, utter sincerity and truthfulness. Oh, give me this wisdom. Sprinkle me with the cleansing blood and I shall be clean again. Wash me and I shall be whiter than snow. . . . Don't keep looking at my sins—erase them from your sight. Create in me a new, clean heart, O God, filled with clean thoughts and right desires. Don't toss me aside, banished forever from your presence. Don't take your Holy Spirit from me. Restore to me again the joy of your salvation, and make me willing to obey you.
Psalm 51:1-12, TLB

Don't get used to sin

JACK AND WENDY were hungry, but Mother was gone to the store. "Hey, there's candy up in the cupboard," said Wendy. "Let's sneak some. Mother will never know."

Jack looked uncertain. "Doesn't that make you feel guilty?" he asked.

Wendy shook her head. "Nah. At first I felt guilty, but it doesn't bother me anymore."

Jack still hesitated, but when he saw his sister eating a chocolate bar, he just couldn't resist. The two finished their candy, carefully threw away the wrappers, and went outside to play in the snow.

After a while their feet were wet and cold, but they wanted to finish the snow fort they were building. They refused to give in and go back indoors. For some time they kept on working. When Mother arrived home, she called them inside. She was shocked when she saw how wet and cold their feet were. "Why didn't you come inside when your feet got cold?" she scolded.

"We wanted to finish our fort," Wendy replied. "Besides, they didn't feel so cold after a while, Mom!"

Mother looked grim. "That sensation of cold was meant to be a warning to you. If you had stayed out much longer, you might have gotten frostbite. The most dangerous time is not when your feel cold, but when you stop feeling it." She rubbed their feet gently and added, "It reminds me of sin. We're in danger if our conscience stops bothering us when we do something wrong."

When Mother left the room, the children looked at each other, remembering the candy they had eaten.

"I sure feel my feet now," commented Jack. "Now that they're getting warmed up, they hurt. And my conscience hurts, too."

"Mine, too," agreed Wendy. "And it's going to hurt more when we tell Mother about the candy we took. But I'm sure we'll feel better afterward!"

HOW ABOUT YOU? Are there habits or activities in your life that made you feel guilty in the past but not anymore? You may have changed, but God's standards of right and wrong haven't. Confess your sin, and be willing to follow the "pricking" of your conscience and of the Holy Spirit. Don't let yourself become "numb" to sin! S.K.

TO MEMORIZE: *"Create in me a new, clean heart, O God, filled with clean thoughts and right desires"* Psalm 51:10 (TLB).

FEBRUARY

2

Wonderfully Made

FROM THE BIBLE:

Then God said, "Let Us make man in Our image, according to Our likeness; let them have dominion over the fish of the sea, over the birds of the air, and over the cattle, over all the earth and over every creeping thing that creeps on the earth." So God created man in His own image; in the image of God He created him; male and female He created them. Then God blessed them, and God said to them, "Be fruitful and multiply; fill the earth and subdue it; have dominion over the fish of the sea, over the birds of the air, and over every living thing that moves on the earth." . . . Then God saw everything that He had made, and indeed it was very good. So the evening and the morning were the sixth day.
Genesis 1:26-28, 31, NKJV

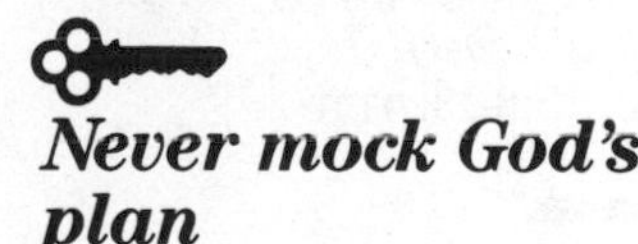

Never mock God's plan

STAN REACHED for a book, opened it curiously, then muttered, "Oh no! Fred gave me this book to read, but I didn't know it was like this!"

"Hmmm," Dad murmured. "I think maybe we should all have a talk next time Fred is here."

The next evening Fred came to see Stan's new pups. While they were outside, the boys and Stan's dad talked about the billions of stars and how God knows each one by name. "But these aren't his greatest works of creation," said Dad. "Come inside, boys. I want to show you something." They went into the house, and Dad showed them a picture.

"It's just a man," said Stan.

"Yes," agreed Dad, "but man is the greatest of all creation. His spine is a series of 33 rings with 150 joints, so he can bend his back in any direction, yet it's capable of supporting five hundred pounds."

"And look at the heart," Fred put in. "It's no larger than a fist, yet it pumps blood at the rate of around four thousand gallons a day."

Dad grinned. "Right! Now look at your hands. Do you notice that the palms are sort of skidproof so you can get a grip on things? And think of all your fingers can do.

"We didn't even mention the brain, or lungs, or other things," said Dad, "but we've seen enough to know that this great handiwork of God is nothing to laugh about."

Fred was surprised. "What do you mean, 'laugh about'?"

Dad explained. "When God made the world, Fred, He made it to continue. God wants man to continue, too. He planned for a man and a woman to love, marry, and have a family. But there are people who make jokes, pictures, books, or movies which mock God's plan for us. To have anything but pure thoughts about our bodies is evil and sinful in God's sight."

As Fred was getting ready to leave, Stan ran to get the book Fred had given him. "I . . . I don't want it," stammered Fred. "Just burn it. You know, it kinda scares me that I made fun of God's work. I'll ask Him to forgive me."

HOW ABOUT YOU? Are you ever tempted to make fun of what God created and planned? He doesn't want only your heart. He also wants your body to be used in His service. A.L.

TO MEMORIZE: *"I will praise You, for I am fearfully and wonderfully made"* Psalm 139:14 (NKJV).

FEBRUARY

3

Higher Ways

FROM THE BIBLE:

This plan of mine is not what you would work out, neither are my thoughts the same as yours! For just as the heavens are higher than the earth, so are my ways higher than yours, and my thoughts than yours. As the rain and snow come down from heaven and stay upon the ground to water the earth, and cause the grain to grow and to produce seed for the farmer and bread for the hungry, so also is my Word. I send it out and it always produces fruit. It shall accomplish all I want it to, and prosper everywhere I send it. You will live in joy and peace. The mountains and hills, the trees of the field—all the world around you—will rejoice. Where once were thorns, fir trees will grow; where briars grew, the myrtle trees will sprout up. This miracle will make the Lord's name very great and be an everlasting sign [of God's power and love].

Isaiah 55:8-13, TLB

Trust God's higher ways

A CHILL WIND whipped through the cemetery and stung Curt's face. He tried to listen as the minister read from the Bible. *I wonder if Grandpa went to heaven,* he thought for the hundredth time in the last few days. On the way home, Curt finally asked the question that lay heavy on his heart: "Did Grandpa go to heaven?"

Dad looked sober. "We're not sure, Son. Grandpa never showed any interest when I talked to him about God." Curt felt empty inside when he heard this.

"Grandpa died on his knees beside his bed." Mom spoke in her gentle voice. "Just the day before that, I spent some special time praying that he would receive Jesus as his Savior from sin. We don't know, but it's very possible Grandpa did that just before he died."

Curt felt a little better as he thought that over. Then, with a sigh, he said, "But I wish I knew."

"I do, too, Son. But we'll have to leave Grandpa in God's hands now," Dad said. "We did all we could do. Many times we explained to Grandpa how to be saved, and for years we prayed he would understand and accept God's gift. We were loving and kind to him, always hoping he would see the difference Jesus made in our lives and would want to know Him, too."

"There are some things we'll never know while we're on earth," added Mom. "But we told Grandpa what the Bible says, and God promises that His Word will accomplish what He sends it to do. He also says His ways are higher than ours, and He does all things right."

At home Curt went to his room and rubbed his fingers over the worn leather of a baseball mitt Grandpa had given him. "Dear Lord," he prayed, "You know I loved Grandpa and want him to be in heaven. Thank You that he knew the way. Thank You that You loved him, too, and that You do everything right."

HOW ABOUT YOU? It always hurts when a loved one dies, but it's especially painful when you don't know if the loved one went to heaven. If you're in that position, try not to fret. Rest in the knowledge that God's ways are right. Pray for those who are unsaved. Be kind and loving, and make sure they know the way to be saved. C.Y.

TO MEMORIZE: *"For just as the heavens are higher than the earth, so are my ways higher than yours, and my thoughts than yours"* Isaiah 55:9 (TLB).

FEBRUARY

Beware of the Foe

FROM THE BIBLE:
Dearly loved friends, don't always believe everything you hear just because someone says it is a message from God: test it first to see if it really is. For there are many false teachers around, and the way to find out if their message is from the Holy Spirit is to ask: Does it really agree that Jesus Christ, God's Son, actually became man with a human body? If so, then the message is from God. If not, the message is not from God but from one who is against Christ, like the "Antichrist" you have heard about who is going to come, and his attitude of enmity against Christ is already abroad in the world. Dear young friends, you belong to God and have already won your fight with those who are against Christ, because there is someone in your hearts who is stronger than any evil teacher in this wicked world.

1 John 4:1-4, TLB

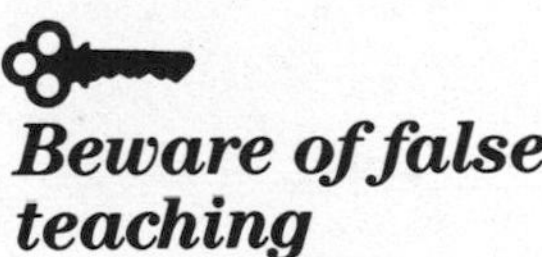

Beware of false teaching

SANDY AND DAD were watching their favorite TV program. After a few minutes a commercial came on. "Look, Dad," Sandy said. "Could we order some of that jewelry for Mom's birthday? She'd love it! They're selling those diamonds and rubies and pearls so cheap—and they're genuine, too. It says so right on the screen, see?"

"There's another word on the screen, too," Dad pointed out. "It's spelled f-a-u-x, and it's pronounced 'foe.' Did you notice that?"

"That's probably a fancy name for the jewelry," Sandy suggested.

"Get the dictionary and look it up," directed Dad.

After she found the word, Sandy looked up in surprise. "It means 'false'!" she exclaimed. "Genuine false stones! Wow!"

"A lot of people will spend their money on that jewelry, and then some jeweler will tell them it's not real," Dad said. He got up and went to answer the doorbell.

"Who was that, Dad?" Sandy asked after her father shut the front door.

"Some people wanting to leave some literature and tell me about their religion," Dad answered. "But I already know what those people believe, and it's false teaching. It fools a lot of people, though."

"How come?" wondered Sandy.

"They remind me of that commercial we just heard," answered Dad. "Remember how good it made the jewelry sound and how easy it was to believe it—until you looked up the word *faux?* Well, these people make their message sound good, too. They even quote Bible verses, and that often fools people who don't check to see if they're using those verses correctly. Some people blindly accept false teaching without studying the Bible to make sure that what they were told is true. We need to know the Bible well so we can be on guard for false teaching."

HOW ABOUT YOU? Are you aware that false teachers may try to get you to believe as they do? Study the Bible to know what is really true. Notice that today's memory verse talks about people who searched the Scriptures *daily.* You do that, too. Don't let false teaching fool you. S.N.

TO MEMORIZE: *"They received the word with all readiness, and searched the Scriptures daily to find out whether those things were so"*
Acts 17:11 (NKJV).

FEBRUARY

5

Second Choice

FROM THE BIBLE:
Remember the former things, those of long ago; I am God, and there is no other; I am God, and there is none like me. I make known the end from the beginning, from ancient times, what is still to come. I say: My purpose will stand, and I will do all that I please. From the east I summon a bird of prey; from a far-off land, a man to fulfill my purpose. What I have said, that will I bring about; what I have planned, that will I do. Isaiah 46:9-11, NIV

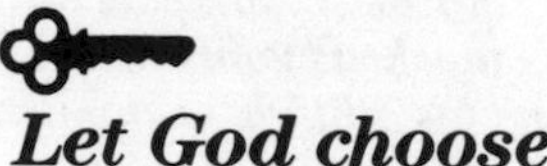

Let God choose

THE SNYDER FAMILY was expecting a new baby. Steve, who was seven, said, "I'm going to pray for a little brother."

"You can tell God how you feel about it, but you really should leave it to God whether to send us a girl or a boy," his parents said. "While we wait, we're going to be looking for a bigger house."

Finding another house was a big job, but finally they found just the one they wanted—their dream house. The rent was a little too high, but they decided they could manage it. Dad called the landlord, only to learn that the house had been rented just an hour before. They were forced to take their second choice. "Didn't you pray that God would let us have the other house?" Steve asked.

Mother answered, "God always answers our prayers, but He doesn't always say yes."

And so they moved. Their new home needed a lot of repair, but the landlord let them do the work for part of the rent. And then, to Dad's surprise, the landlord suggested that they apply the rent toward buying the house. So the Snyders were soon homeowners! "I'm getting our bedroom ready for my brother and me," Steve said proudly.

"Don't be so sure you'll have a brother. I'd rather have a girl," his sister told him.

"It'll be a boy," Steve insisted. "I told you. I prayed."

The big day came. The new baby arrived, and it was a girl! Although Steve was disappointed, he did agree to hold the baby on the way home. As they went down the street, they saw a "For Sale" sign in front of the house they had hoped to rent. "I'm glad we don't live there. I know we could never afford to buy it, and I wouldn't want to move right now!" exclaimed Mother.

"I can see why God didn't let us have that house," agreed Dad. "By the way, Steve, how's the baby doing?"

"She *is* kinda cute," Steve admitted. "She's really my second choice, but I guess she's God's choice for us, so she must be the one best for us."

"I'm sure she is," Mother said, smiling.

HOW ABOUT YOU? Is your second (or even third or fourth) choice sometimes God's choice for you? As today's Scripture says, God knows the end from the beginning. He knows what's best for you. B.W.

TO MEMORIZE: *"I make known the end from the beginning, from ancient times, what is still to come. I say: My purpose will stand, and I will do all that I please"* Isaiah 46:10 (NIV).

FEBRUARY

Taxes! Taxes!

FROM THE BIBLE:
As Jesus was going on down the road, he saw a tax collector, Matthew, sitting at a tax collection booth. "Come and be my disciple," Jesus said to him, and Matthew jumped up and went along with him.
Matthew 9:9, TLB

On their arrival in Capernaum, the Temple tax collectors came to Peter and asked him, "Doesn't your master pay taxes?" "Of course he does," Peter replied. Then he went into the house to talk to Jesus about it, but before he had a chance to speak, Jesus asked him, "What do you think, Peter? Do kings levy assessments against their own people, or against conquered foreigners?" "Against the foreigners," Peter replied. "Well, then," Jesus said, "the citizens are free! However, we don't want to offend them, so go down to the shore and throw in a line, and open the mouth of the first fish you catch. You will find a coin to cover the taxes for both of us; take it and pay them."
Matthew 17:24-27, TLB

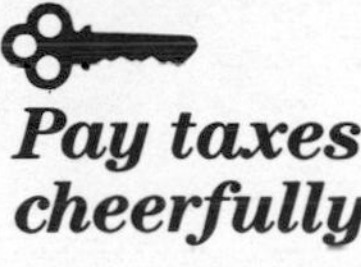

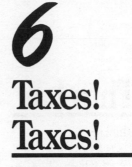

Pay taxes cheerfully

"MOM," GINGER CALLED, "may I take my allowance and go buy some stickers?" Mom agreed, and soon Ginger was at the store.

A smiling sales clerk came to wait on her. "That will be fifty cents for the stickers, plus sales tax."

"Oh no!" groaned Ginger. "I thought I had enough money to buy five stickers, but I forgot about the sales tax! I guess I can only buy four today."

At home again, Ginger and mother had some milk and cookies while Ginger displayed her stickers. "Mom, why do we have to pay taxes?" she asked.

"Taxes are used to pay for many things," answered Mother. "They're used to keep our roads repaired and to pay for teachers, policemen, firemen, and the president of the United States and congressmen. People have paid taxes for a long time. Did you know that people paid taxes in Bible times?"

"They did?" Ginger was surprised.

"That's right," said Mother. "There were taxes on the sale of animals, land, slaves, and produce. There were taxes to support the temple, and there were even road taxes. During the time Jesus lived, the Jews didn't like the tax collectors because they took more money than they should. Some of it went to the Roman rulers, and the tax collectors kept the rest for themselves. But Jesus can change anyone, and He called one of those tax collectors to be one of His disciples."

"Really? Which one?" asked Ginger.

"Matthew," answered Mother. "Besides being a disciple of Jesus, he later wrote one of the Gospels. Because he had been a careful record keeper as a tax collector, it helped him to record many things Jesus taught. And did you know that we have a record of Jesus paying taxes once?"

Ginger thought for a moment. "Oh, I remember!" she exclaimed. "He sent Peter to find money in the mouth of a fish. It was used to pay taxes for himself and Jesus." She paused and grinned. "Well, if Jesus paid taxes, I can, too!"

HOW ABOUT YOU? You hear a lot about taxes these days, don't you? Sometimes they seem unfair, or maybe a bit too high. Try to remember that they are needed for many useful things. And remember that God says we are to pay them. V.L.C.

TO MEMORIZE: *"This is also why you pay taxes, for the authorities are God's servants, who give their full time to governing"* Romans 13:6 (NIV).

FEBRUARY

7

On Thin Ice

FROM THE BIBLE:

Don't do as the wicked do. Avoid their haunts—turn away, go somewhere else, for evil men can't sleep until they've done their evil deed for the day. They can't rest unless they cause someone to stumble and fall. They eat and drink wickedness and violence! But the good man walks along in the ever-brightening light of God's favor; the dawn gives way to morning splendor, while the evil man gropes and stumbles in the dark. Listen, son of mine, to what I say. Listen carefully. Keep these thoughts ever in mind; let them penetrate deep within your heart, for they will mean real life for you, and radiant health. Above all else, guard your affections. For they influence everything else in your life. Proverbs 4:14-23, TLB

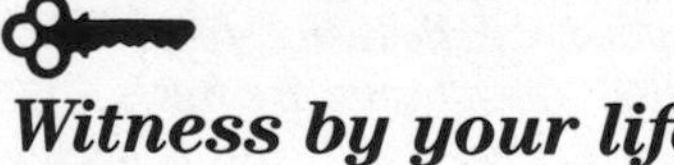

Witness by your life

"I DON'T SEE why I can't go. It seems like a fair exchange," Connie told her mother. "Since Karen is willing to come to church tomorrow if I go with her this afternoon, I think I should.

Mother shook her head. "She wants you to go to a horror movie and then to Peyton's to eat and play electronic games, right? I've explained before why I don't think going to either of those places is the way to win your friend to the Lord."

"But, Mother!" protested Connie. "It will get Karen to come. . . ."

"I said no, Connie," Mother stated firmly. With an angry look, Connie marched off to her room.

Later, with Mother's permission, she spent the afternoon figure skating with some friends at Horn's Lake. When she returned home, she was bursting with excitement. "You know Jack Wolter? He almost drowned! He zipped right past the danger sign toward the middle of the lake. But the ice didn't hold him. One leg went right through into freezing water. I screamed for help!"

Mother was concerned. "Is he all right?"

Connie nodded. "He was hanging onto the ice, half in and half out of the water. He's just lucky the men on duty got there on time!"

"Oh, good!" said Mother. "But why didn't you skate out and rescue him yourself? You took that lifesaving swim class last summer."

Connie looked at her mother in disbelief. "You've gotta be kidding! The men used boards and ropes and stuff to crawl out and reach Jack. If anybody had skated out there, it would have broken more of the ice and made it worse!"

Mother nodded. "I'm glad you had the good sense to know that," she said. "Now think about this—when you see someone in sin, you don't rescue him by joining him. If you do, you might both get trapped in sin."

As Connie heard Mother's words, she remembered their conversation that morning. She would have to find some other way to help Karen.

HOW ABOUT YOU? In order to win a friend to Jesus, are you sometimes tempted to go someplace you should not go or to do something you know is wrong? If you yield to that temptation, you're just fooling yourself—you're not winning your friend. The way to win others to Jesus is through living a pure life before them. Pray for them. H.M.

TO MEMORIZE: *"Do not share in the sins of others. Keep yourself pure"* 1 Timothy 5:22 (NIV).

8

Glowing Coals

FROM THE BIBLE:
Therefore, brothers, since we have confidence to enter the Most Holy Place by the blood of Jesus, by a new and living way opened for us through the curtain, that is, his body, and since we have a great priest over the house of God, let us draw near to God with a sincere heart in full assurance of faith, having our hearts sprinkled to cleanse us from a guilty conscience and having our bodies washed with pure water. Let us hold unswervingly to the hope we profess, for he who promised is faithful. And let us consider how we may spur one another on toward love and good deeds. Let us not give up meeting together, as some are in the habit of doing, but let us encourage one another—and all the more as you see the Day approaching.
Hebrews 10:19-25, NIV

Attend church regularly

"MOM, CAN I go skiing with Jan and her family next Sunday?" asked Amy. She hurried on as she saw her mother begin to shake her head. "Jan and her family go skiing almost every weekend, but they worship God just as well as we do. Jan told me they feel God's presence in nature—in the snow and the hills and everything."

"That sounds good," Mother said, "but I wonder how much you'd even think about God if you were skiing instead of attending church. What Jan's family does is up to them, but you're our responsibility, and Dad and I don't think it's right for us to skip church in favor of skiing."

Amy knew it was useless to argue.

That evening Dad added a log to the fire in the fireplace and stirred it with a poker. Suddenly, with a loud crack, a small ember few out onto the hearth. Amy jumped and then laughed as she watched it glow for a few minutes before slowing fading and turning black.

"Did that scare you?" asked Dad.

"For a minute," said Amy, grinning. "It sure didn't burn long when it got separated from the rest of the logs, did it?"

"No, it didn't," answered Mother thoughtfully. "Amy, does Jan still come to Bible club?"

"Not the last few weeks," answered Amy.

"And what about junior choir?" Amy shook her head. "Any of the church youth activities?"

Again Amy shook her head. "Why?"

"I was just thinking," said Mother, "that the ember that fell from the fireplace is a good illustration of what can happen to God's children when they no longer meet with God's people. That ember was giving light and warmth with the others, but all by itself, it soon grew cold. And God's people, united in fellowship, worship, and prayer, are like the glowing coals. They give and receive strength for everyday living. But, all alone, they often grow cold, too."

Slowly Amy nodded her head. "I'll see if I can get Jan to come back to Bible club," she decided. "It will be a step in the right direction."

HOW ABOUT YOU? Do you worship regularly with God's people? He says you should do that. He knows you need the encouragement and warmth of their fellowship. Together you can do great things for Him. H.M.

TO MEMORIZE: *"Let us not give up meeting together, as some are in the habit of doing, but let us encourage one another"* Hebrews 10:25 (NIV).

FEBRUARY

The Missing Sweater

FROM THE BIBLE:

Judges must always be just in their sentences, not noticing whether a person is poor or rich; they must always be perfectly fair. Don't gossip. Don't falsely accuse your neighbor of some crime, for I am Jehovah. Don't hate your brother. Rebuke anyone who sins; don't let him get away with it, or you will be equally guilty. Don't seek vengeance. Don't bear a grudge; but love your neighbor as yourself, for I am Jehovah.
Leviticus 19:15-18, TLB

Don't accuse falsely

"MOM, I CAN'T find my lavender sweater," wailed Phyllis.

"When was the last time you wore it?" Mother asked.

Phyllis wrinkled her brow. "Last Sunday."

"Maybe you left it at church," Mother suggested. "Call the office and ask if anyone turned it in." But the sweater wasn't there.

"We'll keep looking for it," Mother said. "It will probably show up."

Several times that week, Phyllis searched in vain for her sweater. She wanted to wear it to a Sunday school party at Melissa's house on Friday evening, but now she'd have to choose something else. Arriving at the party, Phyllis stared in amazement at Marci, one of the girls in her class. Drawing Melissa close, she whispered, "Marci's wearing my sweater! She must have picked it up at Sunday school."

"Are you sure?" Melissa whispered back.

"Of course," Phyllis hissed. "She couldn't afford a sweater like that!"

As the girls were talking with Marci later, Melissa said, "That's a pretty sweater, Marci. Where did you get it?"

"My mother bought it at a garage sale," she told them.

"I'll bet," muttered Phyllis. She was angry and told several girls that Marci had stolen her sweater. The party wasn't much fun for her after that.

When Phyllis reached home, her grandmother met her at the door. Phyllis gave her a big hug as Mother said, "You'll be glad to see what Grandma brought you." Mother handed Phyllis her lavender sweater.

"But where did you find this?" Phyllis stammered.

"You left it at my house last Sunday," Grandma told her.

Tears welled up in Phyllis's eyes. "I've made a terrible mistake," she sighed. "I'll tell you about it after I make some phone calls."

HOW ABOUT YOU? Have you ever falsely accused someone? Did you apologize? Next time you're tempted to accuse someone, wait! God says Christians should be slow to speak. He knows that hasty conclusions are often wrong. Hurting others with false accusations is a poor testimony. If you have done that, be sure to apologize. B.W.

TO MEMORIZE: *"Let every man be swift to hear, slow to speak, slow to wrath"* James 1:9.

FEBRUARY

10

How Dumb Are You?

FROM THE BIBLE:

But as for you, continue in what you have learned and have become convinced of, because you know those from whom you learned it, and how from infancy you have known the holy Scriptures, which are able to make you wise for salvation through faith in Christ Jesus. All Scripture is God-breathed and is useful for teaching, rebuking, correcting and training in righteousness, so that the man of God may be thoroughly equipped for every good work.

2 Timothy 3:14-17, NIV

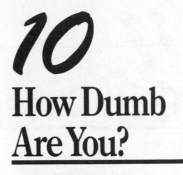

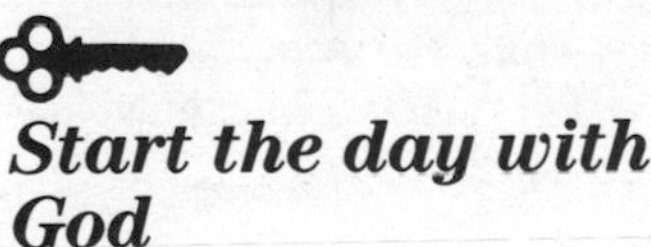

Start the day with God

WHEN BEVERLY was honest with herself, she had to admit that family devotions didn't mean much to her. She especially wished they could skip them on days like today when she was late getting downstairs and had to wait till after devotions to eat breakfast. "How come we have to do this every single day?" she asked when Dad finally ended his prayer. "Shirley's family never has devotions."

Ignoring her question, Dad picked up the cereal box and held it toward her. Then he pulled it back. "Oh, maybe you don't want breakfast," he said.

"Of course I want breakfast!" Beverly exclaimed. "I'm starving! Besides, our nutrition teacher says it's the most important meal of the day."

"I see. Well, I don't suppose you'll be eating lunch today, will you?" her father asked.

Beverly looked at him in surprise. "Why wouldn't I? You know I always take a sack lunch to school."

"And what about supper?" asked Dad. "Are you planning to eat supper tonight?"

By this time Beverly was beginning to get irritated. "Dad, I always eat supper."

He nodded. "I know you always have, but I wondered if you were thinking of giving up eating on busy days."

Beverly looked first at her mother and then at her dad. "Give up eating!" she repeated. "I'm not that dumb!" Suddenly she stopped. "Oh," she added slowly, "you're trying to tell me that it would be just as dumb to quit having my spiritual food. Right?"

"Right," agreed Dad with a smile. "Reading from the Bible every day is like eating good meals every day. In fact, I think it's good to start the day with God's Word—just like it's important to have a good breakfast."

Beverly flashed a big smile at her dad, then picked up the Bible that was next to her plate. "I guess it would be pretty dumb to go through a day without this," she said.

HOW ABOUT YOU? How dumb are you? You wouldn't be dumb enough to go very long without food for your body, would you? Are you dumb enough to go without food for your soul? It's important to feed upon God's Word each and every day. R.J.

TO MEMORIZE: *"All Scripture is God-breathed and is useful"* 2 Timothy 3:16 (NIV).

FEBRUARY

11

Guard Duty

FROM THE BIBLE:

Heaven can be entered only through the narrow gate! The highway to hell is broad, and its gate is wide enough for all the multitudes who choose its easy way. But the Gateway to Life is small, and the road is narrow, and only a few ever find it. . . . Not all who sound religious are really godly people. They may refer to me as "Lord," but still won't get to heaven. For the decisive question is whether they obey my Father in heaven. At the Judgment many will tell me, "Lord, Lord, we told others about you and used your name to cast out demons and to do many other great miracles." But I will reply, "You have never been mine. Go away, for your deeds are evil." Matthew 7:13-14, 21-23, TLB

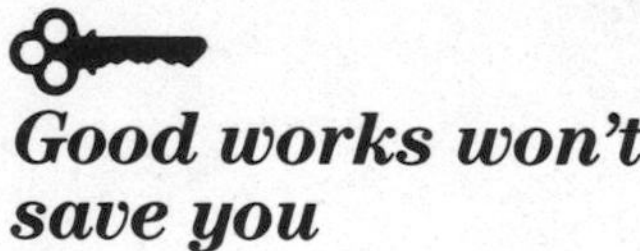

Good works won't save you

SANDY AND BRETT were taking a basket lunch to their father, who worked as a gate guard at a factory in their town. He saw them coming and greeted them as they approached the gate. "Sorry, but you can't get through here without a badge," he said sternly.

Sandy giggled. "Daddy, you know it's us. We brought your lunch."

Dad smiled. "I'll be off for lunch in five minutes. Wait here, and we can talk while I eat."

At lunchtime, they sat under a tree. "Dad, does everyone need to have a badge before you'll let him inside the factory?" Sandy asked as she munched on one of Dad's potato chips.

"Yes," said Dad. "The badge shows they belong here."

"But what if you know a person by name?" asked Brett.

"It makes no difference," Dad said. "He still needs a badge."

"How come?" asked Sandy. "It doesn't seem fair."

"Oh, it is," Dad replied. "The company will issue a free badge to all those who have business inside the factory. It's for their own protection, and the company's, too. It keeps outsiders from hindering our production or from getting hurt by wandering into the wrong place."

"I guess if you really want to be inside, you'll get a badge," Brett remarked.

"Right," Dad replied. "Sometimes people try to sneak in, but that doesn't work." Closing his lunch pail, he added, "This reminds me of the way some people try to get into heaven. In a sense, we need a badge to get into heaven, too—the badge of faith in Jesus Christ. People will try to sneak in by doing good works, or they'll claim God knows them, but that won't work. Accepting Jesus is the only way into heaven." Just then the factory whistle blew. "I must get back to work," Dad said. "See you at supper."

HOW ABOUT YOU? Do you want to go to heaven? You can't get there by your own good works. You must accept Jesus as your personal Savior. Do it today. Tomorrow may be too late! J.H.

TO MEMORIZE: *"But to him who does not work but believes on Him who justifies the ungodly, his faith is accounted for righteousness"* Romans 4:5 (NKJV).

FEBRUARY

12

An Old Piece of Wood

FROM THE BIBLE:

Here is another message to Jeremiah from the Lord: Go down to the shop where clay pots and jars are made and I will talk to you there. I did as he told me, and found the potter working at his wheel. But the jar that he was forming didn't turn out as he wished, so he kneaded it into a lump and started again. Then the Lord said: O Israel, can't I do to you as this potter has done to his clay? As the clay is in the potter's hand, so are you in my hand. Jeremiah 18:1-6, TLB

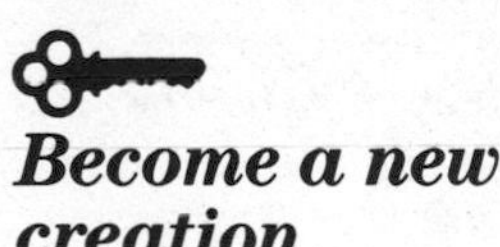

Become a new creation

JASON WAS HELPING his dad pile firewood in the backyard when their neighbor, Mr. Stevens, walked by.

"Looks like you got some walnut here," remarked Mr. Stevens as he stooped down and picked up a piece that Jason's dad had trimmed from a tree in the woods. "Mind if I borrow this for a week?"

"Sure, go ahead," said Dad. Jason wondered why Mr. Stevens would want to borrow the chunk of wood. He could see that Dad was as puzzled as he was.

They found out why exactly one week later. Mr. Stevens stopped by and returned the piece of walnut, except now it wasn't a chunk of firewood—it was a beautifully whittled bufflehead duck! "Wow!" Jason whistled. "Look what you did with just an old piece of wood!"

"We'll put this on our fireplace mantle instead of in the fire," Jason's dad said. "Thanks so much, Mr. Stevens."

The older man smiled. "Come over sometime and see my collection of ducks," he said. "I enjoy carving them. When I work on them and see the old piece of wood change into something beautiful, I like to think of what the Lord did for me. I was an unworthy sinner, living a life of pride and selfishness, yet the Lord took me and made me a new creation in Him!"

"Hmmmm. I never thought of it like that," Jason said, "but I will from now on. Every time I look at the duck made out of firewood, I'll think of how the Lord made the old sinful me into a new creature!"

HOW ABOUT YOU? Have you ever thought that the Lord couldn't love you because you are "so bad"? He tells you in His Word that He loved the whole world (that includes you) so much that He gave His life. He does love you, and if you accept Him as your personal Savior, He will change you into a new creation! L.W.

TO MEMORIZE: *"But now you must . . . put on the new man who is renewed in knowledge according to the image of Him who created him"* Colossians 3:8, 10 (NKJV).

FEBRUARY

13

Bend Your Knees

FROM THE BIBLE:

Listen to my prayer, O God; don't hide yourself when I cry to you. Hear me, Lord! Listen to me! For I groan and weep beneath my burden of woe.

But I will call upon the Lord to save me—and he will. I will pray morning, noon, and night, pleading aloud with God; and he will hear and answer. Though the tide of battle runs strongly against me, for so many are fighting me, yet he will rescue me. God himself—God from everlasting ages past—will answer them! For they refuse to fear him or even honor his commands.

This friend of mine betrayed me—I who was at peace with him. He broke his promises. His words were oily smooth, but in his heart was war. His words were sweet, but underneath were daggers. Give your burdens to the Lord. He will carry them. He will not permit the godly to slip or fall.

Psalm 55:1-2, 16-22, TLB

Give heartaches to God

RICKY FELT so heavy inside. He sat slumped on the stairs as he watched Uncle Bob and Mother carry the furniture from the house. So much had happened lately. His dad had moved out and filed for a divorce. Now he and his mother were moving to a smaller, cheaper house. Ricky had cried and begged and raged, but nothing had changed—except him. He felt hard and bitter. He didn't even try to pray anymore. "God doesn't care, or He wouldn't have let this happen. So why bother talking to Him?" Ricky told himself. But he did feel terribly lonely. Not only did he miss his father, he missed his heavenly Father, too.

Mother patted Ricky's shoulder and smiled as she and Uncle Bob came up the stairs. "She can't be hurting like I am, or she couldn't smile," Ricky thought angrily. "Maybe it's her fault. Maybe she asked him to leave."

"Please help us with this heavy dresser," Mother called.

Scowling and grumbling, Ricky went to help. As he stooped over to lift his end, Uncle Bob exclaimed, "No, no! That's not the way to lift it, Ricky. You'll hurt your back that way. Watch me, and do it this way. Lift your load with your knees, not your back."

Mother sighed deeply. "You know, that's what I've been doing, Bob."

"Good," said Uncle Bob, smiling. "You don't need a backache on top of your heartache."

"I'm not talking about lifting the furniture," said Mother. "I'm talking about my heavy heart. I've been lifting it to God on my knees in prayer. It's the only way I can keep going. I've found it's not the load that can hurt you, it's how you carry it. I don't want to get bitter. I want to keep smiling and trusting God."

"How about you, Ricky?" asked Uncle Bob. "How have you been carrying your heartache? You need to lift that load with your knees, too. Let your heavenly Father help you carry it."

Tears blinded Ricky, but he smiled. "I will, Uncle Bob." Then he bent his knees and lifted his end of the dresser.

HOW ABOUT YOU? Are you carrying a heavy load? Does it seem you have more than your share of troubles? Don't try to carry them alone. Get on your knees and lift your load to the Lord in prayer. He'll help you carry it. B.W.

TO MEMORIZE: *"Cast all your anxiety on him because he cares for you"* 1 Peter 5:7 (NIV).

FEBRUARY

A Special Love

FROM THE BIBLE:

Dear friends, let us practice loving each other, for love comes from God and those who are loving and kind show that they are the children of God, and that they are getting to know him better. But if a person isn't loving and kind, it shows that he doesn't know God—for God is love. God showed how much he loved us by sending his only Son into this wicked world to bring to us eternal life through his death. In this act we see what real love is: it is not our love for God, but his love for us when he sent his Son to satisfy God's anger against our sins.

1 John 4:7-10, TLB

God loves you

"I REALLY DON'T see what's so special about Jesus dying to save people," Bobby said bluntly.

His mother stared at him in amazement. "Why, Bobby!"

"Well, I don't," he repeated. "Lots of soldiers have died so we can be free."

"True, Bobby," agreed Mother, "and I'd say that's special, wouldn't you?"

"Well, sure," said Bobby, "but what I mean is, if I could die to save ten or even five people from hell, I'd do it. At least I think I would. Jesus saved thousands when He died. Amost anyone would be willing to die to save as many people as Jesus did."

His mother regarded him thoughtfully for a minute before she answered. "Bobby, would you die for a thousand grasshoppers?"

A broad grin spread over Bobby's face. "You kiddin'?"

"No, I'm very serious," said Mother. "Don't you suppose we look like grasshoppers in the sight of the Lord?"

Bobby frowned. "I never thought of it like that, Mom."

Bobby's heart pounded and his knees trembled. Somehow he had always pictured God as just another man. It was a bit frightening to think of himself as a little grasshopper with a great big God looming over him.

"But, Bobby," continued Mother, "there's one important difference between how you see a grasshopper and how God sees you. You don't care a thing for the grasshopper, but God loves you! The Bible tells us that while we were still sinners, Christ died for us. Love makes all the difference in the world."

Bobby's eyes misted. "I guess it must."

His mother hugged him. "You know, Bobby, if you had been the only person in the world, Jesus would have died just for you. In fact, He did die for you—for you, personally."

HOW ABOUT YOU? Jesus died for you, too. What love! All the love we talk about on Valentine's Day is nothing compared to the love of Jesus. Do you appreciate what He did for you at Calvary? Have you accepted His gift of salvation? If not, why don't you invite Him right now to be your Savior and to take control of your life. Then thank Him for loving you. B.W.

TO MEMORIZE: *"But God demonstrates His love toward us, in that while we were yet sinners, Christ died for us"* Romans 5:8 (NASB).

FEBRUARY

15

Poisoned Minds

FROM THE BIBLE:

My brethren, do not hold the faith of our Lord Jesus Christ, the Lord of glory, with partiality. For if there should come into your assembly a man with gold rings, in fine apparel, and there should also come in a poor man in filthy clothes, and you pay attention to the one wearing the fine clothes and say to him, "You sit here in a good place," and say to the poor man, "You stand there," or, "Sit here at my footstool," have you not shown partiality among yourselves, and become judges with evil thoughts? . . . But if you show partiality, you commit sin, and are convicted by the law as transgressors. For whoever shall keep the whole law, and yet stumble in one point, he is guilty of all.

James 2:1-4, 9-10, NKJV

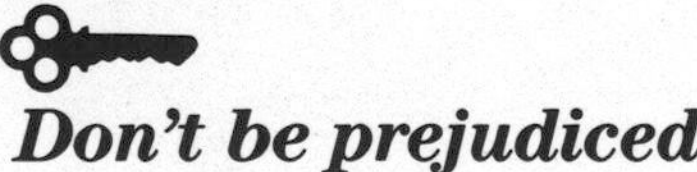

Don't be prejudiced

TOMMY WAS the new boy at school He was an American Indian, and most of the children in his grade had never seen an Indian. His mother greeted him as he arrived home one day. "How was school?" she asked.

"Awful!" answered Tommy. "The kids think Indians wear war paint and feathers and say, 'Ugh! How! Me Big Chief Tommy Hawk.' "

"Oh, Tommy. Has someone been teasing you and calling you 'Big Chief Tommy Hawk'?" asked Mother with a smile.

"It wasn't funny," replied Tommy almost in tears.

Mother was sympathetic. "I know what it's like. I'm an Indian, too. But I'm proud of my heritage," she said. "Tommy, anywhere you live, you will meet people with prejudices."

"What are they?" asked Tommy.

"Prejudices are opinions people form before the facts are known. They include a dislike of people who are different from oneself," Mother told him. "At one time or another, everyone is laughed at. But tell me about the other kids in your class."

"They're mostly just regular kids," answered Tommy. "There's one girl, though, who's different. Her name is Marsha. Every day a chauffeur in a big black Cadillac brings her to school and picks her up. She's a snob!"

"Tommy!" exclaimed Mother.

"Well, she is," Tommy insisted. "She goes around with her nose in the air and never speaks to anyone."

"Tommy," scolded Mother, "you don't even know Marsha, but you're judging her like others judged you."

"But, Mother—" began Tommy.

"There are more kinds of prejudices than just racial prejudices," Mother continued. "Some people are prejudiced against other religions, or against the rich, the poor, or the handicapped. All prejudices are wrong. That's what the Bible is talking about when it says we shouldn't show partiality."

HOW ABOUT YOU? Do you tease or avoid someone of a different race, someone who attends a different church, or someone who is different in other ways? This is not pleasing to God. Ask Him to forgive you, and determine to treat those "different" people just as you would want to be treated yourself. B.W.

TO MEMORIZE: *"If you show partiality, you commit sin"* James 2:9 (NKJV).

FEBRUARY

16

A Cage or a Castle?

FROM THE BIBLE:

Ask, and you will be given what you ask for. Seek, and you will find. Knock, and the door will be opened. For everyone who asks, receives. Anyone who seeks, finds. If only you will knock, the door will open. If a child asks his father for a loaf of bread, will he be given a stone instead? If he asks for fish, will he be given a poisonous snake? Of course not! And if you hardhearted, sinful men know how to give good gifts to your children, won't your Father in heaven even more certainly give good gifts to those who ask him for them?

Matthew 7:7-11, TLB

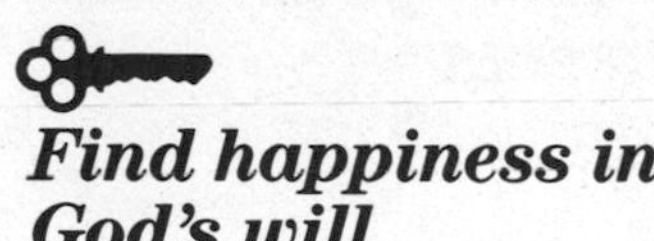

Find happiness in God's will

BRENT CUT doors and windows in an old refrigerator carton, put an old throw rug in it, and climbed inside. Pretty soon, Mother heard little Joey crying from Brent's room. "Mommy!" he sobbed. "Brent won't let me come in his catsul!"

"He keeps messing up the rug and jumping around inside," complained Brent. "I'm afraid he'll wreck it." Mother set Joey in his high chair and gave him some toys.

Later, Mother again heard Joey crying. When she went to investigate, she was surprised to see him crouched inside the big box, crying as he peered out the window. "Brent won't let me out of the cage!" he sobbed.

"Brent!" scolded Mother. "Take that chair away from the door and let Joey out." Brent sheepishly moved the chair, and his little brother scrambled out quickly.

"He kept trying to get in, so I thought if I made him stay in there for a while, he'd get tired of it," explained Brent.

Little Joey scowled. "But he said I was a monkey in a cage. I don't wanna be a monkey."

Mother couldn't help smiling as she hugged him. "An hour ago, he was crying to get into your 'catsul.' Now he couldn't wait to get out!" she remarked.

"That's because I turned it into a cage." Brent grinned. "But it's still the same box. What a joke!"

Mother looked thoughtfully at the castle-turned-cage. "You know, this reminds me of the will of God," she said. "Some people think it's a cage. They feel that if they obey God, they won't ever be happy because they won't get to do what they want to do. But people who know the Lord well consider His will to be the happiest castle on earth. They want to obey Him, because they love Him. It all depends on how you look at it!"

HOW ABOUT YOU? Do you go to church, read the Bible, sing in the choir, and witness to your friends halfheartedly, out of duty or habit? Or do you really enjoy serving the Lord and doing His will? The place that He wants you to serve Him may seem like a "cage" or a "castle," depending on how you look at it. God knows what's best for you. Be happy where He puts you. S.K.

TO MEMORIZE: *"Every good gift and every perfect gift is from above, and comes down from the Father"* James 1:17 (NKJV).

FEBRUARY

17

Old and Honorable

FROM THE BIBLE:

Do not rebuke an older man harshly, but exhort him as if he were your father. Treat younger men as brothers, older women as mothers, and younger women as sisters, with absolute purity. Give proper recognition to those widows who are really in need. But if a widow has children or grandchildren, these should learn first of all to put their religion into practice by caring for their own family and so repaying their parents and grandparents, for this is pleasing to God. 1 Timothy 5:1-4, NIV

Respect your parents

"ANNE, YOU LOOK very thoughtful," commented Mother. "What's on your mind?"

"Oh, I was just reading the strangest story in this book," Anne answered. "It's about a man and his wife. The man's father lived with them. He was old and kind of sick, and his hands shook. When he ate, sometimes he knocked things over, so the wife told her husband to make a wooden bowl for him so he wouldn't break the good dishes. After that, the man got tired of seeing his father spill food at the table, and he made his father take the wooden bowl and sit in the corner behind the stove to eat. That still wasn't good enough. They got tired of cleaning up food, so they made the old man eat out of the kind of grain bin that the animals used."

"Does sound strange," agreed Mother.

"Here's the strangest part of the story," Anne continued. "The couple had a little boy, and one day they saw him whittling, hollowing out a log. The father asked what he was doing, and the little boy said, 'I'm making a trough so it will be ready for you when you're old and come to live with me.' " Anne paused a moment. "Do you think that's a true story?" she asked.

"It's probably not true in fact," answered her mother, "but I know there are many people who don't respect or care for their parents."

Anne nodded. "Connie's grandmother lives with them, and the poor old woman isn't allowed to come out of her room when they have company. Connie says it's because she's had a stroke and talks real funny."

"That really is sad," sighed Mother. "God's Word instructs children to honor their parents, no matter how old they might be. It's important to start showing them respect and honor when you're young. Then it will become a habit, and it will be natural for you to show them love and care when they get old, too."

HOW ABOUT YOU? Do you honor your parents? Do you show respect to your grandparents? To all old people? Do you treat them the way you want to be treated when you grow old? God says you are to respect and honor your parents. You are to do that all your life. Start while you're young, and it will be easier to do when you're older. C.R.

TO MEMORIZE: *"These should learn first of all to put their religion into practice by caring for their own family"* 1 Timothy 5:4 (NIV).

FEBRUARY

18

What We Have

JARED SIGHED as he pushed the door open, pulled the key out, and put it in his pocket. He swung the door shut and locked it. "Tony's lucky—his mom is home baking cookies, but I have to peel potatoes and put dumb old meatloaf in the oven" he said out loud. He talked to himself a lot when he was alone. That way the apartment didn't seem so empty. "I wish I had a pet."

Jared continued to mumble as he did his chores. Soon he heard his mother at the door. "Hi, honey, how was school?"

"OK." Jared didn't look up.

"Thanks for putting the meatloaf in the oven. It sure smells good." She looked at him closely. "Is something wrong?" she asked.

"No."

"Are you sure?" Mom paused on her way toward the stove. "I can tell something's bothering you. Let's talk about it." She put down a dish and hugged Jared. Soon he was telling her all his troubles, especially how he hated coming home to an empty house.

Mom sighed. "We talked about this before, and you know I have to work," she said. "I'd rather be home, but I have no choice. I wish you could have a pet, but the landlord won't allow that." Her shoulders slumped. Then she sat up straight. "Jared, you have something many of your friends don't have—you have Jesus," she reminded him. "That's more important than anything else in the world. When we have to do without things we want, I think it helps to remind ourselves of what we do have. Let's make a list. I'll start." Mom picked up a pen and paper. "We have a place to live."

"And clothes," Jared added.

Mom wrote it down. "You can go to school, and I have a job," she said. "What else?"

"Friends." Jared started to smile.

"We have a church where we can worship God."

Jared sniffed the air. "We have meatloaf." He grinned. "Let's set the table. I'm hungry!"

HOW ABOUT YOU? Do your friends have something you wish you had? Instead of thinking of those things, make a list of what you have. Learn to be content in your circumstances and even give thanks for them. As you do, you'll find they don't seem quite so bad anymore. V.L.C.

TO MEMORIZE: *"Give thanks in all circumstances, for this is God's will for you in Christ Jesus"* 1 Thessalonians 5:18 (NIV).

FROM THE BIBLE:

Do you want to be truly rich? You already are if you are happy and good. After all, we didn't bring any money with us when we came into the world, and we can't carry away a single penny when we die. So we should be well satisfied without money if we have enough food and clothing. But people who long to be rich soon begin to do all kinds of wrong things to get money, things that hurt them and make them evil-minded and finally send them to hell itself. For the love of money is the first step toward all kinds of sin. Some people have even turned away from God because of their love for it, and as a result have pierced themselves with many sorrows. Oh, Timothy, you are God's man. Run from all these evil things and work instead at what is right and good, learning to trust him and love others, and to be patient and gentle. Fight on for God. Hold tightly to the eternal life which God has given you, and which you have confessed with such a ringing confession before many witnesses. 1 Timothy 6:6-12, TLB

Count your blessings

FEBRUARY

Give Them a Chance!

FROM THE BIBLE:
I thank my God upon every remembrance of you, always in every prayer of mine making request for you all with joy, for your fellowship in the gospel from the first day until now, being confident of this very thing, that He who has begun a good work in you will complete it until the day of Jesus Christ. . . . And this I pray, that your love may abound still more and more in knowledge and all discernment, that you may approve the things that are excellent, that you may be sincere and without offense till the day of Christ, being filled with the fruits of righteousness which are by Jesus Christ, to the glory and praise of God.
Philippians 1:3-6, 9-11, NKJV

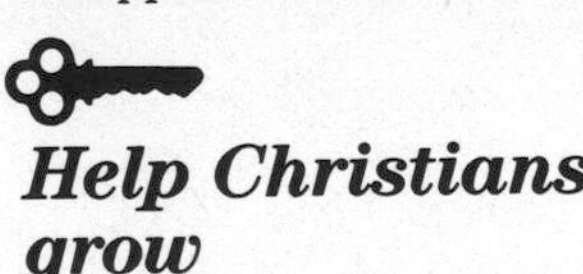

JIMMY SLOUCHED in a kitchen chair. "Hey, Mom," he sighed, "remember I told you that my friend, Pete, accepted Christ last month?"

"Of course I remember," said Mother. "You were really happy and excited about it. But what's wrong now?"

"Well, I saw Pete smoking in the school parking lot today," Jimmy said. "I figured he would quit smoking now that he's a Christian." Jimmy shook his head sadly. "I even heard him use a swear word. Some Christian he turned out to be!"

Mother looked thoughtful. "That's too bad, Jimmy," she began. Just then, they heard a faint cry coming from down the hall. "Your sister's awake," said Mother. "Would you go tell her she can get up from her nap?"

Jimmy stared at Mother. "But Jennifer's only six months old," he said. "You know she can't walk out here by herself."

"Why not?" asked Mother. "After all, I've been carrying her around for a long time. I think it's about time she started walking."

"But . . . but, Mom!" argued Jimmy. "You know that babies can't walk until they're about a year old. Give her a chance to grow up!"

"The same chance you're giving Pete, you mean?" asked his mother. Jimmy looked confused, so after she had gone to get Jennifer, Mother explained. "Babies can't do everything as soon as they're born. They have to grow up gradually. It's the same way with Christians. Some people, after they accept Christ as their Savior, seem to grow very quickly. Others take more time. As they go to church, read the Bible and pray, and fellowship with other Christians, God will help them to grow. But we have to be patient. It takes time!"

"I see," said Jimmy. "I'll try being more of a friend to Pete, and not expect too much of him all at once. And I'll pray that God will help him grow—and me, too!"

HOW ABOUT YOU? You may be tempted to criticize when you see a new Christian falling into sin. But he or she needs help, not criticism. Perhaps you can share some Bible verses that deal with the problem. Then, pray for that person and wait for God to help him or her grow. Making Christians feel discouraged is the devil's work. Your job is to build them up! S.K.

TO MEMORIZE: *"He who has begun a good work in you will complete it until the day of Jesus Christ"* Philippians 1:6 (NKJV).

FEBRUARY

20

An Important Seal

FROM THE BIBLE:
But God's truth stands firm like a great rock, and nothing can shake it. It is a foundation stone with these words written on it: "The Lord knows those who are really his," and "A person who calls himself a Christian should not be doing things that are wrong." In a wealthy home there are dishes made of gold and silver as well as some made from wood and clay. The expensive dishes are used for guests, and the cheap ones are used in the kitchen or to put garbage in. If you stay away from sin you will be like one of these dishes made of purest gold—the very best in the house—so that Christ himself can use you for his highest purposes. Run from anything that gives you the evil thoughts that young men often have, but stay close to anything that makes you want to do right. Have faith and love, and enjoy the companionship of those who love the Lord and have pure hearts.
2 Timothy 2:19-22, TLB

JASON WATCHED as his father made a stamp on several letters with an embosser. "What are you doing, Dad?" he asked.

"This is our company's seal, Jason. It displays our trademark and our motto," explained Dad. "The raised marks make it impossible for anyone to erase it."

"What's your company motto?" asked Jason.

" 'Old-fashioned service with new-fashioned materials,' " said Dad with a smile.

"Do all companies have seals?" Jason wondered.

"Some do," answered Dad. "So do the fifty states. Our Wisconsin seal says, 'Forward.' Our country has a seal, too. It's a Latin phrase that means, 'Out of many, one.' "

Jason grinned. "Hey, that's neat," he said.

"There's another important seal, too, Jason," said Dad. "Take your Bible and look up 2 Timothy 2:19."

Jason got his Bible and quickly turned to the New Testament. He found the verse and read, "Nevertheless the foundation of God standeth sure, having this seal, The Lord knoweth them that are His."

"You see, Jason, when we became Christians we were sealed with the Holy Spirit," said Dad, "and I guess we could say that the motto of our seal is 'The Lord knoweth them that are His.' "

Jason thought about that. "It's kinda like your company's seal, Dad," he decided. "It's something that can't be erased. And when people see that special mark on a letter, they know it's from your business. When we're sealed with the Holy Spirit, people should be able to see that we belong to the Lord!"

HOW ABOUT YOU? Have you ever seen a seal with a motto or a picture representing a country or a business? If you're a Christian, you were sealed with the Holy Spirit when you accepted Christ. You belong to the Lord, and nothing can change that. But, remember, others should be able to see by your life that you have His seal upon you. L. W.

TO MEMORIZE: *"Having believed, you were marked in him with a seal, the promised Holy Spirit"* Ephesians 1:13 (NIV).

The Holy Spirit is our seal

FEBRUARY

21

God's Training School

FROM THE BIBLE:

In everything you do, stay away from complaining and arguing, so that no one can speak a word of blame against you. You are to live clean, innocent lives as children of God in a dark world full of people who are crooked and stubborn. Shine out among them like beacon lights, holding out to them the Word of Life. Then when Christ returns how glad I will be that my work among you was so worthwhile. And if my lifeblood is, so to speak, to be poured out over your faith which I am offering up to God as a sacrifice—that is, if I am to die for you—even then I will be glad, and will share my joy with each of you. For you should be happy about this, too, and rejoice with me for having this privilege of dying for you. Philippians 2:14-18, TLB

Be patient

"HI, MOM." Shelly put her books down. "Hi, Gram."

"Hello, Shelly," said Mom. "I was fixing some coffee for Gram and me. Would you like some juice?"

"Sure," answered Shelly. She went to the refrigerator.

"Why are we all dressed up?" asked Grandma.

"We're having dinner with the Hoyles," Mom replied.

"The Hoyles are so nice. I remember when we spent a week with them at the lake. It was so pretty . . . " Grandma's voice trailed off. Shelly slammed down her glass. She must have heard that story a hundred times! Mom shot a warning look at Shelly. Shelly opened a book.

"Why are we all dressed up?" Grandma asked again, and again Mom answered patiently. "The Hoyles are such nice people," said Grandma. Shelly picked up her book and juice and left the room.

"Mom, how can you be so patient?" Shelly asked later.

"I remind myself that Grandma is sick with Alzheimer's disease and she doesn't remember," Mom said. "It's like a short circuit in the brain. She can't help it."

Shelly frowned. "But how come she has to live here? My friends laugh at her."

"I know it isn't easy sometimes," Mom said, "but we love Grandma, and this is what is best for her."

Grandma came to the bedroom door and smiled. "Why are we all dressed up?" she asked.

Shelly sighed as she glanced at her mom. Then she grinned. "We're having dinner with the Hoyles, Gram."

"They're such nice people. I remember the time we were at the lake together," Grandma said cheerily.

"Tell me about it, Grandma," said Shelly.

HOW ABOUT YOU? Do you need extra understanding or patience with a friend or family member? Ask the Lord to help you develop that patience. As you honor Him by showing love and kindness now, you will also be preparing for whatever ministry the Lord has for you as an adult. V.L.C.

TO MEMORIZE: *"In your patience possess your souls"* Luke 21:19 (NKJV).

FEBRUARY

22

The Mighty Egg

FROM THE BIBLE:

If anyone says "I love God," but keeps on hating his brother, he is a liar; for if he doesn't love his brother who is right there in front of him, how can he love God whom he has never seen? And God himself has said that one must love not only God, but his brother too.

1 John 4:20-21, TLB

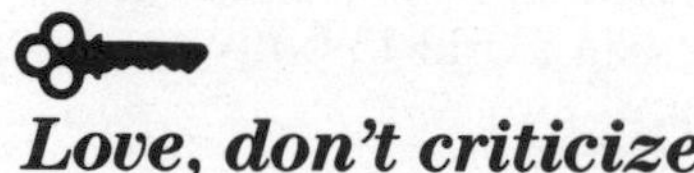

Love, don't criticize

"JOHN! JULIE!" called Mother. "Breakfast is ready!"

"What are we having?" Julie asked as she and John came to the table. "Oh, good! I like eggs!" After thanking God for the food, they began to eat.

"I'm anxious to hear what our new pastor will speak about today," said Dad.

"Whatever it is, I'm sure Mrs. Grady won't like it," mumbled John. "She's always complaining that the sermon is too long or too short or not as good as our old pastor's."

"You should hear the kids in my Sunday school class talk about our teacher when she's not in the room," said Julie. "People sure like to criticize others, don't they?"

"I'm afraid they do, and that's a shame," Mother said with a sigh, "especially among Christians. We who are members of Christ's body should love one another. We get enough criticism from the world without picking on each other!"

Dad held up an egg and gazed at it thoughtfully. "What you've been talking about reminds me of something I read about eggs," he said. "The shell of an egg like this one is strong enough so that the hen can sit on it without breaking it. It protects the chick from many dangers. Because of the rounded shape of the shell, it's quite strong when struck from the outside. But do you know how the small, helpless chick is able to hatch out?"

"It pecks its way out, doesn't it?" asked John.

Dad nodded. "That's right. Although the shell resists pressure well from the outside, it cracks easily when pecked from within. In the same way, a church can resist outside pressure and persecution as long as Christians unite together in love. But when they start picking on one another, their fellowship is easily destroyed."

"That's a good lesson, Dad," said Julie. "I'll have to remember it the next time I'm tempted to criticize someone—especially another Christian."

HOW ABOUT YOU? Are you in the habit of criticizing your pastor, your Sunday school teacher, or others in your church family? You should be especially careful about criticizing Christians. Satan himself is called "the accuser of our brethren" in Revelation 12:10. Don't do his work for him. Remember "the mighty egg"! S.K.

TO MEMORIZE: *"By this all will know that you are My disciples, if you have love for one another"* John 13:35 (NKJV).

FEBRUARY

23

Growing Up

FROM THE BIBLE:

For You have formed my inward parts; You have covered me in my mother's womb. I will praise You, for I am fearfully and wonderfully made; Marvelous are Your works, And that my soul knows very well. My frame was not hidden from You, When I was made in secret, And skillfully wrought in the lowest parts of the earth. Your eyes saw my substance, being yet unformed. And in Your book they all were written, The days fashioned for me, When as yet there were none of them.
Psalm 139:13-16, NKJV

Love the handicapped

JUDY AND BOB were so happy to have a new baby brother. Judy especially like to help Mother take care of little Jimmy. But one day when the children came home from school, they found Dad in deep thought, and Mother was wiping her eyes. "Mother! What's wrong?" Judy exclaimed. "You took Jimmy to the doctor today, didn't you? Is something wrong with him?"

"Yes, Judy, there is," answered Mother. "Jimmy isn't growing normally. He's not doing the things he should be doing at his age. The doctor calls it being developmentally disabled or handicapped. Many people would say he's retarded."

Bob and Judy were stunned! Their baby brother was retarded? How could God allow such a thing to happen? "But why, Mother?" they asked. "Why?"

Dad answered. "We don't know why. We only know that God has a reason—a good reason. Some day, perhaps in heaven, we'll know why. But for now we'll just go on loving him and caring for him."

Judy burst into tears! "Not normal!" she exclaimed. "Jimmy's not normal!"

Dad spoke again. "This is hard to accept," he said, "but God is never unfair. Jimmy needs us more, so we'll love him more. In giving him love and happiness, we'll gain love and happiness, too."

HOW ABOUT YOU? Do you know any handicapped persons? For reasons known only to Himself, God made some people special, with either physical or mental handicaps. Make an effort to smile at them and talk to them. Never stare at them, make fun of them, or say unkind things about them. There are many wonderful, lovable human beings with special problems, and they have much to offer. Remember, God made them. He loves them, and you can love them, too. A.L.

TO MEMORIZE: *"Who gave man his mouth? Who makes him deaf or mute? Who gives him sight or makes him blind? Is it not I, the LORD?"* Exodus 4:11 (NIV).

FEBRUARY

24

Growing Up

(Continued from yesterday)

FROM THE BIBLE:

So get rid of your feelings of hatred. Don't just pretend to be good! Be done with dishonesty and jealousy and talking about others behind their backs. Now that you realize how kind the Lord has been to you, put away all evil, deception, envy, and fraud. Long to grow up into the fullness of your salvation; cry for this as a baby cries for his milk. Come to Christ, who is the living Foundation of Rock upon which God builds; though men have spurned him, he is very precious to God who has chosen him above all others. And now you have become living building-stones for God's use in building his house. What's more, you are his holy priests; so come to him—[you who are acceptable to him because of Jesus Christ]—and offer to God those things that please him. 1 Peter 2:1-5, TLB

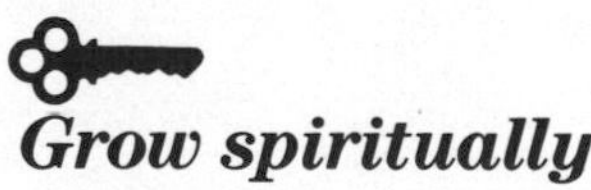

Grow spiritually

AFTER JUDY and Bob learned that their baby brother would never be able to do some of the things most children do, their attitudes toward him seemed to change. Bob played with him more than before and encouraged him to learn new things. But Judy gave him less and less attention. She helped take care of him when she had to, but whenever possible, she busied herself with some other task.

"Judy," said Mother one day, "you used to love to take Jimmy for a ride in the park. Why is it you never want to do that anymore?"

Judy blushed. "It . . . it just isn't the same as before," she stammered.

"What isn't the same, honey?" asked Mother.

"Jimmy!" Judy cried. "Jimmy's not the same! He's not like other babies. Taking care of him isn't fun anymore."

"But Jimmy *is* the same," Mother told her. "He's still the same sweet baby he always was. *You* have changed! You're not the same sweet, happy girl that you were."

"But Mother," objected Judy, "you can't blame me for being disappointed!"

"We were all disappointed," Mother replied, "but we didn't all grow bitter. Judy, you were saved several years ago. If you were growing spiritually, as you should be, you would be concerned about Jimmy instead of yourself. You wouldn't be ashamed. Judy, you are handicapped, too! You see, dear, I have two handicapped children—one mentally handicapped and one spiritually handicapped."

"Oh, Mother," Judy said, her eyes glistening with tears. "I never thought of myself that way! Please forgive me. Here—give Jimmy to me! I'll take care of him. And I'll hug and love him, too. Oh, Jimmy, you *are* sweet!"

Mother smiled. "And so are you, dear—now! You are growing again."

HOW ABOUT YOU? Are you growing spiritually? Are you learning to be more cheerful and to be more kind to your brothers and sisters? Are you being more and more helpful around the house? Growing physically and mentally are important, but we often forget that growing spiritually is even more important. Learn from God's Word what he wants of you. Ask Him to help you grow. A.L.

TO MEMORIZE: *"But grow in grace, and in the knowledge of our Lord and Savior, Jesus Christ"* 2 Peter 3:18.

FEBRUARY

25

A Man of Principle

FROM THE BIBLE:

Happy are all who perfectly follow the laws of God. Happy are all who search for God, and always do his will, rejecting compromise with evil, and walking only in his paths. You have given us your laws to obey: oh, how I want to follow them consistently. Then I will not be disgraced, for I will have a clean record.

After you have corrected me I will thank you by living as I should! Psalm 119:1-7, TLB

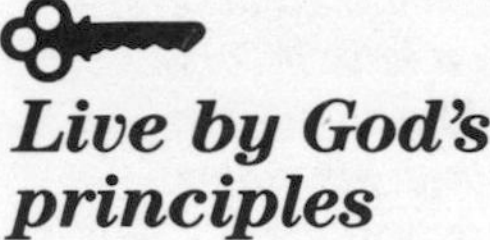

Live by God's principles

"HEY, STEVE! How many raffle tickets do you want?" asked George as the boys walked home from school.

"None. I don't buy raffle tickets."

"I'm not asking you to buy any," George said. "How many do you want to sell? Our class is supposed to sell them to earn money for our class project, you know."

"It doesn't seem right to sell them to other people when I don't believe in them myself," Steve replied.

George scowled. "If you don't sell tickets, you won't be doing your share, Steve," he scolded. "Let me know tomorrow how many you'll take."

Steve sighed. Should he give in and sell the tickets? Other kids in his class were Christians, and it didn't seem to bother them. Maybe he should "do his share," as George said. But he really agreed with Dad's argument that buying raffle tickets was like gambling. He didn't know what to do.

That evening, at a father-son banquet, Steve saw a film on the life of Eric Liddell. Eric, a Scotsman, had been expected to win a gold medal in the 100-meter race during the 1924 Olympics. He refused to run, however, when he learned the race would be held on Sunday. He felt it was important to honor God by keeping a day special for Him. Later, he was able to compete in the 400-meter race and win a gold medal.

After seeing the film, Steve knew what he had to do. "I'd like to try to earn money for our class project by washing cars at home instead of selling raffle tickets," he told his dad.

Dad smiled and nodded. "I'm proud of you," he said. "People may not understand because their principles may not be the same as yours. But you need to do what you believe is right. You know, Son, others ran in that Olympic race and won gold medals, but Eric is the one who is most remembered today. And he's remembered not for running a race but for being a man of principle!"

HOW ABOUT YOU? Are you having trouble making decisions? Don't let anyone talk you into listening to certain types of music, watching questionable TV shows, or doing anything that is against what you believe is right. Learn how God wants you to live, and live that way. Be a person of principles—God's principles—and stick to them. J.H.

TO MEMORIZE: *"Keep the commandments of the LORD your God and walk in His ways"* Deuteronomy 28:9 (NKJV).

FEBRUARY

26

Pretty Package

FROM THE BIBLE:
Judge not, that you be not judged. For with what judgment you judge, you will be judged; and with the same measure you use, it will be measured back to you. And why do you look at the speck in your brother's eye, but do not consider the plank in your own eye? Or how can you say to your brother, "Let me remove the speck out of your eye"; and look, a plank is in your own eye? Hypocrite! First remove the plank from your own eye, and then you will see clearly to remove the speck out of your brother's eye. . . . Therefore, whatever you want men to do to you, do also to them, for this is the Law and the Prophets.
Matthew 7:1-5, 12, NKJV

Don't judge by appearance only

WHEN DOTTIE came into the kitchen, sleepily rubbing her eyes, she found the rest of her family there ahead of her. "Happy birthday!" they shouted. A big smile spread across Dottie's face as she saw gifts piled beside her plate. There was one all done up in rainbow colors, with long, curly streamers. Another had a teddy bear trinket on top. And then there was a plain white envelope. "We thought we'd let you open presents now," said Mother with a smile.

Eagerly, Dottie reached for the package with the teddy bear on top. Inside, she found a cute little notepad and pen. She was surprised to see that it was from her brother. "Thanks, Ned," she said. "I love it." Next, she opened the "rainbow" package. It was from her sister, and it contained a new coloring book and magic markers. "Oh, good!" she exclaimed. "Half of my old markers won't even write anymore." Finally, she reached for the uninteresting white envelope and slowly slit it open. But when she saw what was inside, her eyes widened. "Oh," she squealed, "a kitty? I'm going to get a kitty?" She held out a certificate that read, "Good for one small kitten. With much love, Mom and Dad."

"You and Mom can pick it up after school," said Dad, smiling.

"Oh, thank you! This is the best present I ever had!"

As they went to get the kitten after school, Dottie told her mother all about her day. "We have a new girl in our class," she said, "but she looks kind of sloppy. She could use some new clothes. She combs her hair so funny, too."

"Be careful. Man looks on the outward appearance, but the Lord looks on the heart," Mother reminded her. "You can't tell what's in a package by the wrappings, you know." As they pulled up in front of the pet store, Dottie had to agree. She remembered the contents of the plain white envelope.

HOW ABOUT YOU? Do you make quick judgments when you meet new kids? Do you decide whether you like them by what they wear rather than by what they are? That's not God's way. He judges others—and you—but what He sees inside. Don't judge people just by the way they look. Ask the Lord to help you love them as He does. H.M.

TO MEMORIZE: *"Man looks at the outward appearance, but the LORD looks at the heart"*
1 Samuel 16:6 (NIV).

FEBRUARY

27

Free as the Air

FROM THE BIBLE:

But didn't he earn his right to heaven by all the good things he did? No, for being saved is a gift; if a person could earn it by being good, then it wouldn't be free—but it is! It is given to those who do not work for it. For God declares sinners to be good in his sight if they have faith in Christ to save them from God's wrath. King David spoke of this, describing the happiness of an undeserving sinner who is declared "not guilty" by God. "Blessed, and to be envied," he said, "are those whose sins are forgiven and put out of sight. Yes, what joy there is for anyone whose sins are no longer counted against him by the Lord." Romans 4:4-8, TLB

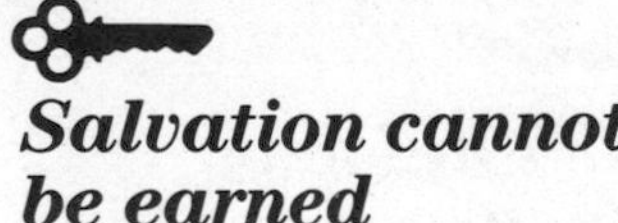

Salvation cannot be earned

"I CAN'T UNDERSTAND Sherri," complained Rachel as she looked down at the candy in her hand. "A couple of days ago she gave me a cute little eraser to pay me back for helping her with her math. Now she gave me this Tootsie Roll to pay me back for a cookie I gave her yesterday. It's not that I don't want the candy, but it's getting so I'm not sure I should ever do anything for her because she always thinks she has to give me something back."

Mother nodded. "Some people are like that. It takes the fun out of doing things for them, doesn't it? But I don't think you should stop helping her."

"I guess so," said Rachel. "But you know, Mom, she even thinks she has to pay God for everything He gives. When we were talking after Bible club the other day, she told me she didn't see how anybody could accept the idea that they could go to heaven just by believing. She said she intends to earn her way by being baptized and joining the church and by living a good, honest life."

"Oh, that is serious!" exclaimed Mother. "Let's pray that she'll see how foolish that is."

A couple days later, Rachel and Sherri conducted an experiment in their science class. By combining several chemicals, they made a gas that smelled just like rotten eggs! "Oh, air! Air! Give me air!" gasped Sherri as she rushed to a window. Rachel, too, eagerly gulped cold air. Suddenly Rachel got an idea. "Hold your breath," she commanded, "until you pay for the air!"

"What! Are you crazy?" asked Sherri.

"But you said you wouldn't take something for nothing, remember?" reminded Rachel. "Yet every day, all day, you breathe the air God gave us and don't pay for it. If you can accept God's gift of air, why is it so hard to accept His gift of salvation?"

"You might be right," Sherri said slowly. "Maybe I better think that over again."

HOW ABOUT YOU? The air that God gives us is a wonderful gift, isn't it? It would be foolish to think we could ever pay for it. Salvation is an even more wonderful gift. You can never earn it. All you can earn is death—being separated from God forever. You must choose. Will you refuse God's gift of salvation, or will you accept it and receive eternal life? H.M.

TO MEMORIZE: *"The wages of sin is death; but the gift of God is eternal life through Jesus Christ our Lord"* Romans 6:23.

FEBRUARY

28

The Homecoming

FROM THE BIBLE:

For we know that when this tent we live in now is taken down—when we die and leave these bodies—we will have wonderful new bodies in heaven, homes that will be ours forevermore, made for us by God himself, and not by human hands. . . . Now we look forward with confidence to our heavenly bodies, realizing that every moment we spend in these earthly bodies is time spent away from our eternal home in heaven with Jesus. We know these things are true by believing, not by seeing. And we are not afraid, but are quite content to die, for then we will be at home with the Lord.

2 Corinthians 5:1, 6-8, TLB

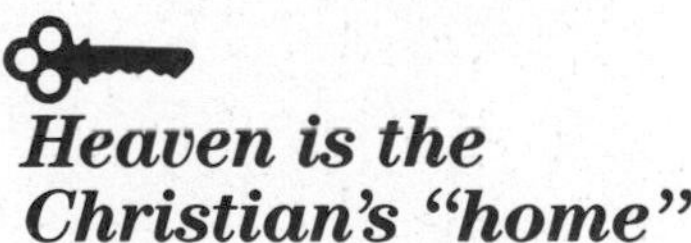

Heaven is the Christian's "home"

LINDA WAS SO SAD. She and her family had just returned from her grandmother's funeral. Already Linda missed Grandma, and so did her brother, Jerry. An older sister, Josie, lived far away. She had a baby only three days old, so she wasn't able to come to the funeral. "Now Grannie will never get to see Josie's baby," Linda cried.

Her parents comforted her. "Try to understand that God knows best," they told her. "You need to stop questioning and trust Him."

One night Linda went to a slumber party. The fun was just beginning when Linda's father telephoned to say she'd have to come home—he had a surprise for her. Linda protested and begged to stay, but Dad was firm and came to pick her up. She was very disappointed. Arriving at home, she unhappily opened the door to the house and heard a familiar voice call, "Surprise!" It was Josie and her husband, Bob, with baby Jane!

"Oooohhh!" breathed Linda. "Oh, let me see the baby! Isn't she cute! She looks just like me."

Jerry laughed. "Ha! You both got red noses, if that's what you mean. Only resemblance I see."

What a happy time they had—visiting, admiring the baby, and just being together! "But I still wish Grannie could have seen Jane," said Linda.

"We all do," answered Dad. "But, Linda, aren't you glad I insisted that you come home from that party?" Linda nodded, and Dad continued. "Having Josie's family come home reminds me of the homecoming that is taking place in heaven because Grandma 'came home.' You know, it's been eight years since she has been with Granddad. And then, there was her baby, who died when he was six years old, and her brother, who was killed in the war, and lots of other relatives and friends who went to heaven before she did."

Linda was thoughtful. "You mean God called her home to heaven just as you called me home tonight?" she asked.

"That's right," Dad said with a smile. "Just think how happy she is in heaven right now."

Linda was beginning to understand. "She's even happier than we are here with our family all together. God does know best, doesn't He?"

HOW ABOUT YOU? Has someone you love gone to heaven? When it hurts, remember how happy he or she is. God knows what is best for you, too. Trust Him. B.W.

TO MEMORIZE: *"For to me to live is Christ, and to die is gain"* Philippians 1:21.

FEBRUARY

The Hitchhiker

FROM THE BIBLE:

Now about brotherly love we do not need to write to you, for you yourselves have been taught by God to love each other. And in fact, you do love all the brothers throughout Macedonia. Yet we urge you, brothers, to do so more and more. Make it your ambition to lead a quiet life, to mind your own business and to work with your hands, just as we told you, so that your daily life may win the respect of outsiders and so that you will not be dependent on anybody.
1 Thessalonians 4:9-12, NIV

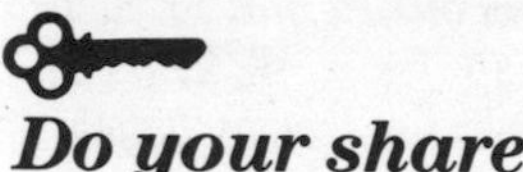

Do your share

"OH, NO!" exclaimed Mother. "Look where they stacked the firewood! I told them to put it on the patio."

"Looks like you get to move the firewood, Son," said Dad as they pulled into the driveway.

"Why me?" demanded Justin. "Why do I get all the dirty jobs around here?"

"I have to work on the car. Mother has to cook dinner, and I hardly think Jennifer can move all that wood." Dad grinned at his small daughter.

"Can too!" argued four-year-old Jennifer. And later, as Justin loaded Jennifer's little red wagon with wood, she announced, "I'm gonna help you."

"Great!" answered Justin sarcastically as he started off with a load. "Wow! This is heavy!"

Jennifer got behind the wagon and started pushing. "See, Justin, I can help."

"Yeah," agreed Justin reluctantly. "That does help." For several loads they worked together. Then Justin noticed that the loads were heavier. "Either I'm getting tired or the wood is gaining weight," he complained.

Dad looked up from his work and grinned. "Look behind you, Son," he suggested. When Justin turned around, he saw Jennifer sitting on top of the wood. "No wonder it's heavier," laughed Dad. "You have a hitchhiker!"

"You get off right now, Jennifer!" ordered Justin.

"Now you can understand how much easier things are when everyone does his fair share," said Dad as he helped Jennifer get down safely. "God's plan for the family is for them to work together. When someone sits down on the job, it's harder for everyone else. Jennifer is small, but when she pushed, your job was easier. When she hitchhiked, it made your job harder."

"Sure did," agreed Jason. "Now, little hitchhiker, start pushing again!"

HOW ABOUT YOU? Do you grumble and complain about doing your share of the work? Perhaps you do have more responsibility than your little brother or sister. That's because you're able to pull a heavier load. Be a good worker, not a hitchhiker. B.W.

TO MEMORIZE: *"Make it your ambition to lead a quiet life, to mind your own business and to work with your hands"* 1 Thessalonians 4:11 (NIV).

MARCH

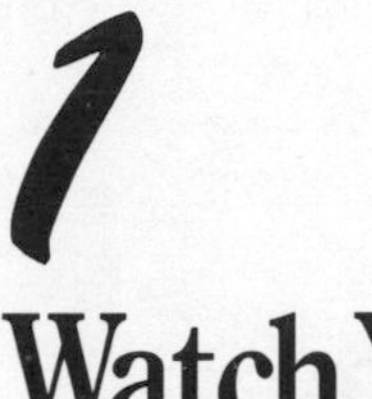

Watch Your Manners

FROM THE BIBLE:

I will sing of your love and
justice;
to you, O Lord, I will sing
praise.
I will be careful to lead a
blameless life—
when will you come to me?
I will walk in my house
with blameless heart.
I will set before my eyes
no vile thing.
The deeds of faithless men
I hate;
they will not cling to me.
Men of perverse heart shall
be far from me;
I will have nothing to do
with evil.
Whoever slanders his neighbor
in secret,
him will I put to silence;
whoever has haughty eyes and
a proud heart,
him will I not endure.
My eyes will be on the faithful
in the land,
that they may dwell with me;
he whose walk is blameless
will minister to me.

Psalm 101:1-6, NIV

"'SCUSE ME." Dave reached right across his sister's plate to get the salt.

"The next time you do that," scolded Nancy, "I'll wipe my knife on your shirt."

"Children!" exclaimed Mother. "Watch your manners! Dave, if you want something, please ask to have it passed."

"But it's quicker to get it myself," Dave retorted.

"It might be quicker, but it's not good manners," said Mother.

As Nancy started to leave the table, Dad stopped her. "Before you leave the table, Nancy, you should asked to be excused."

"Tell you what—let's make a game to help you," Mother suggested. "Each time you use good manners, you get a check mark beside your name. And each time you use bad manners—like reaching in front of someone or interrupting someone when they're talking—we'll erase a check mark. At the end of each week, the winner gets a special treat."

Dave spoke lazily. "You might as well give the prize to Nancy right now! I'll never remember all that!"

"Yes, you will, Dave," Dad replied. "We'll all help you."

The plan worked well. At the end of the first week, Dave was only a few points behind Nancy.

"Hey, this is kinda fun," said Dave after receiving a check mark the next week. "I'll beat you this time, Nancy. I'm getting gooder and gooder at remem—"

"Better and better, not gooder and gooder," Nancy interrupted sarcastically.

"Oops!" Mother erased a mark behind Nancy's name. "You forgot the rule—don't interrupt."

The next day Dave's friend, Bill Jones, invited him to stay overnight, and a few days after that, Mrs. Jones met Dave's mother at the supermarket. "I just want to tell you how well Dave behaved," Mrs. Jones said.

"I felt very proud of you, Dave," Mom said that evening at the dinner table.

HOW ABOUT YOU? Do you usually use your worst manners on your own family? Practicing good manners is important, and the place to begin is at home. Be thoughtful and courteous. Ask the Lord to help you overcome the weaknesses in your manners. C.V.M.

TO MEMORIZE: *"I will walk in my house with blameless heart"* Psalm 101:2 (NIV).

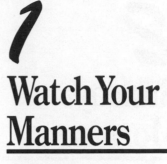

Practice good manners

MARCH

2

Sunday Morning

FROM THE BIBLE:

Give to the Lord the glory due
His name;
Bring an offering, and come
into His courts.
Oh, worship the Lord in the
beauty of holiness!
Tremble before Him, all the
earth.
Say among the nations, "The
Lord reigns;
The world also is firmly
established,
It shall not be moved;
He shall judge the peoples
righteously."
Let the heavens rejoice, and let
the earth be glad;
Let the sea roar, and all
its fullness;
Let the field be joyful, and
all that is in it.
Then all the trees of the woods
will rejoice before the Lord.
For He is coming, for He is
coming to judge the earth.
He shall judge the world
with righteousness,
And the peoples with His
truth.

Psalm 96:8-13, NKJV

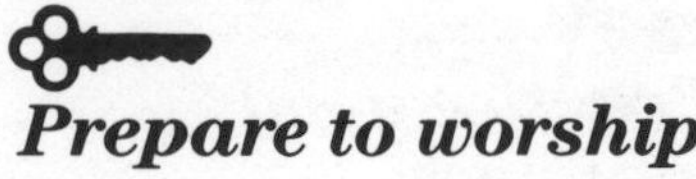

Prepare to worship

THE HUSTLE and bustle each Sunday morning at the Langs' house was becoming an unsettling habit. "Has anyone seen my blue socks?" yelled Steve. Then he scanned his room for his Sunday school book. "I still have to learn my verse. I hope it's a short one this week."

Stacy rolled over in bed when her clock radio went on. "Morning already?" she said with a yawn. "It seems like I just got home from baby-sitting a little while ago." She got up and staggered down the hall pulling on her bathrobe. "Morning," she murmured as she saw Mother emerge from the laundry room, bearing Steve's blue socks. "Would you please turn on the iron? I have to press my dress."

By some small miracle, the Langs made it to church almost on time. They really enjoyed the morning, although Stacy had a little trouble keeping her eyes open during the sermon. Dad commented about their hectic morning as they rode home from church. "I'm embarrassed about being late for Sunday school so often," he said. "Our Sunday mornings seem to be getting more and more disorganized, and they definitely don't prepare our hearts for worship. Does anyone have any suggestions?"

"We should get our clothes ready on Saturday," said Mother. "I'm at fault for allowing so much of that problem."

"I should do my Sunday school lesson earlier in the week," admitted Steve.

"I feel badly about being so tired," remarked Stacy. "I'm going to let people know that I can only baby-sit until ten o'clock on Saturdays."

Dad nodded his approval. "And I'll start Sunday morning by playing some good Christian music on the stereo. Waking up to that kind of music may help to prepare our minds to really worship the Lord with our whole hearts."

HOW ABOUT YOU? What was it like at your house last Sunday morning? Were you prepared to worship God and learn from Him when you walked into church? Why not follow the suggestions given in the story? Have your clothes ready on Saturday, learn your memory verse early, and get a good night's sleep. Then you should be alert to learn from God's Word. D.R.

TO MEMORIZE: *"Enter into his gates with thanksgiving, and into his courts with praise"* Psalm 100:4.

MARCH

3

Temporary Permanent

FROM THE BIBLE:

Lord, here in your Temple we meditate upon your kindness and your love. Your name is known throughout the earth, O God. You are praised everywhere for the salvation you have scattered throughout the world. O Jerusalem, rejoice! O people of Judah, rejoice! For God will see to it that you are finally treated fairly. Go, inspect the city! Walk around and count her many towers! Note her walls and tour her palaces, so that you can tell your children. For this great God is our God forever and ever. He will be our guide until we die.

Psalm 48:9-14, TLB

TIM POURED a glass of milk to drink with the snack his mother had left for him because she was out at the beauty salon getting a permanent. Tim was usually hungry after school, but today the food seemed to be as tasteless as sawdust. He sighed as he thought about his troubles. First, he'd lost his science assignment, and his teacher said he would have to do it over. At recess he'd ripped a hole in the knee of his new jeans. His best friend had ignored him all day, and Tim didn't know why. Finally, Tim hadn't understood the afternoon English lesson, but he was too discouraged to ask for help.

"Why the unhappy face?" asked Mother, coming in the door and interrupting his dark thoughts.

"Everything went wrong today," mumbled Tim. As his mother sat down, he noticed her hair. "Your hair looks nice, Mom. Will it always stay this way now?"

Mother laughed. "I wish it would, but after a while it will start to lose its curl," she said.

"Well, why is it called a 'permanent' then?" asked Tim.

Mother smiled. "I think it's misnamed," she replied. She gave Tim a hug. "Many things we call 'permanent' don't last forever. But there's something that does—God's love. It's really permanent. His love goes on and on. Even when things go wrong and it seems He's forgotten us, He really hasn't. His love is still there, strong and true."

Tim smiled. "That's nice to remember after the kind of day I've had," he said. "Thanks, Mom. When I look at your temporary permanent, I'll remember that God's love is really permanent."

HOW ABOUT YOU? When things go wrong, especially one thing after another, it's easy to get discouraged and forget God's love. But God doesn't forget you. His love is there, whether you're feeling it or not. It's an everlasting love. C.Y.

TO MEMORIZE: *"I have loved you with an everlasting love"* Jeremiah 31:3 (NKJV).

God's love is permanent

MARCH

Horn-a-thon

FROM THE BIBLE:
Take heed that you do not do your charitable deeds before men, to be seen by them. Otherwise you have no reward from your Father in heaven. Therefore, when you do a charitable deed, do not sound a trumpet before you as the hypocrites do in the synagogues and in the streets, that they may have glory from men. Assuredly, I say to you, they have their reward. But when you do a charitable deed, do not let your left hand know what your right hand is doing, that your charitable deed may be in secret; and your Father who sees in secret will Himself reward you openly. And when you pray, you shall not be like the hypocrites. For they love to pray standing in the synagogues and on the corners of the streets, that they may be seen by men. Assuredly, I say to you, they have their reward. But you, when you pray, go into your room, and when you have shut your door, pray to your Father who is in the secret place; and your Father who sees in secret will reward you openly.
Matthew 6:1-6, NKJV

Give and serve unselfishly

"MOM, WILL YOU sponsor me for the jump-a-thon our school is having?" Jane waved a piece of paper. "Each of us kids will spend time jumping rope, or on a pogo stick, or on the school's trampoline. People sign this list to donate a certain amount of money for every minute we jump. And the money we raise will go to help hungry people in Africa."

Mother looked at the paper Jane gave her. "I see this is being held on the same day as the church picnic," she said. "I'm afraid you won't be able to go, honey. But it is a good cause, so I'll be sure to give a donation anyway."

"But, Mom!" Jane pouted. "It won't be any fun if I don't get to jump. Besides, the school is giving prizes to the kids who jump the longest, and my teacher said the TV cameras will be there."

"Hold on a minute!" said Mother. "I thought this was to benefit the hungry people in Africa. It sounds like you're more interested in the attention and the prizes." Jane blushed and looked down, and Mother sighed. "Maybe this should be called a horn-a-thon instead of a jump-a-thon."

"What?" asked Jane. "No one will be blowing horns!"

"I'm afraid they might be," replied Mother. "You see, Jesus told us we should give to others quietly and without drawing unnecessary attention to ourselves. In Bible days, Pharisees used to have someone go before them and blow a trumpet as they were on their way to do a good deed. In God's eyes, their giving had no eternal value because it was done out of pride instead of genuine love."

"I see what you mean," Jane admitted. "I guess I have been kind of selfish. Since I can't go to the jump-a-thon, I'll try to earn money by doing yard work after school."

"That's the right attitude!" Mother smiled. "You can start by raking our lawn. I'd rather pay for an hour of work than an hour of jumping any day!"

HOW ABOUT YOU? Do you give and serve the way God wants you to—simply, generously, without expecting reward? Don't seek recognition from others for every good thing you do. Just obey God with the right attitude, and He'll be sure to reward you. S.K.

TO MEMORIZE: *"Do not do your charitable deeds before men, to be seen by them. Otherwise you have no reward from your Father in heaven"*
Matthew 6:1 (NKJV).

MARCH

5

Meat, Milk, and Michael

FROM THE BIBLE:

For though by this time you ought to be teachers, you have need again for some one to teach you the elementary principles of the oracles of God, and you have come to need milk and not solid food. For every one who partakes only of milk is not accustomed to the word of righteousness, for he is a babe. But solid food is for the mature, who because of practice have their senses trained to discern good and evil. Hebrews 5:12-14, NASB

Study God's Word

"SHERRY, HAVE YOU studied your Sunday school lesson and learned your memory verse?" asked Mother, as she heated baby Michael's food.

"No, Mom. I looked at the lesson, but it seemed hard to me. And the memory verse is thirty-six words long. I can't ever learn that!" answered nine-year-old Sherry.

Mother put Michael in his high chair. As she was tying his bib, the telephone rang. "Sherry, will you feed the baby for me?" Mother asked. "I'll answer the phone."

"OK, baby brother," Sherry scolded, "now you are going to eat like a little man. Here, open your mouth! Oh, Michael, don't drool it all down your chin!" Michael kept grinning at her with his mouth full of food. It was messy, but she still thought he looked cute. Suddenly he banged his fist right into the bowl of baby food. Sherry was so startled she screamed. That made Michael cry, and he rubbed his grubby little fist in his eyes. When Mother returned, she found both Sherry and Michael crying. Sherry was trying to clean up the floor. "Oh, Mom, this is gross!" she sobbed. "It sure was easier to give Michael a bottle. Why does he have to eat solid food anyway?"

"Babies need milk," answered Mother, "but as they grow older, they also need solid food to grow strong."

After dinner, Mother again suggested that Sherry study her Sunday school lesson. "But I told you," whined Sherry, "it's too hard!" Mother then reminded Sherry of the day she had asked Jesus to be her Savior. "After three years as a Christian, you should be growing and wanting to learn some of the deeper things about God. Just like Michael has to learn to eat solid food, you ought to be past the 'milk' part of the Bible and on to eating the 'meaty' part. Sometimes it is hard to learn to eat meat, but it's necessary for growth," she explained.

Sherry listened thoughtfully. "OK, Mom," she said finally. "I guess I'll go study my Sunday school lesson and work on that hard memory verse again. I don't want to be a baby Christian forever!"

HOW ABOUT YOU? If you have been a Christian for any length of time, have you grown spiritually? You need to eat the 'meat' as well as drink the 'milk' of God's Word. R.P.

TO MEMORIZE: *"But solid food is for the mature, who because of practice have their senses trained to discern good and evil"* Hebrews 5:14 (NASB).

MARCH

6

The Birth Certificate

FROM THE BIBLE:

But what does it say? "The word is near you; it is in your mouth and in your heart," that is, the word of faith we are proclaiming: That if you confess with your mouth, "Jesus is Lord," and believe in your heart that God raised him from the dead, you will be saved. For it is with your heart that you believe and are justified, and it is with your mouth that you confess and are saved. As the Scripture says, "Anyone who trusts in him will never be put to shame." For there is no difference between Jew and Gentile—the same Lord is Lord of all and richly blesses all who call on him, for, "Everyone who calls on the name of the Lord will be saved." Romans 10:8-13, NIV

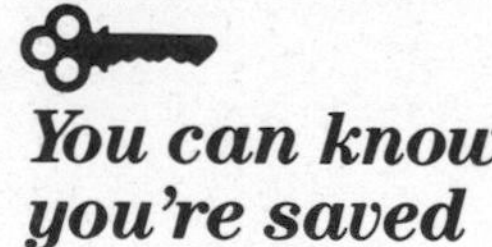

You can know you're saved

"DAD . . . ," Nathan hesitated. "I think I'm saved," he continued. "I've asked Jesus to come into my heart and forgive my sins, but how can I really know God heard me?"

Nathan's dad was delighted that his son was talking his problem over with him. He smiled at Nathan. "Who are your parents?" he asked.

"Why, Dad, you know the answer to that!" Nathan was surprised. "You and Mom are."

"How do you know we are?" Dad continued.

"Well, I just know. You've always been my parents." As Dad opened a desk drawer and took out a piece of paper, Nathan wondered why he was asking such strange questions. Then he saw what Dad was holding in his hand. "That's my birth certificate!" exclaimed Nathan. "It says right on it when I was born. That's proof!"

"And do you believe what the birth certificate says?" Dad asked.

Nathan nodded. "Sure, I do."

"Well, Son, God's Word is just as good as this birth certificate—even better," Dad assured him. "You don't doubt what is written on the birth certificate, and you don't have to doubt anything in God's Word. He says if you accept Jesus as Savior, you're His child. When you accepted the Lord, we made a note of it in your Bible. Let's take a look."

Nathan got his Bible from the shelf, and together they read from the inside cover page, "Nathan accepted the Lord Jesus Christ into his heart on April 10, 1988."

"I think we need to add something here—a verse from God's Word," suggested Dad. After discussing it, Nathan carefully copied Romans 10:13 into the front cover of his Bible. "Now," said Dad, "you can think of this Scripture as another kind of birth certificate—the certificate of your new birth in the Lord Jesus."

Nathan nodded. "Thanks, Dad," he said. "I know I'm saved because God says so."

HOW ABOUT YOU? Do you ever wonder if you're really saved? Carefully study the last page in this book and make sure you've accepted Jesus as your personal Savior. Then pick a verse (such as John 1:12, John 3:16, Acts 16:31, Romans 10:13) which tells you that you now belong to Him. Whenever Satan causes you to doubt it, point to that verse. If you have truly done what it says, you are saved. D.K.

TO MEMORIZE: *"Everyone who calls on the name of the Lord shall be saved"* Romans 10:13 (NIV).

MARCH

7

Please Pass the Peas

FROM THE BIBLE:

For if I preach the gospel, I have nothing to boast of, for necessity is laid upon me; yes, woe is me if I do not preach the gospel! For if I do this willingly, I have a reward; but if against my will, I have been entrusted with a stewardship. . . . For though I am free from all men, I have made myself a servant to all, that I might win the more; and to the Jews I became as a Jew, that I might win Jews; to those who are under the law, as under the law, that I might win those who are under the law; to those who are without law, as without law (not being without law toward God, but under law toward Christ), that I might win those who are without law; to the weak I became as weak, that I might win the weak. I have become all things to all men, that I might by all means save some. Now this I do for the gospel's sake, that I may be partaker of it with you.

1 Corinthians 9:16-23, NKJV

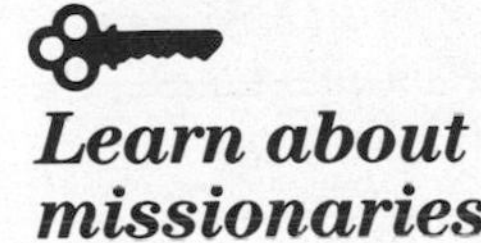

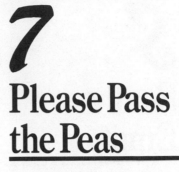

Learn about missionaries

"I KNOW YOU don't care for peas, Josh, but the rest of us do, so I want you to take a few, too," said Mom, handing him the serving dish. Joshua frowned and reluctantly dropped a few peas on his plate. He knew better than to argue.

"Pretend they're something else," suggested Shelly. "Pretend you're a missionary, like in the book I'm reading. The natives have invited you to dinner. They offer you food you've never seen before. If you want them to accept you, you have to eat their food or you'll hurt their feelings."

"You mean they don't have peas in some countries? I'll go there!" Joshua said, grinning, and entering into the game. "What do I pretend these are if they're not peas?"

"Bugs!" laughed Shelly. As Joshua pulled a face, Shelly turned to her mother. "Some night, let's all pretend we're in a different country, Mom. That would be fun!"

"That's a good idea," agreed Mom. "Let's pick a country where our church has a missionary. How about Japan? We could sit on the floor and eat with chopsticks."

"Yeah," agreed Joshua, "or how about Italy? We could have pizza."

"I have an international cookbook," Mom said. "Shelly and I can figure out the menu and do the cooking."

"I can decorate some place mats," offered Joshua. "I'll draw a map on one and pictures showing the country's products and trees or flowers on the others."

Dad leaned back in his chair. "And I'll find out what kind of work the missionary does—whether it's starting churches, working is hospitals, translating the Bible, or whatever. Why don't we have our first missionary dinner a week from Saturday."

"Good," agreed Mom. "Now, Joshua, since you're still in the United States, you need to finish your peas."

HOW ABOUT YOU? Could your family plan a "missions night"? If preparing a whole foreign dinner seems too difficult, perhaps Mom could prepare one special dish or dessert. In any case, find out where the missionaries from your church live and what kind of ministries they have. Learn something about their countries. Doing this will help you to pray intelligently for them. V.L.C.

TO MEMORIZE: *"I have become all things to all men, that I might by all means save some"*
1 Corinthians 9:22 (NKJV).

MARCH

8

Really Empty

FROM THE BIBLE:

And you He made alive, who were dead in trespasses and sins, in which you once walked according to the course of this world, according to the prince of the power of the air, the spirit who now works in the sons of disobedience, among whom also we all once conducted ourselves in the lusts of our flesh, fulfilling the desires of the flesh and of the mind, and were by nature children of wrath, just as the others. But God, who is rich in mercy, because of His great love with which He loved us, even when we were dead in trespasses, made us alive together with Christ . . . that in the ages to come He might show the exceeding riches of His grace in His kindness toward us in Christ Jesus. For by grace you have been saved through faith, and that not of yourselves; it is the gift of God, not of works, lest anyone should boast. For we are His workmanship, created in Christ Jesus for good works, which God prepared beforehand that we should walk in them.
Ephesians 2:1-10, NKJV

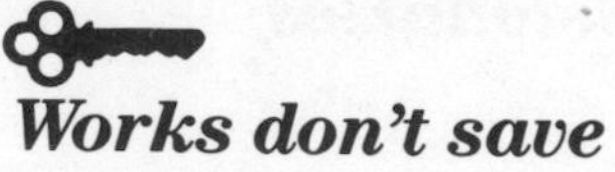

Works don't save

"MOM," SAID JANICE, "can I make some lemonade?"

"I doubt it," teased her brother, Russ. "It takes far more talent than you possess."

"Oh, hush," scolded Janice, "*May* I make some, Mother?"

Mother laughed. "You can, and you may," she said. "I bought several packages of fruit drinks yesterday. Just add the sugar and water."

"I will," agreed Janice. She went to the cupboard and took out the box containing the mixes.

"Stick with lemonade," advised Russ. "It's my favorite."

Janice took out an envelope showing a bright yellow lemon. After carefully measuring sugar into a pitcher, she picked up the lemonade packet. She was going to tear it open, but held it up and inspected it closely instead. She ran her fingers up and down both sides. Then she took a different packet from the box and compared the two, shaking them and feeling them with her hands.

"I was right," declared Russ. "She can't make lemonade. See, she's all confused."

Janice ignored him. "Mother," she said, "I don't think this packet has a thing in it. It feels empty."

Mother took the packet and checked it. "You're right, Janice. It is empty, but don't tear it open. I want to use it as an object lesson for my Sunday school class."

"An object lesson?" asked Janice. "Of what?"

"It reminds me of some people—people who pretend to be Christians," replied Mother. "Like this packet, they look fine on the outside—they're faithful in church, they're generous and kind. Others are often fooled by them."

"Just like you were fooled by this packet when you bought it," said Russ.

Mother nodded. "But God isn't fooled by anyone. He sees their hearts, and He knows they're really empty."

HOW ABOUT YOU? Are you putting on a good front and fooling people? Remember, you're not fooling God. All the fine, nice-looking things you do cannot save you. You need to accept Jesus as your personal Savior, and then you will be a Christian. God wants to make you the "real thing." H.M.

TO MEMORIZE: *"For by grace you have been saved through faith, and that not of yourselves; it is the gift of God, not of works, lest anyone should boast"* Ephesians 2:8-9 (NKJV).

MARCH

A Bad Start

FROM THE BIBLE:

Always be full of joy in the Lord; I say it again, rejoice! Let everyone see that you are unselfish and considerate in all you do. Remember that the Lord is coming soon. Don't worry about anything; instead, pray about everything; tell God your needs and don't forget to thank him for his answers. If you do this you will experience God's peace, which is far more wonderful than the human mind can understand. His peace will keep your thoughts and your hearts quiet and at rest as you trust in Christ Jesus. And now, brothers, as I close this letter let me say this one more thing: Fix your thoughts on what is true and good and right. Think about things that are pure and lovely, and dwell on the fine, good things in others. Think about all you can praise God for and be glad about. Keep putting into practice all you learned from me and saw me doing, and the God of peace will be with you.

Philippians 4:4-9, TLB

Don't be a grumbler!

"MIKE, GET UP! Time to get ready for school," called Mother. Mike pulled the covers over his head and burrowed deeper into the warm cocoon of blankets. He didn't even open his eyes. He was too busy dreaming about being the pilot of a 747. It would be exciting to travel around the world. "Mike," Mother called again. "I told you to get up, and I want you to get up now! Do you hear me?"

"Yes." Mike's voice was muffled by the pillow over his head.

"Mike, I said now!"

Oh, bother! Why do my good dreams always have to be interrupted? Mike thought as he finally stumbled out of bed and into the shower.

"It's raining," he moaned as he entered the kitchen a little later. "Why can't the sun ever shine?" He eyed the breakfast table. "Oh, yuck!" he said with a frown. "Oatmeal! I can't stand oatmeal!"

Just then his sister, Nancy, came to the table. She was chattering excitedly about the field trip her class would be taking that day. "We never go on field trips. I hate school," complained Mike.

"Mike," asked Mother, "would you please give thanks before we eat?"

"Dear heavenly Father," prayed Mike, "thank You for the beautiful day You have given us, and thank You for the good food. In Jesus' name, amen."

"Mike, I think something is very wrong," said Mother as she passed the oatmeal.

Mike looked up in surprise. "What do you mean?"

"You thanked the Lord for the beautiful day, but all you've done so far is grumble," she told him.

Mike thought about that. Yes, he had been grumbling. In fact, he had been out of bed for only half an hour, and he had grumbled the entire time!

"I'm sorry, Lord," he whispered. "Help me to get a new start on this day!"

HOW ABOUT YOU? Do you grumble when Mom calls you in the morning? Do you complain about the food and then thank the Lord for it? Sometimes boys and girls get in the habit of grumbling about everything. The Bible tells you to rejoice. Be a joyful Christian, not a grumbling Christian. L.W.

TO MEMORIZE: *"This is the day the LORD has made; let us rejoice and be glad in it"* Psalm 118:24 (NIV).

MARCH

10

Does It Taste Good?

FROM THE BIBLE:

Oh, how I love Your law!
It is my meditation all the day.
You, through Your commandments, make me wiser than my enemies;
For they are ever with me.
I have more understanding than all my teachers,
For Your testimonies are my meditation.
I understand more than the ancients,
Because I keep Your precepts.
I have restrained my feet from every evil way,
That I may keep Your word.
I have not departed from Your judgments,
For You Yourself have taught me.
How sweet are Your words to my taste,
sweeter than honey to my mouth!
Through Your precepts I get understanding;
Therefore I hate every false way.

Psalm 119:97-104, NKJV

Develop spiritual "taste"

AARON SIGHED and poked at his half-eaten piece of pie. "I don't know why nothin' tastes good today," he said to his grandfather. "I wish my tongue would quit feeling so funny." Aaron had been to the dentist, and one side of his mouth had been numbed so it wouldn't hurt when the dentist drilled on his teeth. When he got home, he felt hungry, but his lunch didn't taste good.

Grandpa chuckled. "Give it a little more time," he advised. "You know there are lots of taste buds on your tongue, and when the dentist numbed your mouth, it numbed those taste buds, too. Why don't you save the pie till later?" Aaron nodded. As he got up to put the pie in the refrigerator, Grandpa reached for his Bible. "Would you like to share a Bible lesson?" invited Grandpa.

Aaron shrugged. "I'm goin' out to play with the guys," he answered, picking up his jacket.

"Spiritual taste buds numbed, too?" asked Grandpa.

Aaron stopped, one arm in his coat sleeve, and looked at his grandfather. "Huh?"

"I remember when you first asked Jesus to be your Savior," answered Grandpa. "You were really excited about it. You wanted to know what God expected of you as a Christian and what promises He gives to His children. You used to sit with me, and we'd read together from God's Word. We'd have some 'spiritual food' together—remember?"

Aaron nodded. He had enjoyed those times. But so many other things demanded his attention lately that reading the Bible seemed less interesting. Maybe Grandpa was right. Maybe his spiritual taste buds were numbed.

Grandpa smiled as Aaron came and sat beside him. "Good," he approved. "The numbness in your mouth will soon go away by itself. But we have to work at getting over spiritual numbness. A good way to start is to get back into God's Word."

HOW ABOUT YOU? Are you less interested in the Bible than you once were? Have your spiritual taste buds been numbed by such things as TV programs, too many parties, personal hobbies, or homework? Don't allow that to happen. Make up your mind to get rid of spiritual numbness. Pray. Read your Bible. Say with the psalmist, "Oh, how I love Your Law!" H.M.

TO MEMORIZE: *"How sweet are Your words unto my taste, sweeter than honey to my mouth"* Psalm 119:103 (NKJV).

MARCH

11

Double Exposure

FROM THE BIBLE:

Don't do as the wicked do. Avoid their haunts—turn away, go somewhere else, for evil men can't sleep until they've done their evil deed for the day. They can't rest unless they cause someone to stumble and fall. They eat and drink wickedness and violence! But the good man walks along in the ever-brightening light of God's favor; the dawn gives way to morning splendor, while the evil man gropes and stumbles in the dark. Proverbs 4:14-19, TLB

Avoid exposure to sin

JEFF WAS ANNOYED. His folks wouldn't let him go to Sam's party because Sam's parents were out of town. Sam's older brother, James, was to chaperone the party, but he didn't have a very good reputation. "Why do my folks have to be so old-fashioned," Jeff muttered to himself. "Everybody else gets to go—even Phil."

The next day was Saturday, and Phil came over to see Jeff. "Did you know that Adam Benton is in the hospital?" he asked. "They think he may have spinal meningitis—and we sat next to him on the bus yesterday! Mom says if he has it, we'll probably have to get shots!"

"Oh no!" groaned Jeff. "How come?"

"Because it's contagious, and we've been exposed," Phil explained. "There are shots that might keep us from getting it, too. It's a very serious disease."

"I sure hope Alan's going to be all right," worried Jeff. "By the way, how was the party last night?"

"Just be glad you didn't go!" exclaimed Phil. "There was a police raid on the house. James and some of his friends were having a drug party and using us younger guys as a cover-up. I didn't like the wild music and the way they were acting. I was scared and left before the police came."

Jeff's mother had been listening. "I was afraid of something like that," she said. "That's why I didn't want you to go, Jeff. I didn't want you to be exposed to sin."

"But we're exposed to sin every day," protested Jeff. "Sin is everywhere."

"That's true," agreed Mother. "And spinal meningitis germs could be anywhere, too. But there's more danger some places than others."

Phil nodded. "We were in more danger sitting next to Alan on the bus than we would have been somewhere away from him," he agreed. "And I was in more danger at the party than you were at home. Wow! Two close calls for me in one day—double exposure!"

HOW ABOUT YOU? Do the places you go, the friends you choose, and the TV programs you watch expose you to sin? Do they encourage you to do such things as drink alcohol, smoke, cheat, swear, or disobey? If so, you are in great danger. You need to avoid these kinds of influences or you may fall into sin. B.W.

TO MEMORIZE: *"A companion of fools suffers harm"* Proverbs 13:20 (NIV).

MARCH

12

Double Exposure

(Continued from yesterday)

FROM THE BIBLE:

Happy are all who perfectly follow the laws of God. Happy are all who search for God, and always do his will, rejecting compromise with evil, and walking only in his paths. You have given us your laws to obey: oh, how I want to follow them consistently. Then I will not be disgraced, for I will have a clean record.

After you have corrected me I will thank you by living as I should! I will obey! Oh, don't forsake me and let me slip back into sin again.

Psalm 119:1-8, TLB

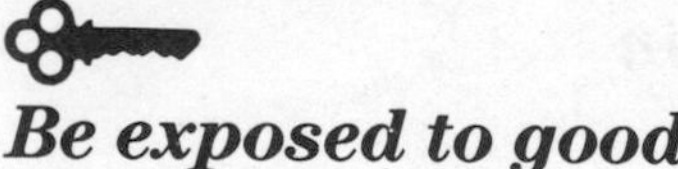

Be exposed to good

JEFF AND PHIL went out to the garage to work on Jeff's bike. Soon Jeff's mother joined them. "Good news, boys," she told them. "Alan's mother just called to say that Alan has some kind of virus infection. He'll be in the hospital for a few days, but he doesn't have meningitis."

"Whoopee!" yelled the boys. "Old Alan's going to be OK! And we don't need to have shots." When they had stopped prancing around, Phil said seriously, "I was just thinking about my double exposure. It's too bad we can't take shots to prevent sin."

Jeff's mother smiled. "There are no shots for that," she agreed. "There is something we can do, though. We can keep our resistance up. You know that we keep up our physical resistance to disease by eating a balanced diet and getting proper rest and exercise. How do you suppose we keep up our spiritual resistance to sin?"

The boys thought about it. "I guess going to church would help," offered Phil.

Jeff nodded. "Yeah, and praying and reading the Bible."

"Good," approved Mother. "And don't forget the importance of good Christian friends, good books, and good music. Expose yourself to these things, and you will be less likely to fall into sin."

HOW ABOUT YOU? Do you regularly attend church and Sunday school where the Bible is clearly taught? Do you listen to music that is honoring to God? Do the books you read draw you closer to Him? Are you faithful in attendance at church activities? Do you seek the companionship of Christian friends? All these things will help build up your resistance to sin. B.W.

TO MEMORIZE: *"He who walks with the wise grows wise"* Proverbs 13:20 (NIV).

MARCH

13

Trash or Treasure?

FROM THE BIBLE:
Listen to me, dear brothers: God has chosen poor people to be rich in faith, and the Kingdom of Heaven is theirs, for that is the gift God has promised to all those who love him. And yet, of the two strangers, you have despised the poor man. Don't you realize that it is usually the rich men who pick on you and drag you into court? And all too often they are the ones who laugh at Jesus Christ, whose noble name you bear. Yes indeed, it is good when you truly obey our Lord's command, "You must love and help your neighbors just as much as you love and take care of yourself." But you are breaking this law of our Lord's when you favor the rich and fawn over them; it is sin. James 2:5-9, TLB

Everyone is valuable

PAM WAS GLAD she and her parents had come to spend a weekend in the country with Aunt Clara and Uncle Bill. With her uncle's permission, she decided to go digging in the old trash pile behind the barn. To her delight, she found an old fruit jar with "1898" stamped on the bottom. Pam took it into the house to show her aunt and mother. "I saw one like it in the antique store, priced at twenty dollars," she told them.

Aunt Clara smiled. "Well, good," she said. "You found it, and you may keep it." Pam squealed with pleasure. Then Aunt Clara asked, "Do you remember Rebecca, who lives across the road? She's coming over this afternoon."

"Oh, no!" groaned Pam. "She's trashy, and kinda . . . well, just plain dumb. She's not my type at all. Besides, she isn't a Christian, and I don't think she ever will be. She doesn't seem like the kind, if you know what I mean."

"Pamela!" scolded her mother. "You aren't acting like a Christian, either. And, no, I don't know what you mean."

Aunt Clara looked thoughtful. "Pam," she said, "go clean that old fruit jar and then bring it back to me." Pam was surprised, but she did as she was told.

"It's quite pretty, now that it's cleaned up," said Aunt Clara later, taking the jar. "Strange, isn't it, that for years it was in the rubbish pile. Until today, no one realized its value and saved it. In a way, Rebecca is like this jar."

"What does it have to do with her?" asked Pam.

"A lot," Aunt Clara told her, "and with me, and with you, too. One day you lay in the trash pile of sin, but God recognized your value. He picked you up, washed you, and gave you a new shine. Rebecca is still lost, but she is very valuable! So valuable that Jesus died for her."

Pam looked ashamed. "I hadn't thought about it like that," she said. "I'm glad she's coming over. Maybe God will use me to help her come to Him so she can be given a new shine, too."

HOW ABOUT YOU? Is there someone that you think is too "trashy" to play with? What does it really matter if his clothes are wrinkled or torn or if he doesn't always use correct English? God looks beneath all that and sees a precious soul. Perhaps by being a friend to that person, God will allow you to uncover the treasure of that soul. B.W.

TO MEMORIZE: *"Judge not according to the appearance"* John 7:24.

MARCH

14

Seedless Oranges

FROM THE BIBLE:

"A farmer went out to sow his seed. As he was scattering the seed, some fell along the path; it was trampled on, and the birds of the air ate it up. Some fell on rock, and when it came up, the plants withered. Other seed fell among thorns, which grew up with it and choked the plants. Still other seed fell on good soil. It came up and yielded a crop, a hundred times more than was sown. . . . The seed is the word of God. Those along the path are the ones who hear, and then the devil comes and takes away the word from their hearts. . . . Those on the rock are the ones who receive the word with joy when they hear it, but they have no root. . . . The seed that fell among thorns stands for those who hear, but as they go on their way they are choked by life's worries, riches and pleasures, and they do not mature. But the seed on good soil stands for those with a noble and good heart, who hear the word, retain it, and by persevering produce a crop."

Luke 8:5-9, 11-15, NIV

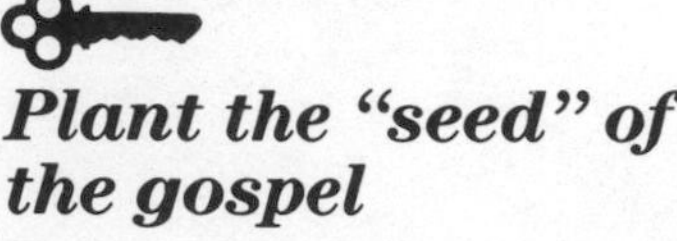

Plant the "seed" of the gospel

"OUR SPEAKER talked about witnessing at school, but he doesn't understand. I can't witness there," said Carl as he prepared potting soil for his school project.

"Oh?" Mother asked, glancing curiously at Carl.

"None of the Christians I know witness there. It's just not a good place to talk about the Lord," said Carl, as he brushed dirt off his hands. "People laugh if you try." He decided to change the subject. "Can we go to the store now and get the oranges for my project?"

"Sure," replied Mother. "I'll get my purse."

After they arrived at the grocery store, Carl and his mother headed for the produce department. "All I can find are seedless oranges," said Carl after a few minutes.

"Let's ask the produce man if he has the kind with seeds," suggested Mother.

When they inquired, the man shook his head. "Sorry. They haven't come in yet this week."

"All seedless oranges," Carl complained in frustration as he and Mother left the store. "How's a guy supposed to grow an orange tree without seeds?"

"That would be a trick!" Mom laughed. "You know," she added thoughtfully, "I wonder if the Lord might be feeling as sad as you."

"Because all the oranges are seedless?" Carl asked.

"No." Mother shook her head. "Because your school has only seedless Christians."

"Seedless Christians?" echoed Carl. "I don't get it."

"You said none of the Christians witness at school," said Mother. "None of them plant the seeds of the gospel. You have the seeds of God's Word, but as long as you refuse to scatter them, you don't witness. You're no more help to the unsaved than if you weren't Christians."

HOW ABOUT YOU? Do you scatter the "seed" of the Word of God? Do you witness for Him at school? Do you tell the kids in your neighborhood about Jesus? God doesn't promise that it will be easy, but He does promise that it will eventually bring results. Let Him spread the gospel through you. He will bless you as you do that. S.N.

TO MEMORIZE: *"He who continually goes forth weeping, bearing seed for sowing, shall doubtless come again with rejoicing, bringing his sheaves with him"* Psalm 126:6 (NKJV).

MARCH

15

Too Many People?

FROM THE BIBLE:

Children are a gift from God; they are his reward. Children born to a young man are like sharp arrows to defend him. Happy is the man who has his quiver full of them. That man shall have the help he needs when arguing with his enemies. Psalm 127:3-5, TLB

Babies are a blessing

WITH SIX CHILDREN in the family, Billy Michaels didn't often have time alone with his parents. One morning he got up early and found his mother working in the kitchen. As he sat munching a bowl of cereal, Billy asked, "Mom, do you ever wish you didn't have all us kids?"

Mother looked at him in surprise. "Of course not!" she said. "Whatever made you ask?"

"Well," replied Billy, "my social studies teacher said that if every couple in the world had only one or two children, all our problems would be solved."

Mother looked thoughtful. "Mr. Rader may be a good teacher, but I doubt that he's a Christian," she said. "Perhaps he doesn't realize that the Bible speaks of children as a 'heritage' and a 'reward.' "

Billy was confused. "But if you and Dad didn't have all of us, there'd be a lot more money to go around."

Mother smiled. "Do you think for a moment that we would trade any of you precious children for a new couch, a car, or a few more hours of free time?"

"I guess not," replied Billy. But what about the things Mr. Rader said?"

"God created this world to provide for the needs of people—all of them," said Mother. "I think the main reason there doesn't seem to be enough to go around is simply our own selfishness. Even today many people are starving, while others have far more than they need."

"Yeah, that's true," agreed Billy.

"Remember when little Christopher was born?" his mother asked. "We all had to 'tighten our belts' to pay the hospital bill, and you other children had to give away your stuffed toys because of his allergies."

"But nobody really minded," Billy said. "We loved him."

"And that's what the world needs—not more things, but more love," said his mother. "We need the kind of love that can only come by knowing Christ as Savior."

HOW ABOUT YOU? Are you worried that there are too many people in the world? Do you think of babies as a problem or a blessing? God is still in control, and He has a plan for every human being. He knows them before they're even born—and He sent His own Son to save them. Let's thank God for the blessing of babies! S.K.

TO MEMORIZE: *"Children are a gift from God"* Psalm 127:3 (TLB).

MARCH

16

Better Late Than Never

FROM THE BIBLE:

Do you not know that your body is a temple of the Holy Spirit, who is in you, whom you have received from God? You are not your own; you were bought at a price. Therefore honor God with your body.

1 Corinthians 6:19-20, NIV

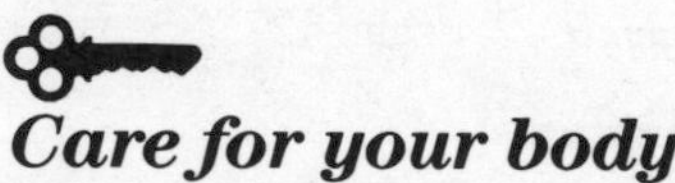

Care for your body

STEVE RAN his tongue over the sore in his mouth. "Maybe I should tell Mom about it," he decided. As soon as Mother saw the sore, she made an appointment with the doctor.

"Do you use smokeless tobacco?" the doctor asked.

"Well, yeah," admitted Steve. For about a year, he and two of his sixth-grade friends had taken turns buying the tobacco from a little store nearby. The man behind the counter had readily sold it to them, asking no questions. The boys met in an old building every afternoon to chew. Then they stuck a piece of gum in their mouths before going home and tried to avoid getting too close to their parents, so they wouldn't smell tobacco.

After finishing the examination, the doctor asked Steve's mother to come in. "This sore is caused from tobacco lying around the gums. Tobacco sometimes changes the cells, causing cancer," he explained to them.

Steve turned white. "You mean I . . . I have cancer?"

"You have what may be the beginning of it, I'm afraid," the doctor replied. "I've seen more and more cases of this since kids have begun using smokeless tobacco. Your sore is still very small, and I think I can get it all out with some surgery."

A few days after his mouth surgery, Steve returned to the doctor's office. "If you don't use tobacco from now on, you may not have any more problems," the doctor said. "But I want you back for check-ups every so often."

As Steve was watching TV that evening, a commercial showed a strong, handsome man taking some smokeless tobacco. "Give yourself some pleasure," said the man, smiling.

"They shouldn't advertise something that can hurt people!" exploded Steve.

"As Christians, we have to be careful not to be influenced by such advertisements," said Dad. "We have to avoid anything that is harmful to the bodies God gave us."

"Too bad I had to learn that the hard way," said Steve, "but better late than never."

HOW ABOUT YOU? Are you fooled by advertisers who make harmful products sound exciting and glamorous? God wants you to stay away from things that harm your body. Don't do anything that could destroy God's wonderful workmanship. C.Y.

TO MEMORIZE: *"Honor God with your body"* 1 Corinthians 6:20 (NIV).

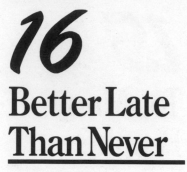

MARCH

17

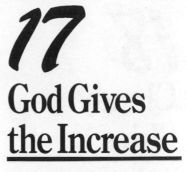

God Gives the Increase

FROM THE BIBLE:
What, after all, is Apollos? And what is Paul? Only servants, through whom you came to believe—as the Lord has assigned to each his task. I planted the seed, Apollos watered it, but God made it grow. So neither he who plants nor he who waters is anything, but only God, who makes things grow. The man who plants and the man who waters have one purpose, and each will be rewarded according to his own labor. For we are God's fellow workers; you are God's field, God's building. By the grace God has given me, I laid a foundation as an expert builder, and someone else is building on it. But each one should be careful how he builds. For no one can lay any foundation other than the one already laid, which is Jesus Christ.
1 Corinthians 3:5-11, NIV

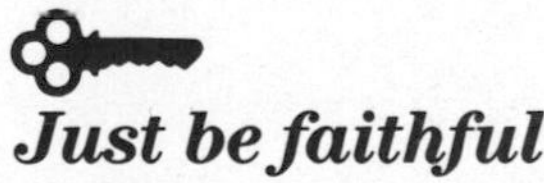

Just be faithful

DARLA WALKED into the house and slammed the door loudly. She looked up to see her father watching her. "My, my," he said in a teasing voice. "Did you mean to slam the door that way or did it slip out of your hand?"

"I meant it," Darla retorted. "I'm mad!"

Dad was concerned. "Care to talk about it?" he asked.

Darla tossed her head. "You'll think I'm awful," she said angrily. "It's about Rhonda Kelly."

"Rhonda Kelly," her father repeated. "She's the girl you've been witnessing to, isn't she?"

Darla nodded. "She just became a Christian," she said in a softened voice.

"That's wonderful!" exclaimed Dad.

"But that's just it," Darla complained, "you know how long I've been witnessing to her, but I didn't even get to lead her to Jesus! Mrs. Noll did."

After a brief silence, Dad said, "And you thought you should be the one to lead her to the Lord. Right?"

"Well, I'm the one who prayed and talked to her," Darla defended. "I even gave her a Bible for her birthday."

Dad smiled ever so slightly. "And that may be the very reason Rhonda was ready to accept Christ at this time."

"But why wouldn't God let me be the one to finally bring her to the Lord?" she asked.

Dad took the Bible off the coffee table. "The Bible tells us that's the way it often works. Let me show you," he said as he turned the pages of the New Testament. "Here in 1 Corinthians Paul said, 'I have planted, Apollos watered; but God gave the increase.' It looks like God allowed you to plant, Mrs. Noll to water, and when He knew it was just the right time, He did the saving."

Darla sat quietly thinking about what her father had said. It really shouldn't matter to her who led Rhonda to Christ. The important thing was that she was now a Christian. And maybe it was because Darla had so faithfully witnessed for all those months.

HOW ABOUT YOU? Are you happy when someone accepts Jesus as Savior, even if others don't give you the credit for your part? Remember, though it is up to you to "plant and water"—to faithfully witness—only God can give the increase. Only He can save. Your part is to be faithful. R.J.

TO MEMORIZE: *"For we are God's fellow workers"* 1 Corinthians 3:9 (NIV).

MARCH

18

Cloudy Skies

FROM THE BIBLE:

O Lord, you have examined my heart and know everything about me. You know when I sit or stand. When far away you know my every thought. You chart the path ahead of me, and tell me where to stop and rest. Every moment, you know where I am. You know what I am going to say before I even say it. You both precede and follow me, and place your hand of blessing on my head. This is too glorious, too wonderful to believe!
Psalm 139:1-6, TLB

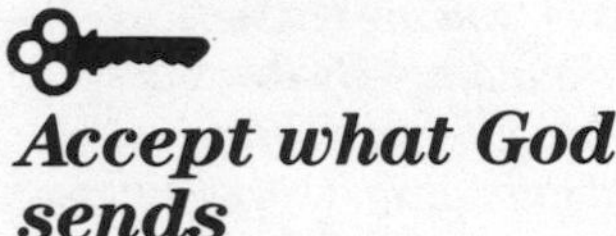

Accept what God sends

SCOTT STARED out the plane window, his thoughts swirling like the thick clouds below. *Why did God allow Mom and Dad to be in that accident,* he wondered. *Going to stay a while with Grandma and Grandpa is nice, but not when it's because Mom and Dad are in the hospital.*

Just then the stewardess arrived with lunch, so Scott turned from the window. "Cheer up," encouraged his big brother, Al, as Scott was given his tray of food. "Eat your chicken. It will help you feel better."

"But I'm not hungry," complained Scott. "I keep thinking about Mom and Dad."

Al gave him a lopsided grin. "I know, Scott. I feel the same way, really. But remember, God cares about us, and He knows what He's doing in our lives."

Scott nodded, but he wasn't sure he agreed. Picking up his fork, he began to eat. When the stewardess came to pick up his tray, he turned with a sigh to the window again. Immediately the sigh became a long whistle. "Look, Al!" he exclaimed. Pressing his nose to the glass, he stared down at the colorful fields and the cars and trucks that looked like tiny toys. "I didn't know it would look like that," he said. "See that train. It looks too tiny! Ohhh! I like this!" Scott's solemn face had brightened.

Al leaned over. "It's great," he agreed. "You know, all that nice scenery was there below the clouds all the time. You just couldn't see it."

"I hadn't thought of that," replied Scott.

"We can think of Mom and Dad's accident in the same way," continued Al. "To us, the whole situation is cloudy, and we can't see anything good in it."

"And you're saying that God can?" asked Scott.

"Right," replied Al. "We've both accepted Jesus as Savior by faith, and we need to also live by faith, accepting what He brings into our lives."

HOW ABOUT YOU? Do you have a "cloudy" outlook? Have things happened in your life that make you think nothing is going to turn out right? Don't let the hard things of life control your attitude. Remember that God knows what he's doing, and His plan is always good, even though you can't see it. Trust Him, and then that trust can help you have the right attitude. G.W.

TO MEMORIZE: *"He knows the way that I take"* Job 23:10 (NIV).

MARCH

Sent, But Not Delivered

FROM THE BIBLE:
For "whoever calls upon the name of the Lord shall be saved." How then shall they call on Him in whom they have not believed? And how shall they believe in Him of whom they have not heard? And how shall they hear without a preacher? And how shall they preach unless they are sent? As it is written: "How beautiful are the feet of those who preach the gospel of peace, who bring glad tidings of good things!"
Romans 10:13-15, NKJV

Deliver God's message

SADLY, THE COWAN family said good-bye to Aniceta. They were leaving their mission work in Mexico for a short furlough. They would miss Aniceta. She had helped them translate the New Testament into her language.

In the days that followed, Aniceta was often in their thoughts and prayers. But how could they let her know she was remembered?

"Let's send a letter," Mark suggested.

"That's a good idea, Mark," agreed Dad. "Mail is not delivered up in the mountains where she lives, but her son, Isauro, lives in town. We could send the letter to him, and he could deliver it to his mother."

Three months later the family returned to Mexico. Immediately they visited Aniceta. She was thrilled. "You are back, good doctor. Praise the Lord. You gone so long. I hear nothing."

"Didn't you get our letter?" Mark asked.

"No letter," Aniceta replied.

The family was puzzled. Why hadn't Aniceta received the letter? Later they visited Isauro in town. He remembered receiving the letter, but had forgotten to deliver it. Mark was disappointed in him and spoke of it on the way home. "Isauro failed us, Dad. He didn't deliver the letter, so Aniceta thought we had forgotten her."

"Yes, Mark," answered Dad. "Isauro didn't intend to be mean, but he neglected his job. You know. I'm afraid we often act the same way."

Mark looked puzzled. "What do you mean, Dad?" he asked.

"God has written a love letter to let people know that He hasn't forgotten them. It's called the Bible. God expects those of us who know Him and love Him to deliver that message to people who haven't heard. Often, out of neglect, we fail to do this," explained Dad. "Many, many people are still waiting to hear that God loves them."

Mark understood. "I'll help all I can, Dad. I'll start by telling Isauro about Jesus again."

HOW ABOUT YOU? Have you received God's message and accepted His Son as your Savior? If so, how long has it been since you told someone else about it? Don't be guilty of failing to deliver God's message to the world. He needs ambassadors who will carry His Word to the world. Can He count on you? J.H.

TO MEMORIZE: *"How beautiful are the feet of those who preach the gospel of peace, who bring glad tidings of good things!"* Romans 10:15 (NKJV).

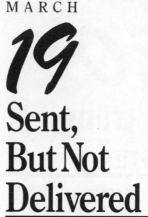

MARCH

20

A Strong Hand

FROM THE BIBLE:
My sheep hear my voice, and I know them, and they follow me: And I give unto them eternal life; and they shall never perish, neither shall any man pluck them out of my hand. My Father, which gave them me, is greater than all; and no man is able to pluck them out of my Father's hand. I and my Father are one. John 10:27-30, KJV

God keeps you

"WANT THIS QUARTER, Terri? You can have it if you can get it." Terri's big brother, Tony, held out a quarter on the palm of his hand. Terri hesitated, knowing how her brother loved to tease, but Tony just stood smiling at her. Slowly she walked toward him. When she was close, she made a sudden, quick lunge for his hand. But just that quickly, Tony's fist closed over the quarter, and the battle was on.

With a lot of laughing and squealing, Terri tried to open Tony's fist. "I got two fingers up," she panted in glee. "I'll get it yet!" But a moment later, Tony's fingers were down again. The quarter was as secure as ever.

Finally Mother intervened. "That's enough," she said. "You know you might as well give up, Terri. Tony's a lot bigger and stronger than you." She turned to her son and added, "You shouldn't always be teasing your sister."

"Teasing her?" Tony slapped his forehead in mock dismay. "I'm not teasing her. I'm just giving her an object lesson like any good brother should do."

"Oh yeah?" asked Terri. "Tell me about it."

"Well, I heard you learning your Sunday school memory verse, see? The one about nobody being able to pluck us out of the Father's hand," explained Tony. "So I just gave you a demonstration of what a safe place a hand can be."

"That's not bad," commented Mother. "Tony is a lot stronger than you, Terri, and God is much stronger than anybody or anything. You couldn't force Tony's hand open, but, of course, there are lots of people who could. But nobody—not even Satan—is strong enough to open God's hand." She smiled at Tony. "Good job, Son."

"Well, now, that's better." Tony grinned at his sister. "And just to show you what a good guy I am, you can even keep this quarter!"

HOW ABOUT YOU? Aren't you glad that, as a Christian, God holds you securely in His hand? You may get discouraged over things that happen, but God loves you and holds you. You are His. You may—and should—feel sad when you disobey, lie, or sin in any way. Satan may tell you that God can't love you anymore. But He does. He still holds you. You're still His. As you ask His forgiveness for what you have done, thank Him for loving you and keeping you safely in His hand. H.M.

TO MEMORIZE: *"No man is able to pluck them out of my Father's hand"* John 10:29.

MARCH

21

God's Mouthpiece

FROM THE BIBLE:

But Moses pleaded, "O Lord, I'm just not a good speaker. I never have been, and I'm not now, even after you have spoken to me, for I have a speech impediment." "Who makes mouths?" Jehovah asked him. "Isn't it I, the Lord? Who makes a man so that he can speak or not speak, see or not see, hear or not hear? Now go ahead and do as I tell you, for I will help you to speak well, and I will tell you what to say."

Exodus 4:10-12, TLB

Be God's mouthpiece

IT WAS YOUTH night at Centerville Church, and the young people were in charge of the entire evening service. They used their talents to serve the Lord as they sang, played instruments, worked in the nursery, put on a skit, ushered, took up the offering, and even preached.

After the special program, Mr. Jenkins approached Connie. "You did a fine job on your ventriloquism," he complimented. "The skit was cute, and it had a good message, too. I'm in charge of a special program that we're planning where I work. Would you do a skit there?"

Connie was so pleased with Mr. Jenkins's comments that she readily agreed. But when she thought about it later, she became apprehensive about what she had done. "I forgot that Mr. Jenkins works at that center for children who have been in trouble with the law," she told her mother. "I can't give a talk there!"

"Why not, dear?" asked Mother. "Those children need to hear the gospel, too."

"But they're so tough," explained Connie. "They aren't church kids. They'll laugh at me. I can't do it—I just can't!"

To Connie's surprise, Mother agreed with her. "You're right, Connie," she said. "They're too tough! Just send your dummy with Mr. Jenkins. Let the dummy handle those kids."

Connie glanced at her mother in surprise. "Mom," she protested, "you know he can't talk without me! I put the words in his mouth. He can't do anything without me."

Mother smiled and nodded. "That's how God works, too," she reminded Connie. "You are His mouthpiece. Without Him your words will be meaningless. It's His power that reaches people and meets their needs. He'll give you His power and the words to say if you ask Him."

"Are you saying I'm God's 'dummy'?" Connie grinned. "You're right, Mom. I will ask for His help. I want to be His mouthpiece. I know that without Him I can do nothing."

HOW ABOUT YOU? Do you speak up for Jesus whenever you get a chance? Are you using your talents to serve Him? If you try to do things in your own strength, you'll fail. Ask Jesus to help. He will give you strength. J.H.

TO MEMORIZE: *"For I will give you a mouth and wisdom which all your adversaries will not be able to contradict or resist"* Luke 21:15 (NKJV).

MARCH

22

Just Carrots?

FROM THE BIBLE:

To everything there is a season, a time for every purpose under heaven: A time to be born, and a time to die; a time to plant, and a time to pluck what is planted; a time to kill, and a time to heal; a time to break down, and a time to build up; a time to weep, and a time to laugh; a time to mourn, and a time to dance; a time to cast away stones, and a time to gather stones; a time to embrace, and a time to refrain from embracing; a time to gain, and a time to lose; a time to keep, and a time to throw away; a time to tear, and a time to sew; a time to keep silence, and a time to speak; a time to love, and a time to hate; a time of war, and a time of peace. What profit has the worker from that in which he labors? I have seen the God-given task with which the sons of men are to be occupied. He has made everything beautiful in its time. Also He has put eternity in their hearts, except that no one can find out the work that God does from beginning to end.
Ecclesiastes 3:1-11, NKJV

Become a well-balanced person

"I JUST GOT another mystery book from the library," Joel told his mother, who was busy in the laundry room.

"I'm glad you enjoy reading," said Mother as she looked up from her work. "By the way, how did the spelling test go?"

"It went OK, I guess," Joel replied sheepishly. He felt guilty because he knew that he had been up late finishing a story, not studying.

All week Joel read so late into the night that he could hardly get up for school in the mornings. He didn't play with his friends, he neglected his chores, and on Sunday morning his Sunday school lesson was not done.

As Joel walked into church on Sunday, his father noticed a mystery book in his son's coat pocket. "I hope you don't plan to read your book in church."

Joel fidgeted. "Could I read between services, Dad?" he asked. Dad shook his head.

As the family sat down for dinner that noon, Mom set a big bowl of carrots on the table. Then she sat down, too. "Is that it?" Joel asked in disbelief. "Where's the rest of the food?"

"The rest?" asked Mother. "Carrots are good for you. I thought you liked them."

"They're OK, but not that many of 'em," said Joel. "What happened to the meat and all the other stuff you always say we need for a balanced diet?"

"Aha!" Dad entered the conversation. "Did I hear the word *balance?* Joel, that word not only applies to food, but it applies to your whole life as well. People can become off balance by doing too much of one thing and neglecting other things. Take reading, for instance. Reading is good, but not when you neglect your body, family, friends, school work, or the Lord to do it."

Joel blushed. "I guess you're right," he admitted. "I should probably try harder to have a 'balanced life.' "

"That's right," said Mom, pulling a pan out of the oven. "You can start by having a good meal!"

HOW ABOUT YOU? Do you spend too much time doing one thing? You should be taking care of your body by getting proper food, sleep and exercise. You should be taking care of your mind by studying, reading good books, and listening in church and Sunday school. you should be spending time with people and also with the Lord. S.N.

TO MEMORIZE: *"And Jesus increased in wisdom and stature, and in favour with God and man"*
Luke 2:52.

JUSTIN GROPED for the doorknob. His eyes were clinched tightly shut. "Eric threw dirt in my face," he sobbed as Mother hurried to let him in. "I can't see! I can't see!"

While she talked calmly, Mother washed the dirt from his eyes. Finally, the last speck was out, and she washed his face. "I'll get even with Eric if it's the last thing I do," Justin threatened.

Mother frowned. "Eric was wrong, but getting even won't accomplish anything."

"It'll teach him not to throw dirt in people's eyes," Justin argued as he went out the door.

At bedtime when Dad read Romans 12:17-21, Justin scowled. "does that mean I'm supposed to be good to Eric to make him ashamed of the way he treated me? Is that how I get even?"

Mother shook her head. "You're not supposed to try to get even. The nineteenth verse says, 'Do not avenge yourselves. . . . Vengence is Mine; I will repay, says the Lord.' "

"How's the Lord going to repay Eric for what he did?" Justin wanted to know. "I hope He gets him really good!"

"Maybe He knows Eric has already suffered enough," Dad replied.

"I'm the one who got hurt!"

"Yes, but Eric has a load of guilt and worry to carry," Dad explained. "He's probably one really scared fellow, wondering how badly you were hurt."

"But the Bible says to heap coals of fire on our enemy's head," Justin pointed out. "Isn't that getting even?"

"That was written before people had matches. If their fire went out, they had to borrow live coals from a neighbor, and they carried these in a pot on their heads," Dad explained. "So this verse is telling you to *help your enemy*. Don't get revenge. Overcome his evil with your good."

"That sounds hard," Justin grumbled.

"Not nearly as hard as it would be to keep fighting with him," Mother reasoned. "Wouldn't you really prefer to have Eric for a friend than an enemy?"

Justin grinned. "I guess you're right about that."

HOW ABOUT YOU? Has someone mistreated you? Are you planning to get even? Ask God to give you a forgiving spirit. Start overcoming evil with good. B.W.

TO MEMORIZE: *"Do not be overcome by evil, but overcome evil with good"* Romans 12:21 (NKJV).

MARCH

23

Getting Even

FROM THE BIBLE:

Repay no one evil for evil. Have regard for good things in the sight of all men. If it is possible, as much as depends on you, live peaceably with all men. Beloved, do not avenge yourselves, but rather give place to wrath; for it is written, "Vengeance is Mine, I will repay," says the Lord. "Therefore if your enemy hungers, feed him; if he thirsts, give him a drink; for in so doing you will heap coals of fire on his head." Do not be overcome by evil, but overcome evil with good. Romans 12:17-21, NKJV

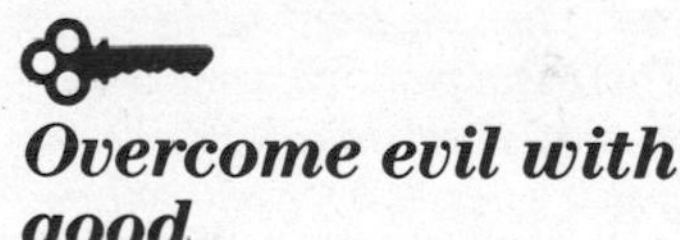

Overcome evil with good

MARCH

24

Here Comes the Sun

FROM THE BIBLE:

And the Lord said to Moses, "I will do the very thing you have asked, because I am pleased with you and I know you by name." Then Moses said, "Now show me your glory." And the Lord said, "I will cause all my goodness to pass in front of you, and I will proclaim my name, the Lord, in your presence. I will have mercy on whom I will have mercy, and I will have compassion on whom I will have compassion. But," he said, "you cannot see my face, for no one may see me and live." Then the Lord said, "There is a place near me where you may stand on a rock. When my glory passes by, I will put you in a cleft in the rock and cover you with my hand until I have passed by. Then I will remove my hand and you will see my back; but my face must not be seen."

Exodus 33:17-23, NIV

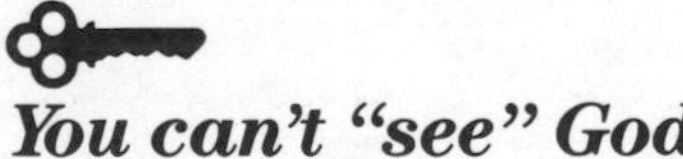

You can't "see" God

PAUL ALWAYS liked to get his grandfather's opinion about questions that came to his mind. As he helped Grandpa in the garden one cloudy spring day, he brought up something that was puzzling him. "I sure find it hard to understand how God can be three different persons and still be only one," said Paul. "My Sunday school teacher says God is a Trinity—that there's the Father, the Son, and Holy Spirit, but they're all one."

"That is hard to understand," Grandpa agreed, "but it is certainly taught in the Bible." He handed Paul a package of radish seeds. "Want to put those in the ground?"

"Sure," said Paul, looking up at the sky. "I sure wish the sun would come out." He opened the package. As he began to sow the tiny seeds, he returned to the subject that was bothering him. "Can you explain the Trinity?"

Grandpa looked up with a smile. "You just mentioned the sun, and it's a good illustration of the Trinity," he said.

"You mean the sun up in the sky?" Paul asked.

"Right," said Grandpa. "It illustrates God the Father. Tell me, has anyone ever seen the sun?"

"Sure," replied Paul.

"Wrong!" objected Grandpa. "No one has really seen that great ball we call the sun, not even astronomers. In fact, it's impossible to look at the sun. What we see is light from the sun, right?"

"I guess that's true," agreed Paul. "And you mean that's like God the Father?"

"Exactly," said Grandpa. "The Bible says no one has seen God the Father. He is so great and glorious that human beings cannot look upon Him. Although we can't see him, we know Him through the Bible and through nature."

As Paul continued to sprinkle radish seeds in the ground, he thought about Grandpa's explanation. "OK. I can see that illustration of God the Father. But what about the Son and the Spirit?"

"I'll get to those in a minute," replied Grandpa. "First, let's water the area we've planted."

HOW ABOUT YOU? Do you have trouble believing in God because you can't see Him? You can't see the sun either, but you certainly don't doubt that it exists. Even though you can't understand everything about God, you can believe what the Bible teaches about Him. G.W.

TO MEMORIZE: *"No one has seen God at any time"* John 1:18 (NKJV).

MARCH

25

Here Comes the Sun

(Continued from yesterday)

FROM THE BIBLE:

Before anything else existed, there was Christ, with God. He has always been alive and is himself God. He created everything there is—nothing exists that he didn't make. Eternal life is in him, and this life gives light to all mankind. His life is the light that shines through the darkness—and the darkness can never extinguish it. God sent John the Baptist as a witness to the fact that Jesus Christ is the true Light. John himself was not the Light; he was only a witness to identify it. Later on, the one who is the true Light arrived to shine on everyone coming into the world. But although he made the world, the world didn't recognize him when he came. Even in his own land and among his own people, the Jews, he was not accepted. Only a few would welcome and receive him. But to all who received him, he gave the right to become children of God. All they needed to do was to trust him to save them.

John 1:1-12, TLB

AS PAUL TURNED on the faucet and pulled the hose over to the garden, the clouds parted to let the sun shine through, "Look, Grandpa!" he exclaimed. "Here comes the sun!"

Keeping a very serious look on his face, Grandpa glanced around the garden. "Do you mean that big ball in the sky is coming down here?" he asked. "Where is it?"

"Oh, Grandpa," laughed Paul, "don't be silly! You know what I mean. It's the sunshine that we see—the sunlight."

Grandpa chuckled. "Right," he agreed, "and your own words can help you understand how the sun illustrates the Trinity."

"What do you mean?" Paul asked.

Grandpa dropped to the grass under a nearby tree and motioned for Paul to join him. "Remember what we said a while ago about not being able to see God?" he asked.

"Sure," said Paul thoughtfully. "Just as we don't actually see the sun, we don't see God the Father."

"Right, but light comes down from the sun, and we see that," responded Grandpa. "And, although we don't see God the Father, Jesus—God the Son—came down to earth from the Father. Men did see Him, and we learn about the Godhead, or the Trinity, by getting to know Jesus, who is the light of the world."

"I think I'm beginning to see what you mean," said Paul.

"We say 'the sun' for both the heavenly body and the light that comes from it. In a sense, they're the same thing," continued Grandpa. "God the Father and God the Son are also one. We call both 'God,' for both are God."

"That takes care of one being two and two being one," said Paul, "but when we talk about the Trinity, there's still a third part to explain."

With a grunt, Grandpa pulled himself to his feet. "Let's get this garden watered," he said, "and we'll talk about it while we work."

HOW ABOUT YOU? Do you think of Jesus as a baby in a manger? As a good man? As a good friend? He's all of that, but also much, much more. He is God! All the great and wonderful things you know about God are also true of Jesus. As you learn about Jesus in the Bible, you will be learning about God. G.W.

TO MEMORIZE: *"I and my Father are one"* John 10:30.

Jesus is God

MARCH

26

Here Comes the Sun

(Continued from yesterday)

FROM THE BIBLE:

If you love me, obey me; and I will ask the Father and he will give you another Comforter, and he will never leave you. He is the Holy Spirit, the Spirit who leads into all truth. The world at large cannot receive him, for it isn't looking for him and doesn't recognize him. But you do, for he lives with you now and some day shall be in you.
John 14:15-17, TLB

Oh, there is so much more I want to tell you, but you can't understand it now. When the Holy Spirit, who is truth, comes, he shall guide you into all truth, for he will not be presenting his own ideas, but will be passing on to you what he has heard. He will tell you about the future.
John 16:12-13, TLB

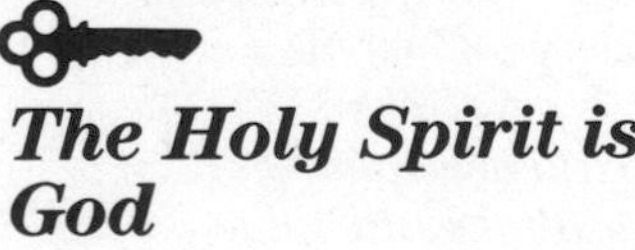

The Holy Spirit is God

"TAKE THE HOSE over to the end of the garden," suggested Grandpa. "Start watering there."

Paul followed instructions and began to give the ground a gentle spray of water. "This will help the seeds sprout," he said confidently.

"You bet," agreed Grandpa as he reached over and smoothed some dirt with a rake. "Do you remember the garden we planted last year?"

"Sure do!" exclaimed Paul. "We had the best radishes and carrots and beans in the whole neighborhood. It was fun to watch everything grow."

"Besides water, what else made them grow?" asked Grandpa.

"Well, I guess it was the sun," replied Paul. "That's what people say, anyway."

"And they're right," agreed Grandpa. "Actually, it's the chemical power of the sun that helps plants grow. That power is very distinct from the actual sun and from the sunlight, yet it is one with them. And when we speak of it, we say 'the sun,' for it is the sun."

"Wow, that's a little hard to understand," said Paul, "but I think you're going to say that the Holy Spirit is like the chemical power of the sun."

"You're catching on," said Grandpa, chuckling, "and you're right about what I'm going to say. The Holy Spirit is one with God the Father and God the Son. He is God the Holy Spirit. He quietly works in our hearts, often unnoticed. But He has a very important part in every life. He gives Christians the power they need to live for God. For the unsaved person, it's the Holy Spirit who makes him realize he needs to accept Jesus."

Turning off the hose, Paul looked at his grandfather with a grin. "You should have been a preacher, Grandpa," he said. "You're always so good at helping me understand the Bible."

HOW ABOUT YOU? Do you know much about the Third Person of the Trinity, the Holy Spirit? If you're a Christian, He lives in your life and helps you understand spiritual truths. Listen to Him and obey. If you're not a Christian, the Holy Spirit is telling you that accepting Jesus as Savior is the most important decision for you to make. Listen to Him and accept Christ. G.W.

TO MEMORIZE: *"For there are three that bear record in heaven, the Father, the Word [Jesus], and the Holy Ghost [or Spirit]: and these three are one"* 1 John 5:7.

MARCH

27

Something Beautiful

FROM THE BIBLE:

For we know in part and we prophesy in part, but when perfection comes, the imperfect disappears. When I was a child, I talked like a child, I thought like a child, I reasoned like a child. When I became a man, I put childish ways behind me. Now we see but a poor reflection as in a mirror; then we shall see face to face. Now I know in part; then I shall know fully, even as I am fully known. And now these three remain: faith, hope and love. But the greatest of these is love.

1 Corinthians 13:9-13, NIV

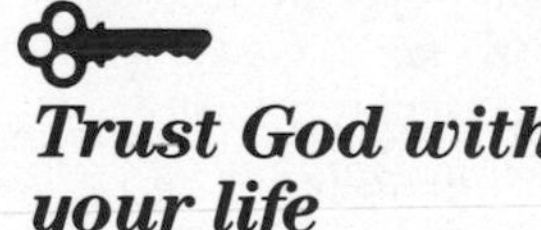

Trust God with your life

NOTHING WAS going right anymore! First, Mother got sick, and no one knew if she would ever get well again. Now Rob had been sent to stay with an uncle and aunt while Dad took Mom to a special doctor in a faraway city. His thoughts were gloomy as he passed the church on his way to school.

"Mornin', young fellow." Old Mr. Barry, the church janitor, was gazing up at the stained glass window that faced the street in front of the church. "I never cease to marvel at the skill of the man who created that window."

Rob looked up. He'd never noticed the window before, and he wasn't impressed now. It was made up of a bunch of dark, dull little pieces of glass, and it wasn't at all pretty. Seeing his frown, Mr. Barry spoke again. "Bet you never saw it with the sun shining through. Tell you what—stop by after school and I'll show you something beautiful. OK?"

As he approached the church on his way home that afternoon, he saw that Mr. Barry was busily raking the church lawn. With a smile, the janitor greeted Rob, and a few minutes later led him into the church sanctuary. "Look!" He turned Rob around to face the stained glass window. It was dazzlingly beautiful as the sun shone brightly through the colored glass. "Quite a change when you see it from this side, isn't there?" continued Mr. Barry. "You know, I sometimes think life is like that. From our point of view it can seem dark and dull, especially when we're going through bad times. But from God's point of view each little part fits together just right."

Rob stared at the window. He saw that even the dark pieces used for Jesus' eyes and a child's curly hair had a beautiful gleam. The artist knew what he was doing when he used each piece. Some day Rob would be able to see that God knew what He was doing, too.

HOW ABOUT YOU? Does life look dull to you? Is it dark and dreary? Perhaps there has been sickness or death in your family. Perhaps your best friend has moved away. Perhaps your parents are separating. What makes up the dark pieces of your life? Try to realize that if you could see it as God does, you would see something beautiful forming. You may not understand until you get to heaven, but God truly is working for your best. H.M.

TO MEMORIZE: *"Now I know in part; then I shall know fully, even as I am fully known"*
1 Corinthians 13:12 (NIV).

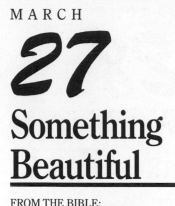

MARCH

28

Watching like a Hawk

FROM THE BIBLE:

I wrote to you as I did so that I could find out how far you would go in obeying me. When you forgive anyone, I do too. And whatever I have forgiven (to the extent that this affected me too) has been by Christ's authority, and for your good. A further reason for forgiveness is to keep from being outsmarted by Satan; for we know what he is trying to do. . . . But thanks be to God! For through what Christ has done, he has triumphed over us so that now wherever we go he uses us to tell others about the Lord and to spread the Gospel like a sweet perfume. As far as God is concerned there is a sweet, wholesome fragrance in our lives. It is the fragrance of Christ within us, an aroma to both the saved and the unsaved all around us.

2 Corinthians 2:9-11, 14-15, TLB

Let God strengthen you

WHILE RANDY and his grandpa were out for a walk one evening, Grandpa spotted a hawk circling above them. "Quick! Get behind this bush," Grandpa said, giving Randy a nudge. "Let's watch this." Screened behind the bush, they watched the hawk sweep down from the sky with lightning speed. The hawk pounced on a mouse, gripped it tightly in its powerful feet, and carried it off.

Randy's mouth hung open in surprise. "How did the hawk see that little mouse?" he asked.

"Hawks have much sharper eyesight than ours," Grandpa explained. "That's where the expression 'watching like a hawk' comes from. That hawk could see the little mouse running in the grass, so he caught his dinner."

"What a terrific aim!" exclaimed Randy. "I'm sure glad I'm too big for a hawk's dinner."

"Way too big," Grandpa chuckled, then he looked serious. "There is an enemy who circles around looking for humans, though. Just as that hawk looks for weaker animals to prey on, Satan looks for weak spots in our lives."

"What do you mean by weak spots?"

"I mean areas in our lives that aren't fully given to God," Grandpa said. "For instance, if a person has a temper and hasn't asked God for help in fighting it, Satan will attack that person through his temper. He'll attack over and over again."

"Could lying and stealing and swearing be weak spots, too?" asked Randy.

Grandpa nodded. "And grumbling and disobedience—all kinds of things. I'll tell you one of my weak spots, Randy."

"You have one?" Randy asked, surprised.

"Sure. One of mine is that I don't help Grandma enough. So when I see I'm neglecting her, I tell God I'm sorry and ask for His help. Then Satan can't attack me in that weak spot. He can watch me like a hawk, but it won't do any good."

"I guess fighting with my sister is a weak spot for me," Randy decided. "I'm going to ask God to help me quit doing that."

HOW ABOUT YOU? What is your weak spot? Arguing? Laziness? Putting things off till later? Talking back? Whatever it is, talk to God about it and ask for His forgiveness and help when you fail. C.Y.

TO MEMORIZE: *"I wrote to you as I did so that I could find out how far you would go in obeying me. . . . A further reason for forgiveness is to keep from being outsmarted by Satan; for we know what he is trying to do"* 2 Corinthians 2:9, 11 (TLB).

MARCH

29

Two Kinds of Sin

FROM THE BIBLE:

Don't just pretend that you love others: really love them. Hate what is wrong. Stand on the side of the good. Love each other with brotherly affection and take delight in honoring each other. Never be lazy in your work but serve the Lord enthusiastically. Be glad for all God is planning for you. Be patient in trouble, and prayerful always. When God's children are in need, you be the one to help them out. And get into the habit of inviting guests home for dinner or, if they need lodging, for the night. If someone mistreats you because you are a Christian, don't curse him; pray that God will bless him. When others are happy, be happy with them. If they are sad, share their sorrow. Work happily together. Don't try to act big. Don't try to get into the good graces of important people, but enjoy the company of ordinary folks. And don't think you know it all! Romans 12:9-16, TLB

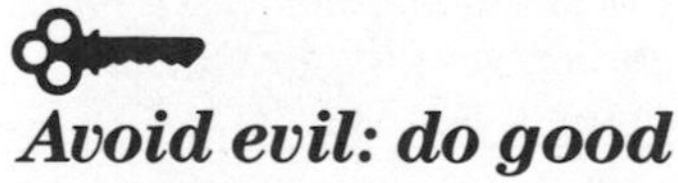

Avoid evil: do good

BILLY WAS HELPING Dad in the workshop, and he thought it would be a good time to ask a question that had been bothering him. "Dad, you're always telling me that it's important to confess our sins when we pray. Right?"

"That's right," Dad replied. "It's important to confess our sins, so our fellowship with God is not disturbed."

Billy sighed impatiently. "I know all that," he said, "but what if I can't think of any sins to confess? There are some days that I never catch myself telling a lie or doing anything else really wrong. So how can I confess anything?"

Dad looked at him seriously, but there was a twinkle in his eye. "I wish I had that problem, Billy," he said. "I can always think of plenty of sins to confess."

"You, Dad?" asked Billy in surprise. "But you're such a good Christian."

Dad laughed. "Thanks for the vote of confidence," he said. "Maybe I don't have much of a problem with 'obvious' sins. But I still sin many times a day. For example, I might have sinful thoughts that no one would know about. Besides, Son, there are actually two kinds of sins."

"Huh?" asked Billy. "I thought sin was sin!"

"In a way it is," agreed Dad, "and all sin displeases God, and it hurts others and ourselves. However, sometimes we sin by doing wrong things, and sometimes by *not* doing things we know we should do. The Bible says that if I know to do good, and don't do it, it is sin."

Billy thought about that. "You mean, when I know Mom needs help in the kitchen but I decide to watch TV instead, it's really a sin?" Dad nodded, and Billy shook his head. "Boy," he exclaimed. "I sure won't have any problem thinking of things to confess any more—and I'll have to make some changes in my life."

HOW ABOUT YOU? Do you confess obvious sins such as stealing, swearing, disobeying your parents, or other things God has said you should not do? You also need to be careful to obey all that God tells you to do. Make use of every opportunity He gives you to do good. Right now, stop and think about those things that you know you should do. Then determine to do them as soon as you can. S.K.

TO MEMORIZE: *"Anyone, then, who knows the good he ought to do and doesn't do it, sins"* James 4:17 (NIV).

MARCH

30

Don't Be a Chicken

FROM THE BIBLE:

By that same mighty power he has given us all the other rich and wonderful blessings he promised. . . . But to obtain these gifts, you need more than faith; you must also work hard to be good, and even that is not enough. For then you must learn to know God better and discover what he wants you to do. Next, learn to put aside your own desires so that you will become patient and godly, gladly letting God have his way with you. This will make possible the next step, which is for you to enjoy other people and to like them, and finally you will grow to love them deeply. The more you go on in this way, the more you will grow strong spiritually and become fruitful and useful to our Lord Jesus Christ. But anyone who fails to go after these additions to faith is blind indeed, or at least very short-sighted, and has forgotten that God delivered him from the old life of sin so that now he can live a strong, good life for the Lord.
2 Peter 1:4-9, TLB

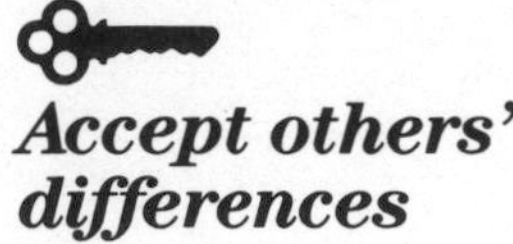

Accept others' differences

RANDY FOLLOWED Grandpa into the chicken coop, and Grandpa closed the door as the chickens crowded noisily around them. Randy scattered a handful of grain over the floor. The chickens scrambled madly for it. But one chicken was having trouble. Every time it tried to eat, it was pecked by the others. Randy saw a small, red spot on the chicken's neck.

"Look, Grandpa!" he exclaimed. "That chicken is hurt!"

Just then a big rooster jabbed the sore on the neck of the chicken, making it even larger. Grandpa picked up the chicken and carried the squawking bird out of the pen. "Come on, old girl. We'll put you in a separate place until your neck heals."

Randy watched as Grandpa rubbed medicine into the sore. "Why do the other chickens peck this one?" he asked.

"Well, Randy, I can't tell you exactly why," answered Grandpa, "but this is typical chicken behavior. They always pick on those who are hurt or different from the rest. And they always peck right at the spot that is already sore or hurt."

"That seems stupid," said Randy.

"Right you are, Randy," said Grandpa. "But do you know that people often do the same thing?"

"They do?" asked Randy, surprised. "How?"

"When others have skin that is a different color, or perhaps their eyes, nose, or ears look a little different, some people make fun of them," explained Grandpa. Randy immediately thought of a boy named Darrin. Some of the other boys teased Darrin about his bright, red-orange hair. Randy was glad now that he had not joined in the teasing—but he hadn't made any effort to be friendly either. "It's too bad when people act like chickens," continued Grandpa.

Randy nodded. When he got home, he was going to invite Darrin to play with him.

HOW ABOUT YOU? Do you accept those who do not look or talk the way you do? Never call them names or tell jokes about them. Remember, that would be acting like a chicken! God wants you to love others and treat them kindly. Perhaps there is a "different" person in your school or neighborhood who needs your friendship. God loves that person. Will you show him or her God's love? C.Y.

TO MEMORIZE: *"A new commandment I give to you, that you love one another; as I have loved you"* John 13:34 (NKJV).

MARCH

31

Follow the Leader

FROM THE BIBLE:

These things command and teach. Let no one despise your youth, but be an example to the believers in word, in conduct, in love, in spirit, in faith, in purity. Till I come, give attention to reading, to exhortation, to doctrine. Do not neglect the gift that is in you, which was given to you by prophecy with the laying on of the hands of the presbytery. Meditate on these things; give yourself entirely to them, that your progress may be evident to all. Take heed to yourself and to the doctrine. Continue in them, for in doing this you will save both yourself and those who hear you.

1 Timothy 4:11-16, NKJV

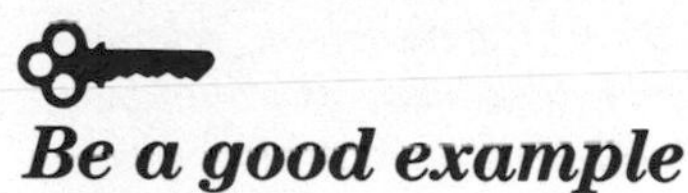

Be a good example

STEVE OFTEN was impatient with his little sister, Karen, because she persisted in trying to follow him wherever he went. She loved to copy whatever he did.

One day Mother sent Steve to Grandpa Wells with some freshly baked cinnamon rolls. Grandpa was happy to see him. As they sat down at the kitchen table to visit and enjoy one of the rolls, there was a knock at the door. "More company?" wondered Grandpa.

"Karen!" exclaimed Steve as the door opened. "Mother is going to be mad at you!" He turned to Grandpa. "Karen thinks she has to go everywhere I go and do everything I do," he complained.

"I reckon that's the highest compliment she could pay you," Grandpa told him. "She looks up to you. You are her example. Where you lead, she will follow."

Steve sighed. "She looks up to me all right. And she follows me like a shadow. Every time I sigh, she sighs and says, 'Me, too.' "

"Then you had better be careful how you sigh," laughed Grandpa.

"Me, too," announced Karen.

Steve laughed. "Oh, come on, little 'Me, Too.' We've got to get home. 'Bye, Grandpa. We'll be back soon."

Steve glanced at Karen as she thrust her hand into his and trotted along beside him. He remembered Grandpa's words about being an example. He had often complained about the way Karen followed him, but he had never realized what a responsibility that put on him. He determined to be the best example for his little sister that he could be. He would need the Lord's help for that.

HOW ABOUT YOU? Real life is a little bit like the game, "Follow the Leader." Everyone is both a follower and a leader. You follow someone and someone follows you. That gives you a double responsibility. First, be sure you are following the right leader—the Lord Jesus. Second, be sure you are setting a good example for those who look up to you and follow you. B.W.

TO MEMORIZE: *"Be an example to the believers in word, in conduct, in love, in spirit, in faith, in purity"* 1 Timothy 4:12 (NKJV).

1

April Birthday!

FROM THE BIBLE:
Follow God's example in everything you do just as a much loved child imitates his father. Be full of love for others, following the example of Christ who loved you and gave himself to God as a sacrifice to take away your sins. And God was pleased, for Christ's love for you was like sweet perfume to him. . . . For though once your heart was full of darkness, now it is full of light from the Lord, and your behavior should show it! Because of this light within you, you should do only what is good and right and true. Learn as you go along what pleases the Lord. Take no part in the worthless pleasures of evil and darkness, but instead, rebuke and expose them. It would be shameful even to mention here those pleasures of darkness which the ungodly do. But when you expose them, the light shines in upon their sin and shows it up, and when they see how wrong they really are, some of them may even become children of light!
Ephesians 5:1-2, 8-13, TLB

Sin hinders your light

"HAPPY BIRTHDAY to you," sang Jerry and Nan as their mother brought the dessert to the table. "Happy birthday, dear Daddy. Happy birthday to you." Dad beamed as Mother set the cake with several candles in front of him. "Blow out the candles," clamored the children, "and don't forget to make a wish."

Dad closed his eyes and thought for a minute. Then he took a deep breath, puffed out his cheeks, and blew! All around the cake the little lights went out. But one of them recovered and burned brightly again. "Oops," said Dad. He tried again. Again the candle flickered and appeared to go out, but when Dad stopped blowing, the flame came right back. Dad tried a third time with the same results. "Hey, wait a minute," said Dad, while the children roared with laughter. He looked at the still burning candle. "Whose idea was it to pull a trick on your old dad?" he growled playfully.

"Jerry got that candle down at Frye's Magic Supplies," laughed Nan. "It's a special candle, and it won't blow out. You have to put it under water to put it out."

"That's what you get for having your birthday on April 1," teased Jerry. "Happy birthday, and Happy April Fool's Day!"

The children each took several turns to see if they could blow out the light. Even Mother tried, but no one could do it. "That special candle reminds me of what God has done for us," said Dad finally. "He has given us the privilege of being lights in this world. When we allow sin to enter our lives, it blows against our lights, causing them to flicker. Sometimes it makes us very ineffective, but let's be sure to thank the Lord that He doesn't allow our lights to go out completely. And let's make up our minds to keep our lights free from sin so they can burn brightly for Jesus."

HOW ABOUT YOU? Is your "light" burning brightly? Or is there sin—such as disobedience, a lie, an unkind act—blowing against it? If there is, it will keep you from being a good testimony for Jesus. Confess that sin, ask God's forgiveness, and shine for Him. H.M.

TO MEMORIZE: *"Let your light so shine before men, that they may see your good works, and glorify your Father which is in heaven"* Matthew 5:16.

JUSTIN PHILLIPS wanted to be a missionary when he grew up, so he was excited when Dr. Cook, a missionary on furlough from Africa, came to visit one evening. As they sat in the living room, Justin asked, "what is it really like in the jungle, Dr. Cook? I'll bet it's exciting."

Justin's sister, Lisa, shuddered. "I think it would be scary, with all those lions and snakes and elephants."

"I'm not chicken!" Justin boasted. "If a big lion came at me, I'd just shoot him with my high-powered rifle. Bam! Bam! Bam!"

Dr. Cook laughed. "I'm glad you're so brave, Justin," he said. "I have seen some dangerous animals in Africa, but not the kind you're thinking of. Our biggest enemies in the jungle are not lions or elephants, but mosquitoes."

"Mosquitoes?" scoffed Justin in unbelief. "How can you even compare a little, dinky mosquito with a big, ferocious lion? Lions are mean and have big teeth and claws. They can kill people."

"It's true that occasionally someone is attacked by a lion in the jungle," responded the doctor, "but it doesn't happen very often. Actually, mosquitoes and other insects kill far more people than the big animals do, for they carry malaria, yellow fever, and other diseases. Many people have had to leave the mission field because of something as small and seemingly insignificant as a mosquito."

At that point, Justin's father spoke up. "We ought to remember that principle when it comes to our Christian lives," he said. "Often it's not the big things that cause us to be discouraged. It's the little things like getting bored or not getting along with people."

"Hmmm. Well, I still want to be a missionary in Africa," said Justin, "but I promise to watch out for those really dangerous animals—the mosquitoes!"

HOW ABOUT YOU? You may think you'd be willing to fight great battles for Jesus' sake, but how are you handling the little problems in your life—friends who tease you, tough homework assignments, a brother or sister you can't get along with, or a parent or teacher who just doesn't seem to understand? Don't let "mosquitoes" keep you from doing God's will. S.K.

TO MEMORIZE: *"I can do all things through Christ who strengthens me"* Philippians 4:13 (NKJV).

Danger: Mosquitoes!

FROM THE BIBLE:

Since we have such a huge crowd of men of faith watching us from the grandstands, let us strip off anything that slows us down or holds us back, and especially those sins that wrap themselves so tightly around our feet and trip us up; and let us run with patience the particular race that God has set before us. Keep your eyes on Jesus, our leader and instructor. He was willing to die a shameful death on the cross because of the joy he knew would be his afterwards; and now he sits in the place of honor by the throne of God. If you want to keep from becoming fainthearted and weary, think about his patience as sinful men did such terrible things to him. After all, you have never yet struggled against sin and temptation until you sweat great drops of blood.

Hebrews 12:1-4, TLB

Overcome "little" faults

APRIL

3

Substitute Teacher

FROM THE BIBLE:

Everyone must submit himself to the governing authorities, for there is no authority except that which God has established. The authorities that exist have been established by God. Consequently, he who rebels against the authority is rebelling against what God has instituted, and those who do so will bring judgment on themselves. For rulers hold no terror for those who do right, but for those who do wrong. Do you want to be free from fear of the one in authority? Then do what is right and he will commend you. For he is God's servant to do you good. But if you do wrong, be afraid, for he does not bear the sword for nothing. He is God's servant, an agent of wrath to bring punishment on the wrongdoer. Therefore, it is necessary to submit to the authorities, not only because of possible punishment but also because of conscience.
Romans 13:1-5, NIV

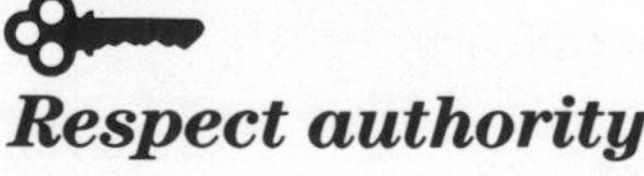

Respect authority

JANE WALKED into the house smiling. "Mom," she called, "we had the best time in school today!"

"What did you do that was so much fun?" asked Mom with a smile. "You're not usually so excited about school!"

"Oh, we had a substitute teacher today. It was so funny!" Jane laughed. "Todd, Mike, and John all switched seats. So all day long she was calling them the wrong names. Then some of the kids told her that our teacher always lets us out for recess early, so we got out fifteen minutes before everyone else! What a dummy!"

Mom frowned. "How was your substitute supposed to know who the kids were?" she asked.

Jane shrugged. "I suppose our teacher left a seating chart for her."

"Well, then, how would she know if the boys were in the right seats or not?" asked Mom. "And how would she know you weren't supposed to be let out early? Has she taught your class before?"

"No," answered Jane. "I guess she couldn't have known, could she?"

"I doubt it," said Mom. "It really wasn't very nice, or funny, to fool her and laugh at her!"

"Well, she's just a sub," said Jane with a shrug. "It doesn't matter."

"Oh yes, it does matter!" exclaimed Mom. "You are under her authority while she's in your class, and you must respect and obey her. It's not only common courtesy. It's a command from God!"

Jane's eyes widened. "It is? I thought the Bible just said to obey your parents."

"It also tells us to obey anyone who is in authority over us," said Mom, "and that includes substitute teachers."

"I suppose she must have felt really bad," said Jane thoughtfully. Suddenly she had an idea. "Mom, will you drive me back to school? I heard our sub say she'd be correcting papers after school, so she should still be there. I could apologize to her."

"That's a great idea!" said Mom. "Let's go now!"

HOW ABOUT YOU? Have you or any of your classmates ever had a little "fun" with a substitute teacher? Have you played tricks and given the substitute a bad day? Did you think it was funny? God didn't. He tells us that we must not only obey our parents, but we must also respect and obey anyone who has authority over us. D.M.

TO MEMORIZE: *"Everyone must submit himself to the governing authorities"* Romans 13:1 (NIV).

APRIL

A Messed-up Messenger

FROM THE BIBLE:

The Holy Spirit said, "Dedicate Barnabas and Paul for a special job I have for them." . . . Afterwards they preached from town to town across the entire island until finally they reached Paphos where they met a Jewish sorcerer, a fake prophet named Bar-Jesus. He had attached himself to the governor, Sergius Paulus, a man of considerable insight and understanding. The governor invited Barnabas and Paul to visit him, for he wanted to hear their message from God. But the sorcerer, Elymas (his name in Greek), interfered and urged the governor to pay no attention to what Paul and Barnabas said, trying to keep him from trusting the Lord. Then Paul, filled with the Holy Spirit, glared angrily at the sorcerer and said, "You son of the devil, . . . God has laid his hand of punishment upon you, and you will be stricken awhile with blindness."

Acts 13:2, 6-11, TLB

DUKE WAS a very smart dog, and Ken and Laura enjoyed sending messages to each other by way of their pet. Ken would fasten a note on Duke's collar and say, "Go to Laura." The faithful dog would trot down the hall to Laura's room. Then Laura would answer the note and tell Duke, "Go to Ken." Duke would obediently return to Ken's room.

One day as he was doing homework in his room, Ken began to get hungry. He thought about the candy Laura had in her room. So Ken wrote a note asking for some, fastened it on Duke's collar, and said, "Duke, go to Laura."

Duke trotted out of the room, and Ken's mouth began to water just thinking about the candy. But he waited and waited, and Duke didn't come back. Ken decided to go check on his messenger. "He never got here," said Laura. "I think he heard Mom open the cupboard door."

Sure enough, Duke had gone to the kitchen, and Mom had let him outside. Now Ken's messenger was running around the backyard in pursuit of a rabbit!

"So much for that messenger," Ken laughed.

"That's the way Christians are sometimes," said Mother with a smile. "We are to be God's messengers, and we agree to the job—but then we get sidetracked."

"Like when I was supposed to play my trumpet in church but didn't get to practice because I was playing baseball," suggested Ken.

"Or when I was supposed to write a letter to a missionary as a Sunday school project and ended up writing to my friend instead," Laura added.

"That's just the kind of thing I'm talking about," said Mother. "The message Ken gave to Duke wasn't important, but the message we have about the Lord *is* important. It takes a serious messenger to deliver a serious message."

HOW ABOUT YOU? Do you sometimes get waylaid when delivering a message for the Lord? Do you get so busy watching TV you don't have time to memorize your Sunday school verse or practice your special music for church? Do you forget to ask your friends to church or to tell them about the Lord because you're so involved talking about other things? Remember, it takes a serious messenger to deliver a serious message. Don't get sidetracked. L.W.

TO MEMORIZE: *"Go into all the world and preach the good news to all creation"* Mark 16:15 (NIV).

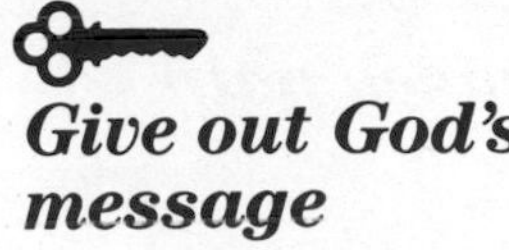

Give out God's message

APRIL

5

Healing the Hurt

FROM THE BIBLE:

As God's messenger I give each of you God's warning: Be honest in your estimate of yourselves, measuring your value by how much faith God has given you. Just as there are many parts to our bodies, so it is with Christ's body. We are all parts of it, and it takes every one of us to make it complete, for we each have different work to do. So we belong to each other, and each needs all the others. God has given each of us the ability to do certain things well. So if God has given you the ability to prophesy, then prophesy whenever you can—as often as your faith is strong enough to receive a message from God. If your gift is that of serving others, serve them well. If you are a teacher, do a good job of teaching. If you are a preacher, see to it that your sermons are strong and helpful. If God has given you money, be generous in helping others with it. . . . Those who offer comfort to the sorrowing should do so with Christian cheer.

Romans 12:3-8, TLB

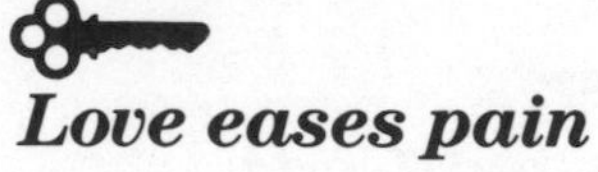

Love eases pain

"LOOK AT the assignment Miss Linda gave us in Sunday school today," said Nancy, handing a paper to her mother.

Before Mother could read the paper, three-year-old Missi came bursting into the room. "Ohhhh! Mommy! Look at my finger. It's bleeding. That flower hurt me!"

A drop of blood almost hid the thorn in Missi's finger. Gently, Mother pulled out the thorn, wiped off the blood, and kissed the finger. Smiling, Missi went back outside.

Mother turned back to the paper Nancy had handed her. "Find a need and fill it; find a hurt and heal it," she read. She smiled at Nancy, "That's a good assignment."

"Sure," groaned Nancy, "except I'm not a doctor. How can I heal someone?"

"Didn't Miss Linda explain that there are different kinds of hurts?" Mother asked.

Nancy nodded. "Yes, she said that besides physical hurts, there are what she called 'mental' and 'spiritual' hurts. But what can I do about those things? I'm just a kid." She sighed. "I know that Karen's folks are getting a divorce. And I know that John's big brother is in jail for pushing drugs. And Mandy's dad is out of work, so she never has money for extra projects at school. But I can't heal their hurts."

"When Missi came crying to me a while ago, I didn't really heal her finger. I just gave her a lot of love, and she forgot the pain," Mother said. "That's what you can do, too. You may not be able to solve anyone else's problems, but with God's help, you can encourage them and make their day brighter. And you can point them to Jesus, the One who really can heal their hurts. Pray about it, and the Lord will show you what you can do."

Nancy smiled. "OK. Maybe it isn't such a hard assignment after all."

HOW ABOUT YOU? Do you know someone who is hurting? God wants to use you to help that person. You can demonstrate God's love by showing that you care. Smile at that person. Talk to him. Pray for him. Share something from God's Word. Try to heal at least one hurt this week. B.W.

TO MEMORIZE: *"Finally, all of you, live in harmony with one another; be sympathetic, love as brothers"* 1 Peter 3:8 (NIV).

"I DON'T KNOW what I'm going to do," Nancy told Kerri as they walked home from school. "Here it is, Thursday, and I still haven't helped heal anybody's hurt."

Kerri shrugged. "Me, either. Guess we'll just have to tell Miss Linda that we're not very good doctors."

Nancy changed the subject. "What did you make on today's math test?"

"Eighty-four," Kerri said with a sigh.

"That's not too bad. Most of the class failed," Nancy comforted her. "Julie didn't get one problem right! I don't know how she got to be in the seventh grade. She's so dumb!"

"It's no wonder she doesn't have any friends. She . . ." Kerri stopped and took a deep breath. "Nancy, how would you feel if you failed in everything and didn't have any friends and everyone called you 'retarded'? You'd hurt, wouldn't you?"

Nancy blinked. "Kerri, you aren't suggesting that we try to heal Julie's hurt, are you?"

Kerri nodded her head solemnly.

"Well, OK," Nancy agreed reluctantly. "Let's stop at her house now and ask if she wants to come over tonight and do homework with us. Then we can tell Miss Linda we did our assignment."

"One evening won't do it," Kerri said wisely. "Do you remember last year when you broke your leg, Nancy? You had to go to the doctor again and again, and it took months for your leg to heal. Julie has been hurting for a long time. It will take lots of care for her wounds to heal."

"Do you mean we'll have to be her friends for a long time?" Nancy asked.

Kerri nodded. "Could be."

Nancy gulped, then smiled. "Here's Julie's house now. Let's get started."

As they walked up on the porch, Nancy added, "I have another idea. We should introduce Julie to Jesus. He's the One who can really heal her hurts."

HOW ABOUT YOU? Do you know someone who needs a friend? Are you willing to be that friend? Be as helpful as you can, and most of all, don't forget to introduce him to your best friend, Jesus. B.W.

TO MEMORIZE: *"A friend loves at all times"* Proverbs 17:17 (NIV).

APRIL

Healing the Hurt

(Continued from yesterday)

FROM THE BIBLE:

Dear brothers, warn those who are lazy; comfort those who are frightened; take tender care of those who are weak; and be patient with everyone. See that no one pays back evil for evil, but always try to do good to each other and to everyone else. Always be joyful. Always keep on praying. No matter what happens, always be thankful, for this is God's will for you who belong to Christ Jesus. Do not smother the Holy Spirit. Do not scoff at those who prophesy, but test everything that is said to be sure it is true, and if it is, then accept it. Keep away from every kind of evil. May the God of peace himself make you entirely pure and devoted to God; and may your spirit and soul and body be kept strong and blameless until that day when our Lord Jesus Christ comes back again.

1 Thessalonians 5:14-23, TLB

Introduce friends to Jesus

APRIL

7

No Letter Today

FROM THE BIBLE:

Bow down Your ear, O Lord,
hear me;
For I am poor and needy.
Preserve my life, for I am holy;
You are my God;
Save Your servant who trusts in You!
Be merciful to me, O Lord,
For I cry to You all day long.
Rejoice the soul of Your servant,
For to You, O Lord, I lift up my soul.
For You, Lord, are good, and ready to forgive,
And abundant in mercy to all those who call upon You.
Give ear, O Lord, to my prayer;
And attend to the voice of my supplications.
In the day of my trouble I will call upon You,
For You will answer me.
Psalm 86:1-7, NKJV

Commune with God daily

"WHERE'S CINDI?" asked Dad as he nodded toward the empty chair at the breakfast table.

"She's washing her hair," Andy replied.

"Again?" asked Dad. "She knows it's time for devotions."

"And she knows we can't wait for her." Mother set orange juice on the table. "What bothers me is that she doesn't seem to care. I think we should change our time for devotions. Maybe right after dinner would work well."

"Bet she doesn't have devotions by herself, either," offered Andy. "Bet she . . ." His voice trailed off when he saw his dad frowning at him.

Mother sighed. "I'll talk to her this afternoon."

After school Cindi sat in the kitchen chatting about the days happenings and looking through the mail that had come. She frowned. "All junk mail and bills," she complained. "I can't understand why Sherry hasn't written me. I always answer her letters right away, but she takes weeks and weeks to answer mine. Some friend she is!"

"You have one friend who might say the same thing about you," suggested Mother.

Cindi looked up. "Who?" she demanded.

"Jesus," Mother replied quietly. "Lately you've been too busy to communicate with Him. Many days He walks away from His 'mailbox' without having received anything from you. Do you suppose He says, 'I wonder why I haven't heard from Cindi'?"

"But, Mother—," Cindi began.

"And I wonder how much of the 'mail' we send Him is junk mail and bills," Mother continued thoughtfully. "How often do we pray, 'Lord, I've done this for You, so You owe me this much'? And how often do we send Him empty, repetitious promises?"

"I guess I'm as bad as Sherry," Cindi said with a sigh. "I've been disappointing the Lord, just as she's been disappointing me. I think I'll go read my letter from God and talk to Him."

HOW ABOUT YOU? Have you been neglecting your "correspondence" with the Lord? Do you expect to receive a quick reply from Him but often go for days without responding to His letter to you? How often is He disappointed because He doesn't hear from you? Make up your mind right now to communicate with Him daily. B.W.

TO MEMORIZE: *"Call to Me, and I will answer you, and show you great and mighty things, which you do not know"* Jeremiah 33:3 (NKJV).

APRIL

Company's Coming

FROM THE BIBLE:

The end of all things is near. Therefore be clear minded and self-controlled so that you can pray. Above all, love each other deeply, because love covers over a multitude of sins. Offer hospitality to one another without grumbling. Each one should use whatever gift he has received to serve others, faithfully administering God's grace in its various forms. If anyone speaks, he should do it as one speaking the very words of God. If anyone serves, he should do it with the strength God provides, so that in all things God may be praised through Jesus Christ. To him be the glory and the power for ever and ever. Amen.

1 Peter 4:7-11, NIV

Entertain cheerfully

"OH, NO," cried Tanya, "not again! All we ever do is have missionaries stay at our house. If it's not missionaries, it's visiting preachers—or even complete strangers, like when people got stranded in the snowstorm last winter!"

"I thought you enjoyed having company," Mother replied.

"Well, sure, once in a while," Tanya admitted. "But other people don't have them as often as we do."

"That's part of our ministry," Dad chimed in.

"Ministry?" Tanya questioned.

"That's right," her father answered. "Mother and I wanted to go to the mission field, but our health didn't permit that."

"So we decided we would open our home to missionaries whenever we could," finished Mother, "and we also want to use our home for a place to witness to others whenever possible."

Tanya had never thought about entertaining people as a "ministry." All she could see was that it meant doing more dishes and often giving up her bedroom to guests. "Does the Bible say you're supposed to have company?" Tanya asked her mother later that evening.

Mother smiled. "You won't find those exact words in the Bible," she said, "but it does say we should be 'given to hospitality.' It also says . . ." Mother picked up her Bible, opened it, and began to read aloud. "Let brotherly love continue. Be not forgetful to entertain strangers: for thereby some have entertained angels unawares."

"Is that like having missionaries come and stay with you while they're in town?" Tanya asked.

Mother nodded. "That's part of it. It's sharing your house and your love with others."

Tanya took a deep breath. "Boy, I didn't know the Bible said anything about having company." She went to her room and picked up things that were scattered around. Suddenly she smiled and called to her mother, "Mom, what time are we going to 'give some hospitality' tonight?"

HOW ABOUT YOU? When you have to help prepare a meal, wash extra dishes, or give up your room because your parents are entertaining, do you grumble about it, or do you think of it as sharing what you have with others? God wants you to share. Will you do it cheerfully for Him? R.J.

TO MEMORIZE: *"Offer hospitality to one another without grumbling"* 1 Peter 4:9 (NIV).

APRIL

Too Much Salt

FROM THE BIBLE:
You are the salt of the earth; but if the salt loses its flavor, how shall it be seasoned? It is then good for nothing but to be thrown out and trampled under foot by men. You are the light of the world. A city that is set on a hill cannot be hidden. Nor do they light a lamp and put it under a basket, but on a lampstand, and it gives light to all who are in the house. Let your light so shine before men, that they may see your good works and glorify your Father in heaven.
Matthew 5 :13-16, NKJV

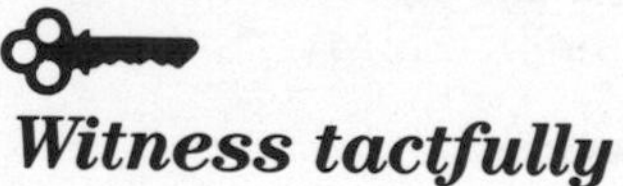

MARK LOOKED up from his plate as he and his family were eating supper. "You know what?" he asked. "Keith sure is stupid. He won't even believe the facts! Since Pastor Hughes talked about witnessing and being the salt of the earth, I decided to witness to Keith. I saw him cheat on a test today. So after school, I told him that he was a sinner going to hell and that he should repent."

"Sounds like you came on a little strong," said Dad. "What else did you tell him?"

"I invited him to come to church," replied Mark, "but he said he already went. Then I told him his church must be a pretty stupid one if he wasn't a Christian yet, and he'd better hurry up and get saved before it was too late."

"Why, Mark!" exclaimed Dad. "If you insult the person you're talking to, he'll just get angry and become completely turned off to the Lord."

"I don't see that I did anything wrong," replied Mark. "If Keith won't listen to reason, then that's his own fault." Mark picked up the salt shaker and started to sprinkle salt onto his food. After just a few shakes, the top fell off, and all the salt came pouring out onto his plate.

"Oh no!" cried Mother. "I must not have put the top on tight when I filled the shaker this afternoon!"

"You know, Mark," Dad spoke up, "that's kind of like what you tried to do with Keith. All that salt on your food has spoiled it. And when you hit Keith with all that talk today, you may have given him too much too fast and spoiled his interest in spiritual things."

Mark looked in dismay at the food on his plate. "I guess you're right, Dad," he admitted. "Keith probably didn't know what I was talking about. I'll apologize tomorrow, and next time I'll try to be kind and tactful."

"Good," said Mother. "Now I'll get you some more food."

HOW ABOUT YOU? Do you witness to your friends? It's important that you do so. You may be the only Christian they know. It's also important to be careful as to how you go about it. Make sure you don't offend people. They have feelings just like you do. Pray about it, and then trust the Lord to give you the right words. D.M.

TO MEMORIZE: *"Let your speech always be with grace, seasoned with salt, that you may know how you ought to answer each one"*
Colossians 4:6 (NKJV).

APRIL

Sidetracked

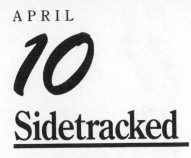

FROM THE BIBLE:
I am always thinking of the Lord; and because he is so near, I never need to stumble or to fall. Heart, body, and soul are filled with joy. For you will not leave me among the dead; you will not allow your beloved one to rot in the grave. You have let me experience the joys of life and the exquisite pleasures of your own eternal presence.
Psalm 16:8-11, TLB

Keep God first

MOTHER WAS TAKING Sara shopping for some new gym shoes, and Sara could hardly wait to get them. As she was picturing them in her mind, she heard a bell clang. A train was going by. As they waited, it moved slower and slower. Finally, it stopped!

"Why would a train stop way out here on the edge of town anyway?" Sara grumbled.

"They're probably sidetracking some cars at the grain elevator," Mother replied.

"Sidetracking? What does that mean?"

"Well, they unfasten some of the cars from the middle of the train, and pull them off onto a side track," replied Mother. "The cars being sidetracked probably are full of grain they've brought to the elevator."

Just then the train backed up a few yards and stopped again. Sara and Mother continued to grumble about the inconvenience of having to wait. After a fifteen-minute delay, they were once more on their way to get the shoes.

The next day was Sunday. Sara suddenly came to attention when something in Pastor Miller's sermon reminded her of the train incident. "Some Christians determine in their hearts that they will serve the Lord and do whatever He wants them to do, but somehow they get sidetracked," he said, "and time is wasted."

Sara remembered how time was lost while the train had backed up and moved so slowly to maneuver the train cars onto the side track. The pastor was continuing. "Sometimes the love of money will sidetrack a Christian from wanting to do God's will. Sometimes it's a desire for fame or pleasure. Whatever keeps us from doing what the Lord wants us to do is wrong."

That evening Sara thought a lot about what Pastor Miller said. She remembered that just last week she had begged Mother to take her to the beach instead of going with her Sunday school class to pass out tracts. Was she allowing herself to be sidetracked? "Dear Jesus," she prayed, "Don't let me get sidetracked out of Your will. Amen."

HOW ABOUT YOU? Have you done what today's memory verse says? Even if you're a Christian, it's sometimes hard to put God first in your life. But when you do, you won't be sorry. Don't let anything sidetrack you from your goal. R.P.

TO MEMORIZE: *"I am always thinking of the Lord; and because he is so near, I never need to stumble or to fall"* Psalm 16:8 (TLB).

APRIL

11

Where the Fish Are

FROM THE BIBLE:

But they all alike began to make excuses. The first said, "I have just bought a field, and I must go and see it. Please excuse me." Another said, "I have just bought five yoke of oxen, and I'm on my way to try them out. Please excuse me." Still another said, "I just got married, so I can't come." The servant came back and reported this to his master. Then the owner of the house became angry and ordered his servant, "Go out quickly into the streets and alleys of the town and bring in the poor, the crippled, the blind and the lame." "Sir," the servant said, "what you ordered has been done, but there is still room." Then the master told his servant, "Go out to the roads and country lanes and make them come in, so that my house will be full. I tell you, not one of those men who were invited will get a taste of my banquet."
Luke 14:18-24, NIV

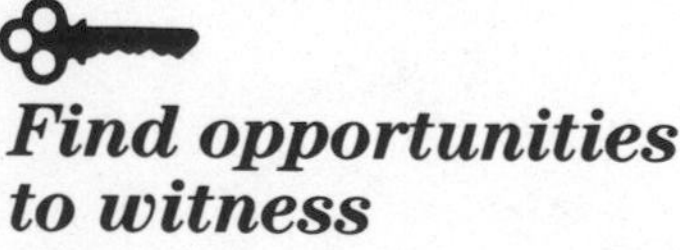

Find opportunities to witness

"OUR SUNDAY SCHOOL contest isn't fair," complained Andy one Saturday morning. "It's called 'Fishing for Jesus,' and we're supposed to bring visitors. But my friends already go to Sunday school, so I don't have anybody to invite. The prize is a fishing rod. I sure could use that!"

"Hmmm." Dad looked thoughtful. "Speaking of fishing, I heard they've been biting lately. Care to go?"

"Whoopee!" yelled Andy. "I'll go get ready."

Mother laughed. "And I'll pack a lunch for you two."

"Good," said Dad. "I'll get the fishing gear. Meet me out in the backyard, Andy, as soon as you're ready."

When Andy ran out the back door a little later, he stopped short and stared. Dad was sitting in a lawn chair, holding his fishing rod, and looking for all the world like he was fishing. His hook lay on the grass, and Dad watched it intently. "Whatever are you doing?" asked Andy.

"Fishing. Shhhh! Don't scare them away."

"Fishing!" exclaimed Andy as he looked at the hook and then looked back at his dad. "What're you talking about? You know there aren't any fish here. C'mon, Dad. Let's go where the fish are."

Dad looked up. "You know," he said, "that's a very good idea." He reeled in his line and got up. "Good thing I wasn't trying to catch the most fish for a contest or something," he observed. "I sure wouldn't have won. But come on. The fish aren't far from here. We'll go to Peerson's Lake."

As Andy and Dad got into the truck, Andy spoke. "I know what you're saying, Dad. You're telling me to go where the 'fish' are for my contest, too."

Dad grinned. "I think you'll find they're not far away."

"Yeah," murmured Andy. "Maybe that new kid down the street would come. And I could ask Mary, who sits across from me at school. I'll make a couple phone calls when we get home."

HOW ABOUT YOU? Do all your friends already know Jesus? It's wonderful if they do, but don't take it for granted. Talk to them about the Lord. But don't limit your witness just to those you know best. Jesus wants you to bring others to Him. Look around. You probably won't have to go very far to be a fisherman for Jesus. H.M.

TO MEMORIZE: *"Come after Me, and I will make you become fishers of men"* Mark 1:17 (NKJV).

APRIL

12

The Wrong Shoes

FROM THE BIBLE:
Try to show as much compassion as your Father does. Never criticize or condemn—or it will all come back on you. Go easy on others; then they will do the same for you. For if you give, you will get! Your gift will return to you in full and overflowing measure, pressed down, shaken together to make room for more, and running over. Whatever measure you use to give—large or small—will be used to measure what is given back to you."
Luke 6:36-38, TLB

Don't criticize and speak evil about each other, dear brothers. If you do, you will be fighting against God's law of loving one another, declaring it is wrong. But your job is not to decide whether this law is right or wrong, but to obey it. Only he who made the law can rightly judge among us. He alone decides to save us or destroy. So what right do you have to judge or criticize others?
James 4:11-12, TLB

LORI SLAMMED down the phone. "Kathy makes me so mad! She's in one of her moods. I almost wish I hadn't invited her over."

"Maybe you can cheer her up," Mother suggested. "She hasn't been a Christian long, and her parents aren't Christians either, you know."

"I get tired of trying to cheer her up," complained Lori. "She used to be lots of fun, but not lately."

Later that evening, the girls came into the living room. "Look, Mother," said Lori, pointing to Kathy's feet. "Kathy has new shoes exactly like mine."

"You must think alike." Mother smiled. "Now, would you like to make cookies?"

By bedtime the girls were having a grand time. The next morning they overslept and had to scurry to catch the bus. "May I go home with Kathy after school, Mother?" Lori called as she ran out the door.

"Yes," Mother answered. "Your dad will pick you up on his way home from work."

That evening when Lori came in with her father, she plopped down on the couch. "Boy, I'm glad to be home. It's so depressing at Kathy's. Her dad was home and in a terrible mood. Little Jason was crying, and Mrs. Mason was at work." Lori took off her shoe and rubbed her heel gently. "Besides, my feet hurt. These new shoes rubbed a blister on my heel."

Mother looked inside Lori's shoe. "I thought you wore a size six. This is size five and a half."

Lori took the shoe from her mother. "No wonder my feet were hurting." She laughed. "Kathy must have worn my shoes all day and I wore hers."

"I've heard that an Indian proverb says, 'Never judge a man until you have walked a mile in his moccasins.' I guess you just walked a day in Kathy's," Mother said, smiling.

Lori nodded. "Yes, and after spending a few hours at her house, I understand her a lot better. I'm going to stop criticizing her and pray for her instead." Lori stood up. "Now I'm going to call her and see how she liked walking in my shoes."

HOW ABOUT YOU? Are you too quick to criticize others when you do not understand their behavior? Perhaps you need to "walk in their shoes" for a while. Try to understand their circumstances better. And don't judge them; pray for them. B.W.

TO MEMORIZE: *"Don't criticize and speak evil about each other, dear brothers"* James 4:11 (TLB).

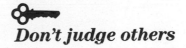

Don't judge others

13

It's Time to Move

FROM THE BIBLE:
Let not your heart be troubled. You are trusting God, now trust in me. There are many homes up there where my Father lives, and I am going to prepare them for your coming. When everything is ready, then I will come and get you, so that you can always be with me where I am. If this weren't so, I would tell you plainly. John 14:1-3, TLB

For we know that when this tent we live in now is taken down—when we die and leave these bodies—we will have wonderful new bodies in heaven, homes that will be ours forevermore, made for us by God himself, and not by human hands. How weary we grow of our present bodies. That is why we look forward eagerly to the day when we shall have heavenly bodies which we shall put on like new clothes.
2 Corinthians 5:1-2, TLB

Death is just a move

JULIE SKIPPED UP the walk and rang the doorbell. Then she burst into the house. "Grannie! Grannie, guess what? Daddy's coming to get us. He's coming tomorrow!"

Grannie sighed as she hobbled into the room. "I thought he was going to wait until school was out before he moved you to the coast."

"He said he couldn't wait any longer. He has to have his family with him." Julie stopped short. "I wish you were really my grandma and could move with us."

"Well, I'll miss you, honey, but you need to be with your father," Grannie said, smiling. "Maybe someday I can visit you."

Later that evening as Mother and Julie packed crates of dishes, the telephone rang. "Hello. . . . Yes. . . . She what?" Mother sank down in a chair and closed her eyes. Julie looked up in alarm. "When? Yes. . . . Yes. . . . Thank you for calling." As Mother hung up the phone, she wiped a tear from her eye. "I have to tell you some sad news, honey," she said. "That was Grannie Wilson's neighbor. They just found Grannie . . . she was sitting in her rocking chair, looking as if she were asleep, but she was dead."

"No, Mama! She can't be," Julie cried out. "I just saw her a few hours ago, and she was fine."

"Perhaps she had a heart attack," Mother said, wrapping her arms around Julie, "and the Lord took her home."

Julie sighed sadly as Mother tucked her in bed later that evening. "I guess Grannie's heavenly Father just couldn't wait any longer to have her with Him. It was time for her to move to His house," she said.

Mother nodded. "Now try to get some sleep, honey. Tomorrow your father is coming."

Julie yawned. "Do you think Grannie was as glad to see her heavenly Father as I will be to see my daddy?"

"I'm sure of it," Mother replied. "I'm sure of it!"

HOW ABOUT YOU? Has someone you love moved to heaven lately? Of course, you will miss that person, but try not to be too sad. Think of the joy he is experiencing, being with his heavenly Father. And someday you can see him again—if you are a child of God. B.W.

TO MEMORIZE: *"Brothers, we do not want you to be ignorant about those who fall asleep, or to grieve like the rest of men, who have no hope"*
1 Thessalonians 4:13 (NIV).

APRIL

14

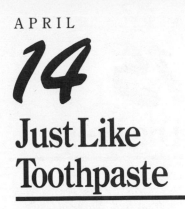

Just Like Toothpaste

FROM THE BIBLE:

Don't be too eager to tell others their faults, for we all make many mistakes; and when we teachers of religion, who should know better, do wrong, our punishment will be greater than it would be for others. If anyone can control his tongue, it proves that he has perfect control over himself in every other way. We can make a large horse turn around and go wherever we want by means of a small bit in his mouth. And a tiny rudder makes a huge ship turn wherever the pilot wants it to go, even though the winds are strong. So also the tongue is a small thing, but what enormous damage it can do. A great forest can be set on fire by one tiny spark. And the tongue is a flame of fire. It is full of wickedness, and poisons every part of the body. And the tongue is set on fire by hell itself, and can turn our whole lives into a blazing flame of destruction and disaster. Men have trained, or can train, every kind of animal or bird that lives and every kind of reptile and fish, but no human being can tame the tongue.

James 3:1-8, TLB

JASON WAS babysitting his little brother, Josh. The afternoon had started out fine, but then the phone rang. It was Jason's friend, Hal, and the boys talked quite a while before Jason returned to the kitchen where he had left Josh. But his brother was no longer there. Suspicious noises were coming from the bathroom, so Jason hurried to see what Josh was up to. Josh was trying desperately to push toothpaste back into the tube.

"You dummy, Josh!" exclaimed Jason. "Why can't you leave things alone? I could swat you!" As he began to clean up the mess, he continued to scold his little brother.

"I'm sorry," whimpered Josh. "I'll put it back."

"You can't," growled Jason. "Once toothpaste is out, it stays out!"

Josh began to cry. "I guess I really am a dummy," he sobbed.

When Jason saw how upset his little brother was, he wished he hadn't been so harsh. "No, Josh," he said, "you aren't a dummy."

"But you said . . . ," began Josh.

Jason rumpled his little brother's hair. "Forget that. I shouldn't have said it in the first place, and I'm sorry."

When their parents arrived, they heard all about the toothpaste episode. "I'm a dummy," confessed Josh with trembling lips.

"I told you you're not," protested Jason, "and I said I was sorry."

"Josh, you were very naughty," said Mother, "and, Jason, you were too hasty with your tongue. I'm glad you apologized, but there's a lesson here. Just like you can't get toothpaste back in the tube, you can't take back words that came out of your mouth. You shouldn't play around with the toothpaste tube, but it's even more important to be careful of the words you say. Make sure they are all pleasing to God."

HOW ABOUT YOU? Do you sometimes say things in anger? Or do you sometimes say things jokingly, but you know they really hurt the one to whom you are talking? Words can never be "unsaid." The Bible says your speech is to be always *with grace*. If you follow this instruction, you won't have to worry about taking back mean words you have spoken. L.W.

TO MEMORIZE: *"Don't use bad language. Say only what is good and helpful to those you are talking to, and what will give them a blessing"* Ephesians 4:29 (TLB).

Speak kindly

APRIL

15

Dig Deep

FROM THE BIBLE:

Our words are wise because they are from God, telling of God's wise plan to bring us into the glories of heaven. This plan was hidden in former times, though it was made for our benefit before the world began. But the great men of the world have not understood it; if they had, they never would have crucified the Lord of Glory. That is what is meant by the Scriptures which say that no mere man has ever seen, heard or even imagined what wonderful things God has ready for those who love the Lord. But we know about these things because God has sent his Spirit to tell us, and his Spirit searches out and shows us all of God's deepest secrets. No one can really know what anyone else is thinking, or what he is really like, except that person himself. And no one can know God's thoughts except God's own Spirit. And God has actually given us his Spirit (not the world's spirit) to tell us about the wonderful free gifts of grace and blessing that God has given us. 1 Corinthians 2:7-12, TLB

Read the Bible thoughtfully

NATHAN YAWNED and blinked. Quickly, his eyes scanned the page of his Bible, then with a sigh he closed the Book. He set it on the nightstand just as Mother came in to say good night. "Does the *plunk-plunk* of the oil well pump ever bother you at night?" she asked as she opened the window a couple of inches.

Nathan shook his head. "No. I guess I'm so used to it, I never hear it. It's been out there behind the barn as long as I can remember."

"But I can remember when it wasn't there," Mother said dreamily. "Before oil was discovered, this farm wasn't worth much. We lived in the old house, and life wasn't nearly as comfortable as it is now. That was when you were a baby." Nathan rearranged the pillow under his head as Mother continued. "Then the oil company asked permission to drill on our land."

"And they struck oil!" Nathan declared. "Not just once but three times!"

"All those years while your grandparents were hardly able to make a living on this farm, there was great wealth under their feet. It wasn't discovered, though, until someone dug deep." Mother emphasized the last two words. "Son, there is also wealth in the Word of God, but you will never find it unless you dig deep. You'll never find the riches of God's Word by merely scanning the pages."

She bent over and kissed him lightly on the cheek before leaving the room. *How does Mother know I haven't been reading carefully?* Nathan wondered as the door closed behind her. He sat up in bed, turned on the lamp, and reached for his Bible. Outside, the pump droned on, *plunk-plunk-plunk-plunk.*

HOW ABOUT YOU? Are you living in spiritual poverty? Do you scan the Word of God and never really think about what you're reading? Read it slowly and carefully. If you're too small to read it by yourself, listen carefully while someone reads to you. Think about what it says. Dig deep. You'll be amazed at the treasures you find. B.W.

TO MEMORIZE: *"O Lord, how great are Your works! Your thoughts are very deep"* Psalm 92:5 (NKJV).

APRIL

16

Love

FROM THE BIBLE:
Love suffers long and is kind; love does not envy; love does not parade itself, is not puffed up; does not behave rudely, does not seek its own, is not provoked, thinks no evil; does not rejoice in iniquity, but rejoices in the truth; bears all things, believes all things, hopes all things, endures all things. Love never fails. But whether there are prophecies, they will fail; whether there are tongues, they will cease; whether there is knowledge, it will vanish away. For we know in part and we prophesy in part. But when that which is perfect has come, then that which is in part will be done away. When I was a child, I spoke as a child, I understood as a child, I thought as a child; but when I became a man, I put away childish things. For now we see in a mirror, dimly, but then face to face. Now I know in part, but then I shall know just as I also am known. And now abide faith, hope, love, these three; but the greatest of these is love.
1 Corinthians 13:4-13, NKJV

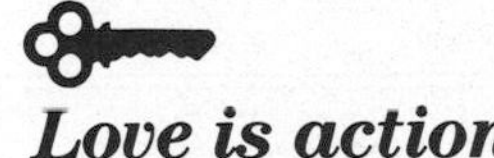

Love is action

HELEN'S FATHER was taking her to choir practice at church when they saw a car with a bumper sticker which read, "Have you hugged your kid today?"

"Hmmph!" Dad snorted. "That stupid bumper sticker always makes me mad! I wonder how many kids have hugged their parents today!"

Just then they arrived at church, and Helen jumped out of the car. But she couldn't forget what her father had said. She had been praying for a long time that he would be saved. *I think I need to show him I love him whether he is saved or not,* she decided.

That afternoon Helen spent nearly an hour cleaning her room and her closet. As she walked to the door with her wastebasket, Dad said, "What's all this? Are you cleaning your room without being told?"

Helen nodded. "I just want you and Mother to know that I am grateful for my nice things and that I love you," she explained. "I thought this would be one way to show you." Dad looked surprised.

After dinner that evening, Helen said, "Mother, I'll do the dishes. Why don't you and Daddy go out in the backyard and relax?"

"What has gotten into that child?" her father murmured as they went out.

When bedtime came around, Helen shyly approached her father. She had quit kissing him and Mother good-night some time ago, but tonight was different. She reached up and hugged him very tightly, laughing as she did so. "See? Here is one kid who has hugged her parents today!" she giggled. She quickly planted a kiss on her mother's cheek and ran up the stairs.

As she reached the top step, however, she overheard her father say to her mother, "You know, Helen is really a wonderful daughter. I think I'll go to church with you in the morning to hear her choir sing."

Helen realized it was love in action that just might win her dad to the Lord.

HOW ABOUT YOU? Have you hugged your parents lately? Have you shown them in other ways that you love them? Maybe you know someone—a parent, a neighbor, a friend—who isn't saved and who may be won over by love in action. What can you do for them? Think about it. R.P.

TO MEMORIZE: *"But the fruit of the Spirit is love"* Galatians 5:22.

APRIL

17

Joy

FROM THE BIBLE:

So be truly glad! There is wonderful joy ahead, even though the going is rough for a while down here. These trials are only to test your faith, to see whether or not it is strong and pure. It is being tested as fire tests gold and purifies it—and your faith is far more precious to God than mere gold; so if your faith remains strong after being tried in the test tube of fiery trials, it will bring you much praise and glory and honor on the day of his return. You love him even though you have never seen him; though not seeing him, you trust him; and even now you are happy with the inexpressible joy that comes from heaven itself. And your further reward for trusting him will be the salvation of your souls. 1 Peter 1:6-9, TLB

Always be full of joy in the Lord; I say it again, rejoice! Philippians 4:4, TLB

Jesus gives real joy

MICHELLE HAD always been very close to her Aunt Katie and often went with her to the park, to the zoo, or just to stay all night at her house. One day Aunt Katie didn't feel very well. The doctors discovered that she had a very fast-growing type of cancer and wouldn't live long.

Michelle was heartbroken, but Aunt Katie smiled happily whenever Michelle went to visit her. "Oh, Aunt Katie," Michelle exclaimed one day, "How can you be so happy? I feel so miserable. Life will just be awful if you go away."

"Michelle, don't be afraid to use the word *die* around me," Aunt Katie answered gently. "I know I'm going to be with Jesus, and I won't have any more pain. I'm eager to go home to heaven, and I'm so glad you're going to join me there one day."

That was the last time Michelle saw her aunt alive, for within a few days, Aunt Katie died. Then came the hours of sitting at the funeral home and meeting all the friends and relatives who came to share words of sympathy. At first Michelle didn't think she could stand all of this. She just wanted to go somewhere and cry her eyes out! She did cry hard—many times! But then she started to remember some of the things Aunt Katie had said to her, especially about going to heaven. She thought of the many happy times they had together, and a smile crossed her face.

I loved her so much, and I'm not happy that she's gone, she thought. *But still, I do feel a certain kind of joy. I know Aunt Katie is at home with Jesus. I know she has no more pain. And I know that she is joyful right now. Besides, even though I miss her, I know I'll see her again when I go to heaven, too.*

HOW ABOUT YOU? Do you feel joy in your heart today, even when things go wrong? When you get blamed for something you didn't do, when you have to go to summer school, when a vacation trip "falls through," when your dog dies, when someone you love dies, there should still be a sense of joy. All these things are temporary, but your salvation through Jesus is eternal. "Happiness" is often found in "happenings." Real joy is found in Jesus. R.P.

TO MEMORIZE: *"But the fruit of the Spirit is love, joy . . ."* Galatians 5:22.

APRIL

18

Peace

FROM THE BIBLE:
Let the peace of heart which comes from Christ be always present in your hearts and lives, for this is your responsibility and privilege as members of his body. And always be thankful.
Colossians 3:15, TLB

Don't worry about anything; instead, pray about everything; tell God your needs and don't forget to thank him for his answers. If you do this you will experience God's peace, which is far more wonderful than the human mind can understand. His peace will keep your thoughts and your hearts quiet and at rest as you trust in Christ Jesus. And now, brothers, as I close this letter let me say this one more thing: Fix your thoughts on what is true and good and right. Think about things that are pure and lovely, and dwell on the fine, good things in others. Think about all you can praise God for and be glad about. Keep putting into practice all you learned from me and saw me doing, and the God of peace will be with you.
Philippians 4:6-9, TLB

THE FIRE ALARM was ringing! As the children got up from their seats, some were saying, "Oh, why do they always have fire drills when it's raining?" But wait! The alarm was not staying on! It was just ringing for a short period of time, stopping, and then starting again. Mrs. Elders said, "Now, children, you know what this means! It's a tornado drill! You all know what to do. Quiet now!"

James went over and opened the windows to equalize pressure inside and out, and Chad closed the curtains so any flying glass would not hit the children. The others filed silently into the hall. They lined up against the inside wall, crouched down with their heads against the wall, and put their arms over their heads to protect themselves.

Kelly began to wonder how long they were going to have to stay in this uncomfortable position, when suddenly she realized that there were many sirens screaming outside. She began to tremble uncontrollably when she heard the principal's voice over the intercom saying, "This is not a drill! I repeat, this is not a drill! A tornado has been spotted. Please remain calm and stay in your positions!"

Some children began to cry out in fear, and Kelly heard several kids say, "I don't want to die!" However, the boy right next to Kelly seemed perfectly calm. "How can you be so calm, Michael?" Kelly asked, her voice shaking. "The whole sky looks so black, and listen to the wind! Why aren't you afraid like the rest of us?"

"I did feel scared at first," Michael answered, "but I know Jesus as my Savior, and I asked Him to help me not to be afraid. Even if I died, I know I would go to heaven. Jesus gives me this peace."

Before long they realized that the tornado had missed their school. The students were allowed to return to their classrooms. Michael would probably never realize what a big effect his calm, peaceful attitude had on the other children.

HOW ABOUT YOU? Do storms frighten you? Are you scared in the dark? Could you just scream if a dog came near? Whatever fear you have, give it to Jesus. This requires a decision on your part. Choose to let God's peace "rule in your heart." It will be a testimony to others who are fearful themselves. R.P.

TO MEMORIZE: *"But the fruit of the Spirit is love, joy, peace . . ."* Galatians 5:22.

Jesus can calm fear

APRIL

Long-Suffering

FROM THE BIBLE:

We can rejoice, too, when we run into problems and trials for we know that they are good for us—they help us learn to be patient. And patience develops strength of character in us and helps us trust God more each time we use it until finally our hope and faith are strong and steady. Then, when that happens, we are able to hold our heads high no matter what happens and know that all is well, for we know how dearly God loves us, and we feel this warm love everywhere within us because God has given us the Holy Spirit to fill our hearts with his love.

Romans 5:3-5, TLB

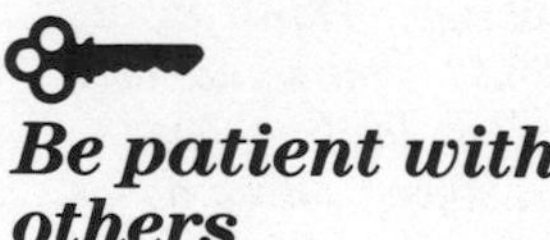

Be patient with others

"DADDY, what does *long-suffering* mean?" asked Tina one evening after Dad had read the verses in Galatians listing the fruits of the Spirit.

"Take the word apart, Tina. *Long* and *suffering*—or suffering long! It's really another word for patience," explained Dad. "Sometimes Jesus allows us to suffer for a long time because of another person. That helps us to develop patience in our lives."

"Oh, you mean like me with Jan, right?" asked Tina, and Dad nodded. Jan, who was a whole head taller than Tina, constantly made fun of her because she was a Christian.

The next day at school Jan shouted, "Everyone be real good! Here comes the perfect Christian. Hail to Tina! Should we bow down?" Tina wondered if it was because Jan was so big and the other kids were afraid of her that they laughed with her, or did they feel that way, too?

At lunch Jan tripped Tina as she was carrying her tray to the table, and Tina got peas and carrots all over her blouse. She wanted so badly to do something back to Jan, but she remembered that she was supposed to be willing to suffer long for the Lord.

After school Tina was surprised when a new girl named Chris came to walk with her. "Tina, why do you just take all this trouble from Jan? Why don't you do something to get even? I know I would! At least talk to the teacher or the principal or something!" Chris urged.

"Well," Tina replied, "I'm a Christian, and the Bible tells me I should be willing to suffer long for Jesus' sake. I'm trying to do what God wants me to do."

Chris looked thoughtful. "I don't understand what you mean, but I sure would like to find out more about your God if He gives you that kind of patience. I have such a terrible temper!" she confessed.

"Daddy!" Tina shouted as she came in from school. "I may not ever lead Jan to Christ by learning long-suffering, but it might help me win Chris for the Lord!"

HOW ABOUT YOU? Do you feel like you have suffered for a long time at the hands of another person? Maybe the Lord is trying to develop the fruit of long-suffering in your life so that you can be an effective witness for Him. R.P.

TO MEMORIZE: *"But the fruit of the Spirit is love, joy, peace, long-suffering . . ."* Galatians 5:22.

APRIL

20

Gentleness

FROM THE BIBLE:

Come to me and I will give you rest—all of you who work so hard beneath a heavy yoke. Wear my yoke—for it fits perfectly—and let me teach you; for I am gentle and humble, and you shall find rest for your souls; for I give you only light burdens.
Matthew 11:28-30, TLB

God's people must not be quarrelsome; they must be gentle, patient teachers of those who are wrong.
2 Timothy 2:24, TLB

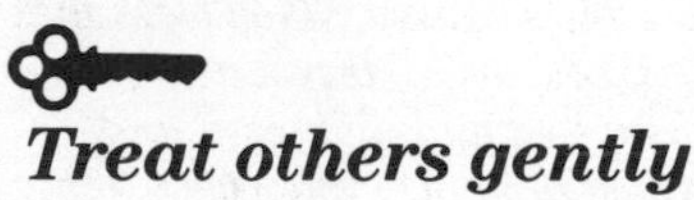

Treat others gently

EIGHT-YEAR-OLD Tim was thrilled. Dad and Mom had just brought home his birthday gift. It was a beautiful brown and white puppy, and Tim loved it with all his heart. He named his dog Sandy and spent hours playing with her. Soon she could fetch a stick and roll over, and she was also learning to mind. Feeding and caring for her was fun. Then one day Tim's Dad brought home a leash and collar for Sandy. "It's about time you taught Sandy to walk sensibly at your side," he said, and a new part of Sandy's training began.

The collar was called a choker, and whenever the puppy pulled at the leash, the choker tightened around her neck. She whined, and Tim knew she didn't like it at all! And he didn't like it either! He complained to Mom about it.

Mother just smiled and said, "Be gentle with her, Son. Give the leash a soft tug when you want her to follow. If you're gentle with her, she'll learn. Remember, you're doing this because you love her. If she learns to walk on a leash now, you'll be able to take her anywhere with you."

Later that evening Tim read some verses from Matthew chapter eleven. When he asked Mom what a 'yoke' was, she explained that it was a burden or problem Jesus might want us to bear for His sake in order to teach us a valuable lesson.

"Is it a little like Sandy's collar and leash?" Tim asked.

"Yes, it is," Mom answered. "As long as Sandy doesn't fight the collar, it's easy on her. And as long as we don't fight the will of God, any yoke Jesus puts on us is easy. He's gentle with us just like you're gentle with your puppy."

"Right," agreed Dad, overhearing the conversation. "And just as you are gentle with Sandy, and Jesus is gentle with us, He expects us to be gentle with others. That's what the fruit of the Spirit called 'gentleness' is all about."

HOW ABOUT YOU? Are you ever guilty of being rough instead of gentle as you deal with other people? When the baby gets into your things and makes a mess, are you gentle in the way you handle him? When a brother or sister accidently breaks something of yours, do you become angry and shout? Remember that Jesus is gentle with us, and He expects us to be the same with our friends. R.P.

TO MEMORIZE: *"But the fruit of the Spirit is love, joy, peace, long-suffering, gentleness . . ."* Galatians 5:22.

APRIL

21

Goodness

FROM THE BIBLE:
Jesus went into the Temple, drove out the merchants, and knocked over the moneychangers' tables and the stalls of those selling doves. "The Scriptures say my Temple is a place of prayer," he declared, "but you have turned it into a den of thieves." And now the blind and crippled came to him and he healed them there in the Temple. But when the chief priests and other Jewish leaders saw these wonderful miracles, and heard even the little children in the Temple shouting, "God bless the Son of David," they were disturbed and indignant and asked him, "Do you hear what these children are saying?"
Matthew 21:12-15, TLB

Love right; hate wrong

AS RACHEL came in from school she slammed the door, threw her books on the couch, and glared at the baby. Mother knew from experience that when Rachel was really mad about something, it was best to let her cool down a while before asking any questions. So she waited until after supper to ask her about it.

"I just can't stand two of my best friends anymore!" Rachel declared, looking angry again. "Mom, they are being absolutely horrid to a new girl in our class just because she's a Mexican. I can't believe that Lisa and Sue can claim to be Christians and yet be so prejudiced against Maria! I know I'm not supposed to get angry with them, but what they're doing is so wrong!" Rachel was on the verge of tears.

Mother put down the dish towel and put her arm around Rachel. "Honey, I'm proud of you for being angry this time! What those girls are doing *is* wrong. Even Jesus became angry when people did wrong things, like when He threw the moneychangers out of the temple. You know, one of the fruits of the Spirit is goodness, and part of being good is to love what is right in the world and hate what is wrong! However, you must remember to hate what Lisa and Sue are doing, not hate Lisa and Sue. Perhaps if you are kind to this girl, they'll see the fruit of goodness in your life and remember that they should have that same fruit in their lives."

Remembering Mother's words, Rachel invited Maria to eat lunch with her the next day at school.

"What are you doing?" whispered Sue. "She isn't like us, Rachel! Leave her alone."

Rachel waited until Maria was across the room before she answered Sue. "I'm just trying to do the good and right thing that I believe Jesus would want us to do," she said.

Lisa and Sue had to admit that Rachel was right. When they followed her example, they found that Maria was not so different after all. Soon all four were good friends.

HOW ABOUT YOU? Are you angered when you see something happening that you know is wrong? Part of the quality of goodness is to love the right and hate the wrong. Ask the Lord to show you the difference. R.P.

TO MEMORIZE: *"But the fruit of the Spirit is love, joy, peace, long-suffering, gentleness, goodness . . ."* Galatians 5:22.

APRIL

22

Faith

FROM THE BIBLE:

Again, the Kingdom of Heaven can be illustrated by the story of a man going into another country, who called together his servants and loaned them money to invest for him while he was gone. He gave $5,000 to one, $2,000 to another, and $1,000 to the last—dividing it in proportion to their abilities—and then left on his trip. . . . After a long time their master returned from his trip and called them to him to account for his money. The man to whom he had entrusted the $5,000 brought him $10,000. His master praised him for good work. "You have been faithful in handling this small amount," he told him, "so now I will give you many more responsibilities. Begin the joyous tasks I have assigned to you." Next came the man who had received the $2,000, with the report, "Sir, you gave me $2,000 to use, and I have doubled it." "Good work," his master said. "You are a good and faithful servant. You have been faithful over this small amount, so now I will give you much more."
Matthew 25:14-15, 19-23, TLB

Be dependable

JIMMY WAS confused. "Mom," he said, "I've been trying to learn the fruits of the Spirit, and the seventh one is faith. I don't understand how that can be one of them since it takes faith to become a Christian in the first place."

Mother smiled. "That's true," she agreed, "but the Bible also tells us to have faith after we're Christians. For example, when we pray, we are to have faith that God will answer. But I think there's something else here, too. Several of the newer translations of the Bible use the word *faithfulness.* Do you understand the word?"

Jimmy nodded. "Dad always says that Tippy is a faithful old dog. I guess that means she's always here when I need her," he said.

Mother laughed. "Yes, we got Tippy to be a companion to you, and she faithfully does her job, doesn't she? In much the same way, we should be faithful in what we do.

The next day Jimmy had a job to do. Mrs. King lived three doors down the street, and she was old and sickly. At the beginning of the summer she had hired Jimmy to take care of mowing her grass for the whole summer. They had made a bargain that Jimmy would mow the lawn every Friday morning, and she would pay him $3.50 each time. Just as Jimmy was putting gas in the mower, some of his friends approached.

"Hey, Jim! A bunch of us are going to play baseball. C'mon," they urged. "We need a good third baseman."

Now there was nothing Jimmy would rather do than play baseball, so he put the gas can away and reached for his mitt. But just then old Tippy came running around the corner of the garage. Stopping, Jimmy thought about his conversation with Mom yesterday. *The fruit of the Spirit is faithfulness,* he remembered. Reaching down, he patted Tippy on the head and called to his friends, "You guys go on! I have a job to do right now."

HOW ABOUT YOU? When someone gives you a job to do, do you do it faithfully, no matter how large or small it is? Perhaps the job God has given you right now is to help Mom, mow the lawn, or be a good student. Are you faithful in whatever it is that He has given you to do? When you stand before Him someday, will you hear the words, "Well done, good and faithful servant?" R.P.

TO MEMORIZE: *"But the fruit of the Spirit is love, joy, peace, long-suffering, gentleness, goodness, faith . . ."* Galatians 5:22.

APRIL

23

Meekness

FROM THE BIBLE:

Don't be selfish; don't live to make a good impression on others. Be humble, thinking of others as better than yourself. Don't just think about your own affairs, but be interested in others, too, and in what they are doing. Your attitude should be the kind that was shown us by Jesus Christ, who, though he was God, did not demand and cling to his rights as God, but laid aside his mighty power and glory, taking the disguise of a slave and becoming like men. And he humbled himself even further, going so far as actually to die a criminal's death on a cross. Yet it was because of this that God raised him up to the heights of heaven and gave him a name which is above every other name.
Philippians 2:3-9, TLB

You younger men, follow the leadership of those who are older. And all of you serve each other with humble spirits, for God gives special blessings to those who are humble, but sets himself against those who are proud. If you will humble yourselves under the mighty hand of God, in his good time he will lift you up. 1 Peter 5:5-6, TLB

Be humble

"MEEK OLD Mr. Martin couldn't hurt a flea," the girls sang as they jumped rope. Dad enjoyed watching them jump and listening to the rhymes they had made up, but this particular rhyme bothered him. Every new verse began with the words, "Meek old Mr. or Mrs. Somebody," and went on to describe how weak that person was.

At dinner Dad asked Shelly to define the word *meek* for him. "Sure," Shelly responded. "It means weak and chicken." Shelly started to laugh as she remembered the rhyme, but then Dad explained that she was wrong.

"Shelly," he said, "in Matthew 11:29, Jesus says that He Himself is meek. Do you think *He* was chicken?"

"Of course not," she answered. "He was braver than anybody! He knew that in coming to this earth He would suffer and go to the cross, but He came anyway." She paused for a moment, then added, "I'll have to be more careful how I use that word."

Dad nodded. "*Humility* is another word for *meekness*," he said. "It's human nature to be proud and to look after ourselves first. But the Bible teaches that all Christians are supposed to strive to be meek. That's why I thought it was important for you children to know the true meaning of the word."

After their discussion, Dad prayed that all of them would try to cultivate this important fruit of the Spirit in their lives. The next day he smiled when he heard Shelly tell her friends, "Hey, we have to change the words to one of our jump-rope rhymes. Let's make it say 'Weak old Mr. Martin' instead of 'Meek old Mr. Martin.' "

HOW ABOUT YOU? Have you always thought that to be meek meant to be weak? God doesn't want you to be weak, but He does want you to be humble. This is another way in which we are to be like Jesus. He left the glories of heaven and became a humble servant for us. Now He is exalted, given a high position and honored. God commands us to be humble, too, and promises that then we will also be exalted one day. R.P.

TO MEMORIZE: *"But the fruit of the spirit is love, joy, peace, long-suffering, gentleness, goodness, faith, meekness . . ."* Galatians 5:22.

STEVE'S eighth-grade American history class was studying the temperance movement of the early 1900s. He learned that this was the time when many people who were opposed to drinking alcohol worked to get laws making its use illegal. They felt this was necessary because people often didn't use temperance (self-control) when drinking, and they drank too much.

As Steve was studying his Sunday school lesson a few days later, he was surprised to find the word *temperance* listed among the fruits of the Spirit. "Mother," he asked, "if the idea of temperance was in the Bible all along, why didn't people do something about it sooner? I mean the temperance movement was only about seventy-five years ago! And why don't we do anything about it now?"

"Well, Steve, you've asked a very good question," Mother replied. "Supporters of the temperance movement used the word *temperance* to mean self-control only with alcohol—in other words, not getting drunk. That's one good meaning of the word, but we also need to show self-control in every other area of our lives! And you're right, we should do something about it now. We should be using self-control every day."

Steve thought he knew what his mother was getting at. She knew that right now drunkenness was not his problem, but eating was another story. Steve loved to eat—and he hated to exercise! Even though we was only in eighth grade, he was already becoming very, very chubby. Some of the kids at school even called him fat! He needed to use temperance, or self-control, when eating.

His mother's words seemed to haunt him after that. Every time he wanted to eat a candy bar or drink another soda, he remembered that he was supposed to show temperance in every area of his life. With the Lord's help and the promptings of the Holy Spirit, Steve reached a much better weight within six months. He had learned that one of the fruits of the Spirit (or evidences of salvation in our lives) is temperance or self-control.

HOW ABOUT YOU? Do you display temperance in every area of your life? Are you tempted to overeat, gossip, or lose your temper? Ask the Lord to help you exercise self-control and say no. Perhaps you love to eat, watch TV, or play ball. Even in those things you need to use self-control. R.P.

TO MEMORIZE: *"But the fruit of the Spirit is love, joy, peace, long-suffering, gentleness, goodness, faith, meekness, temperance"* Galatians 5:22.

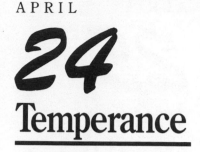

APRIL

24

Temperance

FROM THE BIBLE:

To win the contest you must deny yourselves many things that would keep you from doing your best. An athlete goes to all this trouble just to win a blue ribbon or a silver cup, but we do it for a heavenly reward that never disappears. So I run straight to the goal with purpose in every step. I fight to win. I'm not just shadow-boxing or playing around. Like an athlete I punish my body, treating it roughly, training it to do what it should, not what it wants to. Otherwise I fear that after enlisting others for the race, I myself might be declared unfit and ordered to stand aside.

1 Corinthians 9:25-27, TLB

Let everyone see that you are unselfish and considerate in all you do. Remember that the Lord is coming soon.

Philippians 4:5, TLB

Use self-control

APRIL

25

Instant Everything

FROM THE BIBLE:

Dear brothers, if a Christian is overcome by some sin, you who are godly should gently and humbly help him back onto the right path, remembering that next time it might be one of you who is in the wrong. Share each other's troubles and problems, and so obey our Lord's command. If anyone thinks he is too great to stoop to this, he is fooling himself. He is really a nobody. Let everyone be sure that he is doing his very best, for then he will have the personal satisfaction of work well done, and won't need to compare himself with someone else. Each of us must bear some faults and burdens of his own. For none of us is perfect! Those who are taught the Word of God should help their teachers by paying them. Galatians 6:1-6, TLB

Growth takes time

SINCE MOM and Dad would be gone, Chris would have to get supper for herself and her brother, Doug. "There are TV dinners," Mother was saying. "Just follow the directions on the box. There's instant pudding and brown-'n-serve rolls. You know how to do those."

"And there's a salad in the refrigerator," said Chris.

Mother put on her coat. "Yes, and if you need Dad or me, the phone number is on the table in the dining room."

Chris had no trouble whipping up the meal. Doug even admitted that it was pretty good!

The next day when Chris got home from school, she was very upset with one of her friends. "You know what Sandy did today, Mom?" she exclaimed. "Our teacher didn't collect our homework assignments. Instead, she just asked everyone if they had it done. Sandy told me this morning that she hadn't finished it, but when Miss Derks asked her, Sandy said she had it done! She lied! And she calls herself a Christian!"

"You have to remember that Sandy has only been saved for a little while," responded Mom.

"But, Mom," shrieked Chris, "she lied! You make it sound like it doesn't even matter!"

"I'm not excusing what Sandy did," answered Mom. "I'm just suggesting that you shouldn't be too hard on her. You do wrong things too, you know."

"I know, but that's different. She—"

"Hold on a minute," said Mom. "I'm afraid that in this day and age we get the idea that everything should be 'instant'—like the meal you made last night. The things you fixed were very easy and quick to make because they were all instant foods. But spiritual maturity doesn't come that way. It's more like the salad I made. It takes a lot of time to become mature."

"I get it!" said Chris thoughtfully. "I was expecting too much from Sandy too soon."

HOW ABOUT YOU? Do you have any friends who are new Christians? Remember, when you ask Jesus into your heart, you are instantly saved, but you aren't instantly mature. Be patient with your friends and make sure you set a good example for them to follow. D.M.

TO MEMORIZE: *"Each of us should please his neighbor for his good, to build him up"* Romans 15:2 (NIV).

APRIL

26

God's Patchwork Quilt

FROM THE BIBLE:

As it is, there are many parts, but one body. The eye cannot say to the hand, "I don't need you!" And the head cannot say to the feet, "I don't need you!" On the contrary, those parts of the body that seem to be weaker are indispensable, and the parts that we think are less honorable we treat with special honor. And the parts that are unpresentable are treated with special modesty, while our presentable parts need no special treatment. But God has combined the members of the body and has given greater honor to the parts that lacked it, so that there should be no division in the body, but that its parts should have equal concern for each other. If one part suffers, every part suffers with it; if one part is honored, every part rejoices with it. Now you are the body of Christ, and each one of you is a part of it.
1 Corinthians 12:20-27, NIV

We need one another

JANET'S MOTHER was sewing, and Janet was looking through a box of material scraps. "Mother!" she exclaimed. "Look at this gorgeous blue satin! Can you make me a dress out of this?"

"It *is* pretty," Mother agreed, "but there's not enough to make a dress, or even a blouse." Sadly, Janet laid it back in the box.

Several weeks later when Janet came home from school, she found a large gift-wrapped bundle lying on her bed. When she tore off the wrappings, she found a pretty, handmade, patchwork quilt. It was made with many different colors and designs. Janet squealed with delight. "What a surprise!" she said. "And the border—it's made of that pretty blue satin I liked!"

"It would have been a shame not to be able to use that material for something," said Mother, "so I thought of making a quilt! And while I was sewing it together, do you know what I was thinking?"

"What?" asked Janet.

"God has a patchwork quilt, too—the church!" replied Mother. "Some Christians are young, some are old; some are rich, and some are poor. There are those with many talents and others with just a few. But all of them are necessary in God's church. Together they make a beautiful, finished product, just like this quilt."

"It is beautiful," Janet agreed. "None of the pieces would be of much use by themselves."

"No, they wouldn't," answered Mother. "And there are some Christians who try to make it on their own, without even going to church or making Christian friends. But Christians need one another."

Janet's eyes twinkled. "The next time I feel like a small, unimportant scrap," she said, "I'll just remember that I'm an important part of God's patchwork quilt!"

HOW ABOUT YOU? If you are a Christian, you are an important part of Christ's body, the church. That means you need to serve Him, and serve others, the best way you can. You also need the help that other Christians can give you. So don't be a loner. Go to a church where there are Christians and where the Bible is taught. Get involved! No matter how unimportant you may feel sometimes, God has a special place for you! S.K.

TO MEMORIZE: *"Now you are the body of Christ, and each one of you is a part of it"*
1 Corinthians 12:27 (NIV).

APRIL

27

It Happened to Me

FROM THE BIBLE:

Blessed be the God and Father of our Lord Jesus Christ, the Father of mercies and God of all comfort, who comforts us in all our tribulation, that we may be able to comfort those who are in any trouble, with the comfort with which we ourselves are comforted by God. For as the sufferings of Christ abound in us, so our consolation also abounds through Christ. Now if we are afflicted, it is for your consolation and salvation, which is effective for enduring the same sufferings which we also suffer. Or if we are comforted, it is for your consolation and salvation. And our hope for you is steadfast, because we know that as you are partakers of the sufferings, so also you will partake of the consolation.

2 Corinthians 1:3-7, NKJV

Comfort others with God's love

CHRISTY WAS SORRY when she heard that Nicole's mother had been in a car accident and was in critical condition in the hospital. Many of the children stared curiously at Nicole but stayed away from her because they didn't know what to say. And most of those who did talk to her felt very awkward about it. Christy didn't know Nicole very well, but she could truly understand how Nicole felt because her own dad had been in a serious accident, the year before. There were still some things he couldn't do because of the accident.

At lunchtime Christy sat next to Nicole. "I know how hard it is," she said softly. "My father was in a car wreck last year."

"Oh," sighed Nicole, "then you understand how I feel!"

"Yes, I do," Christy assured her. "Would you like me to pray for your mother right now?"

"Oh, would you?" Nicole's face showed her first smile of the day.

When Christy got home from school that afternoon, she told her dad about Nicole's mother. "I told her that knowing the Lord helped me. She listened to what I had to say, Dad, because she knew I understood how she felt."

Dad smiled and nodded. "It often happens like that, Christy," he said. "In fact, the Bible tells us that because God comforts us during the bad times, we can, in turn, comfort others who are going through bad times. One way we can do this is by telling them about the Lord."

HOW ABOUT YOU? Have you experienced some hard times? Maybe your dad or mom has been seriously sick, or maybe someone close to you has died. The Lord tells us that He will comfort us during any situation, and that we, in turn, can comfort others with His love. Even if nothing really bad has happened to you, you can still pray for those who are going through a tough situation. You can still tell them about God's love. L.W.

TO MEMORIZE: *"Who comforts us in all our tribulation, that we may be able to comfort those who are in any trouble, with the comfort with which we ourselves are comforted by God"*
2 Corinthians 1:4 (NKJV).

APRIL

28

The Doctor Knows Best

FROM THE BIBLE:

But be doers of the word, and not hearers only, deceiving yourselves. For if anyone is a hearer of the word and not a doer, he is like a man observing his natural face in a mirror; for he observes himself, goes away, and immediately forgets what kind of man he was. But he who looks into the perfect law of liberty and continues in it, and is not a forgetful hearer but a doer of the work, this one will be blessed in what he does.
James 1:22-25, NKJV

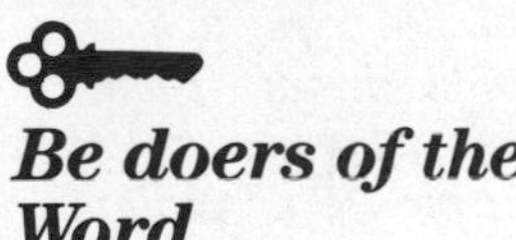

Be doers of the Word

TOMMY WALTERS and his parents went to visit Aunt Eva, who was almost eighty years old. They had heard she was sick, and Tommy's parents hoped they would be able to cheer her up. Aunt Eva certainly needed it! "I feel just miserable," she said. "That new doctor hasn't done me a bit of good. It's been a waste of money to go to him. I sure can't recommend him to others."

"Why, that's too bad," said Tommy's mother. "Didn't he give you any medicine?"

"Well, yes," said Aunt Eva, "but the pills didn't seem to help, so after a few days I stopped taking them. Besides, they were hard to swallow."

"What about your diet?" Mr. Walters asked. "Did he say anything about that?"

"He told me to cut down on salt," answered Aunt Eva, "but I can't stand food without lots of salt on it."

"What about exercise?" asked Mrs. Walters.

Aunt Eva just laughed. "That's the craziest thing of all," she said. "The doctor told me to go for a walk at least once a day. At my age? Ridiculous!"

Mr. and Mrs. Walters tried to persuade Aunt Eva to follow the doctor's instructions, but she shook her head sadly. "It wouldn't help," she said.

On the way home Tommy said, "Isn't Aunt Eva funny? She thinks her doctor is no good. But she didn't do a thing he told her. No wonder she's not getting any better!"

"Yes, it is funny—and sad," replied Mother.

Nodding in agreement, Dad spoke slowly. "A lot of Christians are like that, too. They look to God for help, but they disobey His commands. Then when they get discouraged and unhappy, they think it's God's fault. The worst part about it is that they are a poor testimony to others who need to accept Christ as Savior."

"I sure don't want to turn people away from Christ," said Tommy. "I want to do what He tells me. Then everyone will see what a great 'Doctor' He really is."

HOW ABOUT YOU? When you have problems, do you blame God? But stop and think—have you obeyed all of His commands? Do you read the Bible? Pray? Attend a good church? How about sinful habits that you need to get rid of? Don't be like Aunt Eva. Follow the Doctor's orders—He always knows best! S.K.

TO MEMORIZE: *"But be doers of the word, and not hearers only"* James 1:22 (NKJV).

APRIL

29

God's Erasure

FROM THE BIBLE:

What happiness for those whose guilt has been forgiven! What joys when sins are covered over! What relief for those who have confessed their sins and God has cleared their record. There was a time when I wouldn't admit what a sinner I was. But my dishonesty made me miserable and filled my days with frustration. All day and all night your hand was heavy on me. My strength evaporated like water on a sunny day until I finally admitted all my sins to you and stopped trying to hide them. I said to myself, "I will confess them to the Lord." And you forgave me! All my guilt is gone. Psalm 32:1-5, TLB

Confess; God forgives

NATHAN TOSSED and turned. There seemed to be rocks in his bed. Through the wall came the faint *clickity-clack* of his mother's typewriter. But Nathan knew it was not the noise which kept him awake. It was the lie he had told that kept poking his conscience.

He punched the pillow and snuggled deeper into the covers. He squeezed his eyes tightly shut. But he could not turn off the little voice in head. *Better go tell your mother you're sorry. Tell the truth. Tell the truth.* Nothing could hush the voice. *Tell the truth. Tell the truth.*

Finally Nathan gave up. He scrambled out of bed and stumbled into the next room. His mother looked up in surprise as he burst into sobs. "What's the matter, Son? Did you have a bad dream?"

Nathan shook his head. "No," he choked. "I . . . I told you a lie. I said I hadn't been playing in Mr. Field's barn, but I had. I'm sorry." Nathan sniffed loudly. "I won't play there anymore without permission."

His mother put her arm around him. "I'm sorry you lied to me, Nathan, but I'm glad you have confessed. Let me show you something. Look at this word I just typed. What's wrong with it?"

Nathan looked at the sheet in the typewriter. He grinned through his tears. "You made a mistake. You spelled forgive f-o-r-g-e-v-e."

"Now watch," Mother instructed. She touched a switch and pressed a couple of keys.

"Why, now it's spelled right!" Nathan exclaimed.

"My new typewriter has a built-in correction tape. When I make a mistake, all I have to do is back up and correct it," Mother explained. "It reminds me of the way the blood of Jesus erases our sins, Nathan, if we confess them. If I had tried to ignore this mistake, it would have never been corrected. Ignoring our sins doesn't take care of them, either. When we sin, we must do exactly what you just did—confess. When we confess our sins to God, they are forgiven and forgotten.

Nathan yawned. "I sure do feel better. I think I can sleep now."

HOW ABOUT YOU? Are you trying to ignore a sin in your life? Jesus wants to forgive you and erase it. But you have to confess. Why not do it now? B.W.

TO MEMORIZE: *"If anybody does sin, we have one who speaks to the Father in our defense—Jesus Christ, the Righteous One"* 1 John 2:1 (NIV).

APRIL

30

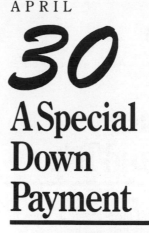

A Special Down Payment

FROM THE BIBLE:

For we know that when this tent we live in now is taken down—when we die and leave these bodies—we will have wonderful new bodies in heaven, homes that will be ours forevermore, made for us by God himself, and not by human hands. How weary we grow of our present bodies. . . . These earthly bodies make us groan and sigh, but we wouldn't like to think of dying and having no bodies at all. We want to slip into our new bodies so that these dying bodies will, as it were, be swallowed up by everlasting life. This is what God has prepared for us and, as a guarantee, he has given us his Holy Spirit. Now we look forward with confidence to our heavenly bodies, realizing that every moment we spend in these earthly bodies is time spent away from our eternal home in heaven with Jesus.
2 Corinthians 5:1-8, TLB

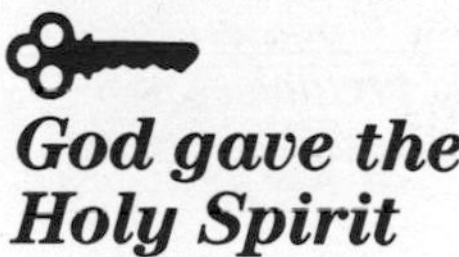

God gave the Holy Spirit

"MARGE, I PROMISED the car salesman that I would bring him the down payment on our new car this afternoon," Mr. Bloss told his wife. "I might as well go now, since I have some free time."

"Can I go, too?" Jennifer asked her dad.

"Sure," he agreed. "Get your jacket on. I'm leaving now."

As Jennifer got into the car she asked, "What's a down payment, Dad?"

"When we were at the car dealer's the other night, your Mom and I talked to the salesman about the kind of car we wanted. We told him what make, what color, and what extras we would like for our car."

"Oh, I remember that," Jennifer said. "You decided on a blue one with power steering."

"Right, but the salesman didn't have a car like that in his showroom, so he'll have to order it from the factory," explained Dad. "That will take a lot of time. To show him I'm serious about buying the car, I'm going to give him a thousand dollars toward the price. Without the down payment, people could just go there and order cars and then not buy them when the cars come."

"Oh, I see," Jennifer said, nodding. "Because you're giving him the thousand dollars, he knows you'll come through with the rest of the payment. He knows you wouldn't want to lose the money."

"Right." After riding in silence for a while, Dad said, "You know, Jennifer, you have a down payment in you."

"In me?" asked Jennifer.

Dad nodded. "That's right. Another word for *down payment* is *deposit.* God tells us in the Bible that He has given every Christian the deposit of the Holy Spirit as a guarantee that we will have a future with God in heaven."

"It really says that?" Jennifer asked in surprise. "I didn't know that! Hey, that's good! God has given me a down payment—the Holy Spirit!"

HOW ABOUT YOU? Do you sometimes wonder about your relationship with the Lord? Did you know that God has given you a promise, or guarantee, that you will some day be with Him? That guarantee is the Holy Spirit. Thank the Lord for giving you a very special down payment! L.W.

TO MEMORIZE: *"He anointed us, set his seal of ownership on us, and put his Spirit in our hearts as a deposit"* 2 Corinthians 1:22 (NIV).

MAY

1

The Band Trip

FROM THE BIBLE:

Remind the people to be subject to rulers and authorities, to be obedient, to be ready to do whatever is good, to slander no one, to be peaceable and considerate, and to show true humility toward all men. At one time we too were foolish, disobedient, deceived and enslaved by all kinds of passions and pleasures. We lived in malice and envy, being hated and hating one another. But when the kindness and love of God our Savior appeared, he saved us, not because of righteous things we had done, but because of his mercy. He saved us through the washing of rebirth and renewal by the Holy Spirit, whom he poured out on us generously through Jesus Christ our Savior, so that, having been justified by his grace, we might become heirs having the hope of eternal life. This is a trustworthy saying. And I want you to stress these things, so that those who have trusted in God may be careful to devote themselves to doing what is good. These things are excellent and profitable for everyone. Titus 3:1-8, NIV

Actions reflect on Jesus

ALL TOO SOON the band trip was coming to an end, and the students from Grace Christian School were getting ready to head for home. "Performing in the band review was really neat. I'm glad we got a 'first' rating," Marsha said. "And staying in this motel was so much fun. I'll never forget it."

"I'm taking home some souvenirs to remind me that I was here," Edna said as she packed a towel with "Shadybrook Motel" woven into it. "Why don't you take one, too?" she suggested, tossing a towel to Marsha.

On the trip home the girls learned that the boys had ended their motel stay with a pillow fight. It had turned into a free-for-all, resulting in torn sheets and a broken lamp. "We almost got caught when the chaperones checked on us," one of the boys told them.

A week after returning home, Mr. Palmbeck, the band director, stood before them with a very solemn look on his face. "I got to know Mr. Hill, the manager at our motel," Mr. Palmbeck said. "I was able to witness to him, and he came to hear us play in the band review. I felt he was quite interested in Christianity. I want to share a letter I just received from him." It grew very quiet in the band room as Mr. Palmbeck read the letter from the motel manager. It told of items missing and ruined motel furnishings.

"Mr. Hill has sent a bill for damages," said Mr. Palmbeck. "We'll pay that, but we can't pay for the damage done to your name, the school's name, or the Lord's name." There was a long silence, then Mr. Palmbeck added, "Your instruments played beautiful music but some of your lives played sour notes. Which notes will Mr. Hill remember? Now I want those who are guilty and who are truly sorry and want to make amends to remain seated. Those who are innocent may leave."

Several students remained with bowed heads while the others filed out.

HOW ABOUT YOU? How do you act away from home? If you are a Christian, you bear Christ's name. Do your actions honor that Name? Are you a testimony for Jesus in the way you behave? Now that you are saved, good works should be a part of your daily life. J.H.

TO MEMORIZE: *"Those who have trusted in God may be careful to devote themselves to doing what is good"* Titus 3:8 (NIV).

MAY

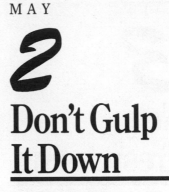

Don't Gulp It Down

FROM THE BIBLE:

How can a young man keep his way pure?
By living according to your word.
I seek you with all my heart;
do not let me stray from your commands.
I have hidden your word in my heart
that I might not sin against you.
Praise be to you, O Lord;
teach me your decrees.
With my lips I recount
all the laws that come from your mouth.
I rejoice in following your statutes
as one rejoices in great riches.
I meditate on your precepts
and consider your ways.
I delight in your decrees;
I will not neglect your word.
Psalm 119:9-16, NIV

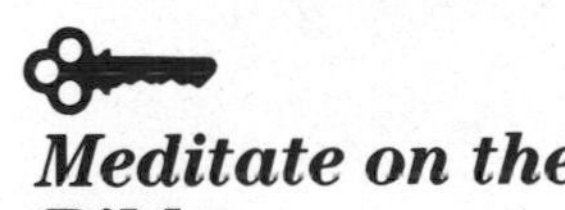

Meditate on the Bible

ALL THROUGH dinner Cal was obviously in a big hurry. He grabbed his milk to wash down the large mouthful of food he took, and he finished long before the rest of the family. "May I be excused?" he asked. "The guys are waiting. We want to go ice skating tonight."

"You'll still have plenty of time to skate after family devotions," answered Dad.

Cal relaxed just a little as Mother passed his favorite dessert—apple pie. But she was dismayed to see it disappear in three large bites. His sister, Karen, had not yet started hers.

"Oh, this dinner was so good, Mother," said Karen. "And the pie looks yummy! Can I save it for after devotions?"

"Sure can," answered Dad, passing Cal a Bible. "Would you read to us from Psalm 119, verses 9-16, Son?" Cal found the place and read the passage as fast as he could. His words tumbled over each other, making them hard to understand. "Hmmm," murmured Dad. "Cal, did you enjoy your dinner tonight?"

Cal was surprised. "Oh, yeah, sure."

"How about you, Karen?" asked Dad.

"It was delicious!" exclaimed Karen. "The chicken was so crispy, and the potatoes were so buttery, and I love corn!"

Dad laughed. "I have a feeling you enjoyed it more than Cal did. Does anyone know why?"

"I can tell you that," said Mother. "Karen took her time, while Cal gulped it down."

Cal looked sheepish as Dad nodded. "Do you know that it's the same with the Word of God? To get as much out of it as possible, we need to take time when we read it. We must not hurry. Food that is gulped isn't well digested; neither does the Bible mean much to us when we hurry through it. Cal, how about reading that passage to us once again. This time let's chew it well—that is, let's take time to think about what we are reading."

Cal nodded as he began to read carefully.

HOW ABOUT YOU? Do you hurry through the Scripture passage each day so you can get on to the story? If you do, you're missing the most important part. Read God's Word carefully—maybe you should read it again *after* the story. Meditate on it as you go through the day and as you go to sleep as well. H.M.

TO MEMORIZE: *"His delight is in the law of the LORD, and in His law he meditates day and night"* Psalm 1:2 (NKJV).

MAY

3

No Trespassing

FROM THE BIBLE:

He was despised and rejected by men, a man of sorrows, and familiar with suffering. Like one from whom men hide their faces he was despised, and we esteemed him not. Surely he took up our infirmities and carried our sorrows, yet we considered him stricken by God, smitten by him, and afflicted. But he was pierced for our transgressions, he was crushed for our iniquities; the punishment that brought us peace was upon him, and by his wounds we are healed. We all, like sheep, have gone astray, each of us has turned to his own way; and the Lord has laid on him the iniquity of us all.

Isaiah 53:3-6, NIV

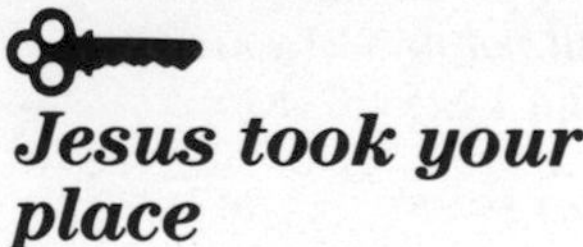

Jesus took your place

TIM AND HIS widowed mother lived on the outskirts of town. Their only near neighbor was grouchy old Mr. Crossley, who had No Trespassing signs on every other fencepost around his farm. But Tim wasn't lonely even though Mother sometimes worked long hours. He had Pudge, a faithful little dog and wonderful companion. He kept Pudge carefully locked inside their yard because Mr. Crossley hated dogs. Besides, Mr. Crossley had been losing chickens lately, and he threatened to shoot any dog he saw on his place.

One day when Tim arrived home, he whistled for Pudge, but there was no happy bark to answer him. As Tim came up the walk, he saw that the gate was open. A package was on the steps, and Tim realized that the postman had come and had failed to close the gate properly. Pudge was gone! Whistling and calling, Tim bounded off in search of his dog. Hearing some barking in the direction of Mr. Cossley's property, Tim headed that way. He arrived just in time to see Mr. Cossley taking careful aim at Pudge. "Stop! Stop!" screamed Tim. He threw himself at his pet just as the gun went off.

Later Mr. Cossley was talking to Mother at the hospital. "I feel just awful!" he said. "I never shot a kid before. He jumped right in the way to save his dog!"

Tim's mother nodded. "I know. He loves Pudge so much! But, thank God, it's only a flesh wound. The doctor says Tim can come home tomorrow." She paused, then added thoughtfully, "You know, Pudge trespassed, but Tim was wounded. This reminds me of myself. I trespassed against God—I sinned. I was doomed to die, but Jesus stepped into my place. The Bible says, 'He was wounded for my transgressions.' He took my place on Calvary's cross—and He took your place, too, Mr. Crossley."

Mr. Crossley was listening intently. "I never realized that anyone loved me that much," he murmured. "I'm going home to take down those No Trespassing signs. Then I'd like to stop at your house and hear more about this."

HOW ABOUT YOU? Do you realize how much Jesus loves you? You, too, have trespassed, or sinned, against God. But Jesus took the punishment you deserve. He was wounded for you. Have you thanked Him and asked Him to be your Savior? Do it today. B.W.

TO MEMORIZE: *"He was pierced for our transgressions"* Isaiah 53:5 (NIV).

KEVIN HELD his ticket for the baseball game tightly in his hand as he approached the gate at the athletic field. Just a little ahead of him, George, a friend from school, appeared to be arguing with one of the men taking tickets. "Sorry, Son," the man was saying as Kevin walked up, "this is a ticket for last week's game. I can't let you in."

"Oh, come on," argued George. "I just grabbed the wrong one by mistake. My dad will pay for a new one when he gets here."

The man shook his head. "You'll have to wait for him."

George bristled. "Don't you know who I am?" he demanded. "My dad's the principal of the high school!"

"How nice," the ticket man replied, "but I have orders."

As Kevin handed his ticket to the man and walked through the gate, he waved to George. "Hey," George yelled, "how come he gets to go in and I don't?"

The man at the gate sighed. "He has a ticket. You don't," he said. "It's that simple. You can be president of the United States, but if you don't have a ticket, you don't get in."

Back home Kevin told his dad about the ticket incident. "Will that man be in trouble because he wouldn't let the principal's son in?" asked Kevin.

Dad shook his head. "The gatekeeper was right," he said. "At a ball game, he doesn't look at the face of the person who wants to get in. He looks at the ticket. If it's the correct one, the person has the right to proceed. If not, he doesn't have the right to go any farther, no matter who he is." Dad reached for his Bible and prepared to read for family devotions. "That's kind of the way God works, too," he added. "Christ, and Christ alone, is our ticket to heaven. God won't look at our faces or at who we are. He will only look to see if we have Christ in our hearts. We'll get into heaven only if we have accepted Him as Savior."

HOW ABOUT YOU? Do you have your "ticket" to heaven? Have you accepted Jesus as your Savior? You can never say, "Look at me, God. I am holy." You can only say, "Look upon Christ, who is my 'ticket' to heaven." If you've never received Him, don't wait. Do it today. H.M.

TO MEMORIZE: *"And be found in Him, not having my own righteousness . . . but that which is through faith in Christ, the righteousness which is from God by faith"* Philippians 3:9 (NKJV).

MAY

Ticket Trouble

FROM THE BIBLE:

. . . though I also might have confidence in the flesh. If anyone else thinks he may have confidence in the flesh, I more so: circumcised the eighth day, of the stock of Israel, of the tribe of Benjamin, a Hebrew of the Hebrews; concerning the law, a Pharisee; concerning zeal, persecuting the church; concerning the righteousness which is in the law, blameless. But what things were gain to me, these I have counted loss for Christ. But indeed I also count all things loss for the excellence of the knowledge of Christ Jesus my Lord, for whom I have suffered the loss of all things, and count them as rubbish, that I may gain Christ and be found in Him, not having my own righteousness, which is from the law, but that which is through faith in Christ, the righteousness which is from God by faith; that I may know Him and the power of His resurrection, and the fellowship of His sufferings, being conformed to His death.
Philippians 3:4-10, NKJV

You need Christ

MAY

5

No Stains

FROM THE BIBLE:
God paid a ransom to save you from the impossible road to heaven which your fathers tried to take, and the ransom he paid was not mere gold or silver, as you very well know. But he paid for you with the precious lifeblood of Christ, the sinless, spotless Lamb of God. God chose him for this purpose long before the world began, but only recently was he brought into public view, in these last days, as a blessing to you. Because of this, your trust can be in God who raised Christ from the dead and gave him great glory. Now your faith and hope can rest in him alone.
1 Peter 1:18-21, TLB

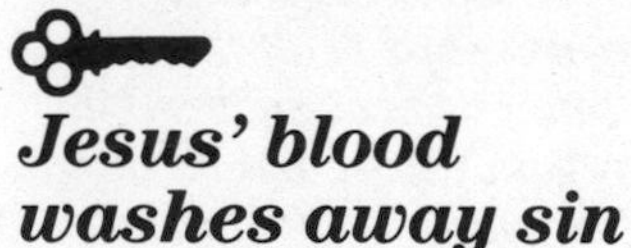

Jesus' blood washes away sin

"NEW AND IMPROVED," read Sandi's mother as she picked up a package of laundry detergent in the supermarket. She grinned at Sandi. "I heard this advertised on TV the other day. It's supposed to be better than ever before—removes the most difficult stains, according to the 'satisfied customer' on the commercial. If you can believe everything you hear, it has never been known to fail."

"Oh, could we try it on my yellow dress? Please?" begged Sandi. "It's got that spot on the sleeve. I try to turn it to the inside a little so it won't show so much, but it doesn't stay in place very well. Maybe this stuff would take it out."

"Well, it's a lot more expensive than the kind I usually use," said Mother, "but I guess you can try it if you want to. Don't get your hopes up too much, though."

They took the detergent home, and Sandi washed out her dress, following the package directions very carefully. She was disappointed with the results. "I can't believe it!" she exclaimed. "They can send men to the moon, but they can't find a way to get out this little spot."

Mother laughed. "That's true," she said. She looked thoughtfully at the dress. "This reminds me of another area where everyone's best efforts fail. Everybody is born a sinner. It's as though the stain of sin is on a person's 'garment of life.' People often try to hide it by being good, and sometimes they can even keep it out of the sight of others. But it's still there. Nothing man can do is able to remove it. There is something that can wash sin away, though. It's the blood of the Lord Jesus Christ, and we don't have to pay a thing for it—Jesus paid it all. Now God offers it freely to all who will admit their need and accept Jesus as Savior. It's the only thing that can cleanse a person's soul."

HOW ABOUT YOU? Are you still trying to cover up your sins or get rid of them through your own efforts? Or have they been washed away by Jesus' blood? If not, won't you admit your failure today and allow Jesus to cleanse your heart and life? H.M.

TO MEMORIZE: *"Unto him that loved us, and washed us from our sins in his own blood . . . to him be glory and dominion for ever and ever"* Revelation 1:5-6.

MAY

6

The Warning

FROM THE BIBLE:
Then I saw a great white throne and Him who sat on it, from whose face the earth and the heaven fled away. And there was found no place for them. And I saw the dead, small and great, standing before God, and books were opened. And another book was opened, which is the Book of Life. And the dead were judged according to their works, by the things which were written in the books. The sea gave up the dead who were in it, and Death and Hades delivered up the dead who were in them. And they were judged, each one according to his works. Then Death and Hades were cast into the lake of fire. This is the second death. And anyone not found written in the Book of Life was cast into the lake of fire.
Revelation 20:11-15, NKJV

Obey God's warning

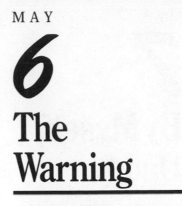

CARRIE AND DAN, who didn't usually attend church, were visiting Uncle Bob and Aunt Ellen. While they were there, they went to Sunday school and church, but they didn't like it much. Pastor Hake's sermon was about hell.

Carrie and Dan made faces at each other. "This is too much!" muttered Dan. "All they do here is try to scare us!"

When they got back to the house, Aunt Ellen said, "Dinner will be ready in half an hour."

"Good!" said Uncle Joe. "That will give me time to try out a new gadget I bought yesterday." He set a box on the table and lifted out a round, white object made of plastic. "What's that for?" asked Carrie. "What does it do?"

"Just wait till I put these batteries in," replied their uncle. "There, all set. We'll see if it works now." He pressed a small, round button on the case. Immediately an earsplitting shriek filled the room! Carrie screamed and jumped back, while Dan covered his ears. Uncle Bob laughed at the look on their faces. He took his finger off the button, and the noise stopped.

"It's a smoke detector," he said. "Whenever there's smoke in the house, the alarm will go off."

"It's awful!" said Carrie. "Why does it have to be so loud and scary?"

"It's supposed to be that way, silly!" Dan said. "Otherwise you might not hear it."

"Right," his uncle replied. "The purpose of this thing is not to scare people. It's to warn them of danger so they can avoid it." He paused, then added thoughtfully, "You know, that reminds me of church this morning. Sometimes we seem to think that sermons about hell are intended to scare us, but actually they are only meant to warn us."

Carrie and Dan looked at each other. Carrie sighed. "Well, that warning this morning did scare me," she said. "I don't want to go to hell. I'd like to be saved."

Dan nodded. "Me, too."

HOW ABOUT YOU? Have you been warned about hell? Did you heed that warning? Hell isn't a pleasant subject, and yes, it is scary! But it is also real. The good news is that you don't need to go there. Accept Jesus as your Savior. Then your name will be written in the Book of Life, and you will spend eternity in heaven. S.K.

TO MEMORIZE: *"And anyone not found written in the Book of Life was cast into the lake of fire"* Revelation 20:15 (NKJV).

MAY

7

By Myself, Daddy

FROM THE BIBLE:

So ever since we first heard about you we have kept on praying and asking God to help you understand what he wants you to do; asking him to make you wise about spiritual things; and asking that the way you live will always please the Lord and honor him, so that you will always be doing good, kind things for others, while all the time you are learning to know God better and better. We are praying, too, that you will be filled with his mighty, glorious strength so that you can keep going no matter what happens—always full of the joy of the Lord, and always thankful to the Father who has made us fit to share all the wonderful things that belong to those who live in the Kingdom of light. For he has rescued us out of the darkness and gloom of Satan's kingdom and brought us into the Kingdom of his dear Son, who bought our freedom with his blood and forgave us all our sins. Colossians 1:9-14, TLB

"Walk" with God's help

SAM ENJOYED helping his little brother, Danny, learn to walk. With a chubby fist wrapped around the helping fingers of his mother, father, or big brother, Danny could run all the way across the living room. But if he let go he nearly always fell down with a thud. "Dad, how long will it be till Danny can walk alone?" Sam asked one day. "Will he always need our help?"

Dad laughed. "No, Son," he replied. "Danny just needs a little more time. I remember when you were learning to walk. Even though you often felt like Danny does, you'd seldom let me help you. If I tried, you'd get angry and say, 'No! By myself, Daddy!' And you'd push at my hands."

Sam grinned. "I can hardly believe I was so stubborn," he said. "Sure you're not mixing me up with somebody else?"

"It was you all right." Dad smiled. "You were very independent. And maybe I should thank you for it because you taught me something."

"I did?" Same was surprised.

Dad nodded. "As I watched you, I saw myself. I was a new Christian, a baby Christian, at that time. And I was trying to walk the Christian life all by myself. I seldom read my Bible or prayed. I rarely went to church. I was accepting no help from my heavenly Father or from any of my brothers and sisters in the Lord. And like you, I was falling. I knew I was a Christian, but I always wanted my own way and had a hard time controlling my temper. As I watched you resist my help, I suddenly realized that I was resisting the Lord's help. In my spiritual life I was saying, 'By myself, Daddy.' It's a lesson I never forgot."

HOW ABOUT YOU? Are you struggling to "walk" as a Christian should? Do you have problems with a temper? Fears? Laziness? Pride? Are you trusting God to help you with these things, or are you stubbornly depending on yourself? No matter how capable you feel, sooner or later you will "fall" spiritually if you try to walk alone. Study God's Word. Meet regularly with other Christians. Take time to pray. You need your heavenly Father's help to be the honest, kind, helpful person He wants you to be. D.M.

TO MEMORIZE: *"Now unto him that is able to keep you from falling, and to present you faultless before the presence of his glory with exceeding joy, to the only wise God our Saviour, be glory and majesty, dominion and power, both now and ever. Amen."* Jude 24–25.

“GUESS WHAT?” Lisa bounded into the room, followed by Amy. “Amy and I are going to give a demonstration at the next 4-H Club meeting.”

“Great,” said Mother. “What will you demonstrate?”

Both girls looked at her with a blank stare, and then burst into peals of laughter. “We hadn't thought about that.” All was quiet as they thought. Then Lisa snapped her fingers. “I know. Let's give a demonstration on flower arranging. Mother has a book that will show us how, and we have lots of flowers in our garden.”

All afternoon the girls studied and practiced arranging flowers. Finally, they came into the living room, carrying a bouquet. “Beautiful!” Mother exclaimed. “I'm amazed at what you've done.”

“We're still working on our speech. We have three weeks to practice,” Lisa said. “May I go with Amy to her Aunt Clara's house tomorrow morning? We want to give this arrangement to her. She's crippled and can't even get out of bed now.” Mother smiled her approval, and the next morning the girls took the flowers to the elderly lady and spent an hour talking with her.

“How did your demonstration go?” Mother asked when Lisa returned home.

“That's not for a few weeks yet,” Lisa replied. She was surprised that Mother had forgotten.

Mother smiled. “I'm talking about the demonstration you performed this morning.” she said. “The flowers you arranged are beautiful, but not nearly as beautiful as the love you girls showed by taking the flowers to Amy's aunt and spending time with her. I'm sure it meant a lot to her. You girls are demonstrating something far more important than flower arranging.”

Lisa raised her eyebrows. “We are?”

Mother smiled. “Yes. A lot of people talk about God's love, but you're demonstrating it by your thoughtfulness.”

HOW ABOUT YOU? Do you show the world the love of God by your actions? Are you kind and thoughtful? Do you help whenever you can? Demonstrate God's love to someone today. B.W.

TO MEMORIZE: *“Let us not love with words or tongue but with actions and in truth”* 1 John 3:18 (NIV).

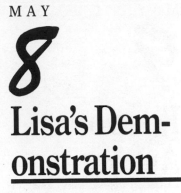

MAY

Lisa's Demonstration

FROM THE BIBLE:

My prayer for you is that you will overflow more and more with love for others, and at the same time keep on growing in spiritual knowledge and insight, for I want you always to see clearly the difference between right and wrong, and to be inwardly clean, no one being able to criticize you from now until our Lord returns. May you always be doing those good, kind things which show that you are a child of God, for this will bring much praise and glory to the Lord.

Philippians 1:9-11, TLB

Demonstrate God's love

MAY

Keep on Asking

FROM THE BIBLE:

Then, teaching them more about prayer, he used this illustration: "Suppose you went to a friend's house at midnight, wanting to borrow three loaves of bread. You would shout up to him, 'A friend of mine has just arrived for a visit and I've nothing to give him to eat.' He would call down from his bedroom, 'Please don't ask me to get up. The door is locked for the night and we are all in bed. I just can't help you this time.' But I'll tell you this—though he won't do it as a friend, if you keep knocking long enough he will get up and give you everything you want—just because of your persistence. And so it is with prayer—keep on asking and you will keep on getting; keep on looking and you will keep on finding; knock and the door will be opened. Everyone who asks, receives; all who seek, find; and the door is opened to everyone who knocks.
Luke 11: 5-8, TLB

Don't give up praying

IT WAS KYLE'S birthday, and right after supper he opened a large present from his parents. "Oh, boy! A chemistry set!" he exclaimed. "It's just what I wanted!"

His parents chuckled. "We know." Mother smiled. "How could we help but know with all the hints you've given?"

"Huh?" asked Kyle innocently. "Have I been hinting?"

"Ever since you saw that chemistry set at Murphy's Department Store, you've been talking about how much you wanted one," Dad said, grinning.

"And when I went out to buy your present," Mother added, "I found a note in my purse that said, 'Don't forget the C.S.! Love, Guess Who.' "

Kyle laughed and turned red. "I guess I have been kind of a pest. I hope you're not mad at me."

"Of course not," replied his father. "You weren't rude about it, just persistent. Actually, we like it when you tell us what you really want."

"I can't wait to show Steve," said Kyle eagerly.

"That reminds me—you were going to pray for an opportunity to witness to Steve," said Dad. "How did that turn out?"

Kyle looked uncomfortable. "Oh, well, I did pray about it for a while, but nothing seemed to happen, so I kinda forgot about it."

"Speaking of prayer," said Mother, "you also said you were going to pray for money to go to the church youth camp this summer. Have you gotten it yet?"

Kyle shook his head. "I saved about ten dollars," he explained, "but I didn't get any more for a long time, so I quit praying about it."

Dad looked serious. "You've learned to be persistent when it comes to asking for birthday presents," he said. "It's a shame you haven't applied this principle to your praying. You see, it pleases God to give His children what they really want and need, but too often we say a halfhearted prayer about something and then forget all about it. Who knows how many wonderful answers to prayer we'd receive if only we kept on asking!"

HOW ABOUT YOU? Is there a problem or a need in your life that you have prayed about? If so, that's fine, but don't forget to keep on praying. In His Word, God sets down several conditions for effective prayer. One of them is persistence. So keep on asking and believing. S.K.

TO MEMORIZE: *"The prayer of a righteous man is powerful and effective"* James 5:16 (NIV).

MAY

10

Imperfect Parents

FROM THE BIBLE:
Slaves, submit yourselves to your masters with all respect, not only to those who are good and considerate, but also to those who are harsh. For it is commendable if a man bears up under the pain of unjust suffering because he is conscious of God. But how is it to your credit if you receive a beating for doing wrong and endure it? But if you suffer for doing good and you endure it, this is commendable before God. To this you were called, because Christ suffered for you, leaving you an example, that you should follow in his steps. "He committed no sin, and no deceit was found in his mouth." When they hurled their insults at him, he did not retaliate; when he suffered, he made no threats. Instead, he entrusted himself to him who judges justly.
1 Peter 2:18-23, NIV

Forgive your parents

JAMIE SMILED happily as Mother gave him permission to go skating with his friends. Just then Dad came in from the backyard. He looked angry. "James Robert," he said, "I've told you at least a dozen times to put the garden tools away when you're done with them. I found these out in the yard. They must have been left out during the last rain." He held up a rusty rake and hoe.

"But, Dad," Jamie said. "I didn't—"

"Don't try to make excuses," his father said sternly. "I'm not going to let you off easy this time. Go to your room till it's time for supper."

As Jamie flopped onto his bed, he brushed away a tear. It was so unfair! Not only would he miss the skating this afternoon, but he was being punished for something he didn't do. How could God let this happen?

It seemed like years before he heard his bedroom door open. His father came in and looked at him sheepishly. "I'm afraid I have to apologize, Son," he said. "I just remembered that I was the last one working in the garden, and I left the tools there when I had to come in for a phone call. Then I forgot all about them. Will you forgive me?"

"I guess so," Jamie mumbled unhappily.

"You know, something like this happened to me when I was a boy," said Dad. "My father gave me a licking for something he thought I had done. I was sore for days!"

"Wow! That's awful," said Jamie. "What did Grandpa say when he found out he was wrong?"

Dad smiled. "He never did find out," he said, shaking his head. "At first I was bitter and questioned God. Then I realized that God wanted me to forgive my father. And that lesson of forgiveness was worth a hundred lickings to me. It's one I've remembered the rest of my life."

"I suppose I shouldn't expect you to be perfect," Jamie said, smiling. "After all, just think of all the things you've forgiven *me* for! I'm going to remember that story so I can tell it to my kids some day. I'm sure *their* father won't be perfect either!"

HOW ABOUT YOU? How do you feel when your parents make a mistake? Do you become bitter and critical? Or do you forgive them and try to learn from the experience? Parents aren't perfect, but God still expects you to love and obey them, for His sake. S.K.

TO MEMORIZE: *"But if you suffer for doing good and you endure it, this is commendable before God"* 1 Peter 2:20 (NIV).

MAY

11

Mothering

FROM THE BIBLE:

Come, you children, listen to me;
I will teach you the fear of the Lord.
Who is the man who desires life,
And loves many days, that he may see good?
Keep your tongue from evil,
And your lips from speaking guile.
Depart from evil, and do good;
Seek peace, and pursue it.
The eyes of the Lord are on the righteous,
And His ears are open to their cry.
The face of the Lord is against those who do evil,
To cut off the remembrance of them from the earth.
The righteous cry out, and the Lord hears,
And delivers them out of all their troubles.

Psalm 34:11-17, NKJV

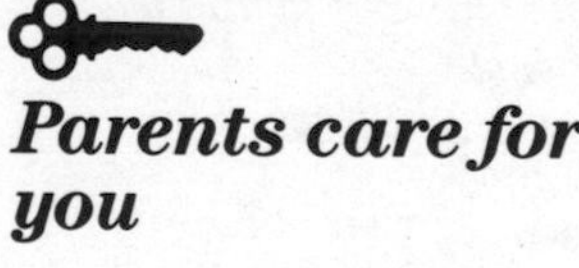

Parents care for you

LIZ GLARED at her mother. "You have no good reason to make me miss Sara's slumber party next Friday," she insisted. "You don't even know her, and I think you're being very unfair."

"Maybe you're right, Liz," admitted Mother. "Perhaps it's because I don't know Sara that I feel you shouldn't go. I'm not trying to ruin your fun. I guess I'm trying to protect you from a possible bad influence. Look, why don't you invite Sara over for dinner sometime? Then I can get to know her better."

Liz agreed to Mother's suggestion, and Sara came the next evening. "You and Sara go ahead and play a game," said Mother after dinner. "I'll clear the table and do the dishes." As she worked, she enjoyed hearing the giggles and chatter of the two girls in the next room.

"Sara seems like a nice girl," said Mother after Sara had been taken home, "but I still feel uneasy about the slumber party. I really need to meet Sara's parents, or at least know more about them, before I can allow you to spend the night there." Liz sighed. She knew there would be no slumber party for her this week.

After school the next day, Liz's dog, GG (short for "Good Girl"), was making a terrible commotion. "Mother, what is wrong with GG?" asked Liz. "Ever since she had her puppies she's been going wild every time someone comes to the door. Make her quiet down! She should know the postman won't hurt her. She never used to bark at him."

"GG isn't going to take any chances with her babies," explained Mother as they settled the dog in kitchen with the puppies. "She'll try to keep anyone who isn't family away from them." She paused, then added, "I guess all mothers are that way, so do please be patient with GG—and me—as we mother our children!"

HOW ABOUT YOU? Do you sometimes wonder why your parents seem so protective of you? Do you feel like they just won't let you grow up? God has given them the great responsibility of keeping you from evil influences. They're just doing their job. Be patient with them. P.R.

TO MEMORIZE: *"Come, you children, listen to me; I will teach you the fear of the LORD"* Psalm 34:11 (NKJV).

MAY

12

No Stepmother Card

FROM THE BIBLE:
Behold, how good and how pleasant it is
For brethren to dwell together in unity!
It is like the precious oil upon the head,
Running down on the beard,
The beard of Aaron,
Running down on the edge of his garments.
It is like the dew of Hermon,
Descending upon the mountains of Zion;
For there the Lord commanded the blessing—
Life forevermore.
Psalm 133, NKJV

Accept what God allows

PAULA JOHNSON was not happy about her father's new wife, and she allowed those feeling to show. "I wish you would try to accept your stepmother for who she is," suggested Dad. "I think you would find her kind and loving."

"I've never said that she wasn't nice," Paula protested. "It's just that she isn't my mother, so I don't know why I have to treat her as if she is."

Paula's father looked at her with sadness. "No, she's not your mother," he admitted. "But your mother is gone, and there is nothing we can do about that. We just have to accept her death as a fact, whether we like it or not."

"But why did you have to bring Marian here?" Paula asked, choking back tears. "And just before Mother's Day!"

Dad nodded understandingly. "Tomorrow is going to be a difficult day for all of us," he admitted. "But just remember, it's going to be a difficult day for Marian, too."

"Marian!" Paula snapped. "Why should this be a hard day for her? You and Kenny both act like you've forgotten all about Mom. Kenny even bought a Mother's Day card!"

"Don't you plan to do that, too?" Dad asked seriously.

Paula shook her head. "They don't make *stepmother* cards," she said with sarcasm.

A light tap on the door interrupted their conversation. It was Marian. "Look what was just delivered," she beamed, bringing in a small plant. "It's lovely. Thank you!" The card that came with it was signed in Kenny's handwriting, and it read "Your new family."

Paula bit her lower lip to keep herself under control. Quickly she slipped out the door. She felt anger building up inside of her, and yet she knew that her anger was wrong. She felt guilty. Somehow, she knew, she would eventually have to accept Marian for who she was—not her real mother, but someone who was willing to step in and take on a new family.

HOW ABOUT YOU? Is there someone you are not accepting? God has brought that person into your life for a purpose. Ask Him to help you to show love, kindness, and thoughtfulness at all times. Look for the good in the situation. It's there. R.J.

TO MEMORIZE: *"Behold, how good and how pleasant it is for brethren to dwell together in unity!"* Psalm 133:1 (NKJV).

MAY

13

No Stepmother Card

(Continued from yesterday)

FROM THE BIBLE:

I will lift up my eyes to the hills—
From whence comes my help?
My help comes from the Lord,
Who made heaven and earth.
He will not allow your foot to be moved;
He who keeps you will not slumber.
Behold, He who keeps Israel
Shall neither slumber nor sleep.
The Lord is your keeper;
The Lord is your shade at your right hand.
The sun shall not strike you by day,
Nor the moon by night.
The Lord shall preserve you from all evil;
He shall preserve your soul.
The Lord shall preserve your going out and your coming in
From this time forth, and even forevermore.

Psalm 121, NKJV

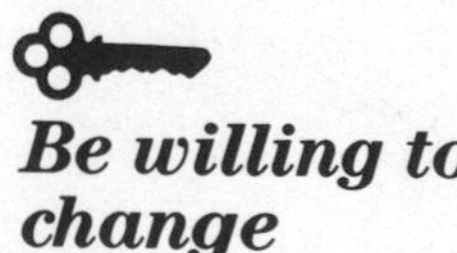

Be willing to change

PAULA WENT outside and called loudly for her brother. She wanted to talk with Kenny and let him know what she thought about his really dumb idea—sending a plant to a woman who wasn't their mother.

"But tomorrow is Mother's Day," protested Kenny. "I thought our new mom should get flowers just like everybody else."

"She's not our mom," Paula retorted. "She's Dad's wife."

Kenny shrugged his shoulders. "Well, she lives here and she's really nice," he said, "so I just wanted to do it."

"But you didn't have any right putting *my* name on that card!" Paula fumed.

"I didn't put your name on the card," responded Kenny. "I just wrote that it was from her new family."

"Well, she thinks I'm in on it," Paula insisted.

"That's what I wanted her to think," Kenny admitted. "You see, I heard her and Dad praying last night. And she asked God to help you to love her soon."

Suddenly Paula felt ashamed—terribly ashamed! Even little Kenny acted more mature than she did. "I'm sorry, Lord," she whispered. "Help me to love as You would." Maybe she wouldn't be able to call Marian "Mother"—at least not right away. But with God's help she was going to be like a daughter, a Christian daughter.

Hurrying into the house, she called for Kenny. "Here," she said, pulling some money from her pocket. "If the 'new family' is going to send flowers, I'd better pitch in and pay for my share." Suddenly Paula felt good inside.

HOW ABOUT YOU? Do you sometimes know your attitude is wrong, but you refuse to change? That makes you unhappy, doesn't it? Admit when you are wrong. Then make a definite effort to correct those wrongs. Remember, God is there to help you. R.J.

TO MEMORIZE: *"My help comes from the* LORD, *who made heaven and earth"* Psalm 121:2 (NKJV).

MAY

14

A Gift for Mother

FROM THE BIBLE:

You children must always obey your fathers and mothers, for that pleases the Lord. Fathers, don't scold your children so much that they become discouraged and quit trying. You slaves must always obey your earthly masters, not only trying to please them when they are watching you but all the time; obey them willingly because of your love for the Lord and because you want to please him. Work hard and cheerfully at all you do, just as though you were working for the Lord and not merely for your masters, remembering that it is the Lord Christ who is going to pay you, giving you your full portion of all he owns. He is the one you are really working for. And if you don't do your best for him, he will pay you in a way that you won't like—for he has no special favorites who can get away with shirking.

Colossians 3:20-25, TLB

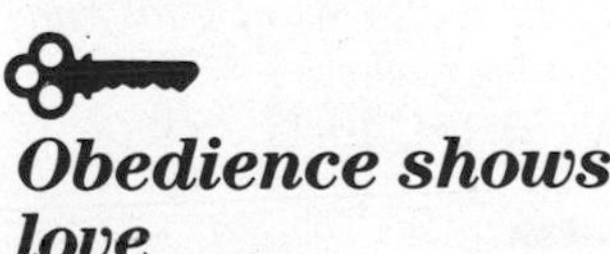

Obedience shows love

ONE SATURDAY morning Dan came storming out of the house. Stomping across the porch, he plopped himself down on the top step. His sister, Nancy, found him there. She suggested that they go and buy their mother a present because the next day was Mother's Day. "Can't," Dan said crossly. "Mom says I can't leave the house."

"Why not?" Nancy asked. "What did you do?"

"Just what she told me," Dan grumbled. "I cleaned my closet. No! She said I had to do it over again and do it right. I told her it was my closet, and it suited me, so it ought to suit her! But she said I was rude and to get busy and do it over. Well, I did, and when I got done, I asked, 'Now does it suit you?' She said my closet did, but not my attitude. So I have to stay home today."

"Oh, Dan," moaned Nancy, "this spoils everything. Look—I'll go ask her if you can go to the store with me."

Nancy went into the house, but when Mother said no, Nancy sassed her mother several times. As a result, she got grounded, too.

After dinner the next day, Mother gave Grandma Pratt, who was spending the day with them, a beautiful sweater. "Mom, we wanted to get you something yesterday," Nancy explained, "but you wouldn't let us go to the store."

"I didn't want a gift from you, children," said Mother.

"You didn't?" asked Dan. "Why not? You gave your mother a present."

"Well, I love her," answered Mother. "How do you show love for someone?"

"Um, give them presents and stuff," stammered Dan.

"Oh, Dan, that isn't right," said Nancy slowly. "It's like Dad read from the Bible last night: 'If you love Me, keep My commandments.' I guess we didn't act like we loved Mom or Jesus yesterday. I'm sorry, Mom—honest I am! I'm going to prove it by acting like I love you. You'll see!"

"Me, too," added Dan. "Will you forgive me?"

"Of course I will," answered Mother.

HOW ABOUT YOU? Can your parents tell by your actions that you love them? Have you told them lately—not by words, but by quick and cheerful obedience—that they are precious to you? Right now ask God to help you obey. A.L.

TO MEMORIZE: *"Children, obey your parents in the Lord: for this is right"* Ephesians 6:1.

MAY

15

Mal-nourished Christians

FROM THE BIBLE:

Say there! Is anyone thirsty? Come and drink—even if you have no money! Come, take your choice of wine and milk—it's all free! Why spend your money on food that doesn't give you strength? Why pay for groceries that do you no good? Listen and I'll tell you where to get good food that fattens up the soul! Come to me with your ears wide open. Listen, for the life of your soul is at stake. I am ready to make an everlasting covenant with you, to give you all the unfailing mercies and love that I had for King David . . . . As the rain and snow come down from heaven and stay upon the ground to water the earth, and cause the grain to grow and to produce seed for the farmer and bread for the hungry, so also is my Word. I send it out and it always produces fruit. It shall accomplish all I want it to, and prosper everywhere I send it.
Isaiah 55:1-3, 10-11, TLB

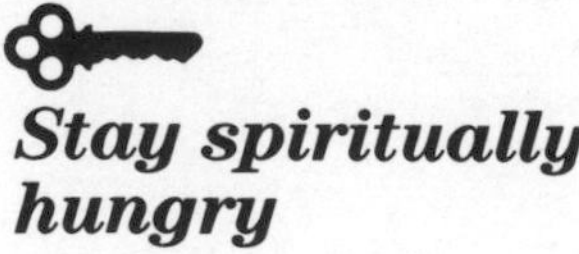

Stay spiritually hungry

KRAIG CALLED his mother into the living room, where he was watching a TV program showing malnourished children in an African country. "They must be so hungry!" he exclaimed. "The man said some people go for a week without food. How do they stand it?"

"Well, in some cases they may not always *feel* as hungry as they actually are," said Mother. "When you don't eat for a long time, the hungry feeling dulls and goes away after a while. So starving people may not *feel* terribly hungry, even though they desperately need food."

That night after dinner Dad said, "Instead of our usual devotions, I thought we could each share something we've learned from our own personal devotions recently. Kraig, why don't you start?"

Kraig squirmed in his chair. "Well, Dad, I guess I haven't been keeping up with my devotions very much lately."

"Why not?" asked Dad.

"I don't know. I guess the Bible's just too hard to understand, and . . ." Kraig hesitated. "And sometimes it's downright boring," he added frankly.

"Kraig," Mother said, "do you remember the starving people we saw on TV today?" He nodded and she continued. "Even though they were starving to death and hadn't eaten for days, they possibly didn't feel terribly hungry. It's the same with the Bible—if you stop reading faithfully, your hunger for God's teaching will fade, even though you need it more than ever. But the more you read it, the more interesting you'll find it, and the more you'll want to continue reading."

"Really?" Kevin asked. "I guess my hunger has been pretty dull lately. I'm going to start reading my Bible to work up my appetite again."

HOW ABOUT YOU? How hungry are you for God's Word? Do you sometimes feel like you don't need to read your Bible? Don't become an undernourished Christian. Be sure to keep your appetite sharp by reading your Bible every day. The more you read it, the more interested in it you'll become. D.M.

TO MEMORIZE: *"Blessed are they which do hunger and thirst after righteousness: for they shall be filled"* Matthew 5:6.

MAY

16

The Race of Life

FROM THE BIBLE:

Endure hardship with us like a good soldier of Christ Jesus. No one serving as a soldier gets involved in civilian affairs—he wants to please his commanding officer. 2 Timothy 2:3-4, NIV

Therefore, since we are surrounded by such a great cloud of witnesses, let us throw off everything that hinders and the sin that so easily entangles, and let us run with perseverance the race marked out for us. Let us fix our eyes on Jesus, the author and perfecter of our faith, who for the joy set before him endured the cross, scorning its shame, and sat down at the right hand of the throne of God.
Hebrews 12:1-2, NIV

Be serious about serving God

"GRANDPA!" Joey called as he burst into the house. "Our school is sponsoring a big race, and I'm going to run in it!"

Grandpa Jones chuckled as he looked up from reading his Bible. "You'd better slow down, or you'll be worn out before the race starts," he teased.

"It's in four weeks," said Joey, "and first prize is twenty dollars! That would buy lots of candy!"

Grandpa looked concerned. "If you're serious about running, you'd better cut down on junk foods," he said. "I ran a few races in my college days, and I remember the coach emphasizing the importance of a good diet."

"My gym teacher said the same thing," said Joey, "and I guess I see his point. But how can I ever live without candy bars and sodas and taco chips for four whole weeks?" He said, groaning. "Couldn't I have them just once in a while?"

"I think you're looking at it the wrong way," replied Grandpa. "There's no law against a runner eating junk food before a race. It's just that if you're really serious about winning, you'll cut out anything that doesn't help you reach your goal."

Joey thought for a moment. "I really do want to win that race," he said finally. "I guess candy and snacks aren't as important to me as the prize. There's really no sense running if I don't do everything I can to try to win."

"That's an important truth," Grandpa said, nodding, "and it can be applied to spiritual things, too. Sometimes I hear you complain because you can't do some of the things your unsaved friends do, Joey. But if we really want to reach the goal—that of becoming like Jesus and serving Him—we won't mind doing without a few harmful or unnecessary activities in order to please the Lord."

"I see what you mean," said Joey thoughtfully. "I need to start being as serious about serving the Lord as I am about winning that race!"

HOW ABOUT YOU? Are there things that keep you from doing your best in your Christian "race"? Places you want to go? TV programs you want to watch? Some things may not in themselves be sinful, but if they keep you from serving the Lord, they're wrong for you. Make up your mind to get serious about serving God. Put away those things that get in the way. S.K.

TO MEMORIZE: *"Let us throw off everything that hinders . . . and let us run with perseverance the race marked out for us"* Hebrews 12:1 (NIV).

17

The Race of Life

(Continued from yesterday)

FROM THE BIBLE:
According to my earnest expectation and hope that in nothing I shall be ashamed, but that with all boldness, as always, so now also Christ will be magnified in my body, whether by life or by death. For to me, to live is Christ, and to die is gain.
Philippians 1:20-21, NKJV

For I am already being poured out as a drink offering, and the time of my departure is at hand. I have fought the good fight, I have finished the race, I have kept the faith. Finally, there is laid up for me the crown of righteousness, which the Lord, the righteous Judge, will give to me on that Day, and not to me only but also to all who have loved His appearing.
2 Timothy 4:6-8, NKJV

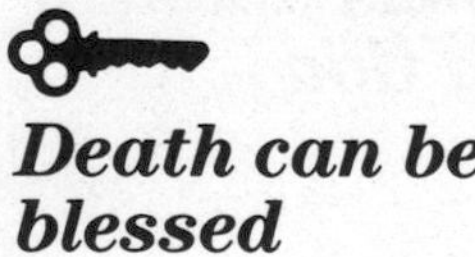

Death can be blessed

THOUGH JOEY didn't win first prize in the big race at school, he did win the ten dollar second prize, and he was glad he had worked so hard to prepare for the race. His happiness did not last long, however, for a few days after the race, Grandpa Jones had to be taken to the hospital. Joey was solemn as he entered his grandfather's hospital room after school one day. "Hi, Joey!" Grandpa said weakly. "It's good to see you!"

"I'm glad to see you, too, Grandpa," replied Joey with a smile. "I sure wish you'd get better and come home. I miss you!"

Grandpa closed his eyes and sighed. "There's nothing I want more than to go home—to my heavenly home, I mean," he said softly.

Joey frowned. "You mean you want to . . . to die? I don't understand."

"You will someday." Grandpa smiled. "When your body is old and worn-out like mine, you'll look forward to having a new body and going to be with Jesus in your new home."

"No!" Joey said, shaking his head. "I don't ever want to get old and sick."

Grandpa Jones smiled at the boy. "Seems awful to you, doesn't it?" he asked. "Do you remember when you ran that race last Saturday? How did you feel when you were almost to the finish line?"

Joey couldn't help grinning. "To tell you the truth, pretty bad," he replied. "My legs were sore, my chest hurt, I was all hot and sweaty, and I wanted a drink of water." Then he added, "But in a way I felt great because I knew the race was almost over, and I knew I had done my best."

"Don't you see, Joey?" said Grandpa gently. "That's exactly how I feel. Even though my body is tired and full of pain, I'm happy because I can see the finish line up ahead. I've been saved by grace through Jesus Christ, and I can't wait to finally see Him and all the wonderful things He has prepared for me."

HOW ABOUT YOU? Do you ever think about growing old and dying? You shouldn't be afraid if you know Jesus as your Savior. Then dying will be just a matter of "crossing the finish line" and receiving a reward for the work you have done for God. S.K.

TO MEMORIZE: *"I have finished the race, I have kept the faith. Now there is in store for me the crown of righteousness, which the Lord, the righteous Judge, will award to me on that Day"*
2 Timothy 4:7-8 (NIV).

MAY

18

Cause for Fear

FROM THE BIBLE:

I, Wisdom, give good advice and common sense. Because of my strength, kings reign in power, and rulers make just laws.
Proverbs 8:14-16, TLB

Blessed be the name of God forever and ever, for he alone has all wisdom and all power. World events are under his control. He removes kings and sets others on their thrones. He gives wise men their wisdom, and scholars their intelligence. He reveals profound mysteries beyond man's understanding. He knows all hidden things, for he is light, and darkness is no obstacle to him.
Daniel 2:20-22, TLB

For this has been decreed by the Watchers, demanded by the Holy Ones. The purpose of this decree is that all the world may understand that the Most High dominates the kingdoms of the world, and gives them to anyone he wants to, even the lowliest of men!
Daniel 4:17, TLB

"MY SOCIAL STUDIES teacher told us to watch that TV special about nuclear war," said Marianne. "We're going to discuss it tomorrow."

"I'm not sure that's a program I'd choose to watch," Mother replied, "but since it's an assignment, we'll watch it together. That way we can answer your questions."

Marianne didn't know much about nuclear warfare before she saw the program. What she saw was scary. She was glad her family was with her. The program showed fire and destruction everywhere, with complete cities, entire buildings, and whole families wiped out in a few seconds by a nuclear blast. Marianne shivered. "Why would men want to destroy each other that way?" she asked, when the show ended.

"I don't know," Dad replied, "but without Christ, man's heart is evil. He thinks only of himself. He wants to control things and run them his way."

"Oh, wow!" Marianne was still shivering. "I don't think I'll be able to sleep tonight!"

"We need to remember that God is in control of everything," Mother reminded her. "Man can do only what God allows him to do. God has the final say as to when and how the world will end."

"That's right," Dad agreed. "That reminds me of the twenty-eighth verse of Matthew, chapter ten. It tells us not to fear those who can kill the body, but rather to fear Him who can destroy the body and soul."

"I guess I thought that was a good verse for missionaries," said Marianne."

"It's a good verse for *all* of us," Dad replied. "It's a warning to those who are not Christians. They have real cause for fear. If someone kills their bodies, their soul will go to hell where they will be in torment forever—much worse than nuclear warfare. For us who are Christians, the verse is a comfort, reminding us that all we can suffer is physical death, and then our souls go to heaven."

"I'm sure glad I'm a Christian," said Marianne. She yawned. "I guess I'll sleep after all."

HOW ABOUT YOU? Does the thought of nuclear warfare frighten you? Remember that nothing can happen without God's permission. But if you're not a Christian, you should be afraid. The day *after* you die will be too late to accept Christ. Salvation is for today. Don't put it off. J.H.

TO MEMORIZE: *"How shall we escape, if we neglect so great salvation?"* Hebrews 2:3.

The unsaved are in danger

MAY

19

Shall I Tell?

FROM THE BIBLE:

Saul now urged his aides and his son Jonathan to assassinate David. But Jonathan, because of his close friendship with David, told him what his father was planning. "Tomorrow morning," he warned him, "you must find a hiding place out in the fields. I'll ask my father to go out there with me, and I'll talk to him about you; then I'll tell you everything I can find out." The next morning as Jonathan and his father were talking together, he spoke well of David and begged him not to be against David. "He's never done anything to harm you," Jonathan pleaded. "He has always helped you in any way he could. Have you forgotten about the time he risked his life to kill Goliath, and how the Lord brought a great victory to Israel as a result? You were certainly happy about it then. Why should you now murder an innocent man? There is no reason for it at all!" Finally Saul agreed, and vowed, "As the Lord lives, he shall not be killed."

1 Samuel 19:1-6, TLB

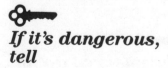

If it's dangerous, tell

DEREK PROBABLY wouldn't have found out about Kevin if he hadn't run out of notebook paper in the middle of his homework that Thursday night. His dad drove him to the drugstore to get some paper, and that's when Derek saw his friend standing on the corner with some other boys—smoking! "Oh, hi," Kevin mumbled, trying to hide the cigarette behind his back.

"Hi," Derek said. Then he walked quickly into the store and found the school supply section, bought what he needed, and ran out the door to meet his dad. But he couldn't get the sight of Kevin out of his mind. Kevin was a Christian!

Derek was just finishing his homework when the phone rang. It was Kevin. "Look, Derek," he said, "just pretend you didn't see me tonight, OK? It doesn't mean anything, you know. I only smoke when I'm with those guys. They think you're really out of it if you don't smoke!"

"Then don't hang around with them!" urged Derek.

"Yeah, well . . . just promise me you won't tell anyone," demanded Kevin, "and I'll work it out."

Derek couldn't promise, and he thought about Kevin the rest of the evening. He prayed about him, too. He didn't usually tell secrets when a friend asked him not to, but this was different. He knew Kevin needed help. He knew Kevin's parents wouldn't want him smoking. He knew it was bad for Kevin's health.

Derek thought of the Bible verse that said Christians were to bear one another's burdens. It was up to him to help Kevin. First, he'd tell Kevin that he'd be willing to go with him to talk to his parents or some other adult. If Kevin said no, then he'd tell Kevin he was going to an adult himself. Yes, there was a time not to break a confidence, but there was also a time when someone had to reach out and help.

HOW ABOUT YOU? Have you ever been in a situation when you couldn't decide whether or not it was right to tell something you knew? If a person shares something with you in confidence, but that "something" is dangerous, you should tell. First, do as Derek planned to do—tell your friend that you must share the problem with an adult. Then offer to go with your friend to get help from a parent, a pastor, or a Sunday school teacher. L. W.

TO MEMORIZE: *"Bear one another's burdens, and so fulfill the law of Christ"* Galatians 6:2 (NKJV).

MAY

20

Cheese and Skates

FROM THE BIBLE:
Since you have been chosen by God who has given you this new kind of life, and because of his deep love and concern for you, you should practice tenderhearted mercy and kindness to others. Don't worry about making a good impression on them but be ready to suffer quietly and patiently. Be gentle and ready to forgive; never hold grudges. Remember, the Lord forgave you, so you must forgive others. Most of all, let love guide your life, for then the whole church will stay together in perfect harmony. Let the peace of heart which comes from Christ be always present in your hearts and lives, for this is your responsibility and privilege as members of his body. . . . And whatever you do or say, let it be as a representative of the Lord Jesus, and come with him into the presence of God the Father to give him your thanks.
Colossians 3:12-17, TLB

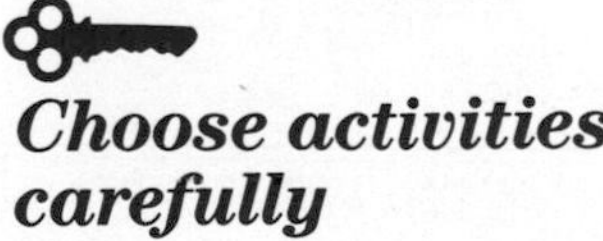

Choose activities carefully

CONNIE SHUDDERED as she watched her father put cheese on the mousetrap and set it. She hated to think of the trap snapping down on a mouse, but she hated the thought of mice living in the house, too. "Dad," she said, "may I go roller-skating with Ellen tonight? They're going to Colewell, and it's only three dollars."

Dad replied, "We've heard that things get pretty wild at that rink sometimes, so we'd rather you didn't go there."

"Oh, you never let me do anything!" stormed Connie. "What's wrong with going skating?"

Dad held up the mousetrap and pointed to the cheese in it. "What's wrong with this cheese?"

"Nothing that I know of," replied Connie, surprised.

"You're right," agreed Dad. "It's perfectly good, wholesome cheese. When a mouse comes along, that's all he'll care about. He won't notice the spring, or the wood, or the wires that make up the trap." Dad took a pencil and touched the cheese. Snap! Connie jumped as the trap closed on the pencil. "And when he takes a bite, he'll be caught," continued Dad. He set the trap aside. "Roller skating is fun and good exercise, and there's nothing wrong with it," he added. "The trouble is, it could lure you into a trap. It could place you in bad company where worldly music influences you, and where your companions would be doing things displeasing to God. From what we hear, there are often fights at the Colewell rink, and drugs and alcohol are widely used. If you want to skate, you can go to the local rink. I haven't heard any bad reports about it."

Connie sighed, but as she looked at the mousetrap, she knew her father was right. Going to the city sounded exciting, but nothing was worth getting caught in a trap.

HOW ABOUT YOU? Do you like to skate? Good—unless it puts you in a place displeasing to the Lord. Do you like to bowl? Fine—unless the people you bowl with tempt you to do wrong things. Do you like to play ball? Great—unless it keeps you from church or some activity where the Lord wants you. Do you like to chatter with friends? Nice—unless they tempt you to gossip or displease God in some way. Make sure the wholesome activity you choose does not lure you into a trap where you'll be tempted to sin. H.M.

TO MEMORIZE: *"Whatever you do, do it all for the glory of God"* 1 Corinthians 10:31 (NIV).

21
The Hibernating Christian

FROM THE BIBLE:
And do this, knowing the time, that now it is high time to awake out of sleep; for now our salvation is nearer than when we first believed. The night is far spent, the day is at hand. Therefore let us cast off the works of darkness, and let us put on the armor of light. Let us walk properly, as in the day, not in revelry and drunkenness, not in licentiousness and lewdness, not in strife and envy. But put on the Lord Jesus Christ, and make no provision for the flesh, to fulfill its lusts.
Romans 13:11-14, NKJV

Always act like a Christian

KEVIN LIVED in two completely different worlds. At home and church he was "Kevin the Christian." He sang in the junior choir, led in devotions, and memorized verses. At school he was "Kevin the Kool Kid." He laughed at dirty jokes, used swear words now and then, and hoped nobody would realize that he went to church and Sunday school. But he wasn't happy with his double life. *I don't even like myself,* Kevin thought as he chopped at the freshly plowed earth in the garden.

"Make that row a little deeper." Dad interrupted his thoughts, and Kevin pushed the hoe blade deeper into the earth. When he brought it up, he exclaimed, "Look here Dad! I just dug up a toad!" Kevin poked at the flabby mass of skin. The toad offered no resistance. "Is he dead?"

"No," said Dad, bending over the toad. "Just sleepy. He's been hibernating, the ground isn't warm enough yet to wake him up.

"Wake up, silly toad." Kevin pushed it with his foot. "I could cut you in two, and you'd just lie there and let me."

"He doesn't realize the danger." Dad leaned on his hoe as he added, "He reminds me of some Christians I know."

Kevin was puzzled. "How?"

"God intended for toads to be cold-blooded. Their blood is always the same as their surroundings. But God did not intend for His children to be cold-blooded. We are not to be controlled by our surroundings."

Kevin looked at the ground.

"Some people act like Christians only when they're with Christians." Kevin could feel his dad's eyes on him. "When they're in the world, surrounded by sin, they hibernate. The sad part is, that like this toad, they're unaware of danger. A hibernating Christian is easy prey for the devil."

Kevin gulped. Was it possible Dad knew more than Kevin had thought? "I see what you mean, Dad." As he dug a hole and put the toad in it to continue his nap, Kevin said, "Good-bye 'Kevin the Kool Kid.' 'Kevin the Christian' just woke up."

HOW ABOUT YOU? Is your walk with the Lord controlled by those around you? Are you living a double life? Be a warm-blooded, faithful Christian, no matter how cold the world around you. B.W.

TO MEMORIZE: *"It is high time to awake out of sleep; for now our salvation is nearer than when we first believed"* Romans 13:11 (NKJV).

MAY

22

Mary's Disciple

FROM THE BIBLE:

Then He said to them all, "If anyone desires to come after Me, let him deny himself, and take up his cross daily, and follow Me. For whoever desires to save his life will lose it, but whoever loses his life for My sake will save it. For what advantage is it to a man if he gains the whole world, and is himself destroyed or lost? For whoever is ashamed of Me and My words, of him the Son of Man will be ashamed when He comes in His own glory, and in His Father's, and of the holy angels. Luke 9:23-26, NKJV

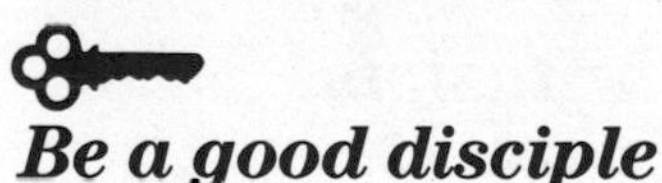

Be a good disciple

"MARY HAD a little lamb, little lamb, little lamb . . . ." Kelli stopped singing as she entered the kitchen. "Hi, Mom. I'm going to play with Josie as soon as I get my Sunday school lesson done, OK?" Mother nodded, and Kelli resumed her song as she went to her room and got out her Sunday school book. "It followed her to school one day, school one day, school one day. . . ." Then there was silence as she got busy with her work.

Soon the song began again. " 'It made the children laugh and play, laugh and play, laugh and play. . . .' Hi, Mom, I'm all done." Kelli stood in the doorway. She grinned at her mother. "Mary had a good disciple, didn't she?"

"A good what?" asked Mother.

"My Sunday school lesson is about the twelve disciples of Jesus. It says a disciple is a follower—and Mary's lamb followed her where she went," explained Kelli. "It was a good disciple."

Mother laughed. "I guess you're right," she agreed. "The lamb was so eager to be with Mary that it followed her right into the school. It didn't seem to be bothered by the children's laughter or jokes."

"Yeah." Kelli nodded solemnly. "We should follow Jesus like that, shouldn't we? We should do what He wants, even if kids at school think we're weird." She stood thoughtfully beside the door. Then she gave a happy little skip. 'Bye, Mom, I'm going over to Josie's now. I'll tell her about being Jesus' disciple and see if she wants to come with me to Sunday school tomorrow."

HOW ABOUT YOU? Do your classmates think you're a little strange when you bow your head and pray before you eat your lunch? Do they laugh if you talk about Jesus? Do they think you're a goody-goody because you go to church and Sunday school regularly? Be a good disciple—a good follower—of Jesus. Do the things that please Him, no matter what anyone says. H.M.

TO MEMORIZE: *"If anyone desires to come after Me, let him deny himself, and take up his cross daily, and follow me"* Luke 9:23 (NKJV).

23

Needed: Small Lights

FROM THE BIBLE:
Whoever can be trusted with very little can also be trusted with much, and whoever is dishonest with very little will also be dishonest with much. So if you have not been trustworthy in handling worldly wealth, who will trust you with true riches? And if you have not been trustworthy with someone else's property, who will give you property of your own?
Luke 16:10-12, NIV

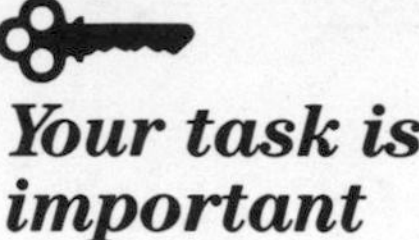

Your task is important

THE CHATTER of the grown-ups surrounded Marcie as she pushed her food around on her plate. Pastor James had come for dinner, and they were discussing their church's campaign to reach every family in their small town with the gospel message. A men's breakfast was being planned, and Dad was going to be master of ceremonies. Mother was going to sing at a women's luncheon. Dick, Marcie's big brother, was going to make posters to advertise a city-wide youth rally. Marcie sighed. *I wish I were big enough to help,* she thought.

Just then, Pastor James turned to Marcie. "Will you invite your friends to our special meetings?" he asked.

Marcie shrugged and nodded. "I suppose," she murmured, "but I wish I could do something important." Discouraged, she excused herself and left the table.

Later that night Mother tucked Marcie into bed. "Don't forget to fix the night-light for me," said Marcie.

"Right," said Mother, snapping off Marcie's bedside light and going out into the hall. "I'm plugging it in right now." Suddenly, a bright light filled the hall, spilling over into Marcie's room.

Marcie jumped out of bed and ran to the door. Instead of the usual little night-light, she saw a bright lamp plugged into the outlet. "Mom, that light's too bright."

Mother turned back. "Why, you're right," she agreed. She turned off the lamp and plugged in the usual night light. "You see," she said, "little lights are needed, just as big ones are. And little jobs need to be done, just as big ones do. Little people, as well as big ones, need to be invited to come to Jesus."

Marcie was thoughtful. "I'll invite all my friends," she decided. "I'll invite my whole class. I'll be a night-light."

HOW ABOUT YOU? Are you too small to preach? To organize meetings? To prepare a dinner? That's all right. Some day the Lord may ask you to do those things. Right now, perhaps you—not your father—can be a friend to the lonesome child down the block. You—not your mother—can invite your teacher and classmates to come to church. Whatever God asks you to do, do it for His glory. H.M.

TO MEMORIZE: *"Whoever can be trusted with very little can also be trusted with much"*
Luke 16:10 (NIV).

MAY

24

Behind Prison Bars

FROM THE BIBLE:
Even as he spoke, many put their faith in him. To the Jews who had believed him, Jesus said, "If you hold to my teaching, you are really my disciples. Then you will know the truth, and the truth will set you free." They answered him, "We are Abraham's descendants and have never been slaves of anyone. How can you say that we shall be set free?" Jesus replied, "I tell you the truth, everyone who sins is a slave to sin. Now a slave has no permanent place in the family, but a son belongs to it forever. So if the Son sets you free, you will be free indeed."
John 8:30-36, NIV

Avoid Satan's trap

BILL COULDN'T get the news report out of his mind. He kept wondering what he would do if he were in prison like the young men he saw in the television documentary. He remembered the picture of a great big room with over fifty beds in it, and he especially remembered the interviews with the men in solitary confinement.

Later as Bill talked with his dad about the TV report, he said, "Boy, Dad, I sure wouldn't want to end up in a place like that!"

"You know, Bill, all those young men in prison probably said the same things when they were your age. I'm sure none of them dreamed that some day they would be in a prison with no freedom." Dad paused for a few moments and then reminded Bill of something they had done the previous week. "You remember when we were having trouble with rats in the barn?"

"Sure," Bill responded. "You went to the hardware store and got the biggest mousetrap I've ever seen."

"That was a rat trap," answered Dad. "I baited it with some cheese and set it in the middle of the barn floor. Those rats we caught never thought about the danger. All they could think about was the good time they would have eating the cheese."

"I see what you mean," Bill interrupted. "Those men in prison never thought about the trouble they would get into when they committed their crimes.

"That's right! Satan baited his trap with things that looked attractive to them," said Dad, "and they were caught. The good news is that God still loves those fellows in prison. I've read of several men who accepted the Lord while behind prison bars."

"But how much better it would have been if they had accepted Christ as Savior while they were young," said Bill thoughtfully. "How much unhappiness they would have avoided if they never had to go to prison at all."

HOW ABOUT YOU? Do you sometimes think it would be fun to see if you could get away with drinking? Trying drugs? Hurting someone? Remember that every criminal behind bars was once young like you, never dreaming he would end up in prison some day. Don't let Satan catch you in his trap of doing "little" bad things now. Accept Jesus as your Savior and pattern your life after Him. Enjoy the freedom He provides. C.V. M.

TO MEMORIZE: *"If the Son sets you free, you will be free indeed"* John 8:36 (NIV).

MAY

25

Tools and Talents

FROM THE BIBLE:

For by the grace given me I say to every one of you: Do not think of yourself more highly than you ought, but rather think of yourself with sober judgment, in accordance with the measure of faith God has given you. Just as each of us has one body with many members, and these members do not all have the same function, so in Christ we who are many form one body, and each member belongs to all the others. We have different gifts, according to the grace given us. If a man's gift is prophesying, let him use it in proportion to his faith. If it is serving, let him serve; if it is teaching, let him teach; if it is encouraging, let him encourage; if it is contributing to the needs of others, let him give generously; if it is leadership, let him govern diligently; if it is showing mercy, let him do it cheerfully. Love must be sincere. Hate what is evil; cling to what is good. Be devoted to one another in brotherly love. Honor one another above yourselves.
Romans 12:3-10, NIV

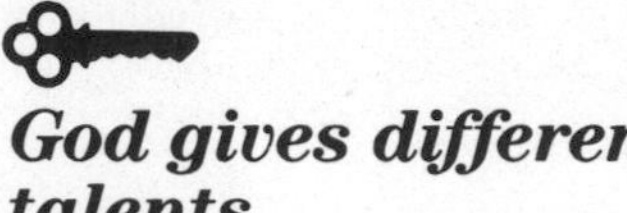

God gives different talents

"DID YOU KNOW Jana refuses to join our choir?" Nan asked her friend Connie. The two girls were having a little chatter session while they baked cookies at Nan's house. "Isn't that terrible? We need all the kids."

Connie sighed. "I know. I asked Mary to help with posters. She said no, too—says she's not artistic."

"It's too bad when no one wants to do things for the Lord," said Nan. As she rummaged through a drawer, her mother walked into the room. "Mom, do you know where the cookie cutters are?"

"Use this," Mother said, handing her a cheese cutter.

"Mother," she laughed, "you can't cut out cookies with a cheese cutter."

"Oh!" Mother acted surprised. "Well, here then," she said, taking a kitchen scissors from the drawer and handing it to Connie.

As Connie held the scissors uncertainly, Nan spoke. "Mother! I don't understand you. You know we need the cookie cutters!"

Mother smiled. "I'm just trying to show you something," she confessed. "You see, in a way, these tools all have the same job—they cut. And yet their jobs are all different—each is good for its own particular purpose." She found a cookie cutter and handed it to Connie. "Christians are something like that. In a way we all have the same task—to glorify the Lord and bring others to Him. But that doesn't mean we all have to do exactly the same thing."

"You heard us talking, didn't you?" asked Nan.

Mother nodded. "Jana's mother told me that Jana doesn't sing well because of a hearing problem. But I've seen some of the pictures she drew, and they were excellent! Maybe she'd like to help you with posters, Connie. As for Mary, I believe her Sunday school teacher said she brought more visitors to class this year than any other person."

"So we should let everyone serve in his own way, right?" asked Connie. "I'll try to remember that." H.M.

HOW ABOUT YOU? Do you think everyone should serve the Lord just the way you do? Remember that the Lord has given different talents to different people. All Christians should serve the Lord, but they may not do it your way. That's OK—just so each one serves God's way.

TO MEMORIZE: *"We have different gifts, according to the grace given us"* Romans 12:6 (NIV).

MAY

26

Kathy's Creation

FROM THE BIBLE:
In the beginning God created the heavens and the earth. . . . God saw all that he had made, and it was very good. And there was evening, and there was morning—the sixth day.
Genesis 1:1, 31, NIV

By faith we understand that the universe was formed at God's command, so that what is seen was not made out of what was visible. Hebrews 11:3, NIV

God created the world

THE HUM OF the sewing machine sounded throughout the house. "My creation is almost ready for you to see," said twelve-year-old Kathy. She had been measuring and cutting and stitching ever since she arrived home from school, only taking time out for supper.

Mother smiled. "I'm eager to see it—whatever it is," she said. "You've certainly spent a lot of time on it."

"Oh, you'll like it," said Kathy as she stood up and shook out the material she was using. "Ta-da! Here it is—my own special creation! It's an apron for Dad to use when he barbeques hamburgers or steak."

"Just what he needs," said Mother, "especially one that has flowered pockets and a polka dot bib."

Kathy laughed. "Some creation, isn't it?"

"You keep saying 'creation,' Kathy, and I know what you mean," said Mother. "But the dictionary says the main meaning of 'create' is 'to cause to exist'—or in other words to make something out of nothing. I like to remember this because it reminds me of God's power. He's the only One who can really create anything in that sense."

Kathy nodded. "I hadn't thought of that," she said as she looked at the apron she was holding. "OK, Mom. I'm a fashion designer, not a creator."

HOW ABOUT YOU? Do you realize what a great thing God did when He created the world and everything in it? When you draw a picture, sew something unusual, or cook some concoction no one ever heard of, remind yourself that you are not creating in the same way God did. Only He can create like that. G.W.

TO MEMORIZE: *"In the beginning God created the heavens and the earth"* Genesis 1:1 (NIV).

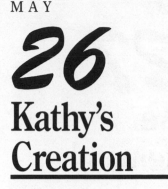

MAY

27

We Remember

FROM THE BIBLE:

Everyone must submit himself to the governing authorities, for there is no authority except that which God has established. The authorities that exist have been established by God. Consequently, he who rebels against the authority is rebelling against what God has instituted, and those who do so will bring judgment on themselves. For rulers hold no terror for those who do right, but for those who do wrong. Do you want to be free from fear of the one in authority? Then do what is right and he will commend you. For he is God's servant to do you good. But if you do wrong, be afraid, for he does not bear the sword for nothing. He is God's servant, an agent of wrath to bring punishment on the wrongdoer. Therefore, it is necessary to submit to the authorities, not only because of possible punishment but also because of conscience. This is also why you pay taxes, for the authorities are God's servants, who give their full time to governing.

Romans 13:1-6, NIV

Be thankful for your country

JANICE WAS AT the Memorial Day parade with her Uncle Phil. Her heart beat with excitement as the fire engines, old cars, bands, and floats came by. Men in uniform carried flags, and Janice saw "VFW" on one. "What is 'VFW'?" she asked her uncle.

"It stands for Veterans of Foreign Wars," Uncle Phil answered. "Remembering the soldiers is the whole reason we celebrate Memorial Day." Janice just shrugged. She didn't know much about soldiers.

After the parade they went to the cemetery where Uncle Phil's friend Don, who died in war, was buried. Uncle Phil carefully placed flowers on his friend's grave. "Doing this helps me remember that Don—and many soldiers—died so you and I can enjoy freedom," he said. "They fought for our country, defending the democratic way of life." Again Janice shrugged. Uncle Phil noticed and decided to be practical. "They died so we have the freedom to be what we want to be and go where we want to go and spend our money the way we'd like—on houses, cars, church, or even on chocolate sodas," he said. "Let's stop at Varney's Ice Cream Village on the way home."

While they sipped cold drinks, Janice was quiet. "Before this, I never realized the meaning of Memorial Day," she said finally. "I mean, I've heard all the fancy words about fighting for democracy and stuff before, but nobody suggested that I had to be grateful to those soldiers for my milkshakes and candy bars and stuff."

Uncle Phil smiled. "It's important to be grateful to those who died for our country," he said, "and it's even more important to be grateful to God. He's the one who has given us the privilege and blessing of living in a free land." Solemnly, Janice nodded.

HOW ABOUT YOU? Does Memorial Day mean more to you than just a day off from school and a nice parade? It should. It's time to remember, with gratitude, those brave men who gave their lives so that you can enjoy so many good things. They're gone now, so you can't thank them. But maybe you know someone who fought for our country alongside those who died. If so, you can thank him. And you can thank God. Be sure to do that. C.Y.

TO MEMORIZE: *"Give everyone what you owe him: . . . if respect, then respect; if honor, then honor"* Romans 13:7 (NIV).

MAY

28

We Remember

(Continued from yesterday)

FROM THE BIBLE:

For this is what the Lord himself has said about his Table, and I have passed it on to you before: That on the night when Judas betrayed him, the Lord Jesus took bread, and when he had given thanks to God for it, he broke it and gave it to his disciples and said, "Take this and eat it. This is my body, which is given for you. Do this to remember me." In the same way, he took the cup of wine after supper, saying, "This cup is the new agreement between God and you that has been established and set in motion by my blood. Do this in remembrance of me whenever you drink it." For every time you eat this bread and drink this cup you are re-telling the message of the Lord's death, that he has died for you. Do this until he comes again.

1 Corinthians 11:23-26, TLB

THROUGH HER thoughts, Janice dimly heard the minister's voice. The Lord's Supper was being served, but Janice had always been bored during that time, and she allowed her mind to wander. She was thinking about the fun she'd had with Uncle Phil on Memorial Day.

After the service Janice looked for her uncle. "Hi, Uncle Phil," she said. "Remember all the things we did on Memorial Day—the parade and going to the cemetery and the ice cream and everything? I'm still thankful to God for my freedom—and my ice cream!"

"Great!" Uncle Phil smiled. "We did have a good time last Monday, didn't we? And today is an even more important memorial day."

"Today?" Janice was puzzled. "What do you mean?"

"Today we celebrated the Lord's Supper, or Communion," said Uncle Phil. "When we do this, we remember that the Lord Jesus died so our souls can be forever free."

"I never thought of this as a 'memorial day,' but I can see that you're right," said Janice. She wished she had listened better during the service. After this she would.

"Be sure to thank God for the freedom He gave you when He washed your sins away," advised Uncle Phil. "Thank Him, too, for all the spiritual blessings and privileges you have because of that freedom."

"I will," promised Janice. "On Monday I learned what I should think about on our country's Memorial Day, and today I learned what I should think about on the Christian's 'memorial day.' That's ever more important—after all, ice cream is good, but heaven is even better."

Uncle Phil grinned. He knew what she meant.

HOW ABOUT YOU? Does the Lord's Supper have meaning for you, or doesn't it hold your interest? Jesus died and paid the price for your freedom from sin. Because of that, you may have your sins forgiven, peace in any circumstance, God's watchful care over you, and best of all, eternity in heaven. You should remember what He's done for you with reverence and thanksgiving. The communion service is a special time for doing that. C.Y.

TO MEMORIZE: *"And you shall know the truth, and the truth shall make you free"* John 8:32 (NKJV).

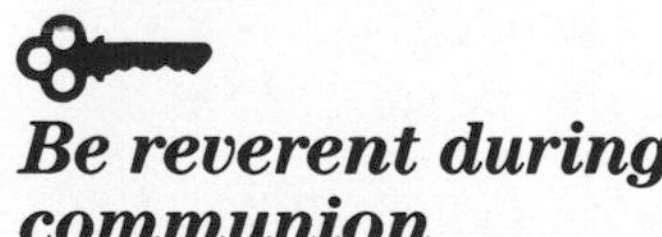

Be reverent during communion

MAY

29

Iron Shoes

FROM THE BIBLE:

And of Asher he said: "Asher is most blessed of sons; let him be favored by his brothers, and let him dip his foot in oil. Your sandals shall be iron and bronze; as your days, so shall your strength be. There is no one like the God of Jeshurun, Who rides the heavens to help you, And in His excellency on the clouds. The eternal God is your refuge, and underneath are the everlasting arms; He will thrust out the enemy from before you, and will say, 'Destroy!' "

Deuteronomy 33:24-27, NKJV

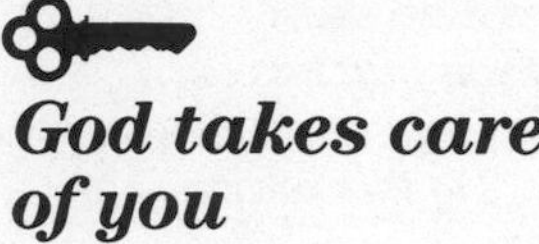

God takes care of you

"I NEED NEW gym shoes. My old ones are all worn-out," announced Kurt as he sat down after dinner one evening.

"So they are!" exclaimed Mother. "I declare, I believe you go through more shoes than a centipede!"

Dad laughed. "Maybe you should have shoes of iron and brass, like Asher, the man we read about in devotions."

Kurt sighed. "My shoes are the least of my problems. Everything is going wrong lately. I can't understand my math, I have to sit between two girls in band, and my friend Ian is moving out of town. Worst of all, Dennis, my best friend, is still in the hospital. They think he might have something serious." Kurt was near tears.

"Oh, that's too bad," sympathized Mother, putting her arm around him.

"You really do need 'iron shoes' to get across those hard places," said Dad soberly, "and they're available!" He smiled at Kurt. "I'm not talking about literal shoes, of course. But, along with the message that Asher would have shoes of iron and brass, the Bible speaks of the greatness of God and the 'everlasting arms' with which He holds His children. I believe He was assuring Asher that he'd not only have the sturdy shoes he needed for the rough and hilly country he'd live in, but that God would also provide the 'spiritual shoes' needed for the battles of life."

"Right," agreed Mother, "and that promise applies to us, too. We can rest in God and trust Him in everything."

"Would you like to pray about your problems right now, Kurt?" asked Dad. Kurt nodded and they prayed together.

"Let's go to town and get those new gym shoes," said Mother when they had finished. "Each time you see them, they'll remind you that God will provide the needed 'shoes' to take care of your other problems, too."

HOW ABOUT YOU? Are your problems piling up? Too much homework? Someone ill? A divorce? A death? Does everything seem to be more than you can bear? God cares. He wants to hold and comfort you in His "everlasting arms." Trust Him to provide whatever you need to face your problems and to help you through them. H.M.

TO MEMORIZE: *"The eternal God is your refuge, and underneath are the everlasting arms"* Deuteronomy 33:27 (NKJV).

MAY

30

Decisions! Decisions!

"I REALLY WANT to take gymnastics," said Alice as she rode with her mother and brother to the grocery store, "but if I do, I'll have to quit the church quiz team."

"Well," said Mother, "I guess you'll just have to weigh the cost and decide which to do."

"The cost?" asked Alice. "The gymnastics lessons are free and so is quiz team."

"I mean the cost in terms of what you have to give up and what you'll receive in return," said Mother. "No matter what you do in life, it always has a price. If you choose the quiz team, it will cost gymnastic lessons and whatever friendships you might enjoy there with the other girls. If you choose gymnastics, it will cost you the enjoyment and value of studying the Bible and meeting new Christian friends."

While they shopped, Alice thought about her problem. Perhaps it might be possible to do both things. "Maybe I could leave gymnastics early and get to quiz practice late. Would that be so bad?" she wondered.

Her little brother, Jimmy, tugged at her sleeve. "Come and show me the candy," he begged, "so I can spend my birthday quarters."

Alice took Jimmy to the candy display, and he chose what he wanted. Then they went to the cashier, but the little boy suddenly shoved his money way down inside his pocket and held the candy in his other hand. "Jimmy, you have to give the money to the lady," Alice whispered.

Jimmy stubbornly shook his head. "Want to keep it," he muttered.

"Well, do you want to put the candy back?" asked Alice.

"No! I want it. Want my quarters, too!" Jimmy cried.

The cashier smiled. "We'd all like to do that—buy things and still keep our money.

Alice nodded. She understood how Jimmy felt. She was learning that it wasn't easy to wisely count the cost of her choices, but decisions did have to be made.

HOW ABOUT YOU? Do you have difficult choices to make? Pray about decisions. Then count the cost. What will you give up and what will you gain by your choice? There's always a price for choices and actions, but there are rewards, too. Choose the way you believe will please the Lord. C.R.

TO MEMORIZE: *"Choose for yourselves this day whom you will serve"* Joshua 24:15 (NKJV).

FROM THE BIBLE:
Now therefore, fear the Lord, serve Him in sincerity and in truth, and put away the gods which your fathers served on the other side of the River and in Egypt. Serve the Lord! And if it seems evil to you to serve the Lord, choose for yourselves this day whom you will serve, whether the gods which your fathers served that were on the other side of the River, or the gods of the Amorites, in whose land you dwell. But as for me and my house, we will serve the Lord. . . . If you forsake the Lord and serve foreign gods, then He will turn and do you harm and consume you, after He has done you good." And the people said to Joshua, "No, but we will serve the Lord!" So Joshua said to the people, "You are witnesses against yourselves that you have chosen the Lord for yourselves, to serve Him." And they said, "We are witnesses."
Joshua 24:14-22, NKJV

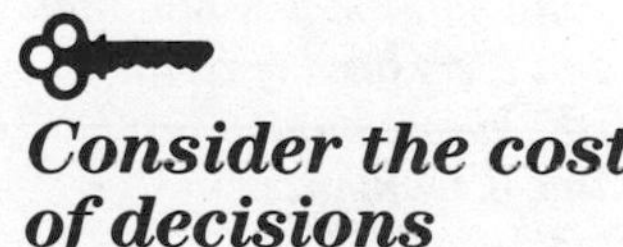

Consider the cost of decisions

MAY

31

Ugly but Beautiful

FROM THE BIBLE:

Dear brothers, don't be too eager to tell others their faults, for we all make many mistakes; and when we teachers of religion, who should know better, do wrong, our punishment will be greater than it would be for others. If anyone can control his tongue, it proves that he has perfect control over himself in every other way. We can make a large horse turn around and go wherever we want by means of a small bit in his mouth. And a tiny rudder makes a huge ship turn wherever the pilot wants it to go, even though the winds are strong. So also the tongue is a small thing, but what enormous damage it can do. A great forest can be set on fire by one tiny spark. And the tongue is a flame of fire. It is full of wickedness, and poisons every part of the body. And the tongue is set on fire by hell itself, and can turn our whole lives into a blazing flame of destruction and disaster. Men have trained, or can train, every kind of animal or bird that lives and every kind of reptile and fish, but no human being can tame the tongue.

James 3:1-8, TLB

Be "blind" to outward appearance

KEITH NUDGED JERRY and pointed to the lady coming down the walk. She had a lovely face, but she was wearing dark glasses and was accompanied by a large dog in a special harness. "Did you ever in your life see such an ugly mutt?" Keith said with scorn.

But Jerry, who loved dogs, just shrugged. He realized that the lady was blind, and he knew this must be a seeing eye dog. He had read about them in school but had never actually seen one in action. "I think he's neat," Jerry said. "He takes that lady wherever she wants to go."

To the boys' surprise, the lady stopped and spoke to them. "I heard you discussing my dog," she said. "This is Shawnee, and he's been taking me places for six years now. He's saved my life twice that I know of, and probably more times that I don't know about. He's always there when I need him, and he's a good listener, too."

"Wow," murmured Jerry.

The lady smiled. "I've been told that Shawnee is not a pretty dog," she said, "but even if he's the ugliest thing in the world to look at, he's still beautiful to me."

"I can see why you think that," agreed Keith.

"Yes," murmured the lady. "I'm very blessed."

"Blessed!" Keith blurted out. "But you're blind!"

The lady nodded. "Yes, but the accident that took away my physical sight gave me a different kind of sight. I no longer judge animals or people on what they look like. I'm blind to all that. Instead, I look at what they're like on the inside. That's what counts, not the outside."

After chatting a few minutes longer, the boys headed homeward. "That lady sure was nice," said Jerry, "and so was her dog. I'm going to try to never make fun of the way another person looks again."

"Me, too," agreed Keith. He grinned and added, "I won't even make fun of how a dog looks."

HOW ABOUT YOU? Do you ever laugh at people because they don't look as nice as you do? Do you look down on them because of scars or other physical handicaps? In a sense, God is "blind" to outward appearances. He cares about what is on the inside. That should be your concern, too. Never laugh at anyone for what he looks like. He may be more beautiful than you on the inside. D.M.

TO MEMORIZE: *"You, only You, know the hearts of all the sons of men"* 1 Kings 8:39 (NKJV).

JUNE

The Open Umbrella

FROM THE BIBLE:

The law of the Lord is perfect,
reviving the soul.
The statutes of the Lord are trustworthy,
making wise the simple.
The precepts of the Lord are right,
giving joy to the heart.
The commands of the Lord are radiant,
giving light to the eyes.
The fear of the Lord is pure,
enduring forever.
The ordinances of the Lord are sure
and altogether righteous.
They are more precious than gold,
than much pure gold;
they are sweeter than honey,
than honey from the comb.
By them is your servant warned;
in keeping them there is great reward.

Psalm 19:7-11, NIV

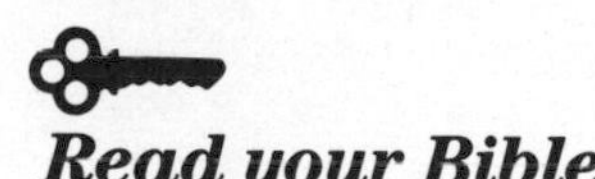

AS JERRY LEFT Mike's house, Mike's mother handed him a large paper bag. "Here are a few things your mother can put in her garage sale tomorrow," she said.

"Thanks," Jerry replied. Taking the bag in his arms, he started town the street. Before long, he felt something hit his face. A raindrop! "Oh, no!" he moaned. Clutching the bag tightly, he started to run, but soon he was soaked to the skin. Then the wet paper bag broke, scattering items over the ground. Jerry quickly gathered everything up in his arms and ran the rest of the way home, stopping several times to pick up objects that kept slipping from his grasp. When he finally reached his house, Mother looked at him in surprise.

"Why, Jerry, you're soaking wet! And what are all those things you're carrying?" she asked.

Jerry dumped his wet armload onto the table. "Just some things that Mike's mom sent over," he gasped. "See, there's a tennis racket, a book, and some shoes, and—" Jerry stopped short and stared at the table. There lay a new, green, perfectly good umbrella.

Mother laughed. "You mean you carried this umbrella all the way home in the rain, without even opening it?"

Jerry was embarrassed. "I guess I didn't even think of using it," he said with a grin. "I just thought of it as something I had to carry." He went to his room to change into dry clothes. When he came back, Mother was staring at the umbrella thoughtfully as she wiped it with a towel.

"You know, Son," she said, "God has used this incident to speak to me about something I haven't been using as I should—my Bible. Oh, I carry it back and forth to church on Sundays, but I'm reminded that it won't do me any good unless I open it and read it for myself."

"That goes for me too, Mom," said Jerry.

"How about reading a passage together right now?" suggested Mother.

"OK," said Jerry. "Then I'll clear the table!"

HOW ABOUT YOU? Do you have a Bible? Do you carry it with you to church? That's fine, but a closed Bible won't do you any good. It must be opened and read in order to help you. If you haven't been reading God's Word like you should, why not start today? You'll be glad you did! S.K.

TO MEMORIZE: *"The commands of the LORD are radiant, giving light to the eyes"* Psalm 19:8 (NIV).

JUNE

2

The Snapping Turtle

FROM THE BIBLE:

A fool gets into constant fights. His mouth is his undoing! His words endanger him. What dainty morsels rumors are. They are eaten with great relish! . . . Those who love to talk will suffer the consequences. Men have died for saying the wrong thing! . . . There are "friends" who pretend to be friends, but there is a friend who sticks closer than a brother.
Proverbs 18:6-8, 21, 24, TLB

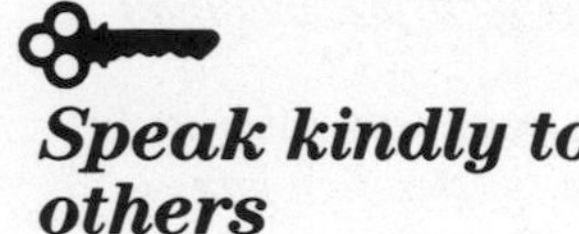

Speak kindly to others

LINDY LAY ON HER BED, sniffing. "Go away!" she snapped when her father tapped on her door.

"Don't you want to go fishing with me?" asked Dad.

Quickly, Lindy jumped to her feet and brushed at the tears with her fingers. "Oh, I do! Wait for me!"

Later as they sat on the riverbank waiting for the fish to bite, Dad asked, "Has something been bothering you, Honey?"

"Oh, Daddy," wailed Lindy, "nobody wants to be my friend anymore."

"Do you have any idea why?" Dad asked.

"No!" snapped Lindy. "They're all hateful!"

"Everybody?" Dad raised his eyebrows.

"Yes, everybody!" Lindy declared. "I—oh! Get away! Get away!"

"What is it?" Dad rushed to her side. A few feet away a turtle was glaring at her and snapping furiously. "Not a very friendly fellow, is he?" laughed Dad. "Leave him alone, Lindy, and he won't hurt you."

Lindy shuddered. "I don't like snapping turtles. Let's move. The fish aren't biting here anyway."

"Lindy," said Dad when they were settled in a new spot, "could it be that everyone is leaving you alone because you've been acting like a snapping turtle—glaring and snapping at anyone who dares to cross your path?"

"But, Daddy," Lindy began, "I—"

"No, let me finish," Dad interrupted. "When that turtle started snapping at us, what did we do?"

"We got out of his way," Lindy answered.

"And that's what your friends are doing—getting out of your way and leaving you alone," Dad replied. "The Bible says to have friends, you must be friendly."

The next day when Lindy came home from school, she was smiling. "You were right, Daddy," she said. "When I stopped snapping at my friends, they stopped getting out of my way."

HOW ABOUT YOU? Have people been avoiding you? Is it because you've been snapping at them? God's Word is filled with practical wisdom, and one thing it teaches is that your tongue can cause you all kinds of trouble. Check your attitude and your tongue. Ask God to help you use it to make friends instead of driving people away. B.W.

TO MEMORIZE: *"I said, 'I will watch my ways and keep my tongue from sin,' I will put a muzzle on my mouth"* Psalm 39:1 (NIV).

JUNE

3

Pass the Potatoes

FROM THE BIBLE:
Be careful not to do your "acts of righteousness" before men, to be seen by them. If you do, you will have no reward from your Father in heaven. . . . But when you give to the needy, do not let your left hand know what your right hand is doing, so that your giving may be in secret. Then your Father, who sees what is done in secret, will reward you. And when you pray, do not be like the hypocrites, for they love to pray standing in the synagogues and on the street corners to be seen by men. I tell you the truth, they have received their reward in full. But when you pray, go into your room, close the door and pray to your Father, who is unseen. Then your Father, who sees what is done in secret, will reward you. And when you pray, do not keep on babbling like pagans, for they think they will be heard because of their many words. Do not be like them, for your Father knows what you need before you ask him.
Matthew 6:1-8, NIV

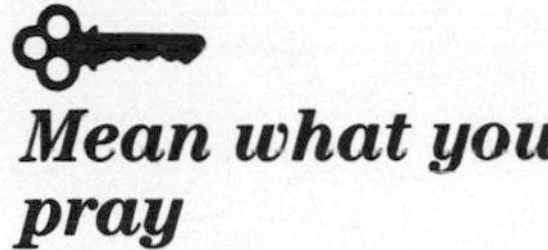

Mean what you pray

"WHY DID IT have to rain today, anyhow?" grumbled Brian when he came into the house after school. "We were supposed to play our first softball game of the season, and it was called off because of this silly storm!"

"I know you were looking forward to today's game," his mother said, "but there will be other games."

"Want to play a game with me?" his sister, Jill, offered.

"No," Brian snapped. "That's boring."

As the family was gathered around the table later, Brian's dad asked him to give thanks for the food. Brian bowed his head, "Dear heavenly Father, thank You for this food and for the beautiful day You have given us. Amen. Pass the potatoes."

"Oh, Brian," Jill said. "You always say the same thing!"

Brian scowled. "You're not supposed to criticize prayers!"

"I'm afraid Jill's right, though," said Mother. "It's become a routine with you. You don't even think about what you are saying."

"I do so," Brian argued.

"Brian, ever since you got home from school you've been complaining about the rain. Then you prayed and thanked the Lord for the 'beautiful' day! Something's wrong!"

Brian looked sheepish. "I guess I didn't think."

"The Bible tells us not to repeat prayers over and over when they have no meaning," said Dad. "I don't think thanking the Lord for the nice day had very much meaning for you, Son. You could have thanked the Lord for sending the rain for the farmers' crops, but it certainly wasn't honest to say you were thankful for the day."

Brian put his fork down. "I know you're right," he admitted. "Shall I pray again?"

Supper waited while Brian again led the family in prayer.

HOW ABOUT YOU? Do you rattle off the same things each time you pray? Wouldn't it become sort of boring if your friends said the same thing every time they talked to you? The Lord desires that you talk to Him about what you're thinking. He is a friend who has done much for you. Think about what you are saying when you pray. L. W.

TO MEMORIZE: *"And when you pray, do not keep on babbling like pagans, for they think they will be heard because of their many words"*
Matthew 6:7 (NIV).

JUNE

Owe No Man

FROM THE BIBLE:

My son, if you become surety for your friend, if you have shaken hands in pledge for a stranger, you are snared by the words of your own mouth; you are taken by the words of your mouth. So do this, my son, and deliver yourself; for you have come into the hand of your friend: go and humble yourself; plead with your friend. Give no sleep to your eyes, nor slumber to your eyelids. Deliver yourself like a gazelle from the hand of the hunter, and like a bird from the hand of the fowler.
Proverbs 6:1-5, NKJV

Render therefore to all their due: taxes to whom taxes are due, customs to whom customs, fear to whom fear, honor to whom honor. Owe no one anything except to love one another, for he who loves another has fulfilled the law. Romans 13:7-8, NKJV

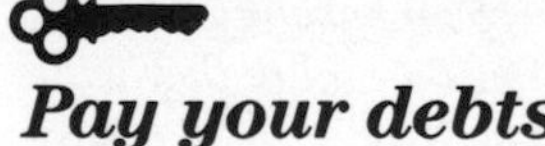

Pay your debts

"ALLOWANCE TIME!" Dad said as he entered his son's room.

Mark looked up and sighed. "Oh, OK," he said. "Just put it on the dresser. I'll get it in a minute."

"What's wrong?" Dad asked "Usually you're quite eager to get your allowance."

"What's the use?" said Mark sadly. "I can't buy anything with that money, anyway."

"Tell me about it," Dad said.

So Mark explained. "A few weeks ago, I was at the video arcade with Scott. I ran out of money, so he loaned me some. I meant to pay him back the next day, but I never got around to it." Dad frowned as Mark went on. "They had a sale on cassette tapes at the music shop. The clerk said I could buy a tape and pay half then and the other half later. I figured it would be only a week till I could pay the rest." He sighed. "But the next Saturday all the guys were going out for ice cream, and I didn't want to be left out, so . . ."

"So you spent your allowance on ice cream instead," finished Dad.

Mark nodded. "Yeah," he said glumly, "and now I owe so much money, that it'll be weeks before I have any to spend on myself."

"I hope you learned a lesson from all this," said Dad solemnly. "Its a biblical principle that it's best to go without something until you have the money to pay for it. You should borrow money only when it's absolutely necessary, and then you should repay it as quickly as possible."

"I guess you're right, Dad," admitted Mark. "I didn't even enjoy those things as much as I thought I would. What should I do now?"

"Divide your allowance between those you owe," Dad suggested, "after you take out your church offering, of course. Tell each one you'll be paying more every week. I think they'll be agreeable about waiting for the rest."

"Sounds good, Dad," Mark said as he picked up his money. "By the way, do you have any odd jobs I could do? I want to pay off my debts as quickly as I can!"

HOW ABOUT YOU? Have you been in the habit of borrowing money—a quarter here or a dollar there? Many people, even adults, have gotten into trouble because they borrowed money. It's far better to wait—and work—for the things you want. You'll be happier if you do. S.K.

TO MEMORIZE: *"Owe no one anything except to love one another"* Romans 13:8 (NKJV).

JUNE

5

Daily Benefits

BRAD RUBBED his eyes hard with his fists. He was not a baby. Just because he couldn't go to summer camp was no reason to cry. He stuffed the application in his pocket, straightened his shoulders, and entered the house.

"Is that you, Dave?" called his mother.

"Naw, it's just me," Brad called from the hall.

"I thought it might be your dad. He's gone to apply for a job." Mrs. Nelson smiled at her son.

"Won't do any good. He applied for a hundred already," Brad mumbled.

"Sooner or later he'll be sure to find one," Mother replied positively.

"Probably later, much later," Brad answered. Under his breath he added, ". . . after summer camp." Then he blurted out, "Why doesn't God give Dad a job? We're God's children. I thought He took care of His children."

Mother nodded. "He does. The bills are paid. We still have our home. We have each other. There may not be money for extras like summer camp, Brad, but God has given us many benefits."

"I can't see—" Brad stopped as Dad burst in.

"I got it!" He swung his wife around and around. "I got the job! The pay is good, and the benefits are great!"

"Put me down," Mother laughed. "Oh, God is so good."

"What are benefits?" Brad questioned.

"You might call them added blessings," Dad explained. "I mean things like health insurance, a retirement plan, paid holidays, and sick leave."

"What did you mean when you said God has blessed us with many benefits, Mom?" Brad looked puzzled.

"I was talking about health, love, joy, eternal life, the promise that He will supply all our needs—things like that," she explained. "Every day He gives us benefits."

HOW ABOUT YOU? Are you so busy looking at what you do not have, that you forget to be thankful for what God has given you? Every day we receive benefits (added blessings) from the Lord. You may not always have as much money as you want, but there are many things more important than money. Right now make a list of at least five benefits God has given to you. B.W.

TO MEMORIZE: *"Blessed be the Lord, who daily loadeth us with benefits"* Psalm 68:19.

FROM THE BIBLE:
I bless the holy name of God with all my heart. Yes, I will bless the Lord and not forget the glorious things he does for me. He forgives all my sins. He heals me. He ransoms me from hell. He surrounds me with lovingkingness and tender mercies. He fills my life with good things! My youth is renewed like the eagle's!
Psalm 103:1-5, TLB

Don't forget the benefits

JUNE

6

An Unjoyful Sound

FROM THE BIBLE:

Shout with joy before the Lord, O earth! Obey him gladly; come before him, singing with joy. Try to realize what this means—the Lord is God! He made us—we are his people, the sheep of his pasture. Go through his open gates with great thanksgiving; enter his courts with praise. Give thanks to him and bless his name. For the Lord is always good. He is always loving and kind, and his faithfulness goes on and on to each succeeding generation. Psalm 100, TLB

Choose good music

AS ERIC AND DARRIN worked together painting a raft they had built, Darrin started singing. "Where in the world did you learn that?" Eric asked.

"Oh, it's on the latest album by the Mid Knight Witches," answered Darrin. "I bought it yesterday at the mall."

Eric looked up. "But you're a Christian!"

"So? The Bible doesn't say you can't listen to Mid Knight Witches' songs," replied Darrin. "Besides, I don't pay attention to the words."

Eric looked surprised. "You must pay some attention to them. You just got the record yesterday, but you already know the words. Listen to what you're singing—'I'm going to steal you, kill you, chill you.' Those words sound awful brutal."

"They don't mean anything, Eric," protested Darrin.

"They must mean *something,*" retorted Eric. "It wouldn't be a hit song if they didn't!"

The conversation with Darrin still bothered Eric that night. As he sat down to supper, he told his parents what Darrin had said. "That's interesting," said Dad. "I just read an article in last night's paper about the Mid Knight Witches. The lead singer was quoted as saying he enjoyed the power the group had over young people's minds. He also said that violence was one of their major themes."

Eric was thoughtful for a few moments, and then he said, "Darrin told me that the Bible doesn't say anything about listening to Mid Knight Witches' music, but it does! The Lord tells us to make a joyful noise, and the Mid Knight Witches' album certainly isn't joyful!"

"It also says we are to make melody in our heart to the Lord," his mother reminded him. Eric smiled and nodded. He had some important verses to show Darrin!

HOW ABOUT YOU? What kind of music do you listen to on your radio? What kind of record albums do you buy? Do you think rock music is OK because you don't pay any attention to the words? Be careful! Often the lyrics in rock songs are not pleasing to the Lord. There are many good songs that are fun to sing. Listen to the right kind of music! L. W.

TO MEMORIZE: *"Speak to one another with psalms, hymns, and spitiual songs. Sing and make melody in your heart to the Lord."* Ephesians 5:19 (NIV).

JUNE

7

Smile, God Loves You

FROM THE BIBLE:

If you live that kind of life, you'll not limp or stumble as you run. Carry out my instructions; don't forget them, for they will lead you to real living. Don't do as the wicked do. Avoid their haunts—turn away, go somewhere else, for evil men can't sleep until they've done their evil deed for the day. They can't rest unless they cause someone to stumble and fall. They eat and drink wickedness and violence! But the good man walks along in the ever-brightening light of God's favor; the dawn gives way to morning splendor, while the evil man gropes and stumbles in the dark. Listen, son of mine, to what I say. Listen carefully. Keep these thoughts ever in mind; let them penetrate deep within your heart, for they will mean real life for you, and radiant health. Above all else, guard your affections. For they influence everything else in your life.

Proverbs 4:12-23, TLB

BRUCE DIDN'T FEEL like getting up, but he finally dragged himself out of bed, feeling more and more crabby as he dressed. He had a big frown on his face by the time he came to the breakfast table where his sister, Carin, and his parents were smiling and talking cheerfully. Sliding onto his chair, Bruce scowled. "Not oatmeal again!"

"How about eggs, then?" suggested Mom.

The frown on Bruce's face deepened. "I hate eggs, I hate oatmeal, I hate school, I hate everything," he growled.

The cheerful look left Carin's face, and the corners of her mouth drooped. "I hate a few things myself," she announced, "like this shirt. Do I have to wear it?"

Mom looked dismayed. "But it's practically new!" she exclaimed. "I thought you liked it."

"I like it," said Dad. He turned to Bruce. "I like yours, too. By the way, how about going to a ball game tonight?"

"Bruce always get to do things," complained Carin. "Mom, why can't we do something for once, like go shopping?"

"And get another shirt you don't like," sneered Bruce.

Mom sighed, and Carin glared. "Oh, you big—"

"Whoa!" called Dad. "Hold on here!" He turned to Bruce. "It occurs to me that we were all sitting happily at the table until you came with that big frown on your face. Your gloom has spread over the whole family."

"That's true," agreed Mom. "No part of your body can influence others as much as your face."

Bruce lifted his head. "I never thought of it that way."

As Mother set bowls of hot cereal before them, Dad added, "Since our faces affect others so much, wc should keep them as bright and cheerful as possible. You know the expression, 'Smile, God loves you.' That's really good advice. Before we eat this morning, let's ask the Lord to give us happy hearts so we are better able to smile."

HOW ABOUT YOU? Do you spread happiness and good will with a cheerful face? Or do you spread unhappiness and depression with scowls and frowns? What you feel in your heart usually shows on your face, so it's important to keep your heart right with the Lord. Before facing the world each day, spend time with God. C.Y.

TO MEMORIZE: *"A happy heart makes the face cheerful"* Proverbs 15:13 (NIV).

Spread happiness

JUNE

8

The Counselor Hunt

FROM THE BIBLE:

I can never be lost to your Spirit! I can never get away from my God! If I go up to heaven, you are there; if I go down to the place of the dead, you are there. If I ride the morning winds to the farthest oceans, even there your hand will guide me, your strength will support me. If I try to hide in the darkness, the night becomes light around me. For even darkness cannot hide from God; to you the night shines as bright as day. Darkness and light are both alike to you.

Psalm 139:7-12, TLB

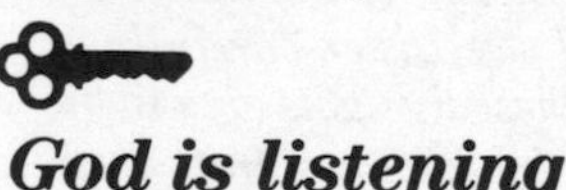

God is listening

JAMIE WAS having a wonderful time at camp with her best friend, Dawn. Every day there were new things to do, new games to play, and new friends to make. Their counselor, Mary, was just like a friend to the girls, and they had many good times together.

During supper one evening the counselors disappeared from the dining hall one by one. Then Mr. Ken, the camp director, explained that the counselors were hiding and the campers had a half hour to find them.

"Where shall we look first?" asked Jamie as they ran out of the building.

"Why don't we try looking near our cabin?" said Dawn. "Maybe Mary's somewhere around there."

Half an hour later, eighty-six kids and most of the counselors were grouped around the dining hall. Mr. Ken rang the bell, which was the signal for the counselors who hadn't been found to come out of hiding. Jamie and Dawn were astonished to see Mary pop out of a garbage can nearby.

"We must have walked right past there a dozen times," Jamie moaned. "I never even thought someone might be hiding in an old garbage can!"

Mary giggled. "I heard you going by once. I thought for sure you'd hear me laughing!"

When the girls in the cabin gathered for devotions that evening, Mary talked about the counselor hunt. "I heard some of you going by while I was hiding in that trash barrel. In fact, I heard what a lot of kids were saying. I don't think some of them would have talked the way they did if they had known a counselor was nearby," she said. "You know, when I was in that garbage can, I think I got a little idea of how God must feel when people forget He's listening. It's important to remember that He can always hear. He's always there even though we can't see Him."

HOW ABOUT YOU? How do you talk when there are no parents, teachers, or other adults around? When you're with your friends, do you say words that you're careful to avoid when your parents are with you? Make sure your speech is clean no matter who is nearby. God can hear you even when you're all alone. He's always listening! D.M.

TO MEMORIZE: *"Can anyone hide himself in secret places, so I shall not see him? says the LORD. Do I not fill heaven and earth?"*
Jeremiah 23:24 (NKJV).

JUNE

Darkness or Light

FROM THE BIBLE:
His life is the light that shines through the darkness—and the darkness can never extinguish it. God sent John the Baptist as a witness to the fact that Jesus Christ is the true Light. John himself was not the Light; he was only a witness to identify it. Later on, the one who is the true Light arrived to shine on everyone coming into the world. But although he made the world, the world didn't recognize him when he came.
John 1:5-10, TLB

Walk in God's light

MOTHS FLUTTERED around outside the screen door, so Michael quickly closed it as he came in. Suddenly his cat, Fluffy, spied a moth fluttering around the lamp. Fluffy couldn't reach the moth, but he watched intently as it circled the lampshade. "The moth wants the light, and Fluffy wants the moth," Dad said, chuckling.

"What makes moths want the light?" asked Michael.

"It's something God built into them," answered Dad. "They fly at night, so they have to find food at night. Most night-blooming flowers are white, and the white shows up in the darkness, especially when the moon is out. The moths are attracted by the light flowers."

"So the fact that they want light helps them find food?" asked Michael.

"That's right." Dad nodded. "The moth gets his food, and while he's at it, he's setting a good example for you."

"For me?" echoed Michael in surprise. "How?"

Dad smiled. "Well, the Bible tells us that God is perfectly holy. He is pure, wise, glorious, and perfect. From Him we get everything we need. God wants us to stay close to Him and away from the darkness. We need the light of God just as the moth needs the light to find the flowers. What would you say about a moth who hungrily flew around in the dark and wouldn't come to the light flowers for food?"

"I'd say something was wrong with a moth like that," answered Michael.

"Yet some people stay away from God and stumble around in darkness, spiritually," said Dad.

"You'd think people would at least know as much as moths!" Michael said with a grin.

HOW ABOUT YOU? Do you know that staying close to God is what the Bible calls "walking in the light"? Forgetting about God and going your own way is like "walking in the darkness." Stay in the light by reading your Bible, praying, obeying God, and keeping Him in your thoughts. C.Y.

TO MEMORIZE: *"For you were once darkness, but now you are light in the Lord. Walk as children of light"* Ephesians 5:8 (NKJV).

JUNE

10

Doing Your Best

FROM THE BIBLE:

Young men, listen to me as you would to your father. Listen, and grow wise, for I speak the truth—don't turn away. For I, too, was once a son, tenderly loved by my mother as an only child, and the companion of my father. He told me never to forget his words. "If you follow them," he said, "you will have a long and happy life. Learn to be wise," he said, "and develop good judgment and common sense! I cannot overemphasize this point." Cling to wisdom—she will protect you. Love her—she will guard you. Getting wisdom is the most important thing you can do! And with your wisdom, develop common sense and good judgment. If you exalt wisdom, she will exalt you. Hold her fast and she will lead you to great honor; she will place a beautiful crown upon your head. My son, listen to me and do as I say, and you will have a long, good life.
Proverbs 4:1-10 TLB

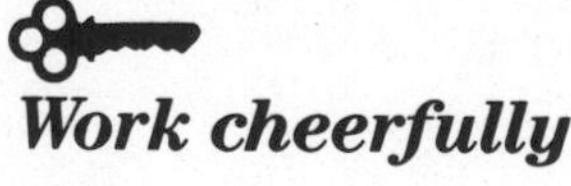

Work cheerfully

"OH, YUCK! I hate this job," mumbled Corrie. She slammed the bathroom door. Every Saturday morning it was one of her chores to scrub the bathroom, and she absolutely detested it. She opened the window and stared out into the backyard. It wasn't fair! Her brother, Ryan, was playing outdoors. (Ryan had jumped right out of bed and gotten his chores done while Corrie was still moping around. But she didn't think about that.)

"Yuck and double Yuck!" Corrie groaned as she knelt down to scour the tub. "Why can't Mom do this? She has longer arms, so it would be easier for her to reach the other side of the bathtub." She scoured for a few seconds, then she stood up and looked in the mirror. Next she got out the brush and tried styling her hair a different way—anything to forget cleaning the bathroom.

Sometime later Mother poked her head through the doorway. "Corrie, this is a twenty-minute job," she said, "and you've been in here an hour already!"

Corrie started scouring again, but she didn't enjoy it at all. She stopped scrubbing. Everything was quiet except for her dad and mother talking in the living room.

"Don't forget," she heard her mother say, "next week Corrie's orthodontist bill is due. That's another hundred."

"Right, and we need to send in her summer camp fee before the end of the month."

"She really needs some new tennis shoes, too," Mom added. "Her old ones are ripped."

Corrie felt badly. All the bills her parents were talking about were for her. She looked around the bathroom. "I'm sorry, Lord," she prayed silently. "I'm sorry I grumbled so much about a little job. Dad and Mom do so much for me, and I know cleaning the bathroom is one of the ways I can show them how much I appreciate their love. Help me not to complain about my chores anymore."

HOW ABOUT YOU? Do you have regular chores you are to do each week? Do you sometimes complain and grumble about them? Your dad and mom do a lot for you. They feed you and clothe you and provide a place for you to live. Thank the Lord for your parents. Show them how much you love and appreciate them by cheerfully helping around the house. L.W.

TO MEMORIZE: *"Honour thy father and mother; which is the first commandment with promise"* Ephesians 6:2.

JUNE

11

Two Buckets

FROM THE BIBLE:
Nevertheless, God's solid foundation stands firm, sealed with this inscription: "The Lord knows those who are his," and, "Everyone who confesses the name of the Lord must turn away from wickedness." In a large house there are articles not only of gold and silver, but also of wood and clay; some are for noble purposes and some for ignoble. If a man cleanses himself from the latter, he will be an instrument for noble purposes, made holy, useful to the Master and prepared to do any good work. Flee the evil desires of youth, and pursue righteousness, faith, love and peace, along with those who call on the Lord out of a pure heart. 2 Timothy 2:19-22, NIV

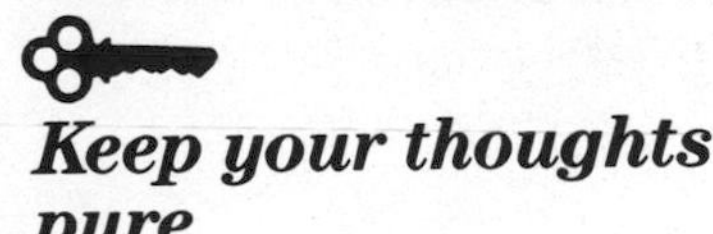

Keep your thoughts pure

"I'LL GO GET some water," volunteered Carl, grabbing the bucket and heading for the spring. He and his parents were spending a weekend at a cottage on Rainbow Lake, and they were really "roughing it." Soon Carl returned with the fresh water. "This is fun," he shouted.

"Since it's so much fun, why don't you go get another bucketful?" suggested Dad. "Here's a bucket you can use."

Carl looked at it. "But, Dad, this thing is filthy!" he exclaimed. "You don't want to drink out of this dirty old bucket, do you?"

"Oh no!" answered Dad. "Mother and I will use the clean one, but I thought you might want to use this one. Since you don't care what you put in your mind, I didn't think you'd care what you put in your stomach, either."

"My mind?" Carl asked.

"Mother just told me that when she was packing for you this morning, she found some magazines and joke books which are nothing less than dirty," Dad explained. Carl looked guilty as Dad continued. "When I was a boy on the farm, we had two buckets. One was the water bucket. The other was the slop bucket, which we kept on the back porch. We put all the garbage in it. Every night it was my job to carry it out to the pigs. We didn't even try to keep the slop bucket clean." He paused, then added slowly, "Your mind can be a water bucket or a slop bucket."

"I'm really sorry. I knew I was wrong," admitted Carl. "What should I do now?"

"Ask the Lord to forgive you," Dad replied. "His blood will wash away the filth of sinful thoughts. Then stay away from evil influences—like dirty books, bad pictures, or the wrong crowd. Turn off the TV set when necessary."

"From now on," said Carl, "I'm going to be as careful about what I put in my mind as I am about what I put in my stomach. I certainly don't want my mind to be a slop bucket!"

HOW ABOUT YOU? What are you putting into your mind? Has it become a slop bucket? Memorize today's long verse, and ask the Lord to help you do what it says. B.W.

TO MEMORIZE: *"Finally, brothers, whatever is true, whatever is noble, whatever is right, whatever is pure, whatever is lovely, whatever is admirable—if anything is excellent or praiseworthy—think about such things"* Philippians 4:8 (NIV).

JUNE

12

Caught in a Trap

FROM THE BIBLE:

In those days when you were slaves of sin you didn't bother much with goodness. And what was the result? Evidently not good, since you are ashamed now even to think about those things you used to do, for all of them end in eternal doom. But now you are free from the power of sin and are slaves of God, and his benefits to you include holiness and everlasting life. For the wages of sin is death, but the free gift of God is eternal life through Jesus Christ our Lord. Romans 6:20-23, TLB

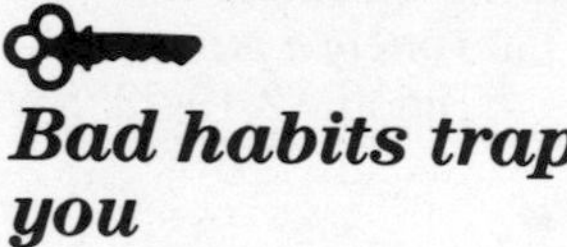

Bad habits trap you

RON REYNOLDS and his Uncle George were buddies. Ron could talk to Uncle George about anything that was on his mind—like he did the day they were out in the woods looking for berries. "Did you ever smoke, Uncle George?" Ron wanted to know.

"Nope, never did," his uncle answered.

"How come?" Ron asked.

A smile crossed Uncle George's face. "First, because I knew if I ever got caught, my dad would give me a good thrashing! Later, because I knew it was bad for me."

"Most of the guys in my class smoke," continued Ron.

"And does it look pretty tempting to you?" asked Uncle George.

"Well, the guys say it's fun, and they look kinda neat when they take a big drag, and—hey!" Ron interrupted himself. "Look here! A mink in one of Mr. Hobson's traps! And it has chewed on the leg that's in the trap."

"That's not unusual," replied Uncle George. "Animals sometimes chew a leg clean off trying to get loose."

"Poor, dumb animal—just for that smelly piece of fish," mused Ron. "I don't suppose it ever dawned on him that the trap holding the fish could hurt him."

"It reminds me of your friends at school," said Uncle George. "They go after those smelly cigarettes, not thinking about the harm they can do to their bodies, or of how hard it can be to get rid of the habit."

"Some people aren't much smarter than dumb animals, are they?" asked Ron. "I sure don't want to get trapped like that."

HOW ABOUT YOU? Are you being lured into a trap by cigarettes, drugs, or alcohol? They can only do you harm. They can even kill you! If you have been trapped, you will need help to overcome these habits. Seek help from your parents, Sunday school teacher, or pastor—and most important, ask Jesus to set you free. B.W.

TO MEMORIZE: *"Sin, when it is full-grown, brings forth death"* James 1:15 (NKJV).

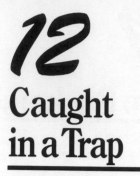

JUNE

13

To Rain or Not to Rain

KEN AWOKE TO the sound of rain beating against his window. "Oh no!" he exclaimed. "If this ran keeps up, Dan and I won't be able to go to Fun Island this afternoon."

After breakfast Ken's little brother, Timmy, tugged at his hand. "Play with me," he begged.

At the same time Ken's sister, Taryn, approached him with a book in hand. "Oh, please, Ken," she said, "You promised to help me with my math sometime, remember? This is a perfect time to do it."

"I can't please you both," Ken said with a sigh, "but Taryn does need help. I'll play with you later, Timmy."

Just then there was a knock on the door. It was Dan. "Isn't this rain awful?" Ken complained.

"We need the rain, though," replied Dan. "We've been praying for it for weeks. It's been so dry that the farmers' crops were drying up."

"But it could ruin our day, and you don't even sound sorry," complained Ken. "I'm praying that it'll stop so we can still go."

"Ken's praying that it will stop, and you're praying that it won't. So whose prayer will God answer?" asked Timmy, who had been listening. "He can't give you both what you want, can He?"

Ken looked at his little brother. Suddenly he remembered that a few minutes earlier, he had had to decide whether to do what Timmy wanted or what Taryn wanted. Now he thought about his prayer and about Dan's. Somehow, he thought it wouldn't be hard for God to decide what to do. He knew God had given guidelines for prayer, and one of those was that we should not pray selfishly. Another was that we should pray according to God's will. He didn't understand all about prayer, but he knew he hadn't prayed with the right attitude.

Forgive me, Lord, for being selfish, he prayed silently. Aloud he said, "I guess I hope He answers Dan's. God will give us another sunny day for our trip."

HOW ABOUT YOU? Do you want things to go your way no matter what hardships it brings to others? We cannot expect God to give us what we want when we pray with that attitude. Learn to pray unselfishly, asking God to send you what He knows is best. A.L.

TO MEMORIZE: *"You ask and do not receive, because you ask amiss"* James 4:3 (NKJV).

FROM THE BIBLE:
We believe men who witness in our courts, and so surely we can believe whatever God declares. And God declares that Jesus is his Son. All who believe this know in their hearts that it is true. If anyone doesn't believe this, he is actually calling God a liar, because he doesn't believe what God has said about his Son. And what is it that God has said? That he has given us eternal life, and that this life is in his Son. So whoever has God's Son has life; whoever does not have his Son, does not have life. I have written this to you who believe in the Son of God so that you may know you have eternal life. And we are sure of this, that he will listen to us whenever we ask him for anything in line with his will. And if we really know he is listening when we talk to him and make our requests, then we can be sure that he will answer us. 1 John 5:9-15, TLB

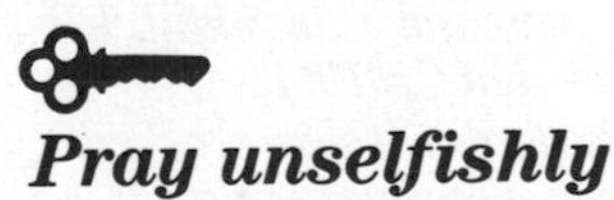

JUNE

14

A Letter for You

FROM THE BIBLE:

But now you must also put off all these: anger, wrath, malice, blasphemy, filthy language out of your mouth. Do not lie to one another, since you have put off the old man with his deeds, and have put on the new man who is renewed in knowledge according to the image of Him who created him, where there is neither Greek nor Jew, circumcised nor uncircumcised, barbarian, Scythian, slave nor free, but Christ is all and in all. Therefore, as the elect of God, holy and beloved, put on tender mercies, kindness, humbleness of mind, meekness, longsuffering; bearing with one another, and forgiving one another, if anyone has a complaint against another; even as Christ forgave you, so you also must do. But above all these things put on love, which is the bond of perfection. And let the peace of God rule in your hearts, to which also you were called in one body; and be thankful. Let the word of Christ dwell in you richly in all wisdom, teaching and admonishing one another.
Colossians 3:8-16, NKJV

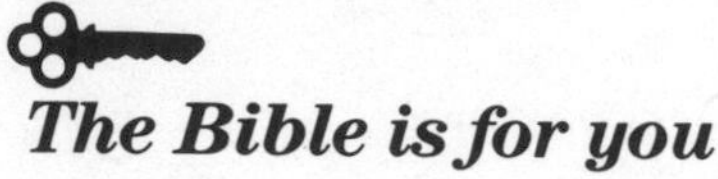

The Bible is for you

"EAT A WELL-BALANCED meal, get to bed early, and be sure to—" Kim's reading aloud was interrupted when her brother, Tom, snatched the paper from her hand.

"Hey," he protested, "who said you could read my mail?"

"It was just lying here on the table," said Kim. "Who's it from anyway?"

"My track coach," replied Tom. "There's an important track meet tomorrow, so he sent a letter to everybody on the team. He's really pushing for us all to follow what he calls the 'basic rules for health and fitness.' "

"What else does he tell you?" asked Kim.

Tom grinned at his sister and held out the letter. "Here," he offered, "you can have all this good advice."

Kim looked at the letter. "I'll read it," she said, "but the advice is for you. I wouldn't want to miss my pizza party at church tonight."

Kim went to her party and had a wonderful time with her friends. Before dismissing the group, Pastor Blake led them in a time of devotions. "How many of you like to get mail?" he asked. All hands went up. "What do you do when you get a letter?" he continued.

"Open it," the children chorused. "Read it."

Pastor Blake nodded and held up his Bible. "This is God's letter to you," he said. "Do you read it very often? And do you apply what God says to your own life, or do you read it as though you were reading someone else's mail?" He paused while the children thought that over.

It was easy for Kim to see what Pastor Blake was getting at. When she had read the track coach's letter to Tom, she hadn't thought much about the advice it contained because that was directed to him. *But do I read the Bible that way, too?"* she wondered. *I'm going to be careful, after this, to see what God is telling me.*

HOW ABOUT YOU? When you read today's Scripture, did you think, *Oh, my friend should read this* or *My brother ought to pay attention to that*? Don't read the Bible as if it were someone else's mail. Realize that it is God's letter to you. Go back over the verses you read today and see what good advice God is giving *you*. H.M.

TO MEMORIZE: *"Let the word of Christ dwell in you richly in all wisdom"* Colossians 3:16.

JUNE

15

Smelly Presents

FROM THE BIBLE:

Once we, too, were foolish and disobedient; we were misled by others and became slaves to many evil pleasures and wicked desires. Our lives were full of resentment and envy. We hated others and they hated us. But when the time came for the kindness and love of God our Savior to appear, then he saved us—not because we were good enough to be saved, but because of his kindness and pity—by washing away our sins and giving us the new joy of the indwelling Holy Spirit whom he poured out upon us with wonderful fullness—and all because of what Jesus Christ our Savior did so that he could declare us good in God's eyes—all because of his great kindness; and now we can share in the wealth of the eternal life he gives us, and we are eagerly looking forward to receiving it. Titus 3:3-7, TLB

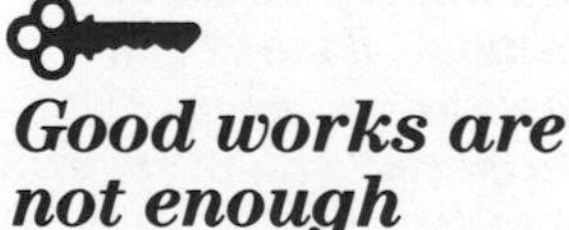

Good works are not enough

LITTLE SARAH HIGGINS had shut herself in her room and warned everyone else to stay out. Finally she came into the living room where the rest of the family was watching television. She held an armful of paper-wrapped bundles. "Look!" she cried happily. "I made you all some presents!"

As she handed out the packages, her brother Ted wrinkled up his nose. "Something stinks!" he said. Then he sniffed at the present in his hand. "I think it's this—whatever it is." Unwrapping the package, he found a small object made from an old newspaper. It was yellow and slightly damp, and it smelled terrible!

"See? It's an airplane," announced Sarah. "We learned to fold them in nursery school. And I made one for Ann, too. And see, I folded hats for Mommy and Daddy."

"They're very nice," said Mother with a faint smile. "But, uh, tell me, Sarah, where did you get the newspapers to make them?"

"Oh, I found them in the basement."

"Oh no!" groaned Dad. "I've been meaning to take those to the dump. It's damp by that window, and the papers must have gotten wet. That's why they smell so bad."

"Don't you like my presents?" Sarah wailed.

Mother tried to soothe her hurt feelings. "Come on, honey, I'll find you some nice construction paper. Then we can make some new presents."

After the two had left the room, Ted and Ann quickly scooped up the smelly papers to take out to the garbage can. "Sarah really did mean well. I'm afraid she was surprised when we weren't overjoyed by her presents," sighed Dad. "She thought they were so nice, and we see them as smelly junk. It reminds me of a verse in Isaiah: 'Our righteousnesses are as filthy rags.' Some people think they can please God just by doing their best. But the things we do that look so good to us God sees as filthy rags. Until we let Christ wash away our sins with His blood, all our good works are no better than those smelly presents of Sarah's."

HOW ABOUT YOU? Do you think God will be pleased with the good things you try to do? If you haven't trusted Jesus as your Savior, God won't accept your good works. They look—and smell—like "filthy rags" to Him. Ask Jesus to save you and give you a clean heart. S.K.

TO MEMORIZE: *"But we are all as an unclean thing, and all our righteousnesses are as filthy rags"* Isaiah 64:6.

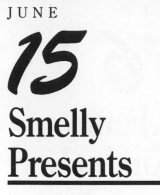

JUNE

16

A Funny Kind of Love

FROM THE BIBLE:

And have you quite forgotten the encouraging words God spoke to you, his child? He said, "My son, don't be angry when the Lord punishes you. Don't be discouraged when he has to show you where you are wrong. For when he punishes you, it proves that he loves you. When he whips you it proves you are really his child." Let God train you, for he is doing what any loving father does for his children. Whoever heard of a son who was never corrected? If God doesn't punish you when you need it, as other fathers punish their sons, then it means that you aren't really God's son at all—that you don't really belong in his family. Since we respect our fathers here on earth, though they punish us, should we not all the more cheerfully submit to God's training so that we can begin really to live? . . . Being punished isn't enjoyable while it is happening—it hurts! But afterwards we can see the result, a quiet growth in grace and character.

Hebrews 12:5-11, TLB

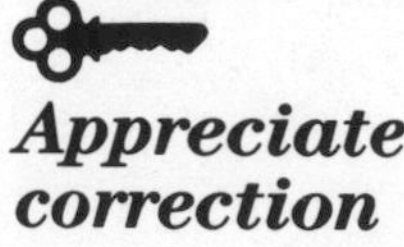

Appreciate correction

RANDY SAT on the front porch, sniffling. "It was just a little fib," he told Buffy, who sat whining at his feet. "Sure wasn't bad enough for a spanking. 'I'm doin' this because I love you.' " He mimicked his mother's voice. "Funny kinda love that is!"

Buffy licked his master's hand in sympathy. Then he jumped up and ran to the gate as Johnny and his dog, Marcus, came into the yard. "What's the matter with you?" Johnny asked as he plopped down beside Randy.

"Nothin'," Randy answered shortly. Then he added, "My mom gave me a spanking because I told a little lie."

"My mom never spanks me," Johnny bragged.

"Maybe that's why you're always in trouble at school," Randy snapped.

At that moment the mailman came into the yard, and the two dogs went out the gate. Down the street they raced. "Come back here, Marcus!" Johnny yelled as he started after his dog.

Randy went to the gate and called, "Buffy, come here!" Buffy stopped as though he had seen a red light. He turned and came back to Randy while Johnny continued down the street, begging his dog to stop. Once Marcus ran right in front of a car. He went three blocks before he decided to let Johnny catch him.

Johnny came back gasping for breath and carrying Marcus. "Boy, Buffy sure is well-trained," he admitted. "How'd you do it?"

"I spanked him with a rolled-up newspaper when he didn't obey," Randy told him. "I hated to do it, but Dad said that was part of my responsibility. He soon learned to obey."

"I couldn't do that to Marcus," Johnny said. "I love him too much to spank him."

"He almost got run over because he didn't come when you called," Randy reminded Johnny. "I love Buffy, too, that's why I spa—" Randy stopped as he remembered what his mother had said. Maybe her love wasn't such a funny kind, after all. Maybe it was Johnny's kind of love that was strange.

HOW ABOUT YOU? Do your parents spank you and then tell you they love you? They are telling you the truth. God says it's their responsibility to train you and even spank you when you need it. They know that a little correction now can save you a lot of trouble later. B.W.

TO MEMORIZE: *"For whom the LORD loves He corrects; just as a father the son in whom he delights"* Proverbs 3:12 (NKJV).

JUNE

17

A Better Person

FROM THE BIBLE:
Young men, in the same way be submissive to those who are older. All of you, clothe yourselves with humility toward one another, because, "God opposes the proud but gives grace to the humble." Humble yourselves, therefore, under God's mighty hand, that he may lift you up in due time. Cast all your anxiety on him because he cares for you. 1 Peter 5:5-7, NIV

Be glad for correction

ADAM WATCHED his father cut branch after branch off the fruit trees in the backyard. "Won't that ruin the trees?" he asked after a time.

Dad stepped away from his work. "Just the opposite," he replied. "If I do this now, these trees will grow into straight, strong, and productive trees."

"That doesn't make sense to me," Adam retorted.

Dad grinned. "Neither do the spankings I give you from time to time, but they're necessary."

Adam scratched his head in wonderment. "What do the spankings have to do with pruning trees?" he asked.

"Well, you may not agree," Dad answered, "but they make you a better person just as pruning results in better trees. When you take something that doesn't belong to you, as you did this morning, a spanking is important."

Adam remembered what happened that morning. He had taken a baseball which belonged to the boy next door. As a result, he had been punished.

"It's like I told you," Dad continued. "If I let you get away with stealing little things now, you may grow up and try to steal bigger things. The punishment you'd get then would be a whole lot worse than what I give you."

Deep down, Adam knew his father was right. It seemed strange to think that he was "lucky" to be punished now, but he supposed it was true. His thoughts were interrupted as his father spoke again. "I punish you because I love you, Son. That's why I want to correct you while you're young. You're something like the trees I'm pruning. If you let the bad things in your life be cut away, you will grow to be a better person."

Adam nodded. Though it hurt a little now, he knew it would pay off later.

HOW ABOUT YOU? Do you get angry when you are corrected? Try to realize that it is helpful. It is done because someone loves you and wants you to be the very best person you can possibly be. R.J.

TO MEMORIZE: *"No discipline seems pleasant at the time, but painful. Later on, however, it produces a harvest of righteousness and peace"* Hebrews 12:11(NIV).

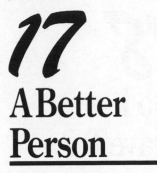

JUNE

18

Do I Have To?

FROM THE BIBLE:

There was a man of the Pharisees named Nicodemus, a ruler of the Jews. This man came to Jesus by night and said to Him, "Rabbi, we know that You are a teacher come from God; for no one can do these signs that You do unless God is with him." Jesus answered and said to him, "Most assuredly, I say to you, unless one is born again, he cannot see the kingdom of God." Nicodemus said to Him, "How can a man be born when he is old? Can he enter a second time into his mother's womb and be born?" Jesus answered, "Most assuredly, I say to you, unless one is born of water and the Spirit, he cannot enter the kingdom of God. That which is born of the flesh is flesh, and that which is born of the Spirit is spirit. Do not marvel that I said to you, 'You must be born again.' "
John 3:1-7, NKJV

You must be born again

DAVE WIPED his hands in the dirt. Then he rubbed them on his shirt and gripped his bat tightly. He had just taken a practice swing when he heard his mother's voice. "Dave," she called, "it's time to come in and do your reading."

"Aw, Mom," Dave moaned, "do I have to right now?" By the look on his mother's face, he knew that he did.

It was summer, and Dave's teacher had suggested that he read one story each day to help improve his reading. But although Dave sat down, he didn't read. He watched a fly climbing up the wall. "Mom, what if I clean my room instead?"

"No, Dave, you *must* read that story," answered Mother. "The only way you'll get to go outside is to finish reading that story."

Dave counted the tiles on the ceiling. "What if I wash the dishes?" Mother shook her head. "What if I write a letter to Grandma?"

"No," said Mother. "Just read your story."

Dave turned back to the story and read two lines. "Mom, I'll take out the trash."

"No, Son, I want you to obey me and read that story. That's the one thing you *have* to do," said Mother, "and then you may go outside." She sat down beside him. "Do you know what this reminds me of? Most people want very much to go to heaven. God has clearly told us there is only one way to get there. John 3:3 says, 'Except a man be born again, he cannot see the kingdom of God.' Some people say, 'But, God, I'll be so good.' God says, 'No, you must be born again.' They say, 'I'll join the church and I'll give money.' God says, 'No, you must be born again.' 'I'll obey the Ten Commandments. I'll be baptized.' 'No, you *must* be born again.' "

"And God won't change His mind, will He?" said Dave. "Those people are sure foolish—even more foolish than I am." He knew his mother wouldn't change her mind, either, so he settled down to read. In fifteen minutes he was outdoors again.

HOW ABOUT YOU? Are you one of those people who try different ways to gain eternal life? Do you think you can be saved by being good, getting baptized, or going to church? These are good things, but they are man's ways, not God's ways. They do not lead to eternal life. You must accept Jesus as Savior and be born again. N.G.H.

TO MEMORIZE: *"Most assuredly, I say to you, unless one is born again, he cannot see the kingdom of God"* John 3:3 (NKJV).

JUNE

How Can You Tell?

FROM THE BIBLE:
He who believes in the Son of God has the witness in himself; he who does not believe God has made Him a liar, because he has not believed the testimony that God has given of His Son. And this is the testimony: that God has given us eternal life, and this life is in His Son. He who has the Son has life; he who does not have the Son of God does not have life. These things I have written to you who believe in the name of the Son of God, that you may know that you have eternal life, and that you may continue to believe in the name of the Son of God.
1 John 5:10-13, NKJV

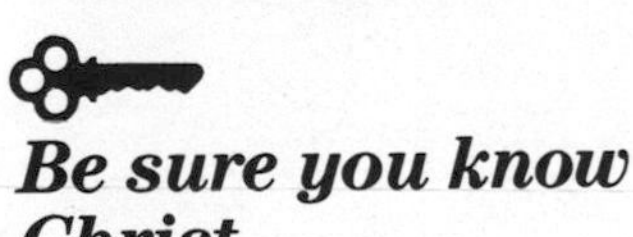

Be sure you know Christ

UNCLE JOE was working in his garden one afternoon when Timmy came to visit. After talking about the weather and the best fishing spots, Timmy said, "You know, I asked Jesus to be my Savior a long time ago, but sometimes I don't feel like a Christian. How can I tell if I am one?"

Uncle Joe smiled as he bent down by a row of tiny green sprouts and pointed to one of them. "That's a beet plant," he said. "But how can you tell, Timmy?"

"Well, if you planted beet seeds there, then what's growing there is probably a beet plant."

"Good!" said Uncle Joe. "And the seed that produces Christians is the gospel. Did anyone explain it to you before you accepted Christ?"

"Oh, sure," said Timmy. "My Bible Club teacher showed me that I'm a sinner and need to depend on Christ and His death on the cross to save me."

Uncle Joe continued. "There's another way we can tell this is a beet plant—by the company it keeps. Once in a while one will be found out of the row, but usually it's in a row with the rest of the beet plants. In the same way, Christians usually are found with other Christians."

"Well, I have made a lot of Christian friends," said Timmy, "and I don't like to miss church. What's another way to tell what kind of plant that is?"

"That's easy—by the fruit it bears," replied his uncle. "If this is truly a beet plant, then eventually it will produce a beet. In the same way, Christians are known by their fruit—good works which come as a result of their faith in Christ."

"I know the best reason of all to know it's a beet plant," said Timmy. "You said it was, and I believe you."

Uncle Joe smiled. "And God tells us in His Word that if we receive Jesus as Savior, we are His children. Also, His Spirit dwells in us and tells us that we belong to Him, although it's not in words we can hear. We must believe what He says."

HOW ABOUT YOU? Do you ever wonder if you're really saved? Make sure you understand the gospel and that you have trusted Jesus Christ to be your own Savior from sin. Remember—it's not what you do that saves you—it's what Christ did for you on the cross. S.K.

TO MEMORIZE: *"These things have I written to you who believe in the name of the Son of God, that you may know that you have eternal life"*
1 John 5:13 (NKJV).

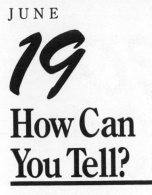

JUNE

20

No Doubt About It

FROM THE BIBLE:

Jesus answered and said to him, "If anyone loves Me, he will keep My word; and My Father will love him, and We will come to him and make Our home with him. He who does not love Me does not keep My words; and the word which you hear is not Mine but the Father's who sent Me. These things I have spoken to you while being present with you."
John 14:23-25, NKJV

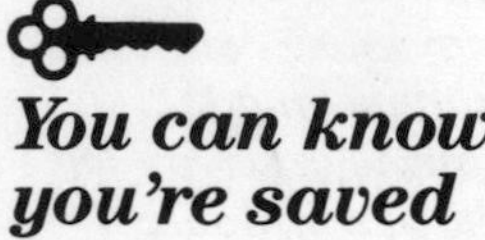

You can know you're saved

"MOM," called Jon, "can I walk with Mrs. Emmet to the store? She says I can help carry her groceries home."

Mother smiled as she gave her approval. "It's nice you're so eager to do that," she teased. She knew that on such excursions, Mrs. Emmet treated Jon to an ice cream cone.

As Jon walked beside his elderly neighbor, he chatted about the various things he hoped to do during the summer. "Tell me, Jon, are you a Christian?"

Jon shrugged. "I sure hope so," he said. "I guess I am."

They turned in at the ice cream shop. As Jon took the first lick of his double dip chocolate fudge ice cream cone, his friend Rollie came in. "Hi, Jon," greeted Rollie. "Ya got an ice cream cone?"

To Jon's surprise, Mrs. Emmet answered for him. "He sure hopes so," she said. Both boys looked at her rather strangely as she added, "He guesses so, at any rate." The boys chatted a minute, and then Jon and Mrs. Emmet went on their way.

"Why did you say I hoped I had an ice cream cone?" Jon asked as they walked along. "I have one—no hoping or guessing about it."

Mrs. Emmet laughed. "That was rather silly of me, wasn't it?" she agreed. "Almost as silly as your saying you 'hoped' and 'guessed' you were a Christian." She paused while Jon thought about that. "You see, Jon," she added, "when you have something, you don't need to hope you have it. You don't need to guess about it. You can know for sure. The question is, Do you believe in the Lord Jesus Christ?"

Slowly Jon nodded. "Last summer I asked Him to forgive me and to save me," he said. "I really meant it, too, but sometimes I feel like maybe I should do something more."

"There's nothing more you can do," Mrs. Emmet assured him. "The Bible says that if you believe in Jesus, you have eternal life—you're a Christian. There's no doubt about it."

HOW ABOUT YOU? Are you a Christian? You don't have to hope so or guess so. You can know. Jesus paid the price for your sin. Accept what He has done for you. Take Him as your Savior. When you do that, you *have* eternal life. H.M.

TO MEMORIZE: *"He who has the Son has life; he who does not have the Son of God does not have life"* 1 John 5:12 (NKJV).

JUNE

21

Don't Fence Me In

FROM THE BIBLE:

Therefore submit yourselves to every ordinance of man for the Lord's sake, whether to the king as supreme, or to governors, as to those who are sent by him for the punishment of evildoers and for the praise of those who do good. For this is the will of God, that by doing good you may put to silence the ignorance of foolish men—as free, yet not using your liberty as a cloak for vice, but as servants of God. Honor all people. Love the brotherhood. Fear God. Honor the king.

1 Peter 2:13-17, NKJV

Rules help you

"I'M SO TIRED of rules," complained Matt, as he was reading the paper one evening. "It's always, 'If you don't do this, you can't do that,' and, 'First things first.' That's all I hear at home, at school, at church, even at play! When I grow up I'm going to be my own boss and do exactly as I please! But guess what? Even dogs are no longer free! It says here that they have to be confined to their owner's property. Tag won't like being fenced in."

"No, but that old rabbit in Mr. Pate's garden is sure going to be relieved," Mother said, laughing. "Tag has been giving him fits lately."

Matt was right—Tag didn't like being fenced, and time after time he dug out of the yard. One day when Matt and his mother came home from town, they discovered that Tag was missing once again. "That Tag!" exclaimed Matt. "I even took the paper out and read the law to him, and I gave him a stern lecture about the big, bad dogcatcher. But he keeps digging out every time our backs are turned. I'll go find him."

But Tag was not to be found. A neighbor had seen the dogcatcher picking him up. Matt was in tears. "We can get him back, can't we?" he asked.

"Oh yes," Mother said, "but he'll just get out again."

"If only he could understand that the yard is a place of safety and protection for him!" sighed Matt. "Then he would know why we fence him in."

"You're right," agreed Mother, "and you know, Matt, we're a little like Tag. We sometimes feel 'fenced in' too—fenced in by rules we don't like. But God has given us parents, teachers, policemen, yes, even rules, to provide safety and protection for us."

"That makes sense," agreed Matt slowly. "I guess we do need rules and laws. But what about Tag, Mom?"

The solution to the problem was found when Dad came home. He made arrangements to pick up Tag and take him out to Uncle Frank's farm. "We'll miss him, but we can visit him," he said. "There he can run free."

HOW ABOUT YOU? Do you rebel at having rules you must follow? You never outgrow the "dos" and "don'ts" of living. All your life there will be those who "have the rule over you." God says to obey them. B.W.

TO MEMORIZE: *"Obey them that have the rule over you"* Hebrews 13:17.

JUNE

22

The Right Tools

FROM THE BIBLE:

These are God's messages to Jeremiah the priest (the son of Hilkiah) who lived in the town of Anathoth in the land of Benjamin. The first of these messages came to him in the thirteenth year of the reign of Amon's son Josiah, king of Judah. . . . The Lord said to me, "I knew you before you were formed within your mother's womb; before you were born I sanctified you and appointed you as my spokesman to the world." "O Lord God," I said, "I can't do that! I'm far too young! I'm only a youth!" "Don't say that," he replied, "for you will go wherever I send you and speak whatever I tell you to. And don't be afraid of the people, for I, the Lord, will be with you and see you through." Then he touched my mouth and said, "See, I have put my words in your mouth!"

Jeremiah 1:1-2, 4-9, TLB

God gives strength

JEREMY WAS UPSET. "I can't do it," he muttered as he pedaled his bike into the garage. "I'm just a kid."

Dad looked up from his workbench. "Jeremy, I'd like you to help paint the lawn furniture this afternoon."

"OK," Jeremy replied. "Just give me the paint and brushes." As they got to work, Jeremy poured out his worries. "Brian Parker wasn't in school today, Dad," he said, "and some of the kids said his mother is going to die. I should go see him, but I'm afraid to. I don't know what to say to him." Jeremy sniffed loudly. "I just can't do it."

"I understand how you feel, Jeremy," said Dad, "but Brian needs you. In difficult situations like this you often don't have to say anything. Just be there and listen."

"But, Dad, I'm just a kid," choked Jeremy.

"That's what the prophet Jeremiah said, but God told him that was no excuse," Dad reminded him. "You know, when I asked you to paint the lawn furniture just now, I supplied all the tools and the paint for you to do the job. When God has a job for us, He always supplies whatever is necessary to get the job done, too. He gives us the grace to do it." Jeremy still looked doubtful. "Mother and I will go with you after dinner," suggested Dad. "Will that help?"

Jeremy grinned. "It sure will."

Later as they returned from the Parkers', Jeremy said, "You were right, Dad. I'm glad I went. Brian needed me."

HOW ABOUT YOU? Is there something you feel God wants you to do, like visit a sick person or witness to a friend? Have you been saying, "But I'm just a kid. I can't do that"? If God asks you to do a job, He will give you the necessary tools to handle it. Stop making excuses and go do it. You'll feel a lot better after you do. B.W.

TO MEMORIZE: *"My grace is sufficient for you, for my power is made perfect in weakness"* 2 Corinthians 12:9 (NIV).

JUNE

23

Just a Mite

FROM THE BIBLE:
As he looked up, Jesus saw the rich putting their gifts into the temple treasury. He also saw a poor widow put in two very small copper coins. "I tell you the truth," he said, "this poor widow has put in more than all the others. All these people gave their gifts out of their wealth; but she out of her poverty put in all she had to live on."
Luke 21:1-4, NIV

Serve in love

IT WAS DON'S ambition to be a missionary to a foreign country some day, but it seemed to take so long to grow up! Sometimes he wondered if he'd ever be big enough to serve the Lord.

When Don arrived at school, he asked his friend, Bob, to go with him to Bible study during the noon hour. He was delighted when Bob accepted the invitation. But he sighed when the missionary offering was taken at the club meeting. He so wished that he had a dollar to give.

After supper Don happily went with his father to Mr. Baker's house. He liked the old gentleman, so while Dad fixed a leaky faucet, Don sat and talked with Mr. Baker. "I wish I could be a big help to others like my dad is," Don said wistfully.

Mr. Baker looked surprised. "Why, Don, I think you're a very helpful person. Isn't it a useful thing to make an old man like me happy by talking with me?" he said, chuckling.

This time Don looked surprised. "Yeah," he said slowly, "but I'd like to be able to give lots of money to help missionaries, and most of all, I'd like to be a missionary myself. Then I'd really be helpful to God and others."

"Ever hear of the 'widow's mite'?" asked Mr. Baker.

"A mite is a bug, isn't it?" Don asked.

Mr. Baker slapped his knee and laughed. "There is such an insect as a mite, but I was thinking of another meaning of the word," he said. "It can mean a small amount of something. The phrase 'a widow's mite' comes from a story Jesus told about a widow who dropped just two small coins in the collection box. Jesus said that in God's sight she gave more than people who put in larger amounts because she gave all she possibly could."

Don sat quietly thinking about what Mr. Baker had said. He didn't have to grow up before he could serve God after all! Right now he could give "a widow's mite."

HOW ABOUT YOU? Does the amount of money you can give seem very small? Do the things you do for Jesus seem little and not worth much? God looks at your heart and counts the smallest acts done in love as special gifts from you. Even a friendly smile given to a lonely person is a precious gift to God. He sees the love for Him that's in your heart. Serve Him now. C.Y.

TO MEMORIZE: *"Let all that you do be done in love"* 1 Corinthians 16:14 (NASB).

JUNE

24

A Noisy Witness

FROM THE BIBLE:

Then he said to all, "Anyone who wants to follow me must put aside his own desires and conveniences and carry his cross with him every day and keep close to me! Whoever loses his life for my sake will save it, but whoever insists on keeping his life will lose it; and what profit is there in gaining the whole world when it means forfeiting one's self? When I, the Messiah, come in my glory and in the glory of the Father and the holy angels, I will be ashamed then of all who are ashamed of me and of my words now." Luke 9:23-26, TLB

Talk about Jesus

JOANNE WENT to the store for her mother. Her two-year-old sister Lena, who like riding in the grocery cart, went with her. As they rounded a corner in the store, they saw an elderly lady standing in the aisle. She was busy rummaging through her purse, looking for coupons. All of a sudden the woman's purse slipped out of her hand, and coins, coupons, and other items went flying everywhere! Joanne hurried over to help pick up the things. "Oh, thank you so much," said the lady. "Most young people wouldn't stop to help an old lady like me. Why did you do it?"

Joanne knew this was a good opportunity to tell the lady about Jesus, but she was embarrassed. "Uh . . . . . . I guess I just like helping people," she managed to say. Then she walked away quickly, pushing her cart in front of her.

After a while, Lena got tired of looking at all the packages. So she began singing her favorite song: "Jesus Loves Me." Louder and louder she sang, "Jesus loves me, dis I know, for da By-ba tell me so!"

Joanne saw that people were looking and smiling at them, and she felt her face turn red. "Hush, Lena! Don't be so noisy!"

Soon the lady that Joanne had helped walked up to her. "I heard what the little one was singing," she said. "You must be a Christian!"

"Well . . . uh . . . yes, I am," Joanne mumbled. The woman smiled. "I thought there was something different about you, and now I know what it is. My neighbor is a Christian, too, and she's always trying to talk to me about Jesus. I think maybe I'll listen more next time."

After the lady walked away, Joanne said to her sister, "Lena, you're a sweetheart! I've been wrong to keep quiet about my Christianity. And I'm going to buy you a great, big sucker for showing me how important it is to be a 'noisy witness'!"

HOW ABOUT YOU? Are you embarrassed to have someone notice that you're a Christian? Perhaps you are a "silent witness"—you try to show by your life and actions that you're a Christian. That's good, but talking is important, too. Others won't be persuaded to come to the Lord unless they know why you do the things you do. Don't be ashamed to talk about Jesus. Be a "noisy witness"! S.K.

TO MEMORIZE: *"Whoever is ashamed of Me and My words . . . the Son of Man will also be ashamed of him"* Mark 8:38 (NASB).

JUNE

25

Ready or Not

FROM THE BIBLE:
First, I want to remind you that in the last days there will come scoffers who will do every wrong they can think of, and laugh at the truth. This will be their line of argument: "So Jesus promised to come back, did he? Then where is he? He'll never come! Why, as far back as anyone can remember everything has remained exactly as it was since the first day of creation."
But don't forget this, dear friends, that a day or a thousand years from now is like tomorrow to the Lord. He isn't really being slow about his promised return, even though it sometimes seems that way. But he is waiting, for the good reason that he is not willing that any should perish, and he is giving more time for sinners to repent.
2 Peter 3:3-9, TLB

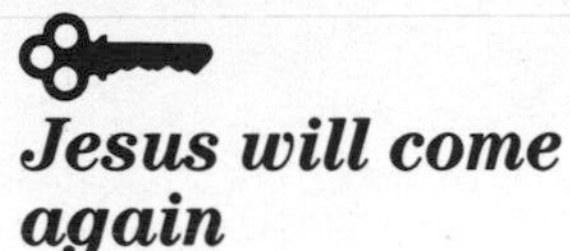

Jesus will come again

"PLEASE CALL Crystal and then sit down for breakfast, Kevin," said Mother.

"Sure," agreed Kevin with a grin. "What shall I call her? Lazybones? Or Sleepyhead?" He went to the stairway. "Crystal!" he called. "Fire! Get up! There's a fire," he paused, "under the bacon," he added softly. He laughed as his sister came pounding down the stairs.

"What? Where? Oh, you're not funny, Kevin,'" scolded Crystal when she saw he was joking. "You scared me!"

Dad looked up from his newspaper. "Talk about being scared," he said, "listen to this. 'Doomsday Prophet Warns End of World Coming Next Tuesday!' This article will scare a lot of people."

"That's silly," scoffed Kevin. "People have been saying that as long as I can remember."

Crystal was wide-eyed. "Is the world really going to end next Tuesday, Daddy?" she asked.

Dad smiled at Crystal. "No, the world won't end Tuesday, but the Lord Jesus might come before then."

"My history teacher says his grandmother was afraid to go to sleep when she was little because she thought the Lord was coming any minute," Kevin told them. "He says people have been saying that for hundreds of years, and he's not so sure Jesus will ever come."

"Kevin," said Mother, "the very fact that people are doubting is a sign of Jesus' soon return. The Apostle Peter wrote that in the last days scoffers would be questioning Jesus' promise, because the world continues as it always has. Then he points out that God doesn't count time the way we do, and that He surely will keep His promise."

"One thing is certain," added Dad, "no man knows the day or hour when Jesus will come. It could be sooner than Tuesday. Then again, it could be next year or years later. Only God knows. We need to be ready for Him anytime."

HOW ABOUT YOU? Do you think that because Jesus hasn't come yet, it isn't going to happen? He's patiently waiting, giving people more opportunities to be saved. But time is running out. You may be sure that when the time is right according to God's timetable, Jesus *will* come. B.W.

TO MEMORIZE: *"Therefore you also be ready, for the Son of Man is coming at an hour when you do not expect him"* Matthew 24:44 (NKJV).

JUNE

26

Balloons for All

FROM THE BIBLE:

Hearing that Jesus had silenced the Sadducees, the Pharisees got together. One of them, an expert in the law, tested him with this question: "Teacher, which is the greatest commandment in the Law?" Jesus replied: " 'Love the Lord your God with all your heart and with all your soul and with all your mind.' This is the first and greatest commandment. And the second is like it: 'Love your neighbor as yourself.' All the Law and the Prophets hang on these two commandments."

Matthew 22:34-40, NIV

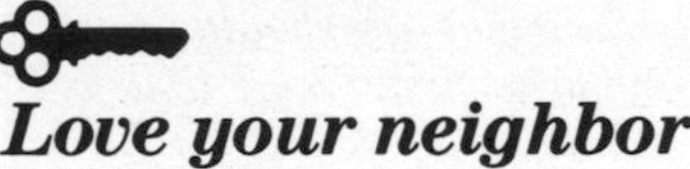

Love your neighbor

HARDY'S DEPARTMENT STORE was having a grand opening, and Mother had let Mike walk downtown to see what was going on. He was especially fascinated as he watched a clown at the front of the store blowing up helium balloons and giving them away to each child who asked for one. Mike wanted one, too! He also knew his little sister Sara would love one. But Sara was sick, and Mike noticed that no child was allowed to have more than one balloon, so he couldn't get one for her. Well, she could look at his. Marching up to the clown, he asked politely, "May I have a balloon, please?"

"Sure thing," boomed the clown. "What's your favorite color?"

"Blue," answered Mike without hesitation. Then, as the clown began to fill a blue balloon, Mike made a sudden decision. "Please, sir, may I have a red one instead? It's for my little sister. She's sick, and she likes red."

The clown looked at him in surprise. "Well, well," he said, as he continued to fill the blue balloon. He handed it to Mike and then took a red one. "The rule is one balloon to a child, but we're going to make an exception. Every girl should have a brother like you! Enjoy your balloons!"

Sara was delighted with her balloon, and when Mother heard the story, she was delighted, too. "I'm so pleased—not just because you both got a balloon, but because you were willing to give up your own balloon so Sara could have one," she told Mike. "I know God is pleased, too. You truly followed his command to love your neighbor—in this case, your sister—as yourself."

HOW ABOUT YOU? The Bible teaches that our neighbor may be anyone we come in contact with, not only the person next door. If you're a Christian, you are to love that neighbor as you love yourself. Do you do that? Would you like the biggest piece of candy? Better give it to your neighbor then. Would you like the best seat? Better give it to your neighbor if you love him as yourself. Would you like to choose the TV program? Ride in the front seat of the car? Talk first in class? See how many ways you can find to show that you truly love your neighbor as yourself. It sounds like a hard thing to do, but it will bring you joy. H.M.

TO MEMORIZE: *"Love your neighbor as yourself"* Matthew 22:39 (NIV).

JUNE

27

Balloons for All

(Continued from yesterday)

FROM THE BIBLE:

In the same way, the Spirit helps us in our weakness. We do not know what we ought to pray for, but the Spirit himself intercedes for us with groans that words cannot express. And he who searches our hearts knows the mind of the Spirit, because the Spirit intercedes for the saints in accordance with God's will. And we know that in all things God works for the good of those who love him, who have been called according to his purpose.
Romans 8:26-28, NIV

Keep praying

THOUGH ONE-YEAR-OLD Andy ignored Mike's blue balloon, he seemed to love Sara's red one almost as much as Sara did. He made a pest of himself, pulling on the string and then trying to take hold of the balloon itself. Sara was afraid he would break it. "Boon! Boon!" he screamed indignantly when Mother tied the balloon out of his reach. Finally, Mike had an idea. "May I take him to the store to get one of his own?" he asked. Mother agreed, and away they went with Mike pushing Andy in his stroller.

When they arrived at the store, Andy really got excited as he saw all the balloons waving gaily over his head. The clown smiled when he saw Mike with Andy. "Brought me a new customer, did you?" Turning to Andy, he asked, "And what would you like, young man?"

"Wahyo boon!" shouted Andy, bouncing up and down.

"Well, now, I hope this won't go 'boom' for you too quickly." The clown smiled as he selected a green balloon and handed it to Andy.

"No! Whyyo boon," insisted Andy.

At the clown's puzzled look, Mike laughed. "He says he wants a yellow balloon."

Grinning, the clown handed one to Andy. "I hope your brother and sister appreciate you."

When Dad arrived home, he admired the balloons as Mother put dinner on the table and Mike recounted the day's events. Dad picked up Andy and his "wahyo boon." Putting him in the high chair, Dad said, "It's a good thing for you that your brother can understand you." He paused, then continued, "You know, that reminds me of something God does for us. Often we have trouble praying. We sometimes don't know what to say or even what to ask God for. But God has given us His Holy Spirit to help us and to pray for us. He makes our requests clear and 'just right' before God."

HOW ABOUT YOU? Do you think your prayers are too weak to be of any worth. Does it seem that the prayers of Mom and Dad—or better still, the prayers of pastors—would accomplish more than yours ever could? Don't be discouraged because you can't pray as well as you would like to. If you're a Christian, the Holy Spirit will take your prayers and make them perfect before God's throne. Keep praying. H.M.

TO MEMORIZE: *"We do not know what we ought to pray for, but the Spirit himself intercedes for us"* Romans 8:26 (NIV).

JUNE

28

Do It Yourself

FROM THE BIBLE:

You have heard that it was said to those of old, "You shall not murder," and whoever murders will be in danger of the judgment. But I say to you that whoever is angry with his brother without a cause shall be in danger of the judgment. And whoever says to his brother, "Raca!" shall be in danger of the council. But whoever says, "You fool!" shall be in danger of hell fire. Therefore if you bring your gift to the altar, and there remember that your brother has something against you, leave your gift there before the altar, and go your way. First be reconciled to your brother, and then come and offer your gift.
Matthew 5:21-24, NKJV

Humble yourself

AS MOTHER arranged the new curtains, Aileen looked proudly around her room. "Oh, it's lovely, Mother. I'm going to be an interior decorator when I grow up."

Mother smiled. "Redecorating is fun, isn't it?"

"I'm almost glad we didn't have the money to buy everything new and ready-made," said Aileen. "My quilt and curtains are so unique, and they match the wallpaper perfectly. Even my old bedroom furniture looks nice refinished."

Mother nodded, "Do-it-yourself jobs are hard work, but they're worth the effort. Why don't you call Josie and invite her over to see your room?"

Aileen snorted. "She wouldn't come. She's not speaking to me," she said sarcastically.

Mother raised her eyebrows. "Are you speaking to her?"

"Of course not! She'll have to speak to me first. She's the one who's mad, and I didn't do a thing to her." Tears filled Aileen's eyes. "I asked God to make her apologize to me, but she still hasn't done it."

"Maybe He wants you to apologize to Josie," suggested Mother.

"But I didn't do anything to her!" Aileen wailed.

"Are you sure? It usually takes two to quarrel," Mother reminded her daughter. "We often want God to take care of our problems when there is something He expects us to do for ourselves. One thing He wants us to do, according to His Word, is to 'humble ourselves.' Apologizing is certainly humbling. In any case, remember our Scripture reading this morning? Josie has something 'against you,' so you should go to her."

"But that's hard!" Aileen cried.

Mother nodded. "It's a hard 'do-it-yourself' job, but the results are worth the effort." As Aileen dialed Josie's number, Mother smiled.

Later Aileen proudly showed Josie her room, and Mother heard her say, "Do-it-yourself jobs are usually hard, but they're worth it."

HOW ABOUT YOU? Does God want you to apologize to someone? It's not easy to humble yourself, but it's God's way and it's worth the effort. An apology is a small price to pay for a friend. B.W.

TO MEMORIZE: *"Moreover if your brother sins against you, go and tell him his fault between you and him alone. If he hears you, you have gained your brother"* Matthew 18:15 (NKJV).

JUNE

29

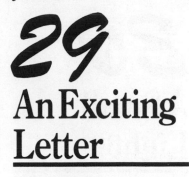

An Exciting Letter

FROM THE BIBLE:

Oh, how I love Your law!
It is my meditation all the day.
You, through Your commandments, make me wiser than my enemies;
For they are ever with me.
I have more understanding than all my teachers,
For Your testimonies are my meditation.
I understand more than the ancients,
Because I keep Your precepts.
I have restrained my feet from every evil way,
That I may keep Your word.
I have not departed from Your judgments,
For You Yourself have taught me.
How sweet are Your words to my taste,
sweeter than honey to my mouth!
Through Your precepts I get understanding;
Therefore I hate every false way.
Psalm 119:97-104, NKJV

Read the Bible

"HOW ARE YOU doing in the Sunday school contest?" Mrs. Anderson asked her daughter.

"Pretty good," said Patty. "I haven't done this week's questions, though, because I left my Bible at church."

"There are other Bibles in the house," Mom reminded her.

"I know, but I don't feel like looking up the answers right now. I'll do the questions later." Patty was glad the mailman came just then. It gave her an excuse to end the conversation. She hurried to the front door and picked up the pile of mail. "Oh, Mom, look! Here's a letter from the Walters, and there's a special note on the front of the envelope that says, 'Good news inside.' May I open it?"

The Walters family and the Anderson family had been close friends for a long time. It had been very difficult for both families when Mr. Walters had been transferred to Oregon. But now Patty was excited. Maybe the good news meant they were coming to visit!

"A letter from the Walters?" Mom seemed to show little interest. "Maybe I'll have time to read it later." She took it and set it on the kitchen counter.

"Later? But why not now?" Patty asked.

"Well, Patty, I have to sweep the floor right now, and then I want to finish the book I've been reading. After that it will be time to start supper. Maybe I can read the letter tonight."

Patty looked at her mother strangely. Suddenly she understood. "I see, Mom. I know the Bible is God's letter to us and that it also contains good news. Yet I keep postponing the time when I'll read it. I'll go do those questions right now!"

Mom smiled as she picked up the letter from the Walters. "Good idea! But I think it will be all right if you wait just long enough to read this letter first!"

HOW ABOUT YOU? Do you study the Bible? Do you read the good things God has to say to you, or do you think "someday when I'm bigger I'll study God's Word"? The Bible is God's letter to you. In it there is good news—how Christ died and rose again and is someday coming back for His own. Be excited about the Bible. L.W.

TO MEMORIZE: *"Oh, how I love Your law! It is my meditation all the day"* Psalm 119:97 (NKJV).

JUNE

30

A Small Light

FROM THE BIBLE:

You are the salt of the earth; but if the salt loses its flavor, how shall it be seasoned? It is then good for nothing but to be thrown out and trampled under foot by men. You are the light of the world. A city that is set on a hill cannot be hidden. Nor do they light a lamp and put it under a basket, but on a lampstand, and it gives light to all who are in the house. Let your light so shine before men, that they may see your good works and glorify your Father in heaven. Matthew 5:13, NKJV

Be a light

GARY AND MELISSA watched from the window as lightning streaked across the sky. An extra brilliant flash seemed to pierce the sky in two. This was followed by a loud crash of thunder. Suddenly it was pitch dark in the house.

"What happened?" cried Gary, stumbling over a footstool in the dark.

"Oh, it's so dark!" Melissa exclaimed. Then she called, "Mom, please come here!"

Mother came into the room with a lighted candle. "The lightning must have knocked the electricity out," she said. "We'll have to see by candlelight for a while—just like in years gone by."

"It's surprising how much light that one little flame gives," said Melissa as they sat watching the flickering light in the otherwise dark room.

Gary was quiet, then blurted out, "You are the light of the world." He grinned as he added, "My Sunday school verse just popped into my mind because of that candle!"

Melissa nodded. "Our teacher said that if we've received Jesus as Savior, He lives in us. When we do things that please Him, others see Jesus in us, so they have light to see Him."

"I always figured that the little bit I could do didn't amount to much," added Gary. "For the first time, I think I know what a lot of difference one small light can make."

"Yeah," agreed Melissa. "Our lives can be lights so the world can see Jesus, just like this candle is a light for us to see things here."

Just then the lights came back on. "I'm glad to have electricity again, but I'll always remember what I learned tonight from the candle," said Gary.

HOW ABOUT YOU? Do you feel as though there's not much you can do to let your light shine for Jesus? That isn't true! Obeying parents and teachers, being kind, showing love, forgiving others, and being patient are just some of the many ways to let your life shine. Anything you are able to do for Jesus is worthwhile. C.Y.

TO MEMORIZE: *"You are the light of the world"* Matthew 5:14 (NKJV).

JULY

It's Boring

FROM THE BIBLE:
So we must listen very carefully to the truths we have heard, or we may drift away from them. For since the messages from angels have always proved true and people have always been punished for disobeying them, what makes us think that we can escape if we are indifferent to this great salvation announced by the Lord Jesus himself, and passed on to us by those who heard him speak? God always has shown us that these messages are true by signs and wonders and various miracles and by giving certain special abilities from the Holy Spirit to those who believe; yes, God has assigned such gifts to each of us.
Hebrews 2:1-4, TLB

Give attention to Bible study

"I WISH I didn't have to go to Sunday school today," Jody sighed as she slowly ate her cereal.

Mother looked at her, surprised. "Why, Jody! What a thing to say! I thought you liked church!"

"I do like church. It's Mrs. Darnell's class I don't like!" Jody explained. "She's so boring! I wish I was back in third grade so I could still be in Mr. Richards's class."

"Mr. Richards was a good teacher," agreed Mother, "and I'm glad you learned so much from him. But Jody, Mrs. Darnell is a good teacher, too. Many children have come to know Christ through her teaching."

"Her class is no fun, though," protested Jody. "I practically fall asleep listening to her!"

"Mrs. Darnell might not be as entertaining as Mr. Richards, but she does know God's Word," insisted Mother. "Remember this, too—nowhere does the Bible say that studying the Scripture is supposed to be 'fun.' Sometimes Bible study is simply hard work." Jody still didn't look convinced. "In 2 Corinthians we're told to bring our thoughts into captivity," continued Mother. "We're to turn them toward the things of Christ."

Jody thought about it. Then she grinned. "OK, Mom. If my thoughts start to wander today, I'll grab hold of them and turn them toward the Lord and not let go! Right?"

"Right!" Mother smiled. "That may sound strange, but we can do that—we can control our thoughts. While in Mrs. Darnell's class, make yourself listen to what she is saying. Be interested in learning about God's Word."

HOW ABOUT YOU? Are you sometimes bored in church or Sunday school? Sometimes it will take concentration on your part to understand the lesson God is teaching, but it will be worth it. Bible study often is hard, but it is important. If you are bored, it could be because you are not capturing your thoughts and turning them toward the Lord. Think about it. L.W.

TO MEMORIZE: *"We take captive every thought to make it obedient to Christ"*
2 Corinthians 10:5 (NIV).

JULY

2

Aunt Sue's Gift

FROM THE BIBLE:

Your word, O Lord, is eternal;
it stands firm in the heavens.
Your faithfulness continues
through all generations;
you established the earth, and
it endures.
Your laws endure to this day,
for all things serve you.
If your law had not been my
delight,
I would have perished in my
affliction.
I will never forget your precepts,
for by them you have preserved
my life.
Save me, for I am yours;
I have sought out your
precepts.
The wicked are waiting to
destroy me,
but I will ponder your
statutes.
To all perfection I see a limit;
but your commands are
boundless.

Psalm 119:89-96, NIV

Know God through the Bible

KEVIN WAVED the brown package excitedly. "Look what came in the mail!" he exclaimed. "I think it's a birthday present from Aunt Sue!" He eagerly ripped the paper off the package. Taking out a book he frowned. "Missionary stories," he said unhappily. Kevin didn't do much reading, and when he did, it was usually a mystery or sports story. Tossing the book on the table, he reached for a sports magazine.

A couple of months later Kevin's family provided dinner for Mr. Jackson, a missionary speaker at their church. Kevin had found the meetings very interesting, but he especially enjoyed talking with Mr. Jackson at home. He listened attentively when Mr. Jackson told a story about a leopard that had once stalked his trail. "Several Indians and I were on our way to preach in one of the villages," said Mr. Jackson. "All day, we were aware of the leopard, and we expected it to attack any moment."

"So what happened?" Kevin's eyes were wide with fear.

"Well," said Mr. Jackson, "surprisingly, the leopard never did attack. It finally just quit following us and left us alone. I find that exciting because I know God was answering the prayers of many of His people back home."

All too soon Mr. Jackson was gone, and Kevin missed him. "Sure wish I could talk to him again and get to know him better," he said a few weeks later. Taking a book from the bookcase, he idly turned the first few pages, then suddenly sat erect. "Mom! This book from Aunt Sue is written by Mr. Jackson!" When bedtime came, he could hardly put the book down. "I feel like Mr. Jackson is a good friend," he said.

"You got to know him through his book." Mother smiled, then looked thoughtful. "You know, Kevin, that's something like God and the Bible. We sometimes feel we don't know God, but it's because we don't read His book—the Bible."

HOW ABOUT YOU? Do you sometimes wish you knew God better—like your Sunday school teacher or your pastor does? Are you willing to do your part to know Him? Be sure to do your Sunday school lessons. And listen to your pastor. There's a book to help you, too—the Bible. Read it daily. Then you'll be getting to know God. G.W.

TO MEMORIZE: *"I delight in your decrees; I will not neglect your word"* Psalm 119:16 (NIV).

JULY

3

Ready for Fishing

FROM THE BIBLE:
From that time Jesus began to preach and to say, "Repent, for the kingdom of heaven is at hand." Now Jesus, walking by the Sea of Galilee, saw two brothers, Simon called Peter, and Andrew his brother, casting a net into the sea; for they were fishermen. And He said to them, "Follow Me, and I will make you fishers of men." Then they immediately left their nets and followed Him. And going on from there, He saw two other brothers, James the son of Zebedee, and John his brother, in the boat with Zebedee their father, mending their nets. And He called them, and immediately they left the boat and their father, and followed Him.
Matthew 4:17-22, NKJV

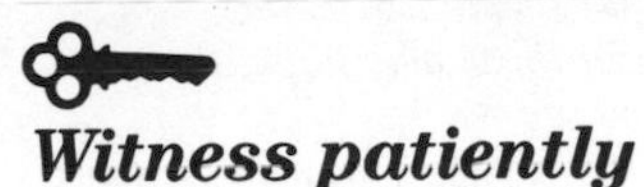

Witness patiently

TRUDY GOT the fishing gear together and put it in the car. This was her first fishing trip with her father, and she was excited. As they traveled to the lake, Trudy told Dad about a girl she had witnessed to last weekend. "But I guess it didn't do any good," she finished. "Carol didn't want to come to Christ."

"Well," Dad replied, "fishing and witnessing are a lot alike, so maybe you'll learn something today."

After they had reached the lake, Dad began to bait his hook. "Will you do mine, too?" Trudy asked. "I don't want to get all messy from handling the worms."

Dad shook his head. "No, honey," he said quietly. "Baiting the hook is part of fishing."

Trudy wrinkled up her nose and finally dug out a worm. She quickly put it on the hook. "Now what?" she asked.

"Now you throw in the line and then sit back and wait," Dad answered.

Trudy followed his instructions, but soon she became restless. "How long do I have to wait?" she asked.

"Until you get a bite," Dad said pleasantly.

Trudy frowned. "I don't like that part," she said, grumbling a little. "I thought you could just throw out the line and get a fish right away."

"No," her father replied. "The fish don't just get up and jump in the boat. You do everything you can, and then you use patience. Lots of patience. When and if you get a bite, you pull in the line, and you may find a fish on the end of it. Now, remember that I told you fishing and witnessing were a lot alike? Do you see why?"

Trudy thought about it, then she nodded. She had talked with Carol about accepting Christ; now she needed to show patience. While she waited, she would pray for Carol every day. Maybe God would let her "pull in the line" someday.

HOW ABOUT YOU? Have you witnessed to someone, thinking they would come to Jesus right away? Sometimes it takes time, patience, persistence, and prayer. Keep witnessing and waiting for God to work. H.M.

TO MEMORIZE: *"Follow Me, and I will make you fishers of men"* Matthew 4:19 (NKJV).

JULY

Consider the Cost

FROM THE BIBLE:

Blessed is the nation whose God is the Lord,
And the people whom He has chosen as His own inheritance.
The Lord looks from heaven;
He sees all the sons of men.
From the place of His habitation He looks
On all the inhabitants of the earth;
He fashions their hearts individually;
He considers all their works.
No king is saved by the multitude of an army;
A mighty man is not delivered by great strength.
A horse is a vain hope for safety;
Neither shall it deliver any by its great strength.
Behold, the eye of the Lord is on those who fear Him,
On those who hope in His mercy,
To deliver their soul from death,
And to keep them alive in famine.
Our soul waits for the Lord;
He is our help and our shield.

Psalm 33:12-20, NKJV

Honor the flag

ON THE FOURTH of July, Tom and his sister, Sally, sat on the curb watching the parade. "There's our school band," said Tom. "Look at old Jack beating on the drum. That drum's almost bigger than he is."

"And look at Old Glory. Isn't she pretty?" said an elderly man who was sitting in a wheelchair.

"Old Glory?" asked Tom. "What's she playing?"

"Don't be silly," giggled Sally. "He means the flag."

"Yes," said the man, "and you two forgot to stand at attention as the flag passed by!"

"But almost no one does that," protested Sally.

"No," agreed the man, "only a few. I imagine they're the ones who know the price of that flag."

"Price? Did that flag cost more than any other flag?" wondered Tom. "Is that a special flag?"

"To me the flag is special,"answered the old man. "If I could stand, I certainly would. I was wounded while fighting for that flag and for what it represents—all the blessings and freedoms we enjoy in this country. I like to believe that I am in this wheelchair today so the flag can go down the street. And no doubt these other folks who stood at attention have also fought for Old Glory or know and love someone who has. They know how much it cost because they helped pay the price."

Tom and Sally felt ashamed. "We're sorry, sir," said Tom. "We didn't realize what our freedom cost. Our flag and our freedom will mean more to us now."

HOW ABOUT YOU? Do you stand at attention when the Pledge of Allegiance is given and when the national anthem is sung? Remember that many brave men and women gave their lives or were wounded so you can enjoy all the blessings your flag represents. Show proper respect for your flag and your country. And be sure to thank God for the privilege of living in a country where He is recognized. As the Pledge of Allegiance says, it is "under God" that you have the liberty which you enjoy. B.W.

TO MEMORIZE: *"Blessed is the nation whose God is the Lord"* Psalm 33:12 (NKJV).

JULY

5

Consider the Cost

(Continued from yesterday)

FROM THE BIBLE:

For you know that it was not with perishable things such as silver or gold that you were redeemed from the empty way of life handed down to you from your forefathers, but with the precious blood of Christ, a lamb without blemish or defect. He was chosen before the creation of the world, but was revealed in these last times for your sake. Through him you believe in God, who raised him from the dead and glorified him, and so your faith and hope are in God. 1 Peter 1:18-21, NIV

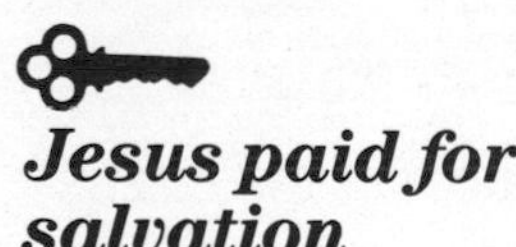

Jesus paid for salvation

WHEN TOM and Sally returned home from the parade, they found their parents having refreshments on the patio. "Can we go to the fireworks tonight?" Tom asked eagerly, as he helped himself to some fruit. "And can Jerry Green go with us?"

"As a matter of fact, we've asked Jerry's family to join us for a picnic before the fireworks," Mom told him. She smiled when he let out a whoop. "Your dad has been witnessing to Mr. Green for some time," she continued.

"That's right," said Dad. "He's interested, but he feels he should do something to earn his salvation—says you can't get something for nothing these days. I'm hoping for another chance to talk with him today. Now, did you enjoy the parade?"

Mom and Dad listened as the children told them about the man in the wheelchair. "We never appreciated the flag and our freedom because it never cost us anything," Sally explained. "But it cost that man a whole lot. And it cost some people even more. Did it cost you anything, Dad?"

Dad looked a bit startled as he answered. "No, it really didn't. I'm glad you shared what you learned. It's so easy for all of us to take our blessings for granted, forgetting that someone paid a big price for them. And you've given me an idea for reaching Mr. Green, too."

"Tell us," suggested Mother.

"As I said, Mr. Green feels that salvation can't be free—that it should cost something," said Dad. "Perhaps I can show him that, although it's free to us—like the liberties we enjoy in America—a big price was paid for it. It cost God His only Son. It cost Jesus His life. We can enjoy the privilege of being a child of God because of the price He was willing to pay for us."

HOW ABOUT YOU? Do you realize that salvation cost a great deal? Jesus had to leave the glories of heaven and live in this sinful world. He had to die on the cross. He had to suffer punishment—all this to pay the price of your salvation. There is nothing more you can do. You must simply believe He paid the price for you and accept the free gift of salvation that He offers. Accept Him today. B.W.

TO MEMORIZE: *"He was chosen before the creation of the world, but was revealed in these last times for your sake"* 1 Peter 1:20 (NIV).

JULY

6

Consider the Cost

(Continued from yesterday)

FROM THE BIBLE:
Husbands, love your wives, just as Christ also loved the church and gave Himself for it, that He might sanctify and cleanse it with the washing of water by the word, that He might present it to Himself a glorious church, not having spot or wrinkle or any such thing, but that it should be holy and without blemish.
Ephesians 5:25-27, NKJV

Appreciate your church

"UP AND AT 'EM, kids!" Dad called up the stairs on Sunday morning.

Tom and Sally soon appeared at the breakfast table, looking sleepy-eyed. "Ooooh! I wish I could sleep in just one Sunday," moaned Sally.

"Yeah," agreed Tom. "Do we have to go to Sunday school and church *every* week? Is church that important?"

"Apparently Christ thought it was important," Dad told them. "The Bible says He loved the church and gave Himself for it. Of course, it's not the *building* that He died for. It's the *people* who make up His church."

"That's right," agreed Mother. "You know, I was just thinking—the privilege of going to church is one of the things we don't appreciate as much as we should. It's interesting how we always value things more if they cost us something."

Tom looked thoughtful. "You mean, like the man in the wheelchair appreciated the flag and our country because he fought for it?" he asked.

"Right," agreed Dad. "We often take living in this country for granted, and we often take the privilege of going to church for granted. But even today—behind the Iron Curtain, for instance—there are those who are making great sacrifices to meet with God's people. Some are even put in prison just because they're Christians."

"In some places people walk for many miles to go to church," added Mother. "Usually they don't have beautiful buildings in which to worship, either, or comfortable benches to sit on. But they come anyway because they love God and want to worship Him."

"All it cost me to go to church is a few minutes sleep," commented Sally. "That's not much, is it?"

"I'm spoiled, too," admitted Tom. "Hey, let's get ready for church."

HOW ABOUT YOU? Do you sometimes grumble because you have to go to church and Sunday school each week? Have you ever stopped to think how little it costs you to go? Have you thanked God for this privilege? Have you thanked Him for your church building? Your pastor? Your Sunday school teacher? Attend services faithfully. Don't take them for granted. B.W.

TO MEMORIZE: *"Christ also loved the church and gave Himself for it"* Ephesians 5:25 (NKJV).

JULY

7

Smart Birds

FROM THE BIBLE:

I have given them your word and the world has hated them, for they are not of the world any more than I am of the world. My prayer is not that you take them out of the world but that you protect them from the evil one. They are not of the world, even as I am not of it. Sanctify them by the truth; your word is truth. As you sent me into the world, I have sent them into the world. For them I sanctify myself, that they too may be truly sanctified.

John 17:14-19, NIV

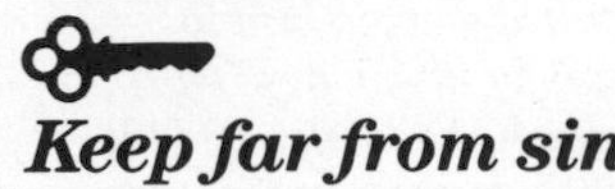

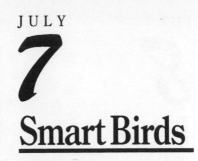

Keep far from sin

BRENT SAT ON the sandy beach, watching his father cast the fishing line out into the water. He enjoyed watching the ocean waves come in and go out again. "Here it is—Saturday," he called to his father, "and I don't have any idea what to talk about in class tomorrow." For several weeks his Sunday school teacher had asked one of the class members to give a testimony, sharing some spiritual lesson he had learned. Brent had said he'd do it this week, but he still hadn't thought of anything to share.

He watched the sandpipers on the moist sand picking for food. Somehow they seemed to sense when the big waves were about to hit, and seconds before the water reached them they flew away. Brent noticed that they returned when the tide went back out, once more finding food. Over and over they repeated the action. Brent laughed. "Those are smart birds," he said. "When the waves go out, they come for food, but when the waves come in, they leave even before the first drop of water can touch their feet."

Dad nodded. "Too bad Christians aren't always that smart." Brent gave him a questioning look. "We live in the world, and we know there is sin all around us," explained Dad, "but we ought to have as much sense as those sandpipers. They know enough to leave before the water gets too close to them. As Christians we should not allow sin to come close to us."

"Sometimes we can't help it if we get pulled into something that's not good," Brent reasoned. "It's not always our fault."

"I know what you're saying," answered Dad. "I've been there, too. But maybe if we had prayed about the situation and looked for God's leading, we would never have gotten close enough to the sin so that there was a danger of being pulled in."

Suddenly Brent realized that this was a lesson he could share with the class. It was also something he wanted to remember all his life.

HOW ABOUT YOU? Do you find yourself trying to get so close to "worldly things" that Satan is able to trap you and pull you under? Or do you try to live so close to God that when temptation comes, you're able to rely on His strength to resist the evil? God's Word teaches us to resist. R.J.

TO MEMORIZE: *"You do not belong to the world, but I have chosen you out of the world"* John 15:19 (NIV).

JULY

8

Little Things

FROM THE BIBLE:

Again, the Kingdom of Heaven can be illustrated by the story of a man going into another country, who called together his servants and loaned them money to invest for him while he was gone. He gave $5,000 to one, $2,000 to another, and $1,000 to the last—dividing it in proportion to their abilities—and then left on his trip. . . . After a long time their master returned from his trip and called them to him to account for his money. The man to whom he had entrusted the $5,000 brought him $10,000. His master praised him for good work. "You have been faithful in handling this small amount," he told him, "so now I will give you many more responsibilities. . . ." Next came the man who had received the $2,000, with the report, "Sir, you gave me $2,000 to use, and I have doubled it." "Good work," his master said. "You are a good and faithful servant. You have been faithful over this small amount, so now I will give you much more."

Matthew 25:14-15, 19-23, TLB

Little things are important

"THERE ARE LOTS of kids at vacation Bible school today," observed Linda as she left the church with her parents.

"Yes, it was a good morning," agreed her father, who was pastor of the church.

"The teachers surely were busy," added Mother. She looked at Linda. "I appreciate all your help, honey."

"I wish I could do more," said Linda as they walked to the parsonage. "I only do little things—like pick up paper after the kids are gone or show the little ones where they have to go. Nothing exciting or important like teaching."

After Linda climbed into bed that evening, Mom handed her a note. "This is from your dad and me," she said, sitting on the bed.

"A thank you note," Linda said, and began reading it out loud, but very slowly. "Thank you linda for your help at vbs each day the little things you do really are important and were proud youre our daughter we love you very much"

Linda was quiet a moment. "Thanks for the note," she said, wrinkling her brow. "It was hard to read, though."

"Oh?" asked Mom, looking surprised. "Why was that?"

"Well, you didn't capitalize words or put periods and commas in the note," Linda answered.

"Oh," Mom said, with a twinkle in her eye, "they're just little things that don't really matter."

"Don't matter!" Linda laughed. "They're little, but they're important."

"That's true," Mom agreed. "And guess what? It's the same with little jobs—especially those done for the Lord. Any time you begin thinking the little things you do aren't important, just think about this note."

"Thanks for the encouragement," Linda said, as Mother tucked the covers around her. "I'm convinced now that little things really do matter!"

HOW ABOUT YOU? Do you sometimes feel as though the jobs you do aren't important? Try to remember that in God's sight it doesn't matter whether a job is big or little, exciting or boring. The most important thing is that you faithfully do it. Whether it's washing dishes, mowing the lawn, or even closing a door for someone, do it in such a way that God Himself would say to you, "Well done." S.N.

TO MEMORIZE: *"Now it is required that those who have been given a trust must prove faithful"* 1 Corinthians 4:2 (NIV).

JULY

The Right Bait

FROM THE BIBLE:
Humble yourselves, therefore, under God's mighty hand, that he may lift you up in due time. Cast all your anxiety on him because he cares for you. Be self-controlled and alert. Your enemy the devil prowls around like a roaring lion looking for someone to devour. Resist him, standing firm in the faith, because you know that your brothers throughout the world are undergoing the same kind of sufferings. And the God of all grace, who called you to his eternal glory in Christ, after you have suffered a little while, will himself restore you and make you strong, firm and steadfast. To him be the power for ever and ever. Amen.
1 Peter 5:6-11, NIV

Resist Satan

LINDA SLAMMED her books down on the table. "That Lonnie!" she exclaimed. "I know he accepted Jesus as his Savior last month, and I know I can't expect him to grow into a mature Christian overnight. But honestly! When I hear the language he uses sometimes, I almost wonder if he's really a Christian after all. It's disgusting!"

Mother looked up from her work. "That's too bad," she said. "Maybe you should speak to him about it. Then be sure to pray for him."

"But, Mother," said Linda, "why would he even want to talk like that? I mean, I can't imagine ever saying those words, even if I weren't a Christian!"

"Perhaps he does it without even thinking—out of habit," suggested Mother. "Or maybe it makes him feel like he's 'one of the guys.' I'm glad that such language is not temptation to you, but the things that tempt you probably don't tempt him."

Linda thought about that. "What do you mean?"

"When Dad went fishing for bluegills last week," asked Mother. "What kind of bait did he use?"

Linda pulled a face. "Yucky red worms," she said. "He says bluegills like them, but if I were a bluegill, I'm sure I'd rather have a nice little minnow. I'd rather eat a fish than a worm any day."

Mother laughed. "But the bluegills wouldn't, and that's my point exactly. A good fisherman knows the right bait to use." She paused. "In a way, Satan is a good 'fisherman.' Maybe he doesn't tempt you to say bad words because he knows they don't appeal to you anyway. Maybe he tempts you instead to, oh, let's say, to be unhappy unless you can have the very latest thing in fashion. Now that probably wouldn't tempt Lonnie at all."

Linda blushed as she recalled how she had pouted when her mother refused to buy her a miniskirt. "You're right," she admitted. "I'm sorry. I'll ask God to help Lonnie—and me."

HOW ABOUT YOU? What bait does Satan place before you? Clothes? Good grades? Sleeping in on Sunday morning? Playing ball instead of going to Bible study? Skipping choir or some other responsibility if you just don't feel like doing it? Satan knows your weakness and will use it to his advantage. But even more important, God is your strength. Ask Him to help you when you're tempted to do wrong. H.M.

TO MEMORIZE: *"The devil prowls around like a roaring lion looking for someone to devour. Resist him, standing firm in the faith"* 1 Peter 5:8-9 (NIV).

JULY

10

The Right Bait

(Continued from yesterday)

FROM THE BIBLE:

Jesus said: "A man was going down from Jerusalem to Jericho, when he fell into the hands of robbers. They stripped him of his clothes, beat him and went away, leaving him half dead. A priest happened to be going down the same road, and when he saw the man, he passed by on the other side. So too, a Levite, when he came to the place and saw him, passed by on the other side. But a Samaritan, as he traveled, came where the man was; and when he saw him, he took pity on him. He went to him and bandaged his wounds, pouring on oil and wine. Then he put the man on his own donkey, took him to an inn and took care of him. The next day he took out two silver coins and gave them to the innkeeper. 'Look after him,' he said, 'and when I return, I will reimburse you for any extra expense you may have.' Which of these three do you think was a neighbor to the man who fell into the hands of robbers?" The expert in the law replied, "The one who had mercy on him." Jesus told him, "Go and do likewise."

Luke 10:30-37, NIV

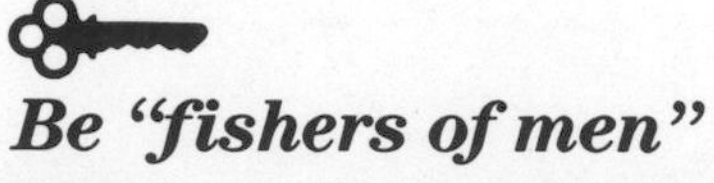

Be "fishers of men"

"HEY, MOM!" Linda climbed into the car after Sunday school and slammed the door. "I'm going fishing this afternoon, OK?" She grinned. "My teacher said I should."

Dad laughed as he started the car. "I can see that there's a catch here somewhere," he said. "Are you going to tell us what it is, or must we guess?"

"Well, our Sunday school lesson was about being 'fishers of men,' " explained Linda. "I remembered the talk Mom and I had this week about using the right bait for fishing, so I told the class about the bait Satan uses to tempt us. We decided it might be a good idea to think about what 'bait' we should use when we 'fish for men,' too."

"Hmmm," murmured Dad. "And did you think of anything more wonderful to offer than what Jesus offers—eternal life?"

"We talked about that," Linda explained. "Mrs. Parsons, our teacher, pointed out that a lot of people live so much 'in the present,' as she put it, that they don't really hear when we talk about something like that. So we decided we should use some other bait to make people want to listen when the way of salvation is explained. Do you know what special bait we plan to use?"

"What?" asked Mother.

"Love," replied Linda. "Mrs. Parsons says that love is the basic bait we should use, but it can take different forms. It's going to take the form of a party this week, and it will be on Saturday. The way of salvation will be explained during our devotional time. We're supposed to bring an unsaved friend, so I plan to start 'fishing' by going to Joy's house and inviting her to the party."

"Good," approved Dad, "but I hope the 'fishing' won't end with the party."

"No." Linda shook her head. "Mrs. Parsons says the party is just a start. Afterwards we still need to offer the 'bait' of loving acts if we want to see our friends come to know Jesus."

HOW ABOUT YOU? Are you "fishing for men"? What are you using for bait? Winning someone to Jesus often begins with being a friend. Something as simple as a cheerful smile, helping with a problem, or sharing a special treat may be the thing that causes a person to listen when you tell him about Jesus or invite him to church. Will you go "fishing" by using a loving act today? H.M.

TO MEMORIZE: *"Love your neighbor as yourself"* Matthew 19:19 (NIV).

JULY

11

Sharing the Right Way

FROM THE BIBLE:

Son of man, I have made you a watchman for the house of Israel; so hear the word I speak and give them warning from me. When I say to a wicked man, "You will surely die," and you do not warn him or speak out to dissuade him from his evil ways in order to save his life, that wicked man will die for his sin, and I will hold you accountable for his blood. But if you do warn the wicked man and he does not turn from his wickedness or from his evil ways, he will die for his sin; but you will have saved yourself.
Ezekiel 3:17-19, NIV

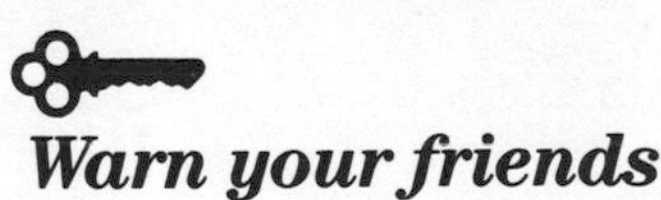

Warn your friends

SALLY WAS UNUSUALLY quiet after she returned home from the evening service at her church. Her pastor had preached about the return of the Lord Jesus, and some of the things he said disturbed her. Oh, she had put her faith in Jesus Christ, and she knew that she was on her way to heaven, but she wondered about her friends. None of them had accepted Jesus as Savior, yet Sally seldom shared God's plan of salvation with her friends.

When Sally went to bed that evening, she tossed and turned for a long time. And when she finally did go to sleep, she had a dream that included her friends. They were all on a hike through one of the dark and dangerous caves in the area. Sally had a descriptive map showing exactly how to walk and where to go to get out safely, but she refused to share it with the others. Some in the group thought they could get out without following her map. In her dream, Sally watched the others start off in many wrong directions, trying to find the way out, but she didn't say anything to them. She looked at her map again and then started out by herself. Finally she reached the exit and waved to the crowd of people waiting for the group.

"Where are the others?" someone asked.

Sally shrugged her shoulders. "They were going all kinds of ways," she replied carelessly.

Sally spotted her pastor standing with the others. "But you knew they were going the wrong way," he stated pointedly. "Why didn't you show them the right way?"

It was then that Sally awoke from her dream. She was glad it was only a dream. She had not been too proud of the way she had withheld the information from her friends. As she remembered her dream, a thought struck her. In the cave her friends were lost. In life they were lost, too. She was glad that she would have another chance to tell them that Jesus is the only Way to heaven.

HOW ABOUT YOU? Do you have some friends who think they'll get to heaven by being good, by going to church, or by being baptized? Are there others who don't seem to be concerned about finding the way at all? Maybe God is giving you another opportunity to share God's way—His Son, the Lord Jesus Christ. Warn them that all other ways lead to eternal death. R.J.

TO MEMORIZE: *"Give them warning from me"* Ezekiel 3:17 (NIV).

JULY

12

A Faithful Friend

FROM THE BIBLE:

Through the Lord's mercies we are not consumed, because His compassions fail not. They are new every morning; great is Your faithfulness. "The Lord is my portion," says my soul, "Therefore I hope in Him!" The Lord is good to those who wait for Him, to the soul who seeks Him. It is good that one should hope and wait quietly for the salvation of the Lord.
Lamentations 3:22-26, NKJV

God is faithful

NED CAREFULLY made his bed, then swept his bedroom floor. "Company's coming," he explained to his dog, Rags, who was watching every move Ned made.

Ned and his family had moved away a year ago, and he had missed his friends very much. But now they were back, and he had invited his old friend, Dan, to come for the weekend. Ned had a big time planned. "I can hardly wait until Dan gets here," he told Rags, reaching down to lovingly ruffle the fur on the dog's neck. Rags pushed his cool, damp nose into Ned's hand, his special way of showing his love.

The lonely year would have been worse without Rags. Ned remembered the time Rags had been hot and dry with fever. Ned had been afraid his dog would die, and he'd prayed that God would make Rags well again. When Rags got better, Ned had thanked God over and over. Since then, his dog's cool, wet nose always made Ned think of God's faithfulness. "Great is Your faithfulness," quoted Ned. "It's just like the Bible says, Rags." The dog wagged his tail as though he fully agreed, nuzzling Ned's hand again with his nose.

Ned jumped at the sound of the telephone and ran to answer it. "Oh, hi, Dan," he said. "You're not coming? Why?" There was a pause. Then, "Your uncle got tickets to the football game? Oh . . . uh, sure. I . . . I understand. Well, OK. 'Bye."

Ned ran into his room with Rags at his heels. He flung himself on his bed. Hot tears streamed down his face. He cried for a long time. Then as he grew quiet, he felt a cool, wet nose push into his hand. He put his arm around the dear, old dog, and he thought of God's love.

"It's true, Rags. God is faithful," he murmured. "My friend disappointed me, but God is here with me just as sure as you are. I didn't get what I wanted this time, but I know God loves me and cares for me just the same."

HOW ABOUT YOU? Has a friend or relative disappointed you? Have you been lonely, sick, or had other trouble? God is always with you. He is faithful and will never leave you. When you're feeling sad, remember God loves you and faithfully cares for you—in good times and in bad. C.Y.

TO MEMORIZE: *"Great is Your faithfulness"* Lamentations 3:23 (NKJV).

JULY

13

Loudmouth Lynn

FROM THE BIBLE:

To hide hatred is to be a liar; to slander is to be a fool. Don't talk so much. You keep putting your foot in your mouth. Be sensible and turn off the flow! When a good man speaks, he is worth listening to, but the words of fools are a dime a dozen. A godly man gives good advice, but a rebel is destroyed by lack of common sense. . . . The good man gives wise advice, but the liar's counsel is shunned. The upright speak what is helpful; the wicked speak rebellion.
Proverbs 10:18-21, 31-32, TLB

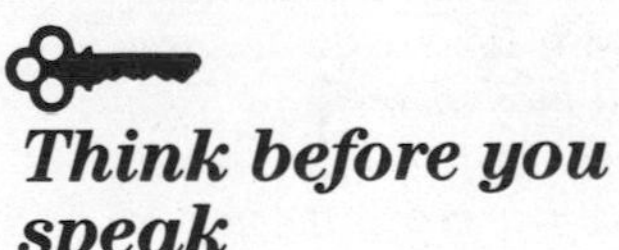

Think before you speak

LYNN REALLY was a sweet little girl, but she had one very bad habit—she talked loud and long! As a result, she had earned the nickname "Loudmouth Lynn."

One day when she was finally getting to the end of a lengthy story, she looked up to see that her mother had returned to her cooking. "Mom!" Lynn wailed. "You're not even listening!"

"I'm listening," Mother assured her, "but I know your stories tend to be somewhat long, so I thought I'd work while I listened. Now before you start again, how about setting the table for supper. Your father should be home soon from his fishing trip with Grandpa."

"Oh, I hope they catch some big ones," said Lynn as she took the plates from the cupboard and headed for the dining room. "Remember the time when . . . " She was still talking as she left the room. Mother sighed. "Loudmouth Lynn" did seem to be a fitting name for her daughter!

Dad arrived home disappointed for he had only caught a few small panfish. Mother cooked them anyway, and Lynn was eager to try them. She found that the meat was delicious, but the fish were full of tiny, white bones.

"I'm tired of picking through these fish to find the good parts," she said finally, pushing her plate away.

Mother nodded. "You know, Lynn, that's the feeling I get sometimes when I'm listening to you talk. Some of the things you say are quite interesting and worthwhile. But the best parts of your conversation are often covered up by silly chatter, complaining, and even gossip. After awhile I get tired of listening for the few things worth hearing."

After a moment, Lynn sighed. "You've told me before that I talk too much, and other people have, too. But I was so busy talking that I didn't really hear what you were saying," she said with a long face.

"Cheer up." Mother smiled. "You don't have to stop talking entirely! Just make sure to take the 'bones' out—your silly, useless speech—before you say anything. You'll find that your speech will be more pleasing to others—and to God as well."

HOW ABOUT YOU? Are you a loudmouth? Do you like to talk and talk? People who talk too much tend to gossip, complain, or exaggerate to get attention. Think before you speak. S.K.

TO MEMORIZE: *"A fool's voice is know by multitude of words"* Ecclesiates 5:3.

JULY

14

Where in the World Is Habakkuk?

FROM THE BIBLE:

How can a young man cleanse his way?
By taking heed according to Your word.
With my whole heart I have sought You;
Oh, let me not wander from Your commandments!
Your word I have hidden in my heart,
That I might not sin against You.
Blessed are You, O Lord!
Teach me Your statutes.
With my lips I have declared
All the judgments of Your mouth.
I have rejoiced in the way of Your testimonies,
As much as in all riches.
I will meditate on Your precepts,
And contemplate Your ways.
I will delight myself in Your statutes;
I will not forget Your word.
Psalm 119:9-16, NKJV

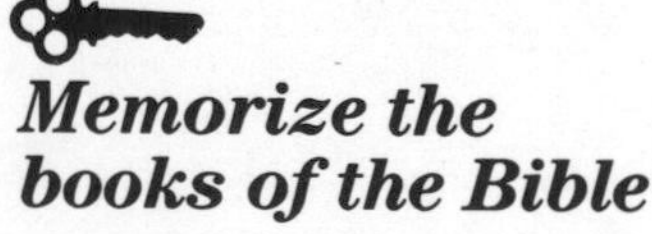

Memorize the books of the Bible

"OK, BOYS," Mr. Paterson said to his Sunday school class, "please turn in your Bibles to Habakkuk, chapter one, verse two."

"You're kidding!" exclaimed David. "Haba-who?"

"That's not really a book, is it?" Jason laughed.

"Sure it's a book," Tim spoke up. "It goes 'Jonah, Micah, Nahum, Habakkuk.' "

"Wow! You sure can rattle those off, Tim," said Jason. "I tried learning them once, but they're just too hard!"

"All those funny-sounding names get me mixed up," agreed David. "It's not worth it to learn them. After all, my Bible has an index."

"It is worth it!" declared Mr. Paterson. "It's difficult to study any book without knowing how to find things in it. Besides, if someone asks you a question about the Bible, you should know where to find the answers. No one will be very patient if you spend a lot of time fumbling around, searching for a particular book."

David shrugged. "If they weren't so hard to say . . ."

Mr. Paterson started teaching, and the boys settled down to listen. At the end of class, however, they had a few minutes to talk before the bell rang. "Hey, Jason, did you get that new comic book?" asked David. "You know, the one about the Tuonical Monster?"

"Sure did," replied Jason. "I have all twenty-seven in that series. They're super!"

"I never even heard of them," said Tim.

"Well, I can tell you what ever single one of them is about," Jason offered.

"Hmmm," murmured Mr. Paterson. "You can do that, yet you can't learn a list of names?"

Jason looked embarrassed. "I never thought about that," he mumbled. "I guess I could learn the books of the Bible." Suddenly he turned to David. "Bet I can learn them quicker than you!"

In answer, David turned to the index in his Bible and began memorizing the list.

HOW ABOUT YOU? Do you know the books of the Bible? Maybe you think it's too hard to learn those "funny-sounding" names. If you learn a little about each book, it will make it easier for you to remember them. It is important to study the Bible, and part of that study is to know the books. L.W.

TO MEMORIZE: *"I have rejoiced in the way of Your testimonies, as much as in all riches"* Psalm 119:14 (NKJV).

JULY

15

The Second Mile

FROM THE BIBLE:
You have heard that it was said, "Eye for eye, and tooth for tooth." But I tell you, Do not resist an evil person. If someone strikes you on the right cheek, turn to him the other also. And if someone wants to sue you and take your tunic, let him have your cloak as well. If someone forces you to go one mile, go with him two miles. Give to the one who asks you, and do not turn away from the one who wants to borrow from you.
Matthew 5:38-42, NIV

Do a little extra

"WILL SOMEONE please volunteer to stay and help me after school?" Mrs. Harris asked her fifth-grade class.

Eric started to raise his hand but remembered his mother was taking him shopping after school.

Gina thought, *I would stay but I'm tired. I'd rather go home and finish the book I started last night. I'll help another time.*

Tony's elbow bent as his hand started up, but a sharp kick from Ricky reminded him that they had scheduled a ball game after school.

Patti raised her hand. "Mrs. Harris, I'll help. May I go call my mother so she won't be worried when I'm late?" Mrs. Harris smiled as she excused Patti to make the call.

The next day when Mrs. Harris made the math assignment, she also pointed to twenty problems on the board for anyone who wished to do them for extra credit. Eric, Tony, and Ricky decided they would not have time to do the extra work. Gina looked at the board and sighed tiredly. She simply did not have enough energy to do any extra work. Patti quickly copied the problems.

And so it went. Time after time, Patti did the little extra, and the other children made excuses.

"Class, the local radio station is planning a special program next week in honor of National Educational Week," Mrs. Harris announced one day. "Each teacher has been asked to choose one student to be interviewed and give a brief report of the class activities." She smiled as the students suddenly looked alert. She had everyone's undivided attention. Each wanted to be selected. "I have chosen Patti Vernon," Mrs. Harris went on. "I'll meet with you after school, Patti. We'll discuss it then."

At lunch Patti was met with jealous glares and catty remarks. "Teacher's pet!" "Apple polisher!" Everyone had forgotten the little extras Patti always did, everyone, that is, except Mrs. Harris.

HOW ABOUT YOU? Do you think pastors, Sunday school teachers, and parents seem to have favorites? How long has it been since you did a little extra for someone else? Like picking up the songbooks or volunteering some help at church? Washing dishes or taking out the trash without being asked? Visiting an absentee or bringing someone to Sunday school? Go the second mile. Do a little bit extra. B.W.

TO MEMORIZE: *"If someone forces you to go one mile, go with him two miles"* Matthew 5:41 (NIV).

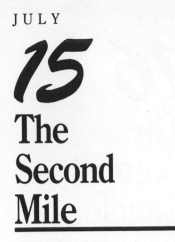

JULY

16

The Scented Candle

FROM THE BIBLE:

Do all things without murmuring and disputing, that you may become blameless and harmless, children of God without fault in the midst of a crooked and perverse generation, among whom you shine as lights in the world, holding fast the word of life, so that I may rejoice in the day of Christ that I have not run in vain or labored in vain.
Philippians 2:14-16, NKJV

Be a sweet witness

"MMMMMM!" Sharla took a deep breath as she closed the front door behind her. "Coconut." She hurried into the kitchen, her nose twitching like a rabbit's. "I want a piece, Mother." Mother looked up from fixing the salad and handed Sharla a carrot. "No, thanks," Sharla laughed. "I don't want a carrot, I want a piece of coconut cake."

A frown wrinkled Mother's forehead. "Coconut cake? I don't have any."

"Are you making coconut pie then?" Sharla opened the oven door. "I smell coconut."

"No, I'm not," Mother answered. Then she grinned. "You smell the coconut candle that's burning, Sharla."

"Ooohhhh! It sure is making me hungry. Well, I guess this will have to do," Sharla said as she picked up a carrot. She sat down at the table and watched as her mother tossed the salad. "Jason witnesses to the kids at school all the time," she said abruptly.

Mother smiled, "That's good."

Sharla frowned. "I don't know if it is or not."

Mother looked up in surprise. "You don't know if it's good or not?" she repeated. "What a strange thing to say."

"It's the way he witnesses," Sharla explained between bites. "He is such a—such a smarty witness. It's like he's bragging because he knows Jesus and the other kids don't. He's not a very good example of a Christian. His attitude is wrong."

"A witness with a wrong attitude is like a floodlight shining in someone's eyes." Mother set the salad on the table. "It blinds people. On the other hand, a witness with a sweet spirit is like a scented candle."

Sharla took a deep breath and smiled. "I know what you mean. Like your scented candle made me hungry, so a sweet witness will cause people to hunger to know Jesus. That's the kind of witness I want to be." Sharla's smile turned to a grin as she added, "And Mother, could we make a coconut cake after dinner?"

HOW ABOUT YOU? What kind of a witness are you? Are you like a floodlight or like a scented candle? Do you blind people with a know-it-all attitude? Or do you cause them to hunger for Christ? B.W.

TO MEMORIZE: *"By this My Father is glorified, that you bear much fruit"* John 15:8 (NKJV).

JULY

17

His Sheep Am I

FROM THE BIBLE:

"Anyone refusing to walk through the gate into a sheepfold, who sneaks over the wall, must surely be a thief! For a shepherd comes through the gate. The gatekeeper opens the gate for him, and the sheep hear his voice and come to him; and he calls his own sheep by name and leads them out. He walks ahead of them; and they follow him, for they recognize his voice. They won't follow a stranger but will run from him, for they don't recognize his voice." Those who heard Jesus use this illustration didn't understand what he meant, so he explained it to them. "I am the Gate for the sheep," he said. "All others who came before me were thieves and robbers. But the true sheep did not listen to them. Yes, I am the Gate. Those who come in by way of the Gate will be saved and will go in and out and find green pastures. The thief's purpose is to steal, kill and destroy. My purpose is to give life in all its fullness. I am the Good Shepherd. The Good Shepherd lays down his life for the sheep." John 10:1-11, TLB

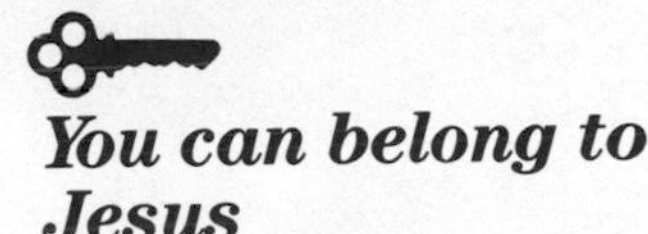

You can belong to Jesus

THUD! The wheels of the plane touched down, and Eric's excitement increased as the plan taxied to the gate. He looked forward to the time he would spend here in Montana. Uncle Joe and Aunt Sue were on hand to meet him, and soon they had driven from the airport to their ranch.

"Can we go see the sheep?" was Eric's first question.

"Sure can," agreed Uncle Joe. That afternoon Eric and his uncle put many miles on the jeep as they traveled up and down the mountain roads.

"I didn't know there were so many sheep in the world," commented Eric. "They all look so fat and woolly!"

"Not all of them," corrected Uncle Joe, and he stopped the jeep along the fence of a neighboring ranch. "Take a good look at those sheep."

Eric was surprised to see a large number of sheep that were very thin. "Oh, Uncle Joe, they look like they may have a disease or something!"

Uncle Joe started the jeep again. "Their owner is away," he sighed, "and the manager doesn't really care about them. He doesn't move them to green pastures or to areas with clean water."

After dinner that evening, Uncle Joe read some verses from John 10. He ended the reading with the verse, "I am the good shepherd: the good shepherd giveth his life for the sheep."

Thoughtfully, Eric spoke. "I think you're really a good shepherd, Uncle Joe," he said. "I'll bet your sheep are glad they belong to you. I guess the people who belong to Jesus are glad, too."

Uncle Joe nodded. "How about you, Eric? Do you belong to Jesus? If you don't belong to Jesus, you belong to Satan, and that means you belong to someone who doesn't really care for you—kind of like the poor, thin sheep down the road."

"Jesus, the Good Shepherd, gave His life so you could belong to Him," added Aunt Sue. "Accept Him as your Savior. Let Him be your Shepherd."

"I'll do that," agreed Eric. Together they bowed their heads to pray.

HOW ABOUT YOU? Do you belong to Jesus, the Good Shepherd, or do you belong to Satan? Jesus loves you and wants to take care of you and guide you. Accept Him as your Savior, and then you can look to Him for care and help, no matter what life may bring. G.W.

TO MEMORIZE: *"The Lord is my shepherd"* Psalm 23:1.

JULY

18

His Sheep Am I

(Continued from yesterday)

FROM THE BIBLE:

Do you want to be truly rich? You already are if you are happy and good. After all, we didn't bring any money with us when we came into the world, and we can't carry away a single penny when we die. So we should be well satisfied without money if we have enough food and clothing. 1 Timothy 6:6-8, TLB

Be content

"ERIC! WAKE UP!" Uncle Joe's loud whisper interrupted Eric's sleep! Rubbing his eyes, Eric glanced at the clock on the nightstand.

"I know it's the middle of the night," Uncle Joe said, chuckling, "but it's raining so hard that there's danger of flooding in the south pasture. The sheep have to be moved. Want to help?"

Three hours later after much hard work, the sheep were high and dry. Eric tumbled back into bed, and Aunt Sue let him sleep late the next morning. While they were eating lunch, Eric learned that Uncle Joe hadn't even gone back to bed. "I went out again to help the ranch hands settle the sheep," explained Uncle Joe.

A few days later Eric and Uncle Joe drove out to see a flock of sheep that had just been moved to a better grazing spot. "Wow!" exclaimed Eric when he saw the rich, green pasture. "Those sheep will never want to leave here!"

Uncle Joe pointed. "See that sheep over by the fence? First thing you know, she'll try to get to the other side, even though it isn't good pasture there. I may not be able to keep her because she teaches her lambs the same tricks."

Eric looked at his uncle in surprise. "Why would she do that when you're such a good shepherd?"

Uncle Joe smiled. "You're never like that, are you?" he asked. "You never want something more when God has already given you many good things, do you?"

Suddenly Eric remembered that just yesterday he had not been content with the way his summer vacation was going. Instead of being happy with the many things he could do on the ranch, he had been crabby when he hadn't been allowed to ride Uncle Joe's favorite horse. And then Aunt Sue had asked him to do the dishes, of all things! At bedtime last night he hadn't even taken time to thank God for a good day, just because he had wanted it to be different. He was a new Christian, but he would try to remember that everything needed in a Christian's life is provided by the Good Shepherd.

HOW ABOUT YOU? Are you a Christian who finds yourself wanting things that God hasn't given you? Do you want a bigger allowance? More clothes? Better health? More permissive parents? Do pray about your needs and your wants, but stay content with what God provides. G.W.

TO MEMORIZE: *"He restores my soul; He leads me in the paths of righteousness for His name's sake"* Psalm 23:3 (NKJV).

JULY

Rescued

FROM THE BIBLE:

And as Moses lifted up the serpent in the wilderness, even so must the Son of Man be lifted up, that whoever believes in Him should not perish but have eternal life. For God so loved the world that He gave His only begotten Son, that whoever believes in Him should not perish but have everlasting life. For God did not send His Son into the world to condemn the world, but that the world through Him might be saved. He who believes in Him is not condemned; but he who does not believe is condemned already, because he has not believed in the name of the only begotten Son of God.

John 3:14-18, NKJV

Jesus rescues sinners

THIRTEEN-YEAR-OLD Hal and his father were walking down Main Street on their way to a baseball game when Hal noticed an unusual display in a shop window. "Hey, Dad, look at that window," he exclaimed. "There's a dog in that cage!" A large hand-lettered sign on the cage read: "Death row! This animal has one more day to live." Hal stopped and looked at the small, brown-eyed puppy inside. "What does the sign mean, Dad?" he asked.

"It's a new program that the animal shelter is trying out," said Dad. "You see, they can't take care of all the stray dogs and cats they find. This display was set up to let people know about the problem and to give the animals one last chance to be adopted out. If no one takes the puppy, he'll have to be put to sleep."

"Put to sleep?" asked Hal. "You mean this little puppy is going to be killed?"

"I'm afraid so, Son," Dad replied.

Hal stared through the glass at the unfortunate puppy. "Poor little guy," he said. "What a shame that such a cute, healthy, little puppy has to be put to sleep!" He turned to his father and wailed, "Oh, Dad, can't we take him home? We can't let him die! Look—he likes us already."

Dad sighed. "We already have a cat and two hamsters," he replied. "Aren't they enough to take care of?"

"But this is different," Hal insisted. "This dog needs us, Dad. It sort of reminds me of Jesus."

"What do you mean?" asked Dad.

"Well, you told me we were already condemned—on 'death row' in a way—before Jesus saved us from our sins," explained Hal. "If Jesus hadn't rescued me, I'd still be on my way to hell. I want to rescue this dog like Jesus rescued me."

Dad nodded his head thoughtfully. Then he smiled. "When you put it that way, how can I refuse?" he said. "If you're willing to take care of this little guy, I'll go in and see if we can take him home tonight. But what about the ball game?"

"Oh, we can go to a baseball game any day. I want to go home and play with my new dog!"

HOW ABOUT YOU? Have you come to the place in your life where you realize that you are a sinner and on your way to hell? If you haven't accepted Jesus as your Savior, you're condemned already. Don't wait till tomorrow. Be saved today! S.K.

TO MEMORIZE: *"He who believes in Him is not condemned; but he who does not believe is condemned already"* John 3:18 (NKJV).

JULY

20

Rescued

(Continued from yesterday)

FROM THE BIBLE:

What then shall we say to these things? If God is for us, who can be against us? He who did not spare His own Son, but delivered Him up for us all, how shall He not with Him also freely give us all things? Who shall bring a charge against God's elect? It is God who justifies. Who is he who condemns? It is Christ who died, and furthermore is also risen, who is even at the right hand of God, who also makes intercession for us. Who shall separate us from the love of Christ? Shall tribulation, or distress, or persecution, or famine, or nakedness, or peril, or sword? As it is written: "For Your sake we are killed all day long; we are accounted as sheep for the slaughter." Yet in all these things we are more than conquerors through Him who loved us. For I am persuaded that neither death nor life, nor angels nor principalities nor powers, nor things present nor things to come, nor height nor depth, nor any other created thing, shall be able to separate us from the love of God which is in Christ Jesus our Lord.
Romans 8:31-39, NKJV

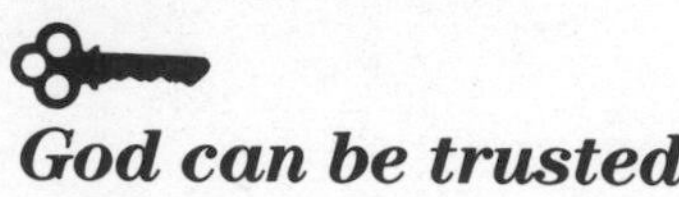

God can be trusted

WHEN HAL and his dad arrived home with the new puppy, Mother lined a box with an old, soft blanket while Dad explained everything. "Come here, Little Guy," Hal called gently. The puppy wobbled across the kitchen floor and sniffed at his new bed. Everyone watched as he turned around and around on the blanket, sniffed at it some more, and finally lay down.

"It's been quite a day for him," Mother said. "What will you name him, Hal?"

"I think I'll call him Little Guy," answered Hal. "That name seems just right for him." Going to the refrigerator, he looked for some meat scraps for the dog. "Say, Mom, can I give him some of this leftover chicken?"

"Well, since there's just that little bit left, I guess he can have it this once," she agreed, "but make sure you take it off the bones, so he won't choke."

Hal set the saucer of meat near the dog, and Little Guy began to eat it greedily. "Uh-oh—there's still a piece of bone in there."

"Take it away from him," Dad said, "or it might get caught in his throat." Hal reached out to pick up the bone, but as he did so, Little Guy growled and snapped at his hand. "Ow!" shouted Hal. "Look at that—he nipped me! I was only trying to help him! Little Guy," he scolded, "you should know you can trust me! It doesn't make sense."

"No, it doesn't," agreed Dad, "but you know, Hal, some Christians don't have any more sense than that dog. They're afraid to trust God completely because they think He's going to take something they love away from them or tell them to do something that will make them unhappy. They forget that it was God who saved them in the first place by sacrificing His own Son, Jesus. That should be proof enough that He only wants what's best for them!"

Hal nodded. "I'd better trust God just like I want Little Guy to trust me."

HOW ABOUT YOU? Are you a Christian, but afraid to trust God with your daily life? Don't be! Remember, God sent His own Son to save your life. He certainly will not change His mind now and try to make you miserable! S.K.

TO MEMORIZE: *"He who did not spare His own Son, but delivered Him up for us all, how shall He not with Him also freely give us all things?"* Romans 8:32 (NKJV).

JULY

21

Rescued

(Continued from yesterday)

FROM THE BIBLE:

But God is so rich in mercy; he loved us so much that even though we were spiritually dead and doomed by our sins, he gave us back our lives again when he raised Christ from the dead—only by his undeserved favor have we ever been saved: and lifted us up from the grave into glory along with Christ, where we sit with him in the heavenly realms—all because of what Christ Jesus did. And now God can always point to us as examples of how very, very rich his kindness is, as shown in all he has done for us through Jesus Christ. Because of his kindness you have been saved through trusting Christ. And even trusting is not of yourselves; it too is a gift from God. Salvation is not a reward for the good we have done, so none of us can take any credit for it. It is God himself who has made us what we are and given us new lives from Christ Jesus; and long ages ago he planned that we should spend these lives in helping others.

Ephesians 2:4-10, TLB

WEEKS PASSED, and Hal's puppy seemed to grow bigger and friskier every day. Hal fed and watered him daily and made sure his fur was clean and brushed. As the dog got older, Hal took him for walks, and often they romped in the woods and streams near their house.

But Little Guy was more than a playmate for Hal. He was taught to help with chores. After Hal had planted some corn in the garden, Little Guy kept the birds away from it. He also barked at rabbits that tried to nibble the lettuce leaves. Little Guy went along when Hal delivered papers. If a paper didn't land right on the porch, he learned to pick it up in his mouth and carry it there. The family knew he was an excellent watchdog, too.

One evening Dad said, "That's some dog you've got there! You're glad you saved him from 'Death Row,' aren't you?"

Hal smiled and patted the dog in his lap. "I sure am!" he said. "You know, I think Little Guy is glad, too. It's almost as though he knows I saved him. He wants to go everywhere with me and seems eager to help me in any way he can."

"I think that's why Little Guy is such a happy dog," said Dad. "He has a loving master who cares for him and whom he can serve. Some dogs are pampered by their owners but never contribute anything in return."

Hal ruffled the dog's fur. "I don't think Little Guy would like sitting on a pillow all day, getting fat. I don't think I would, either."

"Human beings were created to serve God," Dad remarked. "They're never really happy until they do. Some people accept Christ as Savior, and then don't do anything more about it. They sit around on pillows, so to speak, waiting for others to serve them. They have forgotten that they were saved to serve!"

HOW ABOUT YOU? If you are a Christian, are you really serving Christ the way you should? God didn't save you just so you could go to heaven. He wants to use you in this life, too. Get involved in your church. Witness to your friends. Do kind things for your family and others. Read the Bible and pray. Give up your bad habits. It's only right for you to want to serve the One who saved you! S.K.

TO MEMORIZE: *"Therefore, I urge you, brothers, in view of God's mercy, to offer your bodies as living sacrifices, holy and pleasing to God—this is your spiritual act of worship"* Romans 12:1 (NIV).

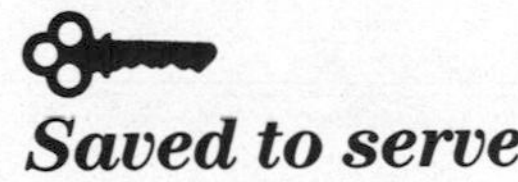

Saved to serve

JULY

22

The Representative

FROM THE BIBLE:
We are therefore Christ's ambassadors, as though God were making his appeal through us. We implore you on Christ's behalf: Be reconciled to God.
2 Corinthians 5:20, NIV

And pray in the Spirit on all occasions with all kinds of prayers and requests. With this in mind, be alert and always keep on praying for all the saints. Pray also for me, that whenever I open my mouth, words may be given me so that I will fearlessly make known the mystery of the gospel, for which I am an ambassador in chains. Pray that I may declare it fearlessly, as I should.
Ephesians 6:18-20, NIV

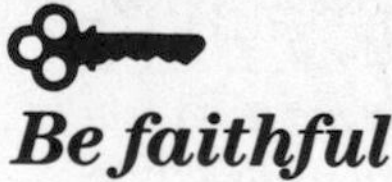

Be faithful

JASON HAD WANTED a paper route ever since he was old enough to qualify. So when Richard asked him to be his substitute, Jason accepted the job excitedly. "Richard's going to be gone a whole month, and I get to keep all the earnings," he told his father that evening.

Each afternoon Jason picked up the papers and hurriedly delivered them to the houses on Richard's route. At the end of the month, he began the job of collecting. This was the part he had been waiting for. He rang the doorbell at the first house. "Collect," he said pleasantly.

The man opened the door and invited him in. "How much do I owe you?" he asked.

"The regular amount," Jason said.

"Oh, I know the regular amount, but I thought you'd want to subtract for the paper that went on the garage roof and the two that fell into the wet flower garden," the man explained. "We weren't able to read any of those."

Jason reluctantly subtracted the price of the three papers and left the house without even saying thanks. Boy, some people were impossible!

At the next house the lady paid for the full month, but she reminded Jason that Richard was always careful to put the paper inside the screen door on rainy days.

By the time Jason returned home, he was not in a very good mood. "Boy, talk about crabby people," he said, telling his dad about what had happened. "Almost everyone complained."

Dad's eyebrows shot up. "Well, Son, those people had a right to expect good service from you, just as they get from Richard," he reminded. "After all, you were his representative."

Jason thought about that. His father's words were almost the same words his Sunday school teacher had used last Sunday. "We are God's representatives here on earth," his teacher explained. "He has a right to expect us to be faithful."

HOW ABOUT YOU? Can the Lord trust you to be His representative? If you're a Christian, all you do and say reflects on the Lord as well as on yourself. If you tell a lie, cheat, snub someone, or do a sloppy job, others may decide that "if that's the way Christians act, I don't care to be one." But a cheerful smile, an honest life, and a job well done is a good testimony for your Lord. R.J.

TO MEMORIZE: *"We are therefore Christ's ambassadors"* 2 Corinthians 5:20 (NIV).

JULY

23

A Picky Witness

FROM THE BIBLE:

So when they met together, they asked him, "Lord, are you at this time going to restore the kingdom to Israel?" He said to them: "It is not for you to know the times or dates the Father has set by his own authority. But you will receive power when the Holy Spirit comes on you; and you will be my witnesses in Jerusalem, and in all Judea and Samaria, and to the ends of the earth." Acts 1:6-8, NIV

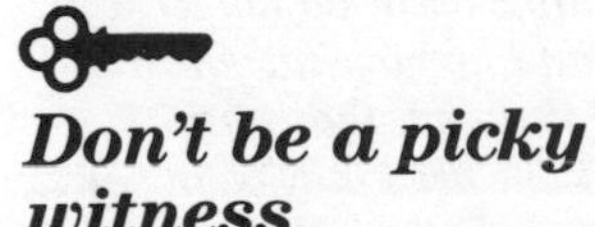

Don't be a picky witness

"I'M GOING to be an overseas missionary when I grow up," said Jason as he watched a small plane circle the Jordan ranch. "A missionary pilot," he added.

"Not me," declared his best friend, Barry. "I'm going to stay right here in the good old U.S.A.! I like . . ." His words were drowned out by the noise of the Piper Cub.

"Crop dusting is dangerous work," Jason shouted. "Look how close he gets to those wires!"

"It's important work," said Barry, as he picked up his ball glove. "One year Dad decided we couldn't afford to spray, and we almost lost everything. The bugs took over."

Again the roar of the plane drowned their words. When the sound had faded, Barry said, "I'm going to show Jose how to hit a baseball. Want to come along?"

Jason frowned. "No! I can't stand that guy. He talks funny. He's dumb, and his clothes are always dirty."

Barry shrugged. "You're not so clean yourself."

Jason looked down at his ragged jeans and dirty hands. "Yeah, but . . ."

"I imagine Jose thinks we talk funny, too," added Barry.

"At least we talk English!" Jason argued. "He speaks a mixture of two or three languages."

"Then he's smarter than we are. We can speak only one," said Barry, and Jason's face turned red. Barry started for the gate, then turned around. "You know, Jason, you called Jose dumb, but you aren't so smart yourself. I think you would be a better crop duster than a missionary pilot. How do you think you can tell people in foreign lands about the love of Jesus when you won't even be friends to a guy who is a little different from you? You're a mighty picky witness."

"I . . . I . . ." Jason dropped his head. His eyes watered. "I never thought about it that way, Barry." Then he looked up. "If you'll wait a minute, I'll go get my ball glove. Maybe Jose will teach me some Spanish."

HOW ABOUT YOU? Do you have visions of doing great things for God some day? What about today? How do you treat those around you? Salvation is for "whosoever will." Are you willing to witness to anyone and everyone? B.W.

TO MEMORIZE: *"And this gospel of the kingdom shall be preached in all the world for a witness unto all nations"* Matthew 24:14.

24

Secret Service

FROM THE BIBLE:

Take heed that you do not do your charitable deeds before men, to be seen by them. Otherwise you have no reward from your Father in heaven. Therefore, when you do a charitable deed, do not sound a trumpet before you as the hypocrites do in the synagogues and in the streets, that they may have glory from men. Assuredly, I say to you, they have their reward. But when you do a charitable deed, do not let your left hand know what your right hand is doing, that your charitable deed may be in secret; and your Father who sees in secret will Himself reward you openly. Matthew 6:1-4, NKJV

God rewards service

MRS. BRIMLEY unlocked the front door and walked wearily into her living room. It had been a long day for her as she worked at the department store. She was very tired, and her feet hurt. Her husband was away on a trip to another city, hoping to find work, so she faced an evening alone. Still, she knew she had to get supper for her children, who were staying with a sitter down the street.

She sniffed the air. Where was that good smell coming from? As she walked into the kitchen, she noticed that the oven was turned on, and the delightful smell of potatoes and ham came out. Mrs. Brimley was startled. *Who could have done this?* she wondered. She saw that the table was set and that the breakfast dishes had been washed. Then on the kitchen counter Mrs. Brimley noticed a small card. It simply said, "I did it in the name of the Lord." There was no signature.

That evening as she ate the lovely supper with her children, she told them about the secret helper. "I bet it was Mrs. James," said David, the youngest.

"No," said Karen, "how could she have gotten in? It must have been Gloria, our sitter."

"But she was with us all day," argued David.

"Children," Mother interrupted, "whoever did all this for us didn't want us to know who he or she is. Don't you think we should respect that wish? It wasn't done for praise. It was done as a service to God, and He'll give the reward. I, for one, am very grateful."

"Well, I'd want at least a thank you if I did all this," insisted David.

Mother smiled. "It's nice to be appreciated for what we do, but which is better, a reward of thanks from people, or a reward from God?"

"Both would be nice." David grinned. "But you're right. A thank you from God is more important."

HOW ABOUT YOU? Can you think of someone for whom you could do a kind deed? Would you be willing to let God receive all the thanks and praise and wait until you reach heaven to get your reward? Acts of Christian service that are done in secret often bring people's attention to God and His workings. Why not be one of God's "secret servants"? Don't wait—do that secret service today. C.R.

TO MEMORIZE: *"Your Father who sees in secret will Himself reward you openly"* Matthew 6:4 (NKJV).

JULY

25

The Hand in the Glove

FROM THE BIBLE:

I am the true vine, and My Father is the vinedresser. Every branch in Me that does not bear fruit He takes away; and every branch that bears fruit He prunes, that it may bear more fruit. You are already clean because of the word which I have spoken to you. Abide in Me, and I in you. As the branch cannot bear fruit of itself, unless it abides in the vine, neither can you, unless you abide in Me. I am the vine, you are the branches. He who abides in Me, and I in him, bears much fruit; for without Me you can do nothing. John 15:1-5, NKJV

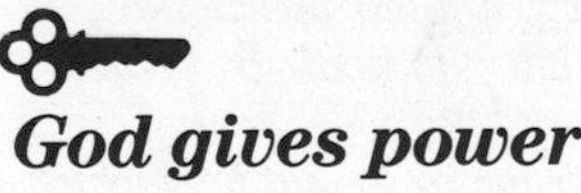

God gives power

"YOU'RE SO QUIET, Son. What's on your mind?" asked Ben's father as he stopped at Ben's room to tell him good night.

Ben put his hands behind his head and stared at the ceiling above his bed. "Oh, I've just been wondering if I should be a missionary."

"You don't seem very excited about the idea," said Dad.

"It seems like such a hard job," said Ben, propping himself up on one elbow. "I have this feeling that I might not be any good at it. What if God calls me to do something I can't do!"

Ben's father thought for a moment, then reached over to Ben's desk and picked up his baseball glove. "What's this?" he asked.

Ben laughed. "Don't be silly, Dad! It's my ball glove."

Dad walked over to the corner of the room. He propped the glove against the wall, found a baseball, and threw it at the glove. Though the ball hit the center of the glove, it rolled to the floor. Dad picked up the glove and looked at it in disgust. "This glove is a total failure," he said, shaking his head.

Ben laughed and laughed. "Oh, Dad, you know it can't catch by itself! It has to have a hand inside."

Dad smiled at Ben. "You're just like this glove," he said. "God has a purpose for your life, Ben, just as there is a purpose for this glove. You put your hand inside the glove to give it guidance and strength—you give it power to catch the ball. In the same way, God will give you power to do whatever He calls you to do. Don't worry, Son, God will never prop you in a corner and leave you alone. It's His mighty hand that does the work when you are willing to be used."

HOW ABOUT YOU? Have you thought about God's plan for your life? Are you learning to accept His guidance and use His power right now? If He asks you to witness to somebody, He'll help you do it. If He asks you to be cheerful when things go wrong, He'll help you with that. If He wants you to do some particular task, He'll help you do it right. Never be afraid of God's calling. He will use you if you are willing. C.R.

TO MEMORIZE: *"I am the vine, you are the branches. He who abides in Me, and I in him, bears much fruit; for without Me you can do nothing"* John 15:5 (NKJV).

JULY

26

Missing Men

FROM THE BIBLE:

But now God has set the members, each one of them, in the body just as He pleased. And if they were all one member, where would the body be? But now indeed there are many members, yet one body. And the eye cannot say to the hand, "I have no need of you"; nor again the head to the feet, "I have no need of you." No, much rather, those members of the body which seem to be weaker are necessary. And those members of the body which we think to be less honorable, on these we bestow greater honor; and our unpresentable parts have greater modesty, but our presentable parts have no need. But God composed the body, having given greater honor to that part which lacks it, that there should be no schism in the body, but that the members should have the same care for one another. And if one member suffers, all the members suffer with it; or if one member is honored, all the members rejoice with it.

1 Corinthians 12:18-26, NKJV

Do your part on God's team

"WANT TO PLAY Foos Ball, Judson?" asked Tim, the camp counselor. "I'll show you how to play."

"Sure!" Judson agreed. "I've wondered how to play this."

"Those handles on your side of the table control your team," explained Tim. "You try to move the ball past my goalie and into the hole in this end of the table. I'll try to stop you and get the ball into your goal."

"I think I'm missing a man on this rod," said Judson. "Isn't it supposed to have two?"

"Yes, but we're even. See, I have a man who has no legs. He can't help his team very much either, can he? I'll put the ball in. Are you ready?"

Judson grabbed the poles. He stared at the ball as it popped onto the table. Then he twisted the rod, making one of his men push the ball toward Tim's men. Tim took careful aim and spun the metal pole. The ball slipped through Judson's defenses, and it shot through the hole where the missing man should have been. Clunk! It fell into the pocket.

"Let's try again," said Judson, picking up the ball and putting it back into play. This time he won the point. "That was fun," exclaimed Judson when the game was over. "Sure wish I had the missing man, though."

"It hurts to have one missing, doesn't it?" agreed Tim. "It reminds me that as Christians we're on God's team. If we're missing from our place in church, we're like the missing man on your pole. If we're in church but not doing what we should be doing for God, we're like the legless figure. The whole team suffers when one person doesn't do his part. Others have to try and fill in the empty area, and sometimes they can't move fast enough."

"That's interesting," said Judson. "I never thought about being on God's team and how important each person is."

HOW ABOUT YOU? Are you on God's team? You are if you're a Christian. How well do you get along with your teammates? Are you in your place each time you're needed? Are you doing what God would like you to do? His team is the best there is, and each team member is needed. Always be ready to do your part. V.L.C.

TO MEMORIZE: *"If one member suffers, all the members suffer with it; or if one member is honored, all the members rejoice with it"*
1 Corinthians 12:26 (NKJV).

JULY

27

Wrong Notes

FROM THE BIBLE:

May the God of peace, who through the blood of the eternal covenant brought back from the dead our Lord Jesus, that great Shepherd of the sheep, equip you with everything good for doing his will, and may he work in us what is pleasing to him, through Jesus Christ, to whom be glory for ever and ever. Amen. Brothers, I urge you to bear with my word of exhortation, for I have written you only a short letter. . . . Grace be with you all.
Hebrews 13:20-22, 25, NIV

God won't give up on you

MARY TOOK her cello out of the hall closet and set up her music stand. "Mother," she called, "I'm going to practice now. Will you set the timer for thirty minutes, please?"

"Sure, Mary," replied Mother. "I'll be listening, too."

As Mary drew her bow across the strings, the notes that came from the cello were shaky and unsure. "I'll never get this right," she wailed. "This song sounds horrible!"

"Try it again," said Mother, coming into the room. With a sigh, Mary did so, and by the end of the thirty-minute practice session the song had definitely improved.

As the family discussed the day's activities that evening, Mary told about a neighborhood ball game. "John lost his temper and went home mad," she said in disgust. "He's a Christian, but he sure blew it today."

"That's too bad," replied Dad. "Try to be patient with him, though. He's still a new Christian."

"Remember that new song you were trying to play on your cello?" Mother asked suddenly.

"Yeah, It still needs a lot of work."

"That's true," agreed Mother, "but it's improving, so don't give up. We all need a lot of improvement in our Christian lives, too, and I'm glad that God doesn't give up on us."

"That's a good thought," commented Dad. "When we accept Jesus, God begins to change us. This takes time, but God has promised that He will continue to work in our lives."

"Right." Mother nodded. "Every time we sin, we sound like a 'wrong note,' and God is not pleased. The harmony we have with Him is gone. But when we confess our sin and ask forgiveness, our friendship with Jesus is like new."

"I'll think about that whenever I practice my cello," Mary said, grinning. "And I'll be more patient with John, too."

HOW ABOUT YOU? Have you or your friends been making "wrong notes" lately? Maybe you've heard the saying, "Be patient, God isn't finished with me yet." Be patient with your friends, too. Ask forgiveness for your own sins. Try each day to learn more from God's Word and grow more like Him. Thank Him for His patient work in your life. J.G.

TO MEMORIZE: *"Be joyful in hope, patient in affliction, faithful in prayer"* Romans 12:12 (NIV).

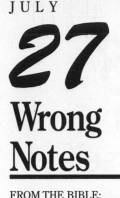

28

Feed Yourself

FROM THE BIBLE:
Teach these things and make sure everyone learns them well. Don't let anyone think little of you because you are young. Be their ideal; let them follow the way you teach and live; be a pattern for them in your love, your faith, and your clean thoughts. Until I get there, read and explain the Scriptures to the church; preach God's Word. Be sure to use the abilities God has given you through his prophets when the elders of the church laid their hands upon your head. Put these abilities to work; throw yourself into your tasks so that everyone may notice your improvement and progress. Keep a close watch on all you do and think. Stay true to what is right and God will bless you and use you to help others.
1 Timothy 4:11-16, TLB

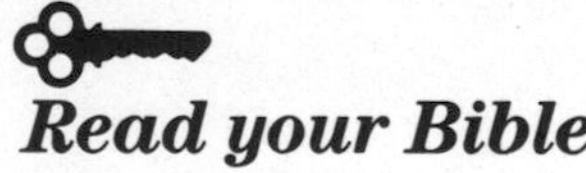
Read your Bible

"MOTHER, LOOK at Nathan," Missi said, laughing. Her one-year-old brother waved his spoon and rubbed mashed potatoes all over his face. He dipped the spoon back into his bowl and then put it to his mouth. "Big boy!" cheered Missi. "You got it all in that time!"

"Soon he'll be eating all by himself," said Mother. She patted his curly head as she reached for a spoon to feed him the last bit of food from his bowl. Then she handed him his glass of milk. "There you go," she said. "You can finish that while Mommy clears the table."

After a busy evening, Mother reminded Missi that it was nearly bedtime. "Did you have your devotions this morning, or do you need to save time for that this evening?" she asked. "If you do, you'd better pick up your game now."

Missi sighed. "Sometimes I think I might as well skip devotions," she said. "I don't understand the Bible very well when I read it by myself anyway. Why can't I just wait till I get bigger—till I'm an adult?"

"Missi, what would you think if Nathan refused to try to feed himself?" asked Mother. "Would you be happy to see that? Do you think Dad and I would be happy?" Missi slowly shook her head. "You're right," said Mother. "We're glad to help him when he needs help, but we're also glad to see him attempt to feed himself—even when he makes a mess—because it's a sign that he's growing. And as he practices, he'll become better at it."

"I know what you're saying," said Missi. "You're saying that as a Christian I should feed myself, too, by reading the Bible for myself."

"That's right," agreed Mother. "God wants to see signs of growth in His children, too. It's fine for you to be fed by going to church and Sunday school and by having devotions with the rest of us, but you also need to feed yourself. Sometimes you may 'miss your mouth' and not understand what you've read. Then you can ask for help. But don't stop trying. Learn to get some spiritual food all by yourself."

HOW ABOUT YOU? Are you learning to feed yourself spiritually? You should be. You may not understand everything, but as you work at it, you'll find you understand more and more. Take time to read God's Word every day. H.M.

TO MEMORIZE: *"We have not stopped praying for you and asking God to fill you with the knowledge of his will"* Colossians 1:9 (NIV).

JULY

29

A Super Songwriter

FROM THE BIBLE:

But the Spirit of the Lord had left Saul, and instead, the Lord had sent a tormenting spirit that filled him with depression and fear. Some of Saul's aides suggested a cure. "We'll find a good harpist to play for you whenever the tormenting spirit is bothering you," they said. "The harp music will quiet you and you'll soon be well again." "All right," Saul said. "Find me a harpist." One of them said he knew a young fellow in Bethlehem, the son of a man named Jesse, who was not only a talented harp player, but was handsome, brave, and strong, and had good, solid judgment. "What's more," he added, "the Lord is with him." So Saul sent messengers to Jesse, asking that he send his son David the shepherd. . . . And whenever the tormenting spirit from God troubled Saul, David would play the harp and Saul would feel better, and the evil spirit would go away.

1 Samuel 16:14-19, 23, TLB

ERIKA SAT at the kitchen window, watching the birds flit around the feeder. "What's on your mind?" her mother asked. "You look thoughtful."

"The church newsletter," replied Erika. "Pastor Hamilton came to our Sunday school class last week and asked us all to do something for next month's issue. Gary is drawing a picture of the church, and Sue is writing a thank you note to all the Sunday school teachers, but I can't think of anything!"

"You like to write poetry," Mother suggested.

"I was thinking about that," agreed Erika. Suddenly she broke into a smile. "I could write a song! And, Mom, maybe Jenny could help me with a tune." Jenny was Erika's older sister, and an accomplished pianist.

"That's a great idea," Mother agreed. "God has always used music and songs."

Erika was already running down the hall to her room. As she got out her pencil and paper, she thought of the birds she had been watching. How beautiful they had looked in the morning sunlight! The red cardinal was her favorite. So Erika started writing a verse to praise God for His creation. She worked all morning and finally had it just the way she wanted. When Jenny saw Erika's lyrics, she agreed to compose a tune. After supper, the girls sang the finished product for their parents.

"My daughters, the songwriters." Dad smiled. "Who knows, maybe songwriting will be your career!"

"Oh, Dad," Erika laughed, "I'm only eleven!"

"Have you heard of the hymnwriter, Issac Watts?" asked Dad. "He started writing poetry when he was very, very young, and in his lifetime wrote over six hundred hymns. Fanny Crosby wrote seven thousand songs of praise to God!"

"Wow!" Erika said. Maybe this would be the first song of many for her. Maybe she would be able to serve the Lord by being a songwriter! That was an exciting thought!

HOW ABOUT YOU? Every Sunday at church you sing different hymns and songs. Have you ever wondered who wrote all that music? It was written by people who had a special God-given talent to express themselves through poetry and music. If you are interested in poetry, practice putting your thoughts about the Lord in rhyme. Perhaps someday a hymnbook will have your name in it! L.W.

TO MEMORIZE: *"O sing unto the LORD a new song; sing unto the LORD, all the earth"* Psalm 96:1.

Use abilities for God

JULY

30

It Still Hurts

FROM THE BIBLE:

The Lord reigns;
Let the peoples tremble!
He dwells between the cherubim;
Let the earth be moved!
The Lord is great in Zion,
And He is high above all the peoples.
Let them praise Your great and awesome name—
He is holy.
The King's strength also loves justice;
You have established equity;
You have executed justice and righteousness in Jacob.
Exalt the Lord our God,
And worship at His footstool;
For He is holy.
Moses and Aaron were among His priests,
And Samuel was among those who called upon His name;
They called upon the Lord, and He answered them.
He spoke to them in the cloudy pillar;
They kept His testimonies and the ordinance that He gave them.

Psalm 99:1-7, NKJV

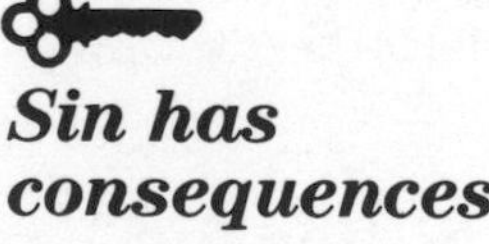

Sin has consequences

OH, HOW TERRY wished he had listened to his mother when she told him not to jump his bike over the ramp he had built with planks of wood. But jumping his bike was fun, so as soon as Mother's back was turned. Terry had done it again. The planks had flown up in his face as he hit the ramp, and then all he could remember was the pain!

"Mom, I'm so sorry," he cried after the doctor set the two broken bones in his arm. "I shouldn't have disobeyed."

Naturally, Terry's mother accepted his apology. But she also reminded him that he had not only disobeyed her—he had disobeyed God. "You need to ask God's forgiveness, too," she said. Terry nodded. After he and Mother prayed together, he felt much better, knowing he was forgiven.

The next morning Terry felt down in the dumps. The pain in his arm had kept him awake much of the night. "I can't stand this pain," he complained to Mother. "My arm hurts so bad. I've prayed and prayed that God would take the pain away, but He doesn't. If He forgave me for disobeying, why doesn't He heal the pain?"

"Oh, Terry, God always is willing to forgive sin," explained Mother, "but He doesn't always take away the consequences of our sin. Because God is a God of justice, sometimes He allows us to face the consequences. He knows that we'll learn our lesson better by having to suffer because of what we've done. The pain in your arm will eventually ease, but just now perhaps God wants you to remember what it cost you to disobey."

HOW ABOUT YOU? Have you ever had to face the nasty consequences of sin? Perhaps you've had to take a zero on a test even though you confessed that you cheated. Or perhaps, like Terry, you've disobeyed your parents and suffered physical injury — even a permanent injury. God always forgives confessed sin, but He does not always remove the consequences of your sins! R.P.

TO MEMORIZE: *"Righteousness and justice are the foundation of Your throne"* Psalm 89:14 (NKJV).

JULY

31

The Family Parrot

FROM THE BIBLE:

You brood of vipers, how can you, being evil, speak what is good? For the mouth speaks out of that which fills the heart. The good man out of his good treasure brings forth what is good; and the evil man out of his evil treasure brings forth what is evil. And I say to you, that every careless word that men shall speak, they shall render account for it in the day of judgment. For by your words you shall be justified, and by your words you shall be condemned.

Matthew 12:34-37, NASB

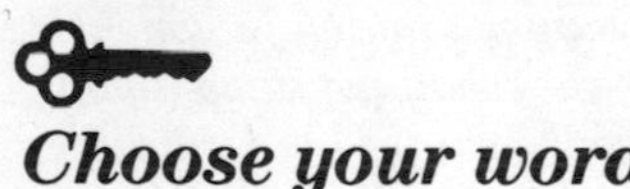

Choose your words wisely

WHEN DAD FINISHED saying the blessing at suppertime, two-year-old Joey called out, "Yay-men!"

Cindy laughed. "Joey's learning new words." Just then Mother lifted the cover from the casserole dish. "Yuck!" Cindy said. "Creamed cabbage. I hate that!"

"Yuck!" came the echo from the high chair. "Hate dat."

Cindy clapped her had over her mouth. "Sorry, Mom! I shouldn't have said that."

Mother nodded as she put some of the food on Joey's plate. "That's right. But now Joey has heard it, and he may add it to his memory."

Dad spoke. "Would you pass the cabbage, please?"

"Pwease!" Joey shouted. "Pwease!" He began to eat heartily, a big smile on his face. "Yuck!"

Cindy laughed. "He doesn't even know what he's saying!"

"That's true." Mother nodded. "Joey is like a parrot. If he hears a word often enough, he learns to say it."

"I don't think he's the only one in the family like that," observed Dad. "I've noticed a few expressions creeping into your speech, Cindy, words you've probably never made an effort to learn. You've just heard them and let them seep into your mind. And frankly, I doubt that you know what they mean."

Cindy blushed as she remembered several times her parents had corrected her language lately. "That's true," she admitted. "I'm surprised myself when I hear the things I say sometimes. I hear kids at school say these things over and over again. I guess, as a Christian, I ought to be careful."

Dad nodded. "We have a big responsibility to spread good words for those around us to hear. And we have a responsiblity to ourselves to repeat only those words we want to become part of our thoughts and hearts."

HOW ABOUT YOU? Are you careful to use only words that you would not be embarrassed to have repeated? Do you think carefully about the meaning of the popular expressions your friends use before you repeat them? Are you embarrassed to have your parents or your pastor hear you using them? God hears them. C.R.

TO MEMORIZE: *"Every careless word that men shall speak, they shall tender account for it in the day of judgment"* Matthew 12:36 (NASB).

AUGUST

Transplanted Tree

FROM THE BIBLE:

Oh, the joys of those who do not follow evil men's advice, who do not hang around with sinners, scoffing at the things of God: But they delight in doing everything God wants them to, and day and night are always meditating on his laws and thinking about ways to follow him more closely. They are like trees along a river bank bearing luscious fruit each season without fail. Their leaves shall never wither, and all they do shall prosper. But for sinners, what a different story! They blow away like chaff before the wind. They are not safe on Judgment Day; they shall not stand among the godly. For the Lord watches over all the plans and paths of godly men, but the paths of the godless lead to doom.

Psalm 1, TLB

Grow spiritually

DAVID CAREFULLY filled the pitcher with water, took it out to the backyard, and gently watered the tiny black spruce tree. In spite of the special care he had been giving the little tree, more and more needles were turning brown each day. "It's not going to live, is it, Mom?" he asked.

"No, David," Mother answered. "I don't think so."

"But I've been taking good care of it!" David said.

"I know, Son," Mother said, smiling. "But remember when you asked Grandpa if you could transplant it? He told you that he didn't think a black spruce would grow in our yard."

"I don't see why not!" David insisted. "Other trees do."

"That's true, but black spruce trees usually grow where it's extremely damp," explained Mother. "We live in a dry area." David and his mother stood looking at the scraggly tree. "You know, David, that seedling reminds me of some Christians."

"Christians?" asked David.

Mother nodded. "Right. To grow in the Lord, they should pray and read their Bibles and be friends with other Christians. Instead, they spend their time in the wrong kind of environment—with people who don't love the Lord. They ignore their Bibles, they don't go to church to learn more about the Lord, they don't take time to pray. Then they wonder why they don't grow spiritually."

"Oh, I get it!" exclaimed David. "It's as important for a Christian to be in the right environment as it is for a tree to be in the right environment." He grinned. "Well, even if this tree doesn't live, I've learned a lesson from it."

HOW ABOUT YOU? Are you growing spiritually? Are you in the right environment? Do your friends love the Lord and live according to what is taught in the Bible? Are you getting nourishment from God's Word? You cannot grow spiritually in the wrong conditions. Make sure you are a healthy Christian! L. W.

TO MEMORIZE: *"Rooted and built up in Him, and established in the faith, as you have been taught, abounding in it with thanksgiving"*
Colossians 2:7 (NKJV).

AUGUST

The Rough Edges

FROM THE BIBLE:

But to obtain these gifts, you need more than faith; you must also work hard to be good, and even that is not enough. For then you must learn to know God better and discover what he wants you to do. Next, learn to put aside your own desires so that you will become patient and godly, gladly letting God have his way with you. This will make possible the next step, which is for you to enjoy other people and to like them, and finally you will grow to love them deeply. The more you go on in this way, the more you will grow strong spiritually and become fruitful and useful to our Lord Jesus Christ. But anyone who fails to go after these additions to faith is blind indeed, or at least very short-sighted, and has forgotten that God delivered him from the old life of sin so that now he can live a strong, good life for the Lord. So, dear brothers, work hard to prove that you really are among those God has called and chosen, and then you will never stumble or fall away.

2 Peter 1:5-10, TLB

"MORNIN', BRIAN. What have you got there?" called Mr. Walker.

"Oh, brother!" Brian muttered under his breath. Aloud he answered, "Good morning, Mr. Walker. This is a porch swing."

"Looks a bit worn-out," Mr. Walker observed. "You fixin' to paint it?"

"Yes, sir," Brian replied.

"Paintin' it white, eh? If it was me I'd paint it green. Match your house better."

Brian took a deep breath. "My mother wants it white."

"You gonna paint wearin' that good shirt, boy? When I was a kid, I only had two shirts to my name."

As Brian dipped his brush into the paint, Mr. Walker grabbed his arm. "Wait a minute there, young 'un. You can't paint yet. Where's your sandpaper?"

Brian jerked his arm free. "I don't need sandpaper."

"Sure you do. Look how that old paint's peelin'. You've gotta sand it down before you put on the new paint."

Brian was about to tell the old man to mind his own business when Mother called him to the telephone. After the phone call, Brian exploded.

"What's wrong now?" Mother asked gently.

"You should paint the porch swing green," Brian mimicked. "You shouldn't wear that good shirt! You shouldn't paint without sanding first."

"Hmmm." Mother nodded. "Pretty good advice. Go change your shirt. And you certainly should sand off the rough spots and peeling paint. If you don't, the new paint will only last a few weeks."

"You're as critical as Mr. Walker."

"Criticism isn't always bad, Brian," explained Mother. "Often it's the sandpaper God uses to knock rough spots off our characters."

"Between you and Mr. Walker, I ought to become a pretty smooth character," Brian teased as he went to change his shirt and look for sandpaper.

HOW ABOUT YOU? Do you resent criticism? It's a sign of spiritual maturity when you can take it with a good attitude. The Lord will often use others to show you where you should change. B.W.

TO MEMORIZE: *"The way of a fool is right in his own eyes, but he who heeds counsel is wise"* Proverbs 12:15 (NKJV).

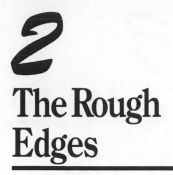

Heed constructive criticism

AUGUST

3

Good Advice

FROM THE BIBLE:

When you arrive in the Promised Land you must be very careful lest you be corrupted by the horrible customs of the nations now living there. For example, any Israeli who presents his child to be burned to death as a sacrifice to heathen gods, must be killed. No Israeli may practice black magic, or call on the evil spirits for aid, or be a fortune teller, or be a serpent charmer, medium, or wizard, or call forth the spirits of the dead. Anyone doing these things is an object of horror and disgust to the Lord, and it is because the nations do these things that the Lord your God will displace them. You must walk blamelessly before the Lord your God.

Deuteronomy 18:9-13, TLB

Don't read horoscopes

DAN EAGERLY OPENED the newspaper and read his horoscope for the next day. No one else in his family read the horoscopes. In fact, Dan's father said it was like witchcraft and that the Bible was against anything that tries to foretell the future. "God is the only One who knows what is in the future," Dad had said. "In the Bible we find all the advice we need on how to live." But the horoscope fascinated Dan.

"You stand a good chance of winning an argument," Dan read in tonight's paper. That sounded good to him. He had lost an argument in the neighborhood ball game just that day. He thought he touched home base before the ball got there, but all the other boys said he was out.

When Dan went to bed, he picked up his Bible, intending to read and pray before going to sleep. But instead, he thought again about his horoscope. He'd sure like to win an argument for once! Putting down his Bible, he turned out the light and settled down to sleep.

The next day the boys played baseball again. When Dan was up to bat, he hit the ball and ran. He got to first base just as Jim, the first baseman, yelled, "Out!"

"I am not out!" protested Dan.

"You are, too," insisted Dan.

"You're lying," said Dan, remembering his horoscope. He decided that he wouldn't give in so easily this time. but Jim didn't give in either—he didn't seem to realize Dan was supposed to win the argument. Before Dan knew it, he had hit Jim. The other boys came running over. To Dan's surprise, they took Jim's side and said Dan couldn't play anymore.

Dan walked slowly away from the ball field. *I never should have believed that dumb horoscope,* he thought. *I guess Dad's right. The Bible does give me better advice.*

HOW ABOUT YOU? Do you read your horoscope to see what kind of day you can expect? It's a dangerous thing to do. Maybe you think you're reading it just for fun, but it's so easy to replace God's Word with words written by people. God wants to be our source of advice, comfort, and help. He sternly forbids the use of things like fortune-telling or witchcraft to try to find out what will happen in the future. Listen to Him and leave the horoscope alone. C.Y.

TO MEMORIZE: *"It is better to trust in the LORD than to put confidence in man"* Psalm 118:8.

AUGUST

No Waves Too Rough

FROM THE BIBLE:

He who dwells in the shelter of
the Most High
will rest in the shadow of the
Almighty.
I will say of the Lord, "He is my
refuge and my fortress,
my God, in whom I trust."
Surely he will save you from the
fowler's snare
and from the deadly pesti-
lence.
He will cover you with his
feathers,
and under his wings you will
find refuge;
his faithfulness will be your
shield and rampart.
You will not fear the terror of
night,
nor the arrow that flies by day,
nor the pestilence that stalks in
the darkness,
nor the plague that destroys
at midday.
A thousand may fall at your
side,
ten thousand at your right
hand,
but it will not come near you.
You will only observe with your
eyes
and see the punishment of the
wicked.

Psalm 91:1-8, NIV

CALVIN STUMBLED into the water. The rolling waves cooled his warm body and relaxed his troubled mind. Because it felt so good and soothing to him, he swam out to deeper water. "I wish I could stay here forever," he sighed, "and not think about anything."

But Calvin had a lot to think about. He had a tumor on his left leg, and in two more days he would be admitted to a hospital where a specialist would perform surgery. It wasn't known yet whether the doctor could remove just the tumor or if Calvin's leg would have to be amputated. Calvin's mind was filled with questions. How would the operation go? What if he lost his leg? Would he ever be able to play ball and run on the track team again?

Little Cindy's shrieks interrupted his thoughts. "Daddy, I can't go swimming here!" she squealed. "The waves are too big! I don't like this ocean. It's scary!"

"Look," Dad said. "The waves aren't too rough for me. They aren't moving me. Here! Take my hand, and we'll swim together. You'll be safe."

Cindy was hesitant. She wanted to swim, but the waves were so big. Then she looked at her dad. He was strong! He would protect her! Cindy put her little hand into her daddy's big hand. Soon she was enjoying the water as it splashed about her.

Calvin swam back to Cindy. "See, Cal," she shouted. "I'm not afraid now. Daddy's holding my hand. He won't let me go."

Calvin smiled at Cindy and at himself. Little Cindy had just taught him a lesson. If she could trust their father in the rolling waves, he could trust his heavenly Father. The days ahead might be rough, but God would hold him and give him strength. That's all he needed to know to give him peace.

HOW ABOUT YOU? Are you facing a difficult time in your life? Are you ready to give up? Don't! Tell Jesus about your struggles. Ask Him for wisdom, and strength, and courage. Ask Him to hold you safely through it all. He will. J.H.

TO MEMORIZE: *"Hold me up, and I shall be safe"* Psalm 119:117 (NKJV).

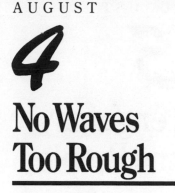

God holds you

AUGUST

5

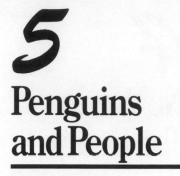

Penguins and People

FROM THE BIBLE:

I will lift up my eyes to the hills—
From whence comes my help?
My help comes from the Lord,
Who made heaven and earth.
He will not allow your foot to be moved;
He who keeps you will not slumber.
Behold, He who keeps Israel
Shall neither slumber nor sleep.
The Lord is your keeper;
The Lord is your shade at your right hand.
The sun shall not strike you by day,
Nor the moon by night.
The Lord shall preserve you from all evil;
He shall preserve your soul.
The Lord shall preserve your going out and your coming in
From this time forth, and even forevermore.

Psalm 121, NKJV

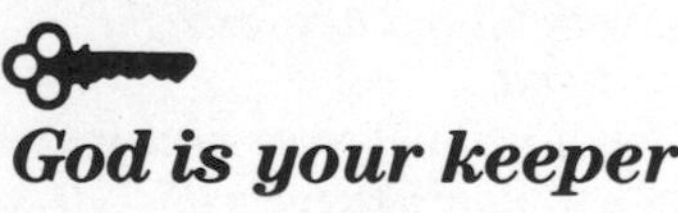

God is your keeper

DIANE WAS SO EXCITED! She and her parents were going on an all-day excursion to the city zoo. She loved watching all the animals, but the penguins were her favorites. She had to laugh at the way they strutted on land, and it was even more fun to watch them swim. Whenever she went swimming herself, Diane would try to imitate the smooth, flowing motions of the funny birds.

That day the tour guide told how the zookeepers kept the penguin room cold so the birds would be comfortable. "Otherwise," explained the guide, "the birds would get sick and possibly die from the change of climate."

During family devotions that evening, Diane's father said, "You know, I keep thinking about those penguins. Remember how careful the zookeepers are in taking care of them?"

Diane nodded. "They have to have certain foods, and just the right temperature, and even special lights!"

"Right," said Dad. "Those who care for them know how to keep the conditions just right so the penguins won't get sick. God does the same thing for us. Just think what would happen if it hailed all the time, or if it suddenly got as hot as an oven. God controls our environment because He knows what conditions we need to live in."

"I never thought of that," said Diane. "I guess God must care an awful lot about us to take care of us so well."

"You're right," replied her father smiling. "God does love us very much. He not only controls our physical environment, but also all the things that come into our lives. He is our Keeper, and He does a perfect job, allowing only what is good for us, whether it seems that way to us or not."

"Yeah," agreed Diane thoughtfully. A twinkle came to her eye. "Hey, Dad, I think we should go to the zoo real often so I'll be reminded of that!"

HOW ABOUT YOU? Did you know that it is God who keeps you day by day? He's the One who provides the air you breathe, the food and water you need, the type of environment in which you can survive. He also provides for your spiritual needs. All the things He allows in your life work together to make you the person you should be. Thank Him for being your Keeper. D.M.

TO MEMORIZE: *"The LORD is your keeper; the LORD is your shade at your right hand"* Psalm 121:5 (NKJV).

AUGUST

No Mistake!

FROM THE BIBLE:
You made all the delicate, inner parts of my body, and knit them together in my mother's womb. Thank you for making me so wonderfully complex! It is amazing to think about. Your workmanship is marvelous—and how well I know it. You were there while I was being formed in utter seclusion! You saw me before I was born and scheduled each day of my life before I began to breathe. Every day was recorded in your Book! How precious it is, Lord, to realize that you are thinking about me constantly! I can't even count how many times a day your thoughts turn towards me. And when I waken in the morning, you are still thinking of me!
Psalm 139:13-18, TLB

LARRY WALKED slowly up to home plate. It was his turn to bat. The pitcher threw the ball, and Larry swung at the air. "Strike one!" the umpire called. The next pitch went right over home plate while Larry just stood there. "Strike two!" the umpire shouted. The third time Larry tapped the ball lightly. He was out before he got halfway to first base.

"Another out!" Bob complained. "And it's all because of Larry. It was a mistake to let him play ball with us."

"He *is* a mistake," Karl joined in.

Gary laughed. "That's for sure."

"Give him a break," urged Adam. "He doesn't have a father to teach him like we do."

"And whose mistake is that?" Gary jeered.

Red-faced, Larry picked up his gear and ran off toward home. He was in such a hurry he didn't even see Mr. Radcliffe walking out to the mailbox to get his mail. Larry collided with him, and the mail scattered. As Mr. Radcliffe bent over to pick it up, he noticed the tears in Larry's eyes. "Hey, you seem a bit shaken," Mr. Radcliffe said. "It's a hot day. Come inside for some lemonade."

Larry hesitated, but he went inside. Soon the incident on the ballfield spilled out. "And it's true—I *am* a mistake," Larry blurted. "I never should have been born! My mother wasn't married when she had me!"

"Larry, you're not a mistake!" Mr. Radcliffe said positively. "Your mother did wrong, yes. But even though she might not have planned your birth, God knew you would be here. Psalm 139 tells us that God knew you and scheduled your days before you were even born."

"Really?" Larry asked hopefully.

"Really," Mr. Radcliffe affirmed as he poured another glass of lemonade. "Don't use the circumstances of your birth as an excuse to be less than what God intended you to be. God loves you and has a wonderful plan for your life."

HOW ABOUT YOU? Don't ever call yourself a mistake! Your birth was no surprise to God. You are very special to Him. You aren't responsible for your parents' actions, but you are responsible for the way you live your life. Make it a life pleasing to God. J.H.

TO MEMORIZE: *"You saw me before I was born and scheduled each day of my life before I began to breathe. Every day was recorded in your Book"* Psalm 139:16 (TLB).

You're not a mistake

AUGUST

7

The Fall

FROM THE BIBLE:

But why do you judge your brother? Or why do you show contempt for your brother? For we shall all stand before the judgment seat of Christ. For it is written: "As I live, says the Lord, every knee shall bow to Me, and every tongue shall confess to God." So then each of us shall give account of himself to God. Therefore let us not judge one another anymore, but rather resolve this, not to put a stumbling block or a cause to fall in our brother's way.
Romans 14:10-13, NKJV

Don't judge others

"I DON'T THINK Anna is a Christian at all," declared Jason as he rode his bike up the driveway. "In fact, I'm sure she's not. She lied to me!" He turned his bike around.

Mother looked up from her flower garden. "I'm sorry to hear that," she replied. "But don't you think you're making an awfully hasty judgment?"

"Well, she's lied before this, too," insisted Jason, "so how can she be a Christian?" He started back down the drive. A moment later his howl pierced the air as he skidded on some loose gravel, lost control of his bike, and fell. "Oh, my elbow," he groaned. "It hurts."

"I'm sure it does," sympathized Mother, who had come running up. "It's all skinned. Come on, we'll go fix it up."

When Jason and Mother went back out a little later, Jason got ready to mount his bike. "Oh," said Mother, taking hold of the handlebars, "you're not going to try to ride again, are you?"

"Sure," Jason replied.

"But, Jason," protested Mother, "I just don't think you can ride. Tell you what—you wait until Dad gets home tonight, and he'll put the training wheels back on for you."

"Mother!" Jason was indignant. "Just because I fell doesn't mean I can't ride!"

"Hmmm," said Mother thoughtfully, "slipping and falling with your bike doesn't mean you're not really a bike rider?" She smiled at Jason. "Well, guess what? Slipping and falling in your Christian life doesn't mean you're not really a Christian either. Did you know that?"

"I . . . I guess you're right," Jason admitted as he thought of what he had said about Anna.

"It does mean you need to confess what you've done and ask God to forgive you," continued Mother. "But be careful not to judge people. Instead, help them get back on the right track."

HOW ABOUT YOU? Are you disappointed in someone who says he's a Christian? Don't judge the person who slips and falls into sin. Leave that to God. Pray for the person. Let him know you love him though you don't like what he did. Let him know that God stands ready to forgive and that you'll forgive him, too. H.M.

TO MEMORIZE: *"But why do you judge your brother . . . for we shall all stand before the judgment seat of Christ"* Romans 14:10 (NKJV).

AUGUST

Wrong Conclusion

ABIGAIL AND STACI slowly walked past Johnny Jake's run-down house. Empty wine bottles could be spotted here and there in the yard and on the porch. Johnny Jake was an alcoholic.

"I bet Johnny Jake doesn't have any friends," said Abigail.

"Not unless they're drunks, too," said Staci.

At that moment Johnny Jake and another man walked out the front door, laughing. "Hey!" exclaimed Abigail. "That's Mr. Horton!"

Staci shook her head in amazement. "You don't think they're friends, do you, Abby?"

"Well," Abigail gulped hard, "they're both laughing, and Mr. Horton was inside that awful house!"

"Could Mr. Horton be an alcoholic, too?"

"He must be if he's a friend of Johnny Jake!" replied Abigail. Staci nodded in agreement.

"Hi, girls!" called Mr. Horton to Abigail and Staci. "Bye, Johnny. I'll see you tomorrow!"

"Oh, great," murmured Abigail.

"Hi, Staci! Hi, Abby!" greeted Mr. Horton. "What's up?"

"We're just going for a walk," mumbled Staci.

"We didn't know you and Johnny Jake were friends," blurted out Abigail.

Mr. Horton smiled broadly. "I've tried to be a friend to him, and that has given me the chance to tell him about Jesus," he said. "Just this morning he asked Jesus to save him and forgive his sins! What's more, Johnny Jake said he'd be in church tomorrow. Praise the Lord!"

Abigail knew she had to explain. "When we saw you at Johnny Jake's house, we thought you must be a drunk, too. I mean . . ." She tried to soften her words. "We thought you must like to drink sometimes. It just seemed like if you were there . . ." She didn't know how to finish.

"I see," said Mr. Horton. "Let this experience be a reminder that you should never jump to conclusions about other people, girls. But now that you know the truth, just praise the Lord! See you tomorrow!"

HOW ABOUT YOU? Are you quick to criticize others? Do you make judgments before you know all the facts? It's better to put off forming an opinion until you're sure you know the whole story. Give others the benefit of the doubt, and leave the judging to the Lord. V.R.

TO MEMORIZE: *"Who are you to judge another?"* James 4:12 (NKJV).

FROM THE BIBLE:
Therefore submit to God. Resist the devil and he will flee from you. Draw near to God and He will draw near to you. Cleanse your hands, you sinners; and purify your hearts, you double-minded. Lament and mourn and weep! Let your laughter be turned to mourning and your joy to gloom. Humble yourselves in the sight of the Lord, and He will lift you up. Do not speak evil of one another, brethren. He who speaks evil of a brother and judges his brother, speaks evil of the law and judges the law. But if you judge the law, you are not a doer of the law but a judge. There is one Lawgiver, who is able to save and to destroy. Who are you to judge another?
James 4:7-12, NKJV

Don't judge others

AUGUST

The Sunday School Lesson

FROM THE BIBLE:

Judge not, that you be not judged. For with what judgment you judge, you will be judged; and with the same measure you use, it will be measured back to you. And why do you look at the speck in your brother's eye, but do not consider the plank in your own eye? Or how can you say to your brother, "Let me remove the speck out of your eye"; and look, a plank is in your own eye? Hypocrite! First remove the plank from your own eye, and then you will see clearly to remove the speck out of your brother's eye.
Matthew 7:1-5, NKJV

Don't judge others

AS STEVE WALKED out of the Sunday school classroom, he was glad Mr. Sanders had taught the lesson about not judging others. Some of the kids were really guilty of doing that.

Theresa Robins, for example. She was always raising her hand to answer all the questions, always acting like a know-it-all. She probably thought that made her a better Christian than anybody else.

Or maybe Mr. Sanders was thinking of Shelley. She always dressed in the latest fashion. She probably thought the rest of the kids were hicks because nobody else wore such expensive clothes.

And then there was Scott. He never listened in class or brought his Bible. But his dad was the chief of police, and Scott probably thought the other kids were just not quite as good as he.

Of course, some of the kids really *weren't* very good—like Lisa. She was always giggling in class. No matter what the subject, Lisa always found a reason to giggle. When Steve stopped to think about it, even his best friend, Tom, wasn't exactly a saint. Tom would whisper all through Sunday school if anyone would listen.

"Wow!" Steve thought as he settled into his seat in church. "that lesson could be good for almost anyone in my class." He took a snapshot of the class from his Bible. "It would even be good for . . ." He stopped suddenly as his eyes fell on his own face smiling back at him from the picture. "Me?" He blushed as he thought about it. Ever since he had left his classroom, he had been judging his classmates, forgetting that he had plenty of faults of his own. He'd better get his own problem—a critical attitude—under control before he worried about the faults of anybody else!

HOW ABOUT YOU? Do you sometimes see all the faults of others and none of your own? In today's Scripture, Jesus is simply teaching that you must check your own life before you try to straighten out others. Don't point out that your sister failed to empty a wastebasket when you forgot to take out the trash. Don't complain about your brother being slow to obey when you're just as bad yourself. Don't grumble about the toys the baby left lying around when you left your bike out in the rain. In other words, as long as you have faults, don't be critical of others. First take care of the sins in your own life. You may find there's no time left to judge anyone else. L.W.

TO MEMORIZE: *"For with what judgment you judge, you will be judged"* Matthew 7:2 (NKJV).

10

A Living Witness

FROM THE BIBLE:
Since you have been chosen by God who has given you this new kind of life, and because of his deep love and concern for you, you should practice tender-hearted mercy and kindness to others. Don't worry about making a good impression on them but be ready to suffer quietly and patiently. Be gentle and ready to forgive; never hold grudges. Remember, the Lord forgave you, so you must forgive others. Most of all, let love guide your life, for then the whole church will stay together in perfect harmony. Let the peace of heart which comes from Christ be always present in your hearts and lives, for this is your responsibility and privilege as members of his body. And always be thankful. Remember what Christ taught and let his words enrich your lives and make you wise. . . . And whatever you do or say, let it be as a representative of the Lord Jesus, and come with him into the presence of God the Father to give him your thanks.
Colossians 3:12-17, TLB

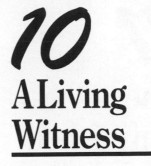

KATHY ARRIVED home from Bible camp just as her family was sitting down for supper. Determined to be a witness, she promptly told them that the best thing about camp was that she had become a Christian. "A Christian?" exclaimed her sister, Kim. "I thought we were already Christians."

"You aren't a Christian just because you call yourself one," began Kathy, and then she noticed that the others were starting to eat. "Oh! Don't eat!" she ordered. "We have to say a prayer first—to thank God for the food!"

"Kathy, if you want to be religious, that's fine," Dad told her, "but don't ask us to join you. Start thanking me for bringing home a paycheck, and thank your mom for fixing meals. Then we'll talk about praying. Now, let's eat."

That evening someone mentioned that the next Sunday was the day for the family reunion. "Sunday!" exclaimed Kathy. "I can't go! I don't want to skip church for some stupid family reunion!"

"If this religion of yours means insulting your family, we want none of it!" growled Dad.

Kathy realized that she had offended her family, and she felt awful. She talked to Pastor Randall about it. After hearing what had happened, he said, "It's great that you're witnessing, Kathy, but by accusing your family and quoting verses at them, maybe you've created a 'holier-than-thou' attitude. Witnessing is more than talking. You must also be a *living* witness. Let your actions and attitude show that Jesus has changed you."

Kathy listened thoughtfully. "I'll try again."

Kathy found many opportunities to be a living witness. She willingly gave in when she and Kim disagreed about which game to play. She mowed the lawn without being told. The climax came when she gave up going to play volleyball with the church youth group in order to help Kim finish a 4-H project that was due the next day. As they finished, Kim turned to her. "I guess I'll go with you to church this week," she said. "I have to see what your religion is all about. It sure changed you."

HOW ABOUT YOU? Have you heard that "actions speak louder than words"? Attitudes also speak louder than words. Watch yourself today. Is your attitude cheerful, humble, and willing? If not, ask God to help you make the needed changes, so you may be a living witness for Him. J.H.

TO MEMORIZE: *"Walk in wisdom toward them that are without"* Colossians 4:5.

Witness through attitudes

AUGUST

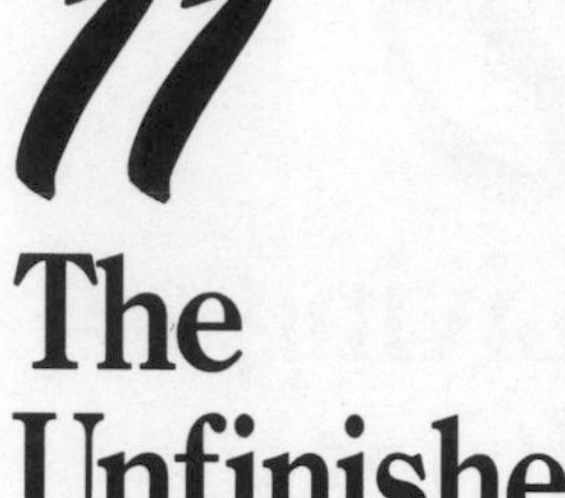

The Unfinished Model

FROM THE BIBLE:

Then I saw a great white throne and Him who sat on it, from whose face the earth and the heaven fled away. And there was found no place for them. And I saw the dead, small and great, standing before God, and books were opened. And another book was opened, which is the Book of Life. And the dead were judged according to their works, by the things which were written in the books. The sea gave up the dead who were in it, and Death and Hades delivered up the dead who were in them. And they were judged, each one according to his works. Then Death and Hades were cast into the lake of fire. This is the second death. And anyone not found written in the Book of Life was cast into the lake of fire.
Revelation 20:11-15, NKJV

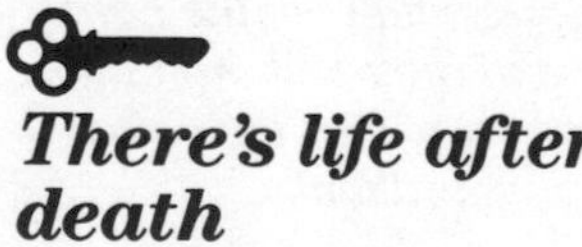

There's life after death

"HAPPY BIRTHDAY, Ken!" exclaimed Anita handing a box to her brother. Ken looked pleased when he opened it and discovered a model airplane.

"Hurry up, kids," exclaimed Mother impatiently. "Your dad will soon be here to take you both for the weekend. You better take your Bibles like he always wants you to do!"

Anita sighed. It seemed to her that Mother was always pushing them out the door, eager for them to be gone. Anita hated the reminder that her mother was divorcing her dad.

Dad tooted the horn. Anita grabbed her suitcase and math book. She sighed again. If she didn't understand fractions soon, she wouldn't pass!

On her way to bed that evening Anita stopped at Ken's room to say good night. She was surprised to see the model in the wastebasket. "It's no good," Ken grumbled when she asked about it. "The pieces don't fit. Now go away!"

That night Anita couldn't sleep. She sat in the dark, brooding over her problems. Life was miserable! Getting up for a drink of water, Anita noticed some pills in the medicine cabinet. She would take the whole bottle and be done with it!

When Anita's father went up to bed, he found her and rushed her to the hospital. The next day, still in the hospital and feeling miserable, Anita shared her feelings with him. "I just wanted to end it all," she sobbed.

"Anita," said Dad gently, "you know that taking your life wouldn't really end it all, don't you? It would end your life on this earth, yes, but there is also life after death. The Bible teaches that when this life is ended, we either go to be with Jesus in heaven or we are punished eternally in hell."

Anita's face was troubled. "Daddy, will you help me make sure I'll go to heaven?"

HOW ABOUT YOU? Have you ever thought things were so awful that you'd like to end it all? If you're a Christian, can you imagine how it would be to face God, knowing that you took things into your own hands? If you're not a Christian, taking your life would be like jumping "from the frying pan into the fire." You would be condemned forever. If you haven't done so, won't you accept Jesus today and trust Him with all your life? J.H.

TO MEMORIZE: *"And another book was opened, which is the Book of Life. And the dead were judged according to their works, by the things which were written in the book"* Revelation 20:14 (NKJV).

AUGUST

The Unfinished Model

(Continued from yesterday)

FROM THE BIBLE:
Haven't you yet learned that your body is the home of the Holy Spirit God gave you, and that he lives within you? Your own body does not belong to you. For God has bought you with a great price. So use every part of your body to give glory back to God, because he owns it. 1 Corinthians 6:19-20, TLB

God gives hope

TWO DAYS after Anita asked Jesus to save her and take charge of her life, she was again talking things over with her father. "I'm glad I'm a Christian now," she told him, "but I still feel so discouraged. I still can't do fractions, and now that I'm in the hospital, I'm missing so much school that I'll probably fail. And you and Mom are still getting divorced. And—oh, I don't know! Everything still seems so hopeless."

"Anita, things may not always go like we want them to," Dad replied, "but life isn't hopeless! God has a plan for us. I don't want the divorce either, but I can't do anything about it unless your mother changes her mind. I want you to know, though, that I love you very much. Your mother loves you, too, and so does Ken. He's been asking about you all the time."

As Dad finished speaking, Ken walked in the door. He held something behind his back. "Surprise!" he exclaimed, holding out the model Anita had given him. It was almost finished. "I just got impatient when I couldn't get it all together right away," he told her sheepishly. "I'm sorry. Doesn't it look great now? It's just about done."

Anita was smiling when Ken left. Dad smiled, too. "Ken's plane does look good," he said, "and your life can be good, too. Anita, the pieces are all there, and with God's help they will work out in time. God is the perfect Creator. He doesn't make junk."

"I guess I gave up too soon," admitted Anita. "I'm ready to work at it agian—with God's help, and yours."

HOW ABOUT YOU? Are there times when you feel like everything and everybody is against you? That isn't true. God loves you very much. Ask Him to help you. There are others who care, too. Seek a Christian adult—perhaps a parent, pastor, or Sunday school teacher—to help you work out your problems. You are very important to them and to God. J.H.

TO MEMORIZE: *" 'I know the plans I have for you,' declares the Lord, 'plans to prosper you and not to harm you, plans to give you hope and a future' "* Jeremiah 29:11 (NIV).

AUGUST

13

Only Bubbles

FROM THE BIBLE:

And no one can ever lay any other real foundation than that one we already have—Jesus Christ. But there are various kinds of materials that can be used to build on that foundation. Some use gold and silver and jewels; and some build with sticks, and hay, or even straw! There is going to come a time of testing at Christ's Judgment Day to see what kind of material each builder has used. Everyone's work will be put through the fire so that all can see whether or not it keeps its value, and what was really accomplished. Then every workman who has built on the foundation with the right materials, and whose work still stands, will get his pay. But if the house he has built burns up, he will have a great loss. He himself will be saved, but like a man escaping through a wall of flames.

1 Corinthians 3:11-15, TLB

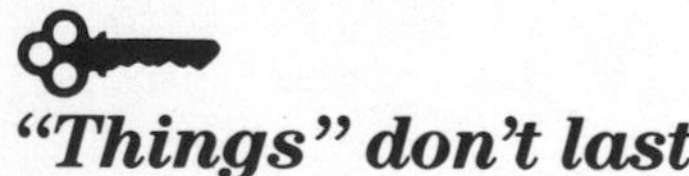

"Things" don't last

"STOP CRYING, Jill. I'll blow more bubbles for you. Here! Watch!" Deborah dipped the red plastic tube into the soap solution, then blew gently. Jill clapped her hands and giggled when the colorful bubbles appeared, but as they drifted away or broke she began crying again.

Deborah sighed. "Can't you understand? Bubbles are pretty, but they don't last." Just then Mother came out on the porch. "Jill bawls whenever the bubbles break," Deborah complained. "She thinks you can play with a bubble just like you play with a beach ball. I'm tired of hearing her cry!"

Mother gave Jill a hug and looked at Deborah. "I wonder if God feels that way sometimes."

"What do you mean?" asked Deborah. "You're thinking of something other than bubbles, aren't you?"

Mother nodded. "Yes, I was remembering how badly I felt when I broke that antique bowl last week," she said. "You know, God's Word tells us that some of the things we treasure most on earth are just like bubbles. In God's sight they're just as worthless and as easily replaced, but we care about them so much! We complain and cry when they are gone."

"I think I understand," responded Deborah. "I did that the time I was sick and couldn't keep my long hair because it was so hard to take care of. I cried and cried when it was cut. That was silly, wasn't it? It grew back, and it's nearly as long now as it was before I got sick."

"And remember how upset Dad and I became when we loaned our new car to Aunt Dori and she got a scratch on it?" reminded Mother. "My, how easy it is to think of 'bubbles' that we cry over. But it's only the loving deeds we do for Christ which will be of value in eternity.

HOW ABOUT YOU? What do you value most in life? Your bicycle? Some jewelry? A favorite toy? Can you recognize it as a "bubble"? God has given you many things to use and enjoy, but don't become too attached to them. Don't spend all your time and energy on "bubbles" that are going to burst and disappear. You may feel badly when that happens, but don't get all upset about it. Remember the old saying, "Only one life, 'twill soon be past. Only what's done for Christ will last." P.R.

TO MEMORIZE: *"For we brought nothing into this world, and it is certain we can carry nothing out"* 1 Timothy 6:7.

AUGUST

Kool Kats?

FROM THE BIBLE:
And we urge you, brothers, warn those who are idle, encourage the timid, help the weak, be patient with everyone. Make sure that nobody pays back wrong for wrong, but always try to be kind to each other and to everyone else. Be joyful always; pray continually; give thanks in all circumstances, for this is God's will for you in Christ Jesus. Do not put out the Spirit's fire; do not treat prophecies with contempt. Test everything. Hold on to the good. Avoid every kind of evil. May God himself, the God of peace, sanctify you through and through. May your whole spirit, soul and body be kept blameless at the coming of our Lord Jesus Christ.
1 Thessalonians 5:14-23, NIV

Test things; keep the good

"I WAS ELECTED to the Kool Kats Klub," Barry proudly announced one night. "Ain't that neat?"

"*Isn't* that neat," corrected Mother. "I'm not so sure it is. What do these particular 'Kats' do?"

Barry shrugged. "They have meetings and talk about stuff and do things together."

"Better check them out before you get involved with them," suggested Dad.

Again Barry shrugged. "I don't see why. They sound neat to me." He looked at the plate of food Mother set before him. "What is this? Why'd you give me so much?"

"It's a new recipe," announced Mother, "and I figured you were hungry."

"Yeah, but what if I don't like it?"

"It's called Continental Hash," said Mother. "Sounds neat, doesn't it? Eat it up."

"Can't tell by the name," insisted Barry. "I'll check it out." He took a very small bite, then tried a little more. "It's good," he said, "but I don't like the mushrooms. Do I have to eat them?"

Mother nodded. "I gave you only a few. If you want another helping, you can avoid them."

"You 'checked it out' so you could take what you found to be good and avoid what was not good," observed Dad. "That's just what the Bible tells us to do. In 1 Thessalonians, Paul says to 'prove'—to test or check out—all things."

Barry looked at his father. "He doesn't mean food."

"I think Paul is warning us about jumping into things we haven't checked out," said Dad.

"Like the Kool Kats," said Barry.

The following evening Barry was rather quiet. "I learned that the Kool Kats aren't so cool," he said. "I talked to one of them, and they showed me a magazine he was taking to the meeting. It was bad! Then he let it slip that they buy cigarettes with part of the club money. I'm glad I found out before I turned over half of my allowance for dues."

"I'm glad you took the Apostle Paul's advice," said Dad.

HOW ABOUT YOU? Are you so eager to join a club, read a popular book, or buy the latest hit record that you plunge ahead without checking to see if it will do you harm or good? Will it help you love the Lord, or will it draw you away from Him? Check it out. Keep only the good. H.M.

TO MEMORIZE: *"Prove all things; hold fast that which is good"* 1 Thessalonians 5:21.

AUGUST

15

I Don't Want to Go!

FROM THE BIBLE:

Then Naomi said to her two daughters-in-law, "Go back, each of you, to your mother's home. . . . May the Lord grant that each of you will find rest in the home of another husband." Then she kissed them and they wept aloud and said to her, "We will go back with you to your people." But Naomi said, "Return home, my daughters." . . . At this they wept again. Then Orpah kissed her mother-in-law good-by, but Ruth clung to her. "Look," said Naomi, "your sister-in-law is going back to her people and her gods. Go back with her." But Ruth replied, "Don't urge me to leave you or to turn back from you. Where you go I will go, and where you stay I will stay. Your people will be my people and your God my God. Where you die I will die, and there I will be buried. May the Lord deal with me, be it ever so severely, if anything but death separates you and me." When Naomi realized that Ruth was determined to go with her, she stopped urging her.

Ruth 1:8-18, NIV

Accept necessary changes

"ENGLAND!" Amanda was stunned. "We're really moving to England?"

"That's right, honey," said Dad. "The company want to start a branch overseas, and they've chosen me to get it started. We'll be living in England for at least five years."

Amanda walked over to the living room window and looked out at the familiar street. She had lived in this same house ever since she was a baby. What would it be like to not only live in a different house, but in a different country? Amanda couldn't imagine. She'd have to leave her friends, her school, and her church. "I don't think I want to move," Amanda whispered in a trembly voice. "I want to stay here." Tears trickled down her cheeks.

Amanda's dad put his arm around her. "You do have a choice," he said. "You can be upset and bitter about moving, or you can look at it as a special experience that very few of your friends will ever have. It's up to you. Remember, too, that no matter where we move, God will be with us, and He promises to take care of us."

As Amanda sat in her room later, she remembered what her dad had said about the choice she had to make. She knew they were going to England whether she liked it or not, so she might as well choose to like it. She certainly didn't want to be bitter and unhappy for five years! Amanda called her best friend, Julie, that very night. "Guess what! We're moving to England!" she said.

Julie almost sounded jealous after Amanda explained. "How neat!" she squealed. "You can send me lots of letters, and I can put the stamps in my stamp collection!"

Amanda smiled. Moving to England would be a good adventure. She was glad she had changed her attitude.

HOW ABOUT YOU? Does your family move a lot? Have you had to change schools? Did you find it hard to make friends at your new school or church? It isn't easy to move away from everything familiar. Remember, though, the Lord promises to be with you anytime and anywhere. You can always talk with Him. So try to see the advantages of living in several different places. Learn to enjoy the unique experiences and the wide array of friends. Be content wherever God places you. L.W.

TO MEMORIZE: *"Now that I speak in regard to need, for I have learned in whatever state I am, to be content"* Philippians 4:11 (NKJV).

AUGUST

16

Blank Paper

FROM THE BIBLE:

All our days pass away under
your wrath;
we finish our years with a
moan.
The length of our days is seventy
years—
or eighty, if we have the
strength;
yet their span is but trouble
and sorrow,
for they quickly pass, and we
fly away.
Who knows the power of your
anger?
For your wrath is as great as
the fear that is due you.
Teach us to number our days
aright,
that we may gain a heart of
wisdom.
Relent, O Lord! How long will
it be?
Have compassion on your
servants.
Satisfy us in the morning with
your unfailing love,
that we may sing for joy and
be glad all our days.
Make us glad for as many days
as you have afflicted us,
for as many years as we have
seen trouble.

Psalm 90:9-15, NIV

Don't waste time

"HELEN," said Mother as she stood in the doorway of her daughter's room one Saturday, "you've spent half the day in here just wasting time. How about doing something constructive, like writing a letter to Grandma Nelson?"

Helen pulled a face but went off to find some writing paper. A few minutes later, Mother heard her shouting in the den. "Jody! Shame on you!" scolded Helen angrily. Mother came in and saw papers spread across the floor. Two-year-old Jody had a black crayon in her hand. "Jody scribbled on all the pages of that new writing tablet," Helen exclaimed. "They're ruined! What a mess!"

As Jody scurried out of the room, Helen bent down and picked up a piece of paper. "Here's one Jody missed. At least there's one good piece left."

But Mother shook her head. "No, the way it is now, it's really no better than the ones Jody scribbled on," she said.

"What do you mean?" asked Helen.

"It's empty," Mother answered. "Nothing has been written or drawn on it which would make it of any real value to anyone. If someone wrote a letter or poem or drew a picture or designed a house on it, then it would be worth something."

Helen grinned. "I'll use it to write Grandma."

"Good." Mother smiled. "A day of your life is like a blank piece of paper, honey. You can use it thoughtlessly with silly or harmful activities, and it would be like these pages Jody scribbled on. Or you can waste it by simply neglecting to use it for anything worthwhile."

"Like I wasted my morning," said Helen thoughtfully. "Well, the day's not over yet, so I still have time to make something out of it. I'll start by writing that letter."

HOW ABOUT YOU? Do you waste time with unnecessary or useless activities or through laziness? If you're a Christian you should be "redeeming the time"—using it carefully in ways that please the Lord. This may include being friendly, helping your mother, studying God's Word, reading a good book, getting needed rest, witnessing to a friend. Start now to make each day of your life worthwhile! S.K.

TO MEMORIZE: *"See then that you walk circumspectly, not as fools but as wise, redeeming the time, because the days are evil"* Ephesians 5:15-16 (NKJV).

AUGUST

17

Over and Over

FROM THE BIBLE:

The proverbs of Solomon son of David, king of Israel: for attaining wisdom and discipline; for understanding words of insight; for acquiring a disciplined and prudent life, doing what is right and just and fair; for giving prudence to the simple, knowledge and discretion to the young—let the wise listen and add to their learning, and let the discerning get guidance—for understanding proverbs and parables, the sayings and riddles of the wise. The fear of the Lord is the beginning of knowledge, but fools despise wisdom and discipline. Listen, my son, to your father's instruction and do not forsake your mother's teaching. Proverbs 1:1-8, NIV

Learn from repetition

"CINDI!" called Mother. "Come in and do your Sunday school lesson. You've been working with King for almost an hour!"

Cindi frowned. "If I don't train King every chance I get, he won't be ready for the show next week," she told her mother. "Besides, I already looked at my lesson. It's the story about Daniel and the lions. I've heard it a million times!"

"I don't think it's been quite that many. It won't take you very long, and you may be surprised—you might learn something new."

"Fat chance!" Cindi grumbled to herself as she plunked down at the table with her Sunday school book and her Bible. Fifteen minutes later she was out the door yelling, "I'm done, Mom! You can check my book. I'll be working with King!"

That evening at the supper table Cindi couldn't stop talking about King and how well he was learning. "I guess it's because I've been teaching him obedience since he was just a puppy. I've made him do things over and over until he got them right."

"You know," said Mother, "like King, you have been taught things since you were very young. You've been taught that God made the world, and that He loves you. All the things you've been learning since you were little are going to help you develop into a fine, mature Christian someday. But, just like King, you have to be taught things over and over. Everything you are learning in church now will be helpful to you in later years."

"So it doesn't really matter if they give us the same lesson all the time?" asked Cindi.

Mother laughed. "You give King the same lessons every day!" she said.

"Yeah, you're right," responded Cindi. "I think I'll do my lesson over this evening. I did it pretty fast this afternoon; maybe I missed something."

HOW ABOUT YOU? Do you get tired of hearing the same Bible stories over and over? Remember, you seldom learn all there is to know by hearing it only once. Thank God for parents and teachers, who patiently teach you God's Word. The knowledge you're gaining now will stay with you for the rest of your life. If you learn your lessons well, you'll be rewarded by being able to use them in later years. D.M.

TO MEMORIZE: *"Apply your heart to discipline, and your ears to words of knowledge"* Proverbs 23:12 (NASB).

AUGUST

18

It Didn't Just Happen

FROM THE BIBLE:
Then God said, "Let the waters teem with fish and other life, and let the skies be filled with birds of every kind." So God created great sea animals, and every sort of fish and every kind of bird. And God looked at them with pleasure, and blessed them all. "Multiply and stock the oceans," he told them, and to the birds he said, "Let your numbers increase. Fill the earth!" That ended the fifth day. And God said, "Let the earth bring forth every kind of animal—cattle and reptiles and wildlife of every kind." And so it was. God made all sorts of wild animals and cattle and reptiles. And God was pleased with what he had done. Then God said, "Let us make a man—someone like ourselves, to be the master of all life upon the earth and in the skies and in the seas." So God made man like his Maker. Like God did God make man; Man and maid did he make them. And God blessed them and told them, "Multiply and fill the earth and subdue it; you are masters of the fish and birds and all the animals."
Genesis 1:20-28, TLB

God created life

BECKY'S science teacher didn't believe in the biblical record of creation. He told the class that all animals evolved from lower forms of life. When Becky asked where the lower forms of life had come from, Mr. Matthews shrugged. "They just happened." Becky was frustrated. She believed God had created the heavens and the earth, but how could she convince her teacher?

That evening after school she had an idea. Her Uncle Bob was a wood carver, and he had made Beck an exquisitely carved cardinal. Carefully she wrapped the wooden bird in several layers of paper, and the next day she took it to school.

When it was time for science class, Becky unwrapped the bird and put it on her desk. The other students admired it, and even Mr. Matthews came back to where she was sitting and looked at the cardinal. "Whoever carved this bird certainly knew what he was doing," he observed. "This is beautiful! Who did it?"

Becky shrugged her shoulders. "Nobody. I woke up this morning, and there it was. It just happened!"

The teacher looked surprised. "You mean you don't know who made it?"

"Nobody made it. I told you it just happened!" insisted Becky.

Mr. Matthews raised his eyebrows. "Sure it did," he said sarcastically. "What are you getting at?"

Becky grinned at him. "Mr. Matthews, you'd think I was silly if I really believed that no one made this wooden cardinal, yet you told me that no one made the real cardinals."

Mr. Matthews gave her a thoughtful look. Becky knew she hadn't convinced him that God created the world, but she silently thanked the Lord that she had at least made the teacher think.

HOW ABOUT YOU? Do your teachers sometimes teach things that go against God's Word? God did create all things, including all life. The Bible teaches that, and you can see evidence of God's creation in the beautiful world around you. Just as it takes a talented artist to create a pretty picture, it took the Master Designer, God, to create the awesome world in which you live. L.W.

TO MEMORIZE: *"I have made the earth, the man and the beast that are upon the ground, by my great power"* Jeremiah 27:5.

AUGUST

19

Everywhere At Once

FROM THE BIBLE:

O Lord, you have searched me
and you know me.
You know when I sit and when
I rise;
you perceive my thoughts from
afar.
You discern my going out and
my lying down;
you are familiar with all my
ways. . . .
You hem me in—behind and
before;
you have laid your hand
upon me.
Such knowledge is too
wonderful for me,
too lofty for me to attain.
Where can I go from your Spirit?
Where can I flee from your
presence?
If I go up to the heavens, you
are there;
if I make my bed in the
depths, you are there.
If I rise on the wings of the
dawn,
if I settle on the far side of
the sea,
even there your hand will
guide me,
your right hand will hold me
fast.

Psalm 139:1-10, NIV

God is everywhere

LARRY AND BOB discussed their Sunday school lesson as they waited for Sunday dinner. "I believe in God as much as you do," Larry declared, "but if He were everywhere, we would see Him. We can't see Him because He's not here. He's up in heaven. He can hear and see us because He's God, but we can't hear and see Him."

"He's here just the same," insisted Bob. "Like Mr. Malloy said, He's onima . . . ominen . . . om . . . "

"Omnipresent." Dad helped him out. "Sounds like you had a good lesson. But Mother has dinner ready, so let's not keep her waiting." After giving thanks, Dad turned to Larry. "Now, what was the disagreement about?"

"Oh, I just think too scientifically to believe that God is everywhere at once," Larry said smugly. He changed the subject. "Can we listen to Children's Bible Hour while we eat? Please?"

"Sure." Mother smiled. "But first, Mr. Science, tell me what makes it possible to hear people on the radio? We can't see them."

Larry grinned. He loved science. "No, not unless they're on TV," he agreed. "You see, there are radio waves, or sound waves, in the air—picture waves, too, and—"

"You don't mean right here in this room, do you?" interrupted Dad, waving his arms around. "I can't see any. I can't *feel* any either. You must mean they're inside the radio and TV sets."

"Nope, they're all around you," stated Larry firmly.

"Well, maybe we'd better skip Children's Bible Hour today, though," suggested Mother. "If we listen, we'll be using up those sound waves, and Jason next door won't be able to listen."

"Oh, Mom," laughed Larry, "he can listen, too. Those same sound waves are over there."

"Just like God!" interjected Bob suddenly. "He's here and next door, and everywhere all at once."

HOW ABOUT YOU? Is it hard to understand that God is omnipresent—everwhere at once? This is part of His greatness. You cannot escape Him. He is there when you tell a lie. He is with you when you're afraid. He is present when you're lonely. What a great God! H.M.

TO MEMORIZE: *"Where can I go from your Spirit? Where can I flee from your presence?"* Psalm 139:7 (NIV).

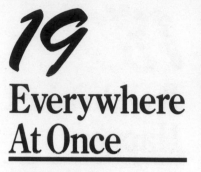

AUGUST

20

The Answered Prayer

FROM THE BIBLE:

Dear brothers, what's the use of saying that you have faith and are Christians if you aren't proving it by helping others? Will that kind of faith save anyone? If you have a friend who is in need of food and clothing, and you say to him, "Well, good-bye and God bless you; stay warm and eat hearty," and then don't give him clothes or food, what good does that do? So you see, it isn't enough just to have faith. You must also do good to prove that you have it. Faith that doesn't show itself by good works is no faith at all—it is dead and useless. But someone may well argue, "You say the way to God is by faith alone, plus nothing; well, I say that good works are important too, for without good works you can't prove whether you have faith or not; but anyone can see that I have faith by the way I act." James 2:14-18, TLB

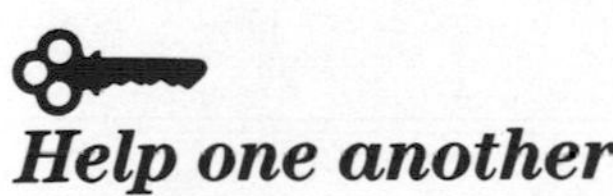

Help one another

CINDY WAS TRYING on her new school clothes when Mother came in. "This skirt and blouse are my favorite of all my new clothes," Cindy said. "And these shoes are exactly what all the girls are wearing."

Mother smiled. "I'm glad you like them. Now come on. It's Joey's bedtime, and we haven't had our family prayer time yet."

When Dad asked for prayer requests, Cindy thought of something. "Let's pray that Sheryl will get some new shoes," she said. "She's worn the same old shoes all summer. They're worn out, but I know they're the only ones she has."

As Cindy prayed for Sheryl, she had a funny feeling that she was forgetting something. She still had that feeling as she put her new clothes and shoes in the closet. Even when she crawled into bed, the feeling stayed with her.

Cindy screwed up her forehead and stared into the dark, trying to remember what she was forgetting. She reviewed the day, starting with breakfast and their daily Bible reading. "If a brother or sister be naked . . . and you say to them, Depart in peace, be you warmed . . . notwithstanding ye give them not those things which are needful . . . what doth it profit?" Dad had read.

Cindy sat right up in bed and laughed. She jumped out of bed and ran into the living room. "Mother, God wants me to answer my own prayer and buy Sheryl's shoes with my baby-sitting money."

Mother looked surprised, then smiled as she said, "Why, Cindy, what a generous idea! We'll go shopping tomorrow."

HOW ABOUT YOU? Are you asking God to do something that you can do yourself? God often uses people to answer prayers, and He may even use you to answer your own prayers. Be ready to obey if God prompts you to do something. B.W.

TO MEMORIZE: *"While we have opportunity, let us do good to all men, and especially to those who are of the household of the faith"* Galatians 6:10 (NASB).

AUGUST

21

A Time to Forget

FROM THE BIBLE:

To everything there is a season, a time for every purpose under heaven: A time to be born, and a time to die; a time to plant, and a time to pluck what is planted; a time to kill, and a time to heal; a time to break down, and a time to build up; a time to weep, and a time to laugh; a time to mourn, and a time to dance; a time to cast away stones, and a time to gather stones; a time to embrace, and a time to refrain from embracing; a time to gain, and a time to lose; a time to keep, and a time to throw away; a time to tear, and a time to sew; a time to keep silence, and a time to speak; a time to love, and a time to hate; a time of war, and a time of peace.
Ecclesiastes 3:1-8, NKJV

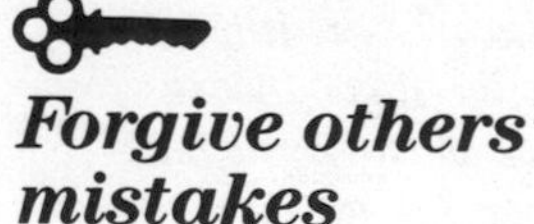

Forgive others' mistakes

"MOM, GUESS what I just heard about our new neighbors. The dad just got out of prison!" Before Mother could reply, Mark rushed on. "He stole a whole lot of money from his employer, and he had to spend five years in prison! I wonder if we should tell Mr. Wilson that he has a thief working for him."

"I'm sure Mr. Wilson knows all about Mr. Smith," Mother replied calmly.

Mark's eyes snapped. "I'm going to be more careful about locking up my bicycle. I told the others guys to watch theirs, too."

"Mark, you should not be talking about Mr. Smith to others. You don't really know anything about it," scolded Mother. "Now, are you going to play at Nathan's?"

"Yeah." Mark nodded. Then he ran down the hall to his big brother's room. As Mother followed she heard him ask, "Brad, can I take your telescope over to Nathan's?"

"No. I can't trust you," snapped Brad. "You lost my calculator last month."

"But I paid for it," Mark reminded him.

"Yeah," admitted Brad, "but if you lose my telescope or break it, it'd take you months to pay for it."

"But, Brad," wailed Mark, "it's not fair to hold that one mistake against me forever."

Mother spoke quickly. "Neither is it fair to hold Mr. Smith's mistake against him," she said. "He has paid for it, and he told your father that he's sorry about it. Jesus said if we want mercy, we must be merciful. If we want to be forgiven, we must be forgiving."

"Oops!" Brad grinned at Mark. "He also said that we should do unto others like we want them to do to us, so I guess I'd better let you borrow my telescope."

HOW ABOUT YOU? When Jesus forgives us for our sins, He forgets them. Is there something about someone that you need to forget? Then do it. How? Stop talking about it and soon you will forget it, too. B.W.

TO MEMORIZE: *"I am He who blots out your transgressions for my own sake; and I will not remember your sins"* Isaiah 43:25 (NIV).

AUGUST

22

What God Won't Share

FROM THE BIBLE:

Don't brag about your plans for tomorrow—wait and see what happens. Don't praise yourself; let others do it!
Proverbs 27:1-2, TLB

As the Scriptures say, "If anyone is going to boast, let him boast about what the Lord has done and not about himself." When someone boasts about himself and how well he has done, it doesn't count for much. But when the Lord commends him, that's different!
2 Corinthians 10:17-18, TLB

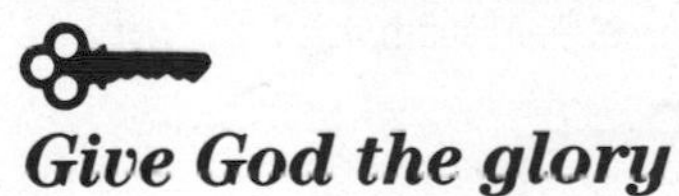

Give God the glory

". . . AND THANK YOU, Lord, that the guys seemed to be so impressed by what I said when I witnessed to them at school," prayed Calvin in his Sunday school class. "Amen."

Several boys exchanged glances as Calvin sat down. Dan nudged Kyle. "I timed him," he whispered. "He prayed for three minutes—and all about what a wonderful witness he was."

Just then their teacher, Mr. Wilbur, asked if anyone had something to share before the lesson began. Again Calvin jumped up. "The Lord just keeps giving me more and more opportunities," he said with a big smile. "It's really exciting! All you guys should witness for the Lord. Next week we're supposed to give an oral report on our favorite book, so I'm going to do mine on the Bible."

After class Mr. Wilbur called Calvin aside. "I'm glad to see your enthusiasm for witnessing," he said, "but I feel that I ought to caution you about one thing. Be careful not to brag when you tell how the Lord is using you. I'd suggest that you talk more about Jesus, less about yourself."

But during the next week, Calvin spent more time talking about the terrific witness his book report would be than he spent working on the report. When he gave the report, he stumbled miserably through it. There were several snickers as Calvin sat down. "Next time, talk about something more familiar to you," his teacher suggested. Calvin blushed with shame.

When Mr. Wilbur asked him how his report had gone, Calvin told him. "I don't understand it! Doesn't God want me to be a good witness?"

Mr. Wilbur nodded. "Yes, but He wants you to glorify Him, not yourself," he said. "Perhaps you just needed a lesson in humility."

In spite of himself, Calvin grinned. "This has been a learning experience," he agreed. "From now on, I'll try to remember that I'm just the instrument. It's God who does the real work."

HOW ABOUT YOU? Are you ever tempted to brag about some good work you've done—or plan to do—for the Lord? Good things done to impress others or to make you feel important often end in failure. It's an honor and a privilege to be used of God, but the glory belongs to Him. It's one thing God won't share! S.K.

TO MEMORIZE: *"I am the LORD: that is my name: and my glory will I not give to another"*
Isaiah 42:8.

AUGUST

23

Calm in the Storm

FROM THE BIBLE:

But now, thus says the Lord, who created you, O Jacob, and He who formed you, O Israel: "Fear not, for I have redeemed you; I have called you by your name; you are Mine. When you pass through the waters, I will be with you; and through the rivers, they shall not overflow you. When you walk through the fire, you shall not be burned, nor shall the flame scorch you. For I am the Lord your God, the Holy One of Israel, your Savior; I gave Egypt for your ransom, Ethiopia and Seba in your place." Isaiah 43:1-3, NKJV

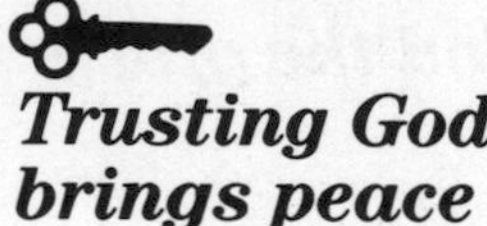

Trusting God brings peace

AS RAIN PATTERED against Dana's bedroom window, two big tears dampened her pillow. The storm inside her heart seemed far greater than the one outside. Her dad had left the family several months ago, and Dana been praying he'd come back to the Lord and rejoin them. But today the awful news had come. Dad was getting married again. Now there was no chance of restoring the family to the way it was.

A few minutes later Dana heard her door opening softly, and Mother came in. "Is the storm bothering you, honey?" asked Mother.

Dana sniffed. "No. I hardly noticed it," she said.

Mother smiled. "That's good. When you were small, you were terribly afraid of lightning."

"I was?" asked Dana. "I don't remember that. I wonder how I got over it."

Mother sat in the rocker next to the bed and stroked Dana's hair fondly. "When there was a bad storm, I used to come and sit in this chair sometimes. For some reason, just having me here seemed to make your fear go away."

Dana looked up at her mother and grinned. "That's funny!" she said. After a moment, she added, "You really don't need to stay in here tonight, Mom. I'll be OK."

"I know you will," replied Mother as she stood up. "You see, I know how upset you've been lately, and I've been praying that God's presence will help you through this tough time. I know I'd never make it without Him, and I hope you'll always remember that He's here to help you. He'll make sure the storms of life never really hurt you."

After Mother had left, Dana looked at the empty rocking chair. She tried to imagine the Lord sitting there, watching over her during this crisis in her life. Suddenly she knew that even though the problems in her life were still there, things were different now because she was trusting God to take care of her. Dana rolled over and was soon sound asleep.

HOW ABOUT YOU? Are there some difficult problems in your life right now? God is able to change your situation, but He may let you go through hard times so that you'll learn to trust in Him completely. Learning to trust God, no matter what happens, is the secret to real happiness. Remember, He's always there! S.K.

TO MEMORIZE: *"You will keep him in perfect peace, whose mind is stayed on You, because he trusts in You"* Isaiah 26:3 (NKJV).

AUGUST

24

Broken Promises

FROM THE BIBLE:

When you make a vow to the Lord, be prompt in doing whatever it is you promised him, for the Lord demands that you promptly fulfill your vows; it is a sin if you don't. (But it is not a sin if you refrain from vowing!) Once you make the vow, you must be careful to do as you have said, for it was your own choice, and you have vowed to the Lord your God.
Deuteronomy 23:21-23, TLB

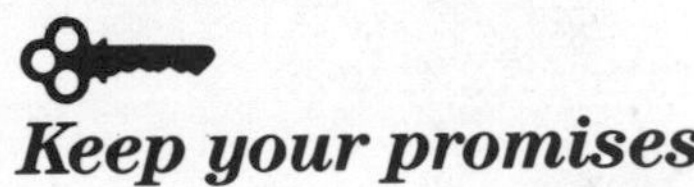

Keep your promises

CHAD LIKED the missionary who was speaking in his church. Mr. Rathbun had told them thrilling stories of his ministry in a foreign land.

"In that country there are many orphan children," Mr. Rathbun was saying. "If we could build a home for them, we could show them love, and it would give us the opportunity to teach them about Jesus and win them to Christ. We are asking Christians to pray earnestly about this home. We're also asking you to give up just one cup of coffee or one bottle of pop or perhaps one candy bar a week and give the price of it to the Lord for this home. If you will do these things, raise your hand." Chad's hand shot right up. He was glad to see many hands raised, including those of his friends, Greg and Gary.

One Saturday a few weeks later the three boys were biking home after ball practice. "I'm hot," said Greg. "Let's get some pop at the gas station."

As they were getting out their coins, Chad exclaimed, "Hey, wait! We promised to give up one pop a week. It's Saturday already, and I haven't given up one this week yet, have you?"

"Nah," said Greg. "I'll give up two next week."

"Yeah," agreed Gary. "I'm too thirsty now."

Chad felt hurt as the boys drank their pop. He wouldn't even take a sip of theirs when they offered it. "I don't see how you can break your promise," he told them.

That evening Chad was very quiet. "Something wrong?" asked Dad.

"Yeah," Chad said. He told his father about his friends and then added, "I was mad all the way home until I remembered I was just as bad as they were. I promised to pray for Mr. Rathbun and the orphanage, but I haven't done it much."

"I'm glad you see your own faults, Chad," Dad told him. "You see, promises aren't to be taken lightly. The Lord says it's better not to make a promise, than to make one and not keep it. Now if you keep your promise, then you can pray that God will work in your friends' hearts so they will want to do their part, too."

HOW ABOUT YOU? Have you made promises to God that you haven't kept? God keeps all His promises, and He expects you to keep yours. Be careful about making promises. Ask God to help you keep the ones you make. A.L.

TO MEMORIZE: *"When you make a vow to God, do not delay to pay it; for He has no pleasure in fools. Pay what you have vowed"* Ecclesiastes 5:4 (NKJV).

AUGUST

25

The Kiwi

FROM THE BIBLE:

Charm is deceitful and beauty is vain, but a woman who fears the Lord, she shall be praised. Give her of the fruit of her hands, and let her own works praise her in the gates.
Proverbs 31:30-31, NKJV

Do not let your beauty be that outward adorning of arranging the hair, of wearing gold, or of putting on fine apparel; but let it be the hidden person of the heart, with the incorruptible ornament of a gentle and quiet spirit, which is very precious in the sight of God.
1 Peter 3:3-4, NKJV

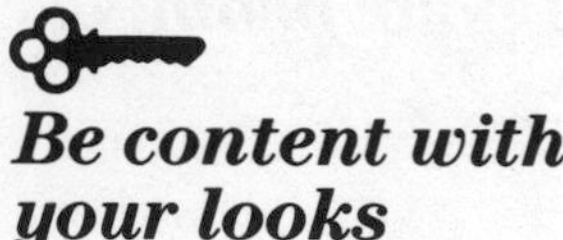

Be content with your looks

LINDSEY FROWNED as she looked at herself in the full length mirror. "I'm ugly," she sighed sadly. "Everyone laughs at me because I'm short and chubby. My eyes are too small and my nose is too big. My nails aren't pretty, either, and my teeth are crooked. I'm ugly, and that's it."

"That's nonsense," Mother said. She and Lindsey's dad had noticed that Lindsey often walked around with slumped shoulders lately and was not her usual friendly, cheerful self. "You're changing," Mother continued, "but you are definitely not ugly. Come on, let's go to the store."

At the store, Mother asked, "Would you get two kiwi for me, please?" She pointed toward the strange, brown fruit.

"I've never seen kiwi before," said Lindsey. "Are you sure you want these funny-looking things?" Mother smiled and nodded as she added some bananas to the basket.

After dinner that evening, Mother set out a colorful bowl of fruit for dessert. "What a pretty green this fruit is, Mom," observed Lindsey, pointing to one of the pieces. She took a bite. "Oh, and it's so good! What is it?"

"It's kiwi," Mom informed her, smiling.

"You're kidding!" Lindsey gulped. "You mean that ugly, fuzzy, brown thing we bought?"

"That's right." Her dad spoke up. "You know, honey, you've been putting too much value on the way things look, lately. You've been especially hard on yourself. Don't forget, the Bible says beauty is vain. Just like with the kiwi, it's what's inside that counts. Keep working on that. Look your best, and then be content with the way you're made. Ever since you've become so concerned about your looks, all your inside sweetness had been covered up. And I really miss my old Lindsey."

"I think I like the old Lindsey better, too," Lindsey said. She grinned at her mother. "You can serve me kiwi, Mom, whenever you think I need a reminder."

HOW ABOUT YOU? Are you unhappy with the way you look? Learn to accept the way God made you, and be content. Most of all, work at becoming a beautiful person inside by living the way God's Word tells you to live. S.N.

TO MEMORIZE: *"Beauty is vain, but a woman who fears the Lord, she shall be praised"*
Proverbs 31:30 (NKJV).

MEOW! MEOW! Mother could hear the cat crying from the living room. "Andy, what are you doing to Muffy?" she asked, walking into the room.

"Nothing, Mom," answered Andy. "I was just petting her, but she turned around to face the other way. When I kept on stroking her, it made her fur all stand up funny, and she didn't like it!"

"I'll be she didn't!" answered Mother with a smile. "I'm sure it makes a cat feel funny to have it's fur rubbed the wrong way. From now on try to be a little more careful."

The next day Andy looked unhappy when he got home from school. "Is something wrong?" asked Mother.

"Just about everybody in my class cheated on a test today," replied Andy. "John asked why I didn't cheat, too. I told him it makes me feel funny to do that kind of stuff—like the time I stole that candy bar. Why do I feel bad about doing things like that when nobody else does?"

"Well, Andy, it's a little like rubbing Muffy's fur the wrong way," Mother replied. "When you do something wrong, the Holy Spirit convicts you about it because you're a Christian. It's as if God were rubbing your fur the wrong way, so you feel uncomfortable. You feel guilty. And you don't feel right again until you turn around and go in the right direction—until you've repented of your sin and confessed it."

Andy's face lit up as he grinned at his mother. "I get it!" he exclaimed.

"When you do what you should," added Mother, "you feel safe and happy instead of guilty and afraid."

HOW ABOUT YOU? Do you feel unhappy and guilty about something you've done? That's the Holy Spirit working to convict you about your sin. It's as though your "fur is being rubbed the wrong way." When you feel guilty about something, confess that sin to God and tell Him you're sorry. You'll feel better when you've done that. D.M.

TO MEMORIZE: *"He who conceals his sins does not prosper, but whoever confesses and renounces them finds mercy"* Proverbs 28:13 (NIV).

26

Turn Around

FROM THE BIBLE:
What happiness for those whose guilt has been forgiven! What joys when sins are covered over! What relief for those who have confessed their sins and God has cleared their record. There was a time when I wouldn't admit what a sinner I was. But my dishonesty made me miserable and filled my days with frustration. All day and all night your hand was heavy on me. My strength evaporated like water on a sunny day until I finally admitted all my sins to you and stopped trying to hide them. I said to myself, "I will confess them to the Lord." And you forgave me! All my guilt is gone. Psalm 32:1-5, TLB

God convicts of sin

AUGUST

27

Guilty Conscience

FROM THE BIBLE:

He came as High Priest of this better system which we now have. He went into that greater, perfect tabernacle in heaven, not made by men nor part of this world, and once for all took blood into that inner room, the Holy of Holies, and sprinkled it on the mercy seat; but it was not the blood of goats and calves. No, he took his own blood, and with it he, by himself, made sure of our eternal salvation. And if under the old system the blood of bulls and goats and the ashes of young cows could cleanse men's bodies from sin, just think how much more surely the blood of Christ will transform our lives and hearts. His sacrifice frees us from the worry of having to obey the old rules, and makes us want to serve the living God. For by the help of the eternal Holy Spirit, Christ willingly gave himself to God to die for our sins—he being perfect, without a single sin or fault.

Hebrews 9:11-14, TLB

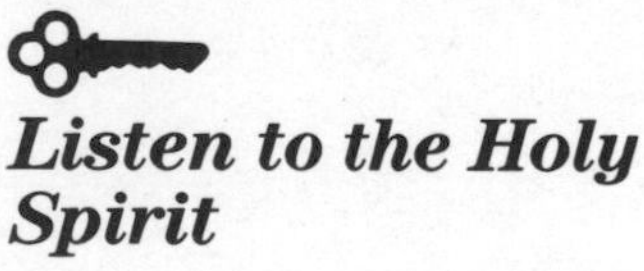

Listen to the Holy Spirit

MICK WHISTLED as he sauntered out of Brown's grocery store. Then with a flying leap, he jumped on his bicycle and raced down the street. Every few seconds he glanced over his shoulder. Only when he was a safe nine blocks from the store did he stop and pull a package of chocolate covered nuts from his pocket. But the candy didn't taste very good after the first few bites. Mick got rid of the rest of the evidence and went home.

"Mick, I'm glad you're home." mother smiled. "Will you run to Brown's store and get me some sugar please?"

"B-B-Brown's? B-b-but I don't feel good," stammered Mick. "Can't Michelle go?" Concerned, Mother agreed.

When Mother answered the phone a bit later, Mick heard her say, "Yes, Mr. Brown." After that he could hear only snatches of the conversation. Soon she hung up, and with a sigh she hurried out to the garage to talk to Dad. Mick could tell she was upset. He felt sicker than ever!

When Dad came in, Mick's feelings poured out. "I didn't think Mr. Brown saw me in the store, but he told Mother, didn't he? Oh, Dad, I don't know what made me do it."

Dad looked puzzled. "Mr. Brown?" he asked. "Mr. Brown told Mother there was a check he had to return to her. It was one a lady had given her at the garage sale. Mr. Brown had cashed it for her, but the bank said it wasn't any good. Now what are *you* talking about?"

"I stole some c-c-candy today," stammered Mick. "I've been scared to death ever since."

Dad shook his head. "You were unhappy and scared because you were trying to run from a guilty conscience. This reminds me of a Bible verse which says, 'The wicked flee when no man pursueth.' That's what you were doing."

"So I didn't have to tell you about the candy at all," said Mick, "but I'm glad I did! I'd hate to spend the rest of my life with a guilty conscience, running from nobody."

"Good," said Dad, "because now you're going to go and pay Mr. Brown for that candy."

HOW ABOUT YOU? God has given each one of us a conscience. If you have accepted Jesus, the Holy Spirit will work through your conscience. Listen to Him. Obey Him. He will keep you from sin. B.W.

TO MEMORIZE: *"The wicked flee when no one pursues"* Proverbs 28:1 (NIV).

AUGUST

28

The Bug Light

"LET'S SIT ON the back porch, Rob, and watch the sun go down," Dad suggested one evening. He walked toward the door, and Rob followed silently. They sat several minutes without talking, then Dad spoke. "Rob, you're usually so cheerful, but you've been very quiet lately."

"Everything's fine—really! We don't need to talk about anything," Rob answered quickly, not looking at his dad.

Soon the sun was down, and the only sound they heard was the *zzzztt!* of the bug light on a post. It cast an eerie blue shadow on the backyard.

Dad decided to try again. "Rob, I hope everything is fine," he said, "but if it isn't, would you talk to me about it? I'm available any time."

"Sure," said Rob as he stared at the bug light.

The next day it was Rob who suggested that they sit on the porch. "Dad, you were right," he said. "Everything isn't fine." Then Rob told how a friend had offered him a cigarette. After saying no a few times, he had smoked one. Since then he had smoked several times, and now he was starting to want a cigarette more often.

Dad put his arm around Rob. "Thanks, Rob, for telling me," he said.

"Last night I watched the bugs fly into that bug light," continued Rob. "They were attracted to the light, not knowing it was drawing them to their death. They got closer and closer and didn't realize they would be harmed. Then I realized that it was the same with smoking. I took the first cigarette because lots of my friends smoked. Then I smoked because I thought it made me feel good. But I'm getting closer and closer to being harmed, too. I could get addicted if I don't stop now."

"Smart thinking, Rob," Dad said. "Sin often looks very pleasant to us. It's easy to get involved in it, but it can destroy us."

"This afternoon I told God I'm not going to smoke again," said Rob quietly.

HOW ABOUT YOU? Has anyone ever asked you to smoke a cigarette? God's Word says Christians are not to defile (do anything to hurt) their bodies. A person who encourages you to smoke or take drugs is not a true friend. Don't try those things—not even once. Keep your body pure for the Lord Jesus. D.K.

TO MEMORIZE: *"Do you not know that your body is the temple of the Holy Spirit who is in you, whom you have from God, and you are not your own?"* 1 Corinthians 6:19 (NKJV).

FROM THE BIBLE:
Don't you realize that all of you together are the house of God, and that the Spirit of God lives among you in his house? If anyone defiles and spoils God's home, God will destroy him. For God's home is holy and clean, and you are that home. Stop fooling yourselves. If you count yourself above average in intelligence, as judged by this world's standards, you had better put this all aside and be a fool rather than let it hold you back from the true wisdom from above. For the wisdom of this world is foolishness to God. As it says in the book of Job, God uses man's own brilliance to trap him; he stumbles over his own "wisdom" and falls. And again, in the book of Psalms, we are told that the Lord knows full well how the human mind reasons, and how foolish and futile it is. So don't be proud of following the wise men of this world. For God has already given you everything you need.
1 Corinthians 3:16-21, TLB

Stay away from sin

AUGUST

29

Breaking Point

FROM THE BIBLE:

First, I want to remind you that in the last days there will come scoffers who will do every wrong they can think of, and laugh at the truth. This will be their line of argument: "So Jesus promised to come back, did he? Then where is he? He'll never come! Why, as far back as anyone can remember everything has remained exactly as it was since the first day of creation." They deliberately forget this fact: that God did destroy the world with a mighty flood, long after he had made the heavens by the word of his command, and had used the waters to form the earth and surround it. And God has commanded that the earth and the heavens be stored away for a great bonfire at the judgment day, when all ungodly men will perish. But don't forget this, dear friends, that a day or a thousand years from now is like tomorrow to the Lord. He isn't really being slow about his promised return, even though it sometimes seems that way. But he is waiting [because] he is not willing that any should perish, and he is giving more time for sinners to repent.

2 Peter 3:3-9, TLB

Jesus is coming

"MOM, IS JESUS really coming back some day?" asked Bob as he and his little sister, Amanda, climbed into the car after church.

"Of course He is," replied Mother. "Why do you ask?"

"My teacher talked about that today," replied Bob. "It seems like I've heard it all my life—from you and Grandpa and at church—but it never happens."

"See what I got in Sunday school," said Amanda, holding up a balloon. "Blow it up for me, Bobby."

Bob took the balloon and blew air into it. "How's this?" he asked. "Shall I tie it for you?"

"Blow it bigger," Amanda instructed, and Bob blew more air into the balloon. He paused and looked at Amanda. "Bigger yet," she told him. Once more Bob blew the balloon bigger.

"There," he said. "That's as big as it will go."

"No," said Amanda crossly. "Blow it more."

"It will burst," warned Bob, but Amanda wouldn't listen. "OK, then," said Bob. Carefully, he blew. Each time he stopped, Amanda insisted that he blow the balloon bigger. Finally it happened! *Bang!*

"It's too bad, honey, but it's your own fault," Mother told Amanda firmly. "Bob warned you." When the little girl had quieted down, Mother turned to Bob. "This reminds me of your question, Son. The Lord hasn't returned because He is patient and loving, wanting everyone to have an opportunity to be saved. That balloon was stretched to the point where it would burst, and Jesus' patience will one day be stretched to the point where the last person who is going to accept Him will do so. Then He will come again."

"So we should be patient, too, shouldn't we?" asked Bob. "OK. I'll try to remember that."

HOW ABOUT YOU? Does it seem strange that people have been talking about the return of Jesus for two thousand years? He has been very patiently giving men and women and boys and girls the chance to accept Him as Savior. But the time will come when He will return as He promised. Do you believe that? It's a wonderful promise. H.M.

TO MEMORIZE: *"He isn't really being slow about his promised return, even though it sometimes seems that way. But he is waiting, for the good reason that he is not willing that any should perish, and he is giving more time for sinners to repent"*
2 Peter 3:9 (TLB).

AUGUST

30
The Messengers

FROM THE BIBLE:
"Now listen to this story: A certain landowner planted a vineyard with a hedge around it, and built a platform for the watchman, then leased the vineyard to some farmers on a sharecrop basis, and went away to live in another country. At the time of the grape harvest he sent his agents to the farmers to collect his share. But the farmers attacked his men, beat one, killed one and stoned another. Then he sent a larger group of his men to collect for him, but the results were the same. Finally the owner sent his son, thinking they would surely respect him. But when these farmers saw the son coming they said among themselves, 'Here comes the heir to this estate; come on, let's kill him and get it for ourselves!' So they dragged him out of the vineyard and killed him. When the owner returns, what do you think he will do to those farmers?"
Matthew 21:33-40, TLB

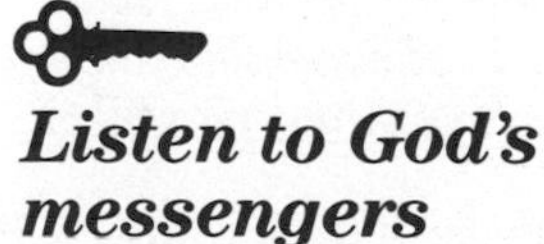

Listen to God's messengers

"I'M TIRED of being preached at all the time!" Matt complained one day. "I get preached at in Sunday school and in church and even at home. It's always 'Do this,' or 'Don't do that.' 'Love your brother,' 'Obey your mother,' 'Pray every day,' "

Dad raised his eyebrows. "Son, God gives us teachers, pastors, and parents to teach and help us," he said.

Matt shrugged. "Maybe so. But it gets to me the way my Sunday school teacher and Pastor Ensey are always telling everyone how to live. Who are they to lay down the laws?"

"They don't lay down the laws," answered Dad. "They're God's messengers. They simply bring His laws to us."

Matt jumped to his feet. "Well, I don't like messengers! Think I'll go for a bike ride." Dad sighed.

The next evening when Matt came in from helping Mr. Bentley at the corner grocery store, his face was as red as his hair. "Some people make me so mad!" he fumed, throwing his cap on the table. "I made a delivery today to old Mrs. Carrington. Mr. Bentley told me to tell her she wouldn't be able to charge anything else to her account until she paid her bill. And would you believe that old lady bawled me out? She called me a smart-aleck teenager. Why should she yell at me? Why doesn't she yell at Mr. Bentley? I'm just the delivery boy. I just took her the message."

A funny look crossed Matt's face when his dad smiled and said, "Well, I seem to remember that you don't like messengers either." Dad paused, then added, "If you don't like the messages your pastor and teacher are giving you, Matt, you should tell God, not the messengers. Right?"

Matt ran his fingers through his hair and said thoughtfully, "I guess I'm just like old Mrs. Carrington. I guess it's not the message or the messengers that are wrong, it's me. I don't know if Mrs. Carrington will ever change, but I'm going to—starting right now!"

HOW ABOUT YOU? Do you gripe and grumble when the preaching convicts you? Or when the teaching applies to you? When others bring you God's message, you had better listen. Don't get mad and pout at them. They are simply the messengers. Listen to them. B.W.

TO MEMORIZE: *"We speak as men approved by God to be entrusted with the gospel"*
1 Thessalonians 2:4 (NIV).

AUGUST

31

Lost Grades

FROM THE BIBLE:

We are only God's co-workers. You are God's garden, not ours; you are God's building, not ours. God, in his kindness, has taught me how to be an expert builder. I have laid the foundation and Apollos has built on it. But he who builds on the foundation must be very careful. And no one can ever lay any other real foundation than that one we already have—Jesus Christ. But there are various kinds of materials that can be used to build on that foundation. Some use gold and silver and jewels; and some build with sticks, and hay, or even straw! There is going to come a time of testing at Christ's Judgment Day to see what kind of material each builder has used. Everyone's work will be put through the fire so that all can see whether or not it keeps its value, and what was really accomplished. Then every workman who has built on the foundation with the right materials, and whose work still stands, will get his pay. But if the house he has built burns up, he will have a great loss. He himself will be saved, but like a man escaping through a wall of flames.

1 Corinthians 3:9-15, TLB

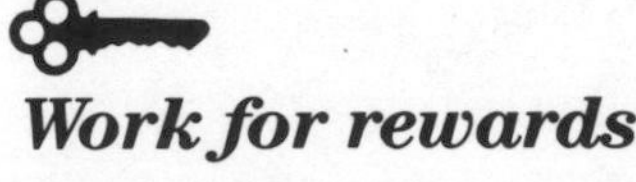

Work for rewards

"MOM, GUESS what happened!" called Mike as he rushed into the house after school. "My teacher's hopping mad!" Mike tossed his cap on a chair and reached for an apple. "Bernie and Pete just think it's so funny. I'll bet they did it!" Mike took a big bite as he headed for his room.

"Whoa!" said Mom. "Did what?"

"Stole my teacher's grade book," replied Mike. "She had this book where she records our grades. She can't find it, and she's sure somebody took it because she had it this morning and now it's gone, and she hasn't decided what to do about it." He stopped, out of breath. "Just think—all our grades are lost!" Mike rolled his eyes, took another bite of his apple, and went to change his clothes.

At suppertime Dad had to hear all about the missing grade book. "I guess we can't get report cards if she doesn't find it," decided Mike.

"Oh, I think Mrs. Cook will manage to come up with some grades," said Mother. "They probably won't be completely accurate, but I'm sure she'll do her best."

"Some of the kids are mad," said Mike, "and some of them think it's funny—especially some of the guys who are always getting bad grades."

Dad nodded. "I guess people who do poorly always like to have their grades cancelled out or forgotten," he agreed. He reached for the Bible. "Read for us tonight, will you, Mike? How about 1 Corinthians 3. Start with verse nine."

Mike took the Bible. "Wow," he said when he had read the verses, "it sounds like God is keeping records, too."

"That's right," Dad said, nodding, "and you can be sure no one will ever be able to steal or destroy God's grade book. His records will be accurate, and He won't fail to reward those Christians who have worked for Him."

"That's neat," murmured Mike. "I wonder if Bernie and Pete know about this?"

HOW ABOUT YOU? Is your name in God's "grade book"? It is if you're a Christian. What kind of grade did you get today? Were you kind? Loving? Helpful? Did you do your best at school? With your chores? With your brothers and sister? Be very careful to please the Lord in your daily life so that some day you may receive His reward. H.M.

TO MEMORIZE: *"Then every workman who has built on the foundation with the right materials, and whose work still stands, will get his pay"* 1 Corinthians 3:14 (TLB).

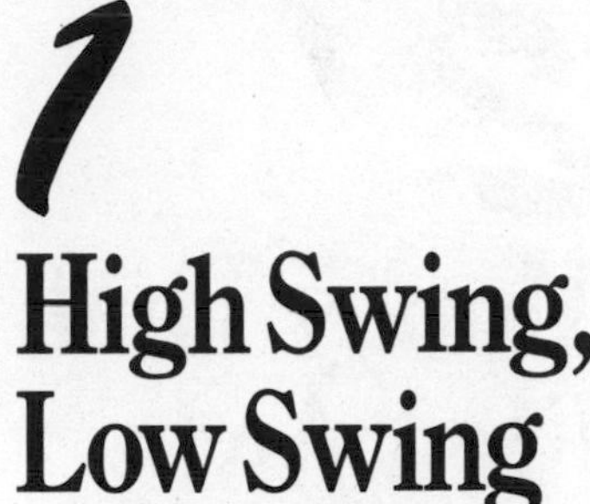

SEPTEMBER

1

High Swing, Low Swing

FROM THE BIBLE:
Your attitude should be the kind that was shown us by Jesus Christ, who, though he was God, did not demand and cling to his rights as God, but laid aside his mighty power and glory, taking the disguise of a slave and becoming like men. And he humbled himself even further, going so far as actually to die a criminal's death on a cross. Yet it was because of this that God raised him up to the heights of heaven and gave him a name which is above every other name, that at the name of Jesus every knee shall bow in heaven and on earth and under the earth, and every tongue shall confess that Jesus Christ is Lord, to the glory of God the Father. Philippians 2:5-11, TLB

Put others first

DAVID AND HIS FRIEND, Billy, went outside during morning recess. It was their first day of second grade, and they looked about the playground with interest. Billy noticed two empty swings on the playground. "Hey! Let's go swing!" he said to David.

"OK!" David agreed.

The boys ran toward the swings, and as they got closer, David realized that one swing was higher than the other. *I want that one,* he thought. *It'll probably go a lot higher than the low one.* So he ran as fast as he could and grabbed the higher swing. The boys scrambled onto their swing seats and pumped themselves higher and higher into the air. After a few minutes, David looked at Billy and frowned. *Billy's going higher than I am,* he thought, so he pumped harder. But no matter how hard David worked, he could not get as high as Billy.

At dinner that evening David told his family all about his first day at school. He also told them what happened on the swings. "I thought the higher swing would go better than the lower one. That's why I wanted it," he admitted.

Dad smiled. "No, the lower swing has longer chains, so it can swing out further and higher than a swing with short chains," he explained.

"You know," commented Mother as she cut some juicy apple pie for dessert, "most people think they'll be happy with the 'first,' the 'biggest,' the 'best,' or the 'most' things in life. But the Bible doesn't teach that. It tells us that as Christians we should think of others before ourselves."

Dad smiled at David. "That's right. Just like that low swing lifted Billy high in the air, God will lift us up if we humble ourselves and put others first."

HOW ABOUT YOU? Are you often interested in getting the best for yourself? That's being selfish. The Bible teaches that Jesus humbled Himself by leaving heaven and becoming a man. It also teaches that Christians should be humble as He was. Put others first instead of putting yourself first. God blesses those who do. S.N.

TO MEMORIZE: *"Humble yourselves in the sight of the Lord, and he shall lift you up"* James 4:10.

2

Money That Flew Away

FROM THE BIBLE:
Do you want to be truly rich? You already are if you are happy and good. After all, we didn't bring any money with us when we came into the world, and we can't carry away a single penny when we die. So we should be well satisfied without money if we have enough food and clothing. But people who long to be rich soon begin to do all kinds of wrong things to get money, things that hurt them and make them evil-minded and finally send them to hell itself. For the love of money is the first step toward all kinds of sin. Some people have even turned away from God because of their love for it, and as a result have pierced themselves with many sorrows.
1 Timothy 6:6-10, TLB

Spend money wisely

IT WAS CARNIVAL TIME! Lucy was so excited she felt that she would burst! She wandered around for a while, looking at all the rides, games, and snack booths. Happy screams came from the roller coaster, and pretty colored lights flashed off and on. And everywhere she went, the smell of hot, buttered popcorn floated through the air. Lucy could hardly wait to try some!

Fingering the five-dollar bill in her pocket, Lucy walked through the midway, where barkers called out to her to try her luck at the games. She stopped at one booth that displayed prizes such as big teddy bears, watches, and radios. Lucy hesitated. Then she decided to try the game just once before she went over to the rides.

Soon Lucy had played the game several times and still had not won a prize. She couldn't resist trying again and again. Before she knew it, she had spent all her money and had won nothing but a cheap plastic toy.

Lucy walked away in a daze. What a gyp! All her money had been spent, and for what? A little plastic toy that she could have bought at the store for a dime! She was still upset when she arrived home and confessed to her parents what had happened. "Boy, was I dumb!" she said. "I spent five dollars, and all I got was a cheap trinket."

"Oh, I don't know," said Mother slowly. "You may have gotten something worth a lot more than that—like a good lesson. What do you think?

"That's right," agreed Dad. "When we buy something without thinking it over, or when our greed causes us to try to get things without earning them, we find that our money takes wings and flies away."

"I wish I'd known that before," said Lucy sadly. "Then the money I had would still be in my pocket instead of flying away!"

HOW ABOUT YOU? Do you love to buy things? Young people are often tempted to spend money foolishly. When you grow up, you'll need to know how to spend money carefully. Now is the time to learn! Get a notebook and write down how you spend your money. Spend it only on things you've planned to buy. Be sure to set aside your offering for God first. Learn to be responsible with the money God has given you. S.K.

TO MEMORIZE: *"For riches certainly make themselves wings; they fly away as an eagle toward heaven"* Proverbs 23:5.

SEPTEMBER

3

The Water's Too Cold!

FROM THE BIBLE:
He who conceals his sins does not prosper, but whoever confesses and renounces them finds mercy. Blessed is the man who always fears the Lord, but he who hardens his heart falls into trouble.
Proverbs 28:13-14, NIV

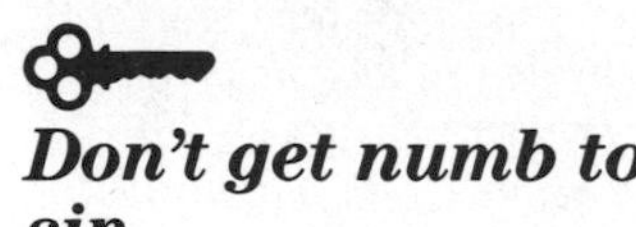

Don't get numb to sin

ROBBIE HAD NEVER cheated on a test before, and he didn't mean to cheat this time either, but somehow his eyes wandered over to Sue's paper. There in plain sight was the word he was trying to spell. Robbie told himself, *I really knew how to spell it. I just forgot for a minute. So it wasn't really cheating.* But deep down inside Robbie knew he had cheated, and it made him feel awful!

The next week when test time came, he again found himself glancing at Sue's paper, this time for more than half of the words. Once more he told himself that he did know many of the words, so it wasn't really cheating. He was just checking his work.

When the next Friday rolled around, Robbie just openly copied many words directly from Sue's paper. Now it only bothered him a little bit.

That weekend Robbie's family went swimming at the lake. As Robbie ran across the beach, Dad yelled, "C'mon in! The water's fine!" But when Robbie's feet touched the water, he stopped quickly. It felt like ice water!

"Oh, Daddy, it's cold!" Robbie exclaimed.

"Not after you get used to it," encouraged Dad.

Robbie took another step and then another. Suddenly he realized he was in over his knees. Maybe his legs were growing numb from the cold! Whatever the reason, he wasn't so cold any more. Finally Robbie took the final plunge and dove into the waves. Now the water didn't seem cold at all, and Robbie was shouting to his mom on the beach, "C'mon in. The water's fine!"

Back home that evening Robbie said, "I wonder why the water at the lake seems so icy cold when you first get in. After you get wet, it's fine!"

Dad nodded thoughtfully. "It's a lot like sin, isn't it, son? At first it really bothers a Christian to sin, but then we get almost numb to it and it hardly bothers us at all. In fact, it feels fine!"

Robbie thought about his cheating at school, and he went to his bedside to do some business with God.

HOW ABOUT YOU? Have you allowed yourself to commit the same sin so often that your spirit is numb to it? Confess and forsake sin at the very beginning. If you don't, it may not bother you after a while. But it's still sin. Don't continue in it. R.P.

TO MEMORIZE: *"Blessed is the man who always fears the LORD, but he who hardens his heart falls into trouble"* Proverbs 28:14 (NIV).

SEPTEMBER

The Golf Lesson

FROM THE BIBLE:
If we live, we live to the Lord; and if we die, we die to the Lord. So, whether we live or die, we belong to the Lord. For this very reason, Christ died and returned to life so that he might be the Lord of both the dead and the living. You, then, why do you judge your brother? Or why do you look down on your brother? For we will all stand before God's judgment seat. It is written: " 'As surely as I live,' says the Lord, 'every knee will bow before me; every tongue will confess to God.' " So then, each of us will give an account of himself to God. Therefore let us stop passing judgment on one another. Instead, make up your mind not to put any stumbling block or obstacle in your brother's way.
Romans 14:8-13, NIV

Show love to everyone

"DID YOU SEE that new kid at school?" Rick leaned on the windowsill as he talked on the phone. "He's strange!" Dad, who was working just outside the window, could hear the conversation. "Yes, I know he's tall, but we don't want him on our team," Rick continued. "He probably doesn't know how to play, and you know he doesn't even speak good English. He looks like a loser to me. Anyway, I have to go. Dad's going to teach me to play golf."

Rick hung up and looked for his father, who was now starting the lawn mower. "Hey, Dad! You were going to teach me to play golf."

Dad stopped the mower. "Well, I decided not to, Rick. You don't look like a very good prospect. You're not dressed like a professional golfer. You don't know any golfer's language. I just think you look like a loser."

"That's not fair!" Rick gasped. "You can't tell what kind of golfer I am by looking at me. Besides, I can learn!"

"Who's the new boy in your school?" he asked.

"Oh, a kid named Ricardo. I think he's Hispanic—he has an accent, and he doesn't look like us, and . . . and . . . You heard me on the phone, didn't you?"

Dad nodded. "Yes, Son, I did. You made a judgment about Ricardo without knowing him, didn't you?"

"Just like you made a judgment about me playing golf," said Rick thoughtfully.

"You know that God tells us not to judge others," said Dad. "What are you going to do about this?"

"I'll have to apologize to Tim for the things I said on the phone." Rick replied. "Then I'll see Ricardo and ask him to come over and shoot baskets. I need to ask God to forgive me, too."

"Good," said Dad. "Now I think we should go see what kind of golfer you really are."

HOW ABOUT YOU? Do you form opinions about others based on how they look or talk? God loves every person in the world so much that He gave His Son to die for them. What can you do to show love for someone different from you? Can you give him a smile? Invite him to play? Include him on your team? Offer a piece of candy? Think of at least one way to share God's love today. D.K.

TO MEMORIZE: *"Therefore let us stop passing judgment on one another"* Romans 14:13 (NIV).

SEPTEMBER

Its Proper Place

FROM THE BIBLE:

Give ear, O my people, to my law;
Incline your ears to the words of my mouth.
I will open my mouth in a parable;
I will utter dark sayings of old,
Which we have heard and known,
And our fathers have told us.
We will not hide them from their children,
Telling to the generation to come the praises of the Lord,
And His strength and His wonderful works that He has done.
For He established a testimony in Jacob,
And appointed a law in Israel,
Which He commanded our fathers,
That they should make them known to their children;
That the generation to come might know them,
The children who would be born,
That they may arise and declare them to their children.

Psalm 78:1-6, NKJV

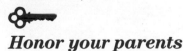

Honor your parents

LYNN WAS EXCITED! She was almost certain she was going to be named captain of the cheerleading squad!

"That's really important to you, isn't it?" her mother asked as they talked about it.

"Important!" Lynn cried out. "Mom, this is the most important thing in my whole life! If I'm elected, all the kids will treat me special!"

"And after you've accomplished this goal, and you get all the kids at school to think of you are something special, then what will you strive for?"

"Mother!" Lynn exclaimed, raising her voice noticeably. "After that I won't need to strive for anything. I'll have it made!"

Lynn's mother took a deep breath and let it out slowly, "That's what worries me, honey. I think it's great to have this opportunity if you don't allow it to go to your head or to replace more important things."

"You just don't want me to make it, do you?" Lynn retorted, a touch of bitterness in her voice.

"That's not what I'm saying at all, but I do want you to think about it carefully."

"What is there to think about?" Lynn countered, trying to keep her voice steady.

"Priorities," her mother said simply. "The Bible says we are to seek 'first the kingdom of God' and to 'set our affection on things above.' " Then Mother went back to the kitchen.

Lynn stood there for a long time. Her mother always did that—always quoted Scripture to her. It made her so mad! Why couldn't Mother just leave her alone? As Lynn sat down on the couch, she noticed her mother's Bible. Suddenly she felt ashamed of herself. She really knew why Mother cautioned her about things and quoted Scripture so often. Just last week in Sunday school they had talked about the responsibility of parents to teach their children the things that God had taught them. And children have a responsibility to listen. Maybe she should think about what Mother had said.

HOW ABOUT YOU? Do you sometimes feel as though your parents are always "preaching" at you? Next time it happens remember that they are doing their best to teach you as they should. Don't be angry with them. Instead, honor them by listening and by thinking about what they say. Ask the Lord to teach you through them. R.J.

TO MEMORIZE: *"Honor your father and your mother, as the LORD your God has commanded you"* Deuteronomy 5:16 (NKJV).

SEPTEMBER

6

Its Proper Place

(Continued from yesterday)

FROM THE BIBLE:

If then you were raised with Christ, seek those things which are above, where Christ is, sitting at the right hand of God. Set your mind on things above, not on things on the earth. For you died, and your life is hidden with Christ in God. When Christ who is our life appears, then you also will appear with Him in glory.
Colossians 3:1-4, NKJV

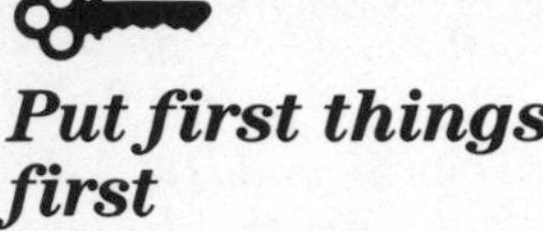

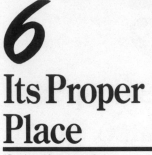

Put first things first

LYNN WAS STILL thinking about her chances of being the cheerleading captain as she and her mother left for a missionary conference at church. But by the time the meeting was over Lynn was no longer thinking about the school group. She had heard about great needs in various places and actually found herself thinking about her responsibility to let people know about Jesus. She remembered once telling her mother she wanted to be a missionary some day, but that was probably just a childish whim. Lynn's thoughts were still on missions as they left the church and even after they reached home.

"Those missionary pictures certainly do something to your heart, don't they?" Mother commented.

"My heart?" Lynn replied.

Mother laughed. "Oh, I mean any person's heart—mine, really."

"They did make me wonder, too," Lynn said at last.

Her mother looked up at her. "About what, honey?"

"Maybe *wonder* isn't the word," Lynn began slowly, "but I've been thinking of what you said this afternoon about needing to keep things in their proper place. Now after seeing those pictures and hearing about all those needy people, being the cheerleading captain just doesn't seem so important anymore."

Just then the telephone interrupted their conversation, and Lynn went to answer it. "Congratulations," a voice said enthusiastically. "You've just been elected captain of the cheerleaders."

Though Lynn was thrilled to get the news, the last few hours had made her realize there were many things in life that were more important than being the captain of the cheerleaders. She would do her best at the job, but some other things would receive equal or more attention. She wondered if perhaps God would call her to the mission field some day after all.

HOW ABOUT YOU? What is most important to you? Is it good grades? Popularity? Athletics? Pretty clothes? Cars or trucks? The list goes on and on. It may be OK for these things to be important in your life, but they should never be most important. Put God and His will first, and other things will fall into their rightful places. R.J.

TO MEMORIZE: *"Set your mind on things above, not on things on the earth"* Colossians 3:2 (NKJV).

SEPTEMBER

7

Size Isn't Everything

FROM THE BIBLE:

I am the true vine, and my Father is the gardener. He cuts off every branch in me that bears no fruit, while every branch that does bear fruit he prunes so that it will be even more fruitful. You are already clean because of the word I have spoken to you. Remain in me, and I will remain in you. No branch can bear fruit by itself; it must remain in the vine. Neither can you bear fruit unless you remain in me. I am the vine; you are the branches. If a man remains in me and I in him, he will bear much fruit; apart from me you can do nothing. If anyone does not remain in me, he is like a branch that is thrown away and withers; such branches are picked up, thrown into the fire and burned. If you remain in me and my words remain in you, ask what ever you wish, and it will be given you. This is to my Father's glory, that you bear much fruit, showing yourselves to be my disciples. John 15:1-8, NIV

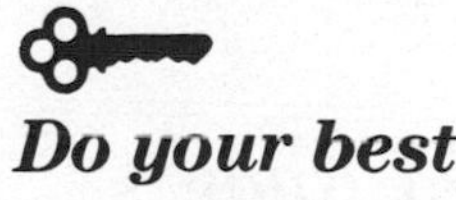

Do your best

"THIS WILL probably be the last picking of tomatoes," said Mart's mother as he followed her into the garden. "It's about time for a frost."

"Yeah," Mart said gloomily.

Mother glanced at him. "What's wrong?" she asked as she started putting tomatoes in her basket.

"Ahhhhh, nothing," Mart mumbled. But Mother knew better, and she had a good idea what the problem was. She had seen Mart measuring himself against the door frame several times lately, and she had heard his friends bragging about how fast they were growing. She knew they sometimes teased him about being the runt of the class.

"Remember when we planted these tomatoes?" asked Mother. "The plants were all the same size." Then she pointed to the smallest plant. "This one didn't grow as fast as the others, but look at the tomatoes on it. It has probably produced more tomatoes than any of the others."

"I don't know how it could," said Mart. "It's about half the size of the others."

"Size isn't everything." Mother stood and stretched. "Some of these plants put all their energy into producing leaves, but this little plant produced fruit. You don't have to be the tallest or biggest to be the most productive."

"Huh! You don't know what it's like to be the runt." He moved some dirt around with his toe.

"Don't worry about being short, Mart," Mother said. "God made us all different in some way, and our goal should be simply to do our best. So you are the shortest." Mother shrugged. "It doesn't matter. You can be the kindest and the friendliest. The important things is to bring forth fruit for God—to do what He wants you to do. And who knows? By next year you may be the tallest."

Mart grinned. "Maybe," he said, "but I doubt it. I know you're right though. I'll try to quit worrying about my size and think more about the things I can do—especially the things I can do for God.

HOW ABOUT YOU? Have you been fretting because you're different from your friends? Remember, we're all different. Don't waste your energy worrying about your size or looks. Think about bearing fruit, doing something for the Lord. What are you going to do today to bear fruit? B.W.

TO MEMORIZE: *"Remain in me, and I will remain in you. No branch can bear fruit by itself; it must remain in the vine"* John 15:4 (NIV).

SEPTEMBER

Homework Solution

FROM THE BIBLE:
Then the multitude rose up together against them; and the magistrates tore off their clothes and commanded them to be beaten with rods. And when they had laid many stripes on them, they threw them into prison, commanding the jailer to keep them securely. Having received such a charge, he put them into the inner prison and fastened their feet in the stocks. But at midnight Paul and Silas were praying and singing hymns to God, and the prisoners were listening to them. Suddenly there was a great earthquake, so that the foundations of the prison were shaken; and immediately all the doors were opened and everyone's chains were loosed. And the keeper of the prison, awaking from sleep and seeing the prison doors open, supposing the prisoners had fled, drew his sword and was about to kill himself. But Paul called with a loud voice, saying, "Do yourself no harm, for we are all here."
Acts 16:22-28, NKJV

A right attitude is important

"THIS SCIENCE experiment is just not working out," Mark moaned. "I've done it four times, and each time it comes out differently."

Dad had just come into the kitchen for a drink of water. "I know schoolwork isn't easy. Remember, I'm taking a night school class."

"Do you like to do your homework?" Mark asked.

"Well, to be honest, not always," Dad said with a chuckle. "It can become frustrating, and when I'm frustrated I might as well forget it. I find that it helps to pray about it before I start."

"Pray?" Mark exclaimed.

"That's right." Dad nodded. "Prayer isn't a magic formula. I know that I have to study. But I do ask the Lord to give me a right attitude. I find that when I have the right attitude, I work much better. And it takes less time, too."

Mark looked at his dad thoughtfully. "I guess maybe I should pray about my science experiment," he decided.

During family devotions that night Dad read the story of Paul and Silas in prison—how they were joyful even though they were chained and uncomfortable. "I've often wondered what would have happened if they had grumbled and complained instead of praying and singing," said Dad. "That wouldn't have been much of a testimony to the other prisoners, and perhaps the jailer would not have been saved at that time. But they had a joyful attitude, and great things happened." He looked at Mark. "Reminds me of some people with homework problems," he said. "When you prayed this afternoon, how did your homework go afterward?"

Mark grinned. "Great things happened then, too," he said. "I calmed down and read the directions again. And I had forgotten one part. I even found it kinda interesting."

Dad nodded knowingly. "God helped Paul to have a right attitude about an unpleasant situation, and He will help us to have a good attitude about schoolwork."

HOW ABOUT YOU? Do you begin your homework with a bad attitude? If so, ask God to change that attitude so you can do your best work for Him. Then try again. A bad attitude keeps you from doing your best. Jesus understands this and wants to help you. J.G.

TO MEMORIZE: *"But at midnight Paul and Silas were praying and singing hymns to God, and the prisoners were listening to them"* Acts 16:25 (NKJV).

SEPTEMBER

Report Cards

FROM THE BIBLE:

And no one can ever lay any other real foundation than that one we already have—Jesus Christ. But there are various kinds of materials that can be used to build on that foundation. Some use gold and silver and jewels; and some build with sticks, and hay, or even straw! There is going to come a time of testing at Christ's Judgment Day to see what kind of material each builder has used. Everyone's work will be put through the fire so that all can see whether or not it keeps its value, and what was really accomplished. Then every workman who has built on the foundation with the right materials, and whose work still stands, will get his pay. But if the house he has built burns up, he will have a great loss. He himself will be saved, but like a man escaping through a wall of flames.

1 Corinthians 3:11-15, TLB

Be ready for report time

STEVE DRAGGED his feet as he headed home. A warm breeze stirred the leaves, and it would be a great night to play ball. But Steve knew he wouldn't be playing tonight, or tomorrow either. *Maybe never,* he thought sadly as he shuffled along. Spunky, a neighbor's dog, noticed him and dashed over for some attention. He raced around Steve and danced in front of him until Steve almost tripped over him. "Go away, you dumb dog!" yelled Steve. He kicked Spunky, and the dog yelped in pain.

Mr. Edwards, who owned the dog, was raking leaves and witnessed the scene. "Steve, what has gotten into you? It isn't at all like you to kick Spunky." Steve hung his head, embarrassed that Mr. Edwards had seen his actions. "What put you in such a bad mood today?" asked Mr. Edwards.

"Teachers," groaned Steve.

"Teachers? Or report cards?"

Steve was surprised. "How'd you know that?" he asked.

"I saw the card sticking out of your pocket," replied Mr. Edwards. "Not so good, huh?"

"No," muttered Steve. "My parents will ground me for sure. They'll say I'm not doing my best."

"Are you?" Mr. Edwards asked.

Steve blushed. "No, I guess not." He paused, then added, "I wish adults got report cards, too. Then maybe they'd be more understanding."

Mr. Edwards smiled. "Well, in a sense those of us who are Christians are earning grades, or marks."

"What do you mean?" asked Steve.

"Well, Christians aren't saved by their works, but they will be judged for the works they do after they're saved," Mr. Edwards explained. "Christians should be concerned about getting 'good grades' in such things as obedience, faith, and love."

"I forgot all about that," said Steve. "I could remind my folks about it, but they'd probably point out that it applies to me, too. Well, guess I'd better get home. I've got a lot of work to do to improve my record—for my parents and for the Lord."

HOW ABOUT YOU? What kind of grades are you getting in your Christian life? Are you trying to be more kind, faithful, and obedient? Some day you will have to give an account. Will you have a good "report card"? J.H.

TO MEMORIZE: *"So then every one of us shall give account of himself to God"* Romans 14:12.

SEPTEMBER

10

Teammates

FROM THE BIBLE:

For now we are all children of God through faith in Jesus Christ, and we who have been baptized into union with Christ are enveloped by him. We are no longer Jews or Greeks or slaves or free men or even merely men or women, but we are all the same—we are Christians; we are one in Christ Jesus. And now that we are Christ's we are the true descendants of Abraham, and all of God's promises to him belong to us.
Galatians 3:26-29, TLB

Christians are your teammates

"GO, JON! GO!" yelled Greg, as he jumped up and down. "Make that touchdown! All right!" He cheered wildly as his teammate scored the first touchdown of the game.

At the dinner table that evening Greg gave his family a blow-by-blow account of the afternoon's game. Over and over they heard the name "Jon" as Greg described the various plays. Finally Greg's sister, Fran, looked at her brother in disgust. "I am sick of hearing about all the wonderful plays Jon made," she declared. "I was under the impression that you didn't even like him, and frankly, I agreed with you. But now all you can do is sing his praises."

"Well, he may not be my favorite person in all the world," admitted Greg. "He's not my best friend or anything, but he's on our team. We're fighting for the same cause. We're both Coreyville Cougars, the 'best in the west!' You should have seen him run this afternoon. Peter passed him the ball, and he was off down the field like a streak. The other team didn't—"

"Oh, help me," moaned Fran. "Here comes another chapter of 'Jon, the Football Player' story."

Mother laughed. "I'm glad you enjoyed your game so much, Son," she said. "It's nice you were able to win, and it's also nice that you've found something to admire in Jon. We should always look for positive things in others."

"I think Greg has given us a good example of how we should view other Christians," observed Dad. "We don't have to like everything about us, and they don't have to like everything about them, and they don't all have to be our best friends. But we should remember that we're on the same team. We're fighting for the same cause—that of winning others to Jesus and bringing glory to God. We should love them, and I believe we can even find something to admire in each of them. We should regard them as teammates."

HOW ABOUT YOU? Is there a fellow Christian whom you dislike? Look for some good quality in him, and then concentrate on that rather than on the things that annoy you. Remember, you both belong to Christ, and that should bind you together. You are teammates. As such, work together to glorify the Lord. H.M.

TO MEMORIZE: *"We are one in Christ Jesus"* Galatians 3:10 (TLB).

SEPTEMBER

11

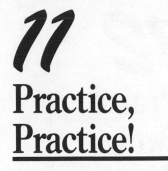

Practice, Practice!

FROM THE BIBLE:
Do all things without murmuring and disputing, that you may become blameless and harmless, children of God without fault in the midst of a crooked and perverse generation, among whom you shine as lights in the world, holding fast the word of life, so that I may rejoice in the day of Christ that I have not run in vain or labored in vain. Yes, and if I am being poured out as a drink offering on the sacrifice and service of your faith, I am glad and rejoice with you all. For the same reason you also be glad and rejoice with me.
Philippians 2:14-18, NKJV

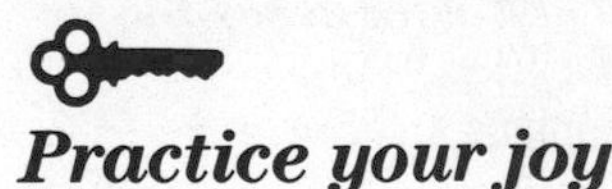

Practice your joy

"PETER, DON'T STOP practicing your trumpet yet! You've only been playing for about five minutes," Mrs. Nelson called from the kitchen.

"But Mom, I've played each of the songs."

"Then play them each again and again, young man. You promised you would practice fifteen minutes every day, without arguing, if we let you join the band," his mother replied.

"But I never get any better at it." Peter grumbled as he picked up the trumpet.

"Peter," said Mother, "some things take lots and lots of practice to be able to do them well. Nothing worthwhile in life comes simply."

Peter remembered hearing those same words a few weeks earlier at school when the band director had met with the sixth graders and their parents to explain the band program. That night it had looked like so much fun to join the band. He had quickly promised to practice fifteen minutes a day, but now the fun had turned into work! He almost wished he could get out of the whole thing. But Dad had paid to rent a trumpet for him, so he knew he had to stick with it.

After dinner that night, the Nelson family read from the letter to the Philippians during family devotions. Then Dad said, "Did either of you children notice a theme to the verses we read?"

Nine-year-old Sara knew. "The same words are used over again and again—*joy* and *rejoice*!"

"Right!" Dad agreed. Then addressing Peter, he asked, "Son, why do you suppose Paul repeated those words—*joy* and *rejoice*—so much?"

"I don't know," Peter answered.

"Maybe joy is a bit like trumpet playing, Peter," Mother suggested. "Maybe it takes practice. We have to practice being joyful over and over, even though we may not feel like being joyful. Some day in the future, rejoicing will get easier for us, just like your trumpet playing will get easier for you. Let's all start practicing joy in this house, OK?"

As Dad closed their discussion with prayer, Peter determined in his heart to practice his trumpet and his joy every day!

HOW ABOUT YOU? Are you often gloomy with your family? When things go wrong do you pout and grumble? If you do, you need to practice finding something to rejoice about. If you're a Christian, Scripture demands that you do this, and the end result is a happier you! R.P.

TO MEMORIZE: *"Rejoice in the Lord alway: and again I say, Rejoice"* Philippians 4:4.

SEPTEMBER

12

Praise Works Wonders

FROM THE BIBLE:
Always be full of joy in the Lord; I say it again, rejoice! Let everyone see that you are unselfish and considerate in all you do. Remember that the Lord is coming soon. Don't worry about anything; instead, pray about everything; tell God your needs and don't forget to thank him for his answers. If you do this you will experience God's peace, which is far more wonderful than the human mind can understand. His peace will keep your thoughts and your hearts quiet and at rest as you trust in Christ Jesus.
Philippians 4:4-7, TLB

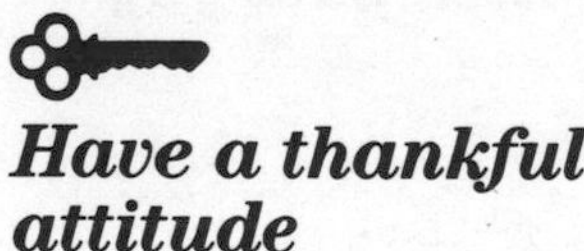

Have a thankful attitude

BETH SLAMMED the door as she came in from school. "What an awful day," she moaned. "Why I was so lucky as to get Mrs. Hodges for two classes a day, I'll never know. She's a grouch! Nobody likes her. Looks like junior high is going to be just awful, thanks to Mrs. Hodges!"

"Remember the verse we read this morning?" reminded Mother. "It says, 'In everything give thanks.' I'm sure the Lord has some lessons to teach you in that class."

"Oh, I'm sure I'll learn lots of lessons before I get out of there," grumbled Beth. "It's, 'Sit up straight. No talking during class. Stay in your seats at all times, blah, blah, blah!' I don't see how I can be expected to give thanks because I have the misfortune of being in Mrs. Hodges's class—not just once, but twice a day."

"No matter what circumstances we find ourselves in, we should always praise the Lord," explained Mother. "He tells us to pray about what is happening and to include thanksgiving in those prayers."

"Well," snorted Beth, "it sure will be hard to praise the Lord in Mrs. Hodges's classes. Just think! I've got to be in her class two hours a day, five days a week, all year long! Oh, I can't stand it! It's too much!" She clapped her hand to her head and fell into a soft chair.

"Now, Beth, don't get dramatic," said Mother, laughing. "If you have to stand it, you can. You can even win Mrs. Hodges's respect and friendship if your attitude is right. Pray about it. I think you'll be surprised."

HOW ABOUT YOU? Have you talked to the Lord about the circumstances you face each day? Perhaps there's a teacher, a classmate, or even a parent that you think you cannot stand. Talk to God about it; pray for that person; ask the Lord to give you a proper attitude toward him. Then thank God for the opportunities and lessons you can learn right where you are. B.W.

TO MEMORIZE: *"Don't worry about anything; instead, pray about everything; tell God your needs and don't forget to thank him for his answers"* Philippians 4:6 (TLB).

SEPTEMBER

13

Praise Works Wonders

(Continued from yesterday)

FROM THE BIBLE:

When a man's ways please the Lord, he makes even his enemies to be at peace with him. . . . He who heeds the word wisely will find good, and whoever trusts in the Lord, happy is he. The wise in heart will be called prudent, and sweetness of the lips increases learning. Understanding is a wellspring of life to him who has it. but the correction of fools is folly. The heart of the wise teaches his mouth, and adds learning to his lips. Pleasant words are like a honeycomb, sweetness to the soul and health to the bones.

Proverbs 16:7, 20-24, NKJV

Give honest praise to others

ONE SATURDAY morning as Beth was working on the lawn her little brother, Brian, came out of the house with Mother. "It worked, Beth! It worked!" Brian called excitedly. "We're going to the store!"

Mother looked puzzled. "What worked?" she asked.

Beth laughed. "Brian was pouting a while ago because he wanted to go to the store, but you had said you were too busy," she explained. "I told him to quit fussing and nagging and start praising you. I told him that if he said nice things about you, you would do nice things for him."

"But she said to tell only the truth," interrupted Brian, "so I did. You're a good housekeeper, and pretty, and a good mama, and I love you."

Mother laughed. "I believe everything you said," she told Brian. She turned to Beth. "Say, I have an idea. This might be the solution to your problem with your teacher, Mrs. Hodges. Why not try telling her the things you do like about her—and keep praying for her, too, of course."

The next Monday when Beth walked into Mrs. Hodges's room, she looked for something nice to say. "That's a pretty dress you have on," she said as she passed Mrs. Hodges's desk. The teacher looked startled but pleased. Later when Beth was having trouble with an assignment, she went to Mrs. Hodges. "You explained this so well in class," she said, "but for some reason I still don't understand. Could you explain it once more?"

As time passed Beth was surprised to find that she was beginning to actually like Mrs. Hodges, and Mrs. Hodges seemed to like Beth, too. She even paid her a compliment now and then. "It's strange," mused Beth. "When you say nice things about people, they say nice things about you, too. Junior high isn't bad after all."

HOW ABOUT YOU? Did you know that praise works wonders? Perhaps it's the answer to your problem with a teacher, a critical neighbor, or a relative that you must endure. Try it—just be careful to always tell the truth. Don't flatter. Ask the Lord to help you see the good things in people, and then be genuine in your compliments. B.W.

TO MEMORIZE: *"When a man's ways please the LORD, He makes even his enemies to be at peace with him"* Proverbs 16:7 (NKJV).

SEPTEMBER

14

The Game of Life

FROM THE BIBLE:
Everyone must submit himself to the governing authorities, for there is no authority except that which God has established. The authorities that exist have been established by God. Consequently, he who rebels against the authority is rebelling against what God has instituted, and those who do so will bring judgment on themselves. For rulers hold no terror for those who do right, but for those who do wrong. Do you want to be free from fear of the one in authority? Then do what is right and he will commend you. For he is God's servant to do you good. But if you do wrong, be afraid, for he does not bear the sword for nothing. He is God's servant, an agent of wrath to bring punishment on the wrongdoer. Therefore, it is necessary to submit to the authorities, not only because of possible punishment but also because of conscience. This is also why you pay taxes, for the authorities are God's servants, who give their full time to governing.
Romans 13:1-6, NIV

Obey those in authority

PAUL STRETCHED and yawned. "I gotta get to bed early tonight," he stated. "Coach's orders. He says it's important to work hard and eat right, but that nothing will take the place of a good night's sleep."

"Well then, by all means get to bed early—after you work hard and eat right, that is," mocked his sister, Alyce. "Be sure to do whatever your football coach says."

"You surely are putting a lot into the game," said Dad. He looked thoughtful. "You know, the game of football reminds me of the game of life. God has provided a big, beautiful field on which to play the game. He created the earth and everything in it."

Alyce grinned. "Oh, and here's an important part—the coaches are our teachers and especially our parents. I bet that's the thing Dad wanted to get across to us."

Dad gave her a playful swat with his newspaper. "You said it, I didn't." He smiled. "You two are getting good at figuring out the lessons I'm trying to teach. Don't forget how important it is to follow the advice of your coaches!"

"Right, Dad." Paul laughed. He stood up and yawned again. "I'm going to do that now by getting to bed. Good night, everybody."

HOW ABOUT YOU? Do you listen to your "coaches" in the game of life? God has given you parents, teachers, pastors, and other Christian leaders and friends to help you make right choices. Listen carefully to what they have to say. God says to obey them. H.M.

TO MEMORIZE: *"Submit yourselves for the Lord's sake to every authority instituted among men"* 1 Peter 2:13 (NIV).

SEPTEMBER

15

The Game of Life

(Continued from yesterday)

FROM THE BIBLE:

Your laws are wonderful; no wonder I obey them. As your plan unfolds, even the simple can understand it. No wonder I wait expectantly for each of your commands. Come and have mercy on me as is your way with those who love you. Guide me with your laws so that I will not be overcome by evil. Rescue me from the oppression of evil men; then I can obey you. Look down in love upon me and teach me all your laws.
Psalm 119:129-135, TLB

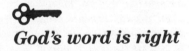

God's word is right

"THAT WAS A GOOD game this afternoon, Paul," observed Dad as they ate dinner. "You did a good job."

"I thought the most exciting part was when the coaches from the two teams got all hyped up over that one play," said Alyce. "For a minute I thought we were going to have a big fight on our hands."

"I was afraid of that, too," agreed Mother. "They didn't calm down until the referee got out a book and looked something up. What book was that?"

"Beats me." Alyce shrugged.

Paul and Dad laughed. "That was the National Football League Rule Book," said Paul. "When there's a disagreement about something, they can look up the rule about it. Whatever the book says that's it! No more arguing."

"It's the final authority in the game of football," said Dad. He paused, then added, "God has supplied a book that is the final authority in the game of life, too."

"This is an easy one," said Paul. "The final authority in life is—"

"The Bible," interrupted Alyce.

Dad nodded. "Sometimes our 'coaches' disagree on something," he said. "A preacher says one thing. A well-known Christian leader says another. A parent or teacher says something different still. It can get very confusing. Then we need to turn to the Bible and see what God says."

"But He doesn't talk about some subjects," said Alyce, "like how fast it's safe to drive or if it's OK for a twelve-year-old girl to wear makeup." She glanced at Mother.

Dad smiled. "No, but He does say we are to obey our civic rulers, so we have to abide by the speed limits they set. And He does say you are to obey your parents, so they'll decided on the makeup issue. God will show us principles to help us in all our decisions. We have to read His Word to know those principles, though." He reached for his Bible. "Let's do that right now."

HOW ABOUT YOU? Do you get confused when there is disagreement among your parents or Christian leaders as to what is right or wrong? Find out what God says about it. He's always right. Look for principles in His Word to guide you in knowing the truth.. H.M.

TO MEMORIZE: *"For the word of the LORD is right"* Psalm 33:4.

SEPTEMBER

16

A Sometimes Friend

FROM THE BIBLE:

If we love other Christians it proves that we have been delivered from hell and given eternal life. But a person who doesn't have love for others is headed for eternal death. Anyone who hates his Christian brother is really a murderer at heart; and you know that no one wanting to murder has eternal life within. We know what real love is from Christ's example in dying for us. And so we also ought to lay down our lives for our Christian brothers. But if someone who is supposed to be a Christian has money enough to live well, and sees a brother in need, and won't help him—how can God's love be within him? Little children, let us stop just saying we love people; let us really love them, and show it by our actions.

1 John 3:14-18, TLB

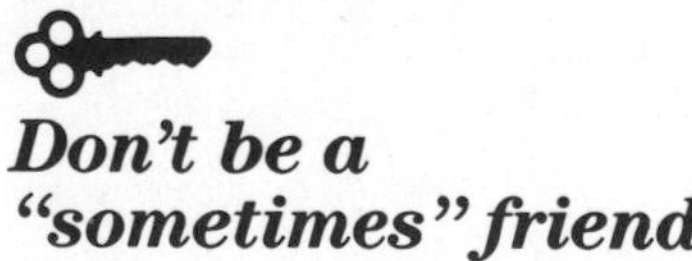

Don't be a "sometimes" friend

DANNY HAD TRIED to be a good friend to Ho, but the boy did not seem to appreciate anything. When the other kids started calling Ho "Slant-eyes," it was Danny who came to his aid. And when the kids at church failed to include Ho in their plans, Danny was the one who had stood up for him. And now look what was happening! Ho seemed to forget that Danny even existed. Now that the kids had finally accepted him, Ho seemed to spend all his spare time with them.

"I'm through helping him," Danny told his dad. "I'll give him a taste of his own medicine. I'm going to ignore him."

At that moment the telephone rang, and Danny hurried to answer it. "Hello, Danny," came a familiar voice on the other end of the line. "This is Ho."

Danny wanted to hang up, but he thought he'd better not be that rude. "Yeah, Ho," he said. "You calling about something special?" After listening a few minutes, Danny said shortly, "I'll see. Can't promise." Then he hung up.

"Was that Ho?" Dad asked.

Danny nodded. "Yeah. He wants me to help him get on the volleyball team. Well, he can just forget that idea. He only calls when he needs something."

Danny's father was quiet for a long time. Finally he spoke. "I wonder if God feels that way when we come to Him," he said soberly. "He probably wants us to come and simply have a friendly talk with Him now and then, but we only seem to call on Him when we need something."

Danny got the message. He wanted to ignore Ho's requests because Ho so often ignored him. But as he thought more, he realized it was a good thing God didn't act that way. God was always there to hear, no matter how much He had been ignored. Danny decided he was going to be more faithful about talking to God. And if he wanted to be like Jesus, he guessed he'd better see what he could do to help Ho, too.

HOW ABOUT YOU? Do you have friends that seem to use you—that talk to you only when they want something? That isn't a nice feeling, is it? Do you ever treat others that way? Do you treat God that way? Don't be a "sometimes friend." Don't use people to get things you want. Talk to God every day. Then, remembering how gracious God is, be patient with your friends, too. R.J.

TO MEMORIZE: *"Love must be sincere. Hate what is evil; cling to what is good"* Romans 12:9 (NIV).

SEPTEMBER

17

Expensive Candy

"GIVE ME THE REST of your allowance," Jim told his little sister, "and then you can have one of these candy bars."

Cindy looked longingly at the candy. "They didn't cost you nearly that much," she argued.

"Doesn't matter." Jim shrugged. "You know Mom won't let you go to the store by yourself, so if you want a candy bar, that's the price." Cindy reluctantly gave Jim the rest of her allowance.

When Cindy heard the bell of the ice cream truck a few days later, she ran to ask Mother if she could buy some. "If you're willing to spend your own money, you can," Mother said. "You get an allowance for things like that."

Cindy burst into tears. "But my allowance is all gone. Jim took it." Cindy told her mother about the candy bar.

Mother called Jim into the room. "I don't like the way you treated your sister," she said. "You charged her far too much for the candy. God's Word has many warnings about greed. It says that the love of money is the root of all evil. That's what causes people to charge unfair prices."

"But she didn't have to buy anything," protested Jim. "I didn't make her give me that money."

"It was a greedy act just the same," insisted Mother. "God never wants us to misuse those who are younger, poorer, weaker, or those who don't have the advantages we do. He wants us to help them and watch out for them. Taking a fair profit is fine, but we must not love money more than people. Now, what could you do to make things right again?"

"I guess I should return Cindy's money, less the price of the candy bar," admitted Jim. Then he grinned. "And I'll even skip the 'fair profit' for my trouble in getting it."

Mother smiled at Jim. "Good for you."

HOW ABOUT YOU? Are you careful to be fair in your dealings with younger brothers and sisters or with small neighborhood children? It's sometimes a great temptation to charge too much from those who don't know the value of money. Even if someone willingly spends the money, the seller is getting money by dishonest means if the item is deliberately overpriced. God tells Christians to "flee" from the temptation to seek the riches of this world. He says to follow after things pleasing to the Lord instead. C.Y.

TO MEMORIZE: *"For the love of money is the root of all evil"* 1 Timothy 6:10.

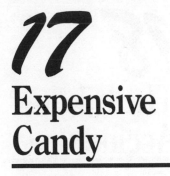

FROM THE BIBLE:

Do you want to be truly rich? You already are if you are happy and good. After all, we didn't bring any money with us when we came into the world, and we can't carry away a single penny when we die. So we should be well satisfied without money if we have enough food and clothing. But people who long to be rich soon begin to do all kinds of wrong things to get money, things that hurt them and make them evil-minded and finally send them to hell itself. For the love of money is the first step toward all kinds of sin. Some people have even turned away from God because of their love for it, and as a result have pierced themselves with many sorrows. Oh, Timothy, you are God's man. Run from all these evil things and work instead at what is right and good, learning to trust him and love others, and to be patient and gentle.

1 Timothy 6:6-11, TLB

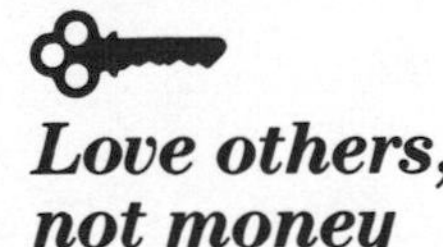

Love others, not money

SEPTEMBER

18

The Bike Accident

FROM THE BIBLE:

Are not two sparrows sold for a penny? Yet not one of them will fall to the ground apart from the will of your Father. And even the very hairs of your head are all numbered. So don't be afraid; you are worth more than many sparrows.

Matthew 10:29-31, NIV

God cares for you

PETE COULD hardly sit still as he and Mom drove to the bike shop. He had been saving money and now had a total of sixty-five dollars. He hoped it would be enough for a new bike. When they arrived at the shop, Pete saw several bikes he liked, including a nice red one on sale for sixty-nine dollars. Pete looked up at Mom, and she smiled. "I'll chip in the rest of the money," she said. "You can buy it." Soon he was the proud owner of the shiny new bike. What fun he was going to have!

The next day as Peter was riding his bike down a steep hill, he started going faster and faster. Suddenly the bike veered wildly out of control! Before he knew what had happened, Pete found himself lying on the pavement beside his bike. He felt pain on his knee and looked down to see blood and dirt covering a scrape as big as a silver dollar. He stumbled to his feet and half ran and half limped as he headed straight for home, pushing his bike along. When he got near the house he began to cry loudly. "Ooohhhh! Oh, Mom," he wailed, "help me!" He sobbed as he limped through the door.

Mom came quickly and gently began to fix Pete's knee. "Why did God let me fall?" he whimpered. "Doesn't he care if I get hurt?"

Mother smiled. "He cares for you even more that I do," she assured him. "Remember last spring when the baby birds fell out of the tree? God says that not one sparrow can fall on the ground without Him knowing it. He also says we are more important to Him than many sparrows. Maybe He let you fall today just so I could teach you that He cares so much." Mom hugged Pete, and then Pete walked back outside, quite pleased with the huge bandage.

HOW ABOUT YOU? When you fall, or even get hurt in your heart, do you know God cares? Do you "run" straight to Him in prayer like Pete ran to Mom? Do you tell God how much you hurt and give Him a chance to help you and show you how much He cares? If you feel hurt or sad right now—for any reason—pray and ask God to help you. C.G.

TO MEMORIZE: *"Are not two sparrows sold for a penny? Yet not one of them will to the ground apart from the will of your Father"* Matthew 10:29 (NIV).

SEPTEMBER

Not Enough Time

FROM THE BIBLE:

This is a faithful saying and worthy of all acceptance. For to this end we both labor and suffer reproach, because we trust in the living God, who is the Savior of all men, especially of those who believe. These things command and teach. Let no one despise your youth, but be an example to the believers in word, in conduct, in love, in spirit, in faith, in purity. Till I come, give attention to reading, to exhortation, to doctrine.
1 Timothy 4:9-13, NKJV

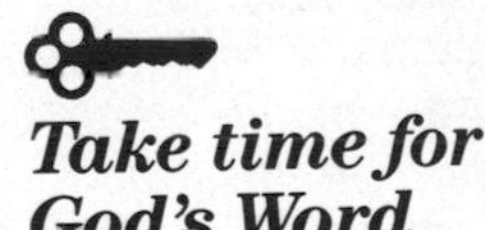

Take time for God's Word

KENNY'S MOTHER called out the window, "Kenny, have you finished your Sunday school lesson? If I remember correctly, you need to read several chapters this week."

"I haven't had time yet," said Kenny as he shot baskets. That had been his answer each time Mother had reminded him of lesson. Now it was Wednesday, and that meant there were only a few days left to do it.

That evening Kenny noticed Mom making some kind of chart. Several times during the week he noticed her writing on it. But when he asked what it was, she told him he'd have to wait till later to find out.

On Saturday night Mom again asked Kenny about his lesson. "Oh, I started it, but I only finished one of the chapters we're supposed to read. It's too long," he complained. "Mr. Powell will just have to understand how busy I am. I don't have time to read all of it."

Mother pulled out the chart. "I've noticed how busy you are, Kenny," she said. "In fact, I've been keeping track. Since Wednesday you have spent six hours watching TV, five hours playing ball, four hours listening to records or the radio, about three hours reading books and magazines, and a couple of hours just lounging around saying, 'I don't have anything to do.' Here, look." With a smile, she handed him the chart.

Kenny blushed as he looked at it. "Wow!" he exclaimed, putting a sports magazine down. "I better go finish my reading right now!"

HOW ABOUT YOU? Do you sometimes claim that you don't have the time to read God's Word? You have the time to do whatever is important to you. Is the Bible important enough to make you willing to give up some of your leisure time in order to read it? It would certainly be worth it. R.P.

TO MEMORIZE: *"Till I come, give attention to reading"* 1 Timothy 4:13 (NKJV).

SEPTEMBER

20

The Wrong Finger

FROM THE BIBLE:

There was a man of the Pharisees named Nicodemus, a ruler of the Jews. This man came to Jesus by night and said to Him, "Rabbi, we know that You are a teacher come from God; for no one can do these signs that You do unless God is with him." Jesus answered and said to him, "Most assuredly, I say to you, unless one is born again, he cannot see the kingdom of God." Nicodemus said to Him, "How can a man be born when he is old? Can he enter a second time into his mother's womb and be born?" Jesus answered, "Most assuredly, I say to you, unless one is born of water and the Spirit, he cannot enter the kingdom of God. That which is born of the flesh is flesh, and that which is born of the Spirit is spirit. Do not marvel that I said to you, 'You must be born again.' "
John 3:1-7, NKJV

You must be born again

"WELL, I'M A CHRISTIAN, that's for sure," Mark told his friend Gordie. "My mom and dad go to church all the time. Dad's on the church board, and Mom teaches Sunday school." He paused, then added, "And last week they both gave testimonies about when they were saved."

"So what?" retorted Gordie. "That doesn't make you a Christian."

"Does too," insisted Mark.

Overhearing the conversation, Mark's mother decided to have a talk with her son. Soon the door opened, and Mark came in. "Mom," he said, holding up a finger, "can I have a Band-Aid?"

Mother looked at the cut on Mark's finger and nodded. "Sure," she said. "I'll get one." After getting the Band-Aid, she tore it open and carefully put it on her own finger. "There," she said. "That should take care of the problem."

Mark stared at his mother. "Mom! It's my finger that's hurt!" he exclaimed. "*I* need the Band-Aid."

"Oh?" Mother looked at him. "You mean the bandage on my finger doesn't help yours?"

"Of course not!" Mark couldn't understand his mother's behavior at all.

"Well, I don't know," she said. "A little while ago I heard you claim that because Dad and I are Christians, you are, too. We took the cure for sin—we accepted Jesus as Savior. If that makes you a Christian, too, then I think this Band-Aid on my finger should also take care of your cut."

Mark stared thoughtfully at his mother. "I guess you're right," he admitted. "I need to accept Jesus myself, don't I? Will you show me how to do that?"

"I surely will," smiled Mother, taking out another Band-Aid to put on Mark's finger. "Let's go talk about it."

HOW ABOUT YOU? Are your parents Christians? Do your grandparents know the Lord, too? Are your relatives saved? Do you come from a Christian home? If you answered yes, that's wonderful. But here's the real question—have *you* accepted Jesus as your own personal Savior? If not, you are not a Christian. Even Nicodemus, a religious ruler, had to be born again. Won't you accept Jesus today? H.M.

TO MEMORIZE: *"You have been born again, not of perishable seed, but of imperishable, through the living and enduring word of God"*
1 Peter 1:23 (NIV).

SEPTEMBER

21

Too Dirty for Heaven

FROM THE BIBLE:

And the city has no need of sun or moon to light it, for the glory of God and of the Lamb illuminate it. Its light will light the nations of the earth, and the rulers of the world will come and bring their glory to it. Its gates never close; they stay open all day long—and there is no night! And the glory and honor of all the nations shall be brought into it. Nothing evil will be permitted in it—no one immoral or dishonest—but only those whose names are written in the Lamb's Book of Life.
Revelation 21:23-27, TLB

Sin can't enter heaven

THE STEVENSONS were getting new carpeting and furniture for their living room. Everyone was excited—even their dog, Buffy! He raced around the room, barking at the men who were carrying out the tattered old couch and chair. And he romped across the faded, threadbare rug just when the workmen were trying to roll it up.

"Dennis," called Mother, "please take Buffy outdoors until the men have finished."

"Oh, all right. Come on, Buffy."

Later that day when everything was done, Dennis came in to take a look. "Wow, Mom! It's great!" he said. "Everything looks so clean and pretty now!"

"Yes, we've been needing new things for a long time," said Mother. Just then Buffy ran into the room. "Oh no!" exclaimed Mother. "Get that dog out of here right now!"

Dennis went over and picked up Buffy. "But Mom, you've always let him come in here before," he said.

Mother looked stern as she replied, "That was when we had our worn-out furniture and that grimy old rug. I want our new things kept clean! Out he goes!"

That night Dad told about a man he had witnessed to during the day. "Jerry couldn't seem to understand that he was a sinner," said Dad. "He kept saying he was no worse than anyone else. He thought he was good enough to make it into heaven without Christ."

"He's like Buffy," observed Dennis. "Buffy thinks he's good enough to be in the living room because he was used to being allowed in our old, worn-out one. But when he tried to go into our new, clean one, Mom kicked him out!"

"Right!" said his father. "We may be 'good enough' for this sinful old world, but God would never let us into His sparkling clean heaven the way we are. Until we let Christ wash away our sin with His blood, we're just 'too dirty' to live in heaven."

HOW ABOUT YOU? Do you think you're "no worse than anyone else"? You may be pretty good by this world's standards, but God's standard is absolute holiness. You can only get into heaven if you let Christ wash all your sins away by His blood. Receive Him today! S.K.

TO MEMORIZE: *"Your eyes are too pure to look on evil; you cannot tolerate wrong"*
Habakkuk 1:13 (NIV).

SEPTEMBER

22

Sincerely Wrong

FROM THE BIBLE:
Therefore Jesus said again, "I tell you the truth, I am the gate for the sheep. All who ever came before me were thieves and robbers, but the sheep did not listen to them. I am the gate; whoever enters through me will be saved. He will come in and go out, and find pasture. The thief comes only to steal and kill and destroy; I have come that they may have life, and have it to the full." John 10:7-10, NIV

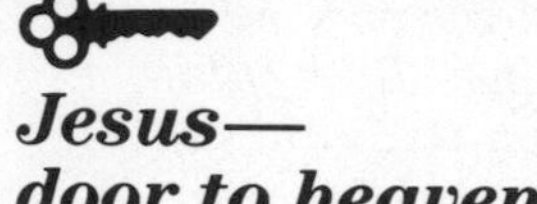

Jesus—door to heaven

"HOW CAN YOU believe that there's only one way to heaven?" Peter asked Carl. "There are lots of good people following different ways to heaven. What's important is just that we make it, one way or another."

Carl spoke firmly. "Jesus says He is the only door to heaven. We can only be saved through Him."

Peter shook his head. "My dad says nobody has all the truth, and a person will go to heaven if he does what he sincerely believes is right. Like, some people worship Buddha. Surely if they're sincere, God will let them into heaven."

"Those people may be sincere, but my minister says they're sincerely wrong," Carl answered. "Jesus is the only door."

The boys changed the subject, but Carl kept praying that he could lead Peter to Jesus. A few days later Peter called Carl. "Want to go over to school with me?" he asked. "I left my trumpet there, and I have to get it so I can practice."

"Sure," agreed Carl, "but I doubt if you can get in. I think the whole school will be locked up by now."

When the boys arrived at the school, they first went to the band room door. It was locked. They tried all the other doors, but everything was locked. Just as they were leaving, a janitor saw them and let them in. They got the trumpet and headed for home.

"Hey, Peter," Carl said, "you really thought some of the doors would be open at school, didn't you?"

"Of course I thought they'd be open," answered Peter. "So what?"

"So you sincerely thought you could get in by yourself, but you were sincerely wrong," stated Carl. "In a way, the janitor was 'the door' for you to get into school. It was only when he opened the band room door that you could get in. Does this remind you of anything?"

Peter grinned. "I guess maybe you're right. I'll have to think about this. Hmmm . . . Jesus is the only door, huh?"

HOW ABOUT YOU? Do you sincerely believe you can get to heaven by being good? Do you think that anyone who earnestly does his best will be OK? Satan wants you to believe that, but Jesus says He is the only door. Trust Him. R.P.

TO MEMORIZE: *"I am the gate; whoever enters through me will be saved"* John 10:9 (NIV).

23

His Life for Mine

FROM THE BIBLE:
Even if we were good, we really wouldn't expect anyone to die for us, though, of course, that might be barely possible. But God showed his great love for us by sending Christ to die for us while we were still sinners. And since by his blood he did all this for us as sinners, how much more will he do for us now that he has declared us not guilty? Now he will save us from all of God's wrath to come.
Romans 5:7-9, TLB

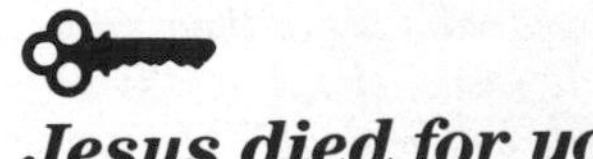

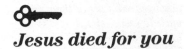

Jesus died for you

PETE ATTENDED Bible club regularly. He enjoyed it, but he just couldn't understand why Jesus would allow Himself to be crucified if He were really God.

One weekend, Mr. Wood, the Bible club leader, took the boys on a camping trip. They visited a lookout tower deep in the woods. Mr. Davis, the forest ranger there, told them about his work and even let them look through his binoculars.

About an hour after the boys left the tower, Mr. Davis detected a small gray cloud of smoke. He immediately reported to headquarters. Men, trucks, and equipment were sent to fight the blaze. Campers were evacuated, but no one was able to locate Mr. Wood and the boys.

At the tower Mr. Davis continued to search the woods. Seeing a sheriff patrol car approaching, he went out on the catwalk to see what was up. "This fire is a bad one, and it's spreading rapidly," the sheriff told him. "You'd better drive out."

"No," insisted Mr. Davis, "I must remain here." And he did. He continued to scan the woods, and suddenly he saw Mr. Wood and the boys! He quickly reported their exact location. Helicopters were sent out, and they were saved!

After their rescue, the sheriff came in. "Boys," he said, "Mr. Davis died in that fire. A power line fell on the tower, and there was an explosion. I'm sorry."

"But why didn't he leave the tower?" asked Pete.

"He stayed to save your lives instead of his own. It was after I tried to talk Mr. Davis into leaving the tower that he spotted you. If he hadn't notified the helicopters, well, you wouldn't be here now."

"He saved us and not himself," said Pete.

"You know, Pete," said Mr. Wood, "this may help you understand how Jesus gave His life for us. He could have saved Himself—but if He had, we could not have been saved from our sins. He was willing to die in our place, but He rose from the dead and is now in heaven. All those who accept Him as Savior will one day go to live with him forever."

"I understand now," Pete said with a nod, "and I do want to be saved."

HOW ABOUT YOU? Do you understand that you cannot save yourself? Have you asked Jesus to be your Savior? Won't you ask Him today? J.H.

TO MEMORIZE: *"I lay down my life. . . . no one takes it from me, but I lay it down of my own accord"* John 10:17 (NIV).

SEPTEMBER

24

The Surprise Package

FROM THE BIBLE:

As they continued onward toward Jerusalem, they reached the border between Galilee and Samaria, and as they entered a village there, ten lepers stood at a distance, crying out, "Jesus, sir, have mercy on us!" He looked at them and said, "Go to the Jewish priest and show him that you are healed!" And as they were going, their leprosy disappeared. One of them came back to Jesus, shouting, "Glory to God, I'm healed!"
Luke 17:11-15, TLB

Don't forget to say "thanks"

"THIS HAS BEEN one of the best birthdays I've ever had," said Jerry as he looked at his gifts. There was a computer game, a magazine subscription, a sweater, a ten dollar check, a new jacket, and a bike.

"Here's one more gift for you." Mother smiled as she handed him a small box.

"Another one?" Jerry was surprised. "I thought I had opened them all." Quickly he ripped the paper off. "What is this? A box of stationery for a boy?"

"A box of thank you notes, complete with stamps," said Mother. "Before you do another thing, sit down here and write thank you notes to everyone who gave you a gift."

"Oh, Mom, I'll do it later," argued Jerry. "I don't have time right now. I want to ride my bike and play with my computer game."

Mother shook her head. "Everyone who bought you a gift spent time and money on you—time and money they could well have used somewhere else. Certainly you have time to sit down and write a short note of thanks to each one."

Jerry grumbled a bit, but he obeyed. Thirty minutes later the notes were written, and Jerry spent the rest of the evening enjoying his gifts.

At bedtime Dad remarked, "Every day the Lord gives us gifts, too, but so often we're in such a hurry to enjoy them that we neglect to tell Him, 'Thanks.' "

"Know what I'm going to start doing?" asked Jerry. "I'm going to start with 'thank you prayers' before I ask the Lord for anything. And I'm going to start right now!"

HOW ABOUT YOU? Have you been putting off writing a thank you note to someone? And what about the Lord? Do you owe Him a "thank you prayer"? Take time to offer your thanks now. You'll be glad you did. L.W.

TO MEMORIZE: *"It is good to give thanks to the LORD, and to sing praises to Your name, O Most High"* Psalm 92:1 (NKJV).

SEPTEMBER

25

Junk Foods

FROM THE BIBLE:

Now that you have purified yourselves by obeying the truth so that you have sincere love for your brothers, love one another deeply, from the heart. For you have been born again, not of perishable seed, but of imperishable, through the living and enduring word of God. For, "All men are like grass, and all their glory is like the flowers of the field; the grass withers and the flowers fall, but the word of the Lord stands forever." And this is the word that was preached to you. Therefore, rid yourselves of all malice and all deceit, hypocrisy, envy, and slander of every kind. Like newborn babies, crave pure spiritual milk, so that by it you may grow up in your salvation, now that you have tasted that the Lord is good. 1 Peter 1:22–2:3, NIV

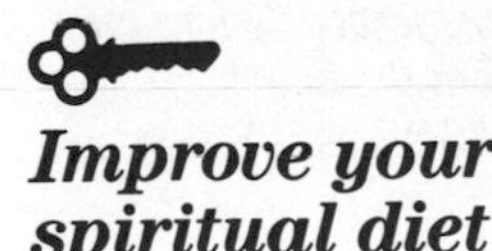

Improve your spiritual diet

"SOMEBODY MUST have decided we shouldn't eat junk food," grumbled Leslie when she came home from school one day. "They're taking the candy and pop machines out of the cafeteria. Now what are we supposed to do if we want something to eat between classes?"

"Won't they put something in their place?" Mom asked.

"Well, yeah," admitted Leslie. "Apples, raisins, milk, and juice."

"Good," approved Mom. "Those are better foods to eat. After all, food affects your health. Do you know there's a Brazilian parrot that changes color, depending on what kind of fish it eats?"

"If I eat candy, will I change color?" laughed Leslie. "Where do you come up with all these odd facts?"

"I learned that when I was in nurses' training. We were taught that we are what we eat." Mom watched as Leslie turned on the TV and spun the dial, then she added, "Did you know that this applies to the mind as well as the physical body?"

"And you classify TV as junk food." Leslie flipped the TV back off and stared at the blank screen.

"Suppose we didn't have television," suggested Mom, "then what would you do instead of plopping yourself down in front of the TV each night?"

Leslie thought about it. "I don't know. Call a friend. Read a book. Maybe even do homework!" She laughed.

"I think that would be considered good food, like apples, raisins, and juices," nodded Mom. "Now, let's see. You need some meat in your diet, too. What do you think that might be?"

"Bible reading," answered Leslie promptly. "And maybe attending church and Sunday school."

"Good," agreed Mom. "Let's both work on improving our diets. You can start by having some milk and crackers while you memorize your verse for Sunday school."

HOW ABOUT YOU? How is your diet? Are there some mental and spiritual junk foods you need to get rid of—things like books or TV programs which use bad language or have ungodly characters and dirty jokes? Are there healthy foods you need to add—like daily devotions and faithful attendance at church? Follow a spiritual diet that is pleasing to the Lord. V.L.C.

TO MEMORIZE: *"Like newborn babies crave pure spiritual milk, so that by it you may grow up in your salvation"* 1 Peter 2:2 (NIV).

SEPTEMBER

26

The Dark Smudge

FROM THE BIBLE:

Therefore, gird your minds for action, keep sober in spirit, fix your hope completely on the grace to be brought to you at the revelation of Jesus Christ. As obedient children, do not be conformed to the former lusts which were yours in your ignorance, but like the Holy One who called you, be holy yourselves also in all your behavior; because it is written, "You shall be holy, for I am holy." And if you address as Father the One who impartially judges according to each man's work, conduct yourselves in fear during the time of your stay upon earth. . . . Since you have in obedience to the truth purified your souls for a sincere love of the brethren, fervently love one another from the heart.

1 Peter 1:13-17, 22, NASB

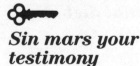

Sin mars your testimony

"OK, SO I probably shouldn't have done it," admitted Jana as she stood before her mother. "But it's just one little thing!"

Mother sighed. "When you joined your friends in making fun of Peter's stutter, you were not only hurting Peter, you were grieving the Lord and hurting your testimony as well. You owe Peter an apology."

Jana shrugged. She supposed maybe she shouldn't have joined in the teasing, but after all, Peter was used to it. Why should anyone get so upset about one little incident? She did plenty of good things—let them remember that!

The whole thing slipped from her mind as she curled up with a storybook, and before she knew it, it was time to get ready for evening church. She decided to wear her favorite light blue dress.

"You look very nice, dear," commented Mother as Jana entered the kitchen. "Here, would you like this last piece of chocolate pie before we leave?"

Jana took it gratefully. Since the church service was so early, they always waited until afterwards to eat supper. This would hold her over until then. As she took the last delicious bite her fork slipped, and a bit of pie filling landed right in the middle of her lap. "Mother!" she wailed. "My dress! Now I'll have to go and change."

Mother surveyed the damage. Yes, there was a chocolate smudge in the middle of the skirt. Mother shrugged. "Why get upset about one little smudge?" she asked. "The rest of the dress looks very nice. Shall we go?"

Jana stared. "But, Mother, the smudge is all you notice when you look at me! I've got to . . ."

Mother smiled. "You're right, of course," she agreed. "Now, I wonder if you can see that a smudge on your testimony is something like a smudge on your clean dress. It's the smudge that stands out, not the clean part."

Jana nodded thoughtfully. She would be sure to apologize to Peter tonight. Little things did count!

HOW ABOUT YOU? Do you think it doesn't matter that you cheated just once? That you snubbed that unattractive person? That you went to a questionable activity? Remember, people are watching you. Even one sin can mar your testimony. Confess that sin to God. Determine with His help to live a holy life before Him and others. H.M.

TO MEMORIZE: *"Like the Holy One who called you, be holy yourselves also in all your behavior"* 1 Peter 1:15 (NASB).

SEPTEMBER

27
Always There

FROM THE BIBLE:

You discern my going out and
my lying down;
you are familiar with all my
ways.
Before a word is on my tongue
you know it completely, O
Lord.
You hem me in—behind and
before;
you have laid your hand upon
me.
Such knowledge is too wonderful
for me,
too lofty for me to attain.
Where can I go from your Spirit?
Where can I flee from your
presence?
If I go up to the heavens, you
are there;
if I make my bed in the
depths, you are there.
If I rise on the wings of the
dawn,
if I settle on the far side of the
sea,
even there your hand will guide
me,
your right hand will hold me
fast.

Psalm 139:3-10, NIV

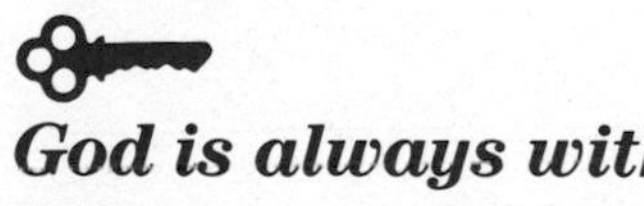

God is always with you

"DON'T BE SCARED, Donnie." Esther comforted her little brother. "Jesus will be with you when you're getting your teeth fixed."

Mother smiled. "That's right," she agreed. Donnie's lip quivered, but he managed a tearful smile as he followed the dentist's assistant into the inner office.

When he came back out, Donnie was smiling. "It didn't hurt too bad," he said.

"See? I told you Jesus would be with you," said Esther as they left the office. "I get to sit in front with Mother," she added, running ahead to the car.

"No! I do!" protested Donnie.

"I said so first," insisted Esther.

"But I had to go to the dentist, so I get the front seat. Mother said so when we left home." Donnie tried to push past his sister and get into the car.

"That was just on the way down here," retorted Esther. She shoved him away, and he shoved back.

Mother pretended not to notice the children fighting. "God is with me today," she sang. "God is with me alway. He's with me when I work, and He's with me when I play. He sees all I do, and He hears all I say. God is with me right now." She emphasized the words "right now." Donnie and Esther looked uncertainly at each other. "Sing it with me, kids," encouraged Mother.

Esther didn't join in the singing. "I know Jesus is with us when we're afraid," she said finally, "or when we need to help with something, but I never thought about Him being with us when we fight. He is, though, isn't He?"

"Oh yes, indeed," answered Mother. "He promised never to leave us. But we often forget that, and then sometimes we act as though we don't know Him at all."

"I'm sorry I was mean to you, Donnie," said Esther. She began to sing the song. "God is with me today. . . ."

HOW ABOUT YOU? If you're a Christian, Jesus is always with you. That's a great comfort when you take a test or go to a new school. It's good to know He's with you when you're home alone or out in the dark. But don't forget, He's there through all the ordinary, routine things you do, too. Will He be pleased with what He sees you do today? Will He be pleased with what He hears? H.M.

TO MEMORIZE: *"The LORD your God, He is the One who goes with you. He will not leave you nor forsake you"* Deuteronomy 31:6 (NKJV).

SEPTEMBER

28

Special Identity

FROM THE BIBLE:

The God who made the world and everything in it is the Lord of heaven and earth and does not live in temples built by hands. And he is not served by human hands, as if he needed anything, because he himself gives all men life and breath and everything else. From one man he made every nation of men, that they should inhabit the whole earth; and he determined the times set for them and the exact places where they should live. God did this so that men would seek him and perhaps reach out for him and find him, though he is not far from each one of us. "For in him we live and move and have our being." As some of your own poets have said, "We are his offspring."

Acts 17:24-28, NIV

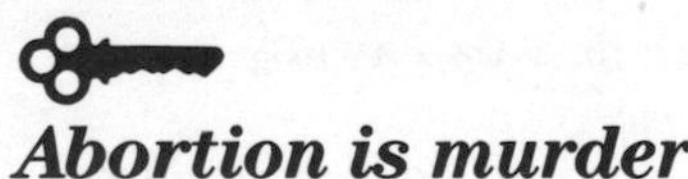

Abortion is murder

CARLA DASHED into the house, waving a paper. "Please, Mom, may I go?" she asked. Her mother read the notice. On Saturday the shopping mall was conducting a free fingerprinting clinic for all children accompanied by a parent. "My teacher says it's real important," Carla said, "in case I need to be identified some time."

"We already know who you are. You're the baby of this family," teased Carla's older brother, David.

Carla ignored him. "May I have it done, Mom?"

"Sure, it's a good idea," said Mother with a smile. "No one else in all the world has fingerprints just like you, Carla. You're one of a kind."

"Whew! That's a relief," laughed David, and then he got serious. "When I did a report on abortion for health class, I found out that a person's fingerprint pattern appears on the fingers four or five months before he's even born. They stay the same throughout his lifetime."

"That shows how special a life is to God," said Mother. "Even before we are born, He forms every little detail in just the way that's best for us. It's sad that so many people regard the life of an unborn baby so lightly that they feel they have the right to end that life just because having a baby would be inconvenient for them."

Carla nodded. "Mrs. Weaver, my Sunday school teacher, is going to have a baby any day now. She told us that the doctors were afraid there might be something wrong. They wanted her to have some tests and then have an abortion if the tests showed the baby would be deformed. But she wouldn't do it. She says God knows just what kind of baby she needs, and whatever He sends will be perfect for her."

"That's great," Mother exclaimed. "To take a life is never right, even if it's a life that is yet unborn and even if we fear it may have some defect. Life and death must be left in the hands of God."

HOW ABOUT YOU? Have you heard that the mother of an unborn child should be allowed to decide whether or not to have her baby? The decision should not be up to the mother. It should be up to God. Abortion—the killing of an unborn baby—is sin. It is murder. Christians should have no part in it. Rather, they should do all they can do to see that it is stopped. J.H.

TO MEMORIZE: *"He himself gives all men life and breath and everything else"* Acts 17:25 (NIV).

SEPTEMBER

29

Special Identity

(Continued from yesterday)

FROM THE BIBLE:

"Before I formed you in the womb I knew you; before you were born I sanctified you; and I ordained you a prophet to the nations." Then said I: "Ah, Lord God! Behold, I cannot speak, for I am a youth." But the Lord said to me: "Do not say, 'I am a youth,' for you shall go to all to whom I send you, and whatever I command you, you shall speak. Do not be afraid of their faces, for I am with you to deliver you," says the Lord. Then the Lord put forth His hand and touched my mouth, and the Lord said to me: "Behold, I have put My words in your mouth. See, I have this day set you over the nations and over the kingdoms, to root out and to pull down, to destroy and to throw down, to build and to plant."
Jeremiah 1:5-10, NKJV

CARLA WAS VERY EXCITED as she and her mother headed for the fingerprinting clinic in a nearby mall. Just the day before her Sunday school teacher had given birth to a healthy baby girl—a perfect baby, even in the eyes of man. "Just think," squealed Carla, "Mrs. Weaver named her baby 'Carlotta'—almost the same as my name! I wonder what she'll be when she grows up."

"I don't know," Mother said, "but God does. He knows who we are before we are born. He has a special plan for our lives. Even before they were born, the Lord chose Jeremiah to be a prophet, Samson to be a Nazarite, and John the Baptist to be a forerunner of Christ."

"That's really neat," said Carla. "Say, Mom, can we buy a gift for Mrs. Weaver and the baby?"

Mother agreed, so after the fingerprinting session, Carla and her mother went shopping for a gift. They chose a pastel colored planter, shaped like a building block. Carla carried it as they went to pick out a plant to put in it. She idly turned it over. "Mom, look at this," she said, pointing to a mark on the bottom of the planter. "Is this a defect?"

Mother examined the planter closely. "That's the artist's initials, Carla," she said. "It identifies its creator."

"Like my fingerprints identify me?" asked Carla.

"Something like that," agreed Mother. "God made you in His image, Carla, and gave you a special identity. He has a plan for your life. Obey Him. Then you'll be a credit to His name."

"I will." Carla nodded. "I want my life to be beautiful and useful like this planter."

HOW ABOUT YOU? Did you know that you are a "designer's special"? God made you as you are for a particular purpose. Smart, not so smart, short, tall. He made you just right. He has a plan for your life. Be willing to accept whatever plans He has for you. You'll be glad you did. J.H.

TO MEMORIZE: *"Before I formed you in the womb I knew you; before you were born I sanctified you"* Jeremiah 1:5 (NKJV).

God has a plan for you

SEPTEMBER

30

Don't Be a Baby

FROM THE BIBLE:

You have been Christians a long time now, and you ought to be teaching others, but instead you have dropped back to the place where you need someone to teach you all over again the very first principles in God's Word. You are like babies who can drink only milk, not old enough for solid food. And when a person is still living on milk it shows he isn't very far along in the Christian life, and doesn't know much about the difference between right and wrong. He is still a baby-Christian! You will never be able to eat solid spiritual food and understand the deeper things of God's Word until you become better Christians and learn right from wrong by practicing doing right. Hebrews 5:12-14, TLB

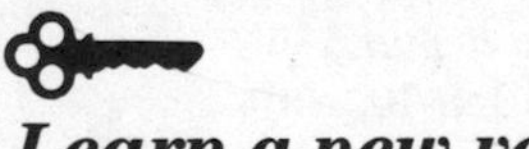

Learn a new verse

EVENING DEVOTIONS were special at the Ryan home. Dad always came up with a unique way to have all the members participate. "Tonight," began Dad, "let's each quote a verse from the Bible. Choose one that has had special meaning to you recently."

Andy started to get fidgety. *Uh-oh,* he thought, *I haven't learned any new verses in a long time.*

Andy listened to his big sister Angela. "Psalm 119:97. Oh, how I love thy law! It is my meditation all the day," she quoted. "This verse reminds me to keep my mind on God during the day."

"A good lesson for all of us," responded Dad. "How about you, Andy? What verse would you like to share?"

Andy took a deep breath and tried not to squirm. "I like John 3:16," he said. "For God so loved the world that he gave his only begotten Son, that whosoever believeth in him should not perish, but have everlasting life."

"You always say the same verse," fussed Angela, rolling her eyes. "Don't you ever learn any new ones?"

"I like John 3:16," said Andy.

"It's an important verse," Mother assured him, "and I'm glad you like it. But it's also important to add new verses to our memories."

"That's right," agreed Dad. "Maybe it would make it clearer to think of it this way: Mother gives Annie baby food, right? But what if she gave all of us strained food?"

"Oh, yuck!" Andy and Angela wrinkled their noses. "Baby food was all we could handle when we were babies," said Andy. "We needed it then. But now we need more solid food so we can grow."

Dad smiled. "See what we're getting at, Son? John 3:16 is an essential verse for salvation—just like strained vegetables are necessary for Annie. But as we grow in our Christian lives, we need to add more solid foods to our spiritual diet so we won't be spiritual weaklings."

"In that case," said Andy, "please pass the Bible. I don't want to be a baby."

HOW ABOUT YOU? Have you learned any new verses lately? Are you adding new truths from the Bible to your spiritual life? It's important to remember verses we learned when we first became Christians, but we also should be learning new things so we can keep on growing. D.R.

TO MEMORIZE: *"Open my eyes, that I may see wondrous things from Your law"* Psalm 119:18 (NKJV).

"A TOTAL FAILURE, that's what I am," Tim muttered as he slowly walked home after school. "When Carl asked why I always go to church, it was a perfect chance to tell him I'm a Christian and that Jesus—not the church—saved me. But I just shrugged and changed the subject. I wish I could talk about the Lord."

That evening Tim heard someone talking in his brother's room. He went to see who was there. "What are you doing?" asked Tim when he saw his brother standing in front of the mirror, talking out loud.

Keith turned around and laughed. "I'm practicing," he said. "Remember when I first started my speech class? I hated it. I never knew how to say what I really wanted to say, and I was scared silly to get up in front of class anyway. But you know what? I kind of like it now!"

"Aren't you scared anymore?" asked Tim.

Keith nodded. "Yeah, but not quite so bad, thanks to my teacher. And I'm getting better."

"How did your teacher help you?"

"He said you have to practice in order to sing or to play a musical instrument well, and you also have to practice to become a good speaker," explained Keith. "He told us to practice, practice, practice, so I do and it works. I may never be a great speaker, but at least I'm improving."

Tim watched as Keith turned back to his mirror and began his speech again. *Practice,* thought Tim as he went to his own room. *That's what I have to do, too.*

When Keith passed Tim's room a little later, Tim was standing in front of his mirror. "I'm a Christian," Tim was saying, "and you can be one, too." He cleared his throat. "I'm a Christian," he repeated, "and you can be one, too." He paused. "The Bible says . . ." Keith smiled and walked on as Tim continued to practice witnessing.

HOW ABOUT YOU? Are you afraid to speak up for the Lord? Do you have trouble knowing what to say? Practice at home first in front of a mirror. Then when you've gotten used to the sound of your own voice talking about the Lord, you may want to practice with a friend or with a parent. It will seem strange at first, but try it. And then speak up for the Lord whenever you have a chance. You can be a witness for Him. H.M.

TO MEMORIZE: *"Men shall speak of the might of Your awesome acts, and I will declare Your greatness"* Psalm 145:6 (NKJV).

OCTOBER

It Does Take Practice

FROM THE BIBLE:

I will praise you, my God and King, and bless your name each day and forever. Great is Jehovah! Greatly praise him! His greatness is beyond discovery! Let each generation tell its children what glorious things he does. I will meditate about your glory, splendor, majesty and miracles. Your awe-inspiring deeds shall be on every tongue; I will proclaim your greatness. Everyone will tell about how good you are, and sing about your righteousness. Jehovah is kind and merciful, slow to get angry, full of love. He is good to everyone, and his compassion is intertwined with everything he does. All living things shall thank you, Lord, and your people will bless you. They will talk together about the glory of your kingdom and mention examples of your power. They will tell about your miracles and about the majesty and glory of your reign. . . . I will praise the Lord and call on all men everywhere to bless his holy name forever and forever.

Psalm 145:1-12, 21, TLB

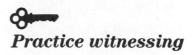

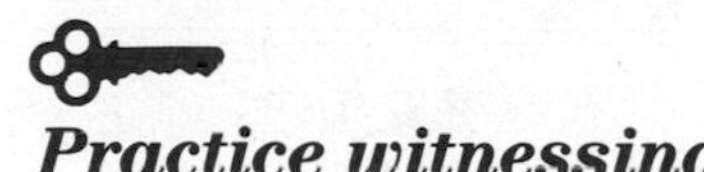

OCTOBER

2

The Gift or the Giver?

FROM THE BIBLE:

The wrath of God is being revealed from heaven against all the godlessness and wickedness of men who suppress the truth by their wickedness, since what may be known about God is plain to them, because God has made it plain to them. For since the creation of the world God's invisible qualities—his eternal power and divine nature—have been clearly seen, being understood from what has been made, so that men are without excuse. For although they knew God, they neither glorified him as God nor gave thanks to him, but their thinking became futile and their foolish hearts were darkened. Although they claimed to be wise, they became fools and exchanged the glory of the immortal God for images made to look like mortal man and birds and animals and reptiles. . . . They exchanged the truth of God for a lie, and worshiped and served created things rather than the Creator—who is forever praised. Amen.
Romans 1:18-25, NIV

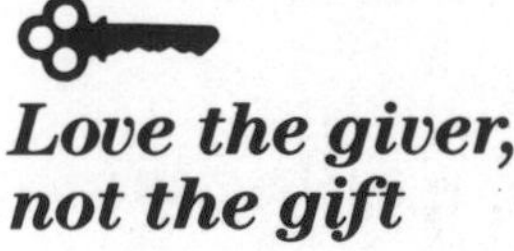

Love the giver, not the gift

DANNY'S UNCLE JACK was driving through town on a business trip and had stopped in for a brief visit. "It sure is good to see you all after so long!" he exclaimed. "I wish I had more time, but I've only an hour before I have to drive on." He handed Danny a package. "Here, Dan—this is a little something I brought for you."

"Oh boy, thanks" said Danny as he tore off the wrapping. Inside was a kit for building a ship inside a bottle. Soon he was busy sorting the pieces and trying to put the model together. Mother suggested a couple of times that he put it aside until later. "Okay," he agreed, but he was having so much fun, he kept right on working. Suddenly he heard Uncle Jack say, "Well, I'm sorry I have to leave so soon."

"Uncle Jack!" exclaimed Danny, looking up from his model. "You're not leaving already, are you?"

"It's been an hour and a half." Uncle Jack smiled. "I really must be going now."

After the goodbyes were said and Uncle Jack's car pulled away from the driveway, Mother turned to Danny with a frown. "Danny, I'm so ashamed of you," she said. "You ignored your uncle the whole time he was here. Why?"

Danny was embarrassed. "Uh—well," he said, "I didn't mean to ignore him. I really was glad to see him, honest. It's just that I got so interested in that model, I sort of forgot he was here. I'm sorry."

"Your uncle was sorry, too," Dad told him. "I could tell he was disappointed when you didn't pay any attention to him."

"But, Dad," said Danny, "didn't he want me to enjoy the gift he got me?"

"Sure," his father replied, "but you got so interested in the gift, you forgot about the giver."

"I guess you're right," Danny said. "It was pretty selfish of me, wasn't it? I think I'll go write a note to Uncle Jack. I want him to know that I really love him more than I love what he gave me."

HOW ABOUT YOU? God has given you many good things to enjoy. Do you sometimes pay more attention to the gifts than you do the Giver? Things should never take the place of God in your life. It's the Giver who really counts! S.K.

TO MEMORIZE: *"Trust in the living God, Who gives us richly all things to enjoy"* 1 Timothy 6:17 (NKJV).

OCTOBER

3

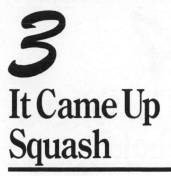

It Came Up Squash

FROM THE BIBLE:

Do not be deceived, God is not mocked; for whatever a man sows, that he will also reap. For he who sows to his flesh will of the flesh reap corruption, but he who sows to the Spirit will of the Spirit reap everlasting life. And let us not grow weary while doing good, for in due season we shall reap if we do not lose heart. Therefore, as we have opportunity, let us do good to all, especially to those who are of the household of faith.
Galatians 6:7-10, NKJV

You reap what you sow

"OH, THIS MEAL looks delicious," said Mike's dad as they began to eat. There was a twinkle in his eye as he looked at Mike. "Please pass the watermelon, Son."

Mike paused with his fork halfway to his mouth. "Watermelon?" He looked around.

"Right there in that bowl in front of you," said Dad.

Mike looked at the bowl heaped full of golden squash. He was about to protest when he looked back at Dad and noticed the smile playing around the corners of his mouth. Suddenly he understood. "Oh, sure, Dad. Here's the watermelon." He laughed as he passed the squash.

"I don't get it," said Mike's sister, Melanie. "Why are you calling the squash 'watermelon'?"

Dad grinned and waited for Mike to explain. "Well, ah, . . . see, I just made a little mistake when we were planting the garden," said Mike, "and Dad won't let me forget it."

"He wanted to plant watermelon," explained Dad, "and I told him he was using squash seeds. But would he believe me? Oh, no! He insisted they were watermelon seeds."

"A perfectly innocent mistake," murmured Mike.

"He said if I'd just be patient and wait until they grew, I'd see for myself," continued Dad, "and here's the finished product." Mike laughed good-naturedly with the rest of the family.

"Whatever a man sows," murmured Mother, "is what he'll also reap. That principle is true, both in a garden and in life. Even as Christians we need to be careful to sow the right kind of seeds."

"That's right," agreed Dad. "If we sow evil, we can expect to reap evil and sorrow. If we sow good things, we can expect to reap the joy and blessing that follow them."

HOW ABOUT YOU? What are you sowing in your life? Are you sowing evil seed, such as lies, disrespect for authority, and unfaithfulness in church? Or are you sowing good seed, such as obedience, cheerful giving, and reverence for the things of God? The things you do now, good or bad, may seem small and unimportant, but little seeds grow. And whatever you sow, you will reap. Make sure you sow things now that you'll want to reap later. H.M.

TO MEMORIZE: *"Do not be deceived, God is not mocked; for whatever a man sows, that he will also reap"* Galatians 6:7 (NKJV).

OCTOBER

The Talking Tools

FROM THE BIBLE:

Yes, the body has many parts, not just one part. If the foot says, "I am not a part of the body because I am not a hand," that does not make it any less a part of the body. And what would you think if you heard an ear say, "I am not part of the body because I am only an ear, and not an eye"? Would that make it any less a part of the body? Suppose the whole body were an eye—then how would you hear? Or if your whole body were just one big ear, how could you smell anything? But that isn't the way God has made us. He has made many parts for our bodies and has put each part just where he wants it. What a strange thing a body would be if it had only one part! So he has made many parts, but still there is only one body. The eye can never say to the hand, "I don't need you." The head can't say to the feet, "I don't need you." And some of the parts that seem weakest and least important are really the most necessary.

1 Corinthians 12:14-22, TLB

Be God's tool

AS RYAN HELPED Uncle Ken replace Grandma Harper's porch floor, his uncle could tell that something had upset him. He was too quiet. "Your friend Jason's really growing as a Christian, isn't he?" Uncle Ken asked.

"Yeah," Ryan answered shortly.

"He's quite a guy," Uncle Ken said as he pulled nails. "His solo with the junior choir was great." Ryan didn't answer. Uncle Ken looked at him curiously. "Have you two been playing tennis lately?"

"Nope!" snapped Ryan.

"You haven't argued with Jason, have you, Ryan?" Uncle Ken probed.

Ryan sighed heavily. "No," he said, "it's just that he does everything better than I do. I used to sing solos in the choir. Now Jason sings them. He's the star student in Sunday school, too. He brings more visitors, learns more Bible verses, even beats me at tennis."

Uncle Ken nodded. "Ryan," he said, "what if the hammer got mad when we laid it down and started using the tape measure? Or what if the saw said, 'I'm tired of cutting boards. If you don't let me pull nails, I won't work'?"

Ryan grinned. "Oh, you know they won't. They have to do what they're made to do."

Uncle Ken put down the hammer and picked up the saw. "You're right," he agreed, "and, as Christians, we're simply tools in God's hands, Ryan. We must do what we are designed to do."

Ryan gulped. "But Jason does everything I do," he said, "only better."

"How many hammers are in my toolbox, Ryan?"

"Two."

"And God doesn't have just one soloist or one witness or one worker," said Uncle Ken. "He has many, and sometimes we have to wait our turn. But when you're a tool, you don't tell the carpenter when you'll work or what you'll do. You simply lie in his hand and let him use you."

"You're right, Uncle Ken. From now on, I'll work or wait, whatever God says."

HOW ABOUT YOU? Do you sometimes question the way God uses you? Do you tell Him what you will do and what you won't do? Surrender your will to God. Be a tool He can use, willing to do whatever He wants you to do. B.W.

TO MEMORIZE: *"In Christ we who are many form one body, and each member belongs to all the others"* 1 Corinthians 12:26 (NIV).

OCTOBER

5

The Uniform Won't Help

FROM THE BIBLE:
He saved us, not because of righteous things we had done, but because of his mercy. He saved us through the washing of rebirth and renewal by the Holy Spirit, whom he poured out on us generously through Jesus Christ our Savior, so that, having been justified by his grace, we might become heirs having the hope of eternal life.
Titus 3:5-7, NIV

Salvation is not by works

"I SEE IT, but I don't believe it!" exclaimed Sally. She stared at her brother who had just come into the room wearing a basketball uniform.

Andy laughed. "The Basket-Masters are putting on an exhibition game at the gym tonight. They were at our school assembly today, and we all drew a number for a door prize. Yours Truly got the lucky number. I get to play with their team for five minutes tonight."

"This is really going to be good. The biggest basketball klutz in the world playing with just about the most famous team in the world!" teased Sally.

And it was good—even better than Sally expected. During the short time Andy was on the floor, the Basket-Masters managed to feed him the ball several times. Once he dropped it; once he passed it to a member of the wrong team; once he even took a shot at the wrong basket. Fortunately, he missed. Andy laughed with his friends and family at all his mistakes.

The following Sunday he visited Sunday school with his friend, Bernie. "So glad you came," Mr. Markham, the teacher said afterwards. They chatted a few minutes, and Mr. Markham asked Andy if he was a Christian.

"Oh, sure," responded Andy. "I go to church all the time. My folks do, too. I've memorized a lot of verses, and I pray a lot, too. I do my best."

Mr. Markham smiled. "Say, I saw you play basketball the other night."

"Oh no," laughed Andy.

"That uniform looked great on you," continued Mr. Markham, "but I noticed that although it made you *look* like a basketball player, it didn't make you one. I wonder if you're also wearing another 'uniform'—that of a Christian. You may look like a Christian, but are you really one? A Christian is someone who has accepted Christ as Savior."

Andy looked puzzled. "I thought I just had to live right. Could you explain that once again?"

HOW ABOUT YOU? Are you really saved? Or are you just 'wearing the uniform'—doing good deeds, going to church obeying parents, trying to live a good life? Wearing the uniform won't help. We are saved through Christ, not through good works. Trust in what He has done for you rather than in what you do yourself. H.M.

TO MEMORIZE: *"He saved us, not because of righteous things we had done, but because of His mercy"* Titus 3:5 (NIV).

OCTOBER

6

As I See It

FROM THE BIBLE:

Do to others as you would have them do to you. If you love those who love you, what credit is that to you? Even "sinners" love those who love them. And if you do good to those who are good to you, what credit is that to you? Even "sinners" do that. And if you lend to those from whom you expect repayment, what credit is that to you? Even "sinners" lend to "sinners," expecting to be repaid in full. But love your enemies, do good to them, and lend to them without expecting to get anything back. Then your reward will be great, and you will be sons of the Most High, because he is kind to the ungrateful and wicked. Be merciful, just as your Father is merciful. Do not judge, and you will not be judged. Do not condemn, and you will not be condemned. Forgive, and you will be forgiven. Give, and it will be given to you. A good measure, pressed down, shaken together and running over, will be poured into your lap. For with the measure you use, it will be measured to you.

Luke 6:31-38, NIV

Understand others' views

"GUESS WHERE Cal Gordon thinks our gym class should go for a field trip," remarked George. He was sitting on the back porch steps with his friend, Frank, watching the clouds float lazily by. "To see a high school football game" continued George, sounding very disgusted at the idea.

"Oh no!" groaned Frank. "It would be lots more fun to go to Sportland, U.S.A. I suppose he'll go around trying to get everybody to vote for the dumb football game. That makes me mad! I can't stand that guy!"

"Me, neither," agreed George. He pointed up at one of the clouds. "Speaking of footballs, that big cloud up there looks just like a foot kicking a football."

Frank looked where George was pointing. "I don't see a football. I see a dog with a bone."

"How about that one?" George pointed again. "That's a dragon with big teeth and a long tail."

"Naw, that's an alligator," said Frank with a grin. "You'd better get glasses." The boys spent the next few minutes pointing out various pictures they saw in the cloud formations. Sometimes they agreed on what the clouds looked like; sometimes they didn't.

"You know, it doesn't bother us that we see different things in the clouds," George said thoughtfully. "It doesn't make us mad that we don't look at them in the same way. Maybe it shouldn't make us mad if people look at other things differently from the way we do, either."

Frank looked at his friend. "You mean Cal, don't you?" he asked. He sighed. "I suppose you're right. I guess there's no law that says he has to like the same things we like. OK, but I'm still going to try to get kids to vote for Sportland, and may the best man win!"

HOW ABOUT YOU? Do you get angry if people disagree with you? You shouldn't. You need to be tolerant of the opinions of others as long as they're not in opposition to the Scriptures. (For example, the Bible teaches that certain things—such as stealing, murder, homosexuality—are wrong. You do not have to accept life-styles that conflict with what God teaches.) People look at many things in different ways. Sometimes there is no definite right or wrong, and you need to agree to disagree. Love people and accept them even if they don't see things exactly as you do. H.M.

TO MEMORIZE: *"Do to others as you would have them do to you"* Luke 6:31 (NIV).

OCTOBER

7

Dumb Ducks

FROM THE BIBLE:

Finally, be strong in the Lord, and in the strength of His might. Put on the full armor of God, that you may be able to stand firm against the schemes of the devil. For our struggle is not against flesh and blood, but against the rulers, against the schemes of the devil. Therefore, take up the full armor of God, that you may be able to resist in the evil day, and having done everything, to stand firm. Stand firm therefore, having girded your loins with truth, and having put on the breastplate of righteousness, and having shod your feet with the preparation of the gospel of peace; in addition to all, taking up the shield of faith with which you will be able to extinguish all the flaming missiles of the evil one. And take the helmet of salvation, and the sword of the Spirit, which is the word of God. With all prayer and petition pray at all times in the Spirit, and with this in view, be on the alert with all perseverance and petition for all the saints.

Ephesians 6:10-18, NASB

ARNIE WATCHED as his big brother, Steve, got ready to go duck hunting. "What are you going to do with those?" asked Arnie, pointing to some painted, wooden ducks on the workbench.

"These are decoys," Steve explained, picking one up. "No self-respecting duck will come near if he sees me standing around with a gun in my hands. So I hide, but I put these fellows out on the lake. From the air, they look real, and when the ducks flying overhead see them, they think to themselves, 'If that's a good spot for my brothers to land, it must be a good place for me.' Then down they come."

"Hmph!" Arnie was scornful. "What dumb ducks!"

That evening Arnie and Steve watched a football game on TV. During a commercial Steve opened a magazine, but he noticed that his younger brother was intently watching a liquor advertisement on the screen. "Don't be a dumb duck," said Steve.

"What are you talking about?"

"Well, I was afraid Satan might be fooling you with the 'decoys' in that commercial," said Steve. "All the people in that ad look as though they're enjoying themselves so much apparently happy and healthy. They're there to entice you to drink. You're not supposed to realize that alcohol causes all sorts of unhappiness—hangovers and meanness and car accidents. You never see a smashed-up car in those ads. You only see the 'decoys'."

"Yeah." Arnie looked over at his brother. "Don't be a dumb duck yourself," he said, pointing to an ad he spotted in his brother's magazine. "The guy in that cigarette ad looks strong and healthy. Don't be fooled just because you don't see him gasping in pain from lung cancer."

"Good thinking." Steve grinned. "Let's both be smart guys, not dumb ducks."

HOW ABOUT YOU? Does Satan fool you by making sin look attractive? He likes to keep you from seeing the ugly side of the picture. A good report card may make cheating seem worthwhile. A candy bar may make stealing look attractive. Being accepted by the other kids may make it seem all right to laugh at a dirty joke. Don't be fooled by the decoys Satan shows you. Sin always ends in sorrow. H.M.

TO MEMORIZE: *"Put on the full armor of God, that you may be able to stand firm against the schemes of the devil"* Ephesians 6:11 (NASB).

Don't be fooled by Satan

OCTOBER

8

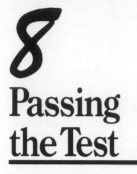

Passing the Test

FROM THE BIBLE:

Then Joseph returned to Egypt with his brothers and all who had accompanied him to the funeral of his father. But now that their father was dead, Joseph's brothers were frightened. "Now Joseph will pay us back for all the evil we did to him," they said. So they sent him this message: "Before he died, your father instructed us to tell you to forgive us for the great evil we did to you. We servants of the God of your father beg you to forgive us." When Joseph read the message, he broke down and cried. Then his brothers came and fell down before him and said, "We are your slaves." But Joseph told them, "Don't be afraid of me. Am I God, to judge and punish you? As far as I am concerned, God turned into good what you meant for evil, for he brought me to this high position I have today so that I could save the lives of many people. No, don't be afraid. Indeed, I myself will take care of you and your families." And he spoke very kindly to them, reassuring them. Genesis 50:14-21, TLB

Be sweet when tested

"TESTS! TESTS! TESTS!" grumbled Steve and Sheila to Gramps Wilson one day. "We hate tests!"

Gramps smiled. "I reckon we all do," he agreed, "but tests are a part of life. Everybody has 'em."

"*You* don't," protested the children. "You're out of school."

But before long Steve and Sheila learned that not all tests are on paper, and not all lessons are learned from a book. The next time Gramps saw them they looked very unhappy. He asked what was wrong. "Might as well tell you," mumbled Steve. "Soon it will be all over town. We found out last night our folks are getting a divorce."

"Oh, Gramps, why did this have to happen?" sobbed Sheila. "If they loved us, they wouldn't do this to us."

"Oh, they do love you," Gramps assured her, "but I don't know just why this happened. It's a test life is giving you."

"Well, I hate tests!" declared Steve. "Why should I have to choose between my mother and dad?' "

"There's not always a quick answer to the questions on life's tests," said Gramps.

As the children talked with Gramps, he reminded them of Joseph, who had been sold into Egypt by his brothers. Joseph faced many lonely hours and difficult situations, but he didn't become bitter. Although he didn't know why things happened as they did, he realized that God allowed them for a reason. He stayed sweet and kind and even forgave his brothers.

"That's what we're going to have to do" Sheila suddenly exclaimed. "We'll have to try to be patient and kind. We don't know why this divorce is happening, but we'll just have to make the best of it."

"Yeah, I guess so," agreed Steve. "Mother and Dad must be pretty unhappy, too."

Gramps nodded. "I'm sure they are," he said. "Try not to be bitter or angry. Look for ways to make things easier for everyone. Ask the Lord to help you 'pass' this test."

HOW ABOUT YOU? Are you facing one of life's tests? A divorce in your family? Loss of Dad's job? Mother going to work? Whatever it is, trust the Lord. Wait to see what He is working out for you. Meanwhile, be patient, sweet and kind. Help those around you pass their tests, too. B.W.

TO MEMORIZE: *"The testing of your faith produces patience"* James 1:3 (NKJV).

OCTOBER

Dirty Hands

FROM THE BIBLE:
But He gives more grace. Therefore He says: "God resists the proud, but gives grace to the humble." Therefore submit to God. Resist the devil and he will flee from you. Draw near to God and He will draw near to you. Cleanse your hands, you sinners; and purify your hearts, you double-minded. Lament and mourn and weep! Let your laughter be turned to mourning and your joy to gloom. Humble yourselves in the sight of the Lord, and He will lift you up. Do not speak evil of one another, brethren. He who speaks evil of a brother and judges his brother, speaks evil of the law and judges the law. But if you judge the law, you are not a doer of the law but a judge.
James 4:6-11, NKJV

Live what you talk

"YOU SURE TOLD old Frazier off," laughed Chuck. "I couldn't have done any better myself."

Derrick shrugged. "So he thinks I cheated on a test? Let him prove it! Just because he's the teacher." His cocky look finished the sentence.

At the bus stop Chuck sighed, "I sure hate to go home. My folks are fighting constantly."

"It was that way at our house, too, before we became Christians," Derrick said. "God really changed our family."

"What do you mean, 'before *we* became Christians'?" Chuck sneered. "*You've* changed? I'd sure have hated to know you *before* that happened."

Derrick's face turned red. "Why you . . ."

Chuck laughed. "See what I mean? You're just like my folks—ready to fight at the drop of a hat."

When Derrick got home, his mother was hanging up the phone. "We're invited to your Aunt Velma's for dinner."

"Oh no! I can't stand to eat there! Have you noticed her fingernails? Her hands are always dirty. And there are cat hairs everywhere."

His mother smiled sympathetically. "Relax. We can't go this time. Dad has to work late."

Later that evening as they sat on the porch, Derrick told his folks about Chuck's problems. "I tried to tell him the Lord Jesus could help his family, but he didn't seem interested." Just then Chuck came up the street on his bike. "Come and join us," Derrick called.

"Derrick sure told old Frazier off in math class today," Chuck bragged. Derrick poked his friend in the ribs, but it was too late. Word for word Chuck repeated the incident. The heavy silence following his story let Chuck know that Derrick's role was not appreciated by his folks, and he left after a short time.

"No wonder Chuck wasn't interested when you witnessed to him," Dad said. "You were offering Jesus, 'the Bread of Life', with dirty hands."

Mother nodded. "No matter how good the food is that Aunt Velma prepares, her dirty hands make it unappetizing. If we offer people the 'Bread of Life' with dirty hands, they will not accept Him."

HOW ABOUT YOU? Have you ever had your friends reject your witness? Check up on yourself. Are you living a Christian life or just talking about it? Are your "hands clean"? B.W.

TO MEMORIZE: *"Cleanse your hands, you sinners; and purify your hearts, you double-minded"* James 4:8 (NKJV).

OCTOBER

10

Different Gifts

FROM THE BIBLE:

There are different kinds of gifts, but the same Spirit. There are different kinds of service, but the same Lord. There are different kinds of working, but the same God works all of them in all men. Now to each one the manifestation of the Spirit is given for the common good. To one there is given through the Spirit the message of wisdom, to another the message of knowledge by means of the same Spirit, to another faith by the same Spirit, to another gifts of healing by that one Spirit, to another miraculous powers, to another prophecy, to another distinguishing between spirits, to another speaking in different kinds of tongues, and to still another the interpretation of tongues. All these are the work of one and the same Spirit, and he gives them to each one, just as he determines.

1 Corinthians 12:4-11, NIV

Be yourself

WHEN THE MARTIN twins came in from school, Mark bounded into the kitchen, and Matt went to his room. "I made all A's on my report card," announced Mark proudly.

Mother hugged him. "Good for you! That makes me very happy. Where's Matt?"

Mark shrugged. "Gone to his room, I guess."

Mother went down the hall. "May I come in, Matt?"

"I guess so," came the muffled reply. "I suppose you want to see my report card." Without looking at Mother, Matt handed it to her.

"Hmmm . . . not too bad," Mother said with a smile.

"And not too *good* either," Matt added angrily. "Mark got all A's. I didn't even make the honor roll."

"Making the honor roll isn't the most important thing in life." Mother sat down beside Matt. "I'm proud of both you and Mark. You're twins, but you're very different, and that's good. Mark loves to read and study. You—"

"Are stupid," Mat interrupted.

"Matt, don't ever say that again" Mother scolded. "You're smart, too, but in a different way from Mark. For instance, when his bike was broken, who fixed it?"

"I did, but there wasn't much wrong with it," Matt said with a shrug.

"You have mechanical abilities that Mark doesn't have. Last year we gave Mark a chess game, and we gave you a set of tools, remember? Did it make you mad because we gave you different birthday gifts?" Mother asked.

"Of course not," Matt exclaimed.

"God gives each Christian different gifts, too," Mother explained. "Remember the verses we read from Corinthians this morning?" Matt nodded, and Mother continued. "Don't think less of your abilities just because they're not like Mark's. Thank God for the talents you have, and use them."

HOW ABOUT YOU? Do you compare your abilities with those others have? You shouldn't do that because God has not given you the same gifts He gave others. Don't try to be anyone else. Be yourself. Use the talents God has given you, and they will grow. B.W.

TO MEMORIZE: *"Each one should use whatever gift he has received to serve others"* 1 Peter 4:10 (NIV).

OCTOBER

11

Ken's Lesson

"SOMETIMES THE Bible uses funny language, Mom," said fourteen-year-old Ken one evening.

"Funny language?" repeated Mother. "In what way?"

"Well, our Sunday school lessons have been about the Bible, and this week we were to read some verses from Jeremiah 15" explained Ken. "There's a verse that talks about 'eating' God's Word."

Mother chuckled. "When you were a baby, there was one time you literally tried to eat the Bible. I wasn't paying any attention to you as you sat on my lap in church. When I looked down, there you were, chewing on my Bible"

They laughed together. "Well, I know I'm not supposed to really eat my Bible," Ken responded, "so what does it mean when it says that?"

Mother thought for a minute, then smiled. "Can you remember when you were smaller and baseball was all you ever wanted to play? You watched baseball on TV, and you always wanted me to buy the cereals with pictures of baseball players. You collected all the baseball cards you could afford. Grandma used to say, 'That boy lives, *eats*, and sleeps baseball twenty-four hours a day'."

"Oh, I see," Ken responded. "So it means to get very involved in the Bible so it becomes the most important thing in my life—even more important than food, I guess."

Just then Ken's older sister, Ellen, walked into the room. She had her nose buried in a book and never even looked up. "Ellen, I've just made oatmeal cookies. Do you want one?" Mother asked. But Ellen was so interested in her book that she didn't even hear.

"I'll take hers," Ken laughed. "She's 'eating' her book right now."

HOW ABOUT YOU? How important is the Bible to you? Do you ever "eat" it—that is, become thoroughly engrossed in it? Make time in your schedule to read the Bible. Find a quiet place and shut other things out of your mind. Ask God to help you understand it. Doing this daily will help you develop a love for the Bible. R.P.

TO MEMORIZE: *"Your words were found, and I ate them, and Your word was to me the joy and rejoicing of my heart"* Jeremiah 15:16 (NKJV).

FROM THE BIBLE:

Oh, how I love Your law!
It is my meditation all the day.
You, through Your commandments, make me wiser than my enemies;
For they are ever with me.
I have more understanding than all my teachers,
For Your testimonies are my meditation.
I understand more than the ancients,
Because I keep Your precepts.
I have restrained my feet from every evil way,
That I may keep Your word.
I have not departed from Your judgments,
For You Yourself have taught me.
How sweet are Your words to my taste,
sweeter than honey to my mouth!
Through Your precepts I get understanding.

Psalm 119:97-103, NKJV

Your words were found, and I ate them, and Your word was to me the joy and rejoicing of my heart; for I am called by Your name, O Lord God of hosts.
Jeremiah 15:16, NKJV

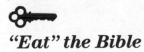

"Eat" the Bible

OCTOBER

12

Forgive Me! Forgive Me!

FROM THE BIBLE:

This is the message which we have heard from Him and declare to you, that God is light and in Him is no darkness at all. If we say that we have fellowship with Him, and walk in darkness, we lie and do not practice the truth. But if we walk in the light as He is in the light, we have fellowship with one another, and the blood of Jesus Christ His Son cleanses us from all sin. If we say that we have no sin, we deceive ourselves, and the truth is not in us. If we confess our sins, He is faithful and just to forgive us our sins and to cleanse us from all unrighteousness.

1 John 1:5-9, NKJV

Accept God's forgiveness

"PLEASE FORGIVE ME. In Jesus name I pray, Amen." There! Darla felt so much better now. She had already asked God to forgive her for lying a few days ago—but every now and then she still felt so guilty that again she'd ask God to forgive her. Now Mother smiled at her, tucked her into bed, and kissed her good night.

The next afternoon Mother suddenly exclaimed, "Oh, Darla, I was supposed to ask if you wanted to go shopping with Grandma this afternoon, and it slipped my mind! Now it's too late, I'm afraid. I'm so sorry."

"Oooh," wailed Darla, "I wanted to go!"

"Can you forgive me?"

Darla nodded. "Sure, Mom. I know you've been busy."

As Darla sat down for supper that evening, Mother looked at her. "Darla," she said. "I am sorry about the shopping trip. Forgive me."

"That's OK." Darla replied. "That ham looks good!"

After supper Darla washed the dishes. As she finished, Mother came into the kitchen. She glanced at Darla and said, "Honey, I do feel badly that you missed the excursion with Grandma. Will you please forgive me?"

"I *told* you—it's OK."

When Darla was ready for bed that night, Mother came to her room. "About the shopping trip, honey. I hope you'll forgive my carelessness."

"Mother! You've apologized for that same thing over and over! You treat me as though you don't believe me when I say I forgave you!"

Mother smiled. "Isn't that just the way you've been treating God?" she asked gently. "You sinned when you lied about where you had been the other day. You were sorry and confessed it to me and to God. I think you know I forgave you. In 1 John 1:9, God says He forgives you, too, yet you feel guilty and confess the same thing again and again. You act as though you don't believe Him."

"You're right," admitted Darla. "God said He would forgive me, and He did!"

HOW ABOUT YOU? Do you still feel guilty after you have confessed a sin to God? Do you continue to ask His forgiveness over and over? He forgave you the first time you sincerely asked Him to. Take Him at His word and claim His promise. H.M.

TO MEMORIZE: *"If we confess our sins, He is faithful and just to forgive our sins and to cleanse us from all unrighteousness"* 1 John 1:9 (NKJV).

OCTOBER

13

Come to Me!

FROM THE BIBLE:

And Jesus prayed this prayer: "O Father, Lord of heaven and earth, thank you for hiding the truth from those who think themselves so wise, and for revealing it to little children. Yes, Father, for it pleased you to do it this way! Everything has been entrusted to me by my Father. Only the Father knows the Son, and the Father is known only by the Son and by those to whom the Son reveals him. Come to me and I will give you rest—all of you who work so hard beneath a heavy yoke. Wear my yoke—for it fits perfectly—and let me teach you; for I am gentle and humble, and you shall find rest for your souls; for I give you only light burdens."

Matthew 11:25-30, TLB

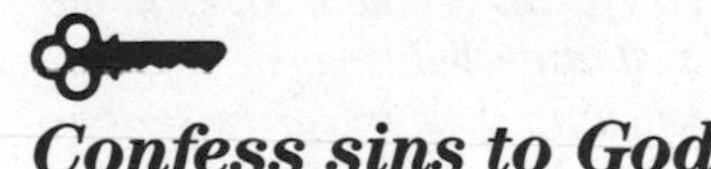

Confess sins to God

GARY FELT a little guilty as he jumped into bed. Earlier at his friends' house he had watched a TV program that he was not allowed to see at home. Now he had decided not to take time to read his Bible or pray. He knew he should, but he really didn't want to. Somehow Bible reading and praying didn't appeal to him tonight, so he went to sleep instead.

After school the next day, Gary idly bounced his ball against the wall of the family room. He knew it was against the rules to play with his ball in the house, but he didn't see why. He tossed the ball again and was horrified at the loud crash which followed. His father's glass-bottled model ship lay shattered on the floor! "Oh no!" Gary cried. He quickly swept up the pieces and threw them out.

At the supper table Gary tried to avoid his father's gaze. "How about a game of chess tonight?" Dad asked. "Maybe I can beat you this time."

"No, I'd rather not play," said Gary.

After Dad suggested a couple of other activities, Gary couldn't keep quiet any longer. "You won't want to play with me when you know what I did," he said. Then he told what had happened.

"I'm disappointed and hurt that you disobeyed me," Dad said, "but I'm glad you told me. I want you to always feel free to come to me, no matter what you've done. I may have to punish you, but I'll never turn you away."

"You're great, Dad," Gary said through his tears.

"Our heavenly Father has set an example for us," Dad replied. "When we confess our sin, He won't turn us away. He wants our fellowship."

As Gary thought about that he knew he had some things he needed to confess to God. His guilt had caused him to avoid Dad's company, and it had caused him to avoid God's fellowship too. He wanted to make things right. He had a great dad, and an even greater God!

HOW ABOUT YOU? When you have done something wrong, do you sometimes avoid God's Word and prayer? Are you ever afraid to come to God because you've sinned? He wants you to come to Him. Confess you sin. He'll forgive you and restore your fellowship with Him. J.H.

TO MEMORIZE: *"Let us therefore come boldly to the throne of grace, that we may obtain mercy and find grace to help in time of need"* Hebrews 4:16 (NKJV).

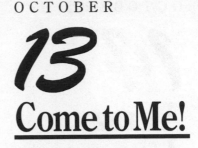

OCTOBER

14

A Crazy Afternoon

FROM THE BIBLE:

You must teach what is in accord with sound doctrine. Teach the older men to be temperate, worthy of respect, self-controlled, and sound in faith, in love and in endurance. Likewise, teach the older women to be reverent in the way they live, not to be slanderers or addicted to much wine, but to teach what is good. Then they can train the younger women to love their husbands and children, to be self-controlled and pure, to be busy at home, to be kind, and to be subject to their husbands, so that no one will malign the word of God. Similarly, encourage the young men to be self-controlled. In everything set them an example by doing what is good. In your teaching show integrity, seriousness and soundness of speech that cannot be condemned, so that those who oppose you may be ashamed because they have nothing bad to say about us.
Titus 2:1-8, NIV

Love children

CARRIE WONDERED if the afternoon would ever end. She was baby-sitting the three Norris children while their mother ran some errands, and things weren't going well. So far Tina unrolled an entire package of paper towels, Tracy spilled a box of cereal, and Tommy kept crying for his mother.

"Can't you make us some popcorn?" Tracy whined.

Carrie shook her head. "No, Tracy. Your mother said you could have some cereal and that was all."

"Please," Tracy begged. "I'm hungry."

"No, but I could read you a story," suggested Carrie.

Surprisingly, Carrie's suggestion worked, and Tommy even stopped crying to listen. By the time Carrie finished reading, Tommy was asleep on the couch. "Girls, let's see how quietly we can walk to the playroom," whispered Carrie, "and I'll help you with that big puzzle."

"Really?" Tracy whispered back. "The big, big one with the three hundred pieces?"

"That's the one," Carrie promised.

They were busily working the puzzle when Mrs. Norris arrived home. "Looks as if everything is under control." She smiled. "Thanks a lot, Carrie."

Later Carrie told her mother about the afternoon. "Once we got busy doing something together, I even enjoyed it," she said.

"Great," approved Mother, "and did you know you got some good training?"

"Good training for what?" asked Carrie.

"In Titus 2, the Lord gives a list of things young men and women are to learn from older men and women," explained Mother. "One of the things is to learn to love your children. Each experience you have in caring for children in a proper way is a step in the right direction."

"Wow," Carrie said, "I didn't realize I was taking a course in loving children this afternoon."

HOW ABOUT YOU? Do you ever take care of younger children? Perhaps you're still too young to baby-sit, but there are probably times when you have the opportunity to entertain a young child for an hour or so. The Lord says that learning to love and care for children is something you should do. Be responsible and caring toward those whom you watch. L.W.

TO MEMORIZE: *"Train the younger women to love their husbands and children"* Titus 2:4 (NIV).

OCTOBER

15

The Broken Promise

FROM THE BIBLE:

Since you have been chosen by God who has given you this new kind of life, and because of his deep love and concern for you, you should practice tender-hearted mercy and kindness to others. Don't worry about making a good impression on them but be ready to suffer quietly and patiently. Be gentle and ready to forgive; never hold grudges. Remember, the Lord forgave you, so you must forgive others. Most of all, let love guide your life, for then the whole church will stay together in perfect harmony. Let the peace of heart which comes from Christ be always present in your hearts and lives, for this is your responsibility and privilege as members of his body. And always be thankful. Remember what Christ taught and let his words enrich your lives and make you wise. . . . And whatever you do or say, let it be as a representative of the Lord Jesus, and come with him into the presence of God the Father to give him your thanks.

Colossians 3:12-17, TLB

AMY WAS SO EXCITED she could hardly sit still. As soon as the car stopped, she jumped out and bounded up the walk. She glanced at her watch—exactly 9:25 A.M., the time she had told Larissa they'd pick her up for Sunday school. Just last evening Larissa had promised to be ready.

Amy rang the doorbell, but no answer. She rang again. Still no answer. Then Amy noticed that the Anderson's car was gone. She stalked back to the car and slammed the door. "She's not home. She didn't even bother to let me know she couldn't come, so we drove clear across town for her. That's rude," Amy stormed. "She broke her promise!"

"Perhaps they had an emergency," suggested Mother.

"She could have called," Amy insisted. To herself she added, *I'll not bother to invite her again.*

Amy was still very angry when she entered her Sunday school classroom. "Good morning, Amy," Miss Mason greeted her. "I missed you yesterday."

Amy's mouth fell open. She had promised to help decorate their classroom, and she had forgotten. "Ooohh, I'm so sorry, Miss Mason," Amy gasped. "I forgot! We went to my grandparent's farm."

Miss Mason smiled gently. "That's all right, Amy. I forget things myself sometimes. Maybe you can help me next month."

Amy nodded. *And maybe Larissa can come to Sunday school next Sunday,* she thought.

HOW ABOUT YOU? Have you even made a promise and then forgotten it? Has anyone broken a promise to you? Did it make you angry? God says if we want forgiveness, we must give it. B.W.

TO MEMORIZE: *"Be kind and compassionate to one another, forgiving each other, just as Christ God forgave you"* Ephesians 4:32 (NIV).

Forgive those who forget

OCTOBER

16

Under the Skin

FROM THE BIBLE:
Try to stay out of all quarrels and seek to live a clean and holy life, for one who is not holy will not see the Lord. Look after each other so that not one of you will fail to find God's best blessings. Watch out that no bitterness takes root among you, for as it springs up it causes deep trouble, hurting many in their spiritual lives.
Hebrews 12:14-15, TLB

Dig out bitterness

DAWN'S TEARS blurred the beauty of the roses she was clipping. She had been lonely and miserable ever since Amy had moved to town. Before that she and Melody had done everything together, but now Melody always wanted Amy included. "So who cares?" she muttered. "I'll find a new friend. I'll—ouch!" Looking at her thumb, she saw a tiny drop of blood. As she rubbed the injured spot, Dawn could feel the thorn under her skin.

"Dawn!" Mother called. "Telephone for you!"

"Coming!" Dawn picked up the roses and went into the house. "Hello . . . Oh, hi, Melody . . . To your house? Now? Who's there? . . . Just you and Amy? Well, I don't think so. Not today. I'm busy. Maybe some other time. Good-bye." Dawn slammed the receiver onto the hook. "Just Amy and me," she mocked. "It's always 'Amy and me.' Since Amy moved to town. . . ."

"Are you going over to Melody's house?" Dawn jumped at the sound of her mother's voice.

"No." As Mother wrinkled her brow, Dawn explained. "Amy's over there. Melody doesn't need me." Then she quickly changed the subject. "Where do you want me to put these roses?"

The next day Dawn's thumb was very sore. It seemed to throb with every pulse beat. "It's that thorn," she remembered. "I forgot to get it out." She showed it to her mother, and after considerable digging and probing, Mother held up a tiny sliver. Dawn was startled by Mother's comments. "Reminds me of Amy," Mother said. "She's just like a thorn in your flesh. She gets under your skin. And you know, honey, if you allow the bitterness you feel about Amy to remain, the hurt will become worse. Why not dig it out and ask the Lord to give you love for Amy?" As Dawn went to her room, she rubbed her thumb. "Lord," she whispered, "it may take some digging and probing, and it may hurt for a bit, but I can't stand this dull ache in my heart any longer. Will you help me?"

HOW ABOUT YOU? Is there something in your heart which causes you to think bitter, hurting thoughts? Does someone get "under your skin?" Is there a relationship in your life which needs healing? Ask the Lord right now to show you how to dig out any resentment and bitterness you feel and to replace those feelings with love. B.W.

TO MEMORIZE: *"Stop being mean, bad-tempered and angry. Quarreling, harsh words, and dislike of others should have no place in your lives"* Ephesians 4:31 (TLB).

OCTOBER

17

Hurt on the Inside

FROM THE BIBLE:
And do not grieve the Holy Spirit of God, by whom you were sealed for the day of redemption. . . . And walk in love, as Christ also has loved us and given Himself for us, an offering and a sacrifice to God for a sweet-smelling aroma.
Ephesians 4:30; 5:2, NKJV

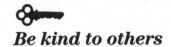

Be kind to others

"LOOK! HERE COMES that retarded girl on her three-wheeled bike," said Jason. "Let's pretend to run into her and see what she does."

Jason and Terry steered their bikes toward the girl. Fear spread across her face as they came closer. "Stop!" she shouted.

"Retard! Retard! You're just a retard," chanted Jason, and Terry joined in. Laughing loudly, they steered away before actually running into the frightened girl.

Just then Mrs. Brown, Jason's Sunday school teacher, came out of her house. Feeling guilty, Jason turned his head away, and before he realized what was happening, he had run into Terry. Down they went, a tangle of boys and bikes! Jason felt a sharp pain where his arm was badly skinned, and Terry was limping when he got up. Mrs. Brown invited them into her house to get cleaned up.

"Do you like to get hurt?" Mrs. Brown asked as she got out the bandages. The boys shook their heads. "How would you have felt," she continued, "if I had come out and pushed you over and then laughed when you got hurt?"

The boys looked at her in wonder. "That would have been mean," Jason answered.

Mrs. Brown nodded. "Yet that's something like what you did to that little girl."

"We didn't touch her," protested Terry. "We just teased her a little. We didn't hurt her."

"You didn't hurt her on the outside," corrected Mrs. Brown, "but you hurt her on the inside. It hurts her to be made fun of because she's retarded." In his heart Jason truly felt sorry. "Jesus taught us to treat others kindly," continued Mrs. Brown. "He treated everyone with love, and He wants us to do that, too."

As the boys got ready to leave, both of them looked ashamed. "We're sorry," they said.

Jason got on his bike, but he turned back. "We'll remember that it hurts to be hurt," he called to Mrs. Brown, "and we won't make fun of that girl again."

HOW ABOUT YOU? Do you sometimes tease others who are different? Teasing can be very painful. Jesus taught us to be kind to everyone, and He lived that way. Be a friend, not a tease, and not a bully. C.Y.

TO MEMORIZE: *"Walk in love, as Christ also has loved us"* Ephesians 5:2 (NKJV).

OCTOBER

18

A Willing Heart

FROM THE BIBLE:
Take heed that you do not do your charitable deeds before men, to be seen by them. Otherwise you have no reward from your Father in heaven. Therefore, when you do a charitable deed, do not sound a trumpet before you as the hypocrites do in the synagogues and in the streets, that they may have glory from men. Assuredly, I say to you, they have their reward. But when you do a charitable deed, do not let your left hand know what your right hand is doing, that your charitable deed may be in secret; and your Father who sees in secret will Himself reward you openly. Matthew 6:1-4, NKJV

Give willingly

JANICE SMILED as she shook the coins out of her piggy bank. "Why, there must be at least two dollars in here," she said happily. She planned to give one dollar for the special missionary offering at church, and that would leave a little more than a dollar to spend on herself. She had worked hard for this money, and was happy to have that much for the offering.

When she arrived at church the next morning, she went straight to her Sunday school room, where several kids were already waiting for the teacher. "Hi, Janice!" Linda greeted her. "Did you remember your offering?"

"Sure did," Janice replied. "Did you?"

As Linda nodded, Katie piped up, "My mom gave me five dollars to put in the offering!"

"My aunt gave me money for my birthday, and I'm going to give five, too," said Jason proudly.

"How about you, Janice?" asked Linda.

Janice blushed. The dollar she was going to give didn't sound like much anymore. "Uh—two dollars," she mumbled. When the offering plate was passed, she dropped the money into it reluctantly.

Later Janice sat glumly as she rode home with her parents. Her mother was surprised at her mood. "You were so eager to get to church this morning," she said. "What happened?"

Janice shrugged and told about the discussion in her Sunday school class. "I don't understand," she said. "I gave twice as much as I had planned to give, so I should be twice as happy, right?"

"Not necessarily," Mother replied. "The dollar you were going to give was of your own free will—a love gift to God. The extra dollar, however, was given just to impress your friends. God is not pleased when we give with an unwilling spirit."

"That's right." Dad nodded. "It really would be better to not even discuss with your friends the amount you plan to give. You should decide what you believe the Lord wants you to give. Then give that amount joyfully and cheerfully."

HOW ABOUT YOU? Do you ever put money in your church offering simply because it's expected of you? Resist that impulse, for God is not pleased with gifts that are given just to impress others. Decide what God wants you to give, and do it with a cheerful, willing heart. Your attitude means more to God than your money does! S.K.

TO MEMORIZE: *"God loves a cheerful giver"* 2 Corinthians 9:7 (NIV).

OCTOBER

From Earth to Heaven

FROM THE BIBLE:

Now we know that if the earthly tent we live in is destroyed, we have a building from God, an eternal house in heaven, not built by human hands. Meanwhile we groan, longing to be clothed with our heavenly dwelling, because when we are clothed, we will not be found naked. For while we are in this tent, we groan and are burdened, because we do not wish to be unclothed but to be clothed with our heavenly dwelling, so that what is mortal may be swallowed up by life. Now it is God who has made us for this very purpose and has given us the Spirit as a deposit, guaranteeing what is to come. Therefore we are always confident and know that as long as we are at home in the body we are away from the Lord. We live by faith, not by sight. We are confident, I say, and would prefer to be away from the body and at home with the Lord.

2 Corinthians 5:1-8, NIV

Christians need not fear death

BECKY WAS OLD enough to understand the reality of death. Her grandmother had died and gone to be with Jesus. But now it was different. Becky herself had a disease that was incurable. Her parents were honest with her when she asked about it, and she knew that unless God worked a miracle she was going to die.

It wasn't that Becky was really afraid. She was a Christian, and she knew that when Christians die they go to be with Jesus. Of course, she was sad when she thought about leaving her mother and father, but even that wasn't the thing that bothered her right now. She was just wondering what it would be like to die—how it would feel.

She decided to mention her feelings to her mother. "Honey," her mother answered after a time, "do you remember when you were a little girl, and you would crawl into bed with Daddy and me?" Becky nodded. Sometimes when she had been afraid in the night, she had climbed into bed with her parents and had felt safe again. "And where would you find yourself in the morning?" Mother asked.

Becky thought about it. "Why, back in my own bed," she said, remembering.

"That's right." Mother smiled. "After you had gone to sleep, Daddy would pick you up in his strong arms and move you to your own bed." Becky's mother suddenly was quiet. "I think that must be what death is like," she said at last. "We go to sleep here on earth and wake up immediately in heaven."

As Becky thought about that explanation, she smiled. It was a beautiful thought. At the right time she would be taken to heaven to be with her Lord forever. When she thought of it that way, it definitely was not something to fear. It was something to look forward to.

HOW ABOUT YOU? Are you afraid of death? If you're a Christian, you don't need to be afraid for someday you, too, will be moved from earth to God's beautiful heaven. The most important thing is to be sure that you are a child of God. Then you can know that at just the right time God will take you to your new home in heaven. Won't that be wonderful? R.J.

TO MEMORIZE: "*We . . . would prefer to be away from the body and at home with the Lord*" 2 Corinthians 5:8 (NIV).

OCTOBER

20

Don't Touch

FROM THE BIBLE:

Do you not know that your bodies are members of Christ? Shall I then take the members of Christ and make them members of a harlot? Certainly not! Or do you not know that he who is joined to a harlot is one body with her? For "The two," He says, "shall become one flesh." But he who is joined to the Lord is one spirit with Him. Flee sexual immorality. Every sin that a man does is outside the body, but he who commits sexual immorality sins against his own body. Or do you not know that your body is the temple of the Holy Spirit who is in you, whom you have from God, and you are not your own? For you were bought at a price; therefore glorify God in your body and in your spirit, which are God's.

1 Corinthians 6:15-20, NKJV

Keep your body pure

PRINCESS PROUDLY purred as the four tiny bundles nestled beside her. As she gently licked their fur, they squirmed closer to her. *Meow, meow,* they cried. As Princess fed them, she closed her eyes. She seemed to be daydreaming when suddenly Kimberly leaned over the kittens' box. Princess's eyes flew open, and she hissed and swatted the air. Kimberly jumped back.

Later when Kimberly checked on the kittens, they were gone! It took Kimberly a whole day to find them. Princess had moved the kittens to the floor of the linen closet. "Pretty clever hiding place," Kimberly said as she reached for a kitten. Princess hissed and swatted at Kimberly again.

Then it happened again. Once more Kimberly couldn't find the kittens. Princess had moved them. "I can't understand her," Kimberly told her mother. "I only want to pet the kittens."

"Princess is being a good mother. She's protective of her kittens right now. She doesn't want to take the chance of someone hurting them."

"I suppose so," said Kimberly reluctantly, "but I thought I could convince her it would be OK."

"Kimberly, this situation reminds me of somethings I want to talk to you about," Mother said. "Princess has a responsibility to protect her kittens, and that's why she won't allow you to touch them. You have a responsibility to protect your body. You see honey, God has given us our bodies. He wants us to keep them pure. Usually, there is nothing wrong with a light touch, a little kiss, or a gentle hug. But certain parts of our body should be clothed and kept private to us. They shouldn't be handled or touched by anyone else outside of marriage. If anyone ever tries to touch your body in an improper way, say no! Do you understand what I'm saying?"

"Yes, I think so, Mother," Kimberly answered soberly. "I'll do what you say. And I'll quit buggin' Princess, too."

HOW ABOUT YOU? Are you keeping your body pure? If someone does something to your body that makes you feel uncomfortable or guilty, tell him or her to stop. Tell God about the problem. Then go to your mother or dad or some other trusted adult and tell that person, too. They will help you handle the situation. J.H.

TO MEMORIZE: *"For you were bought with a price; therefore glorify God in your body and in your spirit, which are God's"* 1 Corinthians 6:20 (NKJV).

OCTOBER

21

Waiters and Waitresses

FROM THE BIBLE:

To you, O Lord, I pray. Don't fail me, Lord, for I am trusting you. Don't let my enemies succeed. Don't give them victory over me. None of those who have faith in God will ever be disgraced for trusting him. But all who harm the innocent shall be defeated. Show me the path where I should go, O Lord; point out the right road for me to walk. Lead me; teach me; for you are the God who gives me salvation. I have no hope except in you. Psalm 25:1-5, TLB

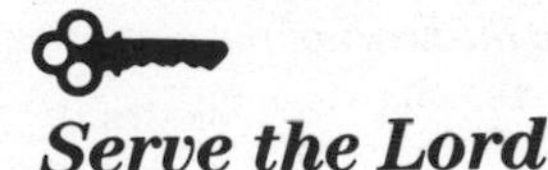

Serve the Lord

THE RESTAURANT hostess led the Blake family to a table and handed them menus. "Your waitress will be with you in a minute. Enjoy your meal," she said. Tim didn't even open his menu. "I know what I want—a cheeseburger, french fries, and a large Coke," he said. "I wish the waitress would hurry. I'm hungry!"

Nancy watched a waitress bring a tray of food to the next table. "I don't think I'd want to be a waitress. It looks like hard work."

"It is," agreed Mother. "A good waitress must be courteous, efficient, and have a good memory."

"And be fast," added Tim. "I wish she would hurry. I don't like to wait, especially when I'm hungry."

"Be patient, Tim." Mr. Blake frowned. "She'll soon be here to wait on us."

" 'On You I wait all the day,' " quoted Nancy. "Do you remember? We read it this morning in our devotions. I hope we don't have to wait for our waitress all day!"

Dad smiled. "It's true that we should patiently wait for the Lord to work things out in His own time," he said, "but can you think of another way we might apply that verse?"

Nancy and Tim looked puzzled as they thought about it. Suddenly Nancy smiled. "I know," she sang out. "We should wait on the Lord all day like the waitress waits on customers all day. We can be the Lord's waiters and waitresses. We can serve Him."

Dad nodded. "Right! While we are waiting *for* Him to come, we wait *on* Him by doing the work He has left us."

"Like praying, witnessing, and helping others," Mom explained.

"I still wish someone would wait on us," Tim grumbled. "I have been waiting for 'hours' to be waited on I'm—"

"May I help you?" interrupted a soft voice.

"You certainly may," Tim said, grinning.

HOW ABOUT YOU? Are you waiting on the Lord while you wait for Him to return to earth? We do not wait on the Lord by sitting and watching the sky. We wait on Him by serving Him, and we serve Him by serving others. Are you a good waiter or waitress? Make plans today to wait on the Lord. B.W.

TO MEMORIZE: *"Wait on the LORD; be of good courage, and He shall strengthen your heart; wait, I say, on the LORD!"* Psalm 27:14 (NKJV).

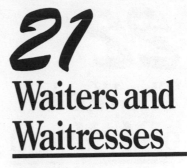

OCTOBER

22

The Words of My Mouth

FROM THE BIBLE:

He provided redemption for his people;
he ordained his covenant forever—
holy and awesome is his name.
Psalm 111:9, NIV

For this is what the high and lofty One says—he who lives forever, whose name is holy: "I live in a high and holy place, but also with him who is contrite and lowly in spirit, to revive the spirit of the lowly and to revive the heart of the contrite." Isaiah 57:15, NIV

This, then, is how you should pray: "Our Father in heaven, hallowed be your name." Matthew 6:9, NIV

Don't use minced oaths

MOTHER HAD CALLED the family to the table, and Carl hurried in to take his place. "Golly! Dinner smells good!" he exclaimed.

"Carl!" exclaimed Mother. "Just yesterday we discussed the seriousness of taking God's name in vain, and already you're back to your old habits."

"I didn't use God's name, Mom," Carl answered. "Why are you getting so excited about nothing?"

Dad spoke up. "I think dinner had better wait for few minutes while you get the dictionary," he said. "Look up *golly* for us, Carl."

Reluctantly Carl did so. "Here it is. It says, 'An exclamation of surprise, a euphemism for God.' What's a euphemism?" he asked.

Mother answered. "It's the use of a word or phrase that is a little less distasteful than another. It's one word substituted for another. In other words, *golly* is just a substitute for *God.* You'll find that the dictionary says the same thing for *gosh,* and you'll find that *gee* is a substitute for *Jesus.*"

"You mean kinda like a nickname?" Carl asked.

"Right," answered Dad. "And God has no nicknames. He has many holy, precious titles, but no nicknames. And I may as well tell you that *heck* is another form of *hell,* and *darn* is a substitute for *damn.*"

"I sure didn't know that," said Carl.

"Yes," Mother said, nodding, "and don't forget that God holds you responsible for the words you use."

"I'll ask God to forgive me again," said Carl, "but how can I stop saying those words? They get stuck in my mind, 'cuz the kids at school say them all the time."

"Jesus will give you strength to overcome them," said Dad. "Everyday pray like David did—that what comes out of your mouth will be acceptable in God's sight. We'll pray for you, too. Now, is everybody hungry?"

HOW ABOUT YOU? Words such as *gee* and *gosh* are called "minced oaths." You may not have been aware that they are substitutes for God's name. Look up each of today's Scripture verses and realize that God's name is holy. Whenever it is used, whether in song or speech, it must be used in a reverent manner. A.L.

TO MEMORIZE: *"Let the words of my mouth, and the meditation of my heart, be acceptable in thy sight, O LORD, my strength, and my redeemer"* Psalm 19:14 (NKJV).

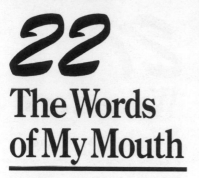

OCTOBER

23

Peace-makers

FROM THE BIBLE:

Come, you children, listen
to me;
I will teach you the fear of the
Lord.
Who is the man who desires life,
And loves many days, that he
may see good?
Keep your tongue from evil,
And your lips from speaking
guile.
Depart from evil, and do good;
Seek peace, and pursue it.
The eyes of the Lord are on the
righteous,
And His ears are open to
their cry.

Psalm 34:11-15, NKJV

Don't be a talebearer

JOY LIKED TAMMY, who lived in a big house and had a "doctor dad." She also like Carol, who was smart and pretty, had no dad, and lived in an average house. But Tammy and Carol didn't like each other, and often Joy felt caught in the middle, with both girls getting mad at her as well as at each other.

One day Joy discussed the problem with her father. "Hmmm," he murmured. "What do you do, Joy, when you hear one of the girls say something unkind about the other? Do you keep it to yourself? Or do you repeat to the girls the things they say about each other?"

Joy flushed. "Well, not too often," she stammered.

"Any repeating of such words is too often, Joy," Dad told her. "The Bible says, 'Where there is no talebearer, strife ceases.' As a Christian, you don't want to be stirring up quarrels between the girls. Now if Tammy says good things about Carol, or if Carol says good things about Tammy, it might be a good idea to repeat that. If they hear that the other has said something good about them, perhaps they'll decide to like one another."

This was a new idea to Joy. "You mean I should start listening for compliments instead of criticism?" she asked.

Her dad smiled. "Could be. Pray about it and keep your eyes and ears open. And determine never to repeat any of the things that would cause anger."

HOW ABOUT YOU? Are you a talebearer? Do you stir up trouble by telling your friends and classmates the unkind things someone has said about them? Today's Scripture reading tells us to seek peace. One way to do that is to keep to yourself any unkind words you may hear someone say about another person. Refuse to be a talebearer. B.W.

TO MEMORIZE: *"Where there is no talebearer, strife ceases"* Proverbs 26:20 (NKJV).

OCTOBER

24

Peace-makers

(Continued from yesterday)

FROM THE BIBLE:

And seeing the multitudes, He went up on a mountain, and when He was seated His disciples came to Him. Then He opened His mouth and taught them, saying: "Blessed are the poor in spirit, for theirs is the kingdom of heaven. Blessed are those who mourn, for they shall be comforted. Blessed are the meek, for they shall inherit the earth. Blessed are those who hunger and thirst for righteousness, for they shall be filled. Blessed are the merciful, for they shall obtain mercy. Blessed are the pure in heart, for they shall see God. Blessed are the peacemakers, for they shall be called sons of God. Blessed are those who are persecuted for righteousness' sake, for theirs is the kingdom of heaven."
Matthew 5:1-10, NKJV

Be a peacemaker

JOY WAS DETERMINED to listen for nice things that Carol and Tammy might say about each other. Then she would tell each of them about it and hope that the two quarreling girls would begin to like one another.

Here's what Joy heard Tammy say: "I hate school, but I suppose Carol likes it since she's the smartest girl in class and is always on the honor roll. It's disgusting!" And: "Here comes Miss America! Look at her hair! It's so pretty! It makes mine look like a haystack. And she thinks she's little 'Miss Homemaker, USA'! Did you know she made the cute skirt she had on yesterday? She makes me sick."

And Joy heard Carol say, "See my new skirt? Of course, it's not as pretty as Tammy's clothes. She has so many, and they look so cute on her. She's so lucky Her dad's a doctor—he's our doctor, and he's great. And she lives in that fancy house."

So Joy decided to "carry tales" again, but this time she carried a different kind of tale—she carried compliments. "Do you know what Tammy said about you?" she asked Carol. "She said you were the smartest girl in the class. And she thinks your hair is pretty. She likes your new skirt, too."

"Really?" Carol was surprised. "Maybe I ought to invite her over."

Then Joy talked to Tammy. "Carol said she thought your clothes are beautiful and look so cute on you," she told her. "And she said she loves your house and thinks your dad is great."

"No kidding? Maybe that's because she doesn't have a dad. Say! I'm going to ask Mom if I can have you and Carol over Friday night. We'll do things with the three of us all the time."

"Great." Joy's dad smiled when she told him what she'd done. "You've been a real peacemaker, Joy. That's a good description for a child of God."

HOW ABOUT YOU? Will you be a peacemaker? Listen for good things about another person, and pass that along. See what a difference it will make. It will please your friends, and it will also please God. It will please you, too, for the Bible calls peacemakers "blessed," or "happy." Find at least one compliment today to carry to someone else. B.W.

TO MEMORIZE: *"Blessed are the peacemakers, for they shall be called sons of God"*
Matthew 5:9 (NKJV).

OCTOBER

25

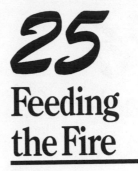

Feeding the Fire

FROM THE BIBLE:

A scoundrel and villain, who goes about with a corrupt mouth, who winks with his eye, signals with his feet and motions with his fingers, who plots evil with deceit in his heart—he always stirs up dissension. Therefore disaster will overtake him in an instant; he will suddenly be destroyed—without remedy. There are six things the Lord hates, seven that are detestable to him: haughty eyes, a lying tongue, hands that shed innocent blood, a heart that devises wicked schemes, feet that are quick to rush into evil, a false witness who pours out lies and a man who stirs up dissension among brothers.

Proverbs 6:12-19, NIV

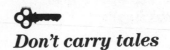

Don't carry tales

TAMI WAS ON the phone when Mother came into the room. ". . . and that's what she said, Staci. She said that you're stupid! But don't tell Marsha that I told you, OK? See you tomorrow."

When Tami hung up the phone, Mother asked, "Why did you tell Staci that Marsha said she was stupid?"

"Because she did," Tami replied quickly. "Staci and Marsha fuss all the time."

Mother raised her eyebrows. "Could it be because you add fuel to the fire?"

"What do you mean?" asked Tami.

"Come into the den." Mother led the way to the fireplace. She pointed at the smoldering fire. "What would happen if I added a log to the fire, Tami?"

"It would get bigger," Tami replied.

"What if I didn't add any wood to it?" Mother asked.

"It would die out," Tami answered.

"Right! And it's like that when there's a quarrel between two people. It usually dies out if there isn't anyone to stir it up and keep it going. God hates talebearing, Tami. And usually it's the talebearer who gets hurt. You—" The ring of the telephone interrupted her.

"I'll get it. It's probably Marsha. She was going to call me." Tami was glad to end the conversation.

Later when Mother called the family to dinner, Tami came to the table with red, puffy eyes. "What's the matter, Tami?" Dad asked.

"Marsha and Staci are going to the riding stables tomorrow." Tami choked back a sob. "Marsha can't invite both of us, 'cuz her mother says we fuss too much when we're all together. So she asked Staci because she's mad at me for telling Staci what she said about her."

"I'm not surprised," Mother said. "Didn't I warn you that it's usually the talebearer who gets hurt?"

HOW ABOUT YOU? Are you tempted to "carry tales"? It's dangerous. Not only will it hurt others, but you'll be hurt yourself. God suggests a better way—He says, "Blessed are the peacemakers." If you know two people who don't get along well, do what you can to keep peace between them. Be a peacemaker, not a talebearer. B.W.

TO MEMORIZE: "*He who covers an offense promotes love, but whoever repeats the matter separates close friends*" Proverbs 17:9 (NIV).

OCTOBER

26

Deadly Arrows

FROM THE BIBLE:

He who passes by and meddles in a quarrel not his own is like one who takes a dog by the ears. Like a madman who throws firebrands, arrows, and death, is the man who deceives his neighbor, and says, "I was only joking!" Where there is no wood, the fire goes out; and where there is no talebearer, strife ceases. As charcoal is to burning coals, and wood to fire, so is a contentious man to kindle strife. The words of a talebearer are like tasty trifles, and they go down into the inmost body.

Proverbs 26:17-22, NKJV

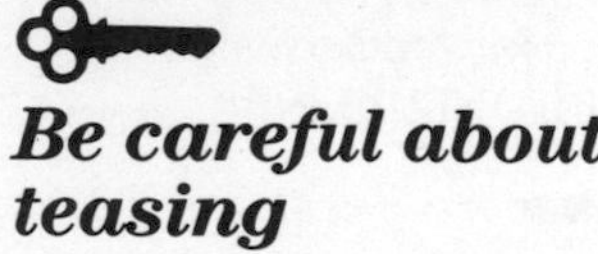

Be careful about teasing

"WHAT'S WRONG, Steve?" Mike asked his friend as they walked home from school.

Steve looked gloomy. "I don't want to tell—you'll laugh."

"Aw, come on. We're friends. Tell me what's bothering you," coaxed Mike.

"Well," said Steve, giving in, "some of the guys learned my middle name is Thomas, which makes me S. T. Bernard. They all started calling me 'Saint Bernard.' They barked at me and everything."

"Don't let it bother you. They'll get over it," consoled Mike. As he thought about it, however, he couldn't resist a joke that came to mind. "Wait till I tell the guys that I 'walk the dog' home from school every day!" he teased.

Steve looked at Mike in disbelief. "You said you wouldn't laugh, and I trusted you" he said, and he began running home as fast as he could.

"Hey, I was only kidding!" Mike called after him. "You know I won't really tell them that!" But Steve was gone.

Several days went by, but Steve refused to talk to Mike or walk home with him. This bothered Mike, but he felt Steve was being stubborn. Then one morning Mike was reading a chapter in his Bible, as he did every day. This time he was reading Proverbs 20. He came to these verses: "Like a madman who throws firebrands, arrows, and death, is the man who deceives his neighbor, and says, 'I was only joking!' "

Uh-oh, thought Mike as feelings of guilt filled his heart. *I've read those verses before, but they never sank in. They're sure sinking in now! I've got to ask Steve to forgive me.* Mike uttered a prayer and quickly got dressed. After a hasty breakfast, he grabbed his books.

"What's the big hurry?" asked his mother as he dashed past her.

"I'll explain tonight," answered Mike. "Right now I've got to see Steve." And he ran all the way to Steve's house.

HOW ABOUT YOU? Are you in the habit of teasing people about things they dislike? God warns that you can deeply hurt them by doing that. If you hurt someone, you should ask his forgiveness. Learn to say things that help people rather than hurt them. S.N.

TO MEMORIZE: *"Like a madman who throws firebrands, arrows, and death, is the man who deceives his neighbor, and says, 'I was only joking!' "* Proverbs 26:18-19 (NKJV).

OCTOBER

27

Deadly Arrows

(Continued from yesterday)

FROM THE BIBLE:

Bless those who persecute you; bless and do not curse. Rejoice with those who rejoice, and weep with those who weep. Be of the same mind toward one another. Do not set your mind on high things, but associate with the humble. Do not be wise in your own opinion. Repay no one evil for evil. Have regard for good things in the sight of all men. If it is possible, as much as depends on you, live peaceably with all men. Beloved, do not avenge yourselves, but rather give place to wrath; for it is written, "Vengeance is Mine, I will repay," says the Lord. "Therefore if your enemy hungers, feed him; if he thirsts, give him a drink; for in so doing you will heap coals of fire on his head." Do not be overcome by evil, but overcome evil with good. Romans 12:14-21, NIV

Don't let teasing upset you

I *GUESS I WOULDN'T like to be called "Saint Bernard" either,* Mike admitted to himself as he hurried to his friend's house to apologize for having teased him. He slowed down as he approached the Bernard home. On the lawn, he saw a handmade sign that said, "Beware of the dog"—and Steve didn't even have a dog! *Uh-oh,* Mike thought. *I wonder who put that sign up. That's gonna make Steve mad. Maybe I should forget about apologizing for now and go to school early.*

Just then the front door opened and Steve came out. "Hi, Mike," Steve greeted him.

"Hi," Mike replied, feeling a little off guard because Steve was smiling and friendly. He decided to get the apology over with. "Look, Steve," he said, "I want to apologize for teasing you the other day. I didn't mean to hurt your feelings, but I did and I was wrong."

"Oh, it's OK," said Steve. "I know I was silly to take the teasing so seriously. I talked to my dad about it last night, and he said I'd better get used to it. He told me the kids used to tease him about his big feet when he was a boy. Some of his friends still do. He said it really helps if a person can play along with the teasing." Steve pointed across the lawn. "How do you like my sign?"

"Your sign?" asked Mike in surprise.

"Yep!" Steve nodded. "I made that. I've decided to take Dad's advice and enjoy being Steven Thomas Bernard from now on."

HOW ABOUT YOU? How do you respond to teasing? Do you get angry and hold a grudge? Getting angry won't stop people from teasing you. It may even make them tease more. God says you are to "bless them which persecute you." So don't let teasing upset you. Learn to laugh at yourself. You'll find you enjoy life more that way, and you'll be following God's instruction to live peaceably with all men. S.N.

TO MEMORIZE: *"Bless them which persecute you: bless, and curse not."* Romans 12:14 (NKJV).

OCTOBER

28

What Are You Thinking?

FROM THE BIBLE:

I plead with you—yes, I, Paul—and I plead gently, as Christ himself would do. Yet some of you are saying, "Paul's letters are bold enough when he is far away, but when he gets here he will be afraid to raise his voice!" I hope I won't need to show you when I come how harsh and rough I can be. I don't want to carry out my present plans against some of you who seem to think my deeds and words are merely those of an ordinary man. It is true that I am an ordinary, weak human being, but I don't use human plans and methods to win my battles. I use God's mighty weapons, not those made by men, to knock down the devil's strongholds.

2 Corinthians 10:1-4, TLB

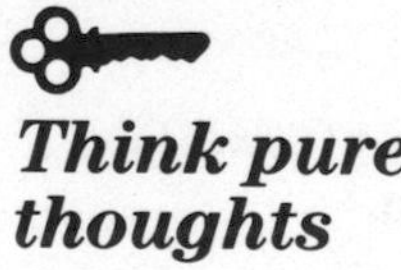

Think pure thoughts

DAVID WAS in the locker room getting ready for gym when he heard some of the boys laughing and joking together. David overheard Ted tell a very dirty joke. The others laughed, but David quickly left the room.

All day the story kept popping back into David's mind. He told God he was sorry he heard it, but still he seemed unable to forget it. This continued for several days. Finally he decided to talk to his father about it. Dad understood. "Satan wants to control your mind," he told David, "so he keeps bringing back the nasty things you see and hear. Now you know the law of space, don't you?"

"Sure," answered David. "No two things can occupy the same space at the same time. We learned that at school."

"Right." Dad smiled. "Take this book, for example. It's lying here on the table, and nothing else can occupy that space until the book is removed. It's the same way with your mind. Fill it and keep it filled with the Word of God and with knowledge that will help you to live a wholesome life. Then no filth can occupy the space which the good things take up."

"I do read my Bible, Dad," David said, "but I still can't forget that joke."

"Well, now comes God's part," said Dad. "When you received Jesus as Savior, you also received the Holy Spirit. He gives you power to overcome evil. Whenever this dirty story pops into your mind, ask for God's Holy Spirit to cleanse your mind, and He will. If you do this, you'll find that you'll think of that story less and less often until finally you forget it."

"Really, Dad?" exclaimed David. "I'm glad!" I felt so guilty remembering that story. I hope I never hear a dirty joke again."

HOW ABOUT YOU? Do you ever have trouble with your thoughts? Following these suggestions will help you. First, avoid situations where you hear or read unwholesome things. Second, fill your mind with good things. Third, ask the Holy Spirit to cleanse your thoughts. Today's Scripture says that through Christ your weapons for fighting Satan are so mighty that you can have victory even over bad thoughts. As you call upon God, He will help you to overcome this problem. A.L.

TO MEMORIZE: *"Blessed are the pure in heart, for they will see God"* Matthew 5:8 (NIV).

OCTOBER

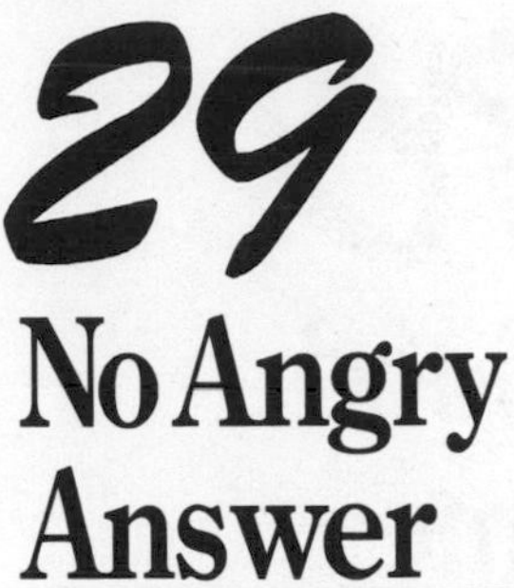

No Angry Answer

FROM THE BIBLE:

A gentle answer turns away wrath, but harsh words cause quarrels. A wise teacher makes learning a joy; a rebellious teacher spouts foolishness. The Lord is watching everywhere and keeps his eye on both the evil and the good. Gentle words cause life and health; griping brings discouragement.

Proverbs 15:1-4, TLB

Don't react with anger

SINCE TODD had become a Christian he had been trying to follow his Sunday school teacher's advice about having devotions each day. So far he hadn't missed many days. One day after reading the Bible and the story from his devotional book, he took time to learn the suggested memory verse: "A gentle answer turns away wrath, but harsh words cause quarrels." After praying he hurried off to school.

The bell rang just as Todd reached his seat. He gave a sigh of relief for he had thought he might be late. As he opened his English book, Beth slipped him a note. It read, "I think you're cute. I love your dimples."

Todd blushed and quickly shoved the paper into his desk, but not quickly enough. Mike, who sat behind him, murmured, "Todd's got a girlfriend," in a singsong voice.

Todd turned angrily, but before he could say anything, the teacher told him to turn around. *I'll tell him off in a note,* Todd told himself. *He always picks on me and I'm tired of it.* As Todd started writing, the verse he had memorized that morning came back to his mind. He crumpled the note and started doing his homework instead.

At lunchtime Mike came up to Todd and started teasing him about having a girlfriend. Todd laughed self-consciously. "Oh, I don't think so," he said. He spoke in a quiet voice because he kept remembering the Bible verse he had learned.

While they ate, Mike continued to bring up the subject, but Todd just smiled and wouldn't show any anger. Finally Mike stopped teasing. He even invited Todd to join his team for a ball game. Todd agreed gladly, and he silently thanked God for the day's memory verse.

HOW ABOUT YOU? How do you react when your family or friends tease you about a mistake you've made? About something you're wearing? About the way you talk? Follow the advice from God's Word. You'll find that a quiet reaction, instead of anger, will make you and others happier.

TO MEMORIZE: *"A gentle answer turns away wrath, but harsh words cause quarrels"*
Proverbs 15:1 (TLB).

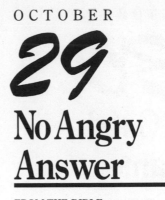

OCTOBER

30

A Good Name

FROM THE BIBLE:

In the city of Joppa there was a woman named Dorcas ("Gazelle"), a believer who was always doing kind things for others, especially for the poor. About this time she became ill and died. Her friends prepared her for burial and laid her in an upstairs room. But when they learned that Peter was nearby at Lydda, they sent two men to beg him to return with them to Joppa. This he did; as soon as he arrived, they took him upstairs where Dorcas lay. The room was filled with weeping widows who were showing one another the coats and other garments Dorcas had made for them. Acts 9:36-39, TLB

Desire a good name

EDNA AND HER grandfather often had long talks. One day she was quite unhappy. "I just hate my name, Grandpa," she said. "I wish I had been given a name that wasn't so old fashioned, like 'Heather' or 'Sarah' or 'Katie.' "

Grandpa smiled. "Well, now, I think 'Edna' is a pretty name," he told her. "Your mom named you after your great-grandmother, whom she dearly loved. She wasn't thinking of how up-to-date or out-of-date your name would be. The name 'Edna' just reminded her of the sweetest person she'd ever known. Your mom really meant well."

"But I have to live with the kids at school, like Jason McCormick and Andy Bristol," she complained. "They keep asking me how things were in the 'olden days.' I think I really will change my name someday. The Bible even says I should."

Grandpa looked surprised. "Where'd you get that idea?"

"The Bible says, 'A good name is rather to be chosen than great riches.' "

"Oh, Edna, that verse isn't talking about changing your name!" Grandpa said. "It's talking about what people think of your character when they hear your name."

"They think of 'old lady,' " Edna pouted.

"Oh," laughed Grandpa, "I doubt that. I'll bet they think of what you are like as a person. Are you friendly, mean, kind, bitter?" Edna shrugged and didn't say anything, but she still scowled. "What do you think of when you hear the name Jason McCormick?" asked Grandpa.

"I think of a boy who picks on girls and calls them names," Edna answered with a hint of anger in her voice.

"Exactly!" Grandpa said, nodding. "Funny that you never mentioned him as a boy with an up-to-date name. It was his personality you described. So even though you don't like your name, try to live in such a way that when people think of Edna Grant, they think happy thoughts. That's what 'a good name' means in that Bible verse."

HOW ABOUT YOU? What do people think of when they hear your name? Do they have good thoughts or bad thoughts? Live your life so people will think of a godly person when they hear your name—one who loves the Lord and lives to please Him. S.N.

TO MEMORIZE: *"A good name is rather to be chosen than great riches"* Proverbs 22:1 (NKJV).

OCTOBER

31

Behind the Mask

FROM THE BIBLE:
Thus says the Lord: "Cursed is the man who trusts in man and makes flesh his strength, whose heart departs from the Lord. For he shall be like a shrub in the desert, and shall not see when good comes, but shall inhabit the parched places in the wilderness, in a salt land which is not inhabited. Blessed is the man who trusts in the Lord, and whose hope is the Lord. For he shall be like a tree planted by the waters, which spreads out its roots by the river, and will not fear when heat comes; but her leaf will be green, and will not be anxious in the year of drought, nor will cease from yielding fruit. The heart is deceitful above all things, and desperately wicked; Who can know it? I, the Lord, search the heart, I test the mind, even to give every man according to his ways, and according to the fruit of his doings."
Jeremiah 17:5-10, NKJV

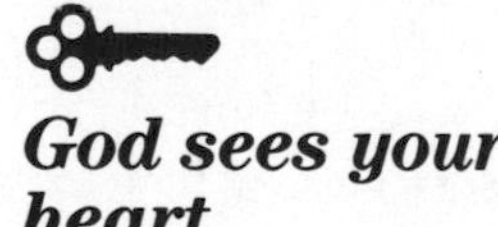

God sees your heart

"TRICK OR TREAT!" rang out the cry all over the neighborhood. Three-year-old Jamie hid behind Mother as she opened the door. He wasn't sure he liked this, but everyone else seemed to be having fun. When he saw a pirate and a tramp on the front porch, he ducked behind a chair. "Come on, Jamie. Don't be afraid," Mother encouraged. "You know these people."

Jamie peeked out—but, no! He certainly didn't know anyone who looked like that!

"Hi, Jamie! Remember me?" called the pirate. That voice sounded familiar, but Jamie still wasn't convinced. The pirate reached up and took off his mask, and the tramp did the same. Why, these were the two big boys who lived in the house next door! Jamie laughed at their funny costumes. When he saw that it was only children all dressed up, he spent the rest of the evening helping Mother pass out candy. Sometimes he would try to guess whose face was beneath the mask.

Finally the last trick-or-treater had come and gone. "It's been a busy evening," said Mother. "We've passed out lots of candy, and with each piece went a good gospel tract. I do hope the boys and girls will read them."

Just then Dad arrived home. "You know," he said to mother, "all those costumes and masks remind me of many people who go around wearing a 'mask' everyday. They try to look like something they're not. They smile and act pleasant. They go to church. They do 'good deeds.' To us they appear to be Christians—but underneath the masks, they have sinful hearts. They need Jesus."

HOW ABOUT YOU? Do you wear a mask only on Halloween, or do you wear one every day? Have you accepted Jesus as your Savior, or do you only pretend to be a Christian? Remember, you may fool others, but you can't fool God. He sees your heart. H.M.

TO MEMORIZE: *"I, the Lord, search the heart"* Jeremiah 17:10 (NKJV).

1

Count on Me

FROM THE BIBLE:

In the name of the Lord Jesus Christ, we command you, brothers, to keep away from every brother who is idle and does not live according to the teaching you received from us. For you yourselves know how you ought to follow our example. We were not idle when we were with you, nor did we eat anyone's food without paying for it. On the contrary, we worked night and day, laboring and toiling so that we would not be a burden to any of you. We did this, not because we do not have the right to such help, but in order to make ourselves a model for you to follow. For even when we were with you, we gave you this rule: "If a man will not work, he shall not eat." We hear that some among you are idle. They are not busy; they are busybodies. Such people we command and urge in the Lord Jesus Christ to settle down and earn the bread they eat. And as for you, brothers, never tire of doing what is right.

2 Thessalonians 3:6-13, NIV

Be helpful

EVERYONE WAS having a good time at the pizza party being held in the church basement. "We need some help cleaning up," Mr. Trenton, the sixth-grade Sunday school teacher, reminded the class toward the end of the evening. "When we planned this party, you all agreed to help with the dishes and with setting the chairs back in order. Remember?"

The kids did remember, but right now they were having too much fun talking and goofing around. They fully intended to help a little later, but one by one they disappeared as their parents came for them. Cindy went into the kitchen to help Mrs. Trenton for a few minutes, but then someone called her, and soon she was laughing and talking again.

At nine o'clock Cindy's dad came to pick her up. He had agreed to drive several other children home, too. "I feel like a bus driver," he told Cindy good-naturedly about forty-five minutes later. They had been to all the corners of town and were once again driving past the church on the way to their own street. "The lights are still on in the church basement," Dad said in surprise. "I guess the Trentons haven't left yet. I wonder if something's wrong." He slowed down and turned into the parking lot.

Cindy knew what was wrong as soon as she and her dad walked into the youth room. Mr. and Mrs. Trenton were still cleaning up the mess that the young people had made. How guilty Cindy felt as she and her dad both pitched in to help!

"I'm so sorry" she apologized. "You two do so much for us, but we sure don't do much for you in return. You can count on me to help clean up next time. I promise!"

HOW ABOUT YOU? Do you enjoy parties at church? Have you even thought about all the work involved in planning a party? What do you do to help? Today's Scripture says that those who won't work shouldn't eat, either. That's true about parties as well as about daily life. Next time adults plan a special event for you, tell them "Thank you" and show them you mean it by doing what you can to help. That's what the Lord would want you to do! L. W.

TO MEMORIZE: *"As for you, brothers, never tire of doing what is right"* 2 Thessalonians 3:13 (NIV).

NOVEMBER

2

Nots and Knots

FROM THE BIBLE:
God spoke all these words: "I am the Lord your God, who brought you out of Egypt, out of the land of slavery. You shall have no other gods before me. You shall not make for yourself an idol in the form of anything in heaven above or on the earth beneath or in the waters below. . . . You shall not misuse the name of the Lord your God, for the Lord will not hold anyone guiltless who misuses his name. Remember the Sabbath day by keeping it holy. Six days you shall labor and do all your work, but the seventh day is a Sabbath to the Lord your God. . . . Honor your father and your mother, so that you may live long in the land the Lord your God is giving you. You shall not murder. You shall not commit adultery. You shall not steal. You shall not give false testimony against your neighbor. You shall not covet your neighbor's house. You shall not covet your neighbor's wife, or his manservant or maidservant, his ox or donkey, or anything that belongs to your neighbor."
Exodus 20:1-17, NIV

God says no for your good

"DON'T TALK TO me about religion, Chad," said Jeff as the boys were leaving school. "You know how I feel about all those 'Thou shalt nots.' It's 'Thou shalt not do this,' 'Thou shalt not do that,' 'Thou shalt not tell a lie even if it keeps you from getting in trouble.' That's crazy; I like my freedom." Pointing to the parking lot, he added, "I've gotta run. My mom's waiting for me."

It's so frustrating, Chad thought as he walked home. *Whenever I mention becoming a Christian or invite Jeff to Sunday school, all he can think of is what we can't do.*

The next Saturday Chad was invited to go boating with Jeff and his father. The wind was blowing and the waves were choppy, but they had fun. When they came back to the dock, Jeff said, "Dad, I'll tie the boat down."

Jeff showed Chad how to make a good knot with the rope to hold the boat to the dock. "But why tie it down?" asked Chad suddenly. "Why not give it its freedom?"

"Are you kidding?" laughed Jeff. "It would drift out into the lake and be lost in no time. Or else it might end up hitting another boat." He lifted the rope and pointed to the knot he had just made. "But this little knot made by Yours Truly will keep all that from happening," he said. "It will protect this boat from harm."

"So," said Chad, "you have your knots and I have mine!"

"What's that supposed to mean?"

"Well, you say you don't want to become a Christian because you say there are too many 'thou shalt nots.' But God tells us not to do certain things—like lie or steal—for our protection, to keep us from ruining our lives or hurting others. Just like that knot in the rope protects your boat."

Jeff looked startled. "That does make sense," he admitted. "I guess I really should learn more about what the Bible teaches."

"How about coming to church with me tomorrow?" Chad suggested. "That's a good place to start." Jeff nodded his agreement.

HOW ABOUT YOU? Are you resentful because of the things God says not to do? He made you, and He knows what will help you and what will hurt you. When He tells you not to do something, it's to keep you from trouble. S.N.

TO MEMORIZE: *"Do not be wise in your own eyes; fear the LORD and shun evil"* Proverbs 3:7 (NIV).

NOVEMBER

3

Only a Dream

FROM THE BIBLE:

My son, preserve sound judgment and discernment, do not let them out of your sight; they will be life for you, an ornament to grace your neck. Then you will go on your way in safety, and your foot will not stumble; when you lie down, you will not be afraid; when you lie down, your sleep will be sweet. Have no fear of sudden disaster or of the ruin that overtakes the wicked, for the Lord will be your confidence and will keep your foot from being snared.
Proverbs 3:21-26, NIV

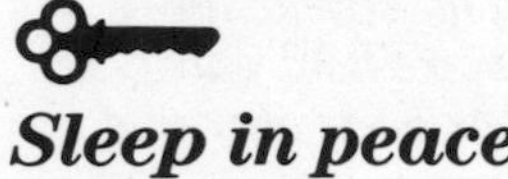

Sleep in peace

SOMETHING WAS chasing Sally, and she ran as fast as she could. She couldn't see what chased her, but it was making all sorts of weird noises, and it was getting closer and closer. Suddenly the road she had been running on seemed to end in midair, and she felt herself falling, falling, as off a high cliff! Then she heard herself screaming as she fell! It was probably her own screaming that woke her up. Yes, Sally had been dreaming!

Her scream also woke her dad, who came into her room and sat on the edge of the bed. "What's the matter, honey?" he asked. Breathlessly and with a shaking voice, Sally told him about the dreadful "thing" that had chased her.

"Calm down, Sally, It was just a dream," comforted Dad.

"I know, but it seemed so real. Where do dreams come from anyway?" Sally wanted to know.

"Well, that's hard to say," replied Dad. "Scientists say that dreams come from deep inside your mind, showing some of the fears that are hidden there. But more often than not, what you think about just before going to sleep has a big effect on your dreams. That's why it's much better to read a good book or some verses from the Bible before going to bed, rather than reading a scary story or watching some horror movie on TV."

Sally had another question. "Does God talk to us through our dreams?"

"Well, in Bible times God often talked to His people through dreams. But now we have the Bible to guide us," answered Dad. "Of course, God can put thoughts into our minds, and we should be careful to listen to what He may be telling us. But we're much better off trusting His written Word for direction in our lives than trusting some dream we've had."

Sally nodded and yawned. "I think I'll try to go back to sleep now. Maybe whatever was trying to catch me is chasing somebody else in their dream." She chuckled as she snuggled under the covers and closed her eyes.

HOW ABOUT YOU? Are you careful about what you put into your mind just before bedtime? Make a habit of reading a few verses from the Bible and praying just before going to sleep. And don't trust your dreams for direction in your life. It's much better to trust what the Bible says! C.V.M.

TO MEMORIZE: *"When you lie down, you will not be afraid; When you lie down, your sleep will be sweet"* Proverbs 3:24 (NIV).

"I'LL NEVER invite Ricky to Sunday school again!" Kevin exploded as he slammed the door behind him. Mother wrinkled her brow. "Why not?" she asked.

"Because he is so mean!" Kevin wiped his eyes with the back of his hand and choked down a sob. His mother sighed. "Kevin, you must not feel angry at Ricky. He doesn't realize—"

She was interrupted by a sharp yip followed by a howl of pain. "It's Mitzy," Kevin cried as he shot out the back door. "She must be hurt!" He found his puppy crouched on the ground, her paw caught under the fence. Every time she moved a sharp barb of wire jabbed her flesh. Kevin reached for the trapped paw.

Grrrrr! growled Mitzy, baring her teeth. Kevin drew back in surprise. "Mitzy! Why are you growling at me?"

Mother reached for the puppy's paw, and Mitzy snapped at her. "Hold her head, Kevin, and talk to her gently. I'll see if I can help."

As Kevin talked softly and patted the whining puppy, Mother carefully freed the paw and examined it. "There's a little cut here, but she'll soon forget about it." She laughed and drew back as Mitzy's wet tongue reached for her. "I guess she's thanking me, but I can do without dog kisses. Kevin, what if we had walked off and left Mitzy when she growled at us?"

Kevin blinked. "She'd still be caught!" he exclaimed. "You know we couldn't do that, Mother. Mitzy needed our help, but she just didn't realize we were trying to help her."

"Neither does Ricky realize what he is doing when he laughs at you for inviting him to Sunday school," Mother said gently. "He does not realize he is caught in the trap of sin and needs your help."

Yip! Yip! agreed Mitzy.

Kevin laughed. "Mitzy's saying, 'Amen.' OK, I'll keep trying," he agreed. "Maybe one day Ricky will thank me, too."

HOW ABOUT YOU? Are you tempted to give up praying for your friends, inviting them to Sunday school, or telling them of Jesus? Never give up on it. Even when they snap back at you, they need your help. Be faithful in your efforts to bring them to Christ. B.W.

TO MEMORIZE: *"Let us not become weary in doing good, for at the proper time we will reap a harvest if we do not give up"* Galatians 6:9 (NIV).

NOVEMBER

Help Needed

FROM THE BIBLE:

How we thank God for all of this! It is he who makes us victorious through Jesus Christ our Lord! So, my dear brothers, since future victory is sure, be strong and steady, always abounding in the Lord's work, for you know that nothing you do for the Lord is ever wasted as it would be if there were no resurrection.

1 Corinthians 15:57-58, TLB

Keep on witnessing

NOVEMBER

5

Two Lists

FROM THE BIBLE:
Hallelujah! Yes, praise the Lord! Praise him in his Temple, and in the heavens he made with mighty power. Praise him for his mighty works. Praise his unequaled greatness. Praise him with the trumpet and with lute and harp. Praise him with the drums and dancing. Praise him with stringed instruments and horns. Praise him with the cymbals, yes, loud clanging cymbals. Let everything alive give praises to the Lord! You praise him! Hallelujah!
Psalm 150, TLB

Give thanks always

PETER PICKED up the ballpoint pen and drew a line down the middle of the paper. His Sunday school teacher had asked the class to bring in a list of things for which they were thankful and a list of things for which they were not thankful. Well, Peter could think of a lot of things he wasn't thankful about. For example, Mother had sent him to his room yesterday because he told a lie. He sure wasn't thankful for punishment. He wrote it down on the list. Opposite, he put down the word *parents*. Yes, he was thankful for them. They took care of him everyday.

Peter looked again at the words *punishment* and *parents*. It didn't seem quite right to be thankful for one and not the other when his parents were the ones who punished him. Maybe he should be thankful that they cared enough to punish him when he did wrong things. He thought about it a while and then finally crossed out *punishment*.

On the "thankful" side, Peter wrote *church*. That was definitely something to be thankful for. It was there he had made his decision to put his faith in Jesus Christ. Suddenly he thought of the memory verse he had to learn before Sunday morning. He hated to memorize. Quickly he wrote down *memorization* on the side of things for which he was not thankful.

A Bible verse popped into Peter's mind—one he had learned way back during his primary Sunday school days. He found himself repeating it word for word. "Giving thanks always for all things unto God and the Father in the name of our Lord Jesus Christ." He even remembered where it was found—Ephesians 5:20.

Well, that verse sure blew the idea of listing things for which he was not thankful. He crossed out the word *memorization*. Then he crossed out the words on the other side of the paper, too. In place of them he wrote in big letters: EVERYTHING!

HOW ABOUT YOU? Are there things you do not thank God for? Maybe you hate to study. Maybe your father lost his job. Or maybe something didn't happen when you wanted it to happen, and you grumbled about it. The Bible says to give thanks for all things. Can you do that? R.J.

TO MEMORIZE: *"Giving thanks always for all things"* Ephesians 5:20 (NKJV).

NOVEMBER

6

The Oilman

FROM THE BIBLE:

The spirit of the Lord God is upon me, because the Lord has anointed me to bring good news to the suffering and afflicted. He has sent me to comfort the broken-hearted, to announce liberty to captives and to open the eyes of the blind. He has sent me to tell those who mourn that the time of God's favor to them has come, and the day of his wrath to their enemies. To all who mourn in Israel he will give—Beauty for ashes; Joy instead of mourning; Praise instead of heaviness. For God has planted them like strong and graceful oaks for his own glory. . . . Let me tell you how happy God has made me! For he has clothed me with garments of salvation and draped about me the robe of righteousness. I am like a bridegroom in his wedding suit or a bride with her jewels.
Isaiah 61:1-3, 10, TLB

Spread gladness

"DAD, MAY I use your oilcan?" Bill's father looked up at his eager, young son. "I want to 'unsqueak' the cupboard doors for Mom. She says the hinges need a little oil and that I can be the 'oilman.' She says if they don't get it soon, they're gong to drive her wild with their squeaking."

Dad laughed as he took the oilcan from the workbench and handed it to Bill. "Then by all means, take it away!"

When Bill returned the oilcan a little later, Dad was still at his workbench. "I oiled the hinges all over the house," Bill reported. "I told Mom that if she heard any squeaks now, she could figure we have mice. She says that will really drive her wild." Bill and his dad laughed together, and then Bill went out to play with his friends.

At dinner that evening Bill shared the neighborhood news. "Todd and Jim are mad at each other again," he said. "They're always fighting. Did you know Mrs. Gentry broke her arm? She fell down her basement stairs. Mr. Snell—that old man at the corner—stood at his window for half an hour and watched us sliding. He's probably got nothing better to do." Bill paused to nibble at his salad.

"I guess the people in our neighborhood could use some oil," observed Dad.

"Oil?" asked Bill. "What do you mean?"

"The Bible speaks of the 'oil of gladness,' and it sounds to me like some of our neighbors could use a little gladness," said Dad. "Since you're the 'oilman' today, I think you should be the one to spread it around the neighborhood."

"Yeah?" Bill looked thoughtful. "I know what I can do," he said, eyeing the dessert on the cupboard. "I can take a piece of pie to Mr. Snell. And I can offer to run errands for Mrs. Gentry. What can I do about Todd and Jim?"

"I don't know," said Mom. "But you're off to a good start. I'm sure you'll think of something."

HOW ABOUT YOU? Do you spread gladness? God's Word says Jesus was anointed with the "oil of gladness," and if you belong to Him, there should be gladness in your heart, too. Will you share that with others? Offer a cheerful smile to help someone feel better. Take time to chat a few minutes with a lonely person. Lend a helping hand. Do it for Jesus. H.M.

TO MEMORIZE: *"You have loved righteousness and hated lawlessness; therefore God, Your God, has anointed You with the oil of gladness"*
Hebrews 1:9 (NKJV).

NOVEMBER

7

Let It Heal

FROM THE BIBLE:

Don't gossip. Don't falsely accuse your neighbor of some crime, for I am Jehovah. Don't hate your brother. Rebuke anyone who sins; don't let him get away with it, or you will be equally guilty. Don't seek vengeance. Don't bear a grudge; but love your neighbor as yourself, for I am Jehovah.
Leviticus 19:16-18, TLB

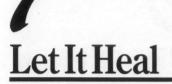

Let hurt feelings heal

"MY FINGER's bleedin' again, Mama!" Jason cried as he ran into the kitchen.

Mother sighed and handed a paper towel to her four-year-old. Jason wrapped it around his finger and watched, fascinated, as the red stain grew. "Jason, if you don't leave that cut alone it will take even longer to heal, and it will leave a scar," Mother scolded. "I wish . . ." The front door slammed, drowning out the rest of her words. Stacy stomped into the room and threw her books on the table.

"Look, Stacy!" Jason held his finger in front of his big sister's face. "My finger's bleedin' again."

"You're not going to get any more sympathy from me," Stacy snorted. "Stop picking it!"

"How was school today, Stacy?" Mother asked.

"Terrible!" complained Stacy. "Jodi thinks she can treat me like an old shoe. Last week she ignored me. This week she wants me to be her friend."

Mother frowned. "I thought Jodi apologized for not inviting you to her slumber party," she said.

"Oh, she did," Stacy said. "Since I had mentioned earlier that we were going to Grandma's, she thought I couldn't come anyway. If she had asked, I would have told her Dad had changed our plans. But did she ask? Oh no! She really didn't want me to come."

"Now, Stacy, that's not fair." Mother looked straight into her daughter's eyes. "You need to stop picking the sore, Stacy, or it will leave a scar that will mar your friendship forever."

Stacy stammered, "But I don't know what you . . ." She paused and looked at her toes. "I do see what you mean, Mom," she finally admitted. "I've been acting just like Jason."

"You cut your finger, Stacy?" Jason asked.

Stacy grinned. "No, but my feelings were hurt."

Jason unwrapped the paper towel from his finger. "Look, Mama. It's stopped bleedin'. Has your sore feelings stopped bleedin', Stacy?"

Mother and Stacy laughed as Stacy gave her answer. "Yes. Everything will be all right now."

HOW ABOUT YOU? Has someone wounded your feelings or hurt your pride? Are you picking the sore, refusing to forgive and forget? Promise yourself right now to stop thinking about your hurt, and let it heal. B.W.

TO MEMORIZE: *"Bear with each other and forgive whatever grievances you may have against one another. Forgive as the Lord forgave you"* Colossians 3:13 (NIV).

NOVEMBER

8 The Thermostat

FROM THE BIBLE:
And so, dear brothers, I plead with you to give your bodies to God. Let them be a living sacrifice, holy—the kind he can accept. When you think of what he has done for you, is this too much to ask? Don't copy the behavior and customs of this world, but be a new and different person with a fresh newness in all you do and think. Then you will learn from your own experience how his ways will really satisfy you. . . . Don't let evil get the upper hand but conquer evil by doing good. Romans 12:1-2, 21, TLB

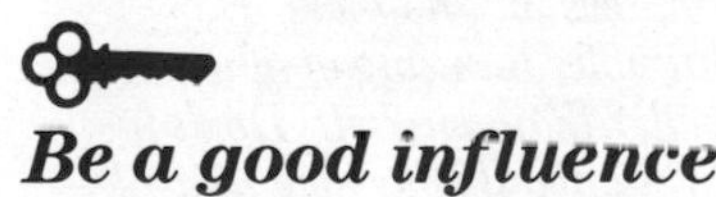

Be a good influence

"WE SURE had fun at school today," said Denny as he sat down at the dinner table. "Mrs. Edwards had to go to the office for something, and everybody ran around and talked while she was gone. She came back mad as a wet hen—said she could hear us way down at the office. Then she told us to sit with our heads on our desks while she went back to the office. When she left, everybody went wild again."

"Including you?" asked Mother.

Denny looked startled. "Well, yeah. Everybody did." He quickly thought of a new topic, hoping to avoid a lecture. "Can I turn the heat up a little? It's so chilly in here that my food is getting cold."

"When the sun goes down, it does get cold pretty fast," agreed Dad. "Go ahead, turn up the thermostat a bit." Denny went to do so. "A thermostat is a great invention," observed Dad when Denny returned to his seat. "It's a controlling device. It doesn't just read the temperature in a room; it does something about it. It tells the furnace when to go on and off. Some people are like thermostats."

"Some people tell the furnace when to go on and off?" asked Denny with a grin.

Dad smiled. "What I meant is that some people do something about what is going on around them," he said. "They control what is happening. They don't just go along with the crowd. Christians should influence those around them instead of being swayed by unbelievers. They should be good examples in the things they say and do."

Denny gulped. "Oh, I guess you're right. Maybe if I had been quiet and stayed in my seat today, some of the other kids would have, too."

"Maybe," agreed Mother. "Next time I suggest that you try it. Meanwhile, I think you owe your teacher an apology, don't you?" Silently, Denny nodded.

HOW ABOUT YOU? Do you go along with the crowd? Do you think the fact that "everybody is doing it" makes it OK for you to follow in their footsteps? If so, you have things backwards. If you're a Christian, you should be like a thermostat. Decide how God would want you to act. Then behave in that manner yourself and influence your friends to follow your example. H.M.

TO MEMORIZE: *"Become blameless and pure, children of God without fault in a crooked and depraved generation in which you shine like stars"* Philippians 2:15 (NIV).

NOVEMBER

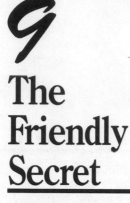

The Friendly Secret

FROM THE BIBLE:

Is there any such thing as Christians cheering each other up? Do you love me enough to want to help me? Does it mean anything to you that we are brothers in the Lord, sharing the same Spirit? Are your hearts tender and sympathetic at all? Then make me truly happy by loving each other and agreeing wholeheartedly with each other, working together with one heart and mind and purpose. Don't be selfish; don't live to make a good impression on others. Be humble, thinking of others as better than yourself. Don't just think about your own affairs, but be interested in others, too, and in what they are doing.

Philippians 2:1-4, TLB

Be friendly

ONCE UPON A time there were three Baars: Mr. Baar, Mrs. Baar, and their daughter, Merry. One day while driving home from church Mr. Baar growled, "I'm never going back there again. No one spoke to me this morning."

Mrs. Baar nodded her head until her curls bobbed. "Me, either! Not one person talked to me."

Merry bounced in the back seat, and in her little, high voice said, "Nobody spoke to me. Let's not go back there."

So they tried other churches, but they were always disappointed when no one paid much attention to them.

One day the pastor from the last church they visited came to their home. "We have so many nice people in our church," he said. "Did you meet any of them?"

Mr. Baar shook his head. "No one talked to me."

"No one welcomed me," added Mrs. Baar.

"Me, either," Merry said in her high little voice. "We squeezed in the backseat just before church started, and we ran out as soon as it ended."

"Ahhh." The pastor smiled. "Perhaps you'd like to try a little experiment. I find that the people who always seem to have a good time with others at church are those who look for someone who seems lonely, and they talk with that person. Would the three of you try that this Sunday?" All the Baars nodded.

That Sunday they went to church a little earlier and looked for someone who seemed friendless. A family stood in the back of the auditorium, looking uncertain as to where they should go. Quickly the Baars went to talk with the family and found they were very nice people. Then they all sat together during the church service.

"This *is* a friendly church," Mr. Baar said later, beaming at the pastor.

"You have found the secret to finding a friendly church," the pastor said. "It's not so much who talks with you as whom you try to talk with."

All the Baars nodded happily.

HOW ABOUT YOU? Do you feel left out and friendless at church? It could be because you don't give others a chance to meet you. If you make an effort to greet others, especially those who seem to be in need of a friendly greeting, you'll find that they usually respond to you. C.Y.

TO MEMORIZE: *"A man who has friends must himself be friendly"* Proverbs 18:24 (NKJV).

NOVEMBER

10

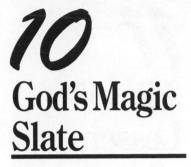

God's Magic Slate

FROM THE BIBLE:

O loving and kind God, have mercy. Have pity upon me and take away the awful stain of my transgressions. Oh, wash me, cleanse me from this guilt. Let me be pure again. For I admit my shameful deed—it haunts me day and night. It is against you and you alone I sinned, and did this terrible thing. You saw it all, and your sentence against me is just. But I was born a sinner, yes, from the moment my mother conceived me. You deserve honesty from the heart; yes, utter sincerity and truthfulness. Oh, give me this wisdom. Sprinkle me with the cleansing blood and I shall be clean again. Wash me and I shall be whiter than snow. And after you have punished me, give me back my joy again. Don't keep looking at my sins—erase them from your sight. Create in me a new, clean heart, O God, filled with clean thoughts and right desires. Don't toss me aside, banished forever from your presence. Don't take your Holy Spirit from me. Restore to me again the joy of your salvation, and make me willing to obey you.

Psalm 51:1-12, TLB

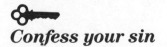

"SEE WHAT I bought, Mother," said Megan excitedly as she took a magic slate out of a sack. She began scribbling on it as they drove home. "Now, look," she said as she lifted the top plastic sheet. "The writing is all gone." As she talked, her brother Andy simply stared out the window. He wasn't hearing the conversation or seeing the scenery.

"Andy!" Mother raised her voice. "This is the third time I've called your name. Is something wrong?"

"No." Andy lapsed into silence again.

And now you've told another lie, his conscience said. *That makes two.*

Andy sighed deeply. *But it was such a little lie,* he argued with his conscience.

"I know something is bothering you, Andy," insisted Mother. "Do you want to talk about it?"

"I told Dad a lie yesterday," Andy blurted out.

Mother was silent for a moment. Then she nodded. "He knows that," she said softly, "but he is waiting for you to confess. He knew it would be much better if you admitted it freely."

Megan, busy with her magic slate, paid no attention to the conversation. She chuckled as she said, "I made a stupid mistake! I put a long tail on a rabbit! Oh, well! I'll just erase it and start over." Again she lifted the top plastic sheet, and like magic, her picture disappeared.

Mother smiled. "When you sin, Andy, it's something like writing the wrong thing on a magic slate," she said. "If you don't do anything about it, it remains there. But if you repent of your sins and confess them to God, He will erase them. Tell both your dad and the Lord what you told me. Let them know you're sorry, and the slate will be clean."

Megan smoothed the plastic sheet on her slate. "This time I'm going to do it right," she announced.

"Me, too, Megan," echoed Andy. "Me, too."

HOW ABOUT YOU? Have you told a lie? Disobeyed? Been sassy? Cheated? Right now, confess to God whatever sin you are aware of in your life and let Him wipe the slate clean. B.W.

TO MEMORIZE: *"I live in a high and holy place, but also with him who is contrite and lowly in spirit"* Isaiah 57:15 (NIV).

Confess your sin

NOVEMBER

11

A Reading Lesson

FROM THE BIBLE:

Are we beginning to commend ourselves again? Or do we need, as some, letters of commendation to you or from you? You are our letter, written in our hearts, known and read by all men; being manifested that you are a letter of Christ, cared for by us, written not with ink, but with the Spirit of the living God, not on tablets of stone, but on tablets of human hearts. And such confidence we have through Christ toward God. Not that we are adequate in ourselves to consider anything as coming from ourselves, but our adequacy is from God, who also made us adequate as servants of a new covenant, not of the letter, but of the Spirit; for the letter kills, but the Spirit gives life.
2 Corinthians 3:1-6, NASB

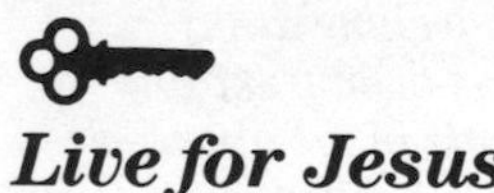

Live for Jesus

MEGAN STOOD at the window, staring at the rain. Her brother listlessly thumbed through a sports magazine. "What can we do, Mom?" asked Megan.

Mother smiled. "I thought you were learning your memory verse for Sunday school."

"I know it already," said Megan. "You are our letter, written in our hearts, known and read by all men."

"Maybe you'd like to help me with this picture album," suggested Mother. "You know most of the people in the pictures, so you might enjoy it."

Megan and Scott joined Mother at the table and began looking at the pictures. "Oh, look!" squealed Megan. "Here's a picture of Scott when he was two. He's wearing some big sunglasses and he looks so funny!"

Scott grinned. "You think that's funny? Well, look at this family reunion picture. You're bald!"

Megan laughed with Scott. "There's Dad's aunt from Ohio," she said. "She looks mad. Remember her?"

"Sure do," muttered Scott. "She was grumpy all day. Complained about everything, didn't she?" He picked up another picture. "This man with the mustache is your uncle, isn't he Mom? I remember how he yelled at me for getting mad at the ball game, and then he got so mad when the coffee was gone at suppertime. He turned red as a beet! What a fake."

"I notice you're both 'reading' people," observed Mother.

"What do you mean?" asked Scott.

"As you saw the people at the reunion, you 'read' one as 'grumpy' and another as 'fake.' "

"Oh, I get it!" exclaimed Megan. "The impression we have of other people is what we 'read' from their lives."

"And what they think of us is what they 'read' from our lives," added Scott. "So we need to make sure they can recognize us as true Christians by the way we live."

HOW ABOUT YOU? How are people "reading" you? Do your face and life show grumpiness or do they show joy and contentment? Are your actions pleasing to Satan, or do they show obedience to authority, love for others, and honesty? Ask God to help you live for His glory. G.W.

TO MEMORIZE: *"You are our letter, written in our hearts, known and read by all men"*
2 Corinthians 3:2 (NASB).

NOVEMBER

12

Through It All

FROM THE BIBLE:

But now, thus says the Lord, who created you, O Jacob, and He who formed you, O Israel: "Fear not, for I have redeemed you; I have called you by your name; you are Mine. When you pass through the waters, I will be with you; and through the rivers, they shall not overflow you. When you walk through the fire, you shall not be burned, nor shall the flame scorch you. For I am the Lord your God, the Holy One of Israel, your Savior; I gave Egypt for your ransom, Ethiopia and Seba in your place." Isaiah 43:1-3, NKJV

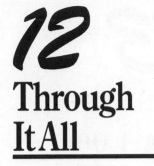

God is with you

STUNNED, BRIAN stared at his dad. He had just learned that his father had a terminal disease, and the doctor could not even promise that surgery would help. "You're not really going to die, are you?" he whispered.

Brian's father didn't answer immediately. "That's something only God knows for sure," he managed at last. "Cancer of this type is usually fatal, but whatever is God's will is what will take place. I need to submit to His will."

"But, Dad," Brian protested, "that's not fair. Mom and I need you, and . . ." His voice trailed off.

"Your mother and I have come to the place where we just want God's will to be done, whatever it is," said Dad. "We're hoping you can come to that place too."

"I'm not sure I can," Brian said honestly. "It seems all wrong."

Brian's father shook his head. "No, Son. God never makes any mistakes. I love you very much, yet it may be God's will for me to leave you." Dad smiled at Brian. "Whenever it seems to be more than you can handle, Son, remember that God loves you even more than I do, and He's with you through it all."

Brian walked away thinking about his father's words. Sure, he knew God was in control of everything. And he knew God never made any mistakes, but . . .

Suddenly Brian stopped. What had Dad said? "God loves you and is with you through it all." With determination in his heart, Brian spoke silently to the Lord. "Help me to trust You for the outcome, no matter what."

HOW ABOUT YOU? How do you react when really hard things come into your life—perhaps loss of a loved one through death or divorce, perhaps an illness of your own? Do you get bitter and angry? Or do you remember that God has promised to go with His children through every difficult time? Trust Him to keep you—you're not alone! And remember that He never makes any mistakes. R.J.

TO MEMORIZE: *"When you pass through the waters, I will be with you; and through the rivers, they shall not overflow. When you walk through the fire, you shall not be burned, nor shall the flame scorch you"* Isaiah 43:2 (NKJV).

NOVEMBER

13

The Way You Look

FROM THE BIBLE:

"But the word of the Lord endures forever." Now this is the word which by the gospel was preached to you. . . . Therefore, laying aside all malice, all guile, hypocrisy, envy, and all evil speaking, as newborn babes, desire the pure milk of the word, that you may grow thereby, if indeed you have tasted that the Lord is gracious. Coming to Him as to a living stone, rejected indeed by men, but chosen by God and precious, you also, as living stones, are being built up a spiritual house, a holy priesthood, to offer up spiritual sacrifices acceptable to God through Jesus Christ.

1 Peter 1:25; 2:1-5, NKJV

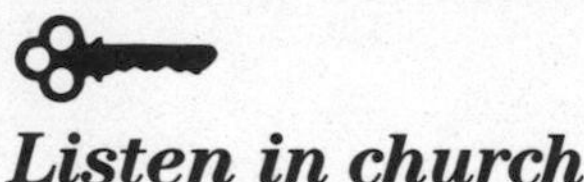

Listen in church

THE CHURCH SERVICE had just begun, and Paul thought of the long hour ahead. He pulled out his Sunday school paper without too much noise, and opened it to an exciting adventure story. Soon he was deep into the story and scarcely noticed what was going on around him. When he finished reading, he sighed and looked up toward the pulpit. Pastor Smith was sitting on the platform, reading the local newspaper!

Pastor Smith was noisily turning the pages of the newspaper now. When it was time to preach, he crumpled the paper loudly and stood up with a grin. "There's a reason for what I was doing," he announced. "Every Sunday I see boys and girls, and even a few adults, hide their faces behind Sunday school papers as soon as the sermon begins. I looked to you the way you look to me."

Pastor Smith was leaving the platform and coming down the aisle. He stopped beside Paul. "The way I looked to you is the way you look to me," he repeated loudly. He shook his finger in Paul's face. "The way I looked to you is the way you look to me!" Pastor Smith was shouting now.

Red-faced, Paul squirmed in his seat. "I'm sorry!"

"Paul! Paul! Wake up!" Someone was shaking him. Quickly he sat up, surprised to find himself in his own bed. "It's time to get up. You must have been dreaming," Mother said.

Paul jumped out of bed. "OK, Mom," he said rubbing his eyes. As he got ready for breakfast, he thought about the discussion at family devotions the evening before. Dad had talked about proper behavior in church. He had suggested that all of them, even the children, would be surprised at what they could learn if they'd try taking notes.

When they left for church that morning, Paul had a small notepad and pencil with him. He reached for it when the sermon began.

HOW ABOUT YOU? How do you look to your pastor? Are you bored in church? Do you complain that the sermon is hard to understand? Take a pad and pencil along next Sunday. Write down the Bible text, the title of the sermon, and one or two important sentences from the sermon. Then look at your notes several times during the week. You'll be surprised how much you can learn from the teaching of God's Word. J.G.

TO MEMORIZE: *"But the word of the Lord endures forever. Now this is the word which by the gospel was preached to you"* 1 Peter 1:25 (NKJV).

NOVEMBER

14

Straight Walls

FROM THE BIBLE:

This is what he showed me: The Lord was standing by a wall that had been built true to plumb, with a plumb line in his hand. And the Lord asked me, "What do you see, Amos?" "A plumb line," I replied. Then the Lord said, "Look, I am setting a plumb line among my people Israel; I will spare them no longer." Amos 7:7-8, NIV

Therefore, prepare your minds for action; be self-controlled; set your hope fully on the grace to be given you when Jesus Christ is revealed. As obedient children, do not conform to the evil desires you had when you lived in ignorance. But just as he who called you is holy, so be holy in all you do; for it is written: "Be holy, because I am holy." 1 Peter 1:13-16, NIV

Live by God's standards

ANDREA COULD hardly wait till Grandpa finished building the playhouse he was making for her. She watched as he raised his arm to the top of the wall he was erecting. In his hand he held a long cord with a weight attached at the bottom. "I know what that is," said Andrea proudly.

Grandpa was surprised. "You do?"

Andrea nodded. "It's a plumb line," she said. "The weight at the end makes the string hang straight down. When you hold it along the wall, you can tell if the wall is straight or not."

"Well, I'm impressed!" exclaimed Grandpa. "Where did a little girl like you learn about plumb lines?"

"In Sunday school," replied Andrea.

Grandpa was even more surprised. "In Sunday school?"

"Yep." Andrea nodded. "My teacher talked about the prophet Amos. She read from the Bible about how God showed him a plumb line and told him He would check the people to see whether or not they were living as they should. He was going to punish them if they didn't measure up to what they should be."

"Very good!" approved Grandpa. He wound up the cord. "Did you talk about the 'plumb line' God uses to measure His children today?"

"My teacher said God tells us in the Bible that He expects us to live godly lives—to be like Him," replied Andrea. "That's hard."

"Yes, it is," agreed Grandpa. "His standard for us is to be holy, just as He is holy. We can't do it without His help. I'm very thankful that He's willing to forgive us when we ask Him and to give us the help we need." He smiled at Andrea. "When your playhouse is finished, would you like a plumb line to hang on one of your walls as a reminder of God's standard for your behavior?"

Andrea nodded. "I'll decorate the weight on the end," she said eagerly. "Can I start now?"

HOW ABOUT YOU? Are you aware of God's standard for Christians? Maybe you think you're better than your neighbors or than other kids in your class. Perhaps you think you behave better than other Christians you know. But God isn't comparing you to any of them. He isn't comparing you to your parents, teachers, or pastor. His standard is Himself. Ask Him to help you measure up and be the person He wants you to be. H.M.

TO MEMORIZE: *"Be holy, because I am holy"* 1 Peter 1:16 (NIV).

NOVEMBER

15

Staying Clean

FROM THE BIBLE:

Don't be teamed with those who do not love the Lord, for what do the people of God have in common with the people of sin? How can light live with darkness? And what harmony can there be between Christ and the devil? How can a Christian be a partner with one who doesn't believe? And what union can there be between God's temple and idols? For you are God's temple, the home of the living God, and God has said of you, "I will live in them and walk among them, and I will be their God and they shall be my people." That is why the Lord has said, "Leave them; separate yourselves from them; don't touch their filthy things, and I will welcome you, and be a Father to you, and you will be my sons and daughters." . . . Having such great promises as these, dear friends, let us turn away from everything wrong, whether of body or spirit, and purify ourselves, living in the wholesome fear of God, giving ourselves to him alone.

2 Corinthians 6:14-18; 7:1, TLB

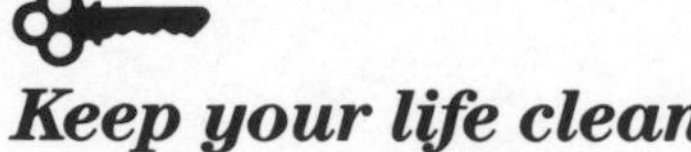

Keep your life clean

"BUT I DON'T SEE how it will hurt me to go to one party!" Marla continued her argument.

Mother sighed. "I repeat: Patti and her friends go places Christians should not go. They have bad habits. Their language is foul—"

"But how can I win them to the Lord if I don't run around with them?" interrupted Marla.

"Being friendly is one thing, Marla. Being best friends is another." Mother looked at the clock. "Call the twins in from play."

Minutes later Marla and the young twins came into the kitchen. "Oh no! Look at you!" Mother scolded the twins. "You had a bath before your naps, and now you're filthy already!"

"We played with Buffy." Shawn grinned.

"Buffy was dirty. He rolled over and over in the mud," Shelly explained. Mother groaned. "You clean Shelly, Marla. I'll take Shawn."

Later at the dinner table Marla asked Dad if she could go to the party at Patti's house. Dad raised one eyebrow. "Is Patti the girl who was over here last week? The one with the loud mouth who was carrying the blaring transistor radio?"

Marla nodded. "She's OK, Dad. Maybe I can win her to the Lord."

"Marla, when the twins went out to play, they were clean. Why didn't they get Buffy clean?" Dad asked.

Marla shrugged. "How should I know?"

"They didn't get him clean because dirt rubs off, not cleanliness. Instead of getting their puppy clean, he got them dirty," Dad said. "We want you to win Patti and her friends to the Lord, but you cannot do it by 'playing in the dirt' with them. You cannot influence Patti by doing what she does or going where she goes. Your life needs to be different—a clean, godly life."

"It's so easy to get dirty, but it takes work to stay clean," Mother added, as she stood up. "Now how about helping me? It even takes work to keep the dishes clean."

HOW ABOUT YOU? Do you try to witness by going along with the crowd? That is not God's way. He says to come out from among them and be separate. You witness best by showing how good it is to be a Christian. B.W.

TO MEMORIZE: *"Let us turn away from everything wrong, whether of body or spirit, and purify ourselves, living in the wholesome fear of God, giving ourselves to him alone"* 2 Corinthians 7:1 (TLB).

NOVEMBER

16

The Sample

FROM THE BIBLE:

For when we brought you the Good News, it was not just meaningless chatter to you; no, you listened with great interest. What we told you produced a powerful effect upon you, for the Holy Spirit gave you great and full assurance that what we said was true. And you know how our very lives were further proof to you of the truth of our message. So you became our followers and the Lord's; for you received our message with joy from the Holy Spirit in spite of the trials and sorrows it brought you. Then you yourselves became an example to all the other Christians in Greece. And now the Word of the Lord has spread out from you to others everywhere, far beyond your boundaries, for wherever we go we find people telling us about your remarkable faith in God. We don't need to tell them about it, for they keep telling us about the wonderful welcome you gave us, and how you turned away from your idols to God so that now the living and true God only is your Master.

1 Thessalonians 1:5-9, TLB

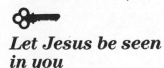

Let Jesus be seen in you

"CAN I GO to the store with you, Mom?" asked Larry. "You need me along to make sure you get the right cereal."

Mother laughed. "Come along," she agreed.

Shortly after arriving at the store, they met Chad, a classmate of Larry's. "Hey, Larry," called Chad, "my mom says I can go to Sunday school with you tomorrow."

"Oh, great!" exclaimed Larry. "It starts at nine-thirty."

"I'll be there. Want to know why?" Without waiting for an answer, Chad rushed on, his words tumbling over each other. "I know I've teased you about being a sissy because you go to Sunday school. But these last few weeks—well, what can I say? You helped me with my paper route and with my homework when I was sick, and you stood up for me when the guys gave me a rough time about striking out three times the other day. Anyway, if it's Jesus who makes you be this way, I want to know more about Him." Chad looked embarrassed after his long speech. "Gotta go," he mumbled, heading for the door. "See ya."

As Larry and his mother turned down another aisle, they saw a lady handing out samples of ice cream bars. "Yummy!" exclaimed Larry, taking a bite of the sample she handed him. "Let's get some of these, Mom."

"It is good," agreed Mother.

"How can the store afford to give away so much ice cream?" asked Larry as they approached the checkout counter. "Look at all the people getting samples now."

Mother smiled. "The samples cause people to want the product, and the store will sell lots of ice cream bars today," she explained. "You know, Larry, this reminds me of you."

"Me?" asked Larry. "What do you mean?"

"You've been a 'sample' Christian," said Mother. "Do you remember what Chad said when we met him? Your life gave Chad a taste of what it means to be a Christian, and now he's wanting more. You've been a good sample."

HOW ABOUT YOU? Do you know that you, too, can be a "sample" for Jesus? People around you need to know what a real Christian is like. They need to see Jesus in you. Your words and actions should cause them to want to know Him. Be the kind of person that Jesus wants you to be. G.W.

TO MEMORIZE: *"In everything set them an example by doing what is good"* Titus 2:7 (NIV).

NOVEMBER

17

A Zoo Full of People

FROM THE BIBLE:

Evil words destroy. Godly skill rebuilds. The whole city celebrates a good man's success—and also the godless man's death. The good influence of godly citizens causes a city to prosper, but the moral decay of the wicked drives it downhill. To quarrel with a neighbor is foolish; a man with good sense holds his tongue. A gossip goes around spreading rumors, while a trustworthy man tries to quiet them.

Proverbs 11:9-13, TLB

Be careful with criticism

JOHNNY AND SUSIE were visiting the city zoo with their mother. "Look at that fat panda bear!" exclaimed Susie. "See how he waddles. Doesn't he remind you of someone?"

"Yeah—old Mrs. Thompkins." Johnny laughed. "And see those funny geese? Look how they strut around with their noses in the air. They remind me of Alice Hayes."

Then they stopped to look at a wide-eyed owl. "Oh, and here's my teacher, Miss Williams," he said. "You know how she looks with those big, thick glasses on."

"Here's an animal that reminds me of someone," Mother said.

Susie read the sign. "A vulture?" she asked. "Who does that remind you of, Mom?"

"Well, a vulture doesn't attack strong, healthy animals. He only preys on those that are sick or injured," explained Mother. "He reminds me of people who like to point out the faults of others, and criticize their weaknesses."

"I-I think I know who you mean," Susie stammered. "You're talking about us, aren't you?"

"That's right." Mother nodded. "I've noticed that you two have a tendency to be critical of others. When you concentrate on their weaknesses, you tend to be blind to their strengths—and also to your own faults."

"But it's not always wrong to tease people, is it?" asked Johnny.

"Not always." Mother smiled. "It's OK to tease once in a while if it's done in the right spirit, and if you're sure you're not hurting someone's feelings. If there's any doubt, don't do it."

"Those doves over there remind me of you, Mom. They're so soft and pretty," Susie said. "And they're so gentle, they wouldn't hurt a fly. We'll try to be more like them and like you, Mom."

"I guess it's not all bad to be like the animals," said Johnny, grinning, "but we'd better get out of this zoo before someone tries to put us in a cage!"

HOW ABOUT YOU? Do you enjoy making fun of others? Make sure that you're not hurting someone's feelings by pointing out their weaknesses. Don't be disrespectful, and remember, you have faults, too! S.K.

TO MEMORIZE: *"A kind man benefits himself, but a cruel man brings trouble on himself"* Proverbs 11:17 (NIV).

NOVEMBER

18

The Paper Route

FROM THE BIBLE:
Then the Lord rose up as though awakening from sleep, and like a mighty man aroused by wine, he routed his enemies and drove them back and sent them to eternal shame. But he rejected Joseph's family, the tribe of Ephraim, and chose the tribe of Judah—and Mount Zion which he loved. There he built his towering temple, solid and enduring as the heavens and the earth. He chose his servant David, taking him from feeding sheep, and from following the ewes with lambs; God presented David to his people as their shepherd and he cared for them with a true heart and skillful hands. Psalm 78:65-72, TLB

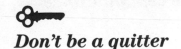

Don't be a quitter

TODD TOSSED his newspaper bag down on the kitchen floor. "I feel like quitting this paper route, Dad," he complained. "It's such a hassle if people aren't home when I go to collect. Besides, I've earned enough to buy the tennis shoes I wanted. I don't really need this job anymore."

Todd could tell by the look in Dad's eyes that he probably wasn't going to be allowed to quit. "You've only had the route for a couple of months, Todd," said Dad. "When your mother and I gave you permission to take this job, we all agreed you would keep it for a year."

"But I didn't know it would be so hard," protested Todd as he slumped onto a kitchen chair. "Besides, what good will it really do me?"

"That's hard to say," said Mother as she joined Dad and Todd at the table. "God uses many different experiences in our lives to develop qualities in us that He can use."

"That's right," agreed Dad. "I'm sure that you remember the story in the Bible about a shepherd boy who became a king."

"Sure. It was David," recalled Todd.

"Psalm 78 says that God took David from being a shepherd of sheep and placed him as a shepherd over his people,"Dad explained. "When he became the king of Israel, he was able to use the principles of leadership and trust in God which he had learned as a shepherd."

"Yeah, but what can I learn from being a paperboy?" asked Todd.

"Responsibility, for one thing," offered Mother. "God wants us to learn to finish what we start."

"You'll learn lots of other things, too," said Dad, smiling. "Just wait and see."

HOW ABOUT YOU? Do you feel like quitting when things get too hard? Maybe you can't see any reason to learn math or to keep your bedroom clean. Even jobs that don't seem to matter are part of God's plan for making you what He wants you to be. Keep at it! D.R.

TO MEMORIZE: *"Therefore, my dear brothers, stand firm. Let nothing move you. Always give yourselves fully to the work of the Lord"*
1 Corinthians 15:58 (NIV).

NOVEMBER

Braces

FROM THE BIBLE:

Young men, listen to me as you would to your father. Listen, and grow wise, for I speak the truth—don't turn away. For I, too, was once a son, tenderly loved by my mother as an only child, and the companion of my father. He told me never to forget his words. "If you follow them," he said, "you will have a long and happy life. Learn to be wise," he said, "and develop good judgment and common sense! I cannot overemphasize this point." . . . Listen, son of mine, to what I say. Listen carefully. Keep these thoughts ever in mind; let them penetrate deep within your heart.

Proverbs 4:1-5, 20-21, TLB

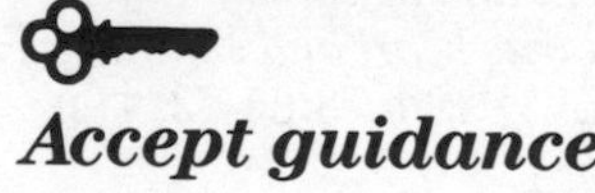

Accept guidance

JERRY PLOPPED down on the bed. He had been sent to his room without dessert! "So I forgot to take out the trash! So I was fifteen minutes late for dinner! So what?" he mumbled. "Every time I turn around someone is telling me to 'do this' or 'don't do that.' "

Later Dad came into Jerry's room. "Son, do you want to help me plant a peach tree?"

"I guess so," Jerry replied slowly.

After they dug a hole and planted the tree, Dad used stakes and twine to make several braces for it. "This will help it grow straight and tall," he explained.

As they walked back to the house, Dad asked, "How are you getting along with the braces on your teeth?"

Jerry shrugged. "All right, I guess. They aren't as bad as I expected. Six other kids in my class have braces on their teeth, too."

"They may be a bit uncomfortable now, but it will be worth it when your teeth are straight," Dad assured him. Then he added thoughtfully, "We put braces on our trees and braces on our teeth."

"Brenda even has a brace on her back. Her spine is curved," Jerry interrupted.

Dad nodded. "God has given us braces for our lives, too," he said. "He wants us to grow straight and strong, spiritually and morally. Right now, Jerry, there are braces around you. Your mother and I have set rules for you, and we make many of your decisions. We also give you certain responsibilities. Sometimes you resent these braces and pull against them, but some day when you're grown, you'll appreciate them."

Jerry raised his eyebrows. "I'd never thought of it like that," he said. After a few minutes he asked, "When are you going to take the braces off the peach tree?"

"When it's strong enough to stand straight and tall by itself," Dad said. Then he smiled and added, "And we'll remove your 'braces,' too, as soon as you prove you can be trusted to stand straight without our help."

HOW ABOUT YOU? Do you feel like every area of your life is controlled by someone else? Do you long for the day you can make your own decisions? Stop pulling at the braces. Thank God for them. Without them you might become a weak, crooked person unable to cope with the storms of life. B.W.

TO MEMORIZE: *"Our sons in their youth will be like well-nurtured plants"* Psalm 144:12 (NIV).

NOVEMBER

20

Star or Sun?

FROM THE BIBLE:

And so they arrived at Capernaum. When they were settled in the house where they were to stay he asked them, "What were you discussing out on the road?" But they were ashamed to answer, for they had been arguing about which of them was the greatest! He sat down and called them around him and said, "Anyone wanting to be the greatest must be the least—the servant of all!"
Mark 9:33-35, TLB

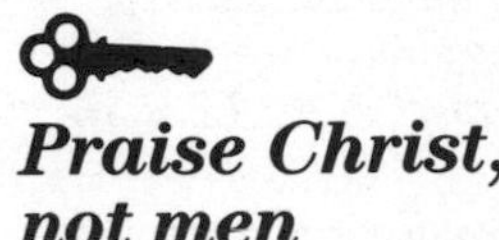

Praise Christ, not men

REVIVAL MEETINGS were being held at Sharon's church, and many people had been saved. Many others had rededicated their lives to God. This all bothered Sharon! You see, her dad was pastor of the church, but for some time nobody had been saved. Then the special evangelist came, and lots of the people to whom her dad had preached every week accepted Jesus under this new man's ministry.

Sharon's father wondered what was bothering her. "You seem awfully quiet lately, honey. Don't you like Reverend Henderson?" he asked after the meeting one evening.

"Yes, but you're every bit as good as he is, Dad!" Sharon responded. "Now all these people are getting right with God under his preaching, and he's getting all the credit. It's not fair!"

Dad was quiet for a moment, then asked her to come with him outdoors. "Now, which star is the brightest in the sky?" he asked.

Sharon gazed upward. "That one up there is," she decided. "Or . . . no, maybe that one way over there. Or is it . . . I don't know! Why do you ask Dad?"

He smiled. "It's hard to decide, isn't it? Now think in the morning when the sun comes up, which star will be the brightest?"

"Well, I don't know," she began. Then she thought of something. "It won't make any difference because the sun is the brightest of all!"

"Exactly," said Dad, "and it's that way in the ministry, too. We sometimes try to decide which preacher is the best, but it doesn't make any difference. When Jesus, God's Son, is preached, He is the best and brightest of all."

HOW ABOUT YOU? Do you think one pastor is better than another because he seems to lead more people to the Lord? Do you think a missionary must not be any good unless he sends back reports of many people being saved? Or maybe you have witnessed to somebody yourself and then thought it was unfair because another person led him or her to Jesus. Be careful Remember that we should not worry who will be greatest in God's kingdom. Jesus will be the greatest of all! R.P.

TO MEMORIZE: *"So neither he who plants nor he who waters is anything, but only God, who makes things grow"* 1 Corinthians 3:7 (NIV).

NOVEMBER

21

Both Glad and Sad

FROM THE BIBLE:

The law of the Lord is perfect,
reviving the soul.
The statutes of the Lord are trustworthy,
making wise the simple.
The precepts of the Lord are right,
giving joy to the heart.
The commands of the Lord are radiant,
giving light to the eyes.
The fear of the Lord is pure,
enduring forever.
The ordinances of the Lord are sure
and altogether righteous.
They are more precious than gold,
than much pure gold;
they are sweeter than honey,
than honey from the comb.
By them is your servant warned;
in keeping them there is great reward.

Psalm 19:7-11, NIV

Memorize God's Word

AS THE MARTIN family gathered for devotions, Dad smiled at Michelle. "I believe it's your turn to say today's Bible verse first."

"More to be desired are they than gold, yea, than much fine gold: sweeter also than honey and the honeycomb," Michelle quoted. "It's found in Psalm 19, verse ten."

"Very good," declared Dad. "Now it's your turn, Aaron."

"More to be . . . uhhh . . . more to be . . . uhhh," Aaron stammered. "I don't know it! I haven't had time to think about it. I don't know why we have to memorize a verse every day anyway!"

"Aaron! You are talking about the Word of God!" Mother was shocked.

"I used to feel the same way when my mother insisted that I memorize the Word of God," Dad said.

"Then why make me memorize it?" Aaron demanded.

"Because I'm older and wiser now," Dad replied. "Let me tell you a little parable I read the other day.

"A young man was walking down a country road when he met a strange-looking old man. After they exchanged greetings, the old man said, 'Pick up some of these stones beside the road and put them in your pocket, and tomorrow you will be both glad and sad.' Curious as to how that could be, the young man picked up a few stones and put them in his pocket. Then he bid the old man a good day. The next day when the young man reached into his pocket, he discovered the stones had turned into precious jewels. There were diamonds, rubies, and emeralds. And so the young man was both glad and sad—glad for the jewels, sad he had not picked up more stones."

Mother nodded. "I like that parable. Learning Bible verses may seem like unnecessary weight to you now, Aaron, but every verse you learn will one day become a precious jewel to you. You will only be sorry you did not learn more."

HOW ABOUT YOU? Perhaps you have not realized the importance of memorizing God's Word. As you learn each verse, you're gaining something very valuable. Do you memorize a Bible verse a day? If not, start today to collect "jewels" from God's Word. B.W.

TO MEMORIZE: *"They are more precious than gold, than much pure gold; they are sweeter than honey, than honey from the comb"* Psalm 19:10 (NIV).

NOVEMBER

22

Thanks for Food Stamps

FROM THE BIBLE:
Shout with joy before the Lord, O earth! Obey him gladly; come before him, singing with joy. Try to realize what this means—the Lord is God! He made us—we are his people, the sheep of his pasture. Go through his open gates with great thanksgiving; enter his courts with praise. Give thanks to him and bless his name. For the Lord is always good. He is always loving and kind, and his faithfulness goes on and on to each succeeding generation. Psalm 100, TLB

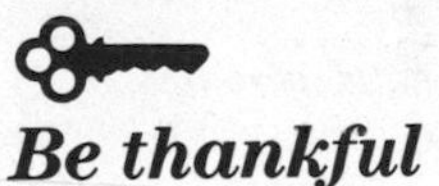

Be thankful

"ALICIA, WOULD YOU go to the grocery store for me?" Mother asked. "We need bread and milk." Mother handed Alicia a book of food stamps. "And don't forget to . . ." She stopped. A look of disgust mingled with anger had covered Alicia's face. "What's the matter?"

"I'm not going to buy anything with those stupid food stamps!" Tears rolled down Alicia's cheeks. "I hate them!"

Mother sighed. "But, honey, you should be thankful we have food stamps. We won't have to use them long, just until I can get a job."

"But it's so humiliating!" Alicia wailed. "Oh, why did Daddy have to have that accident?"

Mother put her arm around Alicia. "This hasn't been easy for any of us, but we can learn from this experience."

"Learn what?" Alicia asked.

"Well, I've learned to be more compassionate," said Mother. "I remember that when things were going well and we had plenty, I often judged those who had less. I even thought they were lazy."

"They probably say that about us now," Alicia sobbed.

Mother sighed. "Perhaps a few people do, but most of them understand and care," she said. "I've also been humbled by this experience. I didn't realize I was so proud. Now I just thank the Lord for these food stamps."

Alicia wiped her eyes and hugged her mother. "I don't like shopping with them, but I will."

Later, Alicia burst into the kitchen, her eyes shining. "Guess what, Mom? As I was paying for the groceries, Mr. Bryant asked if you were still looking for a job. He needs a checker and wants you to call right away."

As Mother picked up the phone, she quoted, " 'But my God shall supply all your needs.' Thank the Lord."

HOW ABOUT YOU? Are you ever ashamed that your family has less than others? Instead of complaining about what you don't have, be thankful for what you do have. God cannot bless an unthankful spirit. But when you thank Him. your blessings will start to multiply. Try it today. B.W.

TO MEMORIZE: *"And my God will meet all your needs according to his glorious riches in Christ Jesus"* Philippians 4:19 (NIV).

NOVEMBER

23

Two Thanksgivings

FROM THE BIBLE:

I will bless the Lord at all times;
His praise shall continually be in my mouth.
My soul shall make its boast in the Lord;
The humble shall hear of it and be glad.
Oh, magnify the Lord with me,
And let us exalt His name together.
I sought the Lord, and He heard me,
And delivered me from all my fears.
They looked to Him and were radiant,
And their faces were not ashamed.
This poor man cried out, and the Lord heard him,
And saved him out of all his troubles.
The angel of the Lord encamps all around those who fear Him,
And delivers them.
Oh, taste and see that the Lord is good;
Blessed is the man who trusts in Him!

Psalm 34:1-8, NKJV

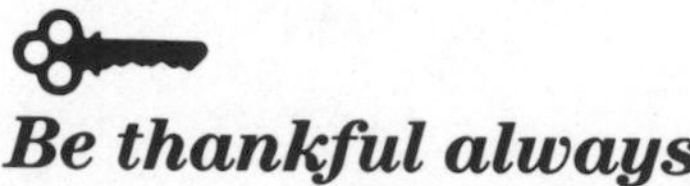

Be thankful always

THANKSGIVING was a joyful time for the Donnelly family. Grandpa and Grandma always came over, and after dinner Grandpa would tell stories. He cleared his throat. "Well, Thanksgiving is a special time for us, but let me tell you about the first two Thanksgivings."

"Two?" the children chorused.

"Yes, the first two." Grandpa nodded. "The second Thanksgiving had a lot of meaning for the Pilgrims. You see, at the first one there was plenty of food due to good weather and a big harvest. The Pilgrims and Indians gathered around and thanked God for their good year. I read that one Indian, named Quadequina, brought deerskin bags full of popping corn, and it filled several bushel baskets when popped."

"Was that the first time the Pilgrims ever ate popcorn?" six-year-old Andrew asked.

"I would think so," chuckled Grandpa. "Their eyes must have really opened wide when those white kernels jumped out of the hot pan." The children laughed while Grandpa shifted in the chair. "The second Thanksgiving was different. It seems they had had a bad year. Many people had died, and others faced possible starvation because of poor crops. But do you know what they did? They set aside a time for Thanksgiving anyway!"

"They were probably thankful just to be alive," suggested Andrew.

"Perhaps," agreed Grandpa, "and they knew that even though their circumstances had changed, God had not! He still loved and cared for them even though it had been a long, hard year." Grandpa paused and looked at the boys. "When we face difficult times, thankfulness doesn't always come easily. We need to recognize that God's hand is still on our lives."

"And remember what happened at the second Thanksgiving," declared Curt.

HOW ABOUT YOU? Have you had a good year with lots of wonderful things happening? Thank God for that. Has it been a hard year with many things going wrong? Thank God anyway. Thank Him for His love, for providing salvation, for the roof over your head, the air you breathe, the land you live in. Look around you, and you'll find many more things for which to thank Him. J.G.

TO MEMORIZE: *"I will bless the* LORD *at all times: His praise shall continually be in my mouth."* Psalm 34:1 (NKJV).

NOVEMBER

24

In God's Sight

FROM THE BIBLE:

Praise the Lord, O my soul;
all my inmost being, praise
his holy name.
Praise the Lord, O my soul,
and forget not all his
benefits—
who forgives all your sins
and heals all your diseases,
who redeems your life from the
pit
and crowns you with love and
compassion,
who satisfies your desires with
good things
so that your youth is renewed
like the eagle's.
The Lord works righteousness
and justice for all the
oppressed.
He made known his ways to
Moses,
his deeds to the people of
Israel:
The Lord is compassionate and
gracious,
slow to anger, abounding in
love.

Psalm 103:1-8, NIV

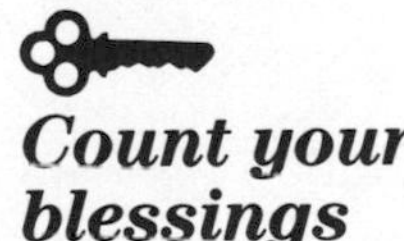

Count your blessings

KAREN SQUEALED with joy as her dad drove into the parking lot at the ice cream store. "Oh, goody! I want a hot fudge sundae with nuts."

Mother shook her head. "It's too near dinner. A single dip cone will be enough."

Karen's mouth tightened. "I don't see why—"

"You heard your mother," interrupted Dad, opening his door. "What flavor do you want?"

"I guess chocolate almond," Karen replied gruffly. As soon as her dad was out of hearing, she spoke again. "I don't see how it would hurt me to have a hot fudge—"

"Karen, how do you suppose you look to God right now?" asked Mother. Karen's mouth fell open. She shrugged, and Mother continued. "Here you sit in a comfortable car, wearing nice, clean clothes. Only three hours ago you had a delicious lunch. Yet you're pouting because you only get one dip of ice cream. Across the ocean—"

"Oh, Mom," interrupted Karen. "I hope you aren't going to start that old stuff about the starving kids in India or some other foreign country!"

"Yes, I am," replied Mother. "At the same time God sees you, He also sees another ten-year-old shivering in the cold, clawing through a garbage can for a bite to eat."

"But I can't do anything about that."

"Remember how you threw a fit last Sunday because Marsha had a new dress and you didn't?" Mother asked. "At the same time God saw you standing before your stuffed closet fussing for a new dress, He saw another girl. She was putting on a faded, patched dress, but she was smiling as she got ready for church."

"Awwww, Mom, you don't know that," protested Karen. "You're just imagining it."

"No, I am not. It happens every day somewhere," Mother replied. "And while you complain about your toys and always ask for more and better, many children around the world are playing with tin cans and rocks and sticks."

Karen looked out the window. She didn't want to see the pictures her mother was painting with words, but she saw them anyway.

HOW ABOUT YOU? How does God see you at this Thanksgiving time? Are you a "spoiled brat" or a thankful child? This would be a good time to count your blessings. B.W.

TO MEMORIZE: *"Praise the Lord, O my soul, and forget not all his benefits"* Psalm 103:2 (NIV).

NOVEMBER

25

Bad Advice

FROM THE BIBLE:
Let me see your kindness to me in the morning, for I am trusting you. Show me where to walk, for my prayer is sincere. Save me from my enemies. O Lord, I run to you to hide me. Help me to do your will, for you are my God. Lead me in good paths, for your Spirit is good.
Psalm 143:8-10, TLB

Take God's advice

LYNN HAD A TOUGH decision to make. Should she go on her class hayride, or should she go to the church party being held the same night? She had prayed about it and really knew in her heart that she should support her church youth group. But the hayride would be Lynn's first class party since attending her new school. She really wanted to go! *I know,* she thought. *I'll ask Connie what she thinks.*

"I think you should go on the hayride," advised her older sister Connie. "The kids might think you're a snob if you don't show up. Besides, you might be able to be a testimony for the Lord there." Lynn was easily convinced. She would go to the school party.

The hayride was rowdy from the start. The kids were keyed up, and some of them carried things too far, roughly pushing each other off the wagon as it moved slowly down the dark country road. One time Lynn fell with a thump to the road. In spite of a bruised knee, she had to jump up quickly and run hard to catch up and climb back on the wagon. She was surprised that the parents who were along to supervise didn't do more to calm things down. Fun was fun, but this was just too rough!

"Hey, look!" shouted one of the boys as he flicked a piece of gravel off his finger. "I have a lethal weapon!" Before anyone could stop them, several kids began pelting each other with stones from the roadside. *Ping!* A stone hit Lynn's glasses, shattering them.

Much later Lynn lay in bed, giving careful thought to the past evening. *Oh, why did I ever ask for Connie's advice,* she thought, *when I knew all the time what the Lord wanted me to do!* Before going to sleep she silently asked Him to forgive her and to help her obey Him.

HOW ABOUT YOU? Has there ever been a time when you knew what *God* wanted you to do, but you kept hoping someone would advise you to do what *you* really wanted to do? Do you know what God wants you to do about that student who doesn't seem to have friends? About showing kindness to that older person? About missing church on Sunday? When you know God's will, do it. Then you can put your name in the place of Ezra's in today's verse. P.R.

TO MEMORIZE: *"For Ezra had prepared his heart to seek the law of the LORD, and to do it"*
Ezra 7:10 (NKJV).

NOVEMBER

26

Who Needs Brothers?

FROM THE BIBLE:
Then his brothers came and fell down before him and said, "We are your slaves." But Joseph told them, "Don't be afraid of me. Am I God, to judge and punish you? As far as I am concerned, God turned into good what you meant for evil, for he brought me to this high position I have today so that I could save the lives of many people. No, don't be afraid. Indeed, I myself will take care of you and your families." And he spoke very kindly to them, reassuring them.
Genesis 50:18-21, TLB

Appreciate brothers and sisters

AS DAD BEGAN to read the Bible during family devotions one morning, Kendra felt a sharp poke under the table. Glaring at her brother, she whispered, "Knock it off, Kyle."

"A friend loveth at all times," Dad read from the book of Proverbs, "and a brother is born for adversity—or hard times."

"You can say that again!" Kendra agreed. "Brothers are good for nothing but giving you a hard time."

"Hold it!" said Dad with a smile. "That's not what the verse is saying. By 'hard times' it means—well, like the time you fell down the stairs, Kendra, and your brother felt so bad he cried harder than you."

"And when you dropped your notebook yesterday," Mother reminded Kendra, "who ran after the papers that went blowing away?"

"Yeah!" Kyle piped up, poking his sister again. "I ran halfway down the street after 'em!"

"And you, young man," Dad continued, catching his son by surprise, "who helped you finish raking the leaves so you could go to the zoo with your friend, Todd?"

"Uh, Kendra," mumbled Kyle. Then he quickly added, "But that verse isn't talking about sisters."

"Oh, yes, it is," said Dad. "It's referring to brothers and sisters. The phrase 'a brother is born for adversity' means that God gave us brothers and sisters—not to bring us trouble—but to be there when trouble comes. You may have some fights at times, we all know that, but you should learn to appreciate each other in spite of those. And thank the Lord for one another as well."

HOW ABOUT YOU? Have you learned to appreciate the brothers or sisters God has given you? Today's Scripture gives the example of Joseph's love for his brothers, even after they had mistreated him. Love your brothers and sisters, and thank God often for them. Did you know He gave them to you to help you through hard times? They're an important part of your life. Be a good brother or sister to them—help them when they need you. S.N.

TO MEMORIZE: *"A brother is born for adversity"* Proverbs 17:17 (NKJV).

NOVEMBER

27

The Bumpy Road

FROM THE BIBLE:

A highway shall be there, and a road, and it shall be called the Highway of Holiness. The unclean shall not pass over it, but it shall be for others. Whoever walks the road, although a fool, shall not go astray. No lion shall be there, nor shall any ravenous beast go up on it; it shall not be found there. But the redeemed shall walk there, And the ransomed of the Lord shall return, and come to Zion with singing, with everlasting joy on their heads. They shall obtain joy and gladness, and sorrow and sighing shall flee away.
Isaiah 35:8-10, NKJV

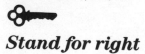

Stand for right

JOE SHUT the front door behind him, but he could not shut out the taunts ringing in his head. He walked slowly down the hall to the room where he heard the whir of his mother's sewing machine. "Did you have a good day, Joe?" asked Mother. Tears filled Joe's eyes, and he shook his head fiercely. Mother pointed at a chair beside the sewing machine. "Sit down and tell me about it."

Joe gulped and sat down. "At lunch some of the guys started telling jokes. Stan told a dirty joke, and I got up and left."

"Good for you," Mother said.

Joe snorted. "Oh, yeah, good for me! Good old Holy Joe! That's what they called me the rest of the day."

"Doing the right thing is not always easy," Mother started taking pins out of a piece of material.

Joe sniffed and ran his thumbnail across a piece of material beside him. He changed the subject. "What are you making?"

"A corduroy jacket for Kim," his mother replied.

"Corduroy sure is bumpy." Joe remembered something. "Did you know they used to make corduroy roads?" Mother shook her head. "Well, they did," Joe continued. "They were made out of logs laid side by side. Imagine riding in a wagon or stage coach down a corduroy road. Bump-bump-bumpity-bump."

As Mother put down her scissors, she chuckled. "It would be rough," she agreed. After a moment she added, "Part of the highway to heaven must be corduroy."

Joe nodded slowly. "It sure must be. I guess I hit a corduroy stretch today. It was pretty bumpy."

"But you made it across." Mother smiled. "You didn't let the rough spots wreck you."

Joe stood up and grinned. "There are worse things to be called that 'Holy Joe! I think I'll go ride my bike a while. There's one stretch of Oak Street that's almost as bumpy as a corduroy road. It's kinda fun to ride on it."

HOW ABOUT YOU? Have you run into some rough roads lately? Maybe you had to go down a different road from your friends. Maybe you had to say no or take a stand against some things they were doing. Living a Christian life is not always easy, but it is always best. B.W.

TO MEMORIZE: *"A highway shall be there, . . . and it shall be called the Highway of Holiness"* Isaiah 35:8 (NKJV).

NOVEMBER

28

Swaying Castle

FROM THE BIBLE:
A truthful witness gives honest testimony, but a false witness tells lies. Reckless words pierce like a sword, but the tongue of the wise brings healing. Truthful lips endure forever, but a lying tongue lasts only a moment. There is deceit in the hearts of those who plot evil, but joy for those who promote peace. No harm befalls the righteous, but the wicked have their fill of trouble. The Lord detests lying lips, but he delights in men who are truthful.
Proverbs 12:17-22, NIV

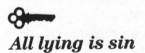

All lying is sin

"THERE!" PETE exclaimed as he finished pounding a nail. "This is the best tree house I've ever seen! I can hardly wait to sleep here. We'll be rocked to sleep, the way this tree sways. It's like being in a swaying castle!"

Vern nodded in agreement. "Let's ask if we can sleep out here tonight," he suggested.

"I know my dad won't let me," said Pete. "He wants to check it out first to be sure it's safe, and I know he won't have time to do that today."

"My dad said the same thing," Vern admitted. "Hey! I know! Let's each ask our folks for permission to spend the night with each other. They'll think we're at each other's houses, but we'll really be sleeping in the tree house."

"I don't know . . ." Pete sounded doubtful, but with Vern's coaxing, he agreed to try it.

Their plan worked, but in the middle of the night they were awakened by a loud crack of thunder! "Hey! I'm getting wet!" yelled Pete. "It's pouring, and the roof is leaking. Come on! Let's get over to my house."

The storm had awakened Pete's parents, too, and they were very surprised when the boys stumbled into the kitchen. "Where have you been? How come you were out in this storm?" Pete's dad asked.

"We . . . ah . . . we were sleeping in the tree house, Dad," answered Pete.

"The tree house? You asked if you could stay at Vern's house overnight."

"Not really," replied Pete. "I just asked if I could spend the night with Vern."

"I see," said Dad. "You used the correct words, but what about your intentions? Since you deceived us in order to sleep in the tree house, you were really disobeying. Do you both see that you were actually lying?"

"Yes," admitted the boys together, and both apologized.

"I'm thankful God protected you tonight," said Dad, "but I'm afraid the tree house will be off-limits until you show us that we can trust you again."

HOW ABOUT YOU? Are you guilty of giving false impressions or of telling "fibs" or "white lies"? God hates every form of lying and deception. He is pleased only when our intentions as well as our words are pure. A.L.

TO MEMORIZE: *"The LORD detests lying lips, but he delights in men who are truthful"*
Proverbs 12:22 (NIV).

NOVEMBER

29

Just a Baby

FROM THE BIBLE:

But, beloved, we are confident of better things concerning you, yes, things that accompany salvation, though we speak in this manner. For God is not unjust to forget your work and labor of love which you have shown toward His name, in that you have ministered to the saints, and do minister. And we desire that each one of you show the same diligence to the full assurance of hope until the end, that you do not become sluggish, but imitate those who through faith and patience inherit the promises.

Hebrews 6:9-12, NKJV

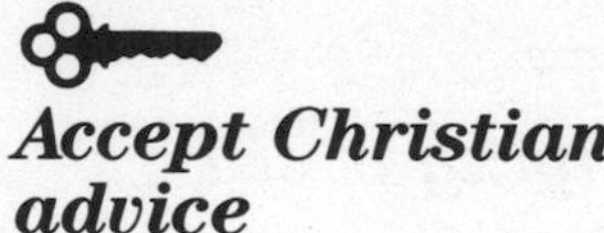

Accept Christian advice

TAMI'S LITTLE brother spied a glittering piece of broken glass on the ground. He picked it up and was about to put it into his mouth when Tami stopped him. Immediately young Troy let out a loud scream that brought Mother out to see what was happening. "I just took this piece of glass away from him," Tami explained.

Mother picked up the little boy. "I'm glad you were watching him," she said to Tami. "You probably saved him from being cut very badly."

Tami shrugged her shoulders. "Yeah, but Troy sure didn't appreciate it. He thought I was being mean."

"That's because he's just a baby," Mother explained, "and babies don't always understand that you're helping them."

Later Tami talked to her mother about a friend. "Karry is mad at me," she said. "At first she was mad because her mom won't let her watch some of the TV shows they used to watch before they were Christians. I agreed with her mom, so now Karry's mad at me, too."

"That's too bad," sympathized Mother. "Try to be patient with her. She's only a baby Christian, you know, and sometimes baby Christians react exactly as Troy did when you took the broken glass away. When someone tries to help them and protect them from dangerous things, they resist and act up because they are not being allowed to live as they want. They often argue and resent guidance from older Christians."

When Tami thought about it, she knew she had been like that, too. She had often thought she knew how to live the Christian life without interference from others, especially from her parents. She hoped she didn't still act that way! She determined in her heart to be more patient with Karry and to not resist or resent the help that older Christians offered to her.

HOW ABOUT YOU? Do you accept the advice and help that is offered to you by your parents? Your pastor? Your Sunday school teacher? They are more experienced in life and know more than you do about the dangers and tricks of Satan. Be open to their guidance. R.J.

TO MEMORIZE: *"Imitate those who through faith and patience inherit the promises"* Hebrews 6:12 (NKJV).

NOVEMBER

30

Leftovers

FROM THE BIBLE:

"A son honors his father, a servant honors his master. I am your Father and Master, yet you don't honor me, O priests, but you despise my name." "Who? Us?" you say. "When did we ever despise your name?" "When you offer polluted sacrifices on my altar." "Polluted sacrifices? When have we ever done a thing like that?" "Every time you say, 'Don't bother bringing anything very valuable to offer to God!' You tell the people, 'Lame animals are all right to offer on the altar of the Lord—yes, even the sick and the blind ones.' And you claim this isn't evil? Try it on your governor sometime—give him gifts like that—and see how pleased he is! 'God have mercy on us,' you recite; 'God be gracious to us!' But when you bring that kind of gift, why should he show you any favor at all? Oh, to find one priest among you who would shut the doors and refuse this kind of sacrifice. I have no pleasure in you," says the Lord of Hosts, "and I will not accept your offerings."

Malachi 1:6-10, TLB

"NOT LEFTOVERS tonight," grumbled Chad as he slid into his chair. "Ugh!"

Mother frowned, and Dad spoke sternly. "That's enough, Chad! Now, let's give thanks."

Chad and Staci picked at their food until Mother asked, "Who wants peach cobbler?"

"I do," the children replied in unison. Staci mumbled to Chad, "At least there's one leftover thing that's good."

As Mother dished out the cobbler, she asked, "What time are we having family devotions, Don?"

"I don't have time this evening," Staci said quickly. "I have a pile of homework."

"And I have to go to Phil's house," Chad added.

"I need to do some research on the Morgan case," Dad said. "Maybe we should skip devotions tonight."

"Yeah," agreed both of the children.

"We skipped devotions last night and the night before," Mother reminded them. "We've been giving God our leftover time . . . that is, when we have any time left over."

Dad raised his eyebrows. "I hadn't thought of that," he admitted, "but you're right. We are guilty—especially me, and I'm sorry."

"I wonder if God likes leftovers any better than we do," said Chad.

"Probably not," replied Mother. "In fact, I'm sure He doesn't. He often rebuked Israel for bringing Him leftover sacrifices."

Dad stood up. "Looks like we need to rearrange our schedule . . . starting right now. Get your Bibles. Family devotions begin in the living room in five minutes."

HOW ABOUT YOU? Do you read your Bible and pray only when you have time? Are you giving God your leftovers? He wants the "firstfruits"—not the "leftovers"—of your time and talents, as well as your money. Make up your mind right now to start putting God first in all things. B.W.

TO MEMORIZE: *"Honor the LORD with your possessions, and with the firstfruits of all your increase"* Proverbs 3:9 (NKJV).

Put God first

DECEMBER

1

The Trickster

FROM THE BIBLE:

About four o'clock in the morning Jesus came to them, walking on the water! They screamed in terror, for they thought he was a ghost. But Jesus immediately spoke to them, reassuring them. "Don't be afraid!" he said. Then Peter called to him: "Sir, if it is really you, tell me to come over to you, walking on the water." "All right," the Lord said, "come along!" So Peter went over the side of the boat and walked on the water toward Jesus. But when he looked around at the high waves, he was terrified and began to sink. "Save me, Lord!" he shouted. Instantly Jesus reached out his hand and rescued him. "O man of little faith," Jesus said. "Why did you doubt me?" And when they had climbed back into the boat, the wind stopped. The others sat there, awestruck. "You really are the Son of God!" they exclaimed.

Matthew 14:25-33, TLB

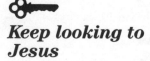

Keep looking to Jesus

"I CAN'T FIGURE out how magicians do those things," said Dave as he and Phil waited outside the library to see the magic show.

"Dave," Phil whispered excitedly, "I think I've got it figured out. Let's do the opposite of what he says! If he says to watch his hands, look at the object he's holding."

Sure enough, the boys were able to see one or two small movements of the magician which gave them clues as to how the tricks were done. But although they tried hard, they couldn't catch on to much of what he was doing. "I still think half the trick is getting the audience to look where you tell them to," said Phil as the boys walked home. "When he holds up his hands and says 'Look here,' it's hard not to do that."

That weekend the boys told their story to their Sunday school teacher. "That's interesting," said Mr. Pierce. "Do you remember the story of Peter walking on the water?"

"Yes," Dave answered. "When he stopped looking at Jesus and looked at the water, he started to sink."

"That's right," said Mr. Pierce. "Satan is a great trickster, you know. He loves to get our attention on anything except the Lord Jesus. If he can get us interested in the bad things he's doing in the world, or even in a good cause, he's happy—just so we don't put our attention on the Lord. Don't be fooled by his methods."

HOW ABOUT YOU? Do you worry so much about things going on in the world—wars, drugs, diseases—that you forget about Jesus Himself? Do you get so busy with schoolwork, a paper route, or even church activities that you don't have time to spend with the Lord? Remember, Satan is a deceiver. He likes you to stay so busy—even with wholesome activities—that you neglect to think about Jesus. Keep your eyes "fixed on Jesus." Read God's Word, pray, think often about your Lord. C.R.

TO MEMORIZE: *"Looking unto Jesus, the author and finisher of our faith"* Hebrews 12:2.

DECEMBER

Sour Lemons

FROM THE BIBLE:

Not that I was ever in need, for I have learned how to get along happily whether I have much or little. I know how to live on almost nothing or with everything. I have learned the secret of contentment in every situation, whether it be a full stomach or hunger, plenty or want; for I can do everything God asks me to with the help of Christ who gives me the strength and power. Philippians 4:11-13, TLB

Look for what's good

As MOTHER put warm, buttery popcorn into bowls, Peter scowled at his sister. "Hey, Mandy! Get out of my chair!" he ordered.

"You always get to sit by the window," replied Mandy. "I want to sit here for a change."

"It's my place," said Peter angrily, but Mandy just stuck out her tongue. "Dad! Make Mandy get out of my chair!" whined Peter, as he tugged at his sister's arm.

Dad and Mother looked at each other and sighed. "Don't you kids ever stop fighting?" asked Dad. "Just sit down over there, Peter, so we can enjoy our snack."

As they crunched their popcorn and sipped glasses of Mother's freshly squeezed lemonade, Dad said, "It seems to me you were fighting over chairs last night, too. Only then wasn't it Peter who wanted to sit in the chair Mandy usually has?" Mandy just shrugged, and Peter nodded sheepishly.

Mother smiled. "I think it's time you children learn to take a sour lemon and make lemonade."

"What do you mean, Mom?" asked Mandy curiously.

Dad laughed. "That's an old saying," he explained. "You see, this good lemonade we're enjoying started out as sour lemons. Mother didn't sit around moaning about how sour they were. She took them and made something good out of them. And instead of complaining about what happens in your life, you should learn to make the best of every situation. Like the Apostle Paul said, we should be content in whatever state or situation we're in."

"Maybe we could say in whatever 'chair' I am," laughed Peter. "I guess I really don't mind sitting over here by the register sometimes. It's nice and warm."

"I like it, too," agreed Mandy, "but it's also nice to sit here by the window. It really doesn't matter that much, does it, Peter?"

"I'm glad that's settled." Mother smiled. "Now how about some more lemonade?"

HOW ABOUT YOU? Do you complain when you don't get what you want? The next time things don't go the way you want them to, stop and look for something good in the situation or do what you can to improve it. Give up your "sour" attitude and enjoy the lemonade! S.K.

TO MEMORIZE: *"Godliness with content is great gain"* 1 Timothy 6:6 (NIV).

DECEMBER

3

OK, So I Goofed

FROM THE BIBLE:

Blessed is he whose transgression is forgiven,
Whose sin is covered.
Blessed is the man to whom the Lord does not impute iniquity,
And in whose spirit there is no guile.
When I kept silent, my bones grew old
Through my groaning all the day long.
For day and night Your hand was heavy upon me;
My vitality was turned into the drought of summer.
Selah
I acknowledged my sin to You,
And my iniquity I have not hidden.
I said, "I will confess my transgressions to the Lord,"
And You forgave the iniquity of my sin.

Psalm 32:1-5, NKJV

All wrong is sin

DOUGLAS JONES did not like to admit that he was a sinner. Whenever he did something wrong, he would shrug his shoulders and say, "OK, so I goofed." One day after he had taken something from another boy's desk, he was ordered to report to the principal's office. When he got there, he saw his mother in the waiting area. "What are you doing here?" he asked, somewhat embarrassed.

"Mr. Sexton called this morning, telling me that you were in trouble again," she told him. "He thought I should be here when he talked with you."

Douglas squirmed as the school principal entered the room. After explaining what had happened, Mr. Sexton looked at Douglas. "I didn't mean to do anything wrong," Douglas told them. "I just goofed again."

Mrs. Jones turned to face the principal. "May I talk with Douglas alone? Just for a moment?"

Mr. Sexton nodded and left the room, closing the door behind him.

"Douglas," Mother said, "did you steal that toy car?"

"I borrowed it, sort of," mumbled the boy after a long silence. "I'll give it back."

"Taking what doesn't belong to you is stealing. What do you have to say for yourself?"

"I already said it," he retorted. "I goofed again."

"Goofed?" Mother asked. "You 'goof' quite often, don't you?" She was quiet for a long time. "You have a real problem, Son," she added finally. "You see, God loves us and promises that when we confess our sins He will cleanse and forgive us. But 'goofs'? Well, He doesn't say He'll wash away our goofs. I don't know what can be done about them. Are you sure they're not really sins?"

Douglas thought about his mother's words. He finally nodded. "I thought it wouldn't sound as bad if I said I goofed," he confessed.

Together they bowed their heads as Douglas admitted his sin and asked Jesus to forgive him. Then after talking with the principal, Douglas also went to tell the other boy he was sorry.

HOW ABOUT YOU? Do you try to cover your sinful actions by calling them something other than sin? You can't cover up sins by calling them "goofs." You do wrong things because you are a sinner. Only when you admit that and confess your sin to God, can you have forgiveness. R.J.

TO MEMORIZE: *"I acknowledge my sin to You, and my iniquity I have not hidden"* Psalm 32:5 (NKJV).

DECEMBER

The Circle

FROM THE BIBLE:

Lord, you have been our
dwelling place
throughout all generations.
Before the mountains were born
or you brought forth the earth
and the world,
from everlasting to everlasting
you are God.
You turn men back to dust,
saying, "Return to dust, O
sons of men."
For a thousand years in your
sight
are like a day that has just
gone by,
or like a watch in the night.
Psalm 90:1-4, NIV

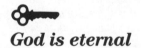

God is eternal

SEVEN-YEAR-OLD Becky was always full of questions—questions like: How many animals were on the ark? How did Jonah keep from drowning in the whale's tummy? How far away are the stars? Can we take a trip to one of them? One day she came to her mother with a real stumper. "Mom, who made God?"

"No one did," Mother answered.

"Then where did God come from?" asked Becky.

Mother shook her head, a bit perplexed as to just how to answer that. "God always was," she said. "I'm afraid I can't explain it so that you can understand. As you grow older, you'll understand it a bit better, but even then it will be hard. You see, our minds are not as great as God's mind, and there are some things we just can't understand. Some day when we get to heaven we'll understand it better. For now, we just have to accept the fact that God always existed."

"But He had to come from *somewhere*," insisted Becky.

Mother took off her wedding ring and handed it to Becky. "I want you to tell me where this ring starts and where it stops," she said.

Becky looked at the perfect circle. "But it doesn't start or stop," she replied. "It's just a circle that doesn't have a beginning or an ending."

"And that's like God, honey. God is eternal. He never had a beginning, and He has no ending." Mother put the ring on her finger as she continued, "You see, we think of our lives in minutes and days and weeks and years. But with God, there is no such thing as time. He is always the same—yesterday, today, and forever."

"Boy, that's really something to think about," Becky said.

Mother set a plate of cookies and a glass of milk on the table. "I think it's time you rested your brain from all those big questions and had some chocolate chip cookies and milk," she said with a smile.

HOW ABOUT YOU? Aren't you glad your God is so great that no human mind can fully understand Him? That's one of the things that makes Him God! Don't try too hard to understand how He could have no beginning. Accept the fact, and thank Him for being so great and so wonderful—and for loving you! C.V.M.

TO MEMORIZE: *"From everlasting to everlasting you are God"* Psalm 90:2 (NIV).

DECEMBER

5

The Whole Parade

FROM THE BIBLE:
Remember the former things, those of long ago; I am God, and there is no other; I am God, and there is none like me. I make known the end from the beginning, from ancient times, what is still to come. I say: My purpose will stand, and I will do all that I please. From the east I summon a bird of prey; from a far-off land, a man to fulfill my purpose. What I have said, that will I bring about; what I have planned, that will I do. Isaiah 46:9-11, NIV

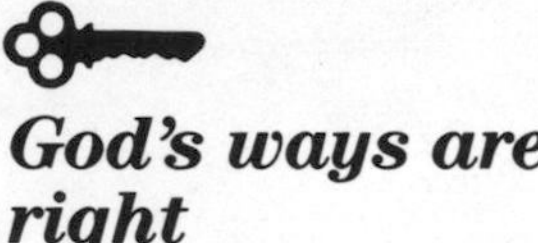

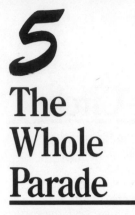

God's ways are right

"WHY, GOD?'" Jolene's heart cried out. Her baby brother, Scott, was adorable, but they had just learned he was deaf.

"Don't blame God, Jolene," Mother had said gently. "His ways are above our ways. We need to trust Him even when we can't understand."

But Jolene wanted to understand. After all, they were Christians. Wasn't God supposed to take care of them? How could her parents be so calm?

"Are you ready to go to the parade, Jolene?" Mother asked as she came into the family room one day. "If we don't hurry, we'll miss part of it." She held out her arms to the baby. "Come to Mother, darling," she said.

"I don't see why you talk to him, Mother. You know he can't hear you!" Jolene said harshly, more angry at herself than anyone else.

Mother sighed. "I've told you, Jolene. It's important that he sees our lips move and feels the vibration of our words. Now brush away the tears and angry thoughts. Let's have a good time. Scott will love the parade."

At the parade people were standing three deep in front of Jolene's family. She squatted down and peered through the legs in front of her. "It would be so much better if I could see it all together instead of one row at a time," she wailed. Dad handed Scott to Mother, and with a swoop, Jolene was on her father's shoulder. She clapped her hands. "Now I can see the whole parade," she said, grinning down at her dad.

All too soon the parade was over and they were on the way home. "Life is a lot like a parade," observed Dad, "and we're like children in the crowd. We can only see one day at a time. But God is above the crowd. He sees the whole parade—the past and the future as well as the present. We wonder why Scott is deaf, but that's because we only see the present. God knows why because He sees the whole picture."

Jolene squeezed her sleeping brother's hand. "I'll try to remember that, Dad," she promised.

HOW ABOUT YOU? Are you questioning God about something that happened in your life? God's ways are far above ours, and His ways are right. Trust Him. He'll take care of you and you can say, "I don't understand, but I believe." B.W.

TO MEMORIZE: *"Trust in the LORD with all your heart and lean not on your own understanding"* Proverbs 3:5 (NIV).

DECEMBER

The Booster Brother

FROM THE BIBLE:

Two can accomplish more than twice as much as one, for the results can be much better. If one falls, the other pulls him up; but if a man falls when he is alone, he's in trouble. Also, on a cold night, two under the same blanket gain warmth from each other, but how can one be warm alone? And one standing alone can be attacked and defeated, but two can stand back-to-back and conquer; three is even better, for a triple-braided cord is not easily broken.
Ecclesiastes 4:9-12, TLB

Help someone

"HELP ME put on my gloves, Kent." Davy struggled, trying to match fingers and glove openings.

Kent groaned. "You're in the first grade. You should be able to help yourself. Who puts your gloves on you after school?"

"My teacher helps me, and she doesn't fuss about it, either." Davy held his hand up to his big brother. "Will you pull me on my sled after school?"

Kent sighed. "Oh, all right."

"Are you boys ready to go to school?" Dad asked as he came into the hall pulling on his coat. "It's a little early, but the roads are a bit slick." He led the way outside and across the snow-packed yard.

As they started to get in the car, Mr. Gleason from next door came toward them. "Got a minute, John? I hate to bother you, but my car won't start. Could you give me a boost?"

"Sure," Dad replied. He backed the car out of the drive and pulled in beside Mr. Gleason's. They boys watched as they men raised the hoods of the cars and attached jumper cables to the batteries. Then Mr. Gleason got in his car and started it.

When the cables had been removed and they were on their way, Davy asked, "Why did you stretch those lines from our car to Mr. Gleason's?"

"We jumped some power from our battery to his. We gave him a boost," Dad explained.

As they pulled into the schoolyard, Kent turned to Dad. "I think I'll run over to Gramps' after school and shovel the walk for him."

"You gonna give Gramps a boost?" Davy asked.

"I guess you could say that," Kent replied.

"Like you gave me a boost with my gloves?" Davy continued. Kent grinned and nodded. "And like you're going to give me a boost on the sled after you help Gramps?" Davy added.

Kent laughed. "Just call me the booster brother," he said as he boosted Davy up on his shoulder and carried him into the school.

HOW ABOUT YOU? Have you given anyone a boost lately? Can you think of someone who needs your help? Run an errand. Write a note. Say some kind words. Listen to someone who is lonely. Give someone a boost today. You'll be glad you did. B. W.

TO MEMORIZE: *"Everyone helped his neighbor, and said to his brother, 'Be of good courage' "*
Isaiah 41:6 (NKJV).

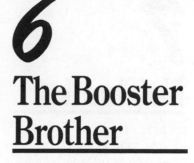

DECEMBER

7

No Thanks

FROM THE BIBLE:

So now, since we have been made right in God's sight by faith in his promises, we can have real peace with him because of what Jesus Christ our Lord has done for us. For because of our faith, he has brought us into this place of highest privilege where we now stand, and we confidently and joyfully look forward to actually becoming all that God has had in mind for us to be. We can rejoice, too, when we run into problems and trials for we know that they are good for us—they help us learn to be patient. And patience develops strength of character in us and helps us trust God more each time we use it until finally our hope and faith are strong and steady. Then, when that happens, we are able to hold our heads high no matter what happens and know that all is well, for we know how dearly God loves us, and we feel this warm love everywhere within us because God has given us the Holy Spirit to fill our hearts with his love.
Romans 5:1-5, TLB

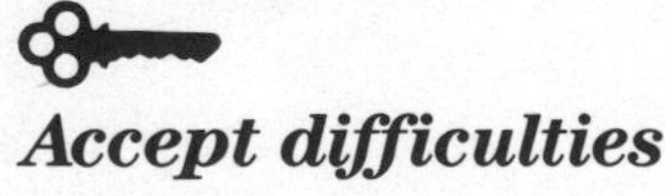

Accept difficulties

"I DON'T WANT to see Dr. Cook," sobbed Kerri. "He always gives me shots."

"He'll give you a shot only if it's needed," said Mother.

"Come on," encouraged the office nurse. "I'll be right with you. Your mom can come, too."

After the doctor examined Kerri, her worst fears came true. "She has an infection," said Dr. Cook. "She needs a shot of penicillin to get on top of it." And in spite of Kerri's wails, the doctor gave her the shot. He also handed Mother a prescription for penicillin tablets, which Kerri had to take for several days.

Mother listened as Kerri prayed before she climbed into bed that evening. "Dear Lord, thank You for Mommy and Daddy," she prayed. "Please bless them. Thank You for the nurse, and bless her. She was so nice to me. Thank You for the pills that will help me get better. Please bless all my friends. In Jesus' name. Amen."

Mother tucked the covers around Kerri. "Didn't you forget someone in your prayer?" asked Mother. "I didn't hear you thank the Lord for Dr. Cook."

"I'm mad at him," replied Kerri with a scowl. "I don't want God to bless him."

Mother sat down on the edge of the bed. "Why did he give you a shot?" asked Mother. Kerri had to admit that it was to make her well again, and Mother had another question. "Do you think he enjoys causing you pain?"

"No." Kerri shook her head.

"So he's not being mean to you, is he?" persisted Mother. "He simply insisted on giving a shot—even though it hurt a little—because it would help you."

"Yes," admitted Kerri. "I . . . I'm sorry I got mad about it. I want to ask God to bless him, too." She climbed out of bed and got back on her knees.

HOW ABOUT YOU? When God lets something come into your life that you don't want or like, do you get angry at Him? God doesn't send unpleasant things—the loss of a friend, a stomachache, lack of money for something special—to hurt you. Ask Him to help you learn from those experiences. Thank Him for hard things and even be joyful in them. H.M.

TO MEMORIZE: *"Consider it pure joy, my brothers, whenever you face trials of many kinds"*
James 1:2 (NIV).

DECEMBER

Why So Snappy?

FROM THE BIBLE:

Finally, all of you, live in harmony with one another; be sympathetic, love as brothers, be compassionate and humble. Do not repay evil with evil or insult with insult, but with blessing, because to this you were called so that you may inherit a blessing. For, "Whoever would love life and see good days must keep his tongue from evil and his lips from deceitful speech. He must turn from evil and do good; he must seek peace and pursue it." 1 Peter 3:8-11, NIV

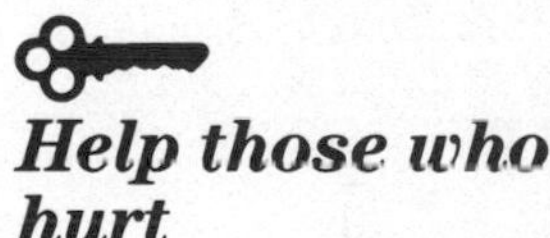

Help those who hurt

ERIN SLAMMED the door behind her. "Oh, that Trena is so hateful!" A tear slipped down her cheek.

Mother looked surprised. "I thought Trena was your best friend," she said.

"She used to be," choked Erin, "but lately she's so touchy. Nothing I do pleases her."

"That's too bad," sympathized Mother, "but try to be patient with her. She hasn't been a Christian very long."

"I know, but I'm getting sick of it." Erin sighed. "I haven't done anything about it yet, but if she doesn't stop snapping at me, I'm going to . . ." The squeal of tires and the loud yipping of a dog sent Erin and her mother running out to the yard. "Oh, Mother! It's Buffy. Someone left the gate open, and he got into the street!" Erin ran to the curb where a young man was bending over the puppy.

"I'm so sorry," he told them. "The dog just ran right out in front of me."

Mother knelt beside the whimpering puppy. As she started to touch him, Buffy snapped at her hand. "It's OK, Buffy. You're going to be all right," she said softly. Once more she reached for him, and again Buffy snapped. "Erin, can you hold his jaws shut?" asked Mother. "I want to see how badly he's hurt before we move him."

Several hours later, they returned from the vet with a stiff and sore puppy. "I'm so thankful Buffy wasn't killed," Erin told her father, who had arrived home from work. "But he sure is snappy."

"That's because he's hurting," Dad told her. He looked up over the top of his newspaper. "Say, do you know the names of Trena's parents? Aren't they Phillip and Lisa?"

"Yes," Erin replied. "Why?"

"Because Lisa Clark is filing for a divorce from Phillip Clark," replied Dad. "Did you know that, Erin?"

"Oh no!" Erin took a deep breath. "Oh, poor Trena! No wonder she's been so snappy lately. She's hurting! I'm so glad I didn't snap back at her."

HOW ABOUT YOU? When someone snaps at you, do you snap back? Or do you stop to consider why he might be acting that way? Before you snap back, ask yourself, "Is he hurting?" If so, he needs your love and kindness to ease the pain. He needs your patience and your prayers. B.W.

TO MEMORIZE: *"Do not repay evil with evil or insult with insult, but with blessing"* 1 Peter 3:9 (NIV).

DECEMBER

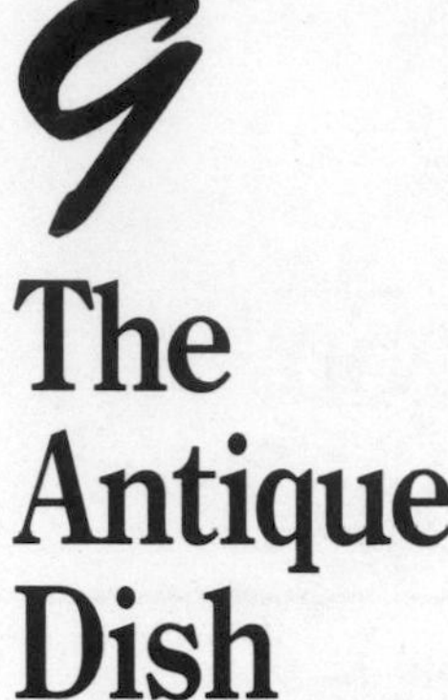

The Antique Dish

FROM THE BIBLE:
Now that you have purified yourselves by obeying the truth so that you have sincere love for your brothers, love one another deeply, from the heart. For you have been born again, not of perishable seed, but of imperishable, through the living and enduring word of God. For, "All men are like grass, and all their glory is like the flowers of the field; the grass withers and the flowers fall, but the word of the Lord stands forever." And this is the word that was preached to you. 1 Peter 1:22-25, NIV

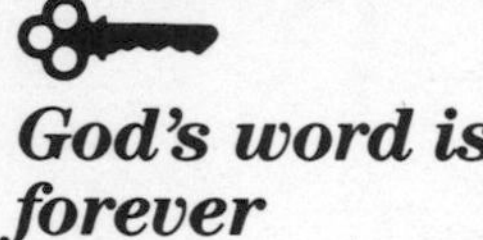

God's word is forever

"HERE WE ARE," said Mother as she pulled the car into a parking space. "Remember that it's important not to handle things in an antique store. They might break."

"I'll remember," Jamie assured her.

Mother used to leave Jamie home when she shopped for antiques. "You're too young, honey," Mother had said. "Antique stores are not for children." But now that Jamie was older, Mother often took her along, and Jamie loved to look at the colorful hand-painted plates, delicate cups and saucers, and sparkling cut-glass bowls and vases.

"Look at this beautiful cheese dish!" Mother exclaimed. "It's not expensive at all, and wouldn't it be pretty on the shelf in the dining room?"

"Oh, Mother, could we get it?" Jamie asked eagerly. Mother agreed, and after paying the shopkeeper, they took it home.

When Mother showed the cheese dish to Dad, Jamie asked, "Do we have to put it on the shelf? Can't we keep it out and use it?"

Mother shook her head. "No, I don't think so," she said. "This dish is very old, and some day it will be valuable. We might chip it if we use it, but it will last a long, long time if we put it where we can just enjoy looking at it."

"I have a riddle for you," said Dad. "What is very, very old, can be used all we want right now, and still will last forever?"

Jamie thought about it. "I can't think of anything that will last forever if it's used," she said. "Give me a clue."

"I read the answer this morning," said Dad. "Look at this." He opened his Bible to 1 Peter. "But the Word of the Lord endureth forever," he read. He smiled and added, "And God wants us to use it over and over, again and again."

"Oh, I didn't think of that!" exclaimed Jamie. "That's a good thing to remember."

HOW ABOUT YOU? Do you read God's Word every day, or is your Bible like the antique dish—sitting on a shelf not being used? The copy you're using may wear out, but God's message will always remain. Learn to live for Him by reading his Word each day. You'll never wear it out. D.K.

TO MEMORIZE: *"Heaven and earth shall pass away: but my words shall not pass away"* Mark 13:31.

THERE WAS A dull thud, and the Taylor's house trembled slightly. Not far away construction workers were using dynamite to make a tunnel through a mountain. "I wish those men were done exploding that stuff!" exclaimed Jessica. She covered her ears with her hands. "It makes me afraid."

"It is noisy, isn't it?" agreed Dad.

"And it crumbles things apart," Jessica added. She had seen films showing how dynamite was used to break up big rocks. "It won't crumble us apart, will it Daddy? I'm scared!" She scooted over on the sofa, close to her father.

"No, honey," Dad assured her. "It's not going to hurt us as long as we stay away from it. You're safe here." Reassured, Jessica went out to play.

Soon she returned to the house. The door slammed behind her, and her face wore a scowl as she flung herself into a chair. "I'll never speak to Rodney again," she fumed. "Never! You know what he said? He said I looked like a monkey. I hate him!" Her words were punctuated by the boom of another explosion at the construction site.

Dad looked up. "You know, Jessica, anger is kind of like dynamite," he said quietly. Jessica stared at him in confusion. "Yes," Dad continued, "it's very much like dynamite. It's loud, it's explosive, and it can hurt people."

Jessica thought about that. "Can it crumble us apart?"

"In a way," answered Dad. "I guess we could say that it crumbles our control. Anger is very powerful, and if we lose control, it hurts us as well as the person with whom we're angry."

"So we should stay away from it, just like we have to stay away from the dynamite?" asked Jessica.

Dad nodded. "That's right. As Christians, we need to let the Lord, not anger, control our actions."

As another explosion rumbled in the distance, Jessica got up from her chair. "I don't like dynamite," she said. "I think I'll go talk with Rodney for a while."

HOW ABOUT YOU? Does anger explode in you? Do you realize the damage it can do, both to you and to others? Next time you feel "ready to explode," say a quick prayer, asking God to help you gain control over the situation. Ask Him to control your life and actions. V.R.

TO MEMORIZE: *"Cease from anger, and forsake wrath"* Psalm 37:8.

DECEMBER

10

Danger: Anger

FROM THE BIBLE:
A wise man is cautious and avoids danger; a fool plunges ahead with great confidence. A short-tempered man is a fool. He hates the man who is patient. . . . A wise man restrains his anger and overlooks insults. This is to his credit. The king's anger is as dangerous as a lion's. But his approval is as refreshing as the dew on grass. Proverbs 14:16-17; 19:11-12, TLB

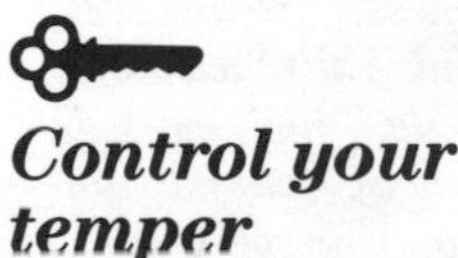

Control your temper

DECEMBER

11

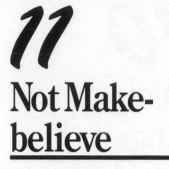

Not Make-believe

FROM THE BIBLE:

O pleasure-mad kingdom, living at ease, bragging as the greatest in the world—listen to the sentence of my court upon your sins. You say, "I alone am God! I'll never be a widow; I'll never lose my children." Well, those two things shall come upon you in one moment, in full measure in one day: widowhood and the loss of your children, despite all your witchcraft and magic. You felt secure in all your wickedness. "No one sees me," you said. Your "wisdom" and "knowledge" have caused you to turn away from me and claim that you yourself are Jehovah. That is why disaster shall overtake you suddenly—so suddenly that you won't know where it comes from. And there will be no atonement then to cleanse away your sins. Call out the demon hordes you've worshiped all these years. . . . You have advisors by the ton—your astrologers and stargazers, who try to tell you what the future holds. But they are as useless as dried grass burning in the fire.

Isaiah 47:8-14, TLB

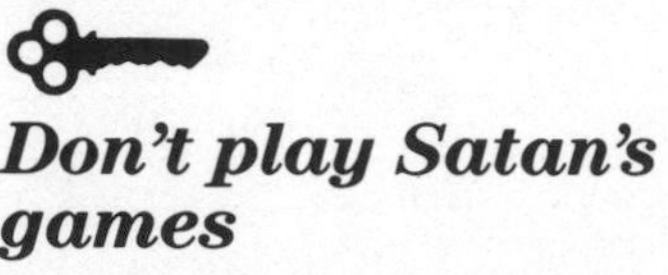

Don't play Satan's games

TIM AND ANDREW grabbed their cereal bowls and milk as they raced into the family room to watch their favorite cartoons. Saturday morning was the only time they were allowed to eat there, and they were happy when Dad brought in the toast and decided to join them. "What are we watching, guys?" Dad asked, pouring milk on his cereal.

" 'Masters of the Sky'," said Tim. "The masters cast evil spells on the invaders of the sky kingdom."

Dad frowned as he listened to the boys introduce each of the cartoon characters and describe the special powers they had. "What's on the other stations, boys? This doesn't sound like something we should be watching."

"Aw, Dad, it's only make-believe," pleaded Tim. "The other cartoons are for babies and scaredy-cats."

"The toy stores have games and dolls taken right from this cartoon," argued Andrew. "How can something that's just fun be so bad?"

"It sounds to me like Satan is up to his old tricks," responded Dad. "He's persuading people that magic and evil spells are only games and make-believe, and that playing around with evil can't hurt them. But Christians have been warned to be on the lookout for his tricks. Evil is not fun and games like in the cartoons. Many people in the Bible were punished for being involved in evil practices."

Andrew sighed. "The guys at school say it's a really exciting program, but I guess we should turn it off then," he admitted.

Tim nodded in agreement as he got up to flip off the TV.

"Why don't we go over to the YMCA and shoot some baskets?" suggested Dad. "It might not match the excitement of your cartoons, but I think it will really be a lot more fun."

HOW ABOUT YOU? Have you ever noticed the evil magic in the TV shows you watch or in the games that you play? Have you read your horoscope just for the fun of it and then found yourself actually believing that it might be true? Satan wants to blend evil with what seems good. Be on the lookout for him! Don't be deceived by his games. D.R.

TO MEMORIZE: *"Satan himself masquerades as an angel of light. It is not surprising, then, if his servants masquerade as servants of righteousness. Their end will be what their actions deserve"* 2 Corinthians 11:14 (NIV).

DECEMBER

Special Place

FROM THE BIBLE:

I will praise You with my whole heart;
Before the gods I will sing praises to You.
I will worship toward Your holy temple,
And praise Your name
For Your lovingkindness and Your truth;
For You have magnified Your word above all Your name.
In the day when I cried out, You answered me,
And made me bold with strength in my soul.
All the kings of the earth shall praise You, O Lord,
When they hear the words of Your mouth.
Yes, they shall sing of the ways of the Lord,
For great is the glory of the Lord.
Though the Lord is on high,
Yet He regards the lowly;
But the proud He knows from afar.
Though I walk in the midst of trouble,
You will revive me;
You will stretch out Your hand against the wrath of my enemies.

Psalm 138:1-7, NKJV

Meet God daily

CLAIRE WAVED as her sister Dottie walked to the car with her boyfriend, Jason. "Where are you going for lunch today?" she asked.

"To that little restaurant called Your Special Spot," Jason replied with a grin, "only we call it 'Our Special Spot' now."

"How come you always go there?" Claire asked.

"We don't always," said Dottie, "but it is our favorite place. It's cozy and quiet—a good place to talk."

"It's where we went on our first date," added Jason, giving Dottie a squeeze, "and it's where we were when I asked your sister to marry me."

Claire went into the house after they left. "Dottie and Jason sure spend a lot of time together," she murmured to herself. "I guess that's because they love each other."

As Claire thought about it, she remembered a sermon she had heard the past Sunday. "If you love the Lord, you should spend time each day with Him," Pastor Grant had said, and Claire was trying to do that. Sometimes it was hard, though. She shared a room with a younger sister, Gayle, and so often when she wanted to have her devotions, Gayle was in the room. *I know!* Claire thought now. *I need a special place for talking to the Lord just like Dottie and Jason have a special place to talk to each other. Where could it be?* She decided to ask her mother.

"That's a great idea!" said Mother after Claire explained what she wanted. "Let's see. I think we could rearrange things in the attic and fix up a private corner for you there. Would you like that?"

Claire nodded. "Can we go take a look?" she asked eagerly. Mother agreed, and they headed for the stairs.

HOW ABOUT YOU? Do you have trouble finding privacy when you want to spend time with the Lord? If possible, find a special place to meet with Him each day. If you have your own room, that may be the best place for you. But maybe you'll need to use a corner in the basement or in a storage room. Perhaps there's a spot you could use in the back of your garage or even in a large closet. Maybe you have a tree house available or a quiet corner of your yard. In any case, it often helps to have a special, quiet place to which you can go to be alone with God. Then be sure to meet Him there each day. H.M.

TO MEMORIZE: *"I will worship toward Your holy temple, and praise Your name"* Psalm 138:2 (NKJV).

DECEMBER

13

The Best for Father

FROM THE BIBLE:

Yours, O Lord, is the greatness, the power and the glory, the victory and the majesty; for all that is in heaven and in earth is Yours; Yours is the kingdom, O Lord, and You are exalted as head over all. Both riches and honor come from You, and You reign over all. In Your hand is power and might; in Your hand it is to make great and to give strength to all. Now therefore, our God, we thank You and praise Your glorious name. But who am I, and who are my people, that we should be able to offer so willingly as this? For all things come from You, and of Your own we have given You. For we are aliens and pilgrims before You, as were all our fathers; our days on earth are as a shadow, and without hope. O Lord our God, all this abundance that we have prepared to build You a house for Your holy name is from Your hand, and is all Your own.
1 Chronicles 29:11-16, NKJV

Give God what is His

MOTHER LOOKED at her watch. "Let's meet here at the Christmas tree in the mall in two hours," she said.

"OK," said Angela. "We'll be here. Come on, Kara. We've got lots of gifts to buy." She studied the Christmas list. "We should buy something nice for Dad first," she suggested. Kara agreed, and soon they were busily looking for just the right presents.

Before long both girls had several packages. They were at the stationery shop looking for their grandmother's gift when the met Kara's Sunday school teacher shopping with her daughter, June. "From the evidence, I can see that you girls are doing your Christmas shopping," said Mrs. Kimball with a smile.

"You sure have a lot of packages," June added. "You must have worked hard to earn enough money to buy all those presents!"

"We didn't actually earn all of the money," Angela said, "and we don't get a regular allowance, so Dad gives us extra money to buy Christmas gifts."

"Oh," June said. "Then you're actually buying your dad a gift with his own money."

"Yep," giggled Kara. "That's why we give him the best present of all. He deserves it, right?"

Mrs. Kimball overheard her daughter's remark and the answer Kara gave. "You're absolutely right," she agreed. "It's too bad we don't always realize that. You know, God gives us our life, strength, time, and talents, yet we often complain about giving those things back to Him. We forget that they really belong to Him, anyway. We're only giving Him what is rightfully His in the first place."

"That's true." Kara nodded, glancing at her watch. "Oh, we have to go or we won't get our shopping done before we have to meet Mom in twenty minutes."

"OK," said Mrs. Kimball. "Happy shopping!"

HOW ABOUT YOU? Do you ever complain about the time it takes to do your Sunday school lesson or go to church? Do you hate to put a whole tenth of your allowance in the offering? Think about it. All the blessings you have today were given to you by God, your heavenly Father. How can you do less than give Him back the best you have to offer? J.H.

TO MEMORIZE: *"For all things come from You, and of Your own we have given You"*
1 Chronicles 29:14 (NKJV).

DECEMBER

14

Onions and Applesauce

FROM THE BIBLE:
Since, then, you have been raised with Christ, set your hearts on things above, where Christ is seated at the right hand of God. Set your minds on things above, not on earthly things. For you died, and your life is now hidden with Christ in God. When Christ, who is your life, appears, then you also will appear with him in glory. Put to death, therefore, whatever belongs to your earthly nature: sexual immorality, impurity, lust, evil desires and greed, which is idolatry. Because of these, the wrath of God is coming. You used to walk in these ways, in the life you once lived. But now you must rid yourselves of all such things as these: anger, rage, malice, slander, and filthy language from your lips. Do not lie to each other, since you have taken off your old self with its practices and have put on the new self, which is being renewed in knowledge in the image of its Creator.
Colossians 3:1-10, NIV

Keep a clean mind

"JENNY WANTS me to come over this evening. May I go?" asked Amy as she and Mother prepared dinner. "There's a movie we want to watch on TV. I wouldn't be late."

"Amy . . ." Mother hesitated. "A paper fell out of your pocket when I was doing the wash today. I thought it was a math paper, but when I looked, I saw that it was a note from Jenny. She mentioned the movie she wants you to come and watch. I had read about that movie, Amy, and it's not a good one for you to see. It's not suitable for a Christian. I can't allow you to go watch it."

"Oh, Mother! Everybody says it's a good story. I'll ignore the bad parts," argued Amy. "It won't hurt me."

"Yes, it will," insisted Mother, "because it might put sinful thoughts into your mind. If you and Jenny want to spend the evening together, see if she can come over here."

Amy didn't argue any more, but she pouted as she helped her mother prepare the food. "Which dish do you want me to put the applesauce in?" she mumbled.

"Take that yellow bowl from the sink," Mother replied. "It just had some chopped onion in it."

"It still has little pieces of onion sticking to it," objected Amy. "I suppose I could wash it."

"No, don't bother," said Mother. "We'll just ignore the onions. The applesauce will be fine in that bowl."

"But, Mother," protested Amy. "We can't put clean food—food that we're going to eat—into a dirty bowl. The applesauce will taste like onions!"

"That's true." Mother nodded. "And, Amy, our minds are more important than our mouths. Just as the onions give a bad taste to the applesauce, the sinful and dirty ideas produced by things we see and hear give a bad flavor to our thoughts."

HOW ABOUT YOU? Are you careful about what you see and hear? There are many things on TV and in books that fill your mind with sinful thoughts. God wants your mind clean so He can speak to you through His Word. Put away the books or magazines that would displease Him. Shut off the TV programs that dirty your thoughts. Ask the Lord to help you keep pure thoughts. D.K.

TO MEMORIZE: *"Put on the new self, which is being renewed in knowledge in the image of its creator"* Colossians 3:10 (NIV).

DECEMBER

15

Say It with Music

FROM THE BIBLE:

Watch out for the false leaders—and there are many of them around—who don't believe that Jesus Christ came to earth as a human being with a body like ours. Such people are against the truth and against Christ. Beware of being like them, and losing the prize that you and I have been working so hard to get. See to it that you win your full reward from the Lord. For if you wander beyond the teaching of Christ, you will leave God behind; while if you are loyal to Christ's teachings, you will have God too. Then you will have both the Father and the Son. If anyone comes to teach you, and he doesn't believe what Christ taught, don't even invite him into your home. Don't encourage him in any way. If you do you will be a partner with him in his wickedness. 2 John 7-11, TLB

Honor God in music

WHEN SHARON'S MOTHER had an emergency operation, Sharon felt—of all things—relief! Now her parents wouldn't be able to attend the PTA meeting at which the school's pop band was performing. Sharon loved to play in the pop band, but she knew her folks wouldn't like the type of music they played. Sharon was caught up in the music. It grew on her, and now she was glad her parents wouldn't be hearing the band.

After the PTA meeting, Sharon was surprised to find her father waiting for her. "Did you hear us play?" she asked anxiously.

Dad nodded. "Mother insisted that I come to hear you," he said. "You know, Sharon, music is a powerful thing. For example, a mother sings a lullaby to quiet and soothe her baby. Now, a march wouldn't affect the baby that way, would it?"

"I guess not," said Sharon. "It would keep him awake."

"My grandfather told me that during the war they had parades where they played marches and patriotic songs," continued Dad, "and young men joined the army in large numbers. A lullaby wouldn't have affected those young men that way, would it?"

Sharon laughed. "Not very likely," she said.

"You know," Dad went on, "even in heathen lands music is used to sway people. And in the same way, our Christian songs move us by their words and music."

Sharon nodded. "I always think of 'How Great Thou Art' when I see beautiful scenery," she said.

"I'm glad to hear that," said Dad with a smile. "God uses music to draw us to Him, and Satan uses music to draw us away from God. Be sure that you're not working with Satan in your music."

Though Dad hadn't actually mentioned the band, Sharon made a big decision. She knew she had been drawn away from God by her deep involvement in the band, and she felt a responsibility to those who might be influenced by her music. She knew she had to quit.

HOW ABOUT YOU? Have you been careful in choosing music to play or listen to? Don't underestimate the powerful effect music has on you. You can sometimes say "praise God," "go to sleep," or "defend your country" more effectively with music than with words. How is the music you hear affecting you? How is your music affecting others? What are you saying with your music? A.L.

TO MEMORIZE: *"Sing forth the honor of His name"* Psalm 66:2.

DECEMBER

16

The Plimsoll Mark

FROM THE BIBLE:

Since we, God's children, are human beings—made of flesh and blood—he became flesh and blood too by being born in human form; for only as a human being could he die and in dying break the power of the devil who had the power of death. Only in that way could he deliver those who through fear of death have been living all their lives as slaves to constant dread. We all know he did not come as an angel but as a human being—yes, a Jew. And it was necessary for Jesus to be like us, his brothers, so that he could be our merciful and faithful High Priest before God, a Priest who would be both merciful to us and faithful to God in dealing with the sins of the people. For since he himself has now been through suffering and temptation, he knows what it is like when we suffer and are tempted, and he is wonderfully able to help us.

Hebrews 2:14-18, TLB

God helps you

GRANDPA BAKER'S hobby was making ship models out of pine and balsa wood. The finished models were works of art. As each of his grandchildren turned twelve, Grandpa would make a ship especially for him. This year Eric had his twelfth birthday, so Grandpa was making Eric's ship.

Finally the night of the birthday celebration arrived. Eric received many nice gifts, and he appreciated them, but everyone knew that Grandpa Baker's gift would be the highlight of the occasion. It was saved until the very last. Carefully, Eric removed the wrapping paper from the box and lifted out the ship. "Wow, this is neat, Grandpa!" He gave his grandfather a hug, then turned to study and admire the ship again. "Grandpa, what's this line on the side of the ship?"

"Oh, that's called a Plimsoll mark, Eric," answered Grandpa. "Years ago, companies would often overload their ships. As a result, the ships would sink easily and lives would be lost. A man named Samuel Plimsoll worked to reform the shipping laws, and a new law was established. It required a mark to be made on each ship. If the water level was above that line, the ship was overloaded and some of the cargo would have to be removed. The mark is now known as the Plimsoll mark.

"Hmmm. I never knew that," said Eric.

"I often think that Christians have a Plimsoll mark, too," Grandpa continued, "and God knows just where it is. He understands exactly how much we can handle in life, and He promises that we'll not be overloaded with greater problems than we can handle with His help!"

As Eric picked up his ship, Mother spoke. "Every time you look at your model ship, Eric, let it remind you of Grandpa's life—and also of God's love and of His promise to help you through any difficulty!"

HOW ABOUT YOU? Do you have such a big problem that it seems there is no solution? Maybe you're tempted to do something wrong, but you want to do it so badly you just don't see how you can help yourself. Talk to God about it. He will be with you through every problem and will help you resist every temptation if you'll let Him. He promised. L.W.

TO MEMORIZE: *"For since he himself has now been through suffering and temptation, he knows what it is like when we suffer and are tempted, and he is wonderfully able to help us"* Hebrews 2:18 (TLB).

DECEMBER

17

Drop the Oars

FROM THE BIBLE:
Then he told this story to some who boasted of their virtue and scorned everyone else: "Two men went to the Temple to pray. One was a proud, self-righteous Pharisee, and the other a cheating tax collector. The proud Pharisee 'prayed' this prayer: 'Thank God, I am not a sinner like everyone else, especially like that tax collector over there! For I never cheat, I don't commit adultery, I go without food twice a week, and I give to God a tenth of everything I earn.' But the corrupt tax collector stood at a distance and dared not even lift his eyes to heaven as he prayed, but beat upon his chest in sorrow, exclaiming, 'God, be merciful to me, a sinner.' I tell you, this sinner, not the Pharisee, returned home forgiven! For the proud shall be humbled, but the humble shall be honored."
Luke 18:9-14, TLB

Simply trust Jesus

"CHUCK CAN'T COME over this afternoon," said Ken. "He has to go with his mom on door-to-door visitation and give out church literature and stuff."

"Is that right?" Mother was interested. "Are Chuck and his family Christians?"

Ken shook his head. "I don't think so. They talk about faith in Jesus, but they don't believe He's God. That doesn't make sense to me. They seem to think they have to do a lot of good works to be saved—like this calling program. And they think they have to be very faithful in church attendance or they won't be saved for sure. I don't understand it. I don't think Chuck does either, but he does whatever he's supposed to—says it can't hurt."

Dad spoke up. "Sounds to me like he needs to drop the oars and catch hold of the rope," he said.

"Drop what oars?" asked Chuck. "What do you mean?"

"There's a river with a big waterfall near the town where I grew up," explained Dad. "Just above the falls the water is very wild and dangerous. It's unsafe for boating, and I remember one time when a man in a rowboat got caught in the swift current. It was pulling him closer and closer to the falls. A crowd gathered on the bank, and people called to him to row harder. He tried his best, but we could see he wasn't going to make it. Then someone threw a rope to him. Do you suppose the crowd continued to encourage him to row? Oh no! Then the cry was, 'Drop your oars! Grab the rope!" He did, and they pulled him to shore." Dad paused, still seeing the scene in his mind. "Like the man in the boat, Chuck needs to stop working to save himself. The only way he can be saved is to stop struggling and just trust Jesus to save him."

HOW ABOUT YOU? Are you struggling to save yourself? Do you hope that going to church, praying, giving, or living a "good" life will save you from your sins and earn a place for you in heaven? It won't. You will be saved only when you stop trying to save yourself and simply trust Christ. Do that today. H.M.

TO MEMORIZE: *"God, be merciful to me, a sinner"* Luke 18:13 (TLB).

DECEMBER

18

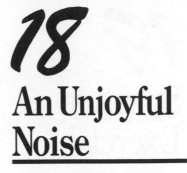

An Unjoyful Noise

FROM THE BIBLE:
It is good to say, "Thank you" to the Lord, to sing praises to the God who is above all gods. Every morning tell him, "Thank you for your kindness," and every evening rejoice in all his faithfulness. Sing his praises, accompanied by music from the harp and lute and lyre. You have done so much for me, O Lord. No wonder I am glad! I sing for joy. O Lord, what miracles you do! And how deep are your thoughts! Unthinking people do not understand them! No fool can comprehend this: that although the wicked flourish like weeds, there is only eternal destruction ahead of them. But the Lord continues forever, exalted in the heavens, while his enemies—all evil-doers—shall be scattered. But you have made me as strong as a wild bull. How refreshed I am by your blessings! I have heard the doom of my enemies announced and seen them destroyed. But the godly shall flourish like palm trees, and grow tall as the cedars of Lebanon.
Psalm 92:1-12, TLB

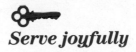

Serve joyfully

BETH PLAYED the flute, and her brother Scott played the clarinet. Since they both did well on their instruments, they were frequently asked to provide special music for church services. One day when they were supposed to be rehearsing a special number for Sunday morning, they couldn't agree on what song to play. "Let's play page 105," Scott suggested.

"Yuck!" Beth exclaimed. "I hate that song!"

"It's a neat song," insisted Scott.

"I always knew you had bad taste," Beth retorted.

"Look who's talking!" he said angrily. "The last time you decided we should play that chorus we learned at camp, and it sounded horrible!"

"Did not!"

"Did!"

"Well, anyhow," said Beth, "I think we should play 'Praise to God.' " Scott snorted, but they played through the song.

"Boring," Scott told his sister when they finished.

"Just forget it, then!" Beth snapped. "I have better things to do than to sit here and argue with you!"

"Wait a minute," said Mother as she walked into the room. "What's going on here? It sounds like war! Why do you two bother to play at all?"

Scott was puzzled. "Because we were asked to play."

Beth knew that wasn't a satisfactory answer. "It's . . . it's our ministry. We hope others will learn about the Lord through our music."

"That sounds good," said Mother, "and I like the words to the song 'Praise to God.' But I certainly didn't hear any praises when you were deciding what number to play."

Mother left the room, and Scott and Beth looked at each other. "Mom's right," Beth said. "First of all, let's pray about our music, and then let's start again."

HOW ABOUT YOU? What is your attitude when you're asked to serve in some way in your church? Do you think of every possible excuse to keep from joining the children's choir? Do you slide down in your seat when your Sunday school teacher asks for someone to pray? The Bible says we are to joyfully serve the Lord. Check your attitude and make sure it's a joyful one! L.W.

TO MEMORIZE: *"Make a joyful noise unto the LORD, all ye lands"* Psalm 100:1.

DECEMBER

19

Spiritual Exercise

FROM THE BIBLE:

Sing a new song to the Lord telling about his mighty deeds! For he has won a mighty victory by his power and holiness. He has announced this victory and revealed it to every nation by fulfilling his promise to be kind to Israel. The whole earth has seen God's salvation of his people. That is why the earth breaks out in praise to God, and sings for utter joy! Sing your praise accompanied by music from the harp. Let the cornets and trumpets shout! Make a joyful symphony before the Lord, the King! Let the sea in all its vastness roar with praise! Let the earth and all those living on it shout, "Glory to the Lord." Let the waves clap their hands in glee, and the hills sing out their songs of joy before the Lord, for he is coming to judge the world with perfect justice.
Psalm 98, TLB

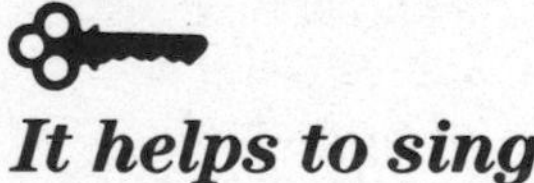

It helps to sing

" 'TIS SO SWEET to trust in Jesus; just to take Him at His Word." The words of the song floated up the stairs. Danny yawned and peeked at the sunlight playing on his bed. "Just to rest upon His promise," the quavering voice rang out over banging pots and pans. Danny grinned. Grandma always sang in the morning. In fact, she always sang. Then he frowned. How could she sing this morning? After yesterday? A sob caught in Danny's throat. "Jesus, Jesus, how I trust Him." Grandma's song continued as Danny got dressed.

At the breakfast table Danny asked, "Grannie, how can you sing this morning?"

Grandma smiled. "Honey, a long time ago I learned to sing when I'm sad and when I'm glad. Your grandfather loved to hear me sing."

"But Grandpa died," Danny blurted out. "We had his funeral yesterday."

"I know," Grandma answered gently, "and I also know he wouldn't want me to stop singing now."

Danny's mother nodded. "And neither do I," she said. She looked at her son. "Singing is good for you, Danny. I read that it clears your lungs and helps your circulation. The article said singing sometimes prevents headaches by speeding blood to the brain, and that it aids your digestive system and prevents ulcers."

"And besides all that, it will ease your heartaches," Grandma added knowingly.

Dad joined the conversation. "Singing is spiritual exercise. We jog to keep our body in shape. We sing for spiritual fitness."

Later as Danny sat on his grandfather's tractor in the field, he sang. "When we all get to heaven, what a day of rejoicing that will be. . . ." And he realized Grandma was right. Singing did help.

HOW ABOUT YOU? Are you sad? Worried? Afraid? Discontented? Sing! Exercise your spirit. Sing unto the Lord, and you will feel better. B.W.

TO MEMORIZE: *"Sing a new song to the Lord telling about his mighty deeds!"* Psalm 98:1 (TLB).

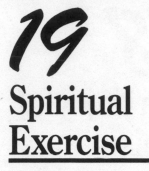

DECEMBER

20

The Right Time

FROM THE BIBLE:
And the Lord God said, "It isn't good for man to be alone; I will make a companion for him, a helper suited to his needs." So the Lord God formed from the soil every kind of animal and bird, and brought them to the man to see what he would call them; and whatever he called them, that was their name. But still there was no proper helper for the man. Then the Lord God caused the man to fall into a deep sleep, and took one of his ribs and closed up the place from which he had removed it, and made the rib into a woman, and brought her to the man. "This is it!" Adam exclaimed. "She is part of my own bone and flesh! Her name is 'woman' because she was taken out of a man." This explains why a man leaves his father and mother and is joined to his wife in such a way that the two become one person. Now although the man and his wife were both naked, neither of them was embarrassed or ashamed.
Genesis 2:18-25, TLB

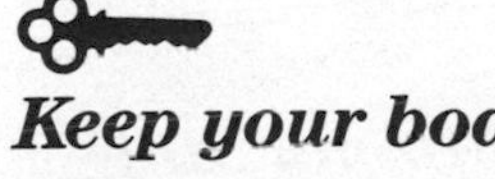

Keep your body pure

MARY LOOKED UP as her mother came into the room. "How about going shopping with me?" asked Mother.

Mary shook her head. "I'll stay home and wrap gifts."

After Mother was gone, Mary began her task. When she looked in Kathleen's room to see if the box of ribbons was there, she saw a package with her name on it. "Ohhh!" she breathed. "Maybe if I'm careful, I can take a peek, and no one will know the difference." Carefully she untied the ribbon and picked at the tape. A small box slid out, and inside it she found a beautiful necklace. Mary swiftly rewrapped the gift. She felt guilty, but she was right about one thing—nobody else knew the difference.

Soon it was Christmas. When Mary opened her package from Kathleen, she tried to act surprised, but it was hard. Having opened it ahead of time spoiled the fun of getting it now. She felt guilty, and she knew Kathleen expected her to be more excited than she was sounding. She was relieved when the phone rang, and she scurried to answer it. But when Mary returned, she was upset. "What's wrong?" asked Mother.

"Patty called," answered Mary. "She says Jane won't be returning to school after Christmas. She's pregnant! She's going to live with an aunt until the baby is born and adopted out."

"How sad," Mother said. "You know, Mary, sexual intimacy between a man and woman is a wonderful gift, but God knew what He was doing when He planned it for marriage. Taking that gift ahead of time has resulted in much unhappiness."

Mary thought about her Christmas gift from Kathleen. It had been wrong to open it ahead of time, and she knew she had to confess what she had done. She thought about Jane, who hadn't waited until marriage to enjoy the gift of intimacy. Mary didn't want to make that mistake. She wanted to follow God's plan.

HOW ABOUT YOU? Television programs, books, and even friends often imply that if you feel like having an intimate sexual relationship, you should do so. That's wrong! God's Word says to wait until marriage or you'll spoil the beauty of it. Wait! J.H.

TO MEMORIZE: *"Flee also youthful lusts: but follow righteousness, faith, charity, peace, with them that call on the Lord out of a pure heart"*
2 Timothy 2:22.

DECEMBER

21

Ordinary but Pretty

FROM THE BIBLE:
However, Christ has given each of us special abilities—whatever he wants us to have out of his rich storehouse of gifts. The Psalmist tells about this, for he says that when Christ returned triumphantly to heaven after his resurrection and victory over Satan, he gave generous gifts to men. Notice that it says he returned to heaven. This means that he had first come down from the heights of heaven, far down to the lowest parts of the earth. The same one who came down is the one who went back up, that he might fill all things everywhere with himself, from the very lowest to the very highest. Some of us have been given special ability as apostles; to others he has given the gift of being able to preach well; some have special ability in winning people to Christ, helping them to trust him as their Savior; still others have a gift for caring for God's people as a shepherd does his sheep, leading and teaching them in the ways of God.
Ephesians 4:7-12, TLB

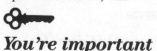

You're important

"I STILL WISH I could sing or act in the Christmas play," Angela sighed. "It would be so nice to be important once in a while—to really be needed instead of just pressing dumb old costumes."

"I've told you—you are important. You are needed," replied Mother patiently. "But you seem determined not to believe that. Well, I'd better get supper ready."

Angela nodded. "I'll set the table," she offered, going to the cupboard. "Mom, can we use the good crystal goblets tonight? They're so pretty!"

"I don't see why not," said Mother. "But before we eat, I want you to take this casserole to old Mrs. Jenkins. Visit with her a little while, too. She's lonely. Tell you what—I'll set the table tonight. Just be back at 5:30 for supper."

When Angela returned home, the family was just sitting down to eat. She slipped into her place and looked at the table in surprise. There were at least three crystal goblets at each place, but no plates. Dad said, "Let's thank the Lord for our food," so she quickly closed her eyes.

When Dad said "Amen," Mother picked up a casserole dish and handed it to Angela. "Help yourself," she invited.

Angela held the casserole uncertainly. "What am I supposed to do with it?" she asked. "Where are the regular plates?"

"Oh," said Mother, "the goblets are so pretty, I thought we'd just use them."

"But we can't use them for this kind of food," protested Angela. "What's going on here?"

"So you admit that we need different 'vessels' for different jobs," said Mother. "That's what I was trying to tell you earlier this afternoon. You see, it's that way in God's kingdom, too. He needs some 'vessels'—some people—to sing, some to preach, some to visit lonely folks. Some jobs appear to us to be 'prettier' than others, but each is as important as the next."

Angela laughed. "OK, I get the point," she said. "But right now ordinary plates sound mighty 'pretty' to me."

HOW ABOUT YOU? Do you feel that the things you're asked to do for the Lord are really unimportant? That's not true. There is no such thing as an unimportant task when it's done for the Lord. H.M.

TO MEMORIZE: *"He will be a vessel for honor, sanctified, useful to the Master"*
2 Timothy 2:21 (NASB).

DECEMBER

22

Made to Be Used

FROM THE BIBLE:

Again, the Kingdom of Heaven can be illustrated by the story of a man going into another country, who called together his servants and loaned them money to invest for him while he was gone. He gave $5,000 to one, $2,000 to another, and $1,000 to the last—dividing it in proportion to their abilities—and then left on his trip. . . . After a long time their master returned from his trip and called them to him to account for his money. The man to whom he had entrusted the $5,000 brought him $10,000. His master praised him for good work. "You have been faithful in handling this small amount," he told him, "so now I will give you many more responsibilities." . . . Next came the man who had received the $2,000, with the report, "Sir, you gave me $2,000 to use, and I have doubled it." "Good work," his master said. "You are a good and faithful servant. You have been faithful over this small amount, so now I will give you much more."

Matthew 25:14-23, TLB

Use your talents

AMBER HURRIED to answer the phone. It was the music director from church, and he wanted her to sing a solo at the Christmas program. "I couldn't," Amber stammered. "The church will be so crowded that night."

"I've heard you sing in the primary department,"said Mr. Bell, "and you did a good job. You have a pretty voice and we could use you." Still, Amber refused to sing.

Mother overheard the conversation. "You do have a lovely voice, dear," she encouraged Amber. "Try it."

"But what if I made a mistake or my voice cracked? I'd rather not sing than do it and make a fool of myself," Amber sputtered. "I'll sing when I'm older."

"So you'll just put your voice on a shelf for now," Mother said as she left to start supper. Amber was puzzled by her mother's remark, but she didn't ask for an explanation. She was just relieved the subject was dropped!

A few days later Amber put the finishing touches on the scarf she was making her grandmother for Christmas. She had recently learned to knit, and the scarf had turned out very well. She just knew Grandma was going to like it. Mother admired it, too. "It's lovely," said Mother. "I suppose Grandma will keep it up on a closet shelf so it will stay nice."

Amber was shocked. "Of course she won't!" she protested. "I made it for her to use, not to put away out of sight!"

"I see." Mother nodded. "And actually you'd be hurt if she didn't use it, wouldn't you?"

"Yeah, I guess I would," admitted Amber. "But why wouldn't she use it?"

"Good question," said Mother. "You're right. She'll use it. But, Amber, this conversation reminds me of your voice. God gave you a special talent to use not to save."

"I never thought of that," Amber said slowly. "I think I'll call Mr. Bell. Maybe it's not too late to accept the solo he asked me to do."

HOW ABOUT YOU? Do you refuse to use your talents from fear of failure? Or because you're too busy? Or because you just don't feel like it? God wants to use you. Don't disappoint Him! J.H.

TO MEMORIZE: *"Our people must learn to devote themselves to doing what is good, in order that they may . . . not live unproductive lives"* Titus 3:14 (NIV).

DECEMBER

23

It Takes Practice

FROM THE BIBLE:
Your laws are wonderful; no wonder I obey them. As your plan unfolds, even the simple can understand it. No wonder I wait expectantly for each of your commands. Come and have mercy on me as is your way with those who love you. Guide me with your laws so that I will not be overcome by evil. Rescue me from the oppression of evil men; then I can obey you. Look down in love upon me and teach me all your laws. I weep because your laws are disobeyed.
Psalm 119:129-136, TLB

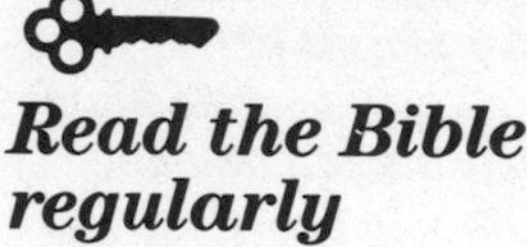

Read the Bible regularly

SCOTT GROANED as he picked himself up from the snow. His feet were in great big boots, and the boots were locked onto two long sticks of wood that wouldn't move properly. You guessed it—Scott was learning to ski. He had saved his money and begged to go along with his big brother, Mike. "Sure, you can come, but I'm warning you—it isn't as easy as it looks," his brother had said with a smile. Scott found that out in a hurry.

"I'm gonna quit. I'll never learn how to ski," Scott said with a frown after falling for the umpteenth time.

"Tell you what," Mike said with a grin, "your lift ticket includes some lessons for beginners. I think they're about ready to start the class. Go join them and get some pointers. It will make it much easier."

The ski instructor gathered the beginning skiers around him and began to teach them some of the basic moves. Then came the first few trips down the "bunny slope," as the easy hill was called. The instructor used a long pole which he held in front of Scott, so he could hold on until he felt a bit steadier. "Hey, this is fun," Scott yelled as Mike watched from the sidelines. "I think I'm ready for the big hill." Just then he lost his balance and fell sideways into the snow. "Oh well, give me a few more lessons and I'll be ready for the big hill," he sighed with a grimace.

As they were heading home at the end of the fun-filled day, Mike said, "You know, Scott, learning to ski well is a little like learning how to understand the Bible better. You told me the other day that you weren't getting much out of your Bible reading. Well, practice helps. The more you ski, the better you'll be. The more you read your Bible, the more you'll understand it. But remember, don't expect miracles right away. Anything worth while takes time—and effort."

HOW ABOUT YOU? Have you gotten discouraged in your Bible reading because you don't seem to understand it the way others do? Maybe they've "practiced" longer than you have! Also, don't start out on the "biggest hills." Read the Gospels and the Epistles before you tackle the books of prophecy. Spend time with a few verses of the Bible every day, and you'll find that the more you read, the better you'll understand. C.V.M.

TO MEMORIZE: *"As your plan unfolds, even the simple can understand it"* Psalm 119:130 (TLB).

DECEMBER

24

The Real Gift

FROM THE BIBLE:

These are the facts concerning the birth of Jesus Christ: His mother, Mary, was engaged to be married to Joseph. But while she was still a virgin she became pregnant by the Holy Spirit. Then Joseph, her fiancé, being a man of stern principle, decided to break the engagement but to do it quietly, as he didn't want to publicly disgrace her. As he lay awake considering this, he fell into a dream, and saw an angel standing beside him. "Joseph, son of David," the angel said, "don't hesitate to take Mary as your wife! For the child within her has been conceived by the Holy Spirit. And she will have a Son, and you shall name him Jesus (meaning 'Savior'), for he will save his people from their sins. This will fulfill God's message through his prophets: 'Listen! The virgin shall conceive a child! She shall give birth to a Son, and he shall be called "Emmanuel" (meaning "God is with us").' "

Matthew 1:18-23, TLB

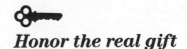

Honor the real gift

AFTER SUPPER on Christmas Eve, little Anna climbed into Mother's lap as Grandpa reached for the family Bible and began to read the familiar Scriptures about the birth of Jesus. Marsha's mind wandered as Grandpa read of the angels, shepherds, and wise men. This would be little Anna's first Christmas, and Marsha could hardly wait to see her excitement as she opened her presents. She just knew Anna would love the little baby doll she and Ted had bought for her!

When Grandpa finished reading, Dad prayed, thanking God for the Savior who came to give them eternal life. Then Marsha and Ted passed out the presents. "Open them, Anna," said Ted.

Anna grinned, but she didn't seem to know what to do. She just looked at the bright wrappings. "Here, open them like this," said Marsha as she pulled off a bow. Anna grabbed the ribbon and put it in her mouth.

"At this rate it will take her all night," Ted muttered.

"Help her a bit," suggested Grandma, and both Ted and Marsha began removing the gift wrappings.

Marsha put the baby doll in Anna's lap. "Baby," said Marsha. "Pretty baby."

Anna looked at the doll. Then she flung it aside and reached for the wrapping paper. She laughed as she crinkled the paper in her fingers and draped the ribbons over her head.

"What a disappointment!" Ted exclaimed. "We give her a really neat gift, and she ignores it! She'd rather play with the wrappings than the doll!"

"Right now, I think the bright trimmings have distracted her," said Mother.

"I wonder if God doesn't feel just as disappointed in us at Christmas time,"commented Grandpa.

"Why?" Ted asked in surprise.

"God sent Jesus to save us from our sins," Grandpa explained. "He's the real gift of Christmas, but too many people ignore Him altogether. They get distracted by the trimmings of Christmas—the presents, lights, gifts, trees, and carols—and they ignore the Savior completely."

HOW ABOUT YOU? What does Christmas mean to you? Do you worship Christ at Christmas time, or do you get caught up in the "trimmings"? Christ is the perfect gift. He gives meaning to life. J.H.

TO MEMORIZE: *"Thanks be to God for His indescribable gift"* 2 Corinthians 9:15 (NKJV).

DECEMBER

25

Same Old Story

FROM THE BIBLE:
And while they were there, the time came for her baby to be born; and she gave birth to her first child, a son. She wrapped him in a blanket and laid him in a manger, because there was no room for them in the village inn. That night some shepherds were in the fields outside the village, guarding their flocks of sheep. Suddenly an angel appeared among them, and the landscape shone bright with the glory of the Lord. They were badly frightened, but the angel reassured them. "Don't be afraid!" he said. "I bring you the most joyful news ever announced, and it is for everyone! The Savior—yes, the Messiah, the Lord—has been born tonight in Bethlehem! How will you recognize him? You will find a baby wrapped in a blanket, lying in a manger!"
Luke 2:6-12, TLB

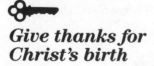

Give thanks for Christ's birth

"TODAY," Mrs. Peters told her Sunday school class, "we're going to review the record of Christ's birth, so please turn to the second chapter of Luke."

Tammy opened her Bible, but as the Scripture was being read, she tuned out her teacher's voice. It wasn't that she didn't like the Christmas story—it was just that she knew it so well. In fact, she believed she could probably teach the class herself! During the last week or so, she had heard the Christmas story in Awana Club, she had read it in a Sunday school paper, and she had seen it acted out on a television program. So while Mrs. Peters talked, Tammy thought about the new bike she expected to receive as a Christmas present.

Finally class was over, and Mrs. Peters closed in prayer. Tammy walked to the main auditorium with Gina, who had been coming to church for only a few months. "Wow! That was a good story!" exclaimed Gina.

Tammy looked at her in surprise. "I've heard it hundreds of times!"

"Well, I've heard it, too," said Gina, "but this is the first Christmas I've been a Christian, so this is the first year I've really understood what it meant. Just think, Tammy! Jesus came to earth for you and me! God must love us a lot to send His only Son to earth to die!"

As Tammy sat down in the pew, she thought about Gina's words. Yes, she understood what God had done. She knew the story almost by heart, but she realized now that she hadn't thought seriously about it for a long time. As a result, she had long ago stopped getting excited about it. But now she saw that Christ's birth was not something she should take for granted. Tammy opened her Bible to the second chapter of Luke once again. She was going to read it for herself while she waited for the church service to begin.

HOW ABOUT YOU? Do you get an "I've heard it all before" attitude when you listen to lessons on the real meaning of Christmas? Do you take Christ's birth for granted because you've heard about it so many times? The Bethlehem story should be familiar to you, but it should also be exciting each time you hear it. If Christ had not come, you would not have a Savior. Read the Scripture again. Really think about the wonderful thing that happened so long ago. Thank God for it. L.W.

TO MEMORIZE: *"The Mighty One has done great things for me—holy is his name"* Luke 1:49 (NIV).

DECEMBER

26

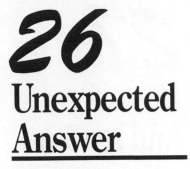

Unexpected Answer

FROM THE BIBLE:

There was a certain man in Caesarea called Cornelius, a centurion of what was called the Italian Regiment, a devout man and one who feared God with all his household, who gave alms generously to the people, and prayed to God always. . . . And Cornelius said, "Four days ago I was fasting until this hour; and at the ninth hour I prayed in my house, and behold, a man stood before me in bright clothing, and said, 'Cornelius, your prayer has been heard, and your alms are remembered in the sight of God. Send therefore to Joppa and call Simon here, whose surname is Peter. He is lodging in the house of Simon, a tanner, by the sea. When he comes, he will speak to you.' So I sent to you immediately, and you have done well to come. Now therefore, we are all present before God, to hear all the things commanded you by God."
Acts 10:1-2, 30-33, NKJV

CHRISTMAS was over. Alan looked at the opened presents which were displayed under the tree. Most of the gifts were more practical than usual because Dad had been out of work quite a bit the past year.

"God surely is good," commented Dad as Mother passed him some fruitcake. "My best Christmas present is that He has provided a job for me. It's an answer to prayer!"

Grandma noticed Alan's frown as he accepted his cake and took it into the family room. "Can I help with a problem, Alan?" she asked.

"God may have answered Dad's prayers," snorted Alan, "but He sure didn't answer mine! I prayed and prayed for a new sled, but all I got was stuff like socks and sweaters. Hardly any toys even! I'm not prayin' any more!"

Grandma asked, "Could it be that you missed God's answer?"

Alan sat up straight, his eyes bright. "Is there another present under the tree?"

"That's not what I mean," she said. "What would you think of your dad if he turned down his job offer and then declared that he wasn't going to pray anymore because God wasn't providing for his family?"

Alan looked disgusted. "That would be silly."

"Yes," agreed Grandma, "yet your mother told me that Mrs. Brown offered you the job of shoveling her walks this winter. It seems you were too busy—playing or reading or doing the many other things you like. You asked God for a sled, and He gave you a chance to earn it. You were too lazy, and now you're blaming God. Isn't that silly?"

Alan stared at Grandma. "Oh!" he said finally. "God did answer, didn't He? I'd better see if Mrs. Brown still needs help." He jumped up and winked at Grandma. "Maybe I can still earn my sled—by next summer!"

HOW ABOUT YOU? Do you pray for things and then refuse to work and earn them? Do you ask God to bless and help Mom and Dad and then look the other way when you see a job you can do to help them? Today's Scripture shows how God sometimes answers prayer by providing a task to be done. Cornelius didn't *just* pray; he sent men to Peter. Don't you *just* pray, either. Pray and then be ready to work. H.M.

TO MEMORIZE: *"Your prayer has been heard . . . send therefore. . . ."*
Acts 10:31-32 (NKJV).

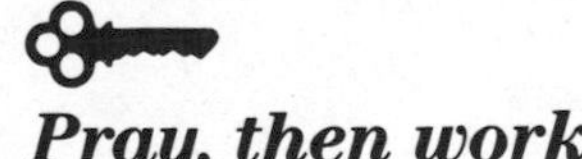

Pray, then work

DECEMBER

27

Born Again and Human

FROM THE BIBLE:

So I tell you this, and insist on it in the Lord, that you must no longer live as the Gentiles do, in the futility of their thinking. They are darkened in their understanding and separated from the life of God because of the ignorance that is in them due to the hardening of their hearts. Having lost all sensitivity, they have given themselves over to sensuality so as to indulge in every kind of impurity, with a continual lust for more. You, however, did not come to know Christ that way. Surely you heard of him and were taught in him in accordance with the truth that is in Jesus. You were taught, with regard to your former way of life, to put off your old self, which is being corrupted by its deceitful desires; to be made new in the attitude of your minds; and to put on the new self, created to be like God in true righteousness and holiness.
Ephesians 4:17-24, NIV

Live as a Christian

"WELL, I SUPPOSE I shouldn't have gotten mad when Kim fell and scratched my bike," admitted Dave as he and Mother drove home from town, "but I think God understands. He knows I'm only human."

"It seems to me you use those words as an excuse too often lately," observed Mother. "I believe you said them when you forgot to do your Sunday school lesson and when you lied about your grade in math and when you—"

"Well, it's true," defended Dave. "I am human."

"But as a Christian, you have God's Word which teaches you a better way," said Mother, turning into the driveway. "Well, here we are, home again."

When Mother and Dave entered the kitchen, they saw the table still cluttered with lunch dishes. The living room was a mess, too, and Kim was sitting in front of the television set. "Didn't you do anything in this house all afternoon?" demanded Mother. "I asked you to clean up the house a bit while I was gone."

Kim shrugged. "I'll pick this stuff up later. I want to finish watching this program now."

"You didn't even clear the table and wash the dishes," said Mother. "Go and do them right now!"

"What a lazy bum," scolded Dave. "And after all Mom does for you!"

"Look who's talking," muttered Kim as she got to her feet. "Besides, I'm only human, you know."

Dave was startled, and Mother looked straight at him as she said, "Nevertheless, I expect you to obey me, Kim, just as God expects obedience from His children. He tells us in His Word what He wants of us. And after all He's done for us, nothing He asks of us is too much."

HOW ABOUT YOU? Do you sometimes make excuses for your sinful behavior? If you're a Christian, you're no longer only human—you're a born again human. God expects you to be honest, helpful, cheerful, kind, and humble. He expects you to study His Word and obey His commands. Ask Him to help you do this. H.M.

TO MEMORIZE: *"Put on the new self, created to be like God in true righteousness and holiness"* Ephesians 4:24 (NIV).

DECEMBER

28

After-Christmas Cookies

"WHAT CAN I DO?" whined Jenny as she moped around the house a few days after Christmas.

"How about playing with your new doll or with some of your new games?" suggested Mother.

"I already did all that," wailed Jenny. "I want something new to do."

Mother sighed. "Come into the kitchen," she said. "We're going to make cookies."

"Mother," pouted Jenny, "we made all kinds of Christmas cookies. Now Christmas is past. How come we're still making cookies?"

"Because we're going to give them away." Mother smiled. "Remember the letdown feeling you had this morning, wishing for something to do? I think other people may have a letdown feeling, too—especially shut-ins and the folks in nursing homes. They had lots of attention before Christmas—carolers, programs, and so on. Now Christmas is past, and they may be feeling lonely. Wouldn't you like to go and cheer them up?"

It was a new idea to Jenny. "Let's do it," she said. "I'll arrange a pretty box of cookies for them, and it'll be like an after-Christmas present."

Jenny's eyes sparkled that evening as she told her father about the calls they had made. "They were so glad to see us!" she exclaimed. "At the nursing home an old man asked me why we were bothering with them *after* Christmas. I didn't know what to say, so I just told him that Jesus loves him after Christmas, too. He said he guessed he should know more about that. Then Mother talked with him, and he was saved! We're going to go see him again . . . all the other people, too!"

Dad laughed at Jenny's breathless account. "That's wonderful!" he exclaimed. He reached for the Bible and turned to Luke 2:15-20. "You remind me of the shepherds. After seeing the baby Jesus, they told others about Him, too. Lets read it together."

HOW ABOUT YOU? Christmas is exciting, isn't it? But that excitement should go on after Christmas as well. Can you think of a way to share Jesus' love with a friend? Can you do something nice for an older person? If you have "seen Jesus"—if you are saved—make it known to others through your words and actions. H.M.

TO MEMORIZE: *"Now when they had seen Him, they made widely known the saying which was told them concerning this Child"* Luke 2:17 (NKJV).

FROM THE BIBLE:
The people who walk in darkness shall see a great Light—a Light that will shine on all those who live in the land of the shadow of death. . . . For unto us a Child is born; unto us a Son is given; and the government shall be upon his shoulder. These will be his royal titles: "Wonderful," "Counselor," "The Mighty God," "The Everlasting Father," "The Prince of Peace." His ever-expanding, peaceful government will never end. He will rule with perfect fairness and justice from the throne of his father David. He will bring true justice and peace to all the nations of the world. This is going to happen because the Lord of heaven's armies has dedicated himself to do it!
Isaiah 9:2, 6-7, TLB

Make Jesus known

DECEMBER

29

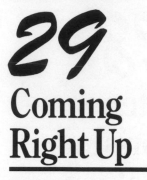

Coming Right Up

FROM THE BIBLE:
Just tell me what to do and I will do it, Lord. As long as I live I'll wholeheartedly obey. Make me walk along the right paths for I know how delightful they really are. Help me to prefer obedience to making money! Turn me away from wanting any other plan than yours. Revive my heart toward you. Reassure me that your promises are for me, for I trust and revere you. How I dread being mocked for obeying, for your laws are right and good. I long to obey them! Therefore in fairness renew my life, for this was your promise—yes, Lord, to save me! Now spare me by your kindness and your love. Then I will have an answer for those who taunt me, for I trust your promises.
Psalm 119:33-42, TLB

Learn God's Word

AS PAM was getting ready for Sunday school, she worked on her memory verse. She read it from her Bible, repeated it to herself several times, and then hurried down to breakfast. But when it was her turn to say it in class, she could only remember a few words. "This happens all the time," she mumbled to herself. "Why is it so hard to learn my memory verse?"

That afternoon Pam heard singing coming from the front porch. Going to investigate, she found six-year-old Anthony sitting on the porch swing, loudly singing the well-known song, "America." Pam laughed. "I heard you singing all the way from the backyard," she said.

Anthony beamed. "That song is right down in my heart," he said. "The words just come right up."

"Come right up?" Pam echoed, not sure she understood.

In answer, Anthony just sang the song again.

As Pam helped with supper that evening, she told her mother what Anthony had said. Mother smiled. "Anthony means that the words come back to his mind so easily because he's heard and sung them so often. I believe his class sings that song every morning at school."

I wish my memory verse would "come right up" when I need it, Pam thought as she headed for her room. She looked at the Bible and the Sunday school book on her dresser. *I guess I've been trying to learn my memory verse the wrong way. I'm going to try a new plan this week.*

Early on Monday morning Pam began studying her memory verse, and she repeated it several times each day during the week. She thought about the words she was saying, and she prayed that God would help her understand them. When it was her turn to recited on Sunday morning, the words "came right up"! Her new plan had worked.

HOW ABOUT YOU? Do you find it difficult to memorize your Sunday school memory verse? Begin studying it on Monday. Each day repeat it several times, think about it, and pray that the Lord will help you understand and memorize it. He will be glad to help you because He wants the Bible to become a part of your life. J.G.

TO MEMORIZE: *"Your Word I have hidden in my heart, that I might not sin against You"* Psalm 119:11 (NKJV).

JOSH STRUGGLED into his pajamas, raced to Elizabeth's bedroom, skidded on the shag rug next to the bed, and dropped to his knees next to his little sister. Elizabeth rolled her eyes and giggled. Josh was always late for bedtime prayers!

Elizabeth squeezed her eyes tightly shut and folded her hands on the bed. Josh also folded his hands and tried to keep his eyes shut. It was Mother's custom to pray with the children before she tucked them in each night. "Dear Lord," she prayed, "please keep my children safe tonight. Help us appreciate things we have and not worry over what we don't have. Thank You, Lord, for our health, our happiness, and our home. Help us to be kind to others." Twice Mother had to pause and wait patiently as Josh picked something off the floor and got back into position. When she finished, she shot Josh a warning glance as he once again dropped whatever he had. Then he prayed briefly, and Elizabeth did, too.

"Thank You for hearing our prayers and being with us always," Mother added in closing. "In Jesus' name. Amen."

Elizabeth hopped into bed as Josh fumbled around with something. "Josh, what do you have there?" asked Mother.

Josh held out a small metal key. "Just this key to my bike lock," he said. "I forgot to put it away after I locked my bike up tonight."

Mother smiled as she took they key. "This is very important, isn't it?" she asked. "You use it to unlock your bike every morning and lock it up every night. And you know, prayer is a key, too. It opens us up to the Lord in the morning and reminds us that we are locked under His protection at night. We must also remember that when we pray, we're in the presence of our great God. That's one reason why it's important to pay attention. We all have a key if we just choose to use it."

"Where's my key?" asked Elizabeth, not understanding.

Mother smiled. "Your key is your prayer to God. It's invisible, but it's very real."

HOW ABOUT YOU? Do you use your key to talk to God? Prayer is a wonderful privilege. As you start a new year, make it your habit to open and close each day with sincere prayer. V.R.

TO MEMORIZE: *"Evening, and morning, and at noon, will I pray, and cry aloud: and He shall hear my voice"* Psalm 55:17.

DECEMBER

30

The Key

FROM THE BIBLE:

But when you pray, go away by yourself, all alone, and shut the door behind you and pray to your Father secretly, and your Father, who knows your secrets, will reward you. Don't recite the same prayer over and over as the heathen do, who think prayers are answered only by repeating them again and again. Remember, your Father knows exactly what you need even before you ask him! Pray along these lines: "Our Father in heaven, we honor your holy name. We ask that your kingdom will come now. May your will be done here on earth, just as it is in heaven. Give us our food again today, as usual, and forgive us our sins, just as we have forgiven those who have sinned against us. Don't bring us into temptation, but deliver us from the Evil One. Amen."

Matthew 6:6-13, TLB

Prayer is a key to God

DECEMBER

31

Throw Out the Junk

FROM THE BIBLE:
So from now on we regard no one from a worldly point of view. Though we once regarded Christ in this way, we do so no longer. Therefore, if anyone is in Christ, he is a new creation; the old has gone, the new has come! All this is from God, who reconciled us to himself through Christ and gave us the ministry of reconciliation: that God was reconciling the world to himself in Christ, not counting men's sins against them. And he has committed to us the message of reconciliation. We are therefore Christ's ambassadors, as though God were making his appeal through us. We implore you on Christ's behalf: Be reconciled to God. God made him who had no sin to be sin for us, so that in him we might become the righteousness of God.
2 Corinthians 5:16-21, NIV

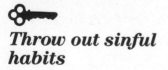

Throw out sinful habits

"JUST THINK, Dad—we get to stay up till two o'clock!" Steve exclaimed as he told his dad about the New Year's Eve party his Sunday school class would be having.

"Sounds great," Dad said. Then, with a twinkle in his eye, he added, "Have I ever told you about the New Year's Eve celebrations we had when I was a boy back in Italy?"

"Did you have a parade or something?" he asked.

"Yes, and fireworks, too," Dad said. "But what happened later that night was the most interesting part of the whole celebration. As midnight approached, people gathered up all their trash, old clothing, boxes, and whatever else they wanted to get rid of. There was a New Year's Eve custom of 'throwing out the old to make way for the new,' so they simply tossed it all out the windows."

"I'd sure hate to be the street cleaner the next day," laughed Steve.

Dad began to look thoughtful. "I think that we, as Christians, could learn a lesson from that strange custom," he said. "The Bible says 'If any man be in Christ, he is a new creature; old things are passed away; behold, all things are become new.' But we sometimes try to 'put on' Christian habits—prayer, attending church, witnessing—without 'putting off' our sinful habits. God cannot bless us and help us to grow until we get rid of the 'old junk' in our lives."

Steve looked thoughtful. "I think you're telling me that even though I've made a resolution to get better grades, God won't help me do it unless I first 'throw out' my sin of laziness."

"Exactly." Dad smiled. "Let's both make a list of some of the 'junk' we need to get rid of."

HOW ABOUT YOU? Do you sometimes wonder why it's so hard to do the right things, to form good habits, or to grow as a Christian? Perhaps there's some "junk" in your life that needs to be thrown out. It might be something like a record collection that is not pleasing to God, immodest clothing, or questionable books and magazines. It might be cigarettes or drugs. Or maybe it's a sin like anger or envy. Whatever it is, get rid of it. God will give you something new and much better to take its place! S.K.

TO MEMORIZE: *"If anyone is in Christ, he is a new creation; the old has gone, the new has come!"* 2 Corinthians 5:17 (NIV).

INDEX
of Topics

INDEX
of Scripture in Daily Readings

INDEX
of Scripture Memory Verses